# *A Tourist Guide to the*

# ANGLO BOER WAR

## 1899-1902

*incorporating*

***Accommodation & Restaurants***
***Museums & Tour Guide Information***

*Compiled by*
**Tony Westby-Nunn**

*"The war declared by the Boers on 11 October 1899 gave the British, in Kipling's famous phrase, 'no end of a lesson'. The British public expected it to be over by Christmas.*

*It proved to be ...*
*the longest – two and three-quarter years,*
*the costliest – over £200 million,*
*the bloodiest – at least 22 000 British,*
*26 000 Boer men, women & children*
*and, 12 000 Native, Coloured & Indian lives lost,*
*and*
*the most humiliating war for Britain between 1815–1914."*

THOMAS PAKENHAM, **THE BOER WAR** *(London: Abacus, 1992)*

WESTBY-NUNN PUBLISHERS CC

But you've come
To the wrong man: there must be many others
Who'd tell the story straight, in the right order
And with a moral too, and better grasp
Of all the politics than I could have.

C. Louis Leipoldt, *'Oom Gert Vertel'* translated from
***The Poetry of the Anglo-Boer War*** by **M van Wyk Smith**.

There is trouble in the Transvaal,
And England wants to know
Whether Mister Kruger or
John Bull shall boss the show.

***Drummer Hodge***, *The Poetry of the Anglo-Boer War* by M. Van Wyk Smith

Most British ministers in 1899 expected the Boer War to be short and swift. Their soldiers had won so many wars in India and Africa that the two republics in the interior of southern Africa - Transvaal and the Orange Free State - did not seem capable of long defying them. A common British attitude to the farmer-armies of these republics was expressed by Alfred Milner, Britain's governor in the Cape Colony and one of the men whose views strongly influenced Britain's to the Boers. At a private luncheon in Cape Town, eight days before the war began, he said in a quizzical manner to the new commander of the British forces: *"Surely these mere farmers cannot stand for a moment against regular troops?"* The Ministry in London was also optimistic. The Chancellor of the Exchequer, Sir Michael Hicks Beach, informed the House of Commons that the 'short war' would cost no more than £11M. The war in fact was not to end for two and a half years, the cost to Britain was more than twenty times the original estimate, and that balance sheet made no allowance for the death of 22 000 British soldiers. At least the British had the compensation of military victory. The Boer republics had also initially believed that they would win, and their ultimate defeat - with 6 000 soldiers killed, thousands of farmhouses and flocks and herds destroyed, leaders banished, and 20 000 of their children and women dead in British 'concentration camps' - was not what they had envisaged. As the Boer politician, Schalk Burger, confessed when the fighting was virtually over: *"It was a 'war of miscalculation'"*.

**The Causes of War** *Geoffrey Blainey*
The Free Press N.Y. 1988

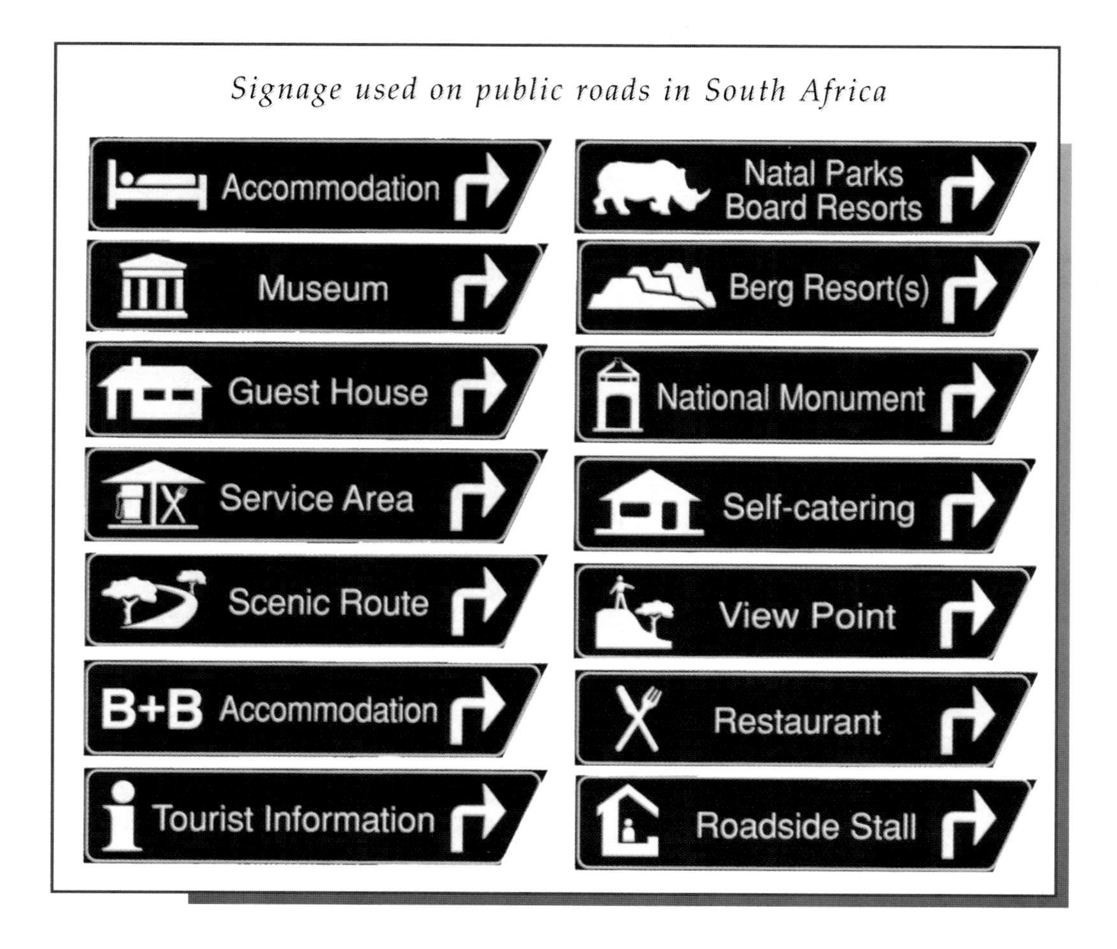

Marking the centenary of the Anglo-Boer War (1899-1902) this guide to the sites of the war has been compiled with visitors and tourists in mind. It is not a comprehensive treatise on the war but, rather, an anecdotal compilation of key sites and aspects of the war – one which does assume an initial interest in the story of the war on the part of the reader. Intended largely for the self-drive visitor or tourist, the guide highlights sites and areas of interest throughout South Africa, giving details on the services available in the areas covered, from accommodation, restaurants and touring options through to museums and collectables. The guide takes a geographical rather than a chronological approach to the sites of the war. Province names within South Africa have changed and we use the new names with reference to the provinces/republics as they were where possible. Wherever relevant, the guide indicates the existence of National Monuments with the use of the *National Monument* symbol. Also included is a recommended reading list for those who may wish to pursue particular points of interest. The following logos as featured against accommodation indicate that they are either of historic interest, Anglo-Boer War interest or are part of an accommodation chain.

*National Monument* logo denotes that the building or product has been proclaimed a National Monument and is of historic interest.

*Cannon* logo refers to an accommodation property that has Anglo-Boer War significance be it historical or informative.

*Portfolio* logo indicates the accommodation establishments that are marketed by Portfolio of Places. For a copy of their guides and additional information contact: Johannesburg (011) 880 3414. Cape Town (021) 686 5400.

***Protea Hotel*** logo covers accommodation properties which form part of the Protea Hotel Group. For central reservations Toll Free 0800 11 9000. For latest directory call (021) 419 5320 or fax (021) 425 2956.

Please support our SATOUR REGISTERED TOUR GUIDES. They have had to attend intensive courses at selected colleges or associations approved by SATOUR (SOUTH AFRICAN TOURIST BOARD), and have had to undergo both written and oral tests to be in a position to supply you with their specialist knowledge on our country and its specific areas.

***Please note: If you are being guided or with a tour where the guide is not a SATOUR REGISTERED TOUR GUIDE, there is a possibility that, in the event of an accident or theft of any personal item, the Insurance company may not be obliged to acknowledge the cover and therefore the claim.*** It is imperative that you assure yourself of the correct credentials of the TOUR GUIDE. The following are examples of the badges in question.

The **BADGE** to be worn by the TOUR GUIDE at all times. (Please, take note of the wording and the shape of the flag as there are occasionally fraudulent copies.)

The **IDENTIFICATION CARD** with photo and tour guide number. Remember: ***Support the Guides with The Knowledge.***

# The Causes of the Anglo-Boer War

The long history of conflict in southern Africa between the expansionist Dutch, later the Afrikaaners, and the colonial British, with the indigenous African population being caught in the middle, is the background to the Anglo-Boer War (1899-1902). Going back to 1652 when the Dutch East India Company established a supply station at the Cape of Good Hope, southern Africa had been a cause of contention between the British and the descendants of these Dutch settlers, the Afrikaaners, or the Boers. During the Napoleonic wars Britain took possession of the Dutch colony at the Cape in 1806 in order to safeguard the sea route to India and beyond. The Afrikaaner people however remained in the majority amongst the white population and the British order for the emancipation of slaves in 1834 precipitated the Great Trek. Between 1835 and 1837 some 5 000 Boers, together with an equal number of black and coloured servants, trekked across the frontiers of the colony to what became known as the Transvaal (across the Vaal River) and the Orange Free State (across the Orange River) and which were recognised by the British as Boer republics in 1852 and 1854 respectively. Meanwhile, in 1843, Britain had created a second colony through the annexation of Natal. In 1877 the British attempted to establish a South African federation with the annexation of the Transvaal. This annexation was reversed in 1881 by Paul Kruger with the defeat of the British at Majuba at the end of the first Anglo-Boer War.

In the meantime, in the global arena, the economic power of 19th Century Britain was being challenged by the rise of Germany and the U.S.A. While Britain's empire had given her a distinct advantage as the world's financial and banking centre, this advantage could only be maintained if further gold reserves could be found to underpin Sterling - the reserves of the Bank of England were running low.

The gold-rich Witwatersrand, part of the Transvaal Republic, was the obvious source. However, not only was this gold supply the preserve of the Transvaal Republic, it was located at very deep levels on the Rand. Mining the gold at these levels required not only complex engineering solutions, but also a government and a society capable of developing the labour force and attracting the capital that such an exercise would entail. The government of the South African Republic (the Transvaal) led by President Paul Kruger, viewed as corrupt and obstructionist by the British, was not considered to be up to the task. As a solution, many in Britain favoured a union of the Transvaal Republic with the Orange Free State; the Cape and Natal under the Union Jack. The British Colonial Office feared the likelihood of such a Union under the flag of the South African Republic, the Vierkleur, rather than the Union Jack. When Lord Milner took over as the British administrator of the Cape Colony in 1897, the Transvaal – with its gold – was the richest and most powerful of the Southern African nations.

*The Executive Council of the South African Republic, 1899,*
Back row: (left to right) A. D. Wolmarans; State Secretary, F. W. Reitz; General Schalk W. Burger; General J.H.M. Kock.
Front row: General P. Joubert; President Paul Kruger; General P.A. Cronje.

Interestingly, the war in South Africa is known by different names. South Africans call it the Anglo-Boer War, the South African War, the Second War of Independence and the Engelse Oorlog (English War). In Canada, Australia, New Zealand and Great Britain it is known quite simply as the Boer War. Even the National Steering Committee for the Centenary calls it The South African War/Anglo-Boereoorlog 1899-1902. A mouthful indeed.

STEVE'S WAR STORIES

It was the issue of the franchise for British subjects living in the Transvaal, known as the Uitlanders (foreigners) that was to be the pretext for the war. Attempts were made to win the franchise for the Uitlanders in the hope that their anticipation in the South African Republic's electoral process would bring about a more enlightened regime. These attempts included lobbying by the "Randlords" (the likes of Rhodes and Beit) and eventually a peace conference in Bloemfontein between Milner (pictured) and Kruger, in May 1899. Ultimately, these attempts failed because even the enfranchising of the Uitlanders would not have brought the Transvaal and its gold under formal British control. The Uitlanders and their grievances had been a pretext and one which worked. The movement of British troops towards the borders of the South African Republic and the Free State provoked Kruger into withdrawing any concession he might have made towards the Uitlanders and on the 11th October 1899, the British Empire was at war with the Boer Republics of the Transvaal and the Orange Free State. In November 1899 the international *"Bankers Magazine"* noted the irony of a situation where the world's leading monetary power was at war with *"a country producing the greater proportion of the world's supply of gold."* ❑

## GOING TO WAR

When war was declared on 11 October 1899, the Boers of the Transvaal and Orange Free State republics had mobilised some 32 000 to 35 000 men. At this time, the British had only about 20 000 troops in the country – although by the end of the war they would have poured more than 400 000 soldiers into South Africa. Before British reinforcements could tip the balance, the Boers planned to invade Natal and the Cape in an ambitious scheme to capture the ports of Durban and Cape Town and the central railway network.

When the Pretoria commando (in which Reitz and his brother served) arrived at Sandspruit, the Boer forces under General Joubert were gathering and the excitement and enthusiasm were intense. At dawn on 12 October, the commandos moved off to invade Natal. *"I shall never forget riding to war with that great host"* Reitz wrote.

*"As far as the eye could see the plain was alive with horsemen, guns and cattle, all steadily going forward to the frontier."*

*Courtesy Volkskas Bank*

# Gold Coinage

*The main cause of the war was Britain's desire for the wealth of the gold mines of the Transvaal. The gold was represented in the form of Ingot and Coinage.*

**BURGHERS STAATSPOND**

The story of the indigenous coinage of our country really begins with the ***1874 Staatspond*** of Thomas Francois Burgers, President of the Transvaal Republic. Following the discovery of alluvial gold at Pilgrim's Rest in the Lydenburg district of the North-Eastern Transvaal in 1873, Burgers sent a quantity of nuggets and gold dust to the Transvaal Consul-General in London with instructions that he should arrange immediately to have coins made from this Transvaal gold of the same value and gold content as the British sovereign. He was to try to have these coins ready in time for the next session of the Volksraad. After some difficulty, a total of **837 of these Burghers Staatsponden** were manufactured by Messrs. Heaton and Sons of Birmingham, using dies which had been especially engraved by L. C. Wyon, engraver at the Royal Mint. At last on 22 September 1874, President Burgers was able to hand **fifty pounds** in Transvaal gold coin to the Chairman of the Volksraad and to seek a formal resolution that they should be declared legal tender in the South African Republic.

**KRUGER COINAGE**

In 1886, gold was discovered on the Witwatersrand and with the considerable economic expansion which followed, the Transvaal Government was persuaded to grant **'The National Bank Concession'** in 1890. As a condition of this concession, the National Bank of the South African Republic undertook to establish a mint in Pretoria to manufacture coins for the Government.

The foundation stone of this Mint which was built on the site of the present General Post Office Building in Church Square, Pretoria, was laid by President Kruger on 6 July 1892. Arrangements had already been made for minting machinery, trained staff and coinage dies to be imported from Germany. Kruger, who was impatient to get his coins into circulation before his imminent election campaign against Joubert and the Chief Justice Kotze, arranged for a preliminary consignment of the new coins to be struck at the Royal Prussian Mint in Berlin. Apart from lesser coins, a **GOLD POND** and **HALFPOND** were to be struck. For the obverse, Prussian Mint engraver, Otto Schultz, produced dies showing the bust of Kruger, facing left. The first batch of these gold coins arrived in Pretoria and Kruger quickly put them into circulation – causing an immediate storm!

On the reverse, the German designer had used a German wagon as the model for the Voortrekker wagon in the central shield of the Republican Coat-of-Arms. The German wagon had two shafts, and front and rear wheels were the same diameter – instead of the single-shafted wagon of the Voortrekkers. The bitter presidential campaign of 1893 was underway and Joubert's supporters were quick to capitalise on this trump card which had been placed so unexpectedly in their hands. In particular they seized on the fact that the designers initials ***'O.S.'***, which had been placed in accordance with minting tradition on Kruger's bust on the obverse of the gold coins, spelt the Dutch word for **ox**. Their candidate, they cried, would surely beat this ***'O.S.'* Kruger** in the race for the presidency!

Consternation reigned in the Kruger camp. Immediate orders were issued for the withdrawal of the coins and instructions were passed to Berlin that new dies were to be prepared immediately showing the correct South African single-shafted tented wagon. Above all, the offending ***'O.S.'***

initials were to be removed from the President's bust. In the event, Kruger beat Joubert by a narrow margin and was returned for a third term as President. In due course new coins bearing the corrected coat-of-arms arrived from Germany and were put into circulation, to be followed later the same year by coins struck at the Pretoria Mint. The error double-shaft is found only on the **POND, HALF-POND** and **FIVE SHILLING PIECE** dated **1892**, but the initials ***'O.S.'*** appear only on the **TWO GOLD COINS**. Operations at the Pretoria Mint continued until 1897. The two gold pieces of the Kruger series were struck each year from 1892 to 1897.

The Mint was closed at the beginning of 1898, but was reopened twenty-one months later when war clouds loomed at the end of September 1899. At that stage it was decided to strike a considerable quantity of gold ponde, but because the 1899 dies had not arrived from Germany, the dies which had been prepared for 1898 had to be used. Between October 1899, and the beginning of June 1900, when the Government evacuated Pretoria ahead of Lord Roberts advancing army, *almost a million gold ponde were struck*, but all were dated either 1898 or 1900.

To mark the war-time reopening of the Mint and to record that it was operating in 1899, a Mint official was instructed to overstamp a few of the ponde. He took a tiny punch of the number ***'9'*** and struck ***'99'*** just under the bust on the obverse of **130 of the ponde dated 1898**. These historic pieces are very valuable today.

During this period special permission was given to Mr. Samuel Marks, one of the financial giants of the early days of the goldfields on the Witwatersrand and a personal friend of the President, to have some threepenny pieces - or *tickeys* - struck in gold. Dies dated 1898 for the complete series of Transvaal coins had previously been received from Germany but had not been used. The obverse and reverse dies for the threepence were, however, taken out of stock, and 215 of what we know today as the '*Sammy Marks Tickey*' dated 1898 were struck in gold for Mr Marks. They were of course not legal tender and did not circulate, but are regarded as rare and interesting pattern coins.

The planned programme for the production of Kruger ponde in 1900 had not yet been completed when the Transvaal Government evacuated Pretoria on 4 June, 1900. At the last minute trusted officials went to the Mint and, in the name of the Government, removed all gold and silver coins still in the Mint office. They also took the small amount of bar gold still in stock, and a quantity of unfinished gold coin blanks. Many of these blanks, some of which had a raised rim and some of which were plain discs, had concentric scraper markings on them and they were all of course of the correct weight of a Kruger pond. They therefore contained a pound's worth of gold. They were later used by the Government as money when supplies of properly minted coins became exhausted. They became known as ***'kaal ponde'*** and circulated to some extent in the Republican army.

**Z.A.R. VELD POND**

The final chapter in the history of the coinage of the Transvaal belongs to the **Z.A.R. VELD POND. 896** of these historic pieces were struck in romantic circumstances from hand-made dies at the ***'Staatsmunt te Velde'*** at Pilgrim's Rest during the closing phase of the Anglo-Boer War, in March and April 1902. Manufactured from gold recovered at the local alluvial diggings, they bear on the obverse the monogram ***'Z.A.R.' '1902'***, and on the reverse the value ***'EEN POND'***. They were properly authorised and ordered by the Republican Government in the field and rank numismatically as ***'siege pieces'***. Their gold content is probably slightly in excess of their face value. ❑

***Indication of value of Boer Gold Coins of Anglo-Boer War period***

| | |
|---|---|
| *1900 Kruger Pond from:* | *S.A. Rands 1 250* |
| *Undated ZAR Pond Blank from:* | *S.A. Rands 4 000–20 000* |
| *1902 ZAR Veld Pond from:* | *S.A. Rands 7 500–25 000* |

***For information on gold coinage, contact:***



**BRITISH COINAGE IN THE FOUR COLONIES**

British coinage had been the legal medium of exchange in the Cape Colony and in Natal since before the middle of the 19th century, and circulated freely alongside the Kruger coinage in the Boer Republics of the Orange Free State and the Transvaal.

During the period of reconstruction which followed the Anglo-Boer War, and which led to the granting of colonial self-government to the two former Republics; the Kruger coinage continued to circulate in both territories. Difficulties were experienced however because increasing numbers of Kruger coins were carried to Natal and parti-cularly to the Cape Colony and caused confusion because they were not legal tender there.

The Government of the Cape of Good Hope was anxious that the entire Kruger coinage should be withdrawn and reminted into British coin, but the Transvaal Colonial Government was in no financial position to welcome the loss which would have devolved upon it. It was acknowledged furthermore, that there was a strong sentimental attachment to the coins of the old Republic in both the Transvaal and the Orange River Colony.

In the event, sentiment won, and when the four colonies came together in 1910 to form the Union of South Africa, Kruger coins were declared legal tender throughout South Africa. To this day they have not been demonetised although they have long since disappeared completely from circulation. ❑

## *The war has turned my wife insane!*

*The war, the war, the bloomin' war, has turned my wife insane.*
*From Kruger to Majuba, she's the Transvaal on the brain.*
*We went to christen our first child, last Sunday week we tried,*
*The parson said "What's this child's name?" and my old gal replied:*
*The baby's name is Kitchener, Carrington, Methuen, Kekewich, White,*
*Cronje, Plumer, Powell, Majuba, Gatacre, Warren, Colenso, Kruger,*
*Cape Town, Mafeking, French, Kimberley, Ladysmith, "Bobs",*
*Union Jack, Fighting Mac, Lyddite, Pretoria, Blobbs.*

The song was written by C. W. Murray and Albert Hall (the famous *Albert Hall* was named in his honour). Sung to the tune by Murphy and published by Francis, Day and Hunter. It sold for 4 shillings a copy and was sung in music halls in England by Charles Bignell.

STEVE'S WAR STORIES

THE CUT-OUT PIECE OF ENGINE BOILER PLATE SHOWS THE HOLE MADE BY A '9-POUNDER' SHELL FIRED INTO THE BOILER OF THE ARMOURED TRAIN, ABOUT THREE Km SOUTH OF KRAAIPAN STATION-70 Km SOUTH-WEST OF MAFIKENG, WHICH WAS PROCEEDING TO MAFIKENG ON THE NIGHT OF THE 12TH OCTOBER 1899 ON THE OUTBREAK OF HOSTILITIES.

THE FEW PIECES OF SHELL SHRAPNEL WERE TAKEN OUT OF THE BOILER OF THE LOCOMOTIVE.

THE SHOT IS REPORTED TO HAVE BEEN THE FIRST FIRED IN THE ANGLO-BOER WAR. CAPTAIN NESBITT WAS IN CHARGE OF THE TRAIN AND HE AND HIS MEN WERE CAPTURED BY THE BOERS AT KRAAIPAN WHERE THE ENGINE WAS WRECKED.

Mafikeng Museum.

## STATISTICS OF THE WAR

Clinically cold, statistics tell the story of an horrific war, and more often than not, take the glamour out of it. Wars still continue around the world, however, no matter what the statistics.

The Anglo-Boer War started on 11 October 1899 and terminated on 31 May 1902, with a loss for the Imperial forces of some 22 664 dead. From 1 June 1902 until the departure of British troops in early 1914 there were an additional 1 718 deaths. Such statistics are meaningless since shortly after the termination of hostilities, deaths occurred as a result of wounds or disease contracted during the war.

Here are some Imperial Forces statistics:

| | | | |
|---|---|---|---|
| Killed in action | 5 570 | Killed by lightning | 69 |
| Died of wounds/injuries | 2 482 | Killed in railway accidents | 194 |
| Died of disease | 13 442 | Murdered | 17 |
| Drowned | 274 | | |

STEVE'S WAR STORIES

*Thomas Pakenham excerpted from* The Boer War

# Events preceding and leading into the War

**1895**

***December 29***

Jameson launches Raid into Transvaal with 500 Chartered Company police from Pitsani and Mafeking.

**1896**

Battle of Doornkop. Jameson surrenders. Arrest and trial of Johannesburg Reform Committee. Rhodes resigns as Prime Minister at the Cape. Cape Enquiry into Raid.

**1897**

London Enquiry into Raid. Sir Alfred Milner takes over as British High Commissioner at the Cape.

**1898**

Kruger elected for fourth term as President of Transvaal.

**1898/9**

Milner back in London for *'holiday'*.

**1899**

***May 31 - June 5***

Bloemfontein Conference

***September***

8 : British Cabinet decides to send 10 000 men to defend Natal
26 : Penn Symons pushes up troops to Dundee
27 : Kruger calls up Transvaal burghers, and persuades Steyn to follow suit in Free State

***October***

7 : British mobilise 1st Army Corps etc. White lands at Durban
9 : Kruger sends ultimatum
11 : Expiry of ultimatum and outbreak of war
14 : Boers begin siege of Kekewich at Kimberley and of Baden-Powell at Mafeking
20 : Penn Symons gives battle at Talana. Moller surrenders
21 : Battle of Elandslaagte
24 : Battle of Rietfontein
30 : *'Mournful Monday'*: Joubert outmanoeuvres White at Battle of Ladysmith (Modderspruit) and Carleton is forced to surrender at Nicholson's Nek
31 : General Buller lands at Cape Town

***November***

2 : White's *'field force'* accepts siege at Ladysmith
15 : Botha wrecks armoured train between Frere and Chieveley
22 : Battle of Willow Grange

23 : End of Botha's and Joubert's raid southward into Natal. Methuen's first battle: Belmont
25 : Methuen's second battle: Graspan
26 : Holdsworth, with *Linchwe's Africans*, attacks Boer laager at Derdepoort
28 : Methuen's third battle: Modder River

*December*

7 : Huter's night raid on *Long Tom* besieging Ladysmith
10 : Gatacre's mishap at Stormberg
11 : Methuen's repulse at Magersfontein
15 : Buller's first reverse: Colenso
18 : Roberts appointed to succeed Buller as C-in-C in South Africa, with Kitchener as Chief of Staff
26 : Baden-Powell's abortive attack on Game Tree Fort
29 : German mail-steamer *Bundesrath* seized by Royal Navy

**1900**

*January*

6 : Boers attack Caesar's Camp and Wagon Hill (Platrand) at Ladysmith
10 : Roberts and Kitchener land at Cape Town
24 : Battle of Spion Kop

*February*

5 : Vaal Krantz captured, then evacuated
11 : Roberts begins great flank march
14 : Buller's fourth attempt to relieve Ladysmith
15 : French relieves Kimberley
18 : Battle of Paardeberg
27 : ***Surrender of Cronje at Paardeberg***
28 : Buller relieves Ladysmith

*March*

7 : Battle of Poplar Grove. Kruger escapes
10 : Battle of Driefontein
13 : **Capture of Bloemfontein**
15 : Roberts first proclamation: amnesty except for leaders
17 : Boer Council of War at Kroonstad
27 : Death of Joubert
31 : De Wet ambushes Broadwood at Sannah's Post

*April*

4 : Surrender of Royal Irish at Reddersburg

*May*

3 : Roberts resumes march to Pretoria
4 : Mahon's relief column sets out for Mafeking
11 : Buller resumes advance
12 : Roberts occupies Kroonstad. Baden-Powell beats off Eloff's attack on Mafeking
14 : Buller outmanoeuvres Boers from Biggarsberg
17 : Mahon and Plumer relieve Mafeking
28 : **Annexation of Orange Free State proclaimed**: renamed Orange River Colony
31 : **Roberts captures Johannesburg.** Piet De Wet captures Spragge and Irish Yeomanry at Lindley

*June*

5 : **Roberts captures Pretoria**. Release of prisoners
7 : Christiaan De Wet's success at Roodewal
11 : Battle of Diamond Hill
12 : Buller turns Drakensberg position and occupies Volksrust

*July*

11 : Surrender of Scots Greys at Zilikat's Nek
15 : Steyn and De Wet escape from Brandwater Basin
21 : Roberts begins advance towards Komati Poort
31 : Surrender of Prinsloo to Hunter in Brandwater Basin

*August*

14 : Ian Hamilton fails to prevent De Wet's escape
27 : Buller defeats Botha at Bergendal (Dalmanutha)
30 : Release of last 2000 British prisoners at Nooitgedacht

*September*

6 : **Buller captures Lydenburg**
25 : Pole-Carew reaches Komati Poort

*October*

19 : Kruger sails for France on board the *Gelderland*
24 : Buller sails for England
25 : Formal proclamation at Pretoria of annexation of Transvaal

*November*

6 : De Wet defeated at Bothaville. Le Gallais killed
29 : Kitchener succeeds Roberts as C-in-C in South Africa. Roberts to succeed Wolseley as C-in-C at home

*December*

13 : De la Rey and Smuts surprise Clements at Nooitgedacht
16 : Kritzinger enters Cape Colony
29 : Helvetia post captured

**1901**

*27 January-26 March*

French's drive in Eastern Transvaal

*January*

31 : Smuts captures Modderfontein. Massacre of Africans

*February*

10 : De Wet's *'invasion'* of Cape Colony
28 : **Abortive Middelburg peace talks between Kitchener and Botha**

*April*

10 : First drive in Northern Free State begins

*May*

8 : Milner sails for leave in England

*July*

18 : First drive in Cape Colony northwards

*August*

7 : Kitchener's proclamation of banishment for Boer leaders captured armed after 15 September
12 : Kritzinger driven out of Cape Colony

*September*
3 : Smuts invasion of Cape Colony via Kiba Drift
5 : Scobell captures Lotter's commando
7 : Smuts cuts up 17th Lancers at Elands River Poort
17 : Botha cuts up Gough's force at Blood River poort
26 : Botha attacks Forts Itala and Prospect

*October*
6 : Botha escapes northward
11 : Execution of Commandant Lotter. Capture of Scheepers
30 : Benson killed at Bakenlaagte

*November*
7 : Ian Hamilton appointed Kitchener's Chief of Staff

*December*
7 : National Scouts inaugurated
16 : Kritzinger captured
23 : Kroonstad-Lindley blockhouse line completed
25 : De Wet captures Yeomanry at Tweefontein

**1902**

*January*
17 : Scheepers executed

*February*
6 : New drive in Eastern Orange River Colony. De Wet breaks out Rawlinson's success

*March*
7 : De la Rey captures Methuen at Tweebosch
24 : First drive in W. Transvaal
26 : **Death of Cecil Rhodes**

*April 4-May 3*
Smuts besieges O'Okiep

*April*
11 : Battle of Rooiwal
12 : **Boer peace delegates' first meeting at Pretoria**

*May*
1 : Last drives in North Eastern Orange River Colony
6 : **Zulu attack on Holkrantz**
11 : End of Ian Hamilton's last drive in Western Transvaal
15 : **First meeting of Boer delegates at Vereeniging**
31 : ***Final meeting at Vereeniging. Surrender terms signed at Pretoria.***

## Love Letters

Sorting through the English Christmas mail taken from a sabotaged train, a letter was found addressed by a titled lady to an army Officer in which she wished her lawful husband *'in hell'*. She mentioned that she had enclosed a cartridge belt embroidered with silk from her petticoat. (Schikkerling, 159).

*Boet Dommisse*

# The Three Fronts

*The strategy planned by the British forces was based on a three pronged offensive which followed the railway lines. The railway lines had to be defended at all costs as they constituted the main arteries for movement of troops, supplies and equipment. The British forces set out from Cape Town, Port Elizabeth and Durban along the three main lines which were the Western Front, the Central Front and the Natal Front. The Boer forces, in the meantime, realised the vital importance of the railway lines and did their utmost to hamper, delay and destroy the British supply columns at strategic points on the lines. In essence, the First Stage of the war was fought along the railway lines, and who ever controlled the railways controlled the balance of power.* *See map on page 18.*

## THE WESTERN FRONT

The British forces, initially under the command of Major General Lord Methuen, advanced along and alongside the railway line from Cape Town to the North, toward Bloemfontein and Pretoria. The first objective was to relieve besieged Kimberley. The Boer forces were commanded by General Piet Cronje and General Koos De la Rey.

| Date | Event | Synopsis |
|---|---|---|
| **1899** | | |
| Oct 12 | Kraaipan | In the first attack of the war the Boers destroyed the rail bridge south of Mafeking. |
| Oct 13 | Mafeking | Defence and later siege of Mafeking. Attack led by Gen. Cronje. Mafeking defended by Lt. Col. Baden-Powell and 2 I/C. Col. Lord Edward Cecil, son of the British Prime Minister the Marquess of Salisbury. |
| Oct 16 | Kimberley | Besieged by Boers under Commandant Wessels. Cecil Rhodes was detained in Kimberley, where the British forces were under Col. R.G. Kekewich. |
| | Matjiesfontein | The Milner Hotel had been recently built by James Logan, and was a base camp for the advancing forces. |
| Nov 23 | Belmont | Methuen's troops, including the Guards Brigade, attacked three hills defended by Boers under General Prinsloo. There were heavy losses on both sides. |
| Nov 25 | Graspan | Also known as Enslin. A major kopje was successfully attacked by troops led by the Naval Brigade. |
| Nov 28 | Modder River | General Koos De la Rey cleverly positioned his forces on the banks of the river bed, shooting down Methuen's advancing troops at ground level. General Methuen was wounded and De la Rey lost his son in this battle. |
| Dec 11 | Magersfontein | The defence of Magersfontein by digging a long trench line in front of the kopje, was planned by De la Rey, Cronje and President Steyn. De la Rey was not present at the battle. After a day's bombardment, the British forces, headed by the *Black Watch,* were led by Major General Andy Wauchope in a night march. It was a stormy night and they were unaware of the Boer trenches. Deployed only 400 metres from the Boer lines, they were mowed down. The battle continued all through a blazing hot day. Casualties, including Wauchope, who was later reburied at Matjiesfontein, were heavy. **This was the second disaster of '*Black Week*'.** |

| Date | Event | Synopsis |
|---|---|---|
| **1900** | | |
| Jan 10 | Cape Town | Field Marshal Lord Roberts and Maj. Gen. F.W. Kitchener arrive to take command and proceed to the Western Front. |
| Feb 15 | Kimberley | Siege relieved by General French. Duration four months. |
| Feb 17 | Paardeberg | General Cronje abandoned Magersfontein and was proceeding toward Bloemfontein. Encamped on the Modder River, he was attacked by Gen. French and surrounded by British troops under Roberts and Kitchener. The siege and battles lasted for 10 days. 4 000 Boers were taken prisoners of war. Many were sick and wounded. The PoWs were transferred to Simon's Town and Cape Town. They were later shipped to St. Helena, Bermuda and Ceylon. |
| Mar 13 | Bloemfontein | Lord Roberts entered the city. |
| Mar 31 | Sannah's Post | General Christiaan de Wet caught General Broadwood's Brigade exposed and helpless, inflicting a heavy defeat. The British fought bravely and four VCs were awarded. |
| Apr 9 | Wepener | Col. Dalgety who commanded 2 000 troops were besieged for seven days by Christiaan de Wet, who departed rapidly when reinforcements arrived. |
| Mar 17 | Mafeking | Relief of Mafeking by French, Plumer and Mahon. Siege lasted almost eight months. |
| Mar 28 | Lindley | Defeat of 13th Battalion by Piet de Wet and Marthinus Prinsloo. |
| May 29 | Doornkop | Lt. Gen. Ian Hamilton and Gen. French defeat Gen. Louis Botha's forces and open up the way to Johannesburg. |
| May 31 | Johannesburg | Lord Roberts enters the city. |
| June 5 | Pretoria | British forces occupy Pretoria, the capital city of the Transvaal. The first phase of the war closes but the Boers refuse to surrender. |

## THE CENTRAL FRONT

Sir Alfred Milner, Governor of the Cape Colony, feared an invasion by the Boers from the sea via Port Elizabeth and East London to defend this border.

| | | |
|---|---|---|
| **1899** | | |
| Dec 10 | Stormberg | Major General Sir William Gatacre undertook a night march from Molteno to attack Stormberg Junction. They lost their way and passed through a valley overlooked by the Kissieberg, which was occupied by the Boers, led by General Olivier. They were gunned down from above, sustaining 90 casualties and losing 600 men as PoWs. **This was the beginning of '*Black Week*'.** |

### Boer Qualities

*"The Boer has three rare qualities, hospitality, bravery, and a sense of humour. He is the most vigorous, resourceful, and intelligent peasant in the world. There is an old-time courtesy and chivalry about him, due to his birth, which takes off his hat when he salutes you; yet, at the same time he will not pamper idle women, nor follow the vagaries of a society that less readily forgives an offence against etiquette than an act of dishonour. He is law-abiding and has a reverend regard for custom, and certainly has the best blood in the colonies".* (Schikkerling, 169)

ROB MILNE

| Date | Event | Synopsis |
|---|---|---|
| **1900** | | |
| Jan | Colesburg | Several battles and skirmishes took place in this area, including Grass Hill, Cybergat and New Zealand Hill. The Boers were under General Olivier and General Schoeman, joined later by General Koos De la Rey. General French, Major Douglas Haig and Major Allenby commanded the British forces. French later made a rapid dash westward – to relieve the besieged Kimberley on 15 February 1900. Immediately he went to initiate the defeat of General Piet Cronje at Paardeberg, where he was joined by Lord Roberts and General Kitchener. |

## THE NATAL FRONT

The line from Durban was the most direct route to the Transvaal. The Boers, commanded by General Piet Joubert, fiercely defended this approach. He was later superseded by General Louis Botha. The British forces led by Lt.-Gen. Sir George White were initially repulsed and besieged in Ladysmith. After several disasters General Sir Redvers Buller was able to relieve Ladysmith on 28 February 1900 and advance to meet up with Lord Roberts near Pretoria on 4 July 1900.

| Date | Event | Synopsis |
|---|---|---|
| **1899** | | |
| Oct 20 | Talana | Battle near Dundee. Boers led by Generals Lucas Meyer and Erasmus engaged British forces, bravely lead by Major General Sir William Penn-Symons who was fatally wounded. Major General J.H. Yule then withdrew to Ladysmith. |
| Oct 21 | Elandslaagte | British troops, led by General Sir John French, successfully engaged Boers under General Kock, after intense fighting, including cavalry charges with lances. However British forces later retired to Ladysmith. |
| Oct 30 | Nicholson's Nek | Lt.-General George White undertook a night march north of Ladysmith. Troops led by Colonel Carleton were ambushed when their mules stampeded. 800 PoWs were taken. Encounters at Tchrengula and Modderspruit, also known as Battle of Farquhars Farm, followed the same day. On 31st White finally withdrew to Ladysmith. The Boers were led by General Louis Botha and his vice-commander Christiaan de Wet. |
| Nov 2 | Ladysmith | The Boer forces surrounded the town, cutting off the rail line to Durban. White's entire British force and the civilian population were besieged until 28 February 1900. The Commander-in-Chief of the Boer's, General Piet Joubert decided not to advance any further. |
| Nov 15 | Chieveley | An armoured train sent out from Estcourt was derailed and ambushed by the Boers who captured 70 prisoners including Winston Churchill, who was a war correspondent for the *'Morning Post'*, but was armed. He later escaped from Pretoria and returned to the Natal Front. |
| Nov 23 | Willow Grange | Louis Botha successfully fended off an attack from the command at Estcourt. |
| Nov 25 | Frere | General, The Rt. Hon. Sir Redvers Buller arrived from Cape Town to command the Natal forces. |
| Dec 15 | Colenso | Buller decided to cross the Tugela River to reach Ladysmith – inexplicably White in Ladysmith was not informed. The British forces advanced on three fronts. On the right flank toward |

PomPom going to the front.

This searchlight train was effective but the armoured train which operated out of Escourt along the same line to Colenso was less highly thought of by the British troops who regarded it as a potential death trap. Whether or not this was so, the fact remains that the fate that befell it on 15 November 1899, became one of the best known stories of the war, for this was the occasion when the train was derailed and Winston Churchill was taken prisoner.

The Boers also made good use of the railways while they could and the line from Pretoria to Delagoa Bay was their only means of contact with the outside world. It was over this line that Kruger travelled when he left Pretoria on 29 May 1900, to move by stages to the Moçambique border at Komatipoort where he finally took leave of the Transvaal and crossed into exile.

With Kruger gone from Pretoria and the British set to enter on 5 June, it was suddenly realised that a considerable amount of gold and currency still remained at the Mint and in the local banks. On the initiative of Jan Smuts this was hurriedly collected and put on a train which got away from Pretoria station just before the British arrived. These were the funds which, incidentally, formed the basis for the legend of the *'Kruger Millions'*.

The last major engagement of the war in which, once again, Smuts was the principal figure, was the siege of O'Okiep in Namaqualand. The siege of this small copper mining town had been in progress for three weeks when, on 24 April 1902, Smuts was summoned to a conference of Boer leaders at Vereeniging to discuss possible peace terms. Smuts and two colleagues were given safe conduct passes by the British and they travelled 100 km down from Steinkopf to Port Nolloth on the Cape Copper Company's narrow gauge railway. There they were taken by ship to Cape Town and from there on by train to the Transvaal. The Treaty of Vereeniging,

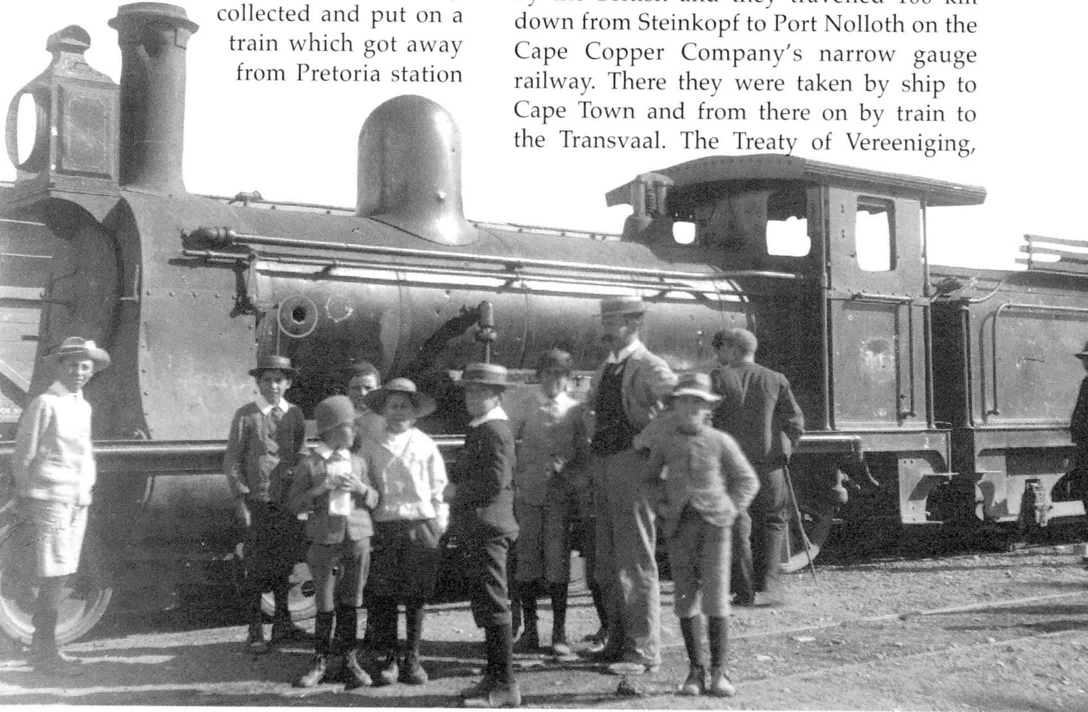

The red circle indicates the first shell fired by the Boers on an armoured train. Refer page 9.

signed in Pretoria, 31 May 1902, brought the war to an end but the war-worn railways were left with the immense task of moving the flood of returning refugees and conveying the troops back to the ports on their return to Britain, New Zealand, Australia and Canada.

Finally, one must not forget the role played by the unsung heroes of the *Railway Pioneer Regiment* whose job it was to repair the lines and protect the trains as best they could. The Regiment was started for the Anglo-Boer War on the 18 December 1899. It was 750 strong by February 1900 and rose to four battalions strength.

The Corps owed its inception largely to Mr. L.G. Seymour, an American engineer, who suggested the enrolment of the many skilled men who were refugees at the Cape from the Johannesburg mines. Major J. E. Capper commanded the Corps and after October 1900 the Corps was employed on Military Police and Outpost duties on the Rand (Gauteng). The strength of the four battalions was over 2 000 men and they were disbanded at the end of the war. ❑

Pictured above: Soldiers alighting from a train.

Below: Soldiers with one of the Naval guns.

## Inaccessible Treasure

The manifest of a train ambushed near Balfour showed that £60 000 were in a safe in the rear compartment. With no explosives left the Boers tried firing into the lock, to no avail.

**Heidelbergers of the Boer War**, *Ian Uys*

## Alcohol

Jack van den Heever and his brother, Gert, lay exposed under the hot summer sun in the veld near Val station (between Standerton and Greylingstad) waiting to blow up a suitable goods train. Their expectations were not in vain as the train which was disabled contained 'fat plunder', and was afterwards known as the 'Whisky' train. Jack was so thirsty that he soon emptied bottles of different types of alcohol, and afterward had to be taken back to camp on the back of a trolley.

**Heidelbergers of the Boer War**, *Ian Uys*

Boers searching for lost ammunition on a deserted British campground.

*Compliments: Morleys Antiques, Cape Tow*

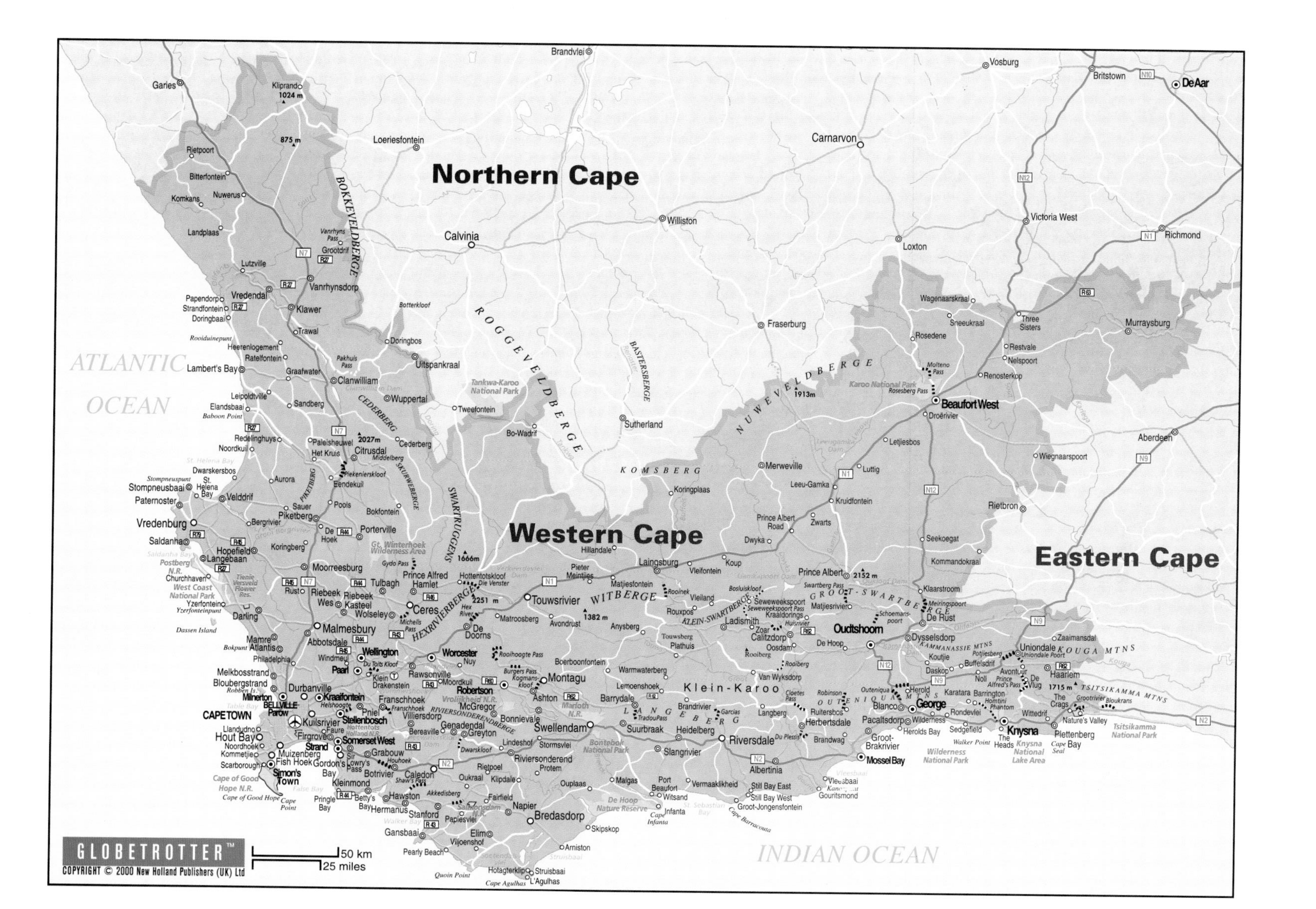
Northern Cape
Western Cape
Eastern Cape
ATLANTIC OCEAN
INDIAN OCEAN
BOKKEVELDBERGE
ROGGEVELDBERGE
BASTERSBERGE
NUWEVELDBERGE
KOMSBERG
CEDERBERG
SKURWEBERGE
SWARTRUGGENS
PIKETBERG
HEXRIVIERBERGE
WITBERGE
KLEIN-SWARTBERGE
GROOT-SWARTBERGE
LANGEBERG
OUTENIQUA MTNS
KAMMANASSIE MTNS
KOUGA MTNS
TSITSIKAMMA MTNS
Klein-Karoo
Tankwa-Karoo National Park
Karoo National Park
West Coast National Park
Bontebok National Park
Wilderness National Park
Knysna National Lake Area
Tsitsikamma National Park
De Hoop Nature Reserve
Cape of Good Hope N.R.
Garies
Brandvlei
Vosburg
Britstown
De Aar
Carnarvon
Loeriesfontein
Calvinia
Williston
Loxton
Victoria West
Richmond
Fraserburg
Sutherland
Beaufort West
Murraysburg
Aberdeen
Vanrhynsdorp
Vredendal
Klawer
Clanwilliam
Citrusdal
Lambert's Bay
Piketberg
Vredenburg
Saldanha
Langebaan
Moorreesburg
Malmesbury
Tulbagh
Ceres
Worcester
Wellington
Paarl
Stellenbosch
Franschhoek
Robertson
Montagu
Touwsrivier
Laingsburg
Prince Albert
Oudtshoorn
George
Knysna
Plettenberg Bay
Mossel Bay
Riversdale
Swellendam
Bredasdorp
Hermanus
Caledon
Somerset West
Strand
Simon's Town
Hout Bay
CAPE TOWN
Bellville
Parow
Durbanville
Ladismith
Calitzdorp
Uniondale
Cape Agulhas
L'Agulhas
Struisbaai
50 km
25 miles
GLOBETROTTER™

*Boet Dommisse*

# War Sites in and about Cape Town

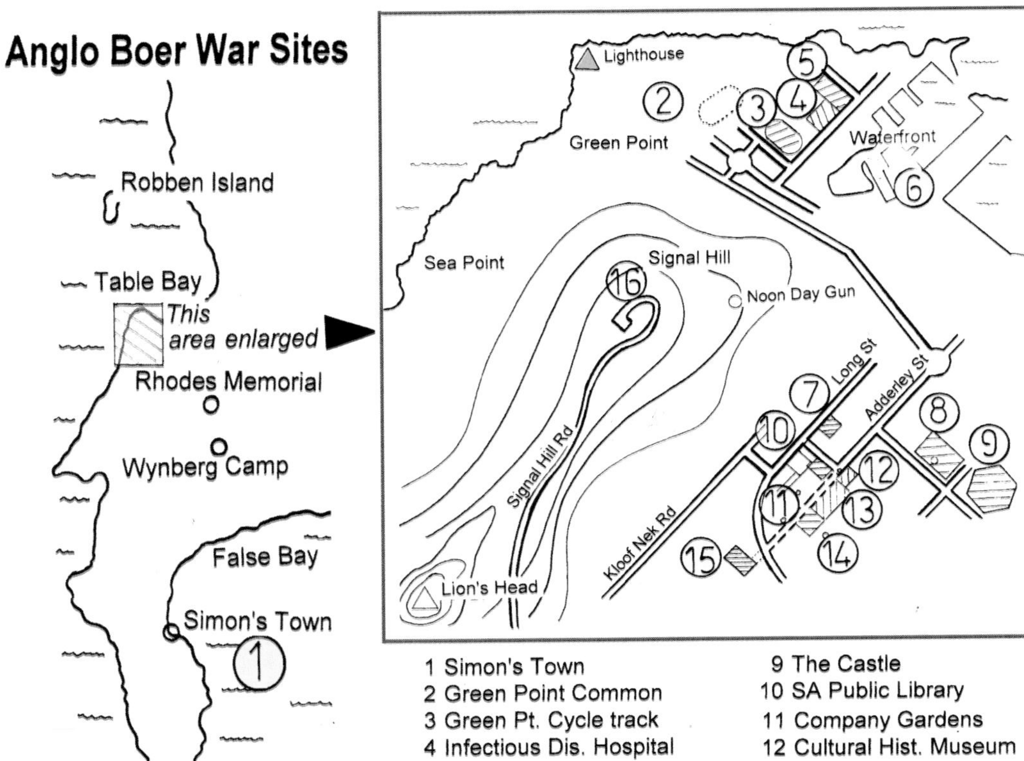


Cape Town was the seat of the Government of the Cape Colony during the Anglo-Boer War. Capetonians were generally very 'pro-British', but there was also sympathy and some support for the Boer Republics. The war brought considerable prosperity to the Cape – produce and other prices rose sharply.

Many arriving troop and supply ships were anchored in Table Bay and, the Alfred Dock (now the *'Waterfront'*) was the port used for the disembarkation of troops arriving from Britain, Canada, Australia and elsewhere. Regiments paraded up Adderley Street and on the Grand Parade, much to the delight of the public who turned out in great numbers to greet them.

An aerial view of Green Point (Circa 1900).

The main troop camps were at **Maitland**, the **Rosebank** showgrounds, and on **Green Point Common**. General Hospitals were established in or near to these camps and No. 1 and No. 2 General (Military) Hospitals were established at **Wynberg**. Some of these buildings are still present in the present Wynberg Military Camp. It was the arrival of large numbers of sick and wounded troops from the front lines that brought home the realities of war to the Cape Town public.

A large Boer prisoner of war camp was established on the **Green Point Cycle Track**, adjacent to the Green Point Common. Most of these Boer PoWs were in transit – to camps in Ceylon, Bermuda, St. Helena and elsewhere. There was a large prisoner of war camp at **Simon's Town** (Bellevue). The best overview of these sites is from **Signal Hill**. This is easily accessible by car or taxi from Kloof Nek along the Signal Hill road, and affords spectacular views over the city, the harbour and Table Bay.

Looking out over **Table Bay** toward **Robben Island** one can picture troop and other ships under steam or sail (or both) at anchor in the bay. In the foreground lies the **Green Point Common**, now sportfields, but in 1899 – 1902, it was the site of large troop encampments, also housing Green Point Camp Hospital. Immediately beyond this, nearer the Waterfront is the **Old Cycle Track**, site of the PoW camp and adjacent to this, the **Infectious Disease Hospital** that was used by the Imperial Military authorities as No. 6 Stationary Hospital. This complex now houses the **Medical Museum** and is well worth a visit. The turreted **New Somerset Hospital** next to this was a civilian hospital during the war.

There is a fine view of the Waterfront complex from **Signal Hill** and one can picture the troops disembarking in the Alfred Dock and marching up Adderley Street with bands playing and flags unfurled! Looking down over the present city several important Anglo-Boer War sites can be identified.

The **Cape Town Castle** (completed in 1679) where the **British Military Command** was sited, has recently been restored and is open to the public. The **Castle Museum** has planned an exhibit of Anglo-Boer War memorabilia and uniforms. Alongside the Castle is the **Grand Parade**, scene of many Military parades and assemblies of the Town Guard. The large statue is of Edward VII, who succeeded Queen Victoria on 22 January, 1901.

On the near side of Adderley Street lies **Green Market Square**, located next to the church tower of the Metropolitan Methodist Church. **Green Market Square** (*now a craft and traders open market*) was the site of many important public meetings and proclamations during the war years. On 3 April 1900 the following Resolution was passed with great enthusiasm at a meeting on this square: *"As British*

*subjects assembled in Cape Town, we desire to express our entire concurrence with the refusal of Her Majesty's Ministers to allow the South African Republic and the Orange Free State to return to their independence, and we hereby declare our solemn conviction that incorporation of those States within the Dominions of the Queen can alone secure peace, prosperity, and public freedom throughout South Africa".*

One of the lions at the Castle entrance.

The **Company Gardens** can be identified as one looks down over the city towards Table Mountain. A walk up **Government Avenue**, which has changed little in the past century, is an excellent way to picture Cape Town in the days of the Anglo-Boer War.

**Government Avenue** commences at the top of Adderley Street. As you enter, the **South African Cultural Museum** is on the left, with Mitford-Barberton's statue of **General Smuts** in front and a statue of **Queen Victoria** in the adjacent grounds of Parliament. **St. George's Cathedral** is on the right and next to this the **South African Public Library**, which has an excellent collection of books, newspapers, etc., relevant to a study of the Anglo-Boer War.

Walking up Government Avenue, the **Company Gardens**, established by Jan van Riebeeck soon after his arrival in 1652, are on the right and there is a fine statue of **Cecil John Rhodes** in the Gardens near the tea-room. The Houses of Parliament are on your left and after this **Tuynhuys**, the official residence of the State President. **Tuynhuys** was Government House during the Anglo-Boer War and was where Sir Alfred Milner received the telegram from Prime Minister Joseph Chamberlain, authorising intervention in the *'Uitlander Question'*. It is also here that the ultimatum from President Paul Kruger was received on 11 October 1899. The main entrance to Tuynhuys is at the top of Plein Street. The **Eternal Flame Memorial** for "*All who fought and died for their Beliefs*", is near this entrance, and also an imposing equestrian statue of **General Louis Botha**. Further up Government Avenue, a more impressionistic statue of **Smuts**, by Harpley, and finally opposite the top gates of the Avenue the grand pillared entrance to the **Mount Nelson Hotel**. Many important and interesting persons stayed here during the war and the Mount Nelson was the venue for many balls and social events.

A visit to **Simon's Town** is essential. On route a visit to the **Rhodes Memorial**, situated on the slopes of Devil's Peak, above the University of Cape Town, is worthwhile. This impressive memorial embodies a powerful equestrian statue *'Energy'* by G.F. Watts, and beneath the bust of Cecil Rhodes are the words Rudyard Kipling wrote on Rhode's death in 1902.

"*The immense and moving spirit still shall quicken and control. Living he was the land and dead his soul shall be her soul*". Such were the sentiments of the British Empire and her colonies at the time. ❑

The Castle with the lions "guarding" the entrance.

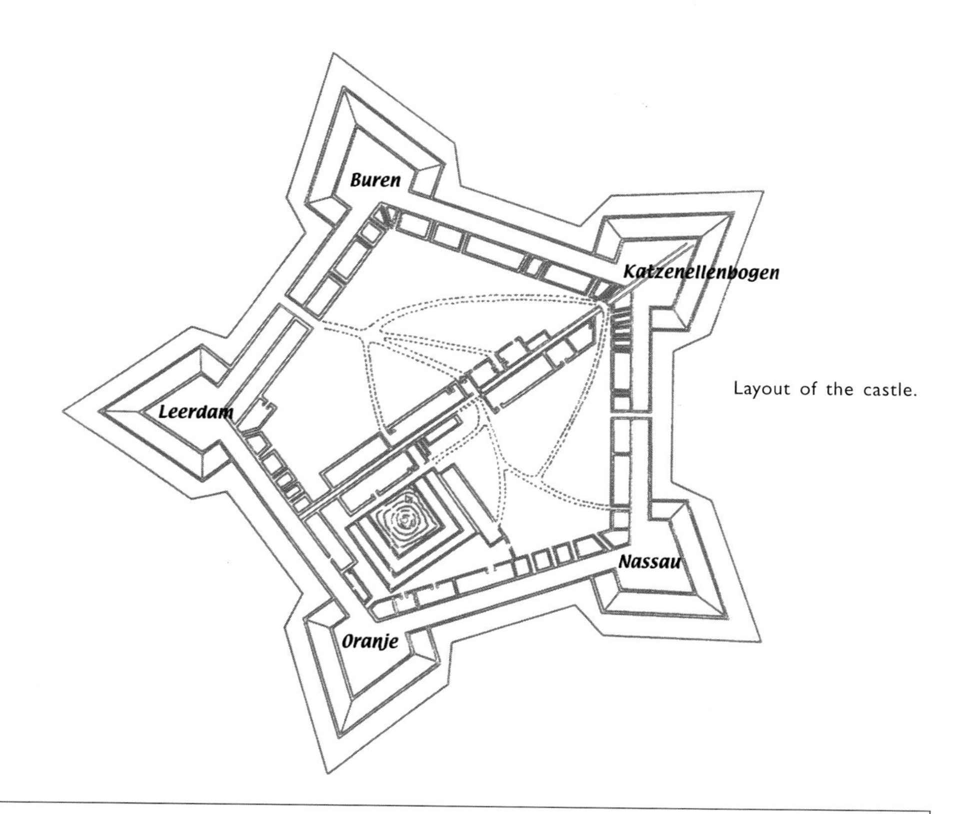


Layout of the castle.

## CAPE BOERS

The finely balanced political situation in the Cape Colony, where the government was against the war, meant that a *'Cape Boer'* was not compelled to fight against the Boer republics. However, if he took up arms on the side of the Boers, this would constitute rebellion and make him (as a British subject) guilty of treason. In spite of this danger, there were several thousand sympathisers in the Cape who felt strongly enough about the Boer cause to join the republican forces during the war.

To start with, the British military authorities were careful to hand the captured Cape rebels over to the ordinary courts. Later in the war, however, hundreds of rebels were sentenced to death by military courts, although the death sentence was confirmed in only 33 cases.

**CAPE TOWN TOURISM**

**Cnr. Berg and Castle Streets, Cape Town City Centre.**

**Tel: (021) 426 4260. Fax: (021) 426 4266. e-mail: captour@iafrica.com**

**Hours: Mon-Fri: 0800hrs - 1800hrs. Sat: 0830hrs - 1400hrs. Sun: 0900hrs - 1300hrs.**

## Historical Places to visit

**Bertram House:** Corner Orange Street & Government Ave. The only surviving brick Georgian house in Cape Town. In 1794 Andries Momsen, the dairyman of the Dutch East India Company, known as *'Momsen de melkboer'* used this land for grazing. John Barker bought it in 1839, and named it after his wife, Ann Bertram Findlay. It has a superb collection of furniture, porcelain and silver. In 1903, Bertram House was annexed to the South African College (**Egyptian Building**), the house later becoming the property of the University of Cape Town. In 1984 it was restored as the **British Colonial House Museum**.

**Bo-Kaap:** The Islam quarter of Cape Town with its brightly coloured houses and mosques. South Africa's first mosque, the *Auwal Mosque* (1794) is in Dorp Street. The **Bo-Kaap Museum** containing the Muslim history of South Africa is at 71 Wale Street. Tel: 424 3846.

**The Castle:** Buitenkant Street. The Castle was first occupied in 1674, and completed five years later. The five bastions were named after Prince of Orange titles; Leerdam, Oranje, Nassau, Buren and Katzenellenbogen. The bell in the turret of the main entrance (1697) was used to ring the hours of the day and raise the alarm. The partition wall known as the *KAT* with its famous *KAT BALCONY* was erected in 1685. The Castle serves as a military base and contains historical objects including the *William Fehr collection of Paintings and Objet d'art.* Fritz Joubert Duquesne and other Boers were imprisoned here before being shipped to the Bermuda PoW camps.

For an excellent Lunch or Dinner visit *De Goewerneur Restaurant* in the Castle. Tel: (021) 461 4895 for reservations

## Collectors of Militaria

Those avid collectors of things militaria and especially 'things from the battlefields' (which is illegal) will be most interested in the going price of shells and fragments of shells in Mafikeng at the time of the Siege in 1899. Solomon Plaatje, in his wonderful Boer War Diary states that a one-pounder maxim shell (Pom-Pom) fetched 10s6d, a 'new' five-pounder shell £2 2s, a seven-pounder shell 15s and an 'Au Sanna' shell (Long Tom) £6 6s. Even a Long Tom base fetched 10s6d at the market place. What price would they fetch now, one wonders?

STEVE'S WAR STORIES

**The City Hall:** Darling Street. The first Victorian building to be erected in Cape Town and was completed in 1905. The clock is said to be a half-size replica of Big Ben. The upper stages of the tower contain 39 bells. The main hall, the home of the Cape Town Symphony Orchestra, is familiar to concert-goers. It has a magnificent organ with 3 165 pipes.

**The Company's Garden:** Upper Adderley Street. Established by Jan Van Riebeeck to supply fresh produce to passing ships. From Van Riebeeck's diary, it was learned that Hendrik Boom prepared the ground for sowing on 29 April 1652. By the time **Kirstenbosch Botanical Garden** was established in 1913 the Company's Garden had become a public pleasure park.

**Cultural History Museum:** Adderley Street. The former slave lodge and the Old Supreme Court. Now housing local and international history, customs and tradition. The only collection of *Postal Stones* in the world. The rear facade of the building was made impressive by the addition of a pediment showing Anreith's version of the British Coat of Arms: *The Lion asleep and the Unicorn looking surprised.*

**Egyptian Building:** Government Avenue. Governor Sir Benjamin D'Urban granted a site for a college building to be built at the top end of the Company's Garden. The college was inaugurated in 1841. The South African College was the forerunner of the University of Cape Town.

**First National Bank Building:** Adderley Street. Sir Herbert Baker designed this building as Barclays Bank in 1936. This was the last building Baker designed in South Africa.

**The Great Synagogue:** (pictured top of page) 84 Hatfield Street, Gardens. Consecrated and opened in 1905. Alongside is the Jewish Museum which was the Old Synagogue opened in 1863 and the first synagogue in South Africa. It was designed in the Egyptian style. *The Synagogue, the Egyptian building and the Paarl Gymnasium are the only three examples of Egyptian Revival buildings in South Africa.*

**Groote Kerk:** Adderley Street. The original building was started in 1678. An outstanding feature is the immense vaulted ceiling with plaster rosettes. The clock tower is the only remaining structure of the original church. A magnificent carved pulpit was installed in 1789. The work of Anton Anreith and carpenter Jan Jacobs Graaf.

It was originally designed to incorporate the figures of *Faith, Hope and Charity* bearing the pulpit. This was rejected by the Kerkraad and *Lions* were chosen. Anreith's reply to this was: *"What do people here know of art forms? All they know about is lions and tigers."*

The flagstones are of Batavian salt-stone which changes colour according to the prevailing weather, darker when stormy and lighter as the weather clears (sic).

**The Houses of Parliament:** Parliament Street. Completed in 1884. The wing housing the new House of Assembly was designed by Sir Herbert Baker. Gallery tickets are available and guided tours are conducted each morning.
Tel: (021) 403 2460/1.

**Noon Gun:** Signal Hill, Bo-Kaap. Originally the gun signalled the time to the ships in Table Bay but it is now fired at Noon each day (except Sundays). It can be reached from Buitengracht Street and Bloem Street.

**Old Mutual Building:** Darling Street. The best example of the *art-deco* period in Cape Town. It was completed in 1939. At first floor level, running round three sides of the building, is a continuous sculptured frieze, depicting the history of South Africa.

**Rust-en-Vreugd:** Buitenkant Street. Was built in 1778. Thibault's influence is noticeable. Anreith was responsible for the baroque carvings of the balcony and doorways.

**St. George's Cathedral:** (pictured right) Wale Street. The foundation stone for the church was laid on St. Georges Day in 1830. It became a Cathedral in 1848. Towards the end of the 19th century it was decided to build a new Gothic cathedral designed by Herbert Baker and Francis Masey. The buttress stone was laid by the Duke of Cornwall and York (later King George V) on 22 August 1901. There are beautiful stained glass windows by Francis Spear and Gabriel Loire.
There are three memorials in the Cathedral to the Boer War.

1 - The apse windows were donated by nursing sisters with the inscription *'To the Glory of God and in the reverent memory of those Army Nursing Sisters who, during the war in South Africa 1899-1902, laid down their lives in performance of their duty'*

2 - Memorial to the 3rd Dragoon Guards.

3 - *'In memory of all ranks of the Cape Mounted Riflemen who fell in action, died of wounds or sickness during the Anglo-Boer War.'*

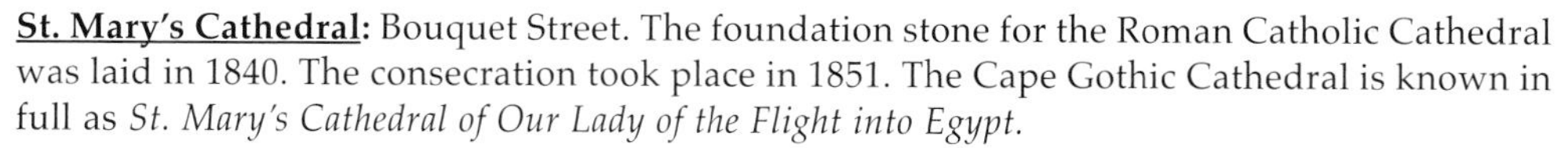

**St. Mary's Cathedral:** Bouquet Street. The foundation stone for the Roman Catholic Cathedral was laid in 1840. The consecration took place in 1851. The Cape Gothic Cathedral is known in full as *St. Mary's Cathedral of Our Lady of the Flight into Egypt.*

**The South African Library:** Company's Gardens. Design based on the Fitzwilliam Museum in Cambridge, it was opened in 1860 by HRH Prince Alfred. It has a large selection of Anglo-Boer War material.

**The South African Museum:** Queen Victoria Street. Includes the **Planetarium** and cultural displays of the San peoples.

**Tuynhuys:** Government Avenue. The Dutch East India Company's Guest House was built in 1700 to accommodate those dignitaries who passed through the Cape and were not housed in the Castle. Today it houses the Cabinet.

## Other Attractions and Activities

**Kirstenbosch National Botanical Garden:** Rhodes Drive, Newlands. The world famous garden of indigenous plants was established in 1913 and covers an area of 528 hectares which includes both a cultivated garden (36 hectares) and a nature reserve. Enjoy the many walks and theme gardens. Walks through the natural forest range from 1,5 km (45 min.) to 7,8 km (three hours). *(General Jan Smuts used to regularly walk up Table Mountain from Kirstenbosch* and there is a Smuts Track which leads to Skeleton Gorge.*)* The restaurant is open daily from 0900 hr to 1700 hr. The restaurant is popular with walkers who enjoy a post-walk breakfast. Summer Concerts are held in an amphitheatre from the first Sunday in December to the last Sunday in March.

Right: Aerial view of Robben Island.

Below: View of Table Mountain, showing Signal Hill on right, photographed from Blaauwberg.

**Robben Island:** A National Monument and National Heritage Site. 2 km x 3,5 km; 9 km north of Green Point.

The name is Dutch and means *'Seal Island'*. It first came to attention when, in 1488, Bartholomew Dias anchored in Table Bay. Van Riebeeck visited the island in September 1652 where he collected seals, penguins and penguin eggs to complement the food supply at the fort. It was used by the Dutch East India Company as a victualling station. In 1845 it became a leper colony and the mentally ill were also housed here. In 1931, the leper barracks were burnt and razed to the ground after the last patient had been removed. For the next 10 years the island was home to the lighthouse-keeper and his family. Shortly before the outbreak of the WWII, the S.A. Army built a harbour and established a base on the island. During the 1950s, the S.A. Navy took over the island and established a naval base - *S.A. Robben Island*. On 1 April 1961, Robben Island was officially taken over by the Prison Services. It gained notoriety as the gaol for those *'considered dangerous'* and for two decades it was where **ex-President Nelson Mandela** was imprisoned. The island has a few historic buildings; and guided tours of the island are available. Booking is essential Tel: (021) 419 1300. To visit the island there are ferries leaving the **Victoria & Alfred Waterfront** on a regular basis.

**Scratch Patch & Mineral World Gemstone:** Dock Road, V&A Waterfront.
Do your own *'scratching'* for gemstones.

**Table Mountain:** (height: 1 086 m) Named *'Taboa da Cabo'* in 1503 by the Portuguese Admiral Antonio de Saldanha. The name appears as *'Ye Table'* about 1613. Weather permitting, visitors can summit (via the Kloofnek Road bus) on the new modern cableway.

**Two Oceans Aquarium:** Dock Road, V&A Waterfront.

**Victoria & Alfred Waterfront:** Table Bay Harbour. Built in 1860, and still a working harbour. The original buildings have been renovated and new buildings built to Victorian style. There are museums, boat-trips, helicopter flips, restaurants, pubs, cinemas, large-screen IMAX cinema, hotels, shops and craft markets. Secure and ample parking above or below ground. Tel: (021) 418 2369.

## Restaurants

**Bayside Café**: 51 Victoria Road, Camps Bay. Beachfront restaurant with great seafood and steaks. Bar upstairs for pre-dinner drinks. Tel: (021) 438 2650.

**Blues:** The Promenade, Victoria Road, Camps Bay. Open from 12 noon. One of the top restaurants for Capetonians and visitors. A large menu to suit all tastes. Relax and enjoy your meal overlooking the beach. Tel: (021) 438 2040.

**Cape Colony Restaurant**: Mount Nelson Hotel, Orange Street, Gardens. One of the most renowned restaurants. Thai, Italian, Classic European and Cape Malay cuisine. Voted as one of the top 10 restaurants in the world.
Tel: (021) 423 1000.

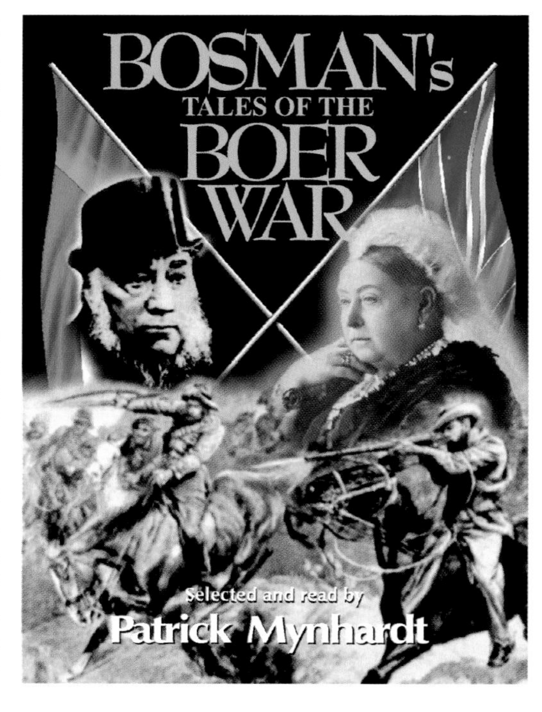


**De Goewerneur Restaurant:** The Castle, Buitenkant Street. For an excellent lunch or dinner in the atmosphere of the Castle with magnificent views of Table Mountain. Cape Malay and traditional food. Tel: (021) 461 4895.

**Quay West:** Cape Grace Hotel, West Quay. Award winning restaurant. Ideally situated close to the V&A Waterfront with magnificent views of the mountain and the marina. A la carte and set menus available on the terrace. Light meals served daily from 1030 hr to 2230 hr.

**Rozenhof:** 18 Kloof Street, Gardens. An ideal venue for lunch or dinner in an elegant Cape Georgian house with relaxing atmosphere providing innovative continental seasonal cuisine. Tel: (021) 424 1968.

**Rustica:** 70 New Church Street. Bistro styled serving rustic Italian food popular with the locals. Tel: (021) 423 5474.



**Serendipity:** 236 Long Street. Possibly the best food in town. Tel: (021) 424 8796.

**Sukhothai Restaurant:** 50 Orange St, Gardens. The finest Thai cuisine in Cape Town.
Tel: (021) 423 4725.

### Tour Guides (Satour Registered)

**Andre de Waal:** (T.0001) PO Box: 995, Bellville.
Tel:(021) 948 666. Fax: (021) 948 3441.
Cell/Mobile: 082 923 6240.

**Arthur Frost:** (T.4629) 81 Upper Orange Street, Oranjezicht. Tel/Fax: (021) 461 2991.
Cell/Mobile: 083 261 9601.

**Stuart Nichols:** (T.0435) 25 Pittosporum Avenue, Thornton. Tel: (021) 54 1669.
Cell/Mobile: 082 921 8986.

**Tony Westby-Nunn:** (T.5419)
158 Buitengracht Street, Cape Town. Tel/Fax: (021) 422 2801. Cell/Mobile: 083 444 4662.

# Protea Hotels : Cape Town & surrounds

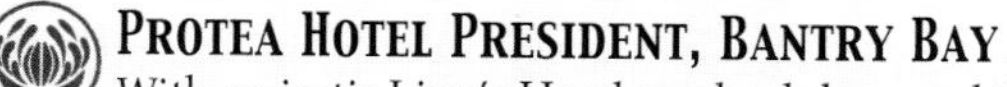

### PROTEA HOTEL PRESIDENT, BANTRY BAY

With majestic Lion's Head as a backdrop and the azure Atlantic Ocean in front, the President Hotel represents the beginning of a new era in comfort and refinement on Cape Town's Platinum Mile. Spacious rooms & suites with sea or mountain views.
349 Rooms from R570 (mtn) & R895 (sea-facing) B&B.
Tel: (021) 434 8111. Fax: (021) 434 9991.
e-mail: petra@presidenthotel.co.za

### PROTEA HOTEL CAPETONIAN, HEERENGRACHT

In the heart of the CBD and close to the V&A Waterfront, the Capetonian is an ideal location for both business and pleasure. Well-appointed air-conditioned stylish rooms. Enjoy the *'On the Square'* restaurant for meals. In-house gym.
170 Rooms from R450 (exec) & R650 (fam) Room Only.
Tel: (021) 419 5670. Fax: (021) 419 7876.
e-mail: res@capetonian.co.za

### PROTEA HOTEL HIDDINGH MEWS, GARDENS

5 mins from the CBD and only 20 mins from the airport. Fully equipped self-catering suites have TV, kitchen, lounge/dining room and telephone. Breakfasts available from *'The Mill'*. Walk to the museums, Parliament and the Company Gardens.
60 Rooms from R430 (std) & R550 (fam) Room Only.
Tel: (021) 462 3099. (021) 462 3326.
e-mail: hiddingh@dockside.co.za

### PROTEA HOTEL PIER PLACE, TULBAGH SQUARE

2 mins from the CBD and only 20 mins from the airport. Fully equipped self-catering suites with TV, kitchen, lounge/dining room and telephone. Breakfast at the *'The Club Room'*; or relax during the day with a book. Health & Racket Club nearby.
56 Rooms from R432 (std) & R486 (sup) Room Only.
Tel: (021) 421 7580. Fax: (021) 421 7591.
e-mail: pierplace@jaywalk.com

### PROTEA HOTEL VICTORIA JUNCTION, CITY CENTRE

Close to the V&A Waterfront and Green Point/Sea Point. Ideally situated for restaurants and clubs. A loft-style hotel with industrial glamour and high-tech creating a *designer hotel.* There are 24 spacious lofts with large windows and views.
172 Rooms from R670 single & R795 double.
Tel: (021) 418 1234. Fax: 418 5678.
e-mail: vicjunct@icon.co.za

# Cape Town

### MOUNT NELSON HOTEL, GARDENS

Opened on 6th March 1899. This splendid hotel, situated in the Gardens suburb at the top of Government Avenue offers all the comforts of a first-class hotel. Steeped in history of the Anglo-Boer War.
226 Rooms from R2640 per room per night.
Tel: 27 (0)21 483 1000. Fax: 27 (0)21 424 7472.
e-mail: nellres@iafrica.com

### CAPE HERITAGE HOTEL, CITY

The Cape Heritage Hotel borders the historical Bokaap of Cape Town. Housing a combination of buildings dating back to 1771, styled in Georgian, Victorian and Cape Dutch architecture, with excellent rooms.
15 Rooms from R390 per person B&B sharing.
Tel: (021) 424 4646. Fax: (021) 424 4949.
e-mail: chrelais@satis.co.za

### CAPE GRACE HOTEL, V&A WATERFRONT

Occupying its own quay in Cape Town's renowned Victoria & Alfred Waterfront with Table mountain as the majestic backdrop, Cape Grace presents an atmosphere of warmth and unpretentious elegance.
102 Rooms from R1900/room per night B&B.
Tel: 27 (0)21 410 7100. Fax: 27 (0)21 419 7622.
e-mail: reservations@capegrace.com

### LEEUWENVOET HOUSE, TAMBOERSKLOOF

Victorian residence, walk to the city. Elegant rooms with fans, telephones, TV and tea trays. Superb breakfasts. Swimming Pool. Mountain and V&A Waterfront nearby. Near restaurants. Secure parking.
12 Rooms from R195 - R250 pp sharing. B&B.
Tel: (021) 424 1133. Fax: (021) 424 0495.
e-mail: stay@leeuwenvoet.co.za

### RADIUM HALL GUEST HOUSE, TAMBOERSKLOOF

This is an 18th century Edwardian home with many original period features. The pressed ceilings are most remarkable. Situated on the slopes of Signal Hill with breathtaking views of Table Mountain.
4 Rooms from R175 per person sharing. B&B.
Tel: (021) 423 5445. Fax: (021) 423 5381.
e-mail: mail@radiumhall.com

# Cape Town

### UNDERBERG GUEST HOUSE, TAMBOERSKLOOF

Homely, quiet and comfortable Victorian double storey manor house of the 'original farm'. Walk to city and Kloof Street restaurants. Bedrooms have TV, phone, bar fridge and tea / coffee making facilities.

10 Rooms from R237,50 - R325 pp sharing. B&B.
Tel: (021) 426 2262. Fax: (021) 424 4059.
e-mail: underberg@nettactive.co.za

### THE CAPE COLONIAL, GARDENS

Victorian double-storey house in Gardens suburb close to the City centre. Offering guests friendly 'home from home' hospitality. Decorated in Cape Colonial style. Bistros, cafés and restaurants nearby.

5 Rooms from R210 pp sharing. R295 single. B&B.
Tel: (021) 423 7382. Fax: (021) 423 7383.
e-mail: safariva@iafrica.com

### LONGWOOD GUEST HOUSE, ORANJEZICHT

Longwood as a Victorian house is a National Monument situated on the slopes of Table Mountain. It was designed by Sir Herbert Baker, and offers distinctive accommodation and true Cape elegance.

7 Rooms from R225 per person sharing. B&B.
Tel: (021) 461 5988. Fax: (021) 461 5953.
e-mail: longwd@iafrica.com

### ORANJEZICHT GUEST HOUSE, ORANJEZICHT

Centally located to the city centre. A gracious Cape Dutch style home offering the visitors tranquility and a welcoming ambience, providing guests with all modern comforts. All rooms have TV and M-Net.

3 Rooms from R235 per person sharing. B&B.
Tel: (021) 461 4614. Fax: (021) 462 4614.
e-mail: reservations@oranjezicht.co.za

### THE VILLA ROSA, SEA POINT

A beautiful Victorian residence, at the foot of Lion's Head. Villa Rosa offers a relaxed and friendly atmosphere with efficient service and delicious breakfasts. Sea Point is on the cosmopolitan Atlantic seaboard.

8 Rooms from R140 - R250 pp sharing. B&B.
Tel: (021) 434 2768. Fax: (021) 434 3526.
Cell: 082 785 3238. e-mail: villaros@mweb.co.za

The Mount Nelson Hotel in 1899.

The opening ceremony of Cape Town's new prestige hotel, the Mount Nelson, had barely passed when Great Britain declared war on the Transvaal and the Orange Free State.

A war was not an affair which would attract the "higher class of traveller" the Mount Nelson was aiming at. Yet the large influx of people to South Africa at the turn of the century, the politicians and soldiers, adventurers, financial speculators and artists who had come from every corner of the globe to take either an active or a passive part in historical events, made the hotel a success far sooner than fame as being a truly great hotel could have spread in more peaceful times.

Sir Redvers Buller made the hotel his *home-from-home.* When Field-Marshall Lord Frederick Sleigh Roberts arrived with Lord Kitchener on 17 January 1900, to take over as Commander-in-Chief from Buller they made the Mount Nelson Hotel their headquarters – and with them, women flocked to South Africa during the war, either seeking adventure in the true or in the romantic sense and became such a nuisance that a complaint was made to Sir Alfred Milner, the Cape Governor, in their regard. They cluttered up the Mount Nelson Hotel and, with their white or light-coloured dresses, parasols and broad-brimmed hats added a flash of colour to the soldiers in mufti, mostly white flannel trousers and navy jackets or blazers, discussing war events, and grey-suited, cigar-smoking individuals who passed the days lazing in the garden.

Cecil Rhodes entertained at the hotel, and Lady Sarah Wilson enjoyed "a room with a view of the bay" for 15 shillings per day with all meals included. H. G. Wells arrived from England to stay at the hotel and Lady Jennie Churchill, Winston's mother was, upon her arrival on the hospital ship *Maine,* invited to a reception given at the Mount Nelson Hotel by a committee of American ladies. *"It was very pleasant,"* Lady Jennie remembered, *"eating strawberries and walking in the pretty garden".*

Winston Churchill, the young war correspondent who wrote his reports for the *Morning Post* in the seclusion of a luxury suite after his spectacular escape from Pretoria's Prisoner of War Camp, paid his tribute to the hotel with the following words: *"It is a most excellent and well-appointed establishment which may be thoroughly appreciated after a sea voyage."*

Arthur Conan Doyle, the creator of *Sherlock Holmes* and an ardent admirer of Kitchener, volunteered to take part in the South African War, but at the age of 40, was turned down. When the wealthy John Langman decided to send out to Lord Roberts a medical unit and travelling hospital, he offered Conan Doyle the job of senior physician. Conan Doyle was delighted at the offer to go to South Africa as a member of the Langman Hospital, as it became known. He sailed with the Langman Hospital on the P&O liner *Oriental,* arriving at sun-drenched Cape Town on 21 March 1900. While awaiting orders, the Langman

Arthur Conan Doyle, photographed in the trenches at the Front.

Hospital was quartered at the Mount Nelson Hotel. After paying official visits to the Boer concentration camps to dispense medicine and offer good cheer, the team was ordered to set sail on the *Oriental* to East London. From there, they took a long and tedious journey to Bloemfontein. After only three months in South Africa, Conan Doyle was released from field duty. At first he had taken ill with typhoid fever and then he suffered from an injury in a soccer match between the doctors and a local team. He stayed again at the Mount Nelson Hotel before returning to England on 11 July, aboard the *SS Briton*, to write a book on the Boer War.

Rudyard Kipling, fascinated by the kaleidoscope of people mingling in Cape Town's streets, arrived at the Mount Nelson Hotel with his suitcases packed with pyjamas. He had founded the 'Absent Minded Beggar' fund and he distributed these pyjamas as gifts to the nurses at Wynberg where all nighties were discarded. His funds thus contributed to the emancipation of the fair sex. In his *Something of Myself*, Rudyard Kipling calls the Cape of Good Hope a "glorious land", to which he gladly gave much of his "life and love". After the Anglo-Boer War had come to an end, Kipling returned for many years to spend the European winter with his family at the sunny Cape.

Every room at the Mount Nelson was booked in advance. Officers in the British Expeditionary Force, while awaiting orders from their commander, passed much of their time in the billiard room. Billiards was a fashionable game and Neville Chamberlain (who was said to have invented snooker) took great delight in challenging Colonel G.F.R. Henderson (Lord Roberts intelligence officer) at the hotel's billiard tables that were built to the specification used in the best London clubs.

Ordinary soldiers, although not being able to stay at the hotel, were highly attracted to its elegant bar. In order to avoid lesser ranks crowding the hotel's facilities and possibly causing disturbance among the celebrities of the time, Emile Cathrein introduced an 'OFFICERS ONLY' rule. This was of course much resented by the soldiers in the British Expeditionary Force. A Canadian private, extremely annoyed that the Mount Nelson luxuries were denied him, shot his way into the bar and its well-stocked shelves. After Lord Roberts had handed over the command to Lord Kitchener at the end of November 1900, the squint-eyed misogynist of Khartoum fame did not even tolerate his officers enjoying the Mount Nelson luxuries.

As a commander of the Egyptian army, in which the bachelor (sic) would have no married officers, he had conquered the Sudan. At the battle of Odurman, 26 000 men, armed with swords and spears, were killed by the field guns of his highly trained men. After the battle, Kitchener dug up the bones of the Mhadi, (the Sudanese religious leader who had opposed him) and carried his skull around with him in a kerosene can, joking that he would use it for a drinking cup.

It is not surprising then that no soldier who served under him loved him. But Kitchener did not seek love. Furiously ambitious, his mastering obsession was to end the war in South Africa as soon as possible by any means which might seem immediately effective, but he mistrusted the officers in the British army, who served the Queen because it was a social fashion and neglected the boring details of their profession.

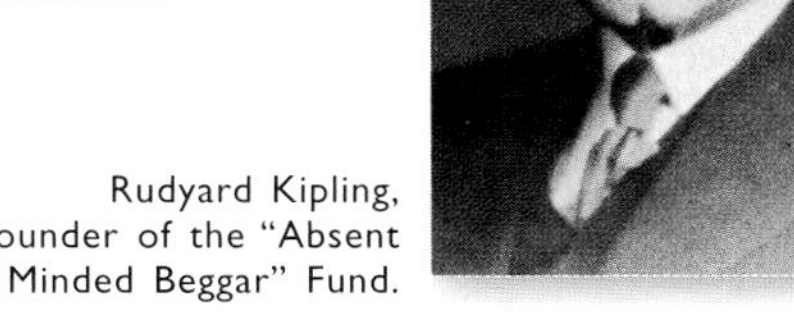

Rudyard Kipling, founder of the "Absent Minded Beggar" Fund.

# MOUNT NELSON HOTEL

Kitchener (pictured right) had inherited his cruelty from his father, a Colonel who, simply because he did not believe in blankets, made his wife sleep under newspapers until she caught pneumonia and died (sic).

A man with this background could not have his officers living in luxury at the Mount Nelson Hotel. Himself a tireless worker, having worked three hours before breakfast, announced that a baggage train would await them the following day to remove them to the lesser delights of Stellenbosch. Having coined the phrase *'to be Stellenbosched'*, which is still in use today, Kitchener made sure that no officer would remain at the Mount Nelson Hotel. However, even the efficient Lord could not keep the British officers away from the Mount Nelson Hotel – as an essential place for social intercourse, it seemed to draw them to its comforts like *moths to a flame*.

On Christmas morning in 1901, high ranking officers were involved in an incident at the hotel which, unbeknown to Kitchener at the time, resulted in an international scandal which would later be debated in the House of Commons in London. Harwicke Foster Stanford, a British journalist, known by the nickname 'Mathilda Chiffon', was the cause of this affair. Standford intruded upon a private party organised by the officers and was subsequently tarred and feathered after a mock court found him guilty. His claims for damages were granted to him by a Cape Town Court and the officers in question duly apologised and returned the negatives of the photographs taken of Stanford, showing him with a wreath of flowers in the fountain in front of the hotel. The fifteen hundred pounds and court costs due to Standford, however, were never paid. Standord's persistent friends saw that the incident was widely covered in all the London newspapers and Lord Kitchener had to order a court-martial. Seven officers were ordered from India and other far-off places to return to London long after the war in South Africa had come to an end. Stanford never received the costs awarded to him in Cape Town but was known for the rest of his life as 'Mathilda Chiffon' who was tarred and feathered at the Mount Nelson Hotel during the South African War.

To the mining magnates of the Rand – cigar-smoking individuals who passed their days lazily in the garden – Britain's military men were a welcome sight. They saw themselves as refugees in the belief that they were enslaved by President Kruger because they had no vote for the First Volksraad. The wealthy 'refugees' thus called their luxurious Mount Nelson Hotel domicile, the 'Helots' Rest' to identify themselves with an underprivileged group of people, with serfs or helots. After the war had come to an end in 1902, the 'helots' returned to their goldmines in the Transvaal and British soldiers were posted to other troublesome areas in the vast Empire. ❑

***Source:*** *The Mount Nelson,* Eric H. Bolsmanu.

## RELIGIOUS SERVICE

A Boer preacher had his flock fervently engaged in prayer when he caught sight of approaching British horsemen. He leapt over his flock and onto his horse before his congregation knew what was happening. A youth caught up to him in their wild flight and said; "Dominee, you forgot to say Amen". (Schikkerling, 280/281).

# The Alphen Hotel – *The Boer 'n Brit*

South Africa, a land of stark contrasts, where the people are no less striking and draw on many different cultures and customs. Although closely related in cultural, historical and religious experience, the Boers and the British developed diverging aspirations. As the years passed these differences turned to an enmity which exploded in 1899 into the Boer War and tore the country asunder. The passions generated by this war affect us even to this day.

As in all civil disturbances, family loyalties were split and the Cloete's of Alphen were no exception. Henry Cloete, although of Dutch descent, backed the British and acted as a British Agent after their emissaries withdrew from Pretoria at the outbreak of hostilities. For this, Queen Victoria gave him the CMG. His wife, Christina Deliana, with her Transvaal background, believed deeply in the Boer cause. Her father, Nikolaas van Warmelo, had established the Hervormede Kerk in the Transvaal and her mother's family, the Maree's, took part in the Great Trek. Small wonder they backed the Boers. This is ardently recalled in two books, those of her brother Dietlof – *'On Commando'* and sister Johanna 'Hansie' Brandt – *'Petticoat Commando'*.

In true Victorian style, Deliana publicly supported her husband and even, on occasion, delivered speeches for him. Privately, though, this strongwilled, independent woman had no intention of helping the British and, in league with her sister 'Hansie', began relaying information to her family in the North. With British leaders like Roberts and Kitchener regularly dining with Henry at Alphen, she had ample opportunity to pick up information. Usually messages were secreted in a hollow oak in the grounds for collection by Boer agents but on one occasion, a novel means was used to relay a return message from Pretoria – Christmas dolls had been sent to the Cloete daughters with a hidden message in the head of the doll for Henry's eldest daughter, Nicolette. That is why Nicolette's doll in the photograph in the Boer 'n Brit, is naked and damaged.

Deliana was not the only Boer sympathiser in the family. Henry's youngest brother, Phillipus Albertus Myburg, known as PAM Cloete, also fought for the Boers. He was captured early in the war and Henry had to intervene to have him sent on parole to England, where he spent the rest of the war living comfortably with his family in Essex and playing cricket for the county.

Today Alphen belongs to the Cloete-Hopkins family and here the Boer and the Brit can be said to have merged. The founder of the Hopkins family in South Africa came from Britain as a cavalry officer in the conflict, fell in love with the country and married a daughter of one of the great Huguenot families. In honouring the Vierkleur and the Union Jack, we remember, mark and close an important chapter in our history. We hope you enjoy the Boer 'n Brit as much as we enjoyed assembling it. ❑

# Pinelands • Newlands • Claremont

### THE COURTYARD AT CAPE TOWN

Country style hotel close to the City. The Courtyard is an original Cape Dutch Manor House and a National Monument that has been renovated. Close to a Golf Course and only 15 minutes from the Airport.
70 Suites from R270/person sharing, room only.
Tel: (021) 448 3929. Fax: (021) 448 5494.
e-mail: cyct.res@citylodge.co.za

### MEDINDI MANOR, ROSEBANK

Gracious Edwardian home built in 1903 and ideally situated for business or holiday. Rooms decorated with period pieces, phone, bar-fridge & satellite TV. 10 mins to City, Airport or Waterfront.
7 Rooms from R400 double. R275 single.
Tel: (021) 686 3563. Fax: (021) 686 3563.
e-mail: manor@medindi.co.za

### THE RED HOUSE, NEWLANDS

The Red House is a gracious early Georgian country house, circa 1729, originally built as a hunting lodge and owned by Lord Charles Somerset. Close to UCT, cricket & rugby grounds. 5 mins from Kirstenbosch.
3 Rooms and 1 Cottage from R375 - R475 pp B&B.
Tel: (021) 683 8000. Fax: (021) 683 8006.
e-mail: info@redhouse.co.za

### VINEYARD HOTEL, NEWLANDS

Originally built by Lady Anne Barnard in 1799, this 4-star Silver Classified hotel is situated in six acres of attractive landscaped parkland in the leafy suburb of Newlands on the banks of the Liesbeeck River.
160 Rooms from R495 (single) to R925 (double).
Tel: (021) 683 3044. Fax: (021) 683 3365.
e-mail: hotel@vineyard.co.za

### HARFIELD COTTAGE GUEST HOUSE, CLAREMONT

Relax in the privacy of this luxurious intimate haven situated in the charming 'Village of Harfield' near Cavendish Square shopping centre and Newlands. Excellent cafés, restaurants and shops close by.
7 Rooms from R235 - R275 pp sharing. B&B.
Tel: (021) 683 7376. Fax: (021) 671 6715.
e-mail: harfield@grm.co.za

## Claremont • Constantia

### TULANA, WYNBERG/CLAREMONT

Built in 1886 by a cousin of JBM Hertzog (general in the Anglo-Boer War). This spacious colonial house with ball room, antiques, art and quality finishes reflect the ambience of gracious living of yesteryear.

6 Double & 1 Single from R325 - R425 pp. B&B.
Tel: (021) 762 8500. Fax: (021) 761 0188.
e-mail: tulana@global.co.za

### THE ALPHEN HOTEL, CONSTANTIA

The home of Cape hospitality since the 18th century at the gateway to the Constantia valley. Relax in the 'Boer 'n Brit' pub, or take a stroll through the valley. Only 15 mins from the City or Simon's Town.

34 Rooms from R795 - R1365. Room only.
Tel: (021) 794 5011. Fax: (021) 794 5710
e-mail: reservations@alphen.co.za

### ARDERNE LODGE, CONSTANTIA

Elegantly furnished and situated close to Cecilia Forest and Kirstenbosch. Arderne Lodge is a graceful Cape vernacular house set in lush gardens filled with Cape flora and breathtaking mountain views.

5 Suites from R400 per person sharing. B&B.
Tel: (021) 794 1672. Fax: (021) 794 4504.
e-mail: hohenort@mweb.co.za

### SNAKEBITE

Looking for supplies in a dark barn, a Boer called *'Swart Lawaai'* (Black Blusterer) received a stinging bite. He was carried outside to die as he was convinced that he had been bitten by a poisonous snake.

Whilst one of his comrades read the Bible to the 'dying man', others went to the barn to see if they could catch the snake. Three men levelled their rifles whilst the fourth investigated a pile of straw with a long pole.

Much to the embarrassment of the 'dying man', they discovered a broody hen which had defended her five eggs with a sharp peck. *'Swart Lawaai'*, after a remarkably short convalescence, recovered his strength, but never his reputation.

Schikkerling, 205.

*Ryno Greenwall*

# Memorabilia of the Anglo-Boer War

A century after the start of the Anglo-Boer War all the combatants are dead, the devastated farms are producing again and the reasons for the war have become obscure and almost forgotten. What remains however, are the thousands of items of memorabilia produced both in the United Kingdom and Europe.

Patriotic fervour whipped up in Britain by the editors of the illustrated newspapers particularly the *Illustrated London News, Graphic, Black & White,* and *Sphere*. The early defeats of Black Week (10 to 18 December 1899), Stormberg, Maggersfontein and Colenso were made to look like victories. An appeal was made to the colonial settlers in New Zealand, Canada, Australia, and civilians alike to volunteer. This they did in their thousands.

Alfred Harmsworth, the owner of *The Daily Mail,* hit upon the idea of *The Gentleman in Khaki,* inspired by Richard Caton-Woodville's painting of a wounded volunteer. Rudyard Kipling, the famous poet, was commissioned to write the poem *Absent Minded Beggar* which was set to music by Arthur Sullivan of Gilbert and Sullivan fame. All manner of items were produced with the logo and the poem which were sold in vast quantities to the public with 25% of the sales being paid over to *The Daily Mail* Fund for the families of the volunteers who had abandoned them and their jobs to go to the Front. Over £350 000 was raised in this manner. The outpouring of pottery, porcelain, glassware,

*The Gentleman in Khaki.*

This Doulton Lambeth blue glaze loving cup with silver rim has medallion of Queen Victoria flanked by Empire flags and the inscription "In Commemoration of the hoisting of the British flag at Pretoria" and "God Save The Queen".

This Copeland porcelain loving cup has three sides containing the inscriptions "1899 Transvaal War 1900"; "Imperial Federation"; "Britannia Tower of Justice"

Two Doulton brown glaze earthenware jugs.
On the left: Wounded Royal Marine "The Handy Man" flanked by Capt. H. Lambton and Capt. P.M. Scott. On the right: Oval print of Lord Roberts flanked by British flags and a lion, kangaroo, ostrich and beaver, and inscription "South Africa 1900".

brass, tin, pewter, plastic, paper, silk and all other household items was quite fantastic. The jewellery manufacturers also produced items in gold, silver and bronze as well as *"sweethearts"*; military insignia made into hat pins, brooches and earrings.

Items bearing the likeness of generals Roberts, Kitchener, White, French, McDonald, Buller and Baden-Powell appeared, and, soon after Bloemfontein and Pretoria (the Boer capitals) were occupied and Ladysmith, Kimberley and Mafeking were relieved, appropriate items were again produced. The demand for these items continued until peace was declared on 31 May 1902. Peace and King Edward VII's coronation coincided, so often the two occasions are commemorated on the same object. Collectors of Coalport, Doulton, Carlton ware, McIntyre, Staffordshire, Foley and Copeland etc., will find several items of this nature as well as those previously discussed.

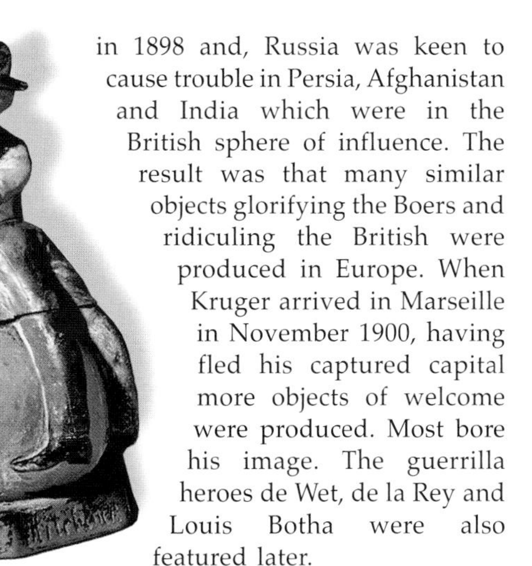

German earthenware tobacco jar of General de Wet holding Lord Kitchener over a globe.

Across the English Channel the Europeans had their own reasons for wishing Edward VII fortune. Germany was still smarting over Queen Victoria's rebuke to her grandson Kaiser Wilhelm for sending a congratulatory telegram to Paul Kruger after the defeat of Jameson and his men in January 1896. France had been humiliated by Britain at Fashoda in 1898 and, Russia was keen to cause trouble in Persia, Afghanistan and India which were in the British sphere of influence. The result was that many similar objects glorifying the Boers and ridiculing the British were produced in Europe. When Kruger arrived in Marseille in November 1900, having fled his captured capital more objects of welcome were produced. Most bore his image. The guerrilla heroes de Wet, de la Rey and Louis Botha were also featured later.

The Golden Age of picture postcards began at the turn of the century – so naturally postcards featured prominently in the Boer War memorabilia. Propaganda, patriotic and other cards showing merely personalities, scenes and events of the war were also produced and collected in their thousands. When Kruger toured Europe, the pro-Boer Committees under the guidance of W.J. Leyds, the two republics' roving ambassador, published cards which purchasers were urged to send to Kruger directly expressing solidarity with his cause.

Cigarette and trade cards which had been in use since the 1880's flourished as well. In England various patriotic series were published. Generals, VC Heroes, even Boer leaders featured; while in Europe manufacturers of chocolate, lace, soap, meat extracts, soda and beer among other diverse

On the left is the President Kruger teapot and on the right, one depicting the Hon. Joseph Chamberlain.

products, had their trade cards which were almost always pro-Boer.

Queen Victoria sent a tin of chocolate to each soldier in South Africa. Each tin had an embossed picture of Victoria and an inscription reading *'South Africa 1900'* and *'I wish you a happy New Year'*.

Following the events of *Black Week*, Queen Victoria decided to send her troops a 1900 New Year's gift of chocolate. She had done the same in the Crimean War nearly 50 years before. The Quaker firms of Rowntree, Cadbury and Fry supplied 130 000 tins. Being pacifists they were reluctant to be involved but relented after a personal appeal from the Queen. The tins are fairly common, but occasionally the full contents remain in their original tinfoil wrapping. These of course are more desirable if not particularly edible.

Postcard: Good-bye Dolly Gray.

Sheet music was a popular commodity, obviously before the record, tape and CD era. Most of the music and lyrics were of a patriotic nature to both Boer and Brit and eminently forgettable but their beautiful lithographic covers were highly collectable and remain so today.

Left:
This board game, produced in France is called *"La Guerre au Transvaal Artillerie Anglaise Planche No. 1101"*. (from a series of children's 'cut-outs' with eight full-colour figures).

Handkerchiefs, both silk and linen, were adorned with battle scenes, heroic generals, and lists of important dates. Often their images were incorporated into the Union Jack or Vierkleur depending on one's political views. Popular and collectable today are the several counter and board games whose main object was to get to Pretoria

Right: This board game called *"How to reach Pretoria. The Great Transvaal War Puzzle."*

Above: A Dutch board game called *"Boer en Rooinekspel"* (Boer and Red-neck Game).

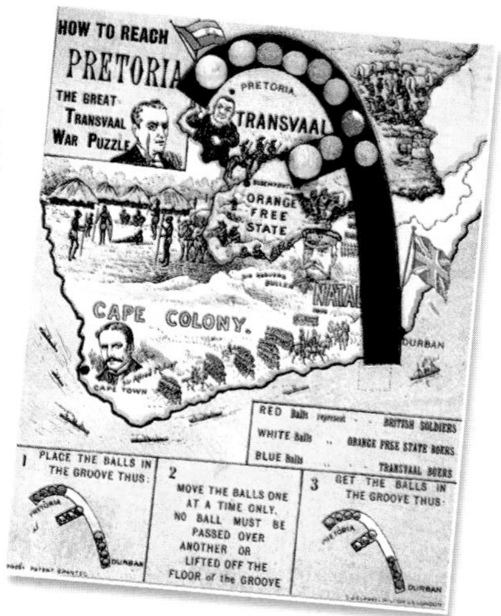

if British or to push *"Tommy"* into the sea if European. Over 37 000 Boers were captured by the British. At first they were housed on ships in False Bay and later on in camps in South Africa. Due to security fears they were sent off to far flung parts of the British Empire and found themselves in India or on the Islands of St. Helena, Ceylon, or Bermuda.

To while away their idle hours they were encouraged to make artefacts of wood, ivory, or metal, or even shells often using only a humble penknife. Some quite exquisite pieces of furniture, chess boards, jewellery, letter openers, snuff boxes, writing boxes and other trinkets were made. These were sold all over the world by charity organisations raising money for the women and children in concentration camps back home. Bermuda being nearest to the United States had a ready market for these items which are today quite sought after. For the numismatist and medal collector the Queen's and King's SA medals are quite desirable as over 26 different combinations of bars were awarded. Besides these medals, tribute medals and medallions were struck to commemorate events or to glorify heroes – often found in silver, bronze, white metal or more rarely in gold. For those interested in this fascinating subject Pieter Oosthuizen's book *Boer War Memorabilia,* which is almost out of print, is a must. There is a tremendous amount of memorabilia about, particularly in England and to a lesser extent in Europe. One merely requires time, patience and luck to find them. ❑

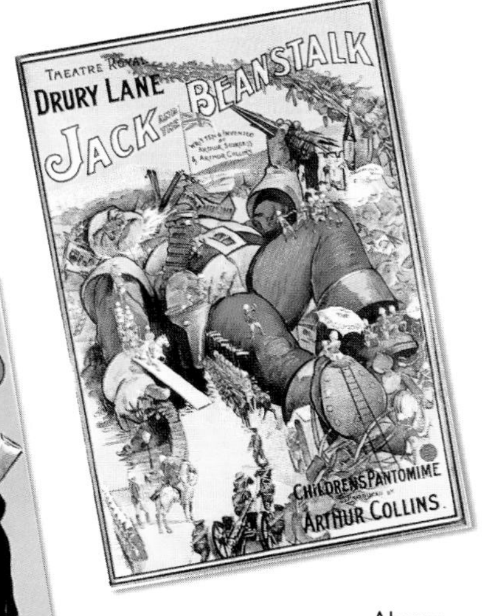


Above:
A poster for the production of *Jack and the Beanstalk* (with President Kruger as Jack).

A French poster with Queen Victoria and President Kruger. *"Si vous toussez prenez Supreme Pilules".*

## Ammunition

It became regular practice for the Boer commandos to follow British columns to replenish their ammunition. The British would not trouble to pick up cartridges which fell from their bandoliers, which could be easily replaced at camp.

Reitz commented that, *"...I doubt if the British ever realised to what an extent the Boers were dependent upon this source of replenishment".* (Reitz, 187 to 188).

Even today, nearly 100 years after the war, it is surprising how many unfired cartridges can be found in the veld.

*Michael Behrens · Tel (021) 761 7263*

# Boer War Relics Walk, Simon's Town

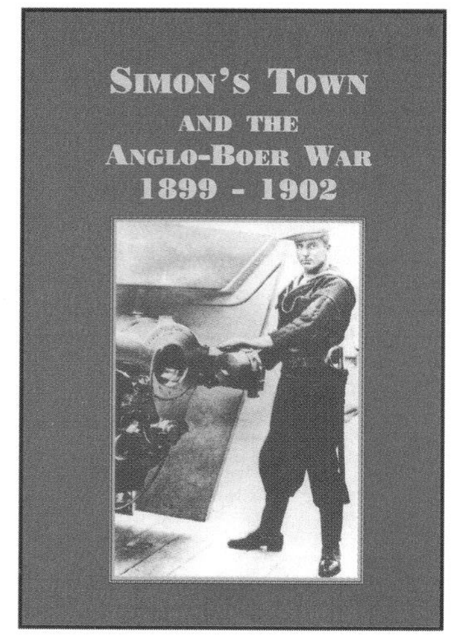


The Cape Peninsula is a bit short on Anglo-Boer War historical sites but much of what there is can be found in Simon's Town so let's take a look at what it has to offer.

The walk should take you about 3 hours (allowing for lingering and looking) starting from Simon's Town Station, - or you could drive to Jubilee Square and start from there - or you could vehicle-hop from point to point. The road along which we will be walking has a maddening way of changing names periodically so for the purposes of this walk I will refer to it simply as the **Main Road**.

**The Station** is a good place to start as this was the scene of departures and returns to and from the Battles at Belmont and Graspan.

Turn left at the Station and head towards the town but when you get to the road coming in at a sharp angle on the right, backtrack along it to the white neo-classical building up on the left. This fine architectural edifice was built circa 1785 and is known as the **Palace Barracks**. (*'Palace'* was probably a sarcastic nickname given to it by the ratings!) Whatever they thought of it, it is a most elegant building and typifies the grace and style of the late eighteenth century. During the Boer War it acquired a new significance when it was used as a hospital and was then referred to as the **Palace Hospital**. It was here that a stout-hearted British lady enters the saga - Mary Kingsley (daughter of famous author Charles Kingsley). As a thumbnail biography of her I

A well-furnished cabin on board one of HM ships.

HM Ship Terrible.

quote, in its entirety, the inscription on a plaque to her memory, which we will see later on this walk:

*'Mary Kingsley was an eminent British woman traveller in Africa. She travelled extensively in West Africa from 1893 to 1895 and her writing and lecturing made her a well-known authority on the region and on colonial questions. In 1900 she came to Simon's Town during the South African War and nursed Boer prisoners in the Palace Barracks. While in Simon's Town Mary Kingsley*

HM Ship Powerful.

The Palace Barrack Hospital, Simon's Town.

*had a room in the British Hotel. She contracted typhus and died on 3 June 1900 aged 37. Mary Kingsley was buried at sea with full military honours.'* The reference to *typhus* is incorrect as she died of typhoid (enteric).

Conditions in the hospital were pretty grim, medical supplies were hopelessly inadequate, while sacking was used for sheets and Mary Kingsley said of it, *"I never struck such a rocky bit of the valley of the shadow of death in all my days as the Palace Hospital"*. She worked tirelessly to bring her patients, both Boer and Brit what comfort she could, and a young Afrikaner once, although wracked with pain, smiled up at her and whispered *"Jy is 'n Engel!"* (You're an angel!) Rudyard Kipling said she was the bravest woman he knew.

Return to the main road and stroll on into the town passing **Admiralty House** on your left, the scene of some socialising between the two factions - senior Boer personnel were occasionally invited to dine there with the Admiral. So full of history is this village that we are going to have to practice great singleness of purpose as we wander along so as not to lose our Boer War focus. Stop when you get to the **British Hotel** (designed by John Parker, built in 1898, and superbly restored in 1992) where you will see the Mary Kingsley plaque previously mentioned. The nurses accommodation at the hospital was so inadequate - four to a room - that Mary Kingsley chose to stay at the hotel much of the time. The solemnity of her requested sea burial was somewhat lightened by the fact that after being committed to the deep, her coffin bobbed afloat and had to be retrieved and weighted down with an anchor before disappearing from view. The **West Dockyard** gates of the Simonsberg Naval Base over the road are worth looking at with their handsome granite posts and intricate ironwork bearing the date 1863 on the left-hand set and 1966 on the replicated right-hand pair.

Further along the road you might like to take a peek at the rather festive looking new **Simon's Town Waterfront** and, well, as you're there why not take in **Jubilee Square** too - it is after all the heart of Simon's Town.

There is a bit of a walk ahead of you now to the burial ground, but on the way on the left when you get to the **Dutch Reformed Church**

The camp in Simon's Town.

you will see the '*Stem Pastori*' sign on the wall of the house below it. This is where '*Die Stem van Suid-Afrika*', now the second part of the National Anthem, was composed by Rev. M.L. de Villiers. The words were written by C.J. Langenhoven.

The house itself, built in 1899, is now the Museum of the National Emblems of South Africa.

You will know when you have reached the cemetery by the sign at the gate - '**Seaforth Old Burying Ground**, established 1813'. There is parking further along on the left-hand side of the road for those who took the easy option. Enter at the gates and walk straight up to the Naval and Military section on the left-hand side at the top. Turn left into Row 15. Towards the end of the row is the grave of Thomas Henry Hall of *HMS Powerful*, who died on 13 October 1899. He was the first serviceman to die in the Boer War. *HMS Powerful* and *HMS Terrible* were en route to and from the far east and both were diverted to Simon's Town with welcome manpower relief at the start of the war. Guns from the '*Terrible*' helped save the day at Ladysmith - they were the British answer to the Boers '*Long Tom*'. I won't list individual graves as this would need a book on its own but do have a look around, many of the tombstone inscriptions tell their own story. A grave in Row 17 commemorates Francis Coleman of *HMS Doris* - he was of the Naval Brigade on land and he died of enteric. *HMS Doris* was, for four years, the flagship of the Commander in Chief, Cape of Good Hope. Another vessel mentioned, in Row 4 is the *Kildonan Castle*. Brand new and built for the Castle Line just before it became the Union Castle Line, it was commandeered by the British Government and hastily converted into a troopship. While in Simon's Town it was used for a while to house 2 000 prisoners of war offshore in January 1901. They were well treated on board and instructions were given to the crew by the Captain, J.C. Robinson, to treat the Boers as '*honourable foes*'.

On your way back down the central avenue you pass through the Memorial area where there are some interesting, and sometimes amusing inscriptions to be read. One ship's surgeon was called Doctor Bones. Continue down and turn right along a path through the Roman Catholic to the Dutch Reformed burial ground. Here you will find a memorial to the Boer Prisoners of War. The Roll of Honour lists 82 names. The majority of Boer deaths were the result of typhoid contracted at the Battle of Paardeberg with the troops confined to a bombarded area where the water had become polluted by the bodies of horses and cattle lying in the river.

Mary Kingsley

Back at the main road turn right for the longest stretch yet and keep walking till you reach Boulders turn-off, and stop at the low rock on the right-hand side with a plaque on it. This was known as the **Post Stone** where the post was delivered - Boer prisoners had to line up here to receive their mail which was passed over their heads down the line. Ahead of you lies the **Simon's Town Golf Course**, the site of the Bellevue Prisoner of War Camp which most of the time held about 1 000 prisoners. Many pastimes and amusements were encouraged and they were allowed to sell their craftware at the camp and in the village - some of them even made a local equivalent of scrimshaw. They also formed a Prison of War Club with membership certificates printed on board and edged in gold.

Carry on down the road and turn right into Links Crescent. When you get to the cul-de-sac follow the path ahead of you to **Windmill Beach**. It was compulsory for the prisoners to take a morning swim here (on a rotation basis), throughout the year and one poor man was taken by a shark on 30 July 1901 - midwinter! The entire area was fenced in with barbed wire as was the path from the camp to the beach. Hard to imagine now. There was a ship's cat that had come with them from one of the prison ships which used to accompany them to the beach every day, but as it wasn't mad about swimming it used to hunt for moles instead. That's it - time to take the hundred year leap back into 2000. If you've walked all the way you now have a long slog back to your car, but you must admit Simon's Town is a delightful town to walk through. ❑

## SIMON'S TOWN TOURISM BUREAU

**St. Georges Street (*the Main Road*), Simon's Town.**
**Tel: (021) 786 2436.**

*Situated 40 km from Cape Town and a pleasant 25 km drive to Cape Point where the two oceans meet. Simon's Town is the Naval Base for the SA Navy. The main street has an array of interesting buildings from the Victorian period as well as a few dating back to the early 1800s. The drive from Simon's Town to Cape Point passes Boulders Beach famous for the Jackass Penguins; and you may see a troop of baboons on the roadside – a regular occurrence.*

### Other activities & places of interest

**Boulders Beach:** Off the Main Road towards Cape Point. Visit the *Jackass Penguins* site at Foxy Beach (entrance fee R10,00) next to Boulders Beach. At Boulders Beach enjoy one of the finest swimming beaches on the coast.

**Just Nuisance Ferry-boat Trip:** (pictured) Take an hour off and learn about Simon's Town and the Naval Harbour with the Just Nuisance boat trip around Simon's Bay. The boat leaves the jetty at the Quayside on the hour every hour from 10:00 hr (weather permitting).

**Just Nuisance Statue:** (pictured) Jubillee Square. Learn all about the famous Great Dane dog who was the *'sailors' friend'* during the Second World War. Have your photo taken at his statue on Jubilee Square.

**SA Naval Museum:** West Dockyard, Court Road. The historic mast house includes a life-size minesweeper and submarine dioramas, as well as a large collection of models and naval relics. (No entrance fee). Tel: (021) 786 4635.

**Simon's Town Museum:** The Residency, Court Road. The building was built for the Dutch Governor in 1777. The museum reputedly has its own ghost. The original slave quarters were housed in the building. It has an excellent and professional collection of artifacts relating to the history of Simon's Town. Well worth a visit. Tel: (021) 786 3046.

### Restaurants

**Bertha's:** Quayside. Enjoy breakfast, lunch or dinner, snacks, coffee – from light meals to fine cuisine. Overlooking the yacht harbour. Tel: (021) 786 2138.

**Black Marlin:** 5 km *en route* to Cape Point. World-renowned for seafood. Cape rock-lobster, linefish, abalone, oysters and mussels. Tel: (021) 786 1621.

**Bon Appétit:** St. Georges Street. French cuisine. Lunch and dinner. The finest food in Simon's Town. Excellent atmosphere and service. Tel: (021) 786 2412

**Django's:** Quayside. Light meals, pancakes, coffee bar and Roastery. Relax on the verandah overlooking the yacht harbour and Quayside jetty. Tel: (021) 786 1431.

**Penguin Point:** Boulders Beach. Breakfast, lunch or dinner. Snacks, coffee and light meals. Overlooking the Penguin colony and False Bay, enjoy a sundowner. Tel: (021) 786 1758.

**Pescados:** St. Georges Street.
Seafood and pizzas. Tel: (021) 786 2272.

**Plymouth Sound:** St. Georges Street.
Home cooking at very reasonable prices.
Tel: (021) 786 2993.

**CAPE POINT NATURE RESERVE:** Sir Francis Drake named it the *"Fairest Cape"*. One of South Africa's great tourist destinations. 7 750 hectares in area. Entry from 0700 hr to 1800 hr. It is one of the most spectacular combinations of sea and mountain scenery in the world. The wildlife that you might be fortunate to see are: Chacma Baboons, Cape Mountain Zebra, Bontebok, Eland, Red Hartebeest and Ostrich. The Reserve is essentially a floral reserve with *fynbos* 'fine bush', the vegetation of the Cape Floral Kingdom. It is a spectacular drive through to the Point. A funicular takes you to the old lighthouse where you can take pictures of the amazing panorama of False Bay stretched out in front of you. You can walk or drive to the *Cape of Good Hope* from the Point. There is an admission charge to enter the Reserve.

The big guns on the beach at Glencairn.

## NOORDHOEK

*At the southern end of Chapman's Peak Drive and famous for its magnificent 6 km beach where walking, horse riding, surfing, and fishing are popular. Visit the Noordhoek Farm Village with its arts & crafts shops, restaurants and cafés. Drive the famous Chapman's Peak Drive to Hout Bay.*

## SCARBOROUGH

*West of Cape Point, this small village is well-known for its restaurants.*

### RESTAURANTS

**Cobbs at the Cape:** Scarborough. Breakfasts, lunches, dinner and teas. Large selection of cakes and gelati. Tel: (021) 780 1480.

**Thorfynns at Monkey Valley:** Noordhoek. Set in a Milkwood forest overlooking the beach. Breakfasts, lunches and candlelit dinners with fine cuisine. Tel: (021) 789 1391.

## COLONA CASTLE, MUIZENBERG

This small hotel of rare distinction is furnished with antiques and offers unsurpassed panoramic views over Muizenberg, the Southern Suburbs and False Bay. Exceptional rooms with luxury touches.

7 Rooms (5 Rooms, 2 Suites) from R225 pp. B&B.
Tel: (021) 788 8235. Fax: (021) 788 6577.
Cell: 082 881 3204. e-mail: colona@link.co.za

## THE BRITISH HOTEL, SIMON'S TOWN

Overlooking the Simon's Town harbour, the British Hotel was home to many British officers during the Anglo-Boer War. It now comprises exclusive self-catering apartments with sea and mountain views.

4 Apartments from R175 pp. Accommodation Only.
Tel/Fax: (021) 786 2214. or (021) 790 4930.
Cell: 083 454 3877. e-mail: british-hotel@iafrica.com

## SIMON'S TOWN QUAYSIDE LODGE

A small elegant lodge overlooking the picturesque harbour and False Bay. Surrounded by the majestic Simons Kloof mountains. Situated at the Quayside Shopping complex. 15 min. walk to see the Penguins.

28 Rooms from R275 - R365 pp room only.
Tel: (021) 786 3838. Fax: (021) 786 2241.
e-mail: info@quayside.co.za

Scene of Simon's Town main street at the turn of the 20th Century.

**SOMERSET WEST TOURIST OFFICE**

**11 Victoria Street, Somerset West. Tel: (021) 851 4022.**

*45 km from Cape Town, this commercial and residential town at the foot of the Hottentots Holland Mountains was founded in 1822 and named after Lord Charles Somerset.*

## Historic Places & National Monuments

**Camphor Trees, Vergelegen, Somerset West:** The historical farm *Vergelegen* lies a few kilometres due east of Somerset West. There are five handsome centuries-old Camphor Trees in front of the house.

**The Dovecot, Meerlust, Faure:** An extract from Prof. G.E. Pearse '... *a short distance from the homestead is an interesting pigeon-house with enclosed courts on either side which were used for cockfighting*'. This is one of the best preserved examples in the Cape.

**Magistrates Court and Police Station:** The only original buildings left in Main Street, Somerset West. Both buildings were declared National Monuments in 1979.

**The Old Bridge:** Built over the Lourens River in 1845.

**Old Nederduitse Gereformeerde Church:** Built in 1820. A number of prominent South Africans are buried here.

**Die Ou Pastorie:** Dating back to 1819, it is now used as a guesthouse and restaurant - .

**Vergelegen:** With its magnificent backdrop of the Hottentots Holland Mountains, is a must for all visitors. Granted to Governor Willem Adriaan van der Stel in 1700, and a historic landmark, the property and its buildings have been extensively restored. There are guided tours to the Wine Cellar, built into the side of Rondekop Hill. Tel: (021) 847 1348.
A walk through the Octagonal Garden and Homestead leads to the *Lady Phillips Tea Garden* where teas and lunches are served on a daily basis. The Tea Garden is open seven days a week. Reservations are advisable Tel: (021) 847 1346. Al fresco lunches are also served at the *Rose Terrace* from November to April. There is an entry fee to Vergelegen of R7,50 per adult and R5,00 for pensioners and children.

## Other activities & attractions

**Arts and Crafts:** The Helderberg has an art route where Helderberg artists and crafters open their homes to the public on the last Sunday of every month. This allows one to meet artists at work in their studios. Brochures are obtainable at the Helderberg Tourism Bureau.

**Beaches:** The long sheltered beaches of False Bay are excellent for swimming, sunbathing and watersport.

**Bay Harbour:** Harbour cruises leave daily from the Gordons Bay harbour.
For bookings Tel: (021) 856 5204.

**The Helderberg Nature Reserve:** One of the Helderberg's greatest treasures. It starts at the foothills of the Helderberg Mountains, where families picnic in the shade of ancient oaks amidst rolling lawns, and reaches up the mountainside to places where hardy fynbos plants cling to the steep slopes. Birds are abundant in the reserve and over 169 species have been recorded. Several species of antelope occur in the reserve and visitors may spot Grey Duiker, Grysbok and Steenbok. Bontebok have also been reintroduced in this reserve.
There are several walks and these are graded from a gentle amble through the lower reaches to longer routes for the more energetic. Walking is the only way to really appreciate all that the Helderberg Nature Reserve has to offer.

**Open-air craft markets:** Somerset West is famous for it's craft markets which are held at Southey's Vines in Main Street on Saturday mornings. The Country Craft Market is becoming well known world-wide for it's many hand-crafted items.

**Sheik Yusuf Kramat (Shrine):** Sheik Yusuf is considered to have founded the Islamic faith in the Western Cape after he was exiled from Batavia by the Dutch in 1694. He died on the farm Zandvliet in 1699, where the Kramat is located today.

**Spookhill:** A visit to this spot often generates intense discussion on whether the fact that cars roll uphill here is an optical illusion or one of the world's great unsolved mysteries. It is found at the top of the Parel Vallei Road in front of Straightway Head Country House.

**Steenbrasdam:** Has several walks around the dams, as well as a picnic area and barbecue (braai) facilities. Permits are needed to enter the dam and can be obtained from Helderberg Municipality Tel: (021) 850 4000; Helderberg Tourism Bureau Tel: (021) 851 4022; Gordons Bay Tourist Centre Tel: 8565204.

**Whale Watching:** Clarens Drive in Gordons Bay is an ideal spot for Whale spotting. An official Whale watching board has been placed *en route* and there are benches provided for eager spotters.

## Stellenbosch Rebels

Many Stellenbosch people were involved with the war in the sense that they had close relatives who were fighting on the Boer side. Thus there was a great amount of secret sympathy with the Boer cause. Three sons of A.P.I. de Villiers of Langverwacht, Kuils River, who had become burghers of the Orange Free State, took part in the war. Their brother, Georg Jacob, was farming on the farm Saxenburg near Kuils River, assisted by his younger brother Attie. In 1900, shortly after his marriage, Georg was holding family prayers one evening when there was a knock on the front door. Attie went to open the door and found two young men there. He invited them in where Georg, with the open Bible before him, said: *"Friends, please sit down, so that we may first finish our devotions, then we can talk further."* In his prayer he interceded fervently for the Boers and especially for his three brothers who were all fighting on the Boer side. After a hymn was sung, the two young men introduced themselves: they were Serfontein and Barry, PoWs who had swum ashore from a ship in Simons Bay during the night. They had made their way inland from the coast and had knocked at the door of Saxenburg in the hope that the inmates would be sympathetic to their cause. The prayer had shown them that they had not made a mistake.

Annie de Villiers hastily prepared food and, during the tasty meal of baked snoek with its roe, homemade noodles and a glass of pontac from the farm, the four started planning an escape route – for the two young men were anxious to return immediately to the Boer forces. This was no easy task as the Cape Colony was under martial law and the National Scouts had posts on all the roads. They also had to rest some time before starting out, but after a few days the escape strategy had been worked out in detail. The two escapees were smartly fitted out in the then Cape fashion (with white straw hats, fine white corded silk shirts and tailored suits) and took on the identity of two De Villiers cousins from Fish Hoek who were going to visit an 'aunt' in Stellenbosch. Supplied with biscuits and biltong they started on the first stage of their journey: the National Scouts at Vlaeberg were quite satisfied to let them through and the Town Guards at Bosman's Crossing had no suspicions whatsoever. At the 'aunt's' home they were warmly welcomed and from there they found themselves sent off on the 'underground' line from farm to farm until they arrived safely with a Boer commando. Later they sent word that they had got through safely and many years afterwards the Serfontein girls who had come to study at Bloemhof school, spent their short vacations at Saxenburg.

## Golf Courses

The Helderberg has three 18-hole golf courses. One is the Gary Player designed *Erinvale Golf Course* which hosted the World Cup Golf Tournament in 1996. Then there is the *Somerset West Country Club* and *Strand Golf Course* where golf equipment can be hired.
*Erinvale Golf Club:* Tel: (021) 847 1906.
*Somerset West Country Club:* Tel: (021) 852 2925.
*Strand Golf Course:* Tel: (021) 853 6268.

## Restaurants

**Chez Michel Restaurant:** 41 Victoria Street, Somerset West. Tel: (021) 851 6069.
**Die Ou Pastorie:** Lourens Street, Somerset West. Tel: (021) 852 2120.
**Die Voorkamer:** Erinvale Hotel, Lourensford Rd, Somerset West. (021) 847 1160.
**Grand Café Amsterdam:** Harbour Island, Gordons Bay. Tel: (021) 856 5359.
**Heidi's German Coffee Shop:** Main Street, Somerset West. Tel: (021) 852 1960.
**Squirrels Coffee Shop:** Bredell Rd, Somerset West. Cell/Mobile: 083 700 8278.
**The Garden Terrace:** The Lord Charles Hotel, Somerset West. Tel: (021) 855 1040.
**The Lady Phillips Restaurant:** Vergelegen Estate, Somerset West. Tel: (021) 847 1334.
**The Village Green Coffee Shop:** Twin Oaks Centre, Somerset West Tel: (021) 851 5089.
**Willowbrook Lodge:** Morgenster Street, Somerset West. Tel: (021) 851 3759.

## Tour Guides (Satour registered)

**Lucia Brits:** (T. 0309). 3 Franz Street, Somerset West, 7130. Tel/Fax: (021) 852 1487.

**Kit Du Plessis:** (T.2538). PO Box 894, Somerset West, 7129. Tel: (021) 852 4435. Fax: (021) 851 2859.

**Yvonne Eppler-Irving:** (T.1595). 522 Helderberg Village, Somerset West, 7129.
Tel/Fax: (021) 855 3839.

**Jean Main:** (T.4359). PO Box 1972, Somerset West, 7129. Cell/Mobile: 082 779 3734.

**Chris Marshall** (T.2050). 23 Harewood Avenue, Somerset West, 7130. Tel/Fax: (021) 855 2218. Cell/Mobile: 082 564 5755.

**STELLENBOSCH TOURISM OFFICE**
**Rhenish Corner, 36 Market Street, Stellenbosch.**
**Tel: (021) 883 3584.**

*When Simon van der Stel took command of the Castle of Good Hope in 1679, the European settlement was still confined to the slopes of Table Mountain. During his first inspection of the cattle outposts of the Dutch East India Company, the commander camped on a small wooded island in the Eerste River. This island was then known as the Wildebosch, but he renamed it Stellenbosch (Stel's Forest) and decided to establish here a colony of free farmers to supply cereals to the Cape.*

*Visiting Dutch East India Company Commissioner-General H.A. van Rheede in 1685 instructed that a village be established. A House of Justice would be located on the island and a Church, as well as dwellings '**for the convenience of the residents**' such as a Minister, Schoolmaster and Smith. A wheat mill was to be erected in addition to a '**fine and proper street**', namely the Wagenweg to the Cape, subsequently Dorp Street. Thus the village of Stellenbosch came into being in 1687 as the first European settlement in the interior of Southern Africa. The historic streets of Stellenbosch still contain examples of the major building periods from the past and the town breathes an old world atmosphere thanks to its stately oak-lined avenues, bordered by babbling water furrows.*

## STELLENBOSCH DURING THE BOER WAR

On becoming Commander-in-Chief of the British Forces at the end of 1900, Lord Kitchener took umbridge at having to share the comforts of the Mount Nelson Hotel in Cape Town with lower ranking officers and ordered the latter to be transported by baggage train to the winelands town of Stellenbosch. Here the British had established a remount camp, in 1898 the year before the war, at *Koelenhof* (the remains of water troughs, a rifle range and graves can still be seen) just outside Stellenbosch, where they acclimatised the horses shipped in for the British army.

One such cargo of 4 500 horses was bought over from North America in the care of an American doctor named William Charles Winshaw, on board the *Laringa* in 1900. Winshaw had met up with the British army's Lieutenant McGuiness who was buying horses in New Mexico and having them delivered to *Koelenhof*. Winshaw went on to join the British army for the duration of the war.

The Stellenbosch depot soon became the largest and best. It also became known for another reason; early in February 1900 complaints were heard that the *Horse Supply Department* was receiving only those men who were unwanted in other sections of the army. Lord Roberts was also eliminating idlers. *Officers who did not come up to scratch were sent to the Remount Camp at Stellenbosch.* By ***Stellenbosching*** them Roberts found a way of dispensing with them without dismissing or formally disgracing them. They could occupy themselves with tasks that would not hamper the war effort. The term ***'to be Stellenbosched'*** became known to the public.

*The late Peter Barlow once mentioned to an aunt that he came from Stellenbosch. She replied "Don't be ridiculous, that is no place to come from – it is a place to go to!"*

# Stellenbosch

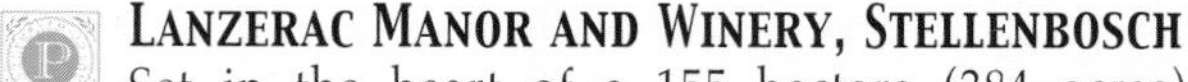

### LANZERAC MANOR AND WINERY, STELLENBOSCH

Set in the heart of a 155 hectare (384 acres) working wine estate, this 5-star luxury hotel is the ideal place to start exploring the Stellenbosch winelands. Purchase wine directly from the Lanzerac Estate.
40 Rooms from R546 - R870 pp Bed & Breakfast.
Tel: 27 (0)21 887 1132. Fax: 27 (0)21 887 2310.
e-mail: info@lanzerac.co.za

### BONNE ESPERANCE, STELLENBOSCH

A stylish decorated Victorian villa, offering warm personal attention. Ideally situated, close to the Wine Estates and excellent Golf Courses. Walk to town and enjoy the ambience of the cafés and restaurants.
15 Rooms from R180 pp sharing. R295 single. B&B.
Tel: (021) 887 0225. Fax: (021) 887 8328.
e-mail: bonesper@iafrica.com

### D'OUWE WERF COUNTRY INN, STELLENBOSCH

Historical Inn built in 1802 situated in the centre of town. Each room has been individually decorated with fully equipped bathrooms. Meals in the a la Carte restaurant. Swimming pool. Free parking.
25 Rooms from R355 pp sharing. Bed & Breakfast.
Tel: (021) 887 4608. Fax: (021) 887 4626.
e-mail: ouwewerf@iafrica.com

### EENDRACHT DORPSHERBERG, STELLENBOSCH

Eendracht Village Hotel is situated in the heart of Stellenbosch and has been rebuilt in the original architectural style on one of the oldest erven (plot) in Stellenbosch. Walk to town, shops and restaurants
11 Rooms from R189 pp. Bed & Breakfast.
Tel: (021) 883 8843. Fax: (021) 883 8842.
e-mail: lutzkor@iafrica.com

### LABRI MANOR, STELLENBOSCH

Set in the heart of Stellenbosch, offering warm friendly hospitality. A Victorian style house with elegantly decorated rooms and antique furnishings. Enjoy delicious breakfasts and high teas.
11 Rooms from R160 - R260 pp sharing. B&B.
Tel: (021) 886 5652. Fax: (021) 887 1501.
e-mail: labriman@mweb.co.za

# Stellenbosch

**VAN DER STEL MANOR, STELLENBOSCH**
Located in Mostertsdrift, part of Stellenbosch, this guest house of elegance and style is situated in the heart of the winelands. Each room at the Van der Stel has its own patio with a scenic view of the mountains. Secure parking.
4 Rooms from R295 pp sharing. R380 single. B&B.
Tel/Fax: (021) 887 4561. Cell: 083 679 0788.
e-mail: vdsmanor@iafrica.com

**KNORHOEK GUEST HOUSE, STELLENBOSCH**
Magnificent, tranquil setting on wine farm with its history and lineage traced back to the 1600's. The Victorian styled bedrooms have TV, M-Net, telephone and tea/coffee facilities. Relax in the sun at the beautiful rock-pool.
7 Rooms from R200 pp sharing. Bed & Breakfast.
Tel: (021) 882 2114/5. Fax: (021) 882 2627.
Cell/Mobile: 082 372 8770.

**SOVERBY GUEST HOUSE, STELLENBOSCH**
Situated on a wine farm next to Spier Estate and a few minutes from Stellenbosch. The homestead circa 1901, has been renovated, and the rooms were the original wine cellars built in 1907. Enjoy this beautiful part of the Cape. Bass fishing.
8 Rooms & 1 Cottage from R160 - R250 pp sharing.
Tel: (021) 881 3838/9. Fax: (021) 881 3433.
Cell/Mobile: 082 925 8785.

## DISCOVERING STELLENBOSCH ON FOOT – HISTORICAL BUILDINGS

**V.O.C. Kruithuis (Powder House):** (1777).
The unique form of this sturdy structure, with its fireproof brick roof (barrel vault) and high enclosing wall, reflects its function as a repository of arms. Above the loft window can be seen the graceful ***'V.O.C. – Cabo'*** monogram of the Dutch East India Company. Now a military museum.

**Rhenish Missionary Church:** (1823), Bloem Street.
Initially a rectangular hall, it was erected on a piece of ground earmarked for a racing clubhouse. The hall served to accommodate the crowds of *'slaves and heathen'* who came to listen to the enthusiastic Amsterdam missionary (and later Voortrekker parson) Erasmus Smit. After the founding in Germany of the Rhenish Missionary Society in 1828, the Rev.Paul Daniel Lückhoff assumed his duties in 1830. The emancipation of slaves in 1838 caused the congregation to grow to the extent that a northern wing was added in 1840. A magnificent baroque pulpit from the Stellenbosch Dutch Reformed Church, carved by Simon Londt of Cape Town in 1853, was ten years later donated when the "Mother Church" was gothicised. Today both the building and the pulpit are declared national monuments.

**Fick House (Burgher House):** (1797), 40 Bloem Street.
This is a modest H-plan house with casement windows, and top and bottom doors (the oldest Cape pattern). The front gable is the oldest neo-classical example in Stellenbosch, and is

characterised by a triangular pediment that rests on a projecting wall and surrounding winged scrolls. After the Rev. Lückhoff had purchased the property in 1839, a school was accommodated in a former part of the house.

**Winelands District Council Building:** (1935), 46 Alexander Street. Modern offices in a neo-Cape style that to some extent overshadow the historical buildings in its vicinity.

**St. Mary's 'On the Braak':**
This was the first neo-gothic building in Stellenbosch, although the whitewashed walls and thatched roof are typical of the Cape style. The cruciform ground plan dates from 1885, while the contemporary stained glass windows commemorate prominent families belonging to the Anglican congregation.

**Wilgenhof:** cnr. Victoria and Ryneveld Street.
*(previously Willow Grange, then The Willows, also The Willows Brandy Distillery)*
This is the first of many historical buildings that became students' housing. Its oblique position reflects the direction of an old wagon road from the village some three centuries ago. In 1880 the homestead was converted into a double storey, later known as *'Bachelors.'* After the **Anglo-Boer War** the outbuildings were consolidated and another storey was added, hence the nickname of *'Bekfluitjie' ('mouth-organ')*; a name that survives in the new three storey residence (1965).

**De Wit House:** (Early 19th century), Plein Street.
The only intact example of an imposing set of five adjoining neo-classical buildings, four of which were double storeys. On the adjoining modern archway is featured the municipal coat of arms, while the latter in turn-abouts on a marble frieze, adjacent to the entrance to the Public Library, commemorating the arrival of the Huguenots in 1688. These tableaux depict their Departure, the Sea Crossing and the Settlement, and were designed and sculpted in 1942 by *Ivan Mitford-Barberton (1896 – 1976).*

**Devonshire House:** (1851), 15 Ryneveld Street.
A restrained early-Victorian double-storey with a pitched roof of Welsh slate. Note the elegant round-headed doors and fine woodwork. It was erected by a descendent of Adriaan van Brakel, builder of the first Drostdy (1687).

**Moederkerk (Dutch Reformed Church):** (1863), Drosdy Street.
The lofty neo-gothic church with its tall spire was the common creation of the idealistic Minister, the Rev. Jan Neethling (statue in the church garden), the German architect Carl Otto Hager, and the English builder James Jardine. The custom of burying the dead inside the church was terminated in 1807 when the first tiled floor was laid. Thereafter family burial vaults were constructed against the graveyard wall.

**Kweekskool (Theological Seminary):** (1905), Dorp Street.
This is the most historical site in town, i.e. the former island named ***'Stellenbosch,'*** in 1679 and which disappeared in the 1770s when the northern watercourses of the Eerste River was filled in. This imposing gabled house in 1859 became the first institution of higher learning in Stellenbosch, with semi-detached apartments on either side for the Professors of Theology. A second storey, added to the building in its centenary year, was designed by architect Hager. This had a flat roof, and portico in front. The present imposing appearance – and the insensitive concrete work detracts from this – dates from 1905 and has the appearance of a Parisian *'Second Empire'* house of the 1860s.

**Kolonieshuis (Colony House):** 2 Ryneveld Street.
This house contains remnants of the oldest dwelling which stood on this site in 1694. Colony houses were built as lodgings for College of Law officials. Stellenbosch's first resident minister, the Reverend Hercules van Loon, lived here for four years before committing suicide in 1704. Subsequently enlarged into a gabled house with ornamental plaster benches at the end of the stoep, as witness the 1834 drawing by the famous astronomer, Sir John Herschel.

**Saxenhof:** 159 Dorp Street.
Named after free burgher and leather tanner Peter Andreas Sachse, to whom the land was granted in 1704. The present double storey dates from 1890 and has an attractive wooden balcony made by the owner, the district surgeon and artistic craftsman J.H. Neethling. The sturdy teak top-and-bottom door with its eighteenth century gabled design (the brass fittings are modern) is the only authentic example of its kind in Stellenbosch and, together with the 1768 front door of the Drostdy, are the oldest in town.

**158 Dorp Street:** An unadorned Victorian double-storey of which it is said that one window was adapted to facilitate the movement of coffins into and from the former funeral parlour inside. The problem of a house situated on the corner of a street was partially resolved by installing a front door to both façades, although the straight parapet and moulding have been omitted on the Andringa Street front.

**135, 133, 129, 127 Dorp Street:** This series of double-storeys were erected with the aid of state subsidies after the great fires of 1803, in order to encourage homeowners to build flat roofed dwellings, rather than the fire prone thatched houses. The best example of this group, two of which were demolished to make way for a road, is *Transvalia (127 Dorp Street)* with its plaster architrave surrounding a fanlight and vertically divided three panelled door.

**Oom Samie se Winkel:** 84/82 Dorp Street.
This was a typical rural shop before chain stores made their appearance. The name relates to Samie Volsteedt, a bachelor and previous owner of the shop, who lived in the house next door.

**Ackerman House:** (1815), 50/48 Dorp Street.
Was radically altered when it had a corrugated roof added, shortly before ***Jan Christiaan Smuts*** was a boarder here while studying at the university. Here too he met his future wife, *Issie Krige,* whose parents lived diagonally across the street in Libertas Parva. 53.

**Libertas Parva (Little Libertas):** 33 – 25 Dorp Street.
This H-plan farm homestead dates from c.1783, judging by its lovely rolling end gables. The present front gable dates from the late Georgian period, when the twin front doors and large pane windows were added. The name refers to the property that was formerly part of the farm Libertas. It presently serves as an important Art Gallery displaying a unique and beautiful panorama of Cape Town, in 1808. The cellar behind houses a Wine and Cork museum with artefacts dating back to the ancient (pre-Christian) era.

**Farm Labourers' Cottages:** Aan de Wagenweg.
Designed by Sir Herbert Baker at the request of Cecil John Rhodes, who owned the nearby farm Vredenburg. Now the *Volkskombuis Restaurant.*

**Wijnhuis:** cnr. Andringa and Church Streets.
This was originally part of a number of early 19th century thatched dwellings which were burnt down in the great fire of 1875. As a result it was much altered and Victorianised. Its interior loft today serves as a *Restaurant and Wine Tasting Centre*. One can see part of one of the original remaining walls at the entrance.

## Restaurants

**Auberge Rozendal:** Omega street. French style cuisine on a wine farm. Tel: (021) 883 8737.

**Avec Mariè:** Plein street. Mediterranean food.Tel: (021) 883 2654.

**Cafè Nouveau:** Plein street. Coffee shop. Tel: (021) 886 6257.

**D'Ouwe Werf:** Kerk street. South African Food. Tel: (021) 887 1608.

**De Soete Inval:** Ryneveld street. Pancakes. Tel: (021) 886 4842.

**De Volkskombuis:** Aan de Wagenweg. Traditional Cuisine. Tel: (021) 887 2121.

**Doornbosch:** Strand street. Italian & French. Tel: (021) 886 6163.

**Evergreen:** De Wet Centre. Health Food. Tel: (021) 886 6071.

**Fishmonger:** Ryneveld street. Fish & Seafood. Tel: (021) 887 7835.

**Hatter's party (coffee bar):** Coffee shop. Tel: (021) 887 3339.

**L'Auberge du Paysan:** French Food.. Tel: (021) 842 2008.

**Mon Doux Plaisir:** Coffee Shop (Belgian chocolate). Tel: (021) 886 5108.

**Mugg and Bean Restaurant:** Coffee Shop. Tel: (021) 883 2972.

**Museum (Ou Kombuis):** Traditional Food. Tel: (021) 887 2902.

**Nino's Italian coffee & sandwich bar:** Tel: (021) 886 5551.

**Panarotti's:** Italian Food. Tel: (021) 886 6123

**Rustic Cafè:** Mediterranean Food. Tel: (021) 883 3545.

**Spier:** Traditional, Mediterranean, Buffet, etc. Tel: (021) 881 3096.

**The Greek Kitchen:** Greek Cuisine. Tel: (021) 887 7703.

**The Little Cake & Coffee Shop:** Coffee Shop. Tel: (021) 883 3629.

## Museums

**Village Museum:** 18 Ryneveld Street.
The museum encompasses nearly 5 000 square metres of the oldest part of the town. Original houses from different periods of Stellenbosch's history have been lovingly restored and furnished to illustrate the development of the town.

**(a)** ***Schreuderhuis:*** This is the oldest restored town house in South Africa, built by Sebastian Schröder and was depicted shortly after its completion on the oldest sketch of Stellenbosch. Note the lead-glazed windows.

**(b) *Blettermanhuis:*** (1789). Built as a retirement house by Magistrate H.L. Bletterman 1795. It was later converted into public service offices and was restored in 1983 and furnished in the "Cape baroque" style from the second half of the eighteenth century.

**(c) *Grosvenor House:*** (c.1803). This was the first and presently only Cape Dutch double-storey in Stellenbosch. The flat roof, covered by plaster (corrugated iron roofs only appear after 1850) is characteristic of this house, as are the top-and-bottom door, small pane single sliding sash-windows and exterior shutters. One can also observe some neo-classical elements in the grooved pilasters and temple-shaped doorframe, with its Biblical palm tree (Psalm 92:13) in the pediment. The restored interior represents the first decades of the 19th century, when J.W. Herold used to live here.

**(d) *Bergh-Huis:*** This was initially an H-plan house. The house was subsequently enlarged and the opening between the pair of side gables became the entrance-hall. The ornate interior represents the home of a well-to-do Stellenboscher of the Victorian era between 1840 and 1880.

## Tour Operators

**Wineland Ballooning:** Daily morning Hot-Air Balloon flights. Tel/Fax: (021) 863 3192.
**Country 'Scapes Tours:** Day Tours of the Winelands and Peninsular. Tel: (021) 881 3707.
**Redwood Tours & Adventures:** Tours to suit the client: Cell/Mobile: 082 443 6480.

## Tour Guides

**Christine Du Toit:** (T.0213). 36 Forelle Crescent, Stellenbosch. Tel/Fax: (021) 887 4085.
**Hildegard Kidd:** (T. 4054). 36 Eastlynne, Die Laan, Stellenbosch. Tel: (021) 887 5727.
**Laetitia Knox-Davies:** (T.0273). 35 Unielaan, Stellenbosch. Tel: (021) 886 5925.
**Sandra Krige:** (T.4073). Uniedal, Stellenbosch. *Historic Walks* daily; *Summer Twilight Walks* and the *Popular Ghost Walks*. Tel/Fax: (021) 887 9150.
**Dries Smit:** (T.1528). 17 Formosa Street, Die Boord. Tel/Fax: (021) 887 2056.

*Oliver Knesl*

# Veterinary Surgeons

There is a monument in Port Elizabeth depicting a horse drinking from a bucket of water held by a kneeling British trooper. The memorial is inscribed as follows: ***'The greatness of a nation consists not so much in the number of its people or the extent of its territory, as in the extent and justice of its compassion. Erected by public subscription in recognition of the services of the gallant animals which perished in the Anglo-Boer War 1899-1902'.***

Jose Burman[1] in his book *'To Horse and Away'* suggests that the Boer War was a high point in the influence exercised by the horse on the development of South Africa. Arguably, without the horse the Boers could not have fought the war, their tactics revolving around the deployment of highly mobile mounted commandos. Similarly, without the horse the British could not have won the war and yet, the true losers of the war were the horses. Of the remounts supplied to the British Army, 63% died (326 000 out of 520 000), most from disease and exhaustion rather than from Boer bullets. By the time the war ended, Basutoland had been drained of her best horses and the Boerperd had been all but eradicated[1].

The horses were not the only losers, as during the war the British Army also suffered a dead loss of 51 000 mules and 195 000 oxen. There were additionally tens of thousands of horses and other stock captured and confiscated from the Boer forces that also perished in British hands. This total excludes the loss of animals which occurred after the war as a result of disease eradication programmes. Stated simply, the average **daily** ***loss of animals experienced by the British Army during the 32 month period of the war itself amounted to 336 horses, 53 mules and 200 oxen.***[2]

State Artillery Barracks, Pretoria, prior to the 1899-1902 War. Sir Arnold Theiler, the principal Veterinary Officer's office was situated extreme left on the ground floor.

> Near Fourteen Streams a lyddite shell exploded at the entrance to a jackal's lair. The jackal bounded out of another entrance and ran off, tail between his legs. (Sophia, 160)
>
> ROB MILNE

Sir Arnold Theiler KCMG and his secretary Mr Pluss in Theilers Office (Daspoort) in September 1899 just prior to the outbreak of the Boer War.

Major General Sir Fredrich Smith, KCMG CB FRCVS, whose *'Veterinary History of the War in South Africa 1899 - 1902'*[2]. was described by Curson[3] as *'a classic in professional literature'* noted in the introduction to his book that *'South Africa has long been regarded as the graveyard of reputations, and amongst those consigned to the scrap heap during the South African War was that of the Veterinary Service of the army.'*

At the outbreak of the war in 1899, the British Army Veterinary Department (AVD) consisted of 63 veterinary officers, five short of peace strength, and possessed no reserve of officers. By reducing the already diminutive veterinary establishment in India and leaving no one in England, except the War Office and Educational Staff, a total of 61 Veterinary Officers could be mustered for the campaign. To add to the problem the Veterinary Officers of the irregular forces were kept distinct and, in order to supply extra numbers, the AVD was forced to create a Civil Veterinary Service[2,3].

Thus, for the duration of the war, there was not a single Veterinary Service under a central administration, but rather several small groups of Veterinary Officers, working independently of each other, with disastrous results. Six separate veterinary commands were in existence, namely: the AVD, which later employed civil veterinary surgeons, the Imperial Yeomanry (operating on a regimental basis), the Natal Volunteer Veterinary Corp and the Canadian, Australian and New Zealand Veterinary contingents[2,3].

On 10 October 1899, there were 19 regular Veterinary Officers in South Africa distributed between Natal and the Cape Colony. Of these 8 were soon besieged at Ladysmith (including the Principal Veterinary Officer for Natal, Colonel Iles Matthews) and one at Mafeking, leaving a dozen for veterinary and remount duties[2,3,4].

On the Boer side the situation was perhaps more incredulous with only two veterinary surgeons on active duty, namely Sir Arnold Theiler KCMG in the Zuid Afrikaansche Republiek (Transvaal) and Otto Henning in the Republiek van de Oranje Vrijstaat (Orange Free State)[4].

Theiler, commissioned as an Officer in the ZAR Staatsartillerie, received orders in November 1899 to report to the Boer forces besieging Ladysmith. His duties were to inspect and maintain the health of the horses of the Boer forces besieging the town.

Major General Sir Frederich Smith, KCMG CB FRCVS.

Lt. Col. Herbert Watkins-Pitchford CMG FRCVS.

Medals from left to right:
The Most Distinguished Order of St. Michael and St. George; Queens South Africa Medal; Natal Rebellion Medal 1906; and Union of South Africa Commemoration Medal 1910.
These medals were awarded to
Lt. Col. Herbert Watkins-Pitchford CMG FRCVS who, as part of the Natal Volunteer Veterinary Corp, was besieged in Ladysmith.

Equipped with a mule-drawn mobile veterinary hospital Theiler tried to busy himself by riding to the various Boer positions to inspect horses. African Horse sickness season was not yet at hand, although Theiler noted a few cases amongst captured British horses. He had hoped to treat interesting war wounds, but few opportunities presented themselves, as most potential cases were simply dispatched with a bullet. Glanders being a stable disease, was hardly present. Occasional outbreaks of scab occurred and there were the ever present masses of ticks. Horses suffered occasionally from heat stroke, laryngitis and conjunctivitis (due to the plague of flies). Overall, however, Theiler and his Swiss staff were bored and rather disillusioned with the haphazard way in which the Boer leadership was conducting the war[5]. Not much is noted of Otto Hennings activities at this time, other than that the Bloemfontein State Veterinarian was also besieging Ladysmith as part of the Orange Free State Commando[4].

Within Ladysmith, Theiler and Henning's former Rinderpest research colleagues, Lt. Col. Herbert Watkins-Pitchford CMG FRCVS and some of the other veterinarians of the Natal Volunteer Veterinary Corp as part of the besieged garrison were facing a situation where typhoid and dysentery were rife and increasing, while food and fodder ran out.[5, 6]

At the start of the siege, Ladysmith contained 5 800 horses, 4 342 mules and 3 800 oxen within the British military camp. The siege effectively deprived the British Army of a Cavalry Brigade consisting of 4 regiments as well as 6 batteries of artillery[1]. As the siege progressed, Lt. General Sir George White was faced with the alternative of dismounting his cavalry or surrendering the town for lack of supplies. He chose the former, with the result that the once proud cavalry regiments contribution to the defence of Ladysmith was horse steaks, horsehair mattresses and a type of Bovril[1]. Quarter Master Sergeant Potter[7], in a private letter, recorded, *"As the siege lengthened it was realised that it would be necessary to use horse flesh as a diet. The Natal Volunteer (Veterinary) Staff therefore set an example by partaking, on 7 January 1900, for the first time, of the flesh of a horse killed by a piece of shrapnel. A few days later this article of food became a regular food ration."* All the while, the British Remount Department was importing masses of horses and mules from all over Europe (as well as Canada, Australia, Argentina and New Zealand) into South Africa. Many of the imported horses simply served as conduits for the introduction of

## Cruelty to animals

The British often destroyed captured enemy livestock by bayoneting them, and some of the soldiers enjoyed performing this terrible task. After they were told to stop killing sheep a British soldier was caught by his officer standing over a sheep that he had just bayoneted. "Under the officer's eye he looked severely at the prostrate beast, and remarked 'I will teach you to attempt to bite a British soldier'". (Schikkerling, 192)

ROB MILNE

Equestrian War Memorial, Port Elizabeth.

Veterinary Lieutenant J. B. Byrne of the Natal Volunteer Veterinary Corp outside his tent in Ladysmith during the Siege.

diseases such as Strangles, Mange, Equine Influenza and Glanders[2,5]. Gilbert May, a Civil Veterinary Surgeon attached to the Army Veterinary Department aboard the *S.S. Morayshire* was responsible for shipping out several consignments of remounts. The *S.S. Morayshire* was fitted to carry 800 horses (each being allocated a space of 10ft x 2ft x 8ft). Posthumus[9] records that in one such consignment, May identified and rejected two animals infected with Strangles. Despite his vigilance, by the time the ship docked in Port Elizabeth Harbour six weeks later, December 1901, 356 cases had occurred. In order to reduce losses, May and other veterinarians assigned to shipping duties were paid a bonus of one shilling per head if losses were under 7,5%, two shillings for losses under 5% and three shillings for losses under 2,5%. Shipping the horses in itself was fraught with difficulty

Entraining Horses at Cape Town, 1900.

as can be seen in the following extract from a letter by Veterinary Lt. George Stevenson who served as the Veterinary Officer for the Canadian unit – Lord Strathcona's Horse. The horses were being shipped from Halifax, Canada, to Cape Town.

*"The first few days the ship rolled considerably and several horses died of sea sickness; following the sea sickness an epidemic of pneumonia affected the horses and from this disease we lost a great number. Although every precaution was taken the disease seemed to spread until nearly every horse on the ship was affected ... at least from 85 to 90%. The isolated ones were not the cause of the disease as they showed no symptoms, nor were they affected with the disease until the voyage was about half over. I held several post-mortems and in every instance found the lungs very badly affected. In my opinion this disease was caused by the horses being brought, as they were, off the range where the mercury stood 35°-40° below zero, from a dry climate to a damp and warmer one.[11]"*

One of the principle causes of large scale horse mortalities once they had been landed in South Africa was the lack of time for rest and acclimatisation that they were allowed before being dispatched to the front. Horses are notoriously susceptible to digestive disturbances which usually manifest as signs of abdominal pain (colic)[8]. Smith[2] records that, *"The British Forces were tied down to certain localities beyond which they could not move; not only did local grazing rapidly become exhausted, but English horses, used to manger-feeding, were as helpless on the veldt as the town-bred soldier. They did not know what was expected from them; when they had purchased a little experience, the grazing had been eaten up by mules and herds of oxen. It seems to have been forgotten that the English troop horse was not a Boer pony. He was a newly arrived foreigner, unaclimatised, ignorant of the country, weak from a long voyage - having had no rest, and had recently left a comfortable stable where he had always been hand fed and kept tied up. He had no experience of hot dusty days and tropical deluges by night, yet he was expected to behave as if immediate adaptation to the methods of the animal of the country were possible."*

To economise, the army – despite vociferous opposition from the Acting Principal Veterinary Officer of the AVD in Cape Town - Colonel Matthews (PVO for Natal) was "holed-up" in Ladysmith with problems of his own – reduced the daily horse ration to 12 pounds grain and grazing, with no regular hay ration. The effect on the horses was calamitous. When Lord Roberts finally arrived in South Africa, Commanding Officers and Veterinary Surgeons complaints about the low ration scale had reached a large proportion. Roberts responded by sending his Acting Principle Veterinary Officer to the front who reported that no grazing was to be had *"within reasonable reach of any of the camps occupied by the western and central forces"* and that the forage in the vicinity of the Orange River had been eaten by locusts. The urgency of the operations at this time, however, resulted in every serviceable locomotive and wagon being used in the effort to relieve Kimberley, with the result that nothing was done to augment the forage ration. The intensive military operations at this time simply exacerbated the forage shortage and, paradoxically, until April 1900 when orders prohibiting this practice were first published, the British columns were implementing a policy of scorched earth which entailed destroying thousands of acres of crops and thousands of tons of grain so as to deny them to the Boer enemy[8]. On the Cape front, the actions of Belmont and Modder River were fought with the British mounted troops possessing 2 300 animals between them, but only two veterinary surgeons, Lts. Todd and Southey, to care for

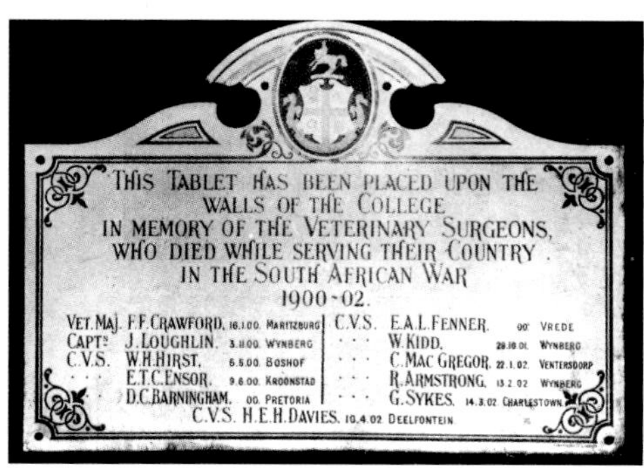


Mural Tablet erected in 1904 by the Royal College of Veterinary Surgeons, London, to the Veterinary Officer's who died during the Anglo-Boer War (1899-1902).

them. The Boers were allowed to retreat unmolested from Modder River, simply because the exhausted state of the British horses made pursuit impossible. Sand colic, with ruptured stomach, was prevalent at the Modder River camp and Veterinary Lieutenant Southey, running the risk of exhausting the limited drugs, he was forced to treat these cases with wood charcoal, which, when suspended in water, acted well in absorbing the gases in the stomach. The charcoal was prepared locally, an ant heap being converted into a receiver, the wood being placed into it and air being excluded as far as possible[2]. During the 30 days of operations between Modder River and Bloemfontein, the Cavalry Division lost 42% of its horses, while approximately one third of the horses in the force as a whole became unserviceable[8]. Throughout the war, these little dramas continued to unfold while inexorably the animal death toll continued to rise. James Hall Masheer served as a Civil Veterinary Officer attached to the 8th Hussars. In a letter to his father on the 4 February 1900 he recorded. *"We are 4 miles north of Bloemfontein ... I've had 3 meals in 4 days ... Camp is 3 inches deep in water, nowhere to lie down and nothing to cover us"*. Of the sick lines he wrote, *"A more ghastly sight I never wish to witness. There were about 500 horses in lines and everyone dead or dying ... no food or water for horses or men, but 3 inches of water on the ground."* Two weeks later the situation was even worse, *"Their lines are a morass of mud and water, right up to their hocks."* By the 13 May 1900 when the 8th Hussars reached Kroonstad they had lost two thirds of their horses, Masheter's own horse having been shot through the chest. His records show that when his brigade covered 350 miles in 34 days they lost 600 out of 1 000 horses.[9]

9th Lancer's going to water their horses at Modder River. Sand colic, with ruptured stomach, was prevalent amongst the horses at the Modder River camp and Veterinary Lt Southey, running the risk of exhausting the limited drugs he had, was forced to treat these cases with wood charcoal.

Smith[2] described South Africa as, *"A country of animal diseases"* and notes, *"Nor did it belie its reputation; never again, let us hope, will a veterinary service have such opportunities for seeing contagious and other diseases on a scale*

## HORSES

The Boers entrusted their lives to their horses. "In peaceful times there never can exist that same strong friendship between man and horse as in time of war, more especially in such a purely equine war as ours." (Schikkerling, 73). On occasion a horse or mule had to be put out of its misery. "And when the beast, in the last stages of exhaustion, could no longer follow and after every device had been tried, rather than leave it to perish of thirst, or be killed by wild beasts he would shoot it, and then sit weeping." (Schikkerling, 73). And from the beast's point of view: "He put four bullets through the beast's head, two from either side, and, as he was coming away, the beast, still living, looked wistfully up at us." (Schikkerling, 49 to 51)

Pictured left: Civilian Veterinary Surgeon J. Irvine-Smith (Commanding Officer) and the Non-commissioned Officer's of A2 Indian Field Veterinary Hospital, De Aar, 1900.

Pictured right: British Officers camp at Daspoort, 1901, on the site of the original Onderstepoort Veterinary Institute where Theiler had his Laboratory.

Pictured left and below: Dippling British Cavalry Horses for Mange, Kimberley 1901.

Pictured below: British Army Camp at Daspoort, 1901, outside Marabastad adjacent to the location of Theiler's original Laboratory at Daspoort.

## PHOTOGRAPHS

The photographs featured in this article are used with courtesy of ***Onderstepoort Veterinary History Museum; Loots Collection,*** South Africa, ***Museumafrica.***

*which baffles imagination. It is simple to speak of twenty to thirty thousand sick horses a month, but the mind is quite unable to grasp the real significance of these numbers."* Remount PARLIAMENTARY PAPER CD 963 (1902), accepted by Smith[2] as an accurate reflection of the prevalence of disease among British Army animals up to the end of June 1900 appears fairly innocuous at first glance. At this time, skin disease is not mentioned, glanders was under control and African Horse Sickness had not extracted a heavy toll during the summer months of the campaign. Biliary fever was not reported and casualties appear to have been caused largely by exhaustion and saddle injuries. In essence, therefore, up to June 1900, nothing in the way of epizootic infections had occurred which could not have been dealt with in a short time, had peace followed the capture of Pretoria. The seeds had, however, been laid for the serious disease problem which was to dominate the Army Veterinary Departments activities for the second two years of the war and by the end of 1900, *"The army was riddled with glanders, while mange cases existed by the thousands"*.[2]

It must be remembered that the AVD had entered the war with ***no*** veterinary hospitals. Early in October 1899, No.6 Field Veterinary Hospital arrived from India, soon being deployed in Ladysmith (9 more were to follow). These small, though highly efficient, hospitals were soon swamped by the stupendous collection of sick and starving horses streaming back from the cavalry, artillery and mounted infantry after the Paardeberg campaign. The army responded by establishing improvised hospitals at Bloemfontein, Kroonstad, Middelburg and Barberton. During the last month of 1900 the army decided to set up one thoroughly equipped hospital at Elandsfontein (Germinston) close to Johannesburg. The site selected was at an altitude of 5 800 feet and thought to be practically free from African Horse Sickness. At this hospital, accommodation was provided for 500 sick horses, and general accommodation for 2 000 more. By the end of May 1902 nearly 50 similar hospitals had been set up, containing nearly 20 000 horses and mules. An additional 8 000 to 10 000 were accommodated on debility farms under Remount control.[2, 3]

The bulk of the cases admitted to the veterinary hospitals and debility farms in the later part of the war consisted of debility and mange cases, although Smith[2] is quick to point out that the class of case admitted to the hospitals and that occurring in the field was markedly different, with many horses succumbing to African Horse sickness, Tulp poisoning and other rapid infections never surviving long enough to be hospitalised. Poisonous plants took a particularly heavy toll on the unaclimatised British Cavalry Horse with 30 or 40 cases of Tulp poisoning within a few hours not unheard of. The Remount depots were established with the primary intention of collecting and distributing locally purchased and imported horses and mules. With the steady stream of injured and debilitated horses flowing back from the front, many Remount depots were forced to double as debility farms and veterinary hospitals. At the close of the war, the depots were also flooded with loot horses, many in a pitiful condition – Mooi River Remount Depot was flooded with such loot horses among which glanders was rife and sarcoptic mange particularly virulent. Actual deaths due to mange and related skin conditions were estimated at tens of thousands, with at least 30 000 carcasses buried at the depot itself.[2,3] In essence, the 2nd Anglo-Boer War was perhaps the most tragic period in the history of veterinary science. The negative publicity that arose from the sickening wastage of horses and mules in South Africa, however, led to an investigation by a parliamentary committee in 1902. The outcome, a warrant signed by King Edward VII in 1903, created the Army Veterinary Corp.

The man elected to lead this reconstituted veterinary arm of the military was none other than Major General Sir Fredrich Smith, KCMG CB FRCVS. Condemning previous failures to apply sound principles of animal management and veterinary science, he set about rebuilding the army veterinarians reputation, succeeding to the extent that the Army Veterinary Corp was conferred the prestigious prefix *'Royal'* in 1918 after an astonishing performance in the 1st World War which saw 78% (two million of two and a half million animals) admitted to military veterinary hospitals during this war return to active duty.[10] ❑

**REFERENCES**


1. Burman, J. 1993. To Horse and Away. Human and Rousseau, Cape Town
2. Smith, F. 1919. A Veterinary History of the War in South Africa 1899-1902. H. & W. Brown, London.
3. Curson, H.H. 1937. The Army Veterinary Service in South Africa 1881 - 1914 (continued). The Jnl of the SAVMA Vol. 8 No.3.
4. Documentation Services, S.A. Defence Force. 1978. The S.A. Army Veterinary Services. The Jnl of the SAVMA Vol 49 No.4 pp 299-308
5. Gutsche, T. 1979. There was a Man - The Life and Times of Sir Arnold Theiler KCMG of Onderstepoort. Howard Timmins, Cape Town.
6. Watkins-Pitchford, H. 1964. Besieged in Ladysmith (A Letter to his Wife Written During the Siege). Shuter & Shooter, Pietermaritzburg.
7. Curson, H.H. 1934. The Veterinary Profession in S.A. : Natal Volunteers (1854 - 1913). The Journal of the SAVMA Vol.5 No.3 pp 157-177.
8. The Marquess of Anglesey F.S.A. 1986. A History of the British Cavalry Vol.4: 1899 - 1913. Leo Cooper, Secker and Warburg, London.
9. Posthumus, P.J. 1983. Past Veterinarians in South Africa. 10th Edition, Privately Published.
10. Dunlop, R.H. & Williams, D.J. 1996 Veterinary Medicine: an Illustrated History. Mosy, N.Y.
11. Clare, M.W. (Ed) 1992. Strathcona's Horse: letters and Weekly Reports between Lt. Col. S.B. Steele and Lord Strathcona and Mt. Royal. Private Publication.


## Aasvoël - Town Crier, Stellenbosch

When the war broke out Koos Bosman, son of Jacobus Petrus Bosman of Rozendal bottelary, was a farm school teacher at Kapokkraal, Bugersdorp, and in November 1899 he joined the Boer forces. He remained in the field almost to the end of the war, but while on campaign with General J.C. Smuts he contracted malaria and was taken to the hospital in Cradock. He recovered after some weeks and was transferred to the local gaol. On 9 March 1902 the magistrate of Cradock sentenced him to death, but the sentence had to be confirmed by Lord Kitchener in Pretoria. He was sent to his home town, where he was imprisoned in the old gaol in Dorp Street. By chance his brother had seen him when he arrived, so his parents and other relatives could visit him. His grandmother, the well-known Annie de Villiers of Villieria, Dorp Street, was given permission to send food to him in gaol.

Understandingly the whole of Stellenbosch was astir as a result of their compatriot who had been sent to his hometown to be fusiladed. One day Aasvoël, the town-crier, announced that the sentence would be executed the next day in public on the Braak.

The next morning five soldiers escorted the prisoner to the Braak where he had to take up position in the midst of a contingent of soldiers. The whole of Stellenbosch was present. The District Commandant read the charge against him as well as the sentence passed in Cradock; but then he opened a sealed envelope and said: *"But your sentence has, by the grace of Lord Kitchener, been commuted to penal servitude for life."*

Bosman was first sent to Worcester but later transferred back to Stellenbosch. Shortly afterwards a government commission reviewed the rebels' cases and Bosman's sentence was commuted to three years in gaol. On 19 March 1903 he was released in terms of the Amnesty Act. Old Aasvoël, mentioned above, was also the man who announced Martial Law in Stellenbosch. As town-crier he used to take up position with his bell on street corners in order to inform the public of all important notices. In June 1901 it was his task to announce that almost all horses were commandeered to be taken to the Remount Camp.

**FRANSCHHOEK TOURISM BUREAU**
**Huguenot Road, Franschhoek 7690.**
**Tel/Fax: (021) 876 3603.**

*Franschhoek, 30 km from Stellenbosch, was originally known as 'Olifants Hoek' after elephants calved in the valley which had food and water. During 1688 and 1690 the land was apportioned to 200 Huguenots fleeing persecution in France. Finding the climate similar to France the Huguenots planted vines. In addition, they brought with them the art of lacemaking and fine fabrics as well as other crafts. Franschhoek is well known for excellent cuisine and accommodation. Time can be spent browsing the shops and antique stores.*

## Boer War Site

There is a display at the Huguenot Memorial Museum on **Marquis Robert de Kersauson de Pennedref *'Robert die Fransman'*.** He was a French Nobleman who came to Pretoria via Lourenço Marques (Maputo) to join the Boer forces. He was sworn in as a Transvaal burgher by President Kruger at Machadadorp on 14 June 1900. He invaded the Cape Colony with Gen.Jan Smuts and while in the Northern Cape he took despatches via German South West Africa (Namibia) to President Kruger in Europe. He rejoined Smuts Commando at Springbok. After the war he returned to France on the same ship as General Maritz. He returned to South Africa after the Second World War and lived on Mr.Max Smuts farm in Franschhoek. His grave is situated between the Huguenot Memorial and the Museum building.

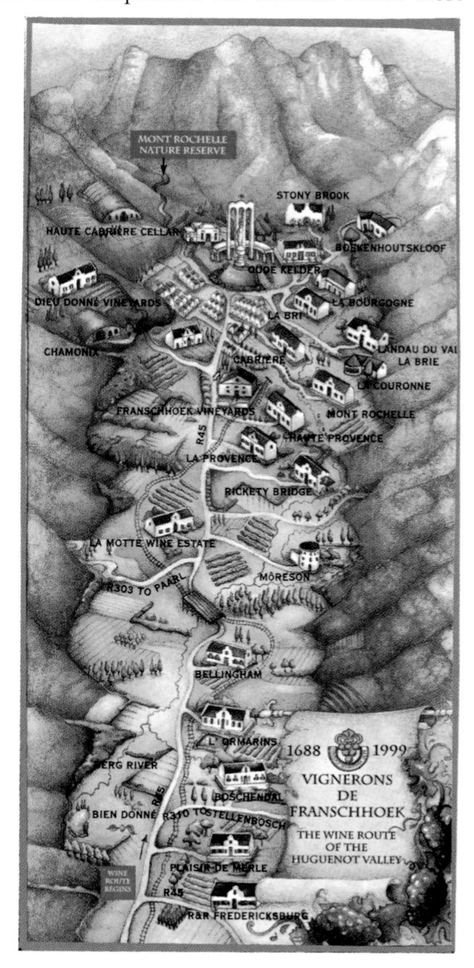


## Attractions

**Bien Donne:** Restored manor house and tours of the orchards. Tel: (021) 874 1864.

**Boschendal Estate:** Cape Dutch manor house. Restaurants. Wine sales. Tel: (021) 874 1031.

**Kei Carpets:** Handknotted carpets and woven products produced on the farm Le Mouillage, La Motte. Tel: (021) 876 2192.

## Wine Estates

**Bellingham:** *"If there was a prize for a cellar showing the most improvement over a short time, it would go to the Bellingham cellar."* says David Hughes, wine correspondent. It says it all. Tel: (021) 874 1011.

**Boekenhoutskloof:** Home of the *Porcupine Ridge* wines and the *Boekenhoutskloof* range of wines. Tel: (021) 876 3320.

**Boschendal:** Produce highly prized wines. Tel: (021) 870 4000.

**Cabriére Estate:** Producers of *Pierre Jourdan* Cap Classique wines. Tel: (021) 876 2630.

**Chamonix:** Award winning wines, Schnapps and a spirit aperitif Kamasutra. Open 7 days a week at the Blacksmith Cottage. Tel: (021) 876 3241.

**La Motte:** Vineyards with noble varieties. Tel: (021) 876 3119.

**L'Ormarins:** Testimony to the excellence of the wines can be found in the 79 trophies and 491 medals awarded locally and abroad. Tel: (021) 874 1026.

**La Provence & Haute Provence:** Gold Medal winning *Angels' Tears* based on the French legend where angels came at night to taste the new vintage and wept for joy at its excellence. Tel: (021) 876 3195.

**Rupert & Rothschild Fredericksburg:** A new cellar with exciting wines. Tel: (021) 874 1648.

### Restaurants

The selection is large, and only a few have been listed below.

**Boschendal Estate:** The following are the eateries at the estate. *Boschendal Restaurant* for a sumptuous buffet luncheon; *Le Café* for light lunches and teas; and *Le pique-nique*, the famous picnic hamper filled with simple country fare in the shade of the lofty pines. And of course the famous *Boschendal* wines are available. Tel: (021) 870 4274.

**Chamonix:** Light lunches, picnics, cakes & teas served under the cool green oaks of the Bistro style restaurant.

**Haute Cabriére:** Cellar restaurant with an unforgettable gastronomic experience. Enjoy the meal with a bottle from the selection of *Pierre Jourdan* wines. Tel: (021) 876 3688.

**La Petite Ferme:** Set high above Franschhoek with views of the valley. Country cuisine accompanied by *La Petite Ferme's* wines. Tel: (021) 876 3016.

**Le Quartier Francais:** Renowned for its innovative cuisine. Tel: (021) 876 2151.

### Museums

**Huguenot Museum:** This museum reflects the history and persecution of the Huguenots in France. Tel: (021) 876 2532.

### Tour Guide

**Gillian Stoltzman:** (T.1517) 12 Akademie Street, Franschhoek 7690. Tel: (021) 876 3643. Fax: (021) 434 9999. Cell/Mobile: 082 893 5387.

### Restaurants

**De Oude Herberg:** Open for breakfast, light lunches, teas and dinners. Tel: (023) 230 0260.

**Paddagang:** 23 Church Street. Situated in a Cape Dutch building. Famous for the authenticity of its traditional Cape dishes. Paddagang also produces an amusing range of *'Padda'* (frog) wines. Open daily from 1030hr - 1600hr. Tel: (023) 230 0242.

**Pieter Potter:** Lunch and dinner from Tuesday to Friday. Saturday: Dinner and Sunday: Lunch. Tel: (023) 230 1626.

**Rijk's Restaurant:** Rijk's Ridge Country House. Tel: (023) 230 1006.

### Museums

**Miniature Houses Museum:** 4 Witzenberg St. Admission: R5.

**Oude Drostdy Museum:** Drostdy Wine Cellar.

**Oude Kerk Volksmuseum:** Church Street. Admission: Adults R5, Children R2.

### Tour Operator

**John Ingram:** Waterval Country Lodge. Tel: (023) 230 0807. Fax: (023) 230 0757.

# Tulbagh

## Rijk's Ridge

Cape Dutch styled accommodation with views across a lake to the mountains. Enjoy the bar and snooker room and visit the town. Each room has a private terrace close to the pool. Classic country cuisine.

12 Suites. 3 Cottages from R250 - R450 pp. B&B.
Tel: (023) 230 1006. Fax: (023) 230 1125.
e-mail: info@rijksridge.co.za

## Waterval Country Lodge

Historic homestead on a 40 acre estate with garden rooms each with its own entrance. Walk to the waterfall and its natural pool, hike or mountain bike or enjoy the large swimming pool. Dinners arranged.

5 Rooms from R215 pp sharing. Bed & Breakfast.
Tel: (023) 230 0807. Fax: (023) 230 0757.
e-mail: waterval@interkom.co.za

## Waterval Bush Camp

Luxury Safari Tents and Log Cabins en-suite in stunning location on a 40 acre estate overlooking farms to superb views of the mountains. Barbeque/braai under the stars at the boma or dinners arranged.

14 tents & log cabins from R150 pp self-contained.
Tel: (023) 230 0807. Fax: (023) 230 0757.
e-mail: waterval@interkom.co.za

**RIEBEEK-KASTEEL & RIEBEEK-WEST TOURIST INFORMATION:**

Voortrekker Road, Malmesbury. Tel: (022) 487 1133.

*Riebeek-Kasteel & Riebeek-West virtually join each other as they are 4 km apart. They are popular and visited by the Capetonians for the various eateries and restaurants. Excellent towns for staying at while exploring the area.*

### Boer War Interest

**General Jan Smuts Birth house:** Visit General Smuts birthplace which is situated on the property of PPC (Pretoria Portland Cement) a kilometre or two outside Riebeek-West. The house has been maintained by PPC who have done an excellent job. There is a small museum in one of the outhouses which portrays the life and times of this great statesman. There is no entrance fee.
**Riebeek Valley Hotel:** The original building was used as a hostel for Boer orphans.
**Wagon Makers Museum:** There is an interesting wagon museum on a farm in the area. The wagons used by the Boers in the area were produced at the farm.

### Accommodation

**Dalmar Country House:** Riebeek-West. Accommodation and meals. Tel: (022) 461 2245.
**The Lodge B&B:** Riebeek-West. Excellent B&B accommodation. Tel: (022) 461 2660.
**Riebeek Valley Hotel:** Riebeek-West. Superb accommodation and meals. Tel: (022) 461 2672.

### Restaurants

**Bishops Pub & Restaurant:** Riebeek-West. Traditional food. Tel: (022) 461 2672.
**Burgundy Snail:** Riebeek-West. Excellent meals in convivial atmosphere. Tel: (022) 461 2713.
**Royal Hotel:** Riebeek-Kasteel. Steaks, seafood and wholesome meals. Tel: (022) 448 1378.
**The Travellers Rest:** Riebeek-Kasteel. Stylish lunches, also vegetarian. Tel: (022) 448 1383.
**Wild Hen Coffee Shop:** Main Road, Riebeek-Kasteel. Coffee, light snacks and lunches.

*Andrew J. McLeod*

# The making of the man ... Jan Smuts

Born in Riebeeck West in the Cape in 1870, Jan Christiaan Smuts becomes the State Attorney for the Transvaal (ZAR) in June 1898 - without doubt becoming a burgher of the republic. It is soon clear that this young man with flaxen hair and a clear, glowing complexion, who could flush like a girl, had a genius lurking inside. However his father is reported to have said, *"He is a poor unhealthy youngster, a queer fellow without much intelligence."*

Even before the Anglo-Boer War broke out he was the right hand man to President Paul Kruger. He was too valuable to the ZAR government to allow him to join the commandos. Nevertheless, he often visited the war zone in Natal during those opening months. He was obviously longing to be part of the action. And why not? He was a young man of only 29 years.

When Lord Roberts was on the point of capturing **Pretoria**, it was the young Smuts who saw to it that the state's gold and some £25 000 in cash was removed from the capital. He played a major role in ghosting away the old president. He joined General Botha in the eastern Transvaal while the Boer forces were planning their new approach to the war. Smuts had recommended all along that the way to tackle Britain was not by large concentrated armies fighting a conventional war but with smaller, self-reliant and fast-moving commandos.

At that stage General Christiaan de Wet was proving just how right Smuts' theory was. He had resounding successes at **Sannaspos** and **Rooiwal**, where his main goal was to disrupt the British war machine.

Smuts was sent to the western Transvaal, together with General Koos de la Rey. To re-organise the commandos and re-motivate the people. Also to impede the British forces. Together the two formed a *'Separate Government'* in order to take quicker decisions. Smuts was still the civil servant, De la Rey the general. But Smuts soon became involved with military matters and he had the best teacher of them all: *The Lion of the West*. From him he learned that you need confidence and audacity. Soon he would philosophy about the lack of confidence in the British officer. However, this young attorney, who was now turning soldier, and who was later to develop the theory of holism, was a philosopher even then. To him the **Magalies Valley** was analogous to the Shenandoah Valley in the United States. And General De la Rey reminded him of General Stonewall Jackson. To him *'the spirit that broods over Magaliesburg is one of profound pathos and melancholy ... a subtle appeal to be at rest and cease from the futility of striving. And yet one heard the Voices which had called mankind to its task of endless endeavour.'*

Smuts was the thinker – withdrawn and analytical of the situation and a lover of nature. He respected valour – he could understand that some burghers surrendered – but he could never accept treason. He would criticise the older generation generals and pay homage to the brave.

He was called to that 'endless endeavour' in October 1900 when, together with General J. De la Rey, General L. Botha and President M.T. Steyn plans were made for the rest of the war. They were camped at the idyllic farm Cyferbult near **Rustenburg**. And if those plans in the end did not work out, he wrote, at least they were not going ahead without a plan. Part of this plan was for him to invade the Cape Colony. Thereby they would divide the concentration of British forces. Now the attorney became a general. He never carried more than a revolver and a sjambuck. He wrote to his wife Isie that *'military life agrees wonderfully with me.'* He and his commando only entered the Cape Colony in September 1901. He leaves a trail of frustration for General John French and his men, who were out to capture him. After months of hardships and narrow escapes he captures **Springbok** and **Concordia** in Namaqualand and lays siege to **O'Okiep copper mine**. His future plans are all worked out. Just then, when all was going well, and he was pleading for more burghers, he was recalled to take part in the Peace negotiations. And that *'unhealthy, queer fellow, without much intelligence'*, came back to the Transvaal - a man broadened in body and mind. A man with confidence and enjoying a ruddy health. Yes, military life did agree with Jan Christiaan Smuts. ❑

***Sources:***


Bateman, P., *Generals of the Anglo-Boer War,* Cape Town, 1977

Hancock, W.K., *Smuts, The Sanguine Years, 1870-1919,* Cambridge 1962

Nattrass, G. & S.B. Spies, *Jan Smuts, Memoirs of the Boer War,* Johannesburg, 1994.


## PAINFUL INTRODUCTION TO THE BOER WAR

The first taste of the Anglo-Boer War for Beaufort West's newly-formed District Mounted Troop unit was a rough one in February 1901. As bands of Boer soldiers moved into the area between Beaufort West and Prince Albert, the British Army deployed the 2nd Brabants Horse, a Colonial regiment, to cut them off and stop them crossing the Swartberg into the southern Cape.

The British ordered the Beaufort West DMT to ride into the Koup to drive the dreaded Commandant Gideon Scheepers toward the more experienced unit but, filled with raw enthusiasm and the hope of capturing the commando from the north, the Beaufort West DMT set off by a round-about route. Suddenly, on 7 February, 15 miles south of Beaufort West on the farm *Kaffersfontein*, they found themselves surrounded by Boers – those who managed to escape later ambushed the Boer soldiers visiting young girls on the farm *Scheurfontein*. Japie Hauptfleisch was killed during this incident. In revenge, a Coloured lad, accused of tipping off the DMT about the presence of Boers, was shot by Hauptfleisch's friends.

*"Thou wears a lion's hide! Doff it!"* – a Boer in British Uniform. COURTESY: MORLEYS ANTIQUES, CAPE TOWN

The troopers of the DMT captured by the commando that day had a rough time. Their clothes and shoes were confiscated and they were forced to walk, barefoot, ahead of the Boer horsemen across the blazing Karoo veld. Not given any food, they lived on left-overs. Eventually they were so weakened, tired and hungry and in such pain they simply straggled along with the commando as it moved through the Prince Albert district. At the end of two weeks they could go no further – they collapsed and simply refused to budge. It seems, however, the commando was only too happy to be rid of them and rode off without a backward glance. One of the DMT troopers remembered the railway line was not far away. With much encouragement his comrades crawled and staggered to the tracks where they managed to board a passing train and soon, in a sad, filthy and dishevelled state, returned back home.

ROSES ROUND UP

**DARLING TOURIST BUREAU**
**Pastorie Street. Tel: (022) 492 3361.**

*75 km from Cape Town. Darling was named after Lieutenant Governor Charles Henry Darling. Darling's environment is a kaleidoscope of vineyards, wheat, dairy, sheep farms and the immense beauty of the wild flowers. it is the mecca of 15 local artists and the famous Mrs Evita Bezuidenhout entertains the 'volk en vaderland' at Evita se Perron. Darling is the centre of a rich dairy farming area and one of the largest fresh-milk producing centres in the country.*

### Boer War Sites

In 1901 the Boers raided deep into the Cape Colony and Darling was the most southerly scene of fighting.

**Hildebrand Monument:** Hildebrand was from Lichtenburg, Transvaal and was killed on 13 November 1901. He was part of Maritz and Wynand Malan's Commando. They penetrated south to within sight of Cape Town. Field Cornet C.B.Hildebrand was killed here and his grave, of the Boer fighters graves, is the closest to Cape Town. From Darling take the road to Yzerfontein and approximately 8 km you will find the road to the memorial on the right-hand side. If you continue on this road to Salamander Bay at the entrance of Saldahna Bay, there are two Naval graves. *(1) Robert Walden of SS Kilburen 4 March 1900. (2) Gunner Jeffries RMA HMS Monarch 15 January 1900.*

**Minature Blockhouse:** Although not a Boer War site. The minature Blockhouse at the cemetery is worth a visit.

### Attractions, Activities & Restaurants:

**Basket Factory:** Open weekdays. Tel: (022) 492 2515.
**Darling Museum:** Pastorie Street. The production of butter is strikingly portrayed with examples of utensils used in earlier days. Tel: (022) 492 3361.
**Duckitt Orchid Nursery:** Open from May to November on the first Saturday of the month. Tel: (022) 492 2606.
**Evita se Perron:** The Railway Station. Restaurant and Show. Tel: (022) 492 2831.
**Wildflower Reserves:** Visit the wildflower reserves. For information contact Tourist Bureau. Tel: (022) 492 3361.
**Zum Schatzi:** Continental cuisine. Tel: (022) 492 3095.

## Darling

### Parrott's Guest House, Darling

Beautifully renovated Victorian house. Luxury accommodation in the quiet West Coast country town of Darling conveniently situated for Cape Town and Cape Winelands. Light suppers are available.
4 Rooms from R185 pp sharing. Bed & Breakfast.
Tel: (022) 492 3430. Fax: (022) 492 3430.
Cell/Mobile: 082 579 7160

**PIKETBERG TOURIST INFORMATION:**

Church Street, Piketberg. Tel: (022) 913 1126.

*Piketberg, 130 km from Cape Town, takes its name from the Piquet Berg or Piketberg, at the foot of which it is situated. This name refers to the posting of military guards (**piquet** or **piket**) against marauding Khoekhoen under Gonnema during the term of office of Governor I. Goske, 1672-1676.*

### Boer War Information

For information on what happened in the area; may I suggest you contact Mrs Du Toit at the Museum. Tel: (022) 913 1126.

### Other Attractions

**Canon:** At the High School. The canon was used during the 1700s to warn farmers of the approach of raiding Khoi-San.
**Dutch Reform Church:** Circa 1882. A striking example of architecture.
**Piketberg Museum:** Hoog Street. Curator is Mrs Du Toit who is extremely knowledgeable of the area; and can show visitors around her Boer War display.

### Accommodation

**De Berge Guest House:** Long Street. 12 rooms with double and twin beds. Tel: (022) 913 2836.
**Dunn's Castle:** Piketberg Area. B&B and self-catering accommodation. Tel: (022) 913 2470.
**Noupoort Guest Farm:** Situated on top of Piketberg mountain with spectacular views. Telephone: (022) 914 5754.

### Restaurants

**Piket Braaihuis:** Steaks and more steaks.
**Winkelshoek Coffee Shop & Restaurant:** Good cuisine. Tel: (022) 913 1092.

**CLANWILLIAM TOURIST BUREAU**
**Old Gaol Museum, Main Road, Clanwilliam.**
**Tel: (027) 482 2024. Fax: (027) 482 2361.**

*Clanwilliam, one of the oldest towns in the country, is rich in history.*
*Situated 232 km from Cape Town, this town offers an historical route, a flower route in season, hiking trails and rock-art viewing.*
*It is also the centre of the* Rooibos Tea *farming area which includes farming of fruit, vegetables and sheep ... plus the well-known* Velskoen *(Veldshoe) factory.*
*The Dam is popular as a water-resort and one of the best in the Western cape for water-skiing.*

## Boer War Activities and Sites

**The Englishman's Grave**

The lonely grave of Lieutenant G V W Clowes *'Die Engelsman se Graf'* beyond the Pakhuis Pass is known to most South Africans in the Western Cape. The very name - the very spot of the grave has an aura of romance and mystery about it. Who is Lt.Clowes and what are the circumstances surrounding his death and grave at the turn to Wupperthal Mission on the road between Clanwilliam and Calvinia over the Doring River.

On the 29 January 1901 Colonel Henry De Beauvoir de Lisle of the Gordon Highlanders supported by Colonel Bethune left Clanwilliam with his column along the Pakhuis Pass with the intention of engaging the Boers in the vicinity of Elandsvlei as small groups had been sighted in the area towards the east of the Pass. They camped for the night at the summit of the Pass and the next day continued to Elizabethfontein where they decided to stay for the night. That same afternoon a small patrol consisting of Captain Gordon, Lieutenant Clowes and two men went ahead to reconnoitre. The terrain is rugged with huge rock outcrops and tailormade for an ambush or surprise attack. The Boers who managed to find cover were hidden from the British patrol and watched them approaching. They held their fire until Capt.Gordon and his men were quite close when the Boers poured in a volley killing Lieutenant Clowes and wounding Captain Gordon in the foot and mortally wounding a Private M Clarke who with Captain Gordon and the fourth trooper managed to get away.

Col.de Lisle deployed his men for an attack on the supposed position of the Boers but they had vanished into the waterless and inhospitable waste towards the east.

During the advance the body of Lt. Clowes was recovered and he was buried close to where he fell. The service was read by Colonel de Lisle and the Gordon Highlanders erected a stone cairn over the grave. De Lisle reached Elandsvlei on 2 or 3 February after a difficult march over rough and precipitous country.

Lieutenant Clowes was born in 1880 and educated at Eton where he was a member of the school choir. He joining the Shropshire Militia in March 1898. In October 1898 he was commissioned into the 1st Battalion of the Gordon Highlanders and sailed with his regiment for South Africa on the *'Cheshire'* on the 9 November 1899 arriving in Cape Town on the 28 November. He was involved in the actions at *Magersfontein, Zand River* and *Thaba Nchu.* Later he joined the Mounted Company of the Regiment under Colonel de Lisle and fought with them at *Doornkop, Pretoria, Diamond Hill* and other engagements.

He received his promotion to a full Lieutenant on the 1 August 1900. He grew up in Hitchin in Hertfordshire and worshiped at St.Mary's Anglican Church in the same town. In the church which dates back to the year 702 and Saxon times, there is a sad collection of brass plaques commemorating the history of his family.

His young sister Kathleen died in 1888 aged 14; his mother Ellie Dorothea Clowes died in 1894 at the age of 41; and his father Winchester Clowes died in 1900. The fourth plaque commemorates the death of the young Lieutenant Clowes. The gravestone on his lonely grave must have been erected by another sister of his - but she too was to experience a life of tragedy and sadness. She married a Lieutenant Colonel Shepherd who was Commanding Officer of the Hertfordshire Yeomanry. In August 1915 he too was killed while marching with his battalion across the dried salt pans at Gallipolli straight into the machine gun fire of the Turks.

When next the winter rains fall and the first warm sunshine of early spring transforms the Pakhuis Pass and the Biedouw Valley into a riot of spectacular colour stop at the lonely *'Engelsman se Graf'* and remember ...

***"For each son of man is a son divine***
***Not just to the mother who calls him 'mine'***
***As he stretches out his stricken hand***
***Wounded to death for the Father Land"***

Private M Clarke died of his wounds and is buried in the Anglican churchyard in Clanwilliam. His grave is in the furthest row from the street.

***Sources:***
M M de Villiers, November 1998.
*'Scars upon my heart'* by Catherine Reilly.
*'An Incident'* by Mary H J Henderson.

OTHER ATTRACTIONS:

**Louis Leipold's Grave:** The ashes of the Afrikaans poet are in a grave at the side of the road on Pakhuis Pass.

**Historical Buildings:** The Old Magistrate's Court (1808); The Dutch Reformed Church (1864) and the Old Gaol (1808).

**Rooibos Tea Tours:** Tel: (027) 482 2155.

**Velskoen Factory:** Tel: (027) 482 2140.

**Wupperthal Moravian Mission Station:** Hidden behind the Cedarberg Mountains. The founder of Wupperthal, Johann Gottlieb Leipoldt, grandfather of poet/writer Dr Louis Leipoldt, started his mission work in the valley in 1830.

# Clanwilliam

**LAMBERTS BAY TOURISM BUREAU**
**Church Street, Lamberts Bay.**
**Tel: (027) 432 1000.**

## Boer War Activities

**HMS Sybille (Boer attack):** The *Sybille* was sent to the West Coast during the Anglo-Boer war after the British had received reports that friends of the Boers in Europe were supplying them with weapons. It was believed that Lambert's Bay was used as the point of disembarkation for the weapons. The rumours were never confirmed but the British warship continued with its reconnaissance of the West Coast. It became the only ship of the Royal Navy to engage the enemy (The Boers) from the sea. While the ship was at anchor in Lambert's Bay, a Boer Commando under the command of General Hertzog came down to the sea and saw the *Sybille*. the Boers opened fire on the ship; who returned the fire. No one was hurt.

**HMS Sybille (The Sinking):** On 15 January 1901 the *Sybille* was lying at anchor in Lamberts Bay. Rumours were rife about the dissention between Captain Williams, commander of the *Sybille*, and his crew. On this evening the Captain and some of his officers went ashore for a party; the sailors were ordered to remain on board. Capt.Williams put his worries aside and surrendered to the spirit of the party - as well as the booze that was flowing. Having become somewhat inebriated he decided to spend the night recovering in someone's loft.

In the meantime, the crew on the *Sybille* decided to have their own party. It was equally jolly and the longer it continued the more hectic it became, until about midnight when one of the crew decided to take a short trip out to sea. This could have been to prove to the Captain that they could do without him!!! Or so they thought.

The *'booze cruise'* turned out to be the last that the *Sybille* was ever to undertake. She was driven on by a strong North wind and the ship struck a reef at about 0200 hr in the morning. A kilometre further on she ran aground and broke in two.

The guns were fired as emergency signals, which at first was thought to be claps of thunder by the people of 'Steenboksfontein'. One of the local inhabitants rode (on horseback) to Lamberts Bay to summon help and arriving at daybreak found that no one was aware that the *Sybille* had

*"The Wreck of the Sybille"*. Courtesy: WOODY NEL. Telephone: (021) 61-3603

left its anchorage. The crew members on board were rescued from the foc'sle of the ship, but two of them drowned during the rescue operation.

The ship had run aground near where the engagement with Hertzog's Commando had taken place. Those members of the crew that landed at Lamberts Bay became entitled to the **Queens Medal CAPE COLONY clasp.!!**

The story continues; as the running aground of the *Sybille* brought much activity to the sleepy community of Steenboksfontein. Engineers from a company in UK came to South Africa to dismantle and salvage the interior fittings of the ship. They were accommodated at 'Steenboksfontein' to the chagrin of the local inhabitants, who were in the main, Boer sympathisers. One of the engineers happened to be Harry Blades, a good looking, charming and friendly young man - but after all a Brit. His work kept him occupied at 'Steenboksfontein' and the burghers treated him with hospitality. At times it was extremely difficult to communicate with him in english. Harry was a frequent visitor to the farmstead (Steenboksfontein Farm) and the *'fat was in the fire'* when the farming community discovered that the reason for the regular visits was the attractive young Maritjie Burger. A courtship between a *boere* girl and a *Brit* was just too much for the *Sandvelders* (the area is known as the Sandveld). However, Harry and Maritjie were not discouraged, and they waited patiently for 6 months until she turned 21 when they got married and left together for England.

## OTHER ATTRACTIONS AND ACTIVITIES

**Bird Island:** Joined to the mainland by a breakwater to protect the fishing fleet in the harbour. Bird Island is a breeding ground for Jackass Penguins and Cape Cormorants.

**Sandveld Museum:** Church Street. Filled with antiques as well as a Dutch Bible reputed to be over 300 years old.

**Whale Watching:** (July–November). The Southern Right Whale can be seen on its annual migration north. Breaching and Lobtailing as they court.

## A QUEEN'S DEATH STUNS THE GREAT KAROO

During the Anglo-Boer War, the news of Queen Victoria's death in 1901 was greeted with deep emotions in the Karoo. British gun salutes echoed across the veld and rumours of battles spread.

Journalist Edgar Wallace received the news at Matjiesfontein and wrote this poignant piece: *"Queen Victoria had ever been a sacred subject among the rank and file of the army. They are very broad-minded the men who serve and love her; Papist or Buddhist or Jew are one with their Protestant selves. They are governed in their thoughts towards her by a love which cannot be commanded."*

*"At Matjiesfontein,"* so writes Wallace, *"a tired postal clerk, pencil in hand, loops up moving tape and transcribes the dots and dashes into plain English. The night is passing; already the clear white glow of morning is turning the lamplight a sickly yellow. Messages have been coming through all night and I who have been listening to the tape-talk am almost as weary as the clerk. Suddenly the clerk drops the festoon of tape and listens to the instrument. He is reading by ear as the chattering sounder speaks. He raises a tremulous hand to his lips to hide a tell-tale quiver.* 'Her Majesty died last night.' *Outside the wind has dropped, the veld was silent and peaceful and the eastern sky was gold and crimson. So I left the clerk with his bowed head on his arm and went and told the men."*

ROSES ROUND UP

# Matjiesfontein
# The *Jewel of the Karoo*

*Visit Matjiesfontein and turn the clock back over 100 years.*

Matjiesfontein village was founded in 1884 by a young enterprising Scot, shipwrecked on his way to Australia. He bought a Karoo farm called *'Tweedside'*, which was on the main railroad to the north. Logan not only developed the farm, but saw the potential in providing a refreshment room at the station for hungry and thirsty travellers. In those days there were no dining cars on trains.

He also found the dry Karoo air, some 1000 metres above sea level, very beneficial for his asthma so he began to develop Matjiesfontein as a Victorian Spa and health resort. With his flair, energy and attention to detail, (he imported lampposts from London), this *'Oasis in the Karoo'* soon became popular with the cream of Cape society and attracted an extraordinary variety of characters - Cecil John Rhodes, Sir Randolph Churchill, the Duke of Hamilton and the Sultan of Zanzibar among them.

Matjiesfontein's most famous resident was writer and feminist Olive Schreiner. Her first novel,*"The Story of an African Farm"*, was set in the Karoo, and gained immediate international recognition. After spending time in Europe, she returned to the Karoo to find relief for her asthma. She loved Matjiesfontein, and lived in a small cottage where she kept up correspondence with a number of English friends, including William Gladstone, George Bernard Shaw and Havelock Ellis.

Olive Schreiner's advanced views on social justice and feminism were almost as controversial for her time as those of her friend Havelock Ellis. He shocked Victorian England with his seven-volume work, *"Studies in the Psychology of Sex"*. Olive's correspondence with Havelock Ellis reveals the great delight she took in Matjiesfontein.

*"Now I am going to put my hat on and go out for a walk over the Karoo. Such a sense of wild exhilaration comes over me when I walk over the Karoo ... I love the Karoo. The effect of this scenery is to make me so silent and self-contained. And it is all so bare, the rocks and the bushes, each bush standing separate from the others, alone by itself."*

During the Anglo-Boer War of 1899-1902, Matjiesfontein was the headquarters of the Cape Command and hosted 12 000 British troops. The hotel was used as a military hospital and its turret became a lookout. Old bully-beef tins and other relics of this time can still be found in the veld.

Matjiesfontein was never again so crowded. And when the national highway bypassed it on its way north, the little village faded into obscurity. Later its unspoilt Victorian charm was restored.

So today, as tourists travel through spectacular scenery to the high plateau of the Karoo, they can stop over in a little Victorian village that looks the same as it did 100 years ago. And, like visitors a century before, they can breathe deeply the air that is like dry champagne. ❑

## REITZ'S TWIN TOWERS OF THE DWYKA

There are four blockhouses in the immediate area of Laingsburg in the Karoo – one just about 12km out of town along the N1 (which you can't miss) and the other three guard the bridges at Ketting and Dwyka stations. The two blockhouses at Dwyka are the **'twin towers of the Dwyka'** referred to by Deneys Reitz in his publication *'Commando'*, while the one at Ketting station is immortalised by Rudyard Kipling in his poem *'Bridge Guard in the Karoo'*. When visiting these blockhouses (along a little used gravel road) remember to take both Reitz's 'Commando' and a copy of Kipling's poem – it all comes to life so vividly when read at the exact spot.

ROSES ROUND UP

PLACES OF INTEREST

**Lord Milner Hotel:** Fountains play in the gardens of the gracious Victorian hotel, fashionable home to distinguished guests at the turn of the century.

**The Laird's Arms:** Enjoy a draft of ale in the festive English country pub, named after the enterprising James Logan, the *'Laird of Matjiesfontein'*, who founded the town in the 1890's.

**Marie Rawdon Museum:** The museum provides a fascinating glimpse into the history of Matjiesfontein, purchased in its entirety in 1968 by Mr David Rawdon and restored to its original Victorian glory.

**Post Office:** During the Anglo-Boer War, correspondents used the little post office's brass telegraph key to send urgent dispatches.

**Olive Schreiner's Cottage:** *"The full African moon poured down its light from the blue sky onto the wide, lonely plain"*. - Evocative opening lines from Olive Schreiner's novel, *"The Story of an African Farm"*.

**The Coffee Shop:** The rich aromas of well-brewed coffee waft through the cosy meeting-place, where visitors can enjoy refresh-ments in a Victorian ambience.

**Chapel:** The snow-capped Swartberg mountains provide an impressive backdrop to Matjiesfontein's small chapel, where worshippers have gathered for a century.

**Railway Station:** In the era before dining cars on trains, James Logan opened a restaurant here and, while the locomotives replenished water, served meals to the passengers.

**Ride in a London Bus:** An unforgettable experience of the Victorian Village from the vantage of an original Red London bus. Original London lamp posts still light Matjiesfontein's main street.

**Losieshuis:** The Losieshuis, James Logan's original Masonic Hotel, is built of corrugated iron and originally formed part of his model village and health resort.

**The Blue Train and Rovos Rail:** Both stop here to allow the passengers to enjoy the atmosphere of Matjiesfontein.

## MERWEVILLE

*A small Karoo village in picturesque surroundings of mountains and plains. It is situated 45 km north-west of Prince Albert Road and 130 km from Beaufort West. It is unspoilt with time and there are charming Karoo cottages and a magnificent Dutch Reform Church.*

### ACCOMMODATION

**The Koup Guest House:** A six-roomed self-catering guest house.
Contact: Hugo Muller on Tel: 02026 ask for 54.

**Die Losieshuis:** Historic boarding house with 7 bedrooms and 3 bathrooms. There are 2 braai areas, a snooker and games room and a social "kuier kamer'.
Contact: Kallie Le Roux on Cell/Mobile: 083 255 6931.

**Lalapanzi (sleep well) in the Karoo:** 2 self-catering houses - locally known as *'The Shop House'* and *'The Bath House'*.
Contact: Cindy Spence on Cell/Mobile: 082 375 1285.

**Nova Vita Farm:** Offering farm holidays, hunting and eco-tourism.
Contact: Suzaan and André Theron on 02026 ask for 1403.

**Banksgate:** Offering farm holidays as well as walks, hikes, rambles, abseiling and eco-tourism.
Contact: Danie and Anette Blom on 02026 ask for 1930.

### BOER WAR SITE

On the outskirts of the village there is a grave of a British soldier who committed suicide.

## MERWEVILLE'S AUSTRALIAN 'ENGLISHMAN'

On the outskirts of town a signpost points the way to 'The Englishman's Grave'. In the nearby veld a tiny marble cross marks the grave of a lieutenant from Australia who served with the British forces during the Anglo-Boer War.

Walter Oliphant Arnot was a member of the 3rd South Australian Contingent. In June 1888, he married Eleanor Frederica Rosevear Seabrook, whom he affectionately called 'Nell'. By 1900 they had four children aged between four and nine.

He served with distinction but died by his own hand on 16 April 1902, leaving a strange note to his wife in his Book of Common Prayer. On a page torn from his pocket book was a map of a road and across it was written: *"This was not for the Boers"* and on the back he wrote: *"I swear before God, whom I am going to meet, that I am innocent"*. It was signed W.O. Arnot.

In his prayer book was a photograph of his wife and between the last page and back cover was a picture of his four children. On the fourth page, written in a shaky hand was: *"I was never in any concern with a Boer or Boer Agent by all we ever had between us good held me and you my darling - goodbye, Walter"*. Also found in a tunic pocket were rail tickets to Matjiesfontein and Laingsburg, a quotation from Shakespeare and letters to his wife and children.

ROSES ROUND UP

## THE JAILER IS JAILED

During the Anglo-Boer War, Van der Byl, a magistrate in the Merweville area, suffered the indignity of being imprisoned in his own farm jail. On a scouting mission one day, Boer Commandant Wynand Malan and his men arrived at the farm. After an altercation with Van der Byl, they locked him in the little farm jail and rode off with the key. Chaos ensued. No duplicate key could be found. With the help of labourers and members of the farming community, they had to break into the jail to free the magistrate. The event forever remained a sore point with Van der Byl, seldom keen to talk about it.

ROSES ROUND UP

Pictured top and left:
Typical families in South Africa at the turn of the 20th Century.

## WHEN COAL WAS THE DRAWCARD

During the Anglo-Boer War a string of tiny coal mines on farms provided fuel for Merweville and several other towns. The coal was transported to town after dark by wagons with well-greased wheels so that as little noise as possible was made. In these isolated communities, dung patties were used as fuel, but so much livestock had been commandeered by the British that these were scarce.

Even though the coal was of a low grade, it nevertheless interested Bernard Israel Nowitz, a Cape Town businessman, so he moved to Merweville and applied for permission to prospect and mine the deposits. The request was turned down, which did not deter him from becoming a member of the local community. Nowitz established a General Dealer's store, married a local girl, joined the Dutch Reformed Church and promptly declared himself a 'Christian Jew'.

Nowitz became a highly-respected and loved member of the community. Soon more Jews followed. Among them were the Katz, Magid, Samuel, Godliep, Lazarus and Solomon families. Some of these men travelled the Karoo as pedlars and speculators before they married local lasses and settled in Merweville.

ROSES ROUND UP

**PRINCE ALBERT TOURISM ASSOCIATION**

**Tel:(023) 541 1366.**

*At the foot of the Swartberg Mountains and 67 km from Oudtshoorn, Prince Albert (after the Prince Consort) obtained municipal status after the Boer War in 1902. There are scenic drives and a variety of local produce to tempt you – sample* ***Witblitz*** *(a potent liqueur) which is made at the museum.*

## Boer War Activities

An extract from the book **Prince Albert and the Anglo-Boer War 1899 - 1902 by Helena Marincowitz.** (Obtainable from the Fransie Pienaar Museum). *'Prince Albert was occupied by the British during the War, while there were skirmishes in Die Gang, and patrols searching for Boer commandos in the mountainous terrain of the region. Gideon Scheepers, the Boer Commandant, has become part of local folklore as a charismatic leader of his commando, who was eventually tried for treason and paid the ultimate price. To me (Helena Marincowitz), after visiting the ruins of the house where Gideon Scheepers was captured and also visiting the graves at Klaarstroom, the war became a reality.*

## Other Attractions

**Fransie Pienaar Museum:** Tel: (023) 541 1172. Worth a visit – interesting displays of the type of equipment used for the Gold Rush at the turn of the 1900s.

**Gamkaskloof 'The Hell':** Known as *The Hell* on account of its inaccessibility. The area was inhabited by the Trekboers over 150 years ago. It is now administered by the Cape Nature Conservation and the historical farmsteads are being restored.

**Stargazing:** Visit the private observatory and enjoy an evening with the stars.

**Swartberg Pass:** Built by Thomas Bain, the pass offers spectacular views of the Swartberg.

**Tour Guide:** Helena Marincowitz. Tel: (023) 541 1366.

# Prince Albert

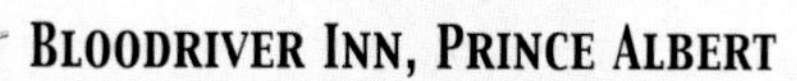

### Bloodriver Inn, Prince Albert

3 1/2 hours from Cape Town and George. Once a Roadside Inn. Close to the bridge that inspired Rudyard Kipling's *"Bridge Guard in the Karoo."* Here Boer Commandant Gideon Scheepers was held prisoner while waiting for a train for Matjiesfontein.

Tel/Fax: (023) 541 1766. Cell: 082 859 5630.

e-mail: lmb@cybertrade.co.za

### Swartberg Country Lodge, Prince Albert

140 year-old Victorian building with spacious comfortable fully equipped rooms. Swimming pool and gardens with relaxing atmosphere and traditional South African cuisine. Explore the romantic Swartberg Pass and area.

18 Rooms from R215 pp sharing. Bed & Breakfast.

Tel: (023) 541 1332. Fax: (023) 541 1383.

e-mail: swartberg@webmail.co.za

## GIDEON SCHEEPERS

Although Gideon Scheepers was executed by a British firing squad, he was not one of the Cape 'rebels'.

Born in the Transvaal, Scheepers was just 17 when he joined the republic's only professional military unit, the *Staats Artillerie*, in 1895. During the South African War he was seconded to the Orange Free State Artillery and promoted to commandant, leading a small commando in the Cape

A fearless and popular leader, Scheepers welded his men into a tight unit. They wrecked trains, burnt the farmsteads of those unsympathetic to the Boer cause and kept the British occupied trying to capture them.

Scheepers was taken prisoner on a farm near Prince Albert and tried by a military court at Graaff-Reinet on more than 30 charges (including murder). Found guilty, he was executed outside the town beside an open grave in January 1902. His body was apparently disinterred by the British during the night and secretly reburied.

Many believed that a British military court was not competent to sentence a non-British prisoner of war to death during the war, and there was an outcry.

# Lieutenant Oats of the Antartic and Gideon Scheepers of Beaufort West

**(From '*The crossed paths of Boer and Brit Folk Heroes*)**

British patrols were sent in pursuit of a Boer commando, which was under the command of **Gideon Scheepers**. One of the British patrols under the command of a **Lieutenant Oats** went down the road to Beaufort West. They were well exposed and presented an ideal target for the Boers who lay in ambush. Six miles from town, on the farm Fairview, Boer bullets began to fly into them and their guide was captured. The patrol took refuge in a dry riverbed where an unhealthy exchange of fire ensued. The captured guide was sent to the beleaguered patrol demanding their surrender, Oats refused and the skirmish continued. Later in the day a second message was sent and again Oats refused the offer to surrender. By noon he had received a bullet in the thigh, it shattered his leg badly. The pinned down group had to wait until dark before they could be rescued. Oat's leg was never the same. Some time later **Gideon Scheepers'** luck ran out and he was captured, tried and executed. Oats, on returning from the epic journey to the South Pole with Captain Robert Scott found that the cold, hunger and exertion of pulling a sleigh for more than three months was too much for his old wound. The old war wound had broken down and the leg was badly swollen.

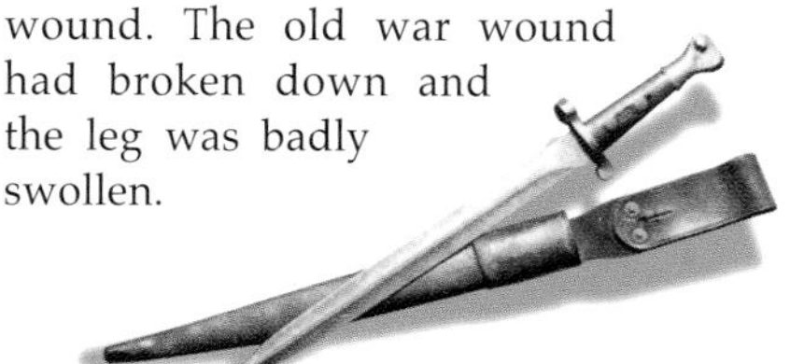

He would go no further and was now a danger to his desperate companions. On 17 March 1912, he stepped out of their tent and into the teeth of a storm with the words, *"I am just going outside and may be some time"*. Both men were Folk Heroes from two different worlds, but are joined by the whine of a bullet in a dry riverbed, far from home. ❑

**BEAUFORT WEST TOURISM BUREAU**
**Museum, cnr. Church and Donkin Streets.**
**Tel: (0201) 5 1488.**

*570 km from Cape Town, Beaufort West is the capital of the Great Karoo. It lies in an arid zone famous for its fossils and flora. There are more than 9 000 species of plants in the Great Karoo. The Karoo National Park on the outskirts of the town on the N1 (5 km south) is well worth a visit and an overnight stay.*

## BOER WAR SITES

**Blockhouse:** Recently renovated to its original splendour. The blockhouse can be found guarding the railway bridge. A worthwhile visit.

**Graves:** Of Boer and British soldiers can be found at the various church cemeteries and graveyards.

**Memorial:** There is a memorial to the convoy which was ambushed by Commandant Malan on its way to Fraserburg in 1902.

## OTHER ATTRACTIONS

**Architecture:** Interesting architecture of Victorian, Georgian and Cape Karoo styles can be seen through out the town.

**Karoo National Park:** Tel: (0201) 5 2828. Highly recommended for overnight or 2 - 3 night stay. There is an abundance of plains game and Black Rhino has recently been introduced to the park. A fascinating fossil route has been laid out close to the Chalets. A bird-hide overlooking a small dam for the ornithologists. Drive around the Park and enjoy the game. Night drives available in open 4x4 vehicles. The chalets look onto an amphitheatre and in the mornings you can see the Springbok casually meander pass your chalet while feeding.

The restaurant supplies good food and wines; otherwise you can 'braai' your own meals outside your chalet. Each chalet is fully equipped as a self-catering unit if required.

**Meiringspoort:** On the road to Oudtshoorn (N12). The 20 kms river gorge is a magnificent drive with view sites where you can stretch your legs and admire the splendour around you.

**The Post Coach House:** 111 Bird Street. Built in 1820 as a town house for a farmer who then left on the Great Trek in 1836.

## RESTAURANTS

**Karoo National Park:** The restaurant has a good menu and a nice selection of wines. Arrive early and have a sundowner on the stoep/verandah overlooking the plain and the mountain range. Pre-book for a Night Drive in an open vehicle. Tel: (0201) 5 2828.

**Matoppo Inn:** (pictured right) Country cuisine. Tel: (0201) 51055.

**Saddles Steak House:** For the steak enthusiast. In the main road.

**Tour Guide: Rose Willis**. Tel: (0201) 51160. Cell/Mobile: 082 926 0474.

# Beaufort West

### Beaufort Manor

Situated in a quiet area, the Beaufort Manor offers tastefully decorated rooms with satellite TV, fan or air-conditioner. Take hiking trails to Bushmen paintings or explore the town museum portraying Chris Barnard.
6 Rooms from R180 pp sharing, R230 single. B&B.
Tel: (023) 414 2175. Fax: (023) 415 2178.
e-mail: droloff@mweb.co.za

### Clyde House Guest House, Beaufort West

This National Monument Victorian-styled house was built in 1839 and used as a Police Station at the time of the Anglo Boer War. All rooms are en-suite. Walk around the lovely, historic town of Beaufort West and visit the museum.
4 Rooms from R140 pp sharing. Bed & Breakfast.
Tel: (023) 414 4083. Fax: (023) 414 4083.
Cell/Mobile: 082 680 2233.

### Matoppo Inn

Situated in a quiet street and located in the heart of the Great Karoo at Beaufort West, Matoppo Inn was once the historic residence of the town's Drostdy. With beautiful Yellowwood floors and high wooded ceilings this was a favourite overnight stop of Cecil John Rhodes.
9 Rooms from R180 - R250 per person room only.
Tel: (023) 415 1055. Fax: (023) 415 1080.

### Lemoenfontein Game lodge

Situated 6,5 km north of Beaufort West, this lodge was built in the 1800's and used for hunting. There are 20 species of game to see including Buffalo, Giraffe and Zebra. Enjoy a hearty bush breakfasts and boma barbecues.
13 Rooms from R200 pp B&B. Dinner available.
Tel: (023) 415 2847. Fax: (023) 415 1044.
e-mail: lemoen@mweb.co.za

### Uniforms

By July 1901, Boer uniforms were getting really interesting. *"He wore knickerbockers, his bulging calves were enclosed in a pair of lady's stockings, and in his hat he sported a white feather. The assemblage looked very much like a cannibal fancy dress meeting. One officer wore a jacket of monkey skin, hair to the outside; another officer a jacket of leopard skin. One looked a cross between Attila the Hun, and Sancho Panza. Others wore odd garments of sheep, goat, and deer skin, and of green baize and gaudily coloured blankets. Quite evidently the apparel does not here proclaim the man. Only last week, a man was decked out in green baize trousers and a dress suit jacket".* (Schikkerling, 250).

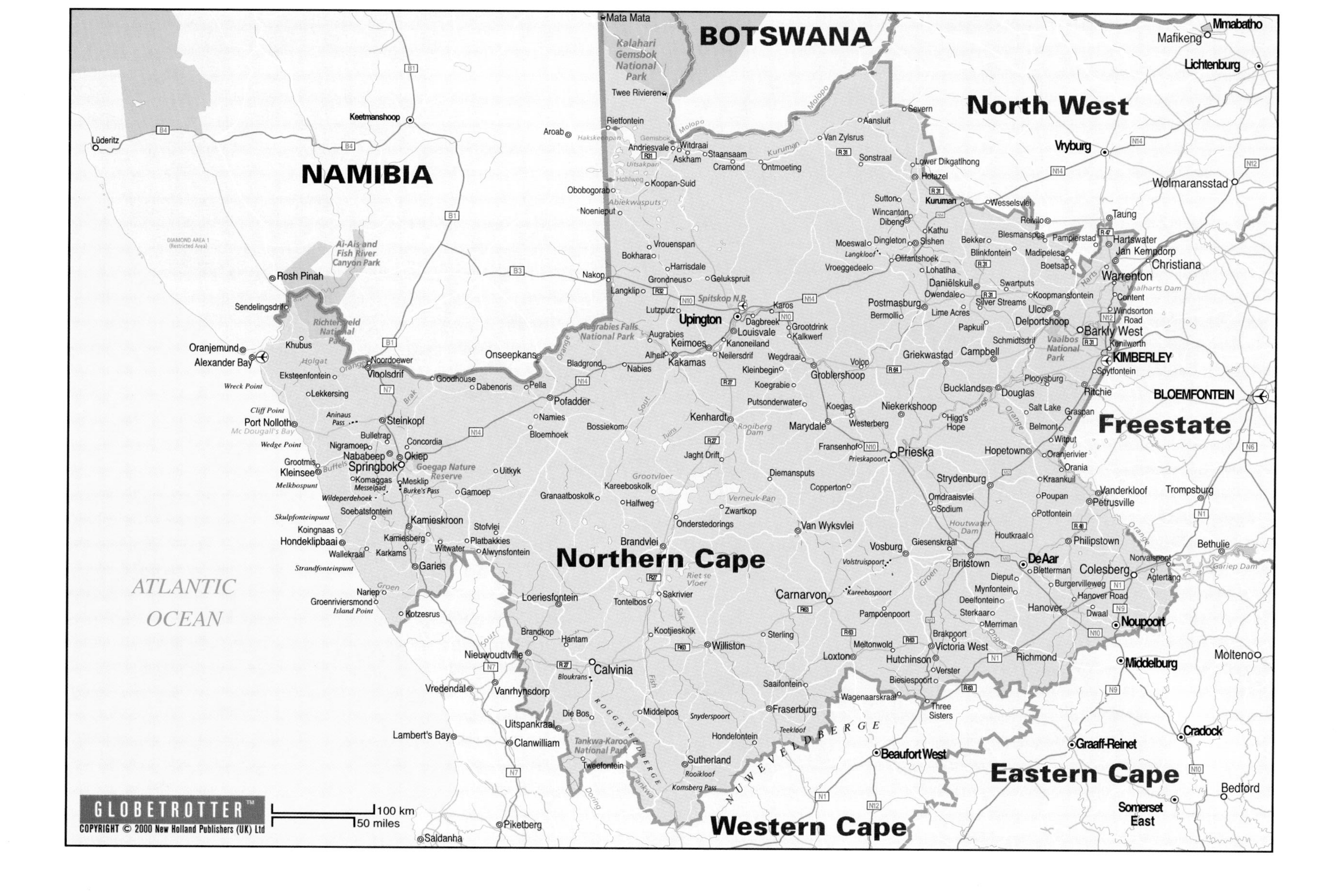

BOTSWANA
NAMIBIA
North West
Freestate
Northern Cape
Eastern Cape
Western Cape
ATLANTIC
OCEAN
Kalahari Gemsbok National Park
Ai-Ais and Fish River Canyon Park
Richtersveld National Park
Augrabies Falls National Park
Goegap Nature Reserve
Vaalbos National Park
Tankwa-Karoo National Park
Spitskop N.R.
Mata Mata
Twee Rivieren
Mafikeng
Mmabatho
Lichtenburg
Vryburg
Wolmaransstad
Keetmanshoop
Lüderitz
Rosh Pinah
Sendelingsdrif
Oranjemund
Alexander Bay
Port Nolloth
Springbok
Okiep
Steinkopf
Vioolsdrif
Noordoewer
Pofadder
Onseepkans
Upington
Keimoes
Kakamas
Kenhardt
Prieska
Kuruman
Postmasburg
Griekwastad
Douglas
Barkly West
KIMBERLEY
BLOEMFONTEIN
Warrenton
Christiana
Jan Kempdorp
Hartswater
Taung
De Aar
Colesberg
Noupoort
Hanover
Richmond
Victoria West
Britstown
Carnarvon
Williston
Calvinia
Fraserburg
Sutherland
Loxton
Vanrhynsdorp
Nieuwoudtville
Vredendal
Clanwilliam
Lambert's Bay
Piketberg
Saldanha
Garies
Kamieskroon
Hondeklipbaai
Beaufort West
Middelburg
Graaff-Reinet
Cradock
Somerset East
Bedford
Molteno
Trompsburg
Bethulie
Brandvlei
Loeriesfontein
Van Wyksvlei
Vosburg
Marydale
Groblershoop
Hopetown
Strydenburg
Petrusville
Philipstown
Three Sisters
NUWEVELDBERGE
ROGGEVELDBERGE
GLOBETROTTER™
100 km
50 miles
COPYRIGHT © 2000 New Holland Publishers (UK) Ltd

# Northern Cape

During the Anglo-Boer War the Northern Cape Province was then part of the Cape Colony. It is an area steeped in history with some of the finest Victorian buildings in original splendour. An unexplored region offering a unique experience to the seasoned and adventurous traveller who enjoys the freedom of wide open spaces, fresh clean healthy air, down-to-earth hospitable and polite people. It has numerous nature reserves, adventure trails, 4x4 routes, hiking, river rafting, and the renowned natural flowers of Namaqualand. It stretches from the Atlantic Ocean to the Kimberley Diamond Fields through the historically famous Great Karoo. Even Sir Malcolm Campbell was taken with the area when he attempted to break the land speed record of 372 km/h in *Bluebird* on 20 March 1929 at Verneukpan near Brandvlei. There is an excellent map (free to tourists) of the province covering the area in detail and indicating where the Battlefield sites are for both the Kimberley and Springbok/ Okiep areas. The map is supplied by the Northern Cape Tourism Authority and can be obtained from them at 187 Du Toitspan Road, Kimberley or telephone (053) 832 2657 or fax (053) 831 2937. ❑

## AUSSIE SAILOR KILLED AT GRASPAN

Midshipman Cymbeline Alonso Edrich Huddart, at just under 19 years of age, was one of the youngest officers to die in the war. From Ballarat in Australia, Huddart joined the *Britannia* (a Naval Training Ship) in 1895, passing out as one of two captains of cadets. He joined the Royal Navy in 1897 and at the time of the battle of Graspan on November 25, 1899, was serving as *Aide de Camp* to Captain Prothero of the Naval Brigade, having served on the flagship of the South African station, HMS *Doris*.

A fellow Naval officer described his death: "At the bottom of the hill he was hit in the arm, and halfway up he was shot in the leg, but he still pressed on. On reaching the top of the kopje he was shot through the stomach, and fell mortally wounded." Australian newspapers stated that Queen Victoria sent her condolences to the family and requested a photograph be sent to her. He was awarded a posthumous Conspicuous Service Cross, which was presented to his mother by King George VI. Initially buried on the battlefied, Huddart was re-interred in Kimberley in the 1960's.

STEVE'S WAR STORIES

During the guerrilla phase of the war, the Boers were compelled to wear captured British uniforms, as this was their only source of clothing. The British issued a proclamation stating that any Boer captured in British uniform would be shot. Reitz maintains that neither the commandos nor the local population were informed that the death penalty attached to the wearing of British uniforms. In fact many of Smuts' men who were taken prisoner were executed for wearing khaki, and his Commando sincerely believed that the British had resorted to shooting prisoners. (Reitz, 236).

*from "Roses Round-up"*

# Colesburg

One of the first districts in the Cape Colony invaded by the Boers was Colesburg. On 14 November 1899, a commando crossed the Orange River and occupied the town. General French was ordered to protect the railway line and push the Boers back to prevent further advances into the Colony. This resulted in several skirmishes. The towns people panicked. Some packed and fled while others stayed behind and dug escape tunnels. The most famous of these tunnels – which leads to a dry water course outside the town – can still be seen at the Methodist Church. Colesberg's museum has a display of Boer War memorabilia and there are ruins of forts and blockhouses on the outskirts of town. Nearby Norvals Pont was the site of a concentration camp where Boer women and children were held between 1901 and 1902. A curious round blockhouse at Noupoort and a tiny Anglican church built by the British soldiers is of great interest to researchers. There are also fort ruins at Richmond, but the one item that never fails to raise a smile is a wooden arm in the Saddle Horse museum. One of the locals, Daan de Kock, lost his lower arm in action at one of the forts. A wooden replacement was fashioned for him but Daan did not care one bit for this device and flatly refused to wear it. These days it is a great novelty. ❏

## Colesburg

**STARSTON STUD, COLESBERG AREA**

This racehorse stud farm is situated 19 km north of Colesberg. Guests can relax with a drink at the 'Gondolier Bar' in the original stable of the famous racehorse. Enjoy horse riding, Orange River canoeing, sunset cruises and explore the British regiments' Boer War camp site.

2 Apartments each sleeps 5 from R95 pp. B&B.

Tel: (051) 753 1351. Fax: (051) 753 1351.

**THE LIGHTHOUSE, COLESBERG**

Offering spaciousness, with stylishly decorated en-suite bedrooms each with a private entrance leading into a tranquil garden setting. All rooms have tea/coffee facilities. Lock-up parking. Ideally located for exploring the Anglo-Boer War sites of the Northern Cape and Free State.

10 Rooms from R95 per person. Room Only.

Tel: (051) 753 0043. fax: (051) 753 0043.

# Kimberley

## Langberg Guest Farm, Langberg

A historic Karoo Game Farm 21km south of Kimberley on the N12. On part of the Magersfontein Battlefield. Battlefield walk on the property. A historic Cape homestead. Game drives & excellent dinners.
5 Rooms from R123 - R218 pp per room.
Breakfast from R28 per person.
Tel/Fax: (053) 832 1001. Cell/Mobile: 083 261 4695.

## Bishops Lodge,

Air-conditioned accommodation with en-suite bathrooms. Optional self-catering is available with lounge area. All rooms are supplied with DSTV. Ideally suited for exploring Kimberley and the Battlefields.
25 Rooms from R200 pp sharing. Bed & Breakfast.
Tel: (053) 831 7876 Fax: (053) 831 7479.
e-mail: bishops@global.co.za

## Milner House,

Set in a tranquil Victorian suburb. Enjoy the relaxed and friendly atmosphere. Close to tourist attractions and restaurants. Pool, TV with M-Net, tea/coffee facilities. Battlefield Tours and Airport transfers.
4 Rooms from R115 pp sharing. Bed & Breakfast.
Tel: (053) 831 6405. Fax: (053) 831 6407.
e-mail: fires@kimnet.co.za

## Kosmos Guest House

Very private rooms with en-suite bathrooms. Secure parking. Enjoy the lovely garden and the evenings with a braai/barbeque at the lapa. Cool down in the sparkling swimming pool after a full day exploring the diamond city, environs and battlefields.
5 Rooms from R170 per person B&B.
Tel: (053) 861 3795. Fax: (053) 861 3795.
Cell/Mobile: 083 270 8305.

## Shalom Guest House

Situated in the historic diamond city of Kimberley, this Bed & Breakfast with comfortable en-suite rooms offers warm hospitality. A perfect base for your visit to the Battlefield Routes of the Northern Cape and the Free State.
3 Rooms from R200 double. R130 single.
Tel: (053) 861 1022. Fax: (053) 861 1022.
Cell/Mobile: 083 283 7790.

# Kimberley

## Diamond Protea Lodge

Centrally situated in Kimberley, the Diamond Protea Lodge offers bedrooms with two double-beds, en-suite bathrooms, remote controlled TV, minibar, fridge and air-conditioning. Perfect for exploring Kimberley and the surrounding areas.
34 Rooms from R325 per room - Room only.
Tel: (053) 831 1281. Fax: (053) 831 1284.
e-mail: dplkim@global.co.za

## Carrington Guest House

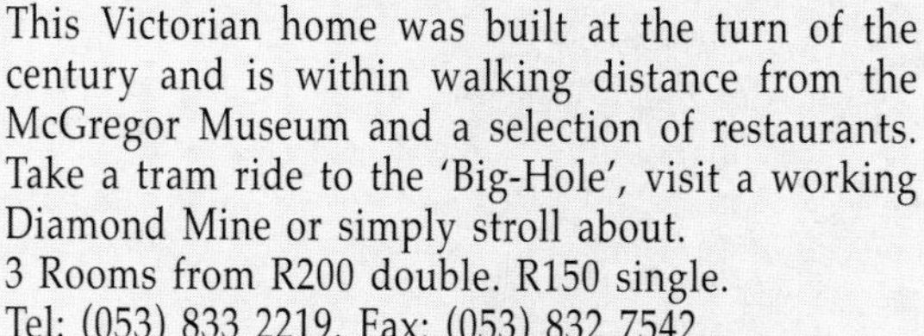

This Victorian home was built at the turn of the century and is within walking distance from the McGregor Museum and a selection of restaurants. Take a tram ride to the 'Big-Hole', visit a working Diamond Mine or simply stroll about.
3 Rooms from R200 double. R150 single.
Tel: (053) 833 2219. Fax: (053) 832 7542.
Cell/Mobile: 083 261 6473.

## Carrington Lodge

Situated in a quiet suburb close to the centre of town and various restaurants. Within walking distance of the Honoured Dead Memorial and the Long Cecil Gun. All rooms at the Lodge have TV and tea/coffee facilities and secure parking is offered.
7 Rooms from R135 pp sharing. Bed & Breakfast.
Tel: (053) 831 6448. Fax: (053) 833 5012.
e-mail: spanhc@kingsley.co.za

## The Palms

This 1920 home is situated in the heart of the Historic Diamond City of Kimberley. It is well placed to explore the Anglo Boer Battlefields. The Palms offers DSTV and M-Net. With a sparkling pool to cool down. Secure parking. Children welcome.
5 Rooms from R125 pp sharing. Bed & Breakfast.
Tel: (053) 831 3485. Fax: (053) 833 2739.
Cell/Mobile: 082 789 2887

When camped near Moordenaar's Poort in the Northern Cape, and hard-pressed by the British, Smut's commando was rendered helpless for a number of hours by a porcupine. It had wandered through the camp at night and stampeded the horses. (Reitz, 211)

## Naries Guest Farm

Naries is an up-market country retreat located in the Spektakelberg mountains, approx 25km due west of Springbok on the Kleinzee road. The 25000 acre farm is dedicated to the protection of stunning flora.
5 Rooms from R270 pp sharing. Dinner B&B.
Tel: (027) 712 2462. Fax: (027) 712 2462.
e-mail: dannyd@intekom.co.za

## Okiep Country Hotel

In the heart of Namaqualand, steeped in the history of copper mines and the Anglo-Boer War. Norman Featherstone at Okiep Country Hotel can take clients on tours of the area. 8 km from Springbok.
19 Rooms from R190 per person.
Tel: (027) 744 1000. Fax: (027) 744 1170 or 744 1170.
e-mail: guilia@mweb.co.za

## Le Must Guest Manor

Situated in the business district of Upington. Georgian styled house with period South African furniture. Bedrooms have air-conditioning, satellite TV with video channel. Canoeing and Swimming.
7 Rooms from R185 pp sharing Bed & Breakfast.
Tel: (054) 332 3971. Fax: (054) 332 7830.
e-mail: lemusttravel@gem.co.za

## Namastat, Springbok

Stay in traditional Namahuts with no electricity or other luxuries. Comfortable beds with bedding and a lamp for lighting, or stay in a wooden cabin.
15 Namahuts and 5 x 4-bed Cabins.
Rates from R45 to R55 per person.
Tel: (027) 712 2435. Fax: (027) 712 1926.
Cell/Mobile: 083 342 6788.

## Protea Hotel Upington, Upington.

Set on the banks of the Orange River. An ideal base for visiting the Namaqualand, the Kalahari Gemsbok Game Reserve and the Augrabies Falls Park. Hire a 4x4 and explore the surrounding area. All rooms with air-conditioning and TV.
53 Rooms from R295 (std) & R325 (suite) Room Only.
Tel: (054) 332 4414. Fax: (054) 332 4486.
e-mail: upthotels@gem.co.za

## Historical Places / National Monuments

**Anglican Church:** This beautifully decorated church was designed by Sophia Gray, wife of Bishop Gray, and was built in 1854.

**Anglo-Boer War Tour:** The Information Office offers a tour of Plateau Camp, Suffolk Hill, Grenadier Guards Rock, Memorial Hill and the military cemetery where more than 400 men from 20 regiments are buried. There is also a week-end tour which includes a visit to Norvals Pont PoW camp and cemetery. **Contact: Belinda Gordon on Tel: (051) 753 0678.**

**Colesburg Kemper Museum:** Murray Street. The museum contains Boer War photographs and artifacts and numerous other interesting displays.

**Horsemill:** Bell Street. One of the country's last working horsemill.

## Restaurants

A guide to the selection of restaurants can be obtained from the Information Bureau.

## Tour Guides

**Belinda Gordon:** Registered Tour Guide. Tel: (051) 753 0678. *Specialising on Boer War activities throughout the area.*

Photographer on the way to the front.

## NOUPOORT TOURIST INFORMATION

Shaw Street, Noupoort. Tel: (049) 562 1056.

Originally spelt *Naauwpoort* and changed in 1963 to Noupoort.

## Boer War Sites

**Anglican Church:** Shaw Street. The church was built by British soldiers during the Anglo-Boer War and it now houses a British Military Museum.

**Blockhouse**: An Anglo-Boer War blockhouse on Hospital Hill. See article on *Blockhouses*.

# Kimberley

A view of Kimberley.

Kimberley is 180 km from Bloemfontein, 485 km from Johannesburg, and 980 km from Cape Town.

In 1866 on the farm De Kalk near Hopetown, a young teenager, Erasmus Jacobs, found a white pebble on the banks of the Orange River. The white pebble became known as *'Eureka'*, a yellow diamond of 21,25 carats. It was the deal made by Schalk van Niekerk, a Hopetown farmer, and a Griqua shepherd Zwartbooi that lead to the great South African diamond rush. Van Niekerk traded all his possessions

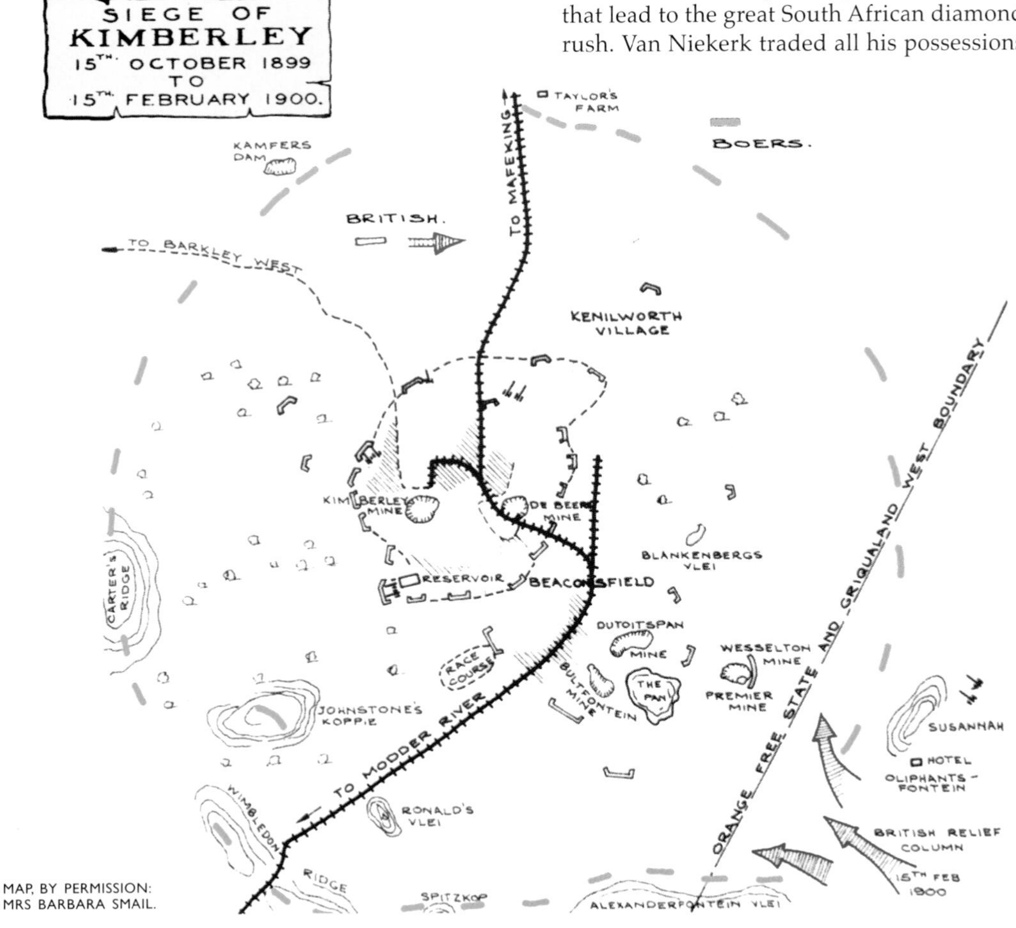


MAP, BY PERMISSION:
MRS BARBARA SMAIL.

for a magnificent 83,50 carat diamond *'The Star of South Africa.'* Sir Richard Southey, the Colonial Secretary at the Cape declared *'this is the rock on which the future success of South Africa will be built'*.

Kimberley developed from a diamond mining camp known as *Colesberg Kopje, De Beers New Rush* and *Vooruitzicht*. In 1873 it was declared a township and in 1877 it attained municipal status and became Kimberley after the Earl of Kimberley. Diamond magnates Cecil John Rhodes and Barney Barnato helped to put Kimberley on the map during the 1880s, and in 1888 the 35 year-old Cecil John Rhodes stabilised the diamond industry while his company De Beers Consolidated Mines Ltd. monopolised the diamond markets of the world. Thus began the development of Kimberley to a historically great city.

**Kimberley and the Anglo-Boer War**:

One of the primary objectives of the Boer command was to isolate the British forces threatening the Republics on their borders. In addition they were to occupy suitable positions in enemy (British) territory where they could halt the advance of British reinforcements from the coast. Hence on 14 October 1899 the Boer forces surrounded Kimberley and *'the Siege of Kimberley'* had started. It lasted a total of 124 days and ended on 15 February 1900. At the outset the garrison under Lieutenant Colonel Kekewich prepared for a Boer attack that never came. The Boers intent on starving the garrison into surrender were content with shelling the town. The shelling created initial chaos and damage; but on the lighter side the shells proved an excellent source of souvenirs. There were a few exciting skirmishes and daily the townsfolk looked south for Methuen's relief column. There were occasions when dispatch riders and black runners managed to sneak through the Boer lines and bring news of the column's early victories.

De Beers Observation Platform

Due to successful skirmishes with the Boers; military confidence in the town was high and on 28 November 1899, Lt.-Col. Scott-Turner, to distract the Boers away from the south, attacked the Boer redoubts on Carter's Ridge with his mounted troops. The Boers were prepared and the attack was brought to a standstill. Scott-Turner and 23 of his troops were killed, and 31 more troops were wounded mostly townspeople. Morale sank. A fortnight later the news of Methuen's defeat at Magersfontein postponed the relief column's advance; and morale sank even further.

Food rationing, unemployment, boredom, continuous bombardment and disease played on the town's occupants. This strained the relationship between Rhodes and Kekewich.

Christmas Day 1899 saw Rhodes give the order to George Labram, Chief Mechanical Engineer of De Beers Consolidated Mines to produce a gun of sufficient size and range to counter the Boer guns. Using among other sources, the Encyclopaedia Britannica, the gun was completed in 24 days and went into action on 21 January 1900. It was called the *'Long Cecil'* after Cecil Rhodes. It opened fire on the Boer laagers creating consternation among the burghers. Retaliation came swiftly and after frantic requests the *'Long Tom'* siege gun was bought into action by the Boers.

Its huge 94-pounder shells had a range of 9 000 m which crumpled the mudbrick and corrugated iron houses, pubs, shops, and the local Stock Exchange.

Terrified women and children were invited by Cecil Rhodes to take shelter down the mines. It was ironic that George

Labram, the developer of the *'Long Cecil'* and hence the reason behind the Boers introducing the *'Long Tom'* to the siege, was killed by a *'Long Tom'* shell while dressing for dinner in his hotel room.

The personality clash between Rhodes (pictured right) and Kekewich, each representing the civilian and military authorities, became a feature of the siege. As Sir Arthur Conan Doyle was to write *"Colonel Kekewich was as much plagued by intrigue within as the Boers without"*. Kimberley was *'Rhodes Town'*, and most of the defences and defenders were supplied by De Beers Company. He considered the military hidebound and incompetent and in one of the messages to Kekewich he stated: *'The only good thing about you soldiers is that you are so loyal to one another and think so much of the military situation: in fact I do believe that if the Almighty God himself were in a fix you would not rescue him if it interfered with your military situation'.*

The situation between the two became so untenable that Rhodes suggested he might surrender the town to the Boers. Lord Roberts, now commanding the relief column, instructed Kekewich in a secret signal to arrest Rhodes. Kekewich did not resort to this drastic measure, but Roberts took the threat seriously and instead of advancing directly on Bloemfontein, he ordered General French's cavalry division to first lift the siege. Swooping round to the east they broke through the Boer defences and reached Kimberley.

The siege was over. Not without a heavy price to pay – no street lamps burnt, few cab horses had escaped the cooking-pot, infant mortality amongst the black population was over 60%. The death rate in the four months was equivalent to a normal year. Large areas of the townships had been flattened, while 483 blacks had died of scurvy. Nine civilians had been killed by Boer shellfire and 42 officers and men in action. Resistance to the Boers occupation had its price. ❑.

Waiting in queue for meat allowance.

## LONG TOM SOUVENIR BROOCH

The well-known Kimberley architect, Fergus Carstairs Rogers, native of Edinburgh, Scotland, who died in 1927, was responsible for the imposing City hall in Kimberley and a recognised water diviner. Rogers was hit by a splinter from a Long Tom shell while standing in the entrance of the Kimberley Club.

He refused to take chloroform as an aid in removing the splinter, preferring instead a tot of whisky. While under the influence of the Scottish beverage he directed his medical doctor friends in extracting the splinter from his leg.

The splinter afterwards was converted into a souvenir brooch and presented to his wife.

STEVE'S WAR STORIES

**KIMBERLEY TOURISM**

**Diamantveld Visitor Centre, Bultfontein Road, Kimberley 8301.**

**Tel: (053) 832 7298. Fax: (053) 832 7211. website: www.kimberley-africa.com**

## Anglo-Boer War Sites & Places of Interest

**Honoured Dead Memorial:** With the *'Long Cecil' Gun*.

**Africana Library:** For their exhibition of books on the War.

**Kimberley Club:** Opposite the Africana Library.

**McGregor Museum:** With its display.

**Nazareth House:** Used as a hospital during the War.

**Cape Police Memorial:** With the gun captured from the Boers in 1900.

**Kamfersdam:** Where the Boer *'Long Tom'* was situated.

**Gladstone Cemetery:** The grave of the first British Officer to die in the War and during the siege.

**West End Cemetery:** With the graves of those killed at the Battlefields, and the Kimberley Concentration Camp Memorial.

**Kimberley Engineering Works:** Where the *'Long Cecil'* was developed.

## Places of Interest & Things to Do

**Big Hole** and **Open Mine Museum village**.

**Kimberley Mine Museum**.

Guided tour of **De Beers Diamond Mine**.
*(Booking essential)*

**Alluvial hand diamond diggings**. *(Booking essential)*

**Diamond Fields:** Archaeological Route and ancient San rock engravings.

Ride an electric tram, from 1914 era, to the Big Hole.

**Freddie Tait Golf Museum**.

**Drive, or stroll around:** And admire the Victorian architecture.

Follow the N12 Anglo-Boer War **Battlefield Route** from Kimberley.

**Kimberley Ghost Trail:** *(Booking essential)* Tel: (053) 831 4006.
*... and many other tours and activities available.*

## Restaurants

**Barnato's:** Dalham Road. Tel: 833 4110

**Mario's:** Du Toitspan Road. Tel: 831 1738

**Safari Steak House:** Market Square. Tel: 832 4621

**Nando's Chicken:** Jones Street. Tel: 831 5258

**Kentucky Fried Chicken:** George Street. Tel: 832 9607

**China Restaurant:** Du Toitspan Road. Tel: 831 4444

The Kimberley Star Medal awarded to thos who participated in the Siege.

A replica of a *Krupp 75mm* at Magersfontein battlefield.

**Mohawk Spur**: Du Toitspan Road. Tel: 832 6472
**Saddles Steak House**: Sidney Street. Tel: 831 5506
**Steers Steak House**: Bultfontein Road. Tel: 831 2092
**Keg & Falcon**: Du Toitspan Road. Tel: 833 2075
**Umberto's Italian**: Du Toitspan Road. Tel: 832 5741
**Pizza Den**: New Park Centre. Tel: 832 2954

### Museums

**Kimberley Mine Museum**: At the Big Hole.
**McGregor Museum**: Atlas Street (pictured below).

**Alexander McGregor Memorial Museum**: Chapel Street.
**Aviation Museum**: 3,5 km from the Airport.
**The Freddie Tait Golf Museum**: 6 km on N12 towards Johannesburg.
**Sol Plaatje Museum**: Angel Street.
**The Africana Library**: Du Toitspan Road.
**Magersfontein Battlefield Museum**: Magersfontein - 32 km from Kimberley.

*Welcome to the Shrapnel Hotel. Enjoy your stay!*

## Bravo Queen Vic!!

On 8 May 1900, Her Majesty, the Queen (VR) has sent to Colonel Kekewich her signed photograph in recognition of his long and resolute defence of Kimberley.

## Tour Operators and Guides

**Steve's Tours:** Operated by Steve Lunderstedt. (T.0374)
***Tour Operator and Guide***. Tel/Fax: (053) 831 4006. Cell/Mobile: (083) 732 3189.
*Guided Tours. Historical Kimberley, Cecil Rhodes tours, the Ultimate Ghost Experience tour, N12 and Free State Battlefield tours.*

**Janet Welsh:** (T.1143) Tel/Fax: (053) 832 8343. Cell/Mobile: (082) 856 2280.
*Guided Tours. De Beers Mines, Historical Kimberley and Museums, Big Hole, Alluvial Diamond diggings, Ghost Trail and N12 Battlefields Route.*

**Yvonne Dreyer:** (T.0434) Tel: (053) 861 4765. Cell/Mobile: (082) 469 0275.
*Guided Tours. Magersfontein and Modder River.*

## Reading Matter

There are a few excellent books on Kimberley and the Anglo-Boer War that have recently been published, which are available from the **Africana Library**, P.O. Box 627, Kimberley 8300 or telephone (053) 830 6247.

*Excellent FREE brochures are available from Kimberley Tourism.*

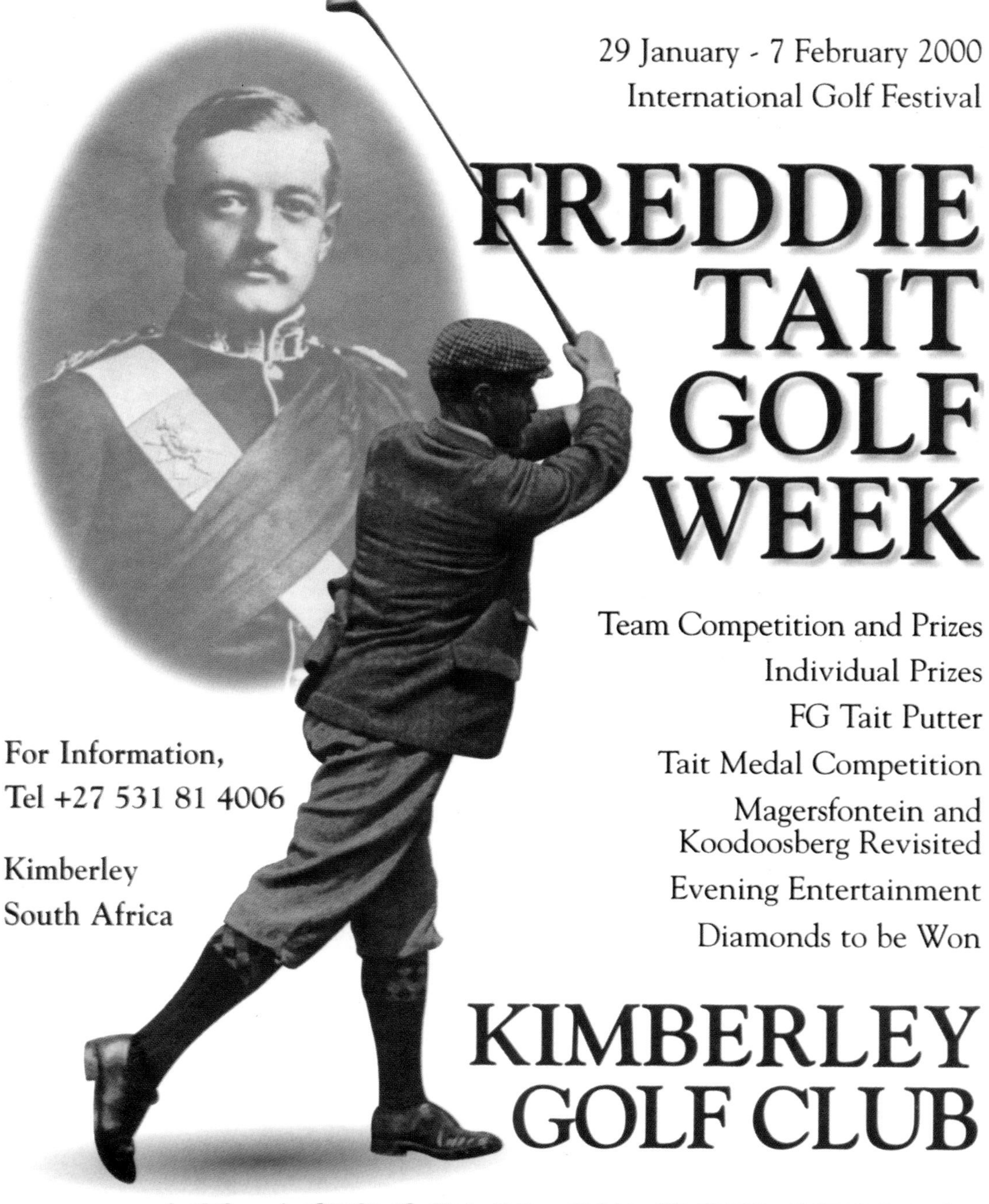
29 January - 7 February 2000
International Golf Festival
FREDDIE
TAIT
GOLF
WEEK
Team Competition and Prizes
Individual Prizes
FG Tait Putter
Tait Medal Competition
Magersfontein and Koodoosberg Revisited
Evening Entertainment
Diamonds to be Won
For Information,
Tel +27 531 81 4006
Kimberley
South Africa
KIMBERLEY
GOLF CLUB

AN AFRICAN EXPERIENCE
Our holes are too big to drive past!
For that hole-in-one visitor information service,
just dial +27 531 82 7298 or write to Tourism Kimberley,
PO Box 1976, Kimberley 8300 e-mail: dvcadmin@kimnet.co.za

# The "Long Cecil" Gun

**"The production of this gun must be considered one of the most remarkable events in the history of beleaguered garrisons"**
*The Times of London*

Dissatisfaction with the superiority of Boer guns over the British guns led to the manufacture of *Long Cecil*.

After research at the Public Libary (now the Africana Library) where amongst other books and documents, the Encyclopaedia Britannica was referred to under the articles on Gunnery, as well as the Treatise on Ammunition, and coupled with the aid of drawings in technical books, George Labram, Chief Mechanical Engineer of De Beers and an USA citizen, together with Mr. E. Goffe, Chief Draughtsman of De Beers, designed the gun. They were assisted by several employees who had previous experience in Woolwich Arsenal and elsewhere.

The Gun was manufactured at the De Beers Workshops - now the Kimberley Engineering Works. The lathe used is still in operation, and also turned gun barrels during World War II. The gun was made out of a solid piece of hammered steel (billet) 10 feet long and 10,5 inches wide. It weighed 2 800 pounds (1 270 kg). Most of the tools used in making the gun had to be especially made.

Cecil Rhodes gave the go ahead to make the gun on 25 December 1899, and George Labram started on 26 December 1899 to plan the gun. The workshops began the gun on 30 December 1899 and it rolled out of the workshops on the evening of 18 January 1900. It had taken 24 days, much of it under shell fire. The foreman in charge was William Berry, who in his own words said: *"The greatest difficulty we were faced with in making the gun was having, first of all, to make the tools necessary to build it."*

On the 19 and 20 January 1900, sighting and slight adjustments were made. On 21 January 1900 the gun went into service and began regular firing.

Cecil Rhodes paid Colonel Chamier a compliment by asking him to be the first to fire the gun, but the Colonel refused the invitation on the ground that it was against military regulations for British artillerymen to fire a gun that was not British-made. Cecil Rhodes asked Colonel Chamier to stand back in a safer position; and turning asked for his cart to be sent to collect Mrs Pickering wife of William Pickering, the Secretary of De Beers. When she arrived Cecil Rhodes asked her to fire the gun. The Kimberley Artillerymen had loaded and sighted the gun on the Boer laager at the Intermediate Pumping Station, some 10 000 yards (7 200 metres) distant. Mrs Pickering fired the gun half a dozen times. Those who observed the effects of the shots through field glasses reported a large number of men running out from the laager. The results were indeed very satisfactory.

The following day a Boer arrived at one of the British outposts carrying a white flag. He produced a note addressed to Colonel Kekewich, demanding to know the reason for firing at a laager occupied by women and children.

Kekewich abruptly told him: *"Women and children have no right to besiege a town. Their place is at home"*.

Sixteen rounds were fired that day of which Rhodes fired eight. It is interesting to note that Sundays were observed as a day of rest – from gun firing – by the Boers.

An interesting story relating to the effect of the *'Long Cecil'* and the Boers: A dispatch rider, with some private correspondence from Boers to their friends, happened to be captured a day or

The "Long Cecil" at the Honoured Dead Memorial (see picture below).

two later, and one of the letters had the following to say: *"I am very glad we have been transferred here (Modder River), because the day before yesterday we were still at the Waterworks enjoying a meal when a big gun shot right into the Waterworks where they have never shot before. You should have seen our people run. I was busy with my sweet-pap (porridge), but had to leave everything and run. It is better here."* The Waterworks (Intermediate Pumping Station) referred to in the letter is 8 000 yards from the nearest defence works of Kimberley and was occupied by the Boers as a laager.

It was later found that a good many Boer families had come to reside in the laagers around Kimberley, expecting that the place could hold out no longer, and that when it was occupied they would be allowed to install themselves in the luxurious homes belonging to the diamond magnates and other wealthy residents. The immediate effect of *Long Cecil's* appearance on the scene was to drive a large number of burghers and their lady friends to seek quarters at a more respectful distance from Kimberley.

The shells also made in the De Beers workshops, weighed 28,1 pounds and could fire 5 miles (8 to 9 km). George Labram, in fact, had had the workshops make shells, charges and fuses since November 1899 for the 2,5 inch guns. The Long Cecil shells had De Beers engraved upon the shell with a diamond cast on the base and some had *With Compts CJR*. The bag that contained the powder charge was made from a good wool serge and was hooped with silk ribbon.

255 shots were fired, the majority at 5 000 yards (3 miles).

George Labram, the developer of the *Long Cecil*, was killed by a *Long Tom* shell only a few days before the relief came while dressing for dinner in his hotel room. His wife was given an annuity by De Beers and his son's education was organised by them. This was all they received!

After the siege the *Long Cecil* was first used in August 1901 at a special exhibition in Cape Town for the Duke and Duchess of Cornwall and York. It was again used in March 1902 at the funeral procession of Cecil John Rhodes in Cape Town. Rhodes' coffin was placed on the gun carriage, the procession going through the streets of Cape Town to the railway station. The gun is now resting in a prominent position in the city forming part of the Honoured Dead Memorial. ❑

George Labram with the 'Long Cecil'.

# The Honoured Dead Memorial

Erected to perpetuate the memory of the British soldiers who gave their lives defending the town from 14 October 1899 to 15 February 1900. Twenty-seven out of 42 soldiers lie within the vault. It is situated on the highest point of Kimberley. The 5 roads leading from the memorial were constructed by Blacks, Asiatics and non-combatants during the siege to afford employment. Dedication took place on 28 November 1904. It was designed by Sir Herbert Baker and its prototype was the Nereid Monument discovered in Xanthos (Asia) in 1840-1842. The Kimberley design was chosen by a committee under C.J. Rhodes. All the stone came from the Matopos in Rhodesia (Zimbabwe). It has a height of 52 feet (16,5 metres) and a weight of over 2 000 tons. It cost over £10 000 to build. There are bronze tablets designed by J Lockwood Kipling, father of Rudyard Kipling. In addition the inscription in the stone is by Rudyard Kipling. ❑

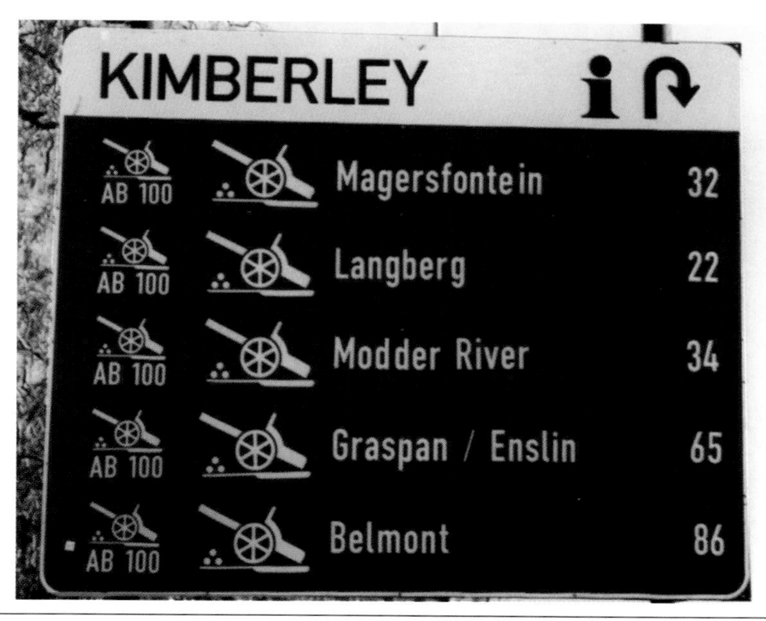


## Treasure discovered

A Boer camped at a farmhouse set out a trail of mielies to capture some chickens, which he succeeded in doing. Later he found a diamond in one of the chicken's stomachs, which he sold for £9. After the war, he secured the right to prospect in the area and to purchase the farm at a nominal price. He successfully mined the diamonds and became a wealthy man. (Schikkerling, 302).

## Kimberley Siege Soup

Not the most appetising of meals, the siege soup dished out during the siege consisted of mangel-wurzel, prickly pear and horse flesh amongst other ingredients.

STEVE'S WAR STORIES

# Sister Henrietta Stockdale

*1847:* ***Born 9 July**, Gringly on the Hill, England.*
*1874:* ***6 March** sailed for South Africa.*
*1878:* *In charge **St. George's Cottage Hospital**. Bloemfontein.*
*1879:* *In charge **Carnavon Hospital**, Kimberley.*
*1891:* *First statutory **registration of nurses** in Cape and the world.*
*1895:* *Opens **St. Michaels Maternity Home** in Kimberley.*
*1899:* ***Siege of Kimberley** from October to February 1900.*
*1911:* ***Died** aged 64 years.*

THE FOLLOWING ARE EXCERPTS FROM A DIARY SHE KEPT DURING THE BOER WAR (WHICH IS PRINTED *VERBATIM* IN THE BOOK *'The Lure of the Stone'*).

***September:***
*They have ceased to light the town after 8pm. Still the world goes on, dancing and racing and playing ...*

***October 23:***
*The lookout is built on top of the big hauling gear of the mine ... the red danger signal floats from it, and very often a little blue flag, which shows that the Colonel (Kekewich) is there, too.*

***November 26:***
*43rd day of siege. The enemy have sent over a thousand shells into the town, costing 10 Pounds each ... Absolutely no one and nothing has been hurt.*

***December 3:***
*49th day of the siege. The Boers planted a 100-pounder over the town ... our brave fellows were all mad to go at it ... darkness fell. 27 wounded ... Col. Turner fell dead at almost the first shot.*

***December 10:***
*Food is getting short. Such numbers of children are dying for want of milk in the intense heat.*

***December 31:***
*This town is in a sad state ... water still holds out ... But, oh, I hope we shall never surrender. No, not until the last inhabitant is dead of starvation.*

***January 17:***
*96th day of the siege. Normally we are allowed an ounce of beef and 3 ounces of horse daily ... Mr. Rhodes has been a great help; he brought 50 pounds with him one day when he called and sent beautiful fruit and vegetables. Three times he has brought us 2 onions. Eggs are 18 Shillings a dozen. It is very kind of Mr. Rhodes ...*

***January 24:***
*De Beers has made an enormous gun which carries seven miles - Long Cecil.*

***January 29:***
*I fear we get more donkey and mule than horse .. Cats are selling for 10 and 12 shillings each.*

***February 4:***
*Things are getting worse and worse ... eggs 30 shillings a dozen and dogs ever so high. Mr. Rhodes still brings us his welcome basket twice a week.*

***February 9:***
*A terrible three days, shelling with hundred pounders ... a poor child was brought in today from a house quite near, dead of course from a house torn to atoms.*

***February 11:***
*Thousands of people are going down the mines to hide in the exhausted chambers.*

***February 22:***
*Thursday afternoon about 5.30 the Relief Column rode in ... some 45000 strong (sic) ... poor women rushed out of cottages with sixpences, shillings, florins and half-crowns, crying and sobbing, pressing them into the soldiers' hands - money was all they had ... I can never tell you the relief and joy ... As darkness fell, they began all sorts of songs and rubbish. I walked down into the midst of them and began to sing 'God save the Queen' ... When they had done we had 'Rule Brittania'.*

<u>*Source:*</u> W.M. & Vincent Buss, *'The Lure of the Stone'*, Howard Timmins 1976.

*Andrew J. McLeod*

# Methuen, the British "bitter-ender"

Paul Sanford, third Baron Methuen of Corsham, was born in Wiltshire, where he also died 87 years later. Lord Methuen was a tall, bony Guardsman, with a full moustache hanging over his lips – the typical Etonian.

He arrived in South Africa as commander of the 1st Infantry Division in early November 1899. He was immediately appointed commander of the Western forces, with the orders to relieve Kimberley and Mafeking. Things happened fast. He arrived at Orange River Station on 12 November. His first contact with Boers was at *Belmont Station* (23 November) and two days later at *Graspan*. Neither of these battles are considered decisive victories for either side.

However, Methuen soon learned that the Boers used different battle tactics. The British faced exceptionally accurate rifle fire, from an enemy who lost themselves among the rocks and shrubs of the veld, and who retired behind the *kopje* as soon as things became too hot. Methuen was a fighter by temperament. He preferred not to direct operations from a safe distance. He approached the third battle - *Modder River* - with his usual self assurance, saying to one of his colonels: *"My dear fellow, I intend to put the fear of God into these people."*

However, one man who would cross his path again, appeared on the scene. General Koos De la Rey of the Western Transvaal. Under his guidance the Boers dug trenches - on the British side of the river. When the British attacked they unsuspectingly walked directly into the Boer gunfire. 70 were killed, 143 wounded. One of the wounded - Lord Methuen himself. And Kimberley was still under siege!!

As his wound healed he prepared for *Magersfontein Kopje*, the only obstacle between him and Kimberley. However he is once again flouted by De la Rey's unexpected placing of his trenches (as well as by his own rigid battle tactics). This turned out to be the second fiasco of '*Black Week*'. This was also where Gen.Andy Wauchope fell, together with 287 other British soldiers.

So, Methuen was not to relieve Kimberley (or Mafeking) after all. Roberts came along and took over. Roberts even demoted Methuen: *"I am resolved that he shall not be entrusted with an independant command."* He was blamed for many of the mistakes made at *Magersfontein*. Yet, as a gentleman of integrity he bore the reproaches in silence: *"There must be a scapegoat, so I must bear my fate like a man."*

Under the command of Lord Roberts and later under Lord Kitchener, Methuen was involved in many of the well known encounters of the war. With three yeomanry battalions he was only one day too late to rescue Col.Spragge's Irish Yeomanry at the humiliating coup at Lindley. He was closely involved in the first '*De Wet-hunt*' along the Magaliesberg. But De Wet escaped over the mountain where no one suspected him to.

Gradually he became a *'forgotten general'*, chasing and scattering De la Rey's and Smut's commandos over the plains of the Western Transvaal, with fluctuating successes. When the war approached its end, Methuen was the senior British general in the field. Senior even to Kitchener. In the British mind he occupied that special place reserved for men who do not give up.

Operating where he did, he was constantly aware of his '*Modder River Rival*' - General de la Rey – and when at last in early March 1902, their forces clashed at Tweebosch, De la Rey took the honours. Methuen was wounded for a second time during a battle against De la Rey and as he lay wounded his fallen horse crushed his leg. There were 200 dead or wounded. Thus De la Rey finds his old adversary laid up in his tent. Wounded, a captive. De la Rey, against the wishes of many of his burghers, sets him free and arranges for him to reach the nearest British Hospital. He even sends a message to Lady Methuen. When other generals returned home, Methuen remained – striving to retrieve the discredit of Magersfontein. He continued to serve his country with unabated constancy and zeal. Forgotten? Without banners and glory. Nevertheless: *'The British Bitter Ender'*. ❑


***Sources:***

Kruger, Rayne, *Good-bye Dolly Gray,* London, 1959.

Baring Pemberton, W. *Battles of the Boer War,* London, 1974.

Pakenham, Thomas, *The Boer War,* London, 1979.

Cecil Rhodes, Scott-Turner with Mr & Mrs Maguire relaxing on the front porch of the hotel.

## TRAGIC STORY

One of the many tragic stories to come out of the Anglo-Boer War must be that of John Henderson, brother of R.H. Henderson, the Mayor of Kimberley when the Siege began in October 1899. He was severely wounded in the head, at Alexandersfontein on 15 February 1900, during the Siege of Kimberley while serving as a Private in the Kimberley Town Guard (No. 2 Schmidt's Breastwork). He was treated by Dr. E.O. Ashe and recovered fully, later joining Lord Tullibardine's Column and remaining with it until hostilities ceased in 1902. He returned for a vacation to Ireland shortly afterwards and was accidentally shot in the head and killed while on a hunting expedition.

STEVE'S WAR STORIES

## DEATH BY FIRING SQUAD

In the cemetery on the outskirts of Hanover is a pyramid of stone marking the single grave of three young men executed in an event that deeply touched the towns people. About 20 km from town a train had been derailed and plundered resulting, shortly afterwards, in three men (who were sleeping in the outside rooms of a nearby farm) being arrested. They were charged with *"maliciously assisting Boer forces"*, robbery and causing the deaths of passengers. Tried on somewhat dubious authority by a military court at De Aar, the three were subsequently shot. To the very end they protested their innocence. In his war reminiscences, General Wynand Malan said that his commando was responsible for the derailment of the train – not the three young men who, in fact, were sent to the farm to collect fodder.

ROSES ROUND UP

Kimberley was the key to the war on the western front, and most of the major and minor battles took place within an hour's drive of the city. Lt.-General Lord Methuen, with a field force of 8 500 troops, which reached 15 000 at Magersfontein, marched 120 km from Orange River Station to relieve Kimberley.

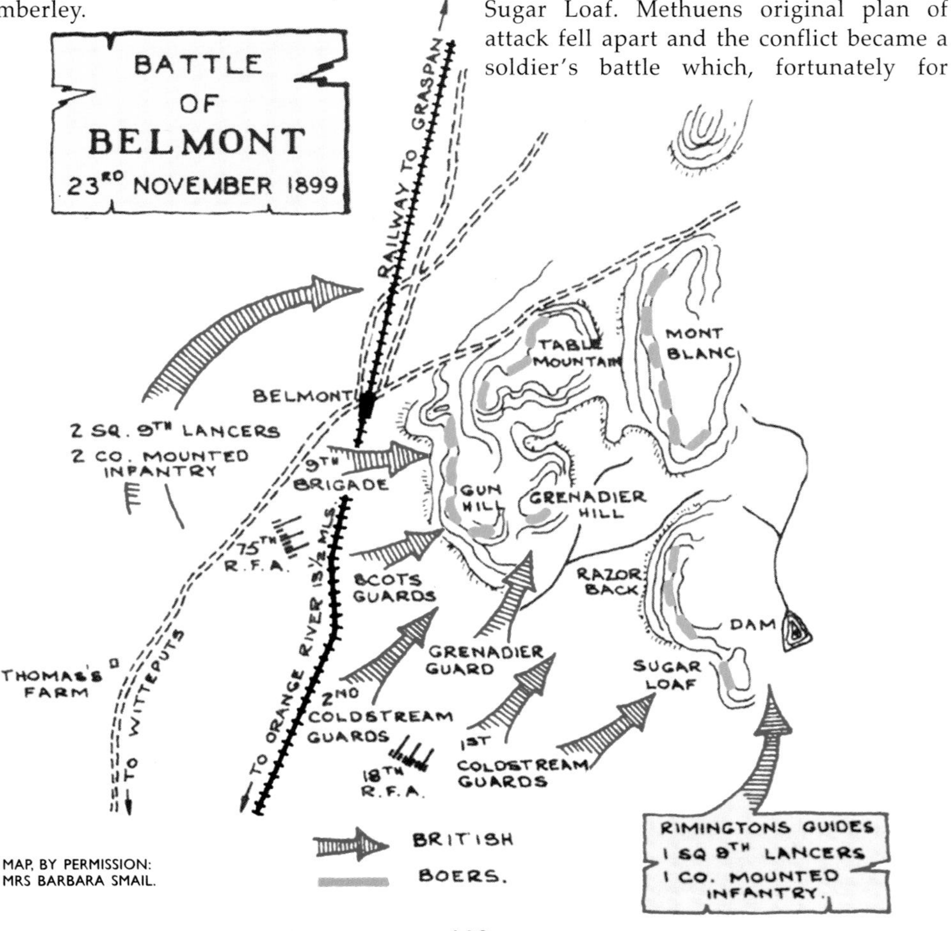


MAP, BY PERMISSION:
MRS BARBARA SMAIL.

***Battle of Belmont: 23 November 1899***

86 km from Kimberley. Methuen's first battle and 30 km from Orange River Station. The British had marched all night and attacked at dawn. The Boers had positioned themselves on Table Mountain, Mont Blanc, Gun Hill, Grenadier Hill, Razor Back and Sugar Loaf. Methuens original plan of attack fell apart and the conflict became a soldier's battle which, fortunately for

Methuen succeeded. The Boers, after pouring a hail of bullets into the British mounted their horses and vanished into the veld. The British lost 75 men, with 220 wounded. 22 Grenadier Guards had been killed.

The Boers lost 15 men, 30 wounded and 36 taken prisoner. Two monuments are located on the battlefield to those who died here; and site-displays provide visitor information.

***<u>Battle of Graspan (Enslin or Rooilaagte) 25 November 1899</u>***

65 km from Kimberley and 16 kms from Belmont. The Boers defeated at Belmont fell back on Graspan where they joined Gen.de la Rey's burghers and occupied kopjes (hills) between the Graspan and Enslin sidings. Methuen commenced the attack by shelling the Boers hoping to move them from their positions. The key to the battle was a short steep kopje, which was on the Boers left flank. Methuen attacked it using the Naval Brigade supported by British infantry. The first British line was barely 600 yards from the kopje when the Boers poured searching fire into it, the British wheeled and prepared for an attack. The artillery plied the kopjes with schrapnel while the troops advanced under fierce fire that swept across the open plain amongst the frontline of the troops. Casualties were high. It was not until the British were within 25 yards of the top that the Boers abandoned the sangers that they had so tenaciously clung. By 1000hrs the whole position was cleared as the Boers retreated.

The British lost 18 men, with 143 wounded. The Boers lost some 19 men, 41 wounded and 43 taken prisoner. Adjacent to the N12 on a low kopje a memorial lists the British troops killed. The Boer losses are recorded on a monument on the eastern kopje.There is a site-display with information.

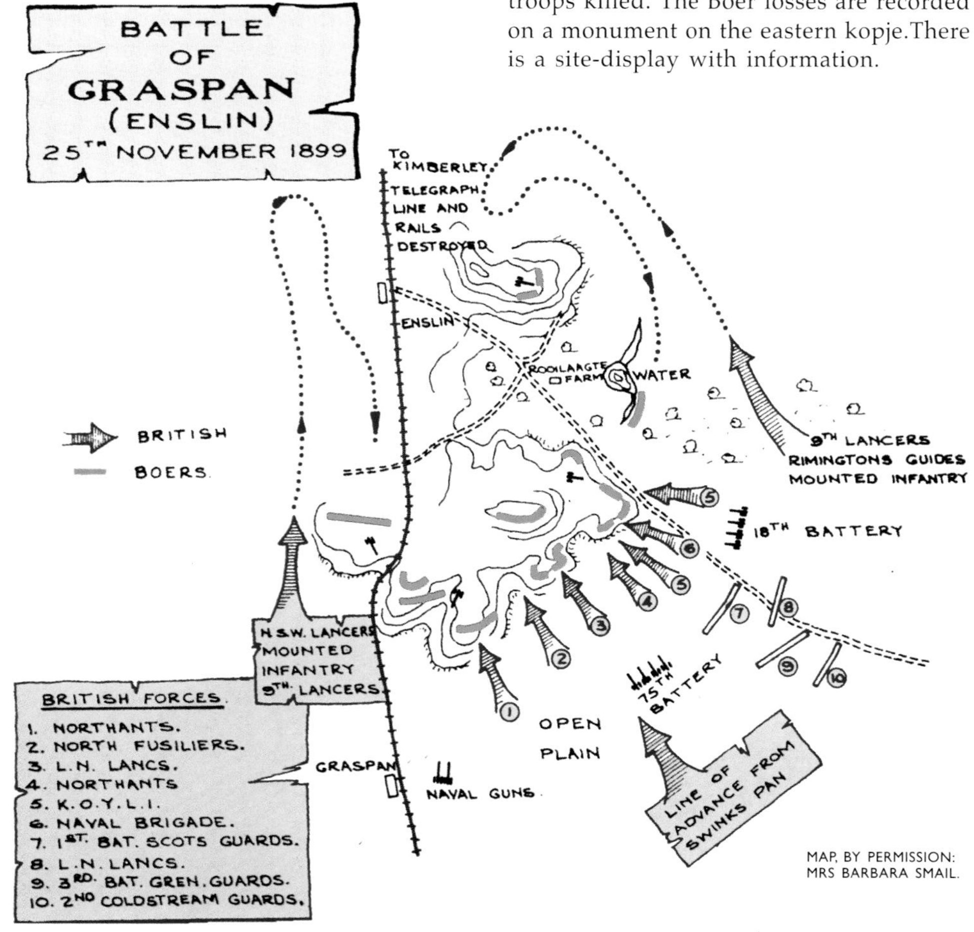

MAP, BY PERMISSION: MRS BARBARA SMAIL.

## Rugby in Kimberley

Although organised sport ceased during the war, "friendly" games were played between various Regiments, and also between civilians and Regiments. Rugby in 1900 was growing in popularity in South Africa, but still a minority sport in comparison to soccer and cricket. Some games played in Kimberley after the lifting of the Siege in February 1900 included a veritable 28-0 hiding dished out to the Royal Munster Fusiliers by a combined Kimberley side, while the self-same Combined Kimberley side just pipped the Mafeking Relief Force 9-8 in what was described as a "tough game" by the Diamond Fields Advertiser.

STEVE'S WAR STORIES

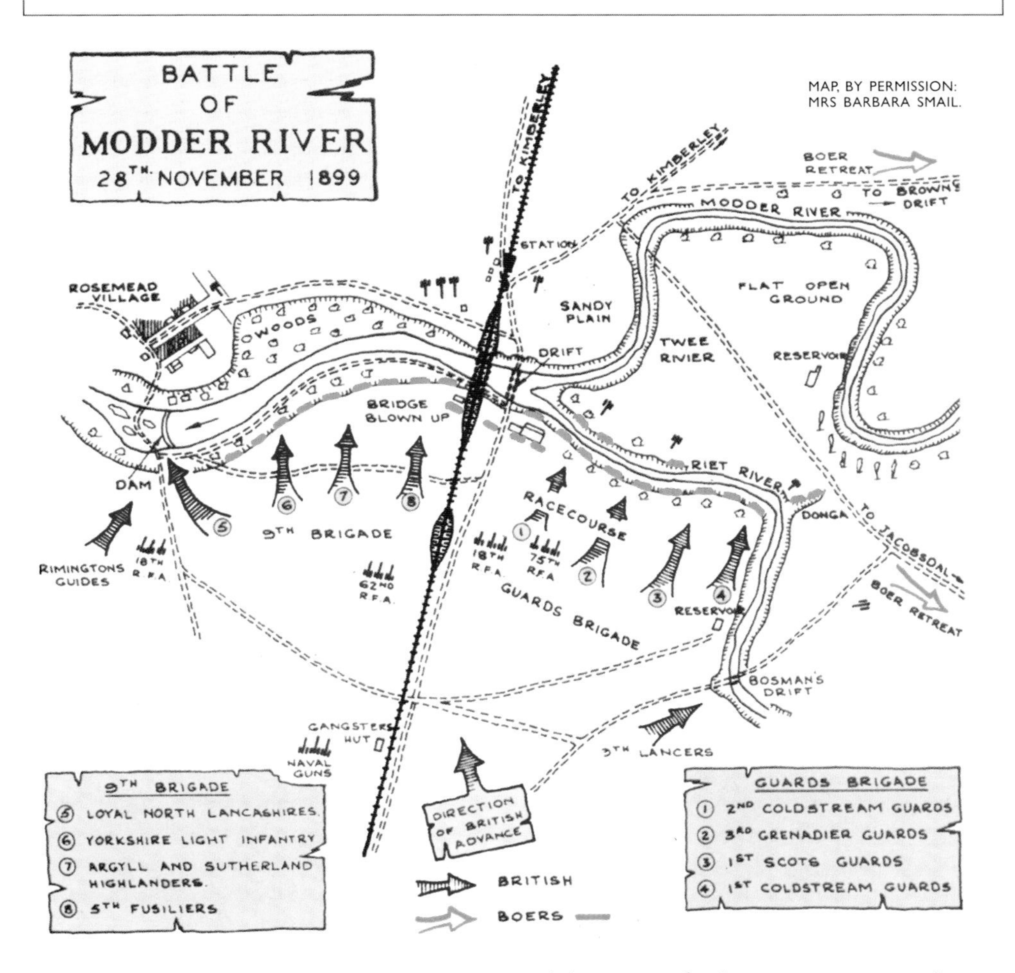


### Battle of Modder River (Twee Riviere) 28 November 1899

34 kms from Kimberley. General de la Rey had seen enough of both Belmont and Graspan to realise it was not so much the lack of courage as lack of judgement in the choice of positions which led to the Boer defeats. High kopjes were no longer impregnable, but actually invited artillery targets, and steep slopes offered cover to an attacking force once it had reached its base.

A position on the level ground would give far better consealment and a more effective field of fire for the flat trajectory of the modern rifles. Modder River offered such a position and the Boers prepared for the next British attack. They waited perfectly concealed in the grass, shrubs and trees on the banks of the river. At 0400 hr on 28 November the British infantry were on the move to the Modder River bridge. Methuen used to encountering the Boers on the hills walked straight into the Boer ambush. His troops came under heavy fire and the duel between the two sides lasted a solid 10 hours. The British were pinned down in the open veld, but a later attack against the Boer right flank proved successful and wading across the Riet River, the British were able to capture Rosemead Village (Ritchie).

The British losses were 70 dead, and 413 wounded; Methuen himself was wounded in the thigh. The Boers lost 16 dead, and 66 wounded with 13 men taken prisoner.

There are two battlefield monuments located after the Jacobsdal/Schutskamma Road turnoff, and two memorials near the rail bridge (that record the British troops who later died at the Modder River camp) and site-displays located at prominent positions on the battlefield.

While at Modder River visit the *Crown & Royal Hotel* where the wounded lay in the passages of the hotel; and the Bar was frequented by the British Troops.

A stone blockhouse constructed in 1901 guards the rail bridge. It has been renovated and is well worth a visit. It has a site-display with information. When you park at the parking area to the blockhouse you will see a full-scale model of a corrugated-iron blockhouse. This is the style of blockhouse that was produced en-mass throughout South Africa during the later half of the war.

Methuen, anxious to proceed towards Kimberley, had no choice but to call a temporary halt as the railway bridge across the Modder River had been demolished by the Boers and needed repair before he could advance. The troops were exhausted after fighting three battles in a row, and he also needed a week for his own wound to heal. It was almost two weeks later before

Blockhouse, Modder River.

Methuen's army was ready to move, having been restored to full strength and increased to 13 000 men with the arrival of a brigade of Highlanders. He had additional artillery and a balloon section. He heliographed Kimberley to say that he was on his way. He had decided on a daring night march on Magersfontein Kopje after an artillery bombardment.

***Battle of Magersfontein 10 & 11 December 1899***

32 km from Kimberley. With the exception of Spionkop, there are few battles in the 1899-1902 Anglo-Boer War that have provoked more embittered controversy than Maggersfontein. The causes of this controversy do not form part of this guide and it is suggested that those interested should read the many books that have been produced on the subject.

The artillery bombardment commenced on the afternoon of 10 December 1899 preceded the night march. The bombardment, aimed at the hills where the Boers were supposed to be, inflicted slight damage (only three Boers wounded) and warned the Boers of an impending attack. They had entrenched themselves at the foot of the hills in narrow trenches. Once again, General Koos de la Rey had come up with an innovative and bold plan of defence.

On 11 December 1899 at first light and in pouring rain, The British forces ,officers and men of the Highlander Brigade who had moved out into the night, the Black Watch leading, followed by the Seaforths, Argylls and Highland Light Infantry, had been marching since midnight, were less than 400 m from the Boer trenches. The Boers opened fire from their concealed trenches with devastating effect. The Highlanders suffered very heavy casualties including Major General Andrew Wauchope, commander of the Highland Brigade, who was killed within the first few minutes of the battle. According to General Kemp his body was found six metres from the Boer trenches. A group of the Seaforths slipped through a gap in the trenches and commenced to work their way around the Boers onto a kopje, from where they could fire down into the trenches from behind. General Cronje with six of his adjutants who had got lost in the rain, were on the same hill and seeing the Seaforths opened fire on them with such accuracy that they had to abandon their plan when the Boers in the trenches realised what was happening behind them. The group of Seaforths were all killed or captured (40 men were taken prisoner). The Seaforths succeeded in surrounding the Scandinavian volunteers (who were sympathetic to the Boer cause) on the left flank of the trenches, and not wanting to be taken by the Scots, they perished to a man. The Highland Brigade spread out in front of the Boer lines on 12 December were to suffer more. The khaki aprons they wore proved no protection as the men lay prone in the sand. The bright metal of their canteen tins was a conspicuous target for the Boers. Efforts were made to rush the Boer trenches from time to time , but to no avail. Being mid-December in the Northern Cape, the men lay exposed to a relentless sun beating down on the bare insides of their knees causing severe blistering which was aggravated by their kilt if they moved. Every move elicited a shot from the trenches usually with deadly accuracy. No back-up plan was in place as Methuen had not envisaged defeat. The soldiers had to suffer the sun and keep their heads down. At 1400 hr the right flank of the Highlanders came under attack led by a

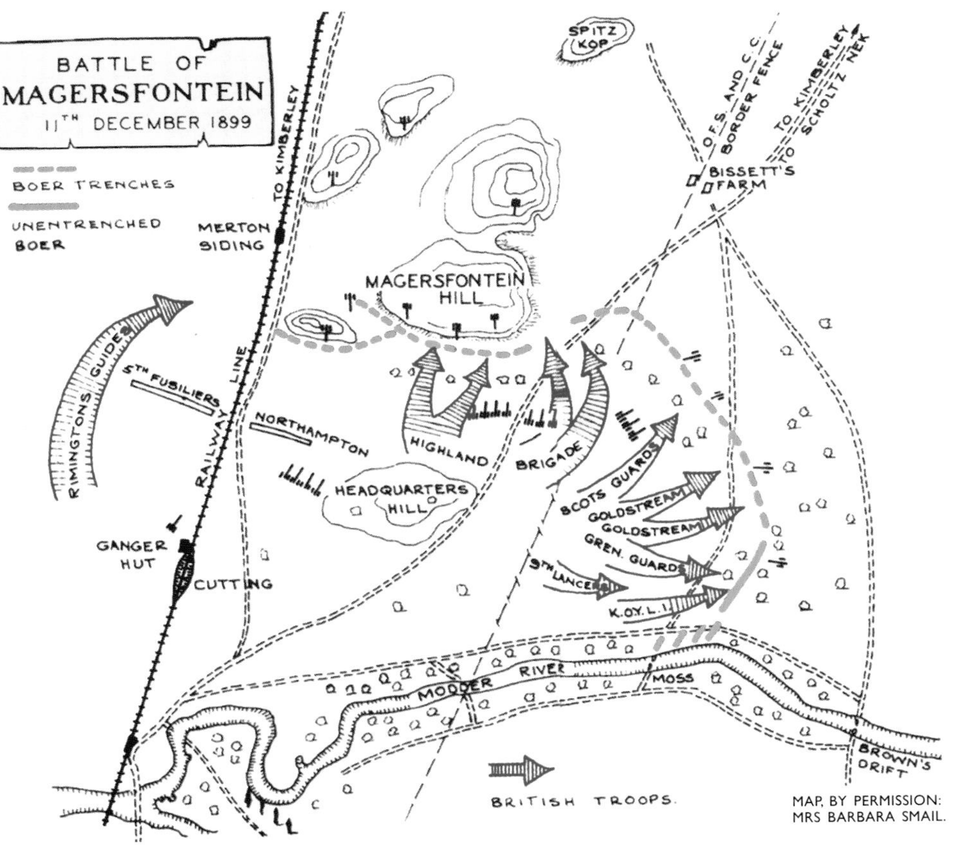

SUPLEMENT to the CAPE TIMES

TUESDAY, DECEMBER 12, 1899.

Second Extra.

# The Battle Described

## TWO DAYS' HEAVY FIGHTING.

## BUT STILL INCONCLUSIVE.

## HEAVY LOSSES ON BOTH SIDES.

[By Telegraph from Our Special Correspondent.
Received and Published December 12th, 5 a.m.

MODDER RIVER, DEC. 12, 9 A.M.

A huge battle, which has raged for a day and a half, commenced on Sunday afternoon at Magersfontein, or Bisset's farm.

At four p.m. on Sunday our artillery shelled the enemy's position till dusk. On Monday morning, at early dawn, Lord Methuen's division, consisting of 8th and 12th Lancers, the Naval Brigade with 4·7 gun, the G Battery R.H.A., 75th, 62nd, 73rd, 18th, and 65th Howitzer Battery, Highland Brigade, Guards Brigade, 9th Brigade in reserve, Mounted Infantry, Remington's Guides, with details of Army Service Corps and the Field Hospital Corps, moved on the enemy's position, which had been very carefully selected and entrenched.

The Highland Brigade were moved t the foot of the kopje while it was yet dark, and chancing on one of the Boer rine pits, paid heavily for the accident, having to retire to cover.

Soon after daylight on Monday our artillery opened fire on the enemy's position such as has seldom, if ever, been seen in modern waarfare.

The guns were excellently placed. "Joe Chamberlain" played long bowls from the west of the position, and from this point round to our centre and right the battery was planted with consummate skill.

From dawn till dusk, with a brief rest at midday, our guns were kept going, playing all the time on what appeared to be the enemy's rifle pits. But as no artillery was brought into play against us, the exact positions were difficult to locate.

The balloon meanwhile from its coign of vantage was giving valuable information.

The searching fire from 38 guns in action gave one the idea that no one can be alive in the trenches; but notwithstanding whenever our front line got within a decent range of the Boer riflemen a different lesson was learned.

The Guards Brigade were told off for a flank movement on the enemy's left, and were deploying to our right with this object in view; but a reinforcement of about two thousand Boers, who took up a very strong position on our right flank effectually stopped what would have been a very paying move on the part of our general, and as nearly as possible turned the day against us.

Towards evening an assault of the position was spoken of by many, but the Boers sticking to their trenches with dogged determination rendered such an undertaking by a tired force too hazardous to attempt.

Lieut. H. H. Cowie, of the Bechuanaland Rifles, well known in the Colonial Office, Cape Town, was here on a visit from De Aar and got attached to the Mounted Infantry for the day.

Major Milton, commanding Mounted Infantry, being knocked over in a hot corner on our right, Cowie rushed to his aid. Whilst holding him in his arms, Cowie got two Mausers through him, and his Commanding Officer received his quietus. Cowie, though dangerously wounded, is very cheerful and looks forward to the day when he may become permanently attached

Our loss is very heavy.

The Boer loss must have been enormous.

One prisoner states 60 Boers were killed by one Lyddite shell.

Although trenches had been used in warfare since at least the sixteenth century, de la Rey's use of trenches at Magersfontein caught the British by surprise. In spite of their observation balloons, the British did not detect a 20km defence line which consisted of trenches, stone sangars, and earthworks. (Bateman, 79).

## THE FIRST AND LAST TIME

Tragically, for many it was to be the first and last time many Boer and British soldiers saw action. Most unusual is the case of Lt-Colonel J.H.C.Coode, commanding officer of the Black Watch who was killed at Magersfontein on 11 December 1899. It was the very first time he had been on active service in a war. Others of the Black Watch killed at Magersfontein who died in their first battle included Captain E.G. Elton, Lt. N.G. Edmonds, Lt. H.C.W. Burton and 2nd-Lt.Drummond.

STEVE'S WAR STORIES

commando from the village of Ficksburg, Orange Free State; and Colonel Hughes-Hallet gave orders to ease back slightly. First in ten then hundreds the Highlanders rose from the ground. The Boers, presented with a better target than ever, fired with the frenzy of men scenting victory. Not all ran for their lives; Captain E.B.B. Towse (the Blind V. C.) of the Gordons won a V. C. for refusing to leave his mortally wounded commander until help came to carry him off.

Officers tried to stem the rush, and nearly succeeded until the Boer guns suddenly opened up, with the first shells falling among the rallying Highlanders. They broke and fled again ... reforming only at nightfall. In the evening the Boers called out to them that all those that could walk might go unmolested on condition that they left their rifles and ammunition. Then Methuen decided to retreat after there was an armistice where the ambulances were brought out and, amid complete silence, moved about the field. British Doctors and stretcher-bearers approaching the Boer lines were guided blindfold so that they could not report on the enemy positions. Methuen began his retreat at noon and by 1600 hr the last of the British troops were back in camp at Modder River. The British losses were upward of 1 000 men killed, wounded and taken prisoner. Boer losses were about 87 killed, 168 wounded and 21 taken prisoner.

*Figures of deaths vary considerably; therefore the numbers referred to in the above battles may not be accurate. References used are: 'Times History', 'Breytenbach' and 'Maurice's Official History.'*

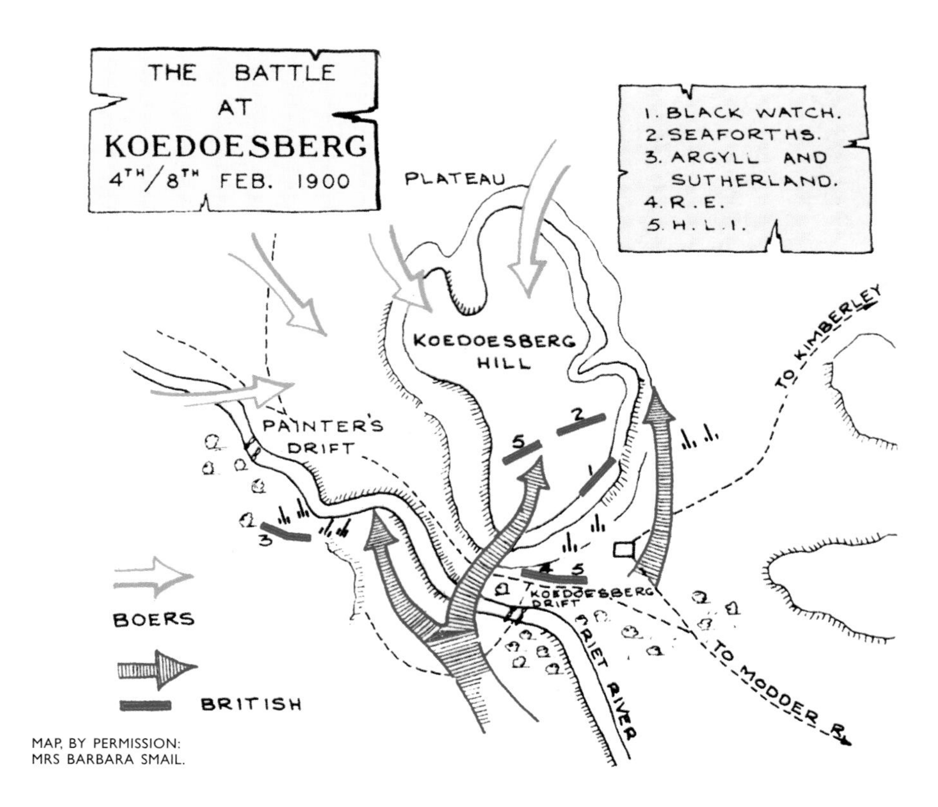

MAP, BY PERMISSION: MRS BARBARA SMAIL.

On the battlefield there are site-displays as well as memorials to the Black Watch, British Grave sites and the Scandinavian Grave sites. You will see the occasional field gun (replica) on the battlefield as well as numerous 'pepper trees'. These trees are significant as they were planted by the Guild of Loyal Women who looked after the original graves where soldiers fell. To enable them to identify the position of a grave they planted 'a pepper tree.' The occasional stone painted white identifies the position where a soldier fell and was buried. Experience the eeriness of the Battlefield where you can imagine the turmoil that took place a hundred years ago.

Visit the Museum on the hill and enjoy a meal at the Magersfontein Restaurant (Tel: 053 831 6711). The memorial near the Museum honours the Scottish dead and the Black Watch and Maj.Gen.Andy Wauchope.

Further along the hills are the Memorial to Eleven Transvalers and the Scandinavian Memorial. A must is the Lookout Post where the entire battlefield is spread out in front of you.

***Battle of Langberg 11 December 1899***

22 km from Kimberley. The Boer right flank crossed the railway line, and the present N12 road, and ended on hills near Langberg Farm. A site-display is featured on a hillock across the railway line; and overlooks the western line of the Magersfontein Battlefield.

***Koedoesberg Drift 5–8 February 1900***

Koedoesberg Drift is a willow shaded depression hidden below the surface of the veld. Koedoesberg Hill dominates the country for many a kilometre around and approaches could easily come under fire from the crest. A fort built on Koedoesberg would be vunerable to being cut off from water; therefore a redoubt was constructed on a small knoll close to the drift. To divert attention away from the eastern British troop build-up; on the night of 2 February 1900 orders were given that a task force was to proceed 20 miles west of Modder River camp to prevent the Boer retirement from Magersfontein via Koedoesberg Drift, and to assist in the construction of a small fort to hold 200 men and prevent Boer re-inforcements going to the south. This force consisted of the Highland Brigade under the command of Gen. MacDonald, two squadrons of the 9th Lancers, 62nd Field Battery and the 7th Co. Engineers. News of the march to Koedoesberg reached De Wet at Magersfontein on the afternoon of 3 February; and Boer forces reached the foot of the hill late that night. During the ensuing days from the 5 - 8 February skirmishes broke out with occasional fierce fighting from the Black Watch, Seaforths and Argyll and Sutherlands. Both sides suffered slight casualties during the actions. Lt. Freddie Tait, a champion British golfer, lost his life on the hill. Their attention distracted by the British at Koedoesberg Drift, the Boers were caught offside, and General French's cavalry relieved Kimberley by breaking through the Boers eastern defences. ❑

**_References_**:
*Goodbye Dolly Gray* by Rayne Kruger.
*Diamond Fields N12 Battlefields Route* produced for Kimberley Tourist Centre.
*The Anglo-Boer War 1899-1902 Kimberley & Diamond Fields* produced by Johann van Schalkwyk

**_Pilcher's Raid 1 January 1900_**

Towards the end of December Boer Commandos crossed the Riet River and a laager was established in the Douglas District under Commandant Scholtz on the farm near Sunnyside Hill, which lay 30 miles north-west of Belmont.

Lt.-Colonel T. D. Pilcher who commanded at Belmont secured permission to raid the Boer force at Sunnyside and if successful to reconnoitre as far as Douglas. His force consisted of 200 Queenslanders, 40 regular Mounted Infantry, one Company of Canadians, two guns of 'P' Battery, R.H.A. (Royal Horse Artillery) to compose his flying column. It was also arranged to send the Greys and several Mounted Infantry up from the Orange River to Marks Drift.

A British force marched west to prevent the Magersfontein Boers crossing the Riet River. Another mobile column was to march from De Aar to Prieska, some 195 km, to damp down the incipient rebellion in that district.

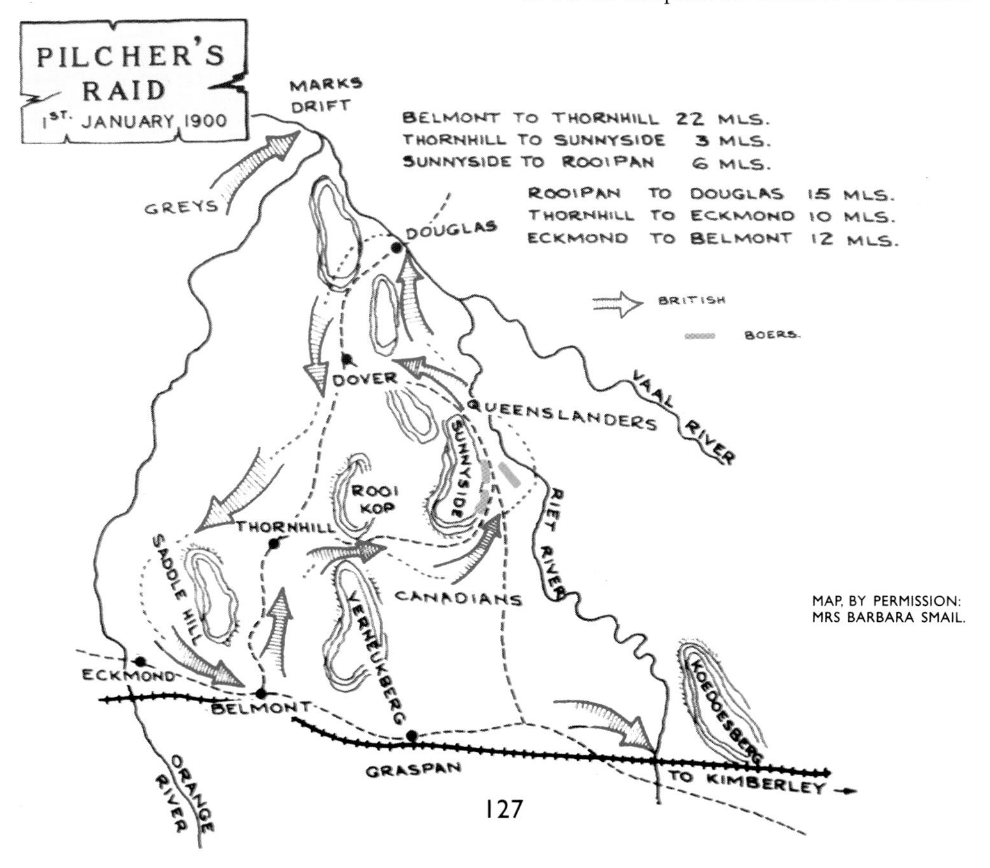

MAP, BY PERMISSION: MRS BARBARA SMAIL.

To ensure surprise in an area full of Boer sympathisers was not easy but by pretending that a march to the east of the railway line, and actually starting a column in that direction on the 30 December 1899, Pilcher provided false information that would be relayed to the Boers at Sunnyside. On the afternoon of the 31 December, he marched his column towards Thornhill. Two Companys of Cornwalls left Belmont with orders to proceed to Thornhill as a support unit.

On 01 January 1900, the British force starting at 0615 hrs and moving in a somewhat circuitous route in order to keep under cover of the small hills, unseen, came within striking distance of the Boers at 1000 hr. The two guns, the Canadians and the regular Mounted Infantry were sent to the north-east to engage the enemy, but not to press home the attack. At 1125 hr the British guns opened fire on the laager. The Boers swarmed onto a kopje in front of the laager and became engaged with the Canadians and Mounted Infantry. As soon as the firing started the Queenslanders carried out an enveloping movement on the Boer right flank. It was not long before it was all over and the Boers surrendered.

On 02 January, Pilcher entered Douglas. By 05 January, he was back at Belmont. **The indirect effects of this raid were not unimportant, as it helped delay the southward spread of rebellion.** ❑

Source:

*Battlefields of the SA War 1899* by J.L. Smail. (with kind permission, Mrs Barbara Smail)

## THE 'BLIND' VICTORIA CROSS

*Towse, Capt. E.B., Gordon Highlanders.*

On 11 December 1889, at the action of Magersfontein, Captain Towse was brought to notice by his commanding officer for his gallantry and devotion in assisting the late Colonel Downman, when mortally wounded, in the retirement, and endeavouring, when close up to the front of the firing line, to carry Colonel Downman on his back; but finding this not possible, Towse supported him until joined by Colonel Sgt. Nelson and Lance-Corporal Hodgson.

On 30 April 1900, Towse, with 12 men, took up a position on Mount Thaba, far away from support. A force of about 150 Boers attempted to seize the same plateau, neither party appearing to see the other until they were but 100 yards apart. Some of the Boers then got within 40 yards of Towse and his party, and called on him to surrender. He at once caused his men to open fire, and remained firing himself until severely wounded (both eyes shattered), succeeding in driving off the Boers.

The gallantry of this officer in vigorously attacking the enemy (for he not only fired, but charged forward) saved the situation, notwithstanding the numerical superiority of the Boers.

*(July 6, 1900)*

*F. L. Mikko Uola*

# Scandinavians in the Anglo-Boer War

Of the Finnish human fates from around the world; those countrymen who participated in the Boer War over 100 years ago form their special totality about which it is difficult to obtain information. Excluding those few Finns on the British side, there were about thirty Finns in the Boer forces. Some of them had immigrated to South Africa for the allure of the gold and diamond fields, others were sailors and adventurers who travelled from one continent to another.

The Scandinavians living in Johannesburg and Pretoria had in the middle of 1899 under unemployment and the risk of war, founded an organisation which was known as ***'Skandivaviska Organisation'***. Its leader was a Swede, *Christer Uggla*, who lived in Pretoria and worked for the Transvaal Railway Company. When the war was imminent there were different opinions among the Scandinavians towards the two sides of the war. Some sympathised with the British while many others were with the Boers.

The first meeting in Johannesburg did not reach any unity about the organisation's opinion to the war. Those who supported the Boers organised another meeting in Pretoria on 12 October 1899. In this meeting it was decided to form a Scandinavian Volunteer Force which would fight on the Boer side. This was accepted by the Transvaal officials. All the Scandinavian warriors received the full Burgher rights and a plot of land was promised for everybody after a successful war, but the soldiers did not get any salaries. The Government, however, gave some money to the corps for equipment and riding horses.

Originally about **65 men joined the Scandinavian Corps** and they were from all the Nordic countries: **Sweden, Denmark, Norway and Finland.** Besides them there were other volunteers which represented other nationalities in the corps. In the original Scandinavian corps there were probably **thirteen Finns.** Most of them were from Pohjanmaa (Bothnia) and all of them had worked at the Transvaal gold mines although they originally represented many occupations. Nearly all of the Scandinavian volunteers were miners but many of them were former sailors. Like all the Boer corps the Scandinavians also elected their Captain. The elected captain was a son of a Swedish missionary *Carl Ludvig Flygare, Natal born Johannes Flygare.* His greatest merit was his knowledge of the Boer language. In Finland it is often wrongly claimed that Flygare was a Finn.

Before their leave for the front between 14 & 17 October the Scandinavians made a parade before the residence of President Paul Kruger where the President made a stimulating speech to them. When leaving for the front the Scandinavians' destination was Mafeking where the Boers had besieged the British forces commanded by Colonel Baden-Powell. On their way to Mafeking the Scandinavians escorted the famous Boer gun *'Long Tom'*.

The Scandinavians participated in small skirmishes in Mafeking but the Boer commander General Piet Cronje opposed any large scale attack against the British occupied town because of vain losses. The Scandinavians protested strongly against Cronje's passive viewpoint because they wanted more active attacking. They complained of Cronje's passivity to Pretoria. It is said that Scandinavians volunteered to everything which was amusing and dangerous. They distinguished themselves in trench digging, blowing up the British mine fields, stealing cattle, etc.

The Scandinavians met their first loss in Mafeking; in an attack on 25 October a Finn, *Johan Johansson*, was badly wounded. Johansson was taken into an ambulance organised by the Scandinavians. It was suggested that Johansson go to hospital in Pretoria but he preferred to stay with his corps. When the strong British army led by Lord Methuen advanced from the south towards another besieged town, Kimberley, the main forces of General Cronje (including the Scandinavians), received the order on 20 November to go toward Kimberley.

On the way they received an additional 15 men – although the corps did not exceed 70 men. The corps arrived at Magersfontein, on 28 November and the slower ambulance unit arrived on 10 December 1899.

The Boer force of about 8 500 men led by Cronje prepared to avert the probable British attack by digging trenches in front of the Magersfontein hills. The Finns in the Scandinavian corps proved to be the best experts with explosives and they distinguished themselves in sabotaging the railway at the British rear.

Monument to Scandanavian volunteers, sympathetic to the Boer cause.

In the evening on 10 December after a severe British artillery bombardment, 52 men of the Scandinavian corps (according to other sources 49 men) were sent to an outpost about 1,5 kilometres in front of the defenses where 10 men stayed with horses. Other Scandinavians were around the whole encampment in different tasks. The night was rainy and chilly. About at four o'clock in the morning the British were seen advancing towards the Boer positions. The Scandinavians received orders to retreat to the main force but *Captain Flygare* decided to let his men fight at the outpost. The corps, however, fought persistently and twenty Scandinavians were killed, among them *Captain Flygare*. Tweny-one were taken prisoners by the British – the majority were badly wounded. Three of the prisoners died within the following days from their wounds. Only four of the Scandinavians at the outpost got safely back to their own side. The Finnish losses were one killed on the battlefield; one who died in captivity (after two days from his wounds); two badly wounded and one captured.

The Boer losses, except for the Scandinavians, were slight. Cronje's troops stayed at Magersfontein for two months until the British succeeded in bypassing the Boers to raise the siege of Kimberley in February 1900.

The Scandinavians had received the supplements of twenty men, (four or five of them Finns), at Magersfontein in January. The Scandinavians formed their own unit which took part in the *Battle of Paardeberg* on the 18 to 27 February 1900. In this battle only two Scandi-navians were killed. Among the wounded were three or four Finns. The whole Boer force surrendered to the British on 27 February. The *Prisoners of War* were sent to Cape Town and from there the largest number were sent to St. Helena where they were released after the war in 1902.

It is worth a mention that in the Scandinavian memorial erected at Magersfontein in 1908, a name *J. Jakobsson* is cut among the Finnish killed. There was no person called *Jakobsson* among the Scandinavians as far as is known, at least not in the lists of the fallen.

There were Scandinavians in the Anglo-Boer War on the Boer side, as members of commandos. There is little information available about the Finns in the Boer commandos. Presumably the names of only a few of them are known. The same applies for the Finns fighting on the British side.

According to the newspaper comments there were about 50 to 60 Finns in Johannesburg when the war broke out. Twenty of these joined the Scandinavian corps while the others either left for Finland or stayed in Johannesburg. The Finns who served in other Boer units probably lived in the Transvaal or Orange Free State but presumably not in Johannesburg or Pretoria.

The year of birth of sixteen Finnish Boer War participants are known. The youngest of these was 22 years old and the oldest 46 years old. ❑

*Apollon Davidson & Irina Filatova*

# The Russians and the Anglo-Boer War

Few people know that the Russians participated in the Anglo-Boer War, that the country sent two medical detachments to South Africa and that the Russian government of the time was keenly interested in the outcome of the War and closely watched the events. How and why did this happen?

More than 200 Russian volunteers fought on the side of the Boers. They came from different sides of the political spectrum, from communists to monarchists, but they shared their sympathy for the Boers. Some thought that the Boers were wonderful democrats because they defended republicanism against the world's most powerful monarchy; others admired their patriotism and their ability to stand up for their Motherland; yet others thought that it was their stand against national oppression that deserved admiration. There were those who hated Britain and whatever it stood for at the end of the 19th century and were ready to fight it whenever the opportunity arose. Whatever the cause with rare exception the Russians fought on the side of the Boers.

*Lieutenant-Colonel Yevgeny Maximov* may have been the most prominent of Russian volunteers. He was, at some stage, Deputy to the Commander of the European Legion, *French Colonel De Villebois-Mareuil*, and later, Commander of a Dutch detachment. More importantly, he made friends with the top leadership of the Boers, could visit President Kruger without ceremony, became at home with Reitz, and befriended President Steyn. His courage and gallantry were respected by the Boers; **he was even elected a Boer field general** - the greatest honour that there could be for a foreigner. After the War President Kruger wrote to Maximov, *"Your services to my Fatherland were of extraordinary importance."*

There were, however, more exotic figures among Russian volunteers than Maximov. A Georgian prince, *Nikolai Bagration*, a relative of a famous Russian general who fought against Napoleon, was one such person. He fought with the French Corps, then joined the European Legion and was taken prisoner in the same battle in which *De Villebois-Mareuil* was killed. *Nikolai Bagration* spent several months on St. Helena. His national dress, his tall and powerful figure, his bodyguards, his good sense of humour and his endurance caught attention of several authors who wrote about the War and earned him much sympathy among his companions.

A Russian woman dressed as a man, came to South Africa in order to find her husband with whom she had had a quarrel and who had decided to find consolation on the battlefields of the Anglo-Boer War. She was rich and well educated. In search of her husband she first fought with the Boers and then worked as a nursing sister in a British hospital. She finally found her husband in a prisoner of war camp in Ceylon and helped him to escape. It could be a legend of fiction despite the fact that mysterious *'Maria Z'* published her memoirs – but a short archival document seems to prove that it was not. *Lieutenant Alexei Ganetsky* organised and led a controversial ***'Russian Commando'***. The Russians constituted a minority in this detachment which was revered for valour by some and denounced for drunken brawls by others.

An experienced military journalist, a future

A group of Russo-Dutch ambulance personnel outside their hospital in Kroonstad.
*Back row, left to right:* Sister van Schermbeek, Brother van Nieuwenhuisen, Sister Meisner, Sister Jacobsen, Sister Cohen and Brother Siestrop.
*Middle row:* Doctor van Leersum, Miss Wessels and Sister Meyer.
*Front row:* Doctor Kukharenko, Sister van Maarsseveen and Sister Ross.

chairman of the Russian parliament who was to receive the abdication the last Russian Tsar, yet another prince - a socialist, a famous pilot, a count - a descendant of Catherine the Great, a future main architect of Soviet Moscow, a future top administrator of Soviet economy – all these people were among Russian volunteers as were officers of the Russian army, Russian Jews, Lithuanian peasants and straightforward adventurers.

Doctors and nurses of the **Russian Red Cross Detachment** and of the **Russo-Dutch Ambulance** (equipped and manned on public donations) worked on the frontline and in the rear, some were taken prisoner and changed their previously unequivocally unfavourable opinion of the British, others went on assisting the Boers as long as the Russian government allowed them, and one, *Dr. Rennenkampf* stayed with De La Rey's Commando until the very end of the War.

The Russian government of the time was highly interested in the events in South Africa. Not only did it collect information about the War wherever it could in Europe but it also sent its military observers to South Africa, both official and unofficial. Official Russian military observers were attached to both fighting sides: two to each. One managed to work on both sides but generally their movement was quite strictly restricted. Unofficial observers - and there is plenty of evidence to prove that some if not many officers among Russian volunteers were exactly this – watched the War from the inside and reported back to St. Petersburg on the latest military technology, tactics, politics, etc.

Even though they did not have high military ranks the government held them in high regard. A volunteer *Lieutenant Yedrikhin*, for example, was invited for a private conversation to the then Minister of War, not even in the office but at home and over the weekend. As a result of this conversation the lieutenant was awarded his normal army salary for all the time he spent in South Africa.

Not all Russians returned home from South Africa. Cap*tains Pokrovsky, Petrov* and *Duplov, Navy Lt. Strolman, Field Coronet Judelowits, Lukas Heyman,* and a young nameless volunteer *'Pavlusha R.'* who had come to South Africa with his girlfriend hoping to stay after the War, were killed. *Captain*

Photograph of Lieutenant-Colonel Yevgeny Maximov.
Compliments: MediaMakers CD *Photo Album of the Anglo-Boer War.*

## Underwear

The personal belongings of the Russian-Dutch ambulance was captured by the British shortly before Pretoria surrendered. In gentlemanly fashion it was returned to St. Petersburg some time later. (Sophia, 191).

*Pokrovsky* is still remembered in South Africa for his pluck. In 1938 his comrades in arms installed a memorial plate for him on the War memorial in Utrecht.

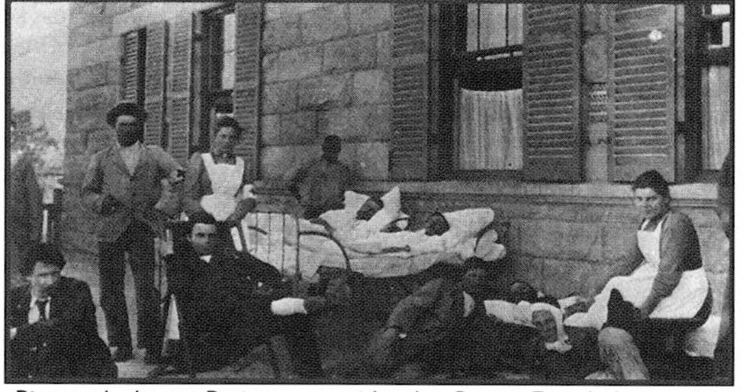

Pictured above: Patients outside the Russo-Dutch hospital in Kroonstad with Sister van Maarsseveen and Sister van Schermbeek.

The Anglo-Boer War remained in the historical memory of the Russian people as an integral part of its image of the turn of the 20th century. This was because of the enormous popularity of the Boer cause in the country. *'The Boers, the Boers and only the Boers'* wrote an annoying contemporary. Songs were sung about South Africa and about the Boers, articles and books published, lectures delivered, plays staged, church services served, presents sent to South Africa and donations collected. Restaurants and pubs, and even dishes and drinks were given *'Boer'* names. This fashion did not last long and the heroes of the Anglo-Boer War were forgotten in Russia's tragedies of the 20th Century. But even during the Second World War Russian soldiers still sung *'Transvaal, Transvaal, my country'* - the only Russian folk song about a foreign country ever. This first line of the song was still remembered in 1960's and 1970s[1]. Did you know that a substantial component of Russian volunteers were Russian Jews who had emigrated to South Africa before the War to escape from *'pogroms'* - physical attacks by the members of Russian chauvinistic organisation *'Black Hundreds'*?

The majority remained neutral, some joined the British, while others supported the Boers. The British took revenge on them indiscriminately: many were deported back to Russia while the war was still on.

[1]**If you want to find out what happened to Russian volunteers after the War, who of the South Africans visited Russia during the War and after it was over and how they were met, what political and diplomatic games Russia played behind the scenes in connection with the war, read *'The Russians and the Anglo-Boer War' by the Apollon Davidson & Irina Filatova (Human and Rousseau, Cape Town, 1998)*** ❑

*Dr M. D. Hayhurst*

# Medical Services in the Anglo-Boer War

The Medical Services of the British Army had a point to prove. The Royal Army Medical Corps (RAMC) had been founded in response to the public outcry of the inhumane and incompetent treatment received by battle casualties in the Crimean War. Despatches written by war correspondents, notably that of ***The Times,*** and the reports of Florence Nightingale, brought to the British public tales of the terrible suffering of the battle casualties. As a result of this public outcry the Military Medical Services were reorganised and the first opportunity to show their improvement was the Anglo-Boer War.

To help them, between 1850 and 1900 there had been substantial advances in medical science. In the Crimean War a Surgeon's work was a cruel, bloody business. Wounds to the head and body invariably proved fatal and wounds to the limb often resulted in amputation performed without any anaesthesia other than brandy or rum or occasional Laudenum. Surgeons were prized for the speed with which they could perform amputations and thus reduce the agony.

Post-operative wound infection was common and fatal. A fracture of the thigh due to a gunshot wound carried a 73% mortality in the Crimea; in South Africa it had dropped to 10%. The warm dry climate of South Africa helped to minimise the risk of infection. By 1900 antisepsis had been developed and good general anaesthesia, which allowed surgeons to take their time with the operation, and thus perform more complicated and intricate surgical procedures. Even injuries to the chest were operated on, although injuries to the abdomen were almost invariably fatal and, indeed, surgeons were ordered not to operate on such cases. Above all, patients had a painless operation, which reduced the chances of post-operative shock and improved survival remarkably. Other technologies available to the medical services were x-rays, which were freely used by both sides in the conflict, and intravenous fluids, which began to replace the previously extremely dangerous doses of Strychnine used in the treatment of shock. Perhaps the most important advance in the management of battle casualties however, was the development of a system designed to get the wounded soldier from the battlefield where he was injured, to immediate medical help and then, when necessary, to increasingly sophisticated levels of medical care, further away from the battlefield. The final level of sophisticated care was repatriation by a hospital ship back to the United Kingdom. This practice of treating and moving severely injured patients down the line to more sophisticated levels of care is carried on today

Above: Wounded being moved by stretcher-bearers at Modder River, Field Hospital.

Wounded being transferred from No. 3 hospital-train to ambulance waggons at Wynberg Station. The waggons have tail-pieces resting on the platform for the easy loading of the wheeled stretchers.

in modern battle, although the means of evacuation has changed from stretcher bearer, and horsedrawn ambulance, and the ambulance train, to the motor ambulance and the helicopter. It could not help everyone. Lt. 'Freddy' Roberts, the son of Lord Roberts, the Commander in Chief of the British Forces in South Africa was wounded by rifle fire in the Battle of Colenso on 15 December 1899. He was evacuated by the stretcher bearers and taken to the local field hospital. Sir Frederick Treves, an eminent Senior Surgeon from London, was asked to give an opinion. Lt. Roberts was shot in the abdomen and a general order existed that no operations were to be performed on these wounds because the chance of success was small. Treves travelled to the front line by special train, examined the patient, and pronounced the prognosis hopeless.

Lord Roberts' son died soon thereafter. The Battle of Colenso was a significant reverse for the British forces and the Force Commander Sir Redvers Buller, despite having to send cables of explanation to London, found time to add a brusque cable to Lord Roberts: *"Your gallant son died today. Condolences. Buller"*.

A soldier wounded on the battlefield was evacuated by stretcher bearers to the local dressing station. His wounds were dressed, bleeding was stopped, pain killing drugs dispensed. Those patients that could, would be returned to the battlefield, those that were unable to fight further would be moved to the Field Hospital. These were situated at a safe distance from the battlefield and manned by Medical Officers, together with medical orderlies. They performed further life-saving operations, such as stopping haemorrhage, splinting fractures, and dressing open wounds. Those patients needing further treatment were taken by horsedrawn ambulance to the Railhead for evacuation.

A more grim task of the Medical Officer was to triage those patients too sick to make the journey. These patients were merely made comfortable. The process of selecting those patients who are unlikely to live and give preference to those patients likely to benefit most from treatment, is a major philosophy

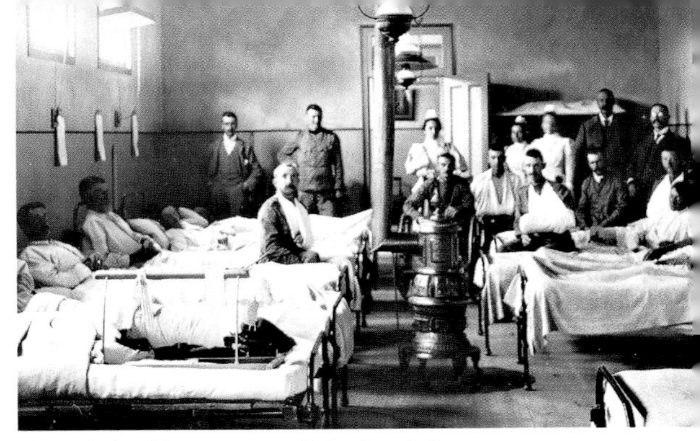

Wounded soldiers in one of the hospitals.

of mass casualty management, but nonetheless, many Doctors have told of the horror and stress of having to make such decisions. One Field Hospital was attached to each Infantry Division and consisted of three Surgeons and a Quartermaster with variable numbers of medical orderlies. The hospitals, since they had to be mobile, were largely tent based, with a large central marquee in which the operating theatre was situated and surrounded by bell tents as hospital wards. They held between one and 200 patients, but of course this depended on the character of the battle. The Field Hospital at Spearmans farm received the wounded from Spion Kop and over the course of two days handled 800 casualties. The medical staff of field hospitals was often bolstered with Civilian Surgeons who were seconded to the medical corps.

Later during the war, as many as eight Civil Surgeons would be added to the three Military Medical Officers in a Field Hospital. The more senior of these Civilian Surgeons were eminent academic staff of teaching universities and included such famous medical personalities as Cheyne, Stokes,

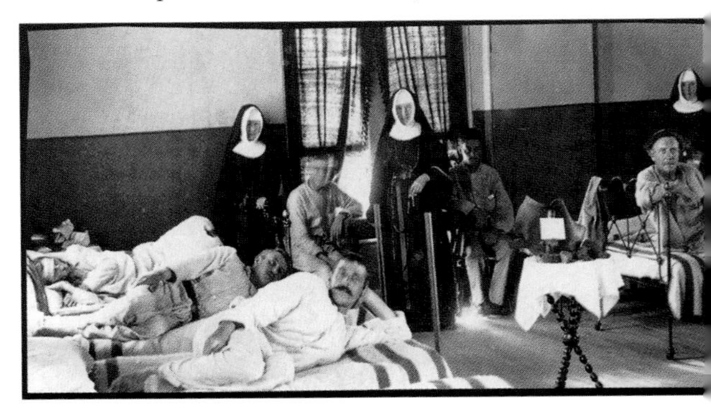

Wounded soldiers being tended to by the Sisters at Nazareth House.

No. 1 General Hospital in Wynberg, Cape.

Looking down between two rows of huts, formerly barracks, towards military gaol.

Cheatle, and many of whom went on to become leaders in their profession and used their experience in the Boer War to provide sound teaching principles for the treatment of battle casualties that persist to this day. The Civil Surgeon, Frederick Treves, who was summoned to a Field Hospital to give an opinion on Lt. 'Freddy' Roberts, was a well-known surgeon from the Westminster Hospital in London, who was perhaps better known for his protection of the *"Elephant Man"*(the subject of a recent film). Of course, things did not go entirely smoothly. The Field Hospital established in Bloemfontein Fort was established without any drugs since they had left them behind (and also had only three bedpans for 200 patients!).

Those patients requiring protracted convalescence or sophisticated treatment were moved from the Field Hospital to the railway line and then by ambulance train to a general hospital. The general hospitals were a more elaborate affair (often in permanent structures with a large component of tent accommodation). The average size being about 500 beds. There were 20 Medical Officers (a quarter were Military surgeons and the remainder civilian) and, since x-rays were a relatively routine investigation, a Radiographer. General hospitals originally were based in Cape Town but as the front moved forward and northward, they were moved to other centres such as Pretoria and Bloemfontein, as well as Ladysmith and Johannesburg. Those wounded in Kimberley on a Thursday would be loaded on to the Ambulance Train on the Friday night and would arrive in Cape Town by Sunday morning.

Surprisingly there were very few fatalities on the train, which attests for the good medical care given en route. However, fatalities on arrival were often considerable – on a particular day one hospital train arriving at No. 1 General Hospital, Wynberg, Cape Town, suffered 22 deaths due to shock.

In order to reduce these casualties, Stationary Hospitals were situated on the Railway line where, if necessary, patients could be offloaded for further treatment. Stationary Hospitals were in fact anything but 'stationary' (moving up and down the railway line as the front moved up and down – they were called stationary because these field hospitals did not move behind advancing or retreating troops). Stationary Hospitals were situated at De Aar, and Noupoort, on the line to Johannesburg, and in Bloemfontein. General Hospitals had an abundance of surgical talent, often from Civilian Surgeons. There were x-rays, electricity and telephones. Quite complex surgical operations such as neurosurgery were undertaken but because of the bureaucracy all operations were conducted under the supervision of a 'responsible officer' – a military surgeon whose job it was

Volunteer Hospital during siege.

Pictured top left:
An x-ray of the hip-joint of a wounded soldier. The bone was not fractured but a Mauser bullet can be seen lodged behind the hip-joint.

Pictured left:
One of the earliest X-ray machines used at Ladysmith.

Pictured below:
Wounded soldiers inside one of the hospital huts. Not mosquito-curtaining – and legs of beds have been place in cigarette tins.

to stand and merely supervise the civilian surgeon and the anaesthetist.

The General Hospitals had quite sophisticated kitchen facilities since many of the treatments of the day were based on various diets according to the patients' sicknesses.

Patients received a diet of milk, beef-tea, chicken and roast meat since these were considered important components of treatment – the convalescent hospitals did not have the facilities to provide these different diets. The presence of volunteer nurses at the general hospitals certainly made a change from the usual medical orderlies found elsewhere. While some of these nurses were attracted rather for the social life of Cape Town, many others were dedicated nurses and some even found their way up to the Field Hospitals, close to the front.

At the other end of the chain were the volunteer stretcher-bearers who assisted the battalion cooks and band members collecting the wounded from the battlefield, to start the chain of survival. These stretcher-bearers removed the wounded from the battlefield, often under heavy enemy fire, and at great personal risk. Many were non-combatants, recruited from the Red Cross and St John's Ambulance Services. Many bearer companies came from other parts of the British Empire, perhaps to show their support of the empire in a less war-like manner than by sending combatant troops. Perhaps the most famous was a group of stretcher-bearers of Indian origin, recruited in Durban where they were active in the Natal Campaign. One of the prominent members of this company was a lawyer, Mahatma Ghandi, who went on to play a dominant role in the subsequent independence of India from the British Empire. His pacifist protest approach in India may well have been fuelled by the horrors of what he witnessed on the battlefields of South Africa.

Arthur Conan Doyle, author of the Sherlock Holmes stories, was a doctor in South Africa. Rudyard Kipling was a newspaper reporter and editor in South Africa during the war. Their reminiscences, plus those of people such as Robert Baden Powell, helped

No. 3 Rondebosch, looking west towards Table Mountain. Note the tree used by convalescents.

formulate the character and up-bringing of the young people of the United Kingdom in the early 20th century. The sites of the general hospitals in Cape Town are well described but few actually remain. No. 1 & No. 2 General Hospital were situated in the Wynberg Military Camp. Many of the buildings used to house the patients are still present – the most interesting building of the old hospital which functioned as the Officer's Club was destroyed by fire in 1998. No. 3 General Hospital and a private hospital, The Portland Hospital, were situated as tent hospitals on the Rondebosch Common, which is still used as common ground today.

A small hospital was situated at McKenzie's Farm, Maitland Military Camp, which now forms part of Youngsfield Military Camp. No. 6 Stationary Hospital came to rest at Green Point Common, where some of the facilities of the newly built City Hospital were used. The common and the City Hospital still stand and the interesting Cape Medical Museum is situated in an outbuilding of the City Hospital. Other Military Hospitals at Woodstock, Maitland and Claremont have, due to ongoing urban expansion, long since vanished. A specific barrack hospital for Boer prisoners of war was established in Simons' Town. This building, the Palace Barrack, still stands.

Of the approximately 448 000 British and Colonial troops involved in the Anglo-Boer War, 5 774 soldiers were killed by enemy action. More than 100 000 casualties were reported and 16 168 died of wounds or disease. As shown, the major cause of death was not from battle wounds but disease – of which typhoid, dysentery and pneumonia were the major culprits. The mortality rate for people wounded in action and reaching medical help was about one-in-ten (comparable to any war since then). Thus, the Anglo-Boer War marked, not only, the beginning of the "modern" war but also the beginning of a scientific approach to the treatment of battle casualties. ❑

## KINDNESS TO THE ENEMY - ON BOTH SIDES

During the guerilla phase of the war, the Boers left their serious casualties behind for the British ambulances. *"Amid all the cruelty of farm burning and the hunting down of the civilian population, there was one redeeming feature, in that the English soldiers, both officers and men, were unfailingly humane. This was so well known that there was never any hesitation in abandoning a wounded man to the mercy of the troops, in the sure knowledge that he would be taken away and carefully nursed, a certainty which went so far as to soften the asperities of the war".* (Reitz, 169).

Two commandos fired at, and badly wounded, an English Officer near Heidelberg. They then dressed his wound and took him to the nearest British camp. Their act of humanity was so appreciated that they were given supper and a bath before leaving the camp. After the war the Officer's parents visited one of the commandos, Leonard Buys, to thank him for saving their son's life.

**Heidelbergers of the Boer War**, *Ian Uys*, 1981

# Doctor's Requirments

***Every thing a doctor may conceivably want ... on the veld or in city!***

*Having been asked by many men going out to South Africa what should be taken with them, the following list is given of the outfit found most useful.*

*A.* Packages as follows:–
*For hold.*–Case containing camp-furniture; case containing bicycle; two Saddle-boxes, tin-lined, at 15/6 (one labelled "For use on voyage", the other only half full).[1]
*For cabin.*–Large Gladstone bag; large kit-bag (Half full); bundle of wraps; Kodak (No. 4 cartridge folding) and field-glasses (Zeiss, No. 7, binocular).

*B.* Contents of above (including articles worn):–
1. *Case of camp-furniture* (mostly as recommended by Director-General):–
Brown canvas Wolseley valise, containing small canteen (full of useful articles for purposes of cooking and eating), hair-pillow in green canvas, treble sack Jaeger blanket, single blanket, cork mattress, nightcap and socks, green canvas bath and bucket, and two large bath-towels. Camp-bed, -table, -chair, -lantern (with candles), -looking-glass, tent-pole -strap with hooks (quite indispensable) and enamelled basin with leather cover (most useful at the front, as a separate package, to contain washing- and shaving-kit, and other small articles).
2. *Wraps*:– Rug; thick Mackintosh sheet 7 ft. by 4ft.; Mackintosh coat and straps; ulster[2] umbrella and stick; riding whip; tripod for kodak.
3. *Two boxes and two bags* for clothes, books, and instruments:–
*(a) Head-gear*– Khaki helmet in case, with blue serge field cap; Panama straw hat; soft grey felt hat; linen cricketing hat; mufti cap.
*(b) Leg-gear*–Two pairs brown boots, patent aluminium trees, two doz. laces and two bottles of polish, buckskin tennis shoes, white canvas shoes at 1/6, evening pumps, felt slippers, Stohwasser gaiters, puttees.
*(c) Outer body-gear*–Khaki drill[3] tunic and trousers, khaki serge do., six linen and two celluloid uniform-collars, thin Bedford-cord riding breeches, dark grey flannel suit, light cloth suit, dress suit, dress jacket, two pr. white flannel trousers, blazer, old Norfolk jacket.
*(d) Under-gear*–three coloured flannel,[4] eight striped cotton, and six white linen shirts, three suits pyjamas, 1 1/2 doz. white collars, four vests, four pr. drawers, nine pr. socks (one dress), suspenders.
*(e) Odds and ends of clothes*–Gloves, two pr. doeskin, two pr. tan riding; ties and bows, seven day, one doz. white evening, one black evening; neck scarves, one silk, one white cashmere, one hunting stock; handkerchiefs, 1/2 doz. bandanna silk, 1/2 doz. white silk, 1/2 doz. white linen; towels, two bath, two hand; braces, two pr. with extra ends; housewife with needles, threads, plain and safety pins, buttons for boots, waistcoats, coats, tunics (brass and leather), trousers and under-clothing, tie-pin, tie-clip, two pr. sleeve-links, three sets shirt-studs, six collar and six odd studs, one doz. collar-pins.
*(f) Toilet articles*–Sponges, safety razor-box and 4 blades, with strop, brushes (hair-, clothes-, shaving-, and 2 tooth-) and comb, 3 cakes soap and shaving-stick, court-plaster, tin vaseline.
*(g) Books & stationery*–TECHNICAL: Erichsen's *Surgery* (2 vols.), Jacobson's *Operations*, Heath's *Anatomy*,[5] Stevenson's *Wounds in War*, Osler's *Medicine*, Manson's *Tropical Diseases*, Whitelegge's *Public Health*.
GENERAL: Bryce's *S. Africa*, 1/2 doz. paper novels, Unicode, Map of S.A.; note-books for this journal, etc.[6]; prose and poetry and music *ad lib.* STATIONERY, ETC.–small leather despatch-case,[7] fountain pen[8] and bottle of ink in wooden case, refill-pencils for case and rubber, two packets foreign note-paper and envelopes, foolscap, two packs cards, visiting cards, elastic bands, paper-clips, etc.
*(h) Medical instruments and sundries*–Surgical dressing-case, case of four thermometers, aseptic tabloid hypodermic case, B.&W.'s pocket 'emergency' tabloid-case, stethoscope, 2 prs. dental forceps,[9] box capsicum dental-plasters, long rectal tube and metal funnel,[10] chloroform drop-bottle and tongue-

forceps, toilet paper, Keating's powder. *(i)* *Other instruments and sundries*–Kodak and field-glasses (as above, *A*), aneroid barometer, pocket luminous compass, 'Bee'-alarm clock, stop-watch and wrist-strap, Webley blued revolver,[11] belt, pouch and ammunition, flask, small Berkefeld filter, aluminium cup, folding knife, fork and spoon in case, four briar pipes, 'baccy for voyage, 500 cigarettes, bicycle-lamp, pump, lock, repair-outfit with cleaning apparatus, key-chain and key-ring, whistle, barbed-wire-nippers, pocket tape-measure. Add to this, gun with 500 cartridges, or a cricket-, golf-, or tennis-outfit according to taste. ❑

NOTES:

1. It would have been better to have had both labelled in this way. You never know what you may not want to use or refer to on the voyage; and, unless thus labelled, boxes were stowed away underneath waggons and ammunition, and all sorts of immoveable things.
2. Afterwards replaced by a grey cavalry coat with plain buttons.
3. Most useful, because cool and washable.
4. This is a minimum.
5. The most important, especially because of pictures.
6. Including Smith's automatic self-registering pocket diary, which was most useful.
7. Most useful at the front.
8. Indispensable.
9. Curved Reed's for upper teeth and Hawksbill Roots for lowers–enough for most work in campaign.
10. For saline injection, in case of internal haemorrhage from wounds.
11. Useful for amusement on board ship; not otherwise.

**Medikit No. 2** *(left) contains, on the front, which is folded down, tins of strapping, packets of dressings, clippers, anvil and hammer for splints of perforated zinc, two triangular metal dressing-dishes, and food-warmer. The drawers of basket, with lids removed here, are full of dressings in paper packets, and tins of milk and bovril for emergencies; with two housewives and roll of dental forceps. Inside the cover are strapped sheets of perforated zinc and two prescription books.*

**Medikit No. 1** *(right) containing medicines and instruments. The lid is raised and the front lowered. On this front are seen from left to right: note-books, candle-lantern, irrigation-tin with rubber tubes and clamps, tin steriliser with lamps and spirit, vulcanite medicine cups and mortars in one, with pestles, and lastly a couple of minim measures. On the ground lies open the box of instruments, from which the tray of knives, etc., in front of it has been taken out. To the left, metal stethoscope, tongue-depressor and hypodermic case. To the right, spoons and box of hypodermic tabloids. These all fit away into compartments under the bottles.*

**SPRINGBOK & OKIEP REGIONAL TOURISM**
**Old Anglican Church, Namakwa Street, Springbok.**
**Tel: (027) 712 2011.**

*Springbok is situated 560 km north of Cape Town. It was founded in 1862 as a copper-mining centre under the name of Springbokfontein. The principal copper mine was at Okiep where copper was first discovered and mined in 1855.*
*Okiep is situated 8 km north of Springbok and 120 km south of the Namibian border.*

## BOER WAR ACTIVITY & SITES, SPRINGBOK

The Namaqualand Copper-Belt was known at the turn of the last century (1900) to be the richest copper mining area in the world. This made Okiep famous during the last phase of the Anglo-Boer War when it was sieged by the Boers under the command of General Jan Smuts for the two months of April - May 1902. When Smuts invaded the Cape Colony in September 1901 the Boers made their way to Namaqualand via Calvinia with the idea of taking the rich copper fields and therefore forcing the British to send their troops to Okiep. This would have left Cape Town open for attack by the Boers. Unfortunately for the Boers this did not happen as in late April 1902 Smuts was called back to Pretoria for the signing of the *Peace of Vereeniging* in June 1902.

One can see the remnants of 12 blockhouses surrounding the area as well as the Boer positions which were situated above Okiep. See ***The Invasion & Relief of Namaqualand***.

## HISTORICAL PLACES, SPRINGBOK

**Blue Mine**: Springbok.The first mine at Springbok – with walking trail offering views of the town.

**Mineshaft**: Carolusberg. Simon van der Stel in 1685 instructed the digging of the shaft. The *'Simon van der Stel Mine'* is at Carolusberg approximately 6 km from Springbok.

**Monument Koppie**: Town Centre, Springbok. Commemorates the Anglo-Boer War.

**Namaqualand Museum**: Springbok. Situated in the Old Synagogue.

**Namastat**: Springbok. Traditional dome-shaped reed hut. (Tel: 027 712 2435). *See Accommodation.*

**Orbicule Hill**: This is a unique geological formation which is only found in Namaqualand and Scandinavia. It contains *Orbicular Diorite*.

**Smelting Furnace**: *National Monument*. To the north of Springbok, unused since 1871.

## HISTORICAL PLACES, OKIEP

In 1873 a 2'6" railway line was operational from Port Nolloth to Okiep. Visitors travelled this line which was used for the transportation of copper to Port Nolloth, which was 147 km from Okiep. At Port Nolloth, all passengers were offloaded from their ships by a large basket which held 4 persons and which was swung onto the jetty.

**Cornish Pump House:** *National Monument* (fully intact steam pump engine) The only remaining pump house of its kind in the southern hemisphere – much of the old mining works remain in Okiep, especially the remains of the old Cornish miners' working.

**Fort Shelton:** On the road between Okiep and Concordia. The main fortification of the Home Guard during the Siege of Okiep.

**Smokestack:** *National Monument*. Built by the Cape Copper Company in 1880.

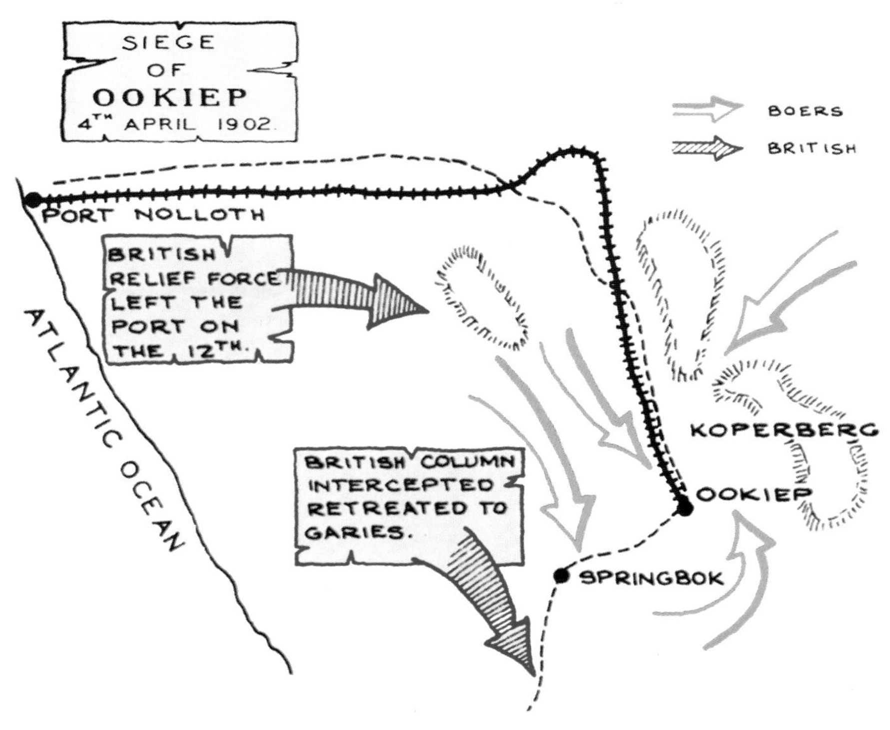


# The Invasion and Relief of Namaqualand

## *Events that took place during the Anglo-Boer War*

**1901**

**20 January:** Colonel W.S. Shelton arrives in Okiep from Cape Town by sea.

**9 August:** Boers forces occupy Van Rhynsdorp under Steenkamp.

**4 September:** General Smuts enters Cape Colony at Kiba Drift, Free State.

**25 November:** Shelton starts preparing for possible siege.

**1902**

**20 January:** Martial Law declared in Namaqualand – Boer patrols reported in Springbok area.

**3 February:** Namaqualand Border Scout - Private S. E. Ramsden shot at Spektakel Pass on Kleinzee road by Cape Rebels (Boers). The grave can be seen next to the road on the pass. *(A farmer and father of 10 children, he was captured by Boers 2 February 1902, shot and buried 25 February where he was shot.)*

**25 February:** The spy Colyn executed by Smuts' Commando at Atties near Van Rhynsdorp.

**18 March:** Lieutenant Charles T. Darter killed at Brandewynskop near Kamieskroon. The grave is next to the road 11.5 km south of Kamieskroon on N7. ***The Darter family owns the grave site.*** *(Lt. Darter – 1st Namaqualand Border Scouts; ex: Gorringers Flying Column; Troop No. 15 Western Province Horse. Entitled to QSA Cape Colony bar.)*

Veldkornet M. Boonzaaier killed in Darter action. His name is on the monument behind the DRC Church at Kamieskroon.

*(Veldkornet Matthys 'Thys' Boonzaaier - General Maritz Commando).*

**21 March:** Garies under siege by Boers.

Photograph depicting the typical clothing of Boer soldiers.

**1 April:** Springbok sacked by Maritz and Reitz forces in 19 hours.

**3 April:** Nababeep sacked and looted. Mines blown up by Boers. Telegraph links with Port Nolloth cut by Smuts. Okiep cut off.

**4 April:** Concordia forces surrender to Smuts without a shot fired. Boers make Concordia their HQ. Boers capture large quantities of dynamite.

**5 April:** *Deneys Reitz delivers a letter from Smuts to Shelton in Okiep ordering them to surrender. Shelton declines, so begins the Siege of Okiep.* The population was 2 000 plus 3 000 refugees with supplies for nearly three months.

**6 April:** Smuts offered an armistice for women and children to leave Okiep. This was turned down by leading women in the community. Boers started sniping at Okiep.

**8-12 April:** Boers attack the blockhouses with rifle fire and dynamite bombs.

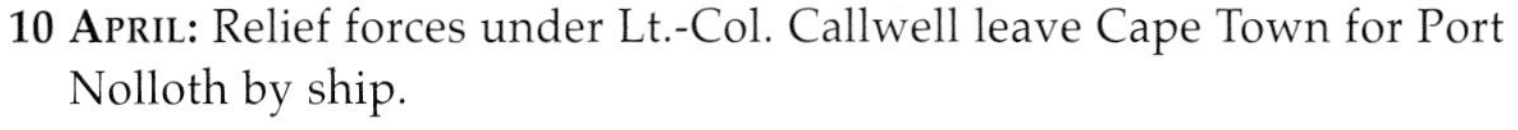

**10 April:** Relief forces under Lt.-Col. Callwell leave Cape Town for Port Nolloth by ship.

**11 April:** Second truce flag from Boers offering women and children safe passage – refused again.

**12 April:** Relief forces arrive at Port Nolloth.

**13 April:** Boer forces launch a fierce attack from Crows Nest. It was repulsed.

**14 April:** Boer force of 120 men repelled from Fort Shelton. Relieving forces attack Boers in hills around Anenous.

*(Anenous Viaducts - located on the decent of the Anenous Pass on the LHS of the road to Port Nolloth. Several remains of Blockhouses and Fortifications which were held by Lt. 'Nuffie' Moffat and Lt. Meynick of the NBS. Their efforts saved the wooden viaducts over which the narrow gauge railway ran to Port Nolloth and assisted in the relief column in their advance).*

**15-22 April:** Relieving forces proceed to occupy area *en route* to Springbok.

**25 April:** 3rd truce and letter from Smuts to Shelton. Shelton refuses.

Colonel Crabbe and Lieutenant Chadwick arrive in Okiep under flag of truce notifying all of peace negotiations.

**26 April:** *Smuts left with Reitz and brother-in-law via Klipfontein/Port Nolloth/ Cape Town for the Transvaal. They were given safe passage to the negotiations.*

**28 April:** Lt. Ironside fires shrapnel bombs at Van Deventer (who was in charge of Boer force in absence of Smuts) and causes serious damage. Boers retreat to Steinkopf.

**29 April:** Boer reinforcements reach Concordia from Upington.

**30 April:** Flag of truce by Boers using railway trolley with wounded NBS.

**29 - 30 April:** Boer forces leave Steinkopf for Concordia.

**31 April:** Maritz sends Pioneer train engine loaded with dynamite from Concordia – train derailed at Brackputs junction outside Okiep.

**1 May:** British occupy Steinkopf.

**3 May:** Boers start evacuating Concordia.

**4 May:** *Relieving British forces enter Okiep. Siege ends.*

**15 May:** ***First meeting between representatives of Boer Republics and British Forces held at Vereeniging.***

Okiep Tribute Medal.

The Irish members of General Smuts' Commando, with their love of explosives, made hand grenades from dynamite pillaged from the copper mines in the Northern Cape. They were used to good effect in capturing the forts defending the town of Springbok. (Reitz 301/304).

Whilst a burgher was engaged in conversation he casually pulled a small Bible from his pocket, out of which he tore a page from the Book of Revelation, and proceeded to roll a cigarette. He remarked that, *"he did not know how to accept the Revelation!"* (Schikkerling, 155).

**PORT NOLLOTH TOURISM**
**The Town Clerk, Port Nolloth.**
**Tel: (027) 851 8739.**

*80 km south of the Orange River mouth. It was founded in 1855 and was named after M S Nolloth, commander of the HMS Frolic, who surveyed the coast in 1854. It was established as a small vessel harbour and railway junction for the copper mining industry. It is now a centre for the small-scale diamond recovery and crayfishing industries. It is also the only holiday resort on the Diamond Coast.*

On 26 April, Jan Smuts, Krige, his brother-in-law and Deneys Reitz set sail on the 'Lake Erie' for Simon's Town as part of their journey to the Transvaal to join the rest of the Boer contingent for the peace talks. This was basically Smuts' last involvement in the Anglo-Boer War.

*Andrew J. McLeod*

# Deneys Reitz, from President's boy to Ragamuffin

He was a teenager in the presidency in Bloemfontein – the third son of Free State President F. W. Reitz. As a boy they spent time in Europe, Britain and Cape Town. When war with Great Britain breaks out his father is the State Secretary for Transvaal (ZAR). At 17 he is recalled from his school in Bloemfontein. Young as he is, he is determined to join the republican forces. What can a father do? The ageing president Paul Kruger even sees to it that he recieves a brand new Mauser Rifle. His name is Deneys Reitz.

He and brother Joubert leave Pretoria for the Natal border by train. The crowds on the station sing the anthem - *'Kent gij dat volk'* - waving *'Vierkleur'* flags. Then starts the hard life. When the first battle - **Talana Hill** - is fought on 20 October 1899, Deneys is with the Pretoria burghers on a hill nearby - ready to fight. This is what he came for. They were to attack Gen. Penn-Symons from the rear but when the moment comes, Gen. Erasmus refuses to move. That day Penn-Symons falls - but the Boers lose their first battle.

A group photograph with Smuts and Reitz

Then starts two and half hectic years for the youngster. He is part of the battles of **Nicholson Nek** and **Spionkop** in Natal. He then moves to the Free State to fight the advance of Lord Roberts to Pretoria. He is always in the thick of the battles, people around him are killed and wounded. Miraculously Reitz soldiers on. Reitz joins the burghers under General De la Rey in the western Transvaal. He takes part in the battle of **Nooitgedacht** on 13 December 1900. For weeks he goes without a horse. But being tied to one group for long is not for this young adventurer. He is prepared to struggle and to suffer (he breaks his leg yet battles on). He is restless and wants action. He moves south, joining up with small groups, fighting together. Often he loses them, but moves on. On to his destination - the **Cape Colony**.

During this time he and his comrades learn to be self-sufficient. They struggle for clothes, horses and ammunition. At one stage near Vet River they follow a column of British for two days, collecting dropped Lee-Metford cartridges. The Tommies did not bother with one or two dropped rounds. They did not lack meat for springbok were plentiful, but coffee, sugar, vegetables they only remember. In mid winter, close to **Bloemfontein**, they were in tattered clothing and threadbare blankets. He then joins up with a group: the *'Rijk Section'* (Dandy fifth) - so called for their tattered clothing. Together they join General Jan Smuts on his invasion of the **Cape Colony**. From the eastern Cape they slip past the British, causing havock as they go. This life suites young Reitz. They land up at **O'Okiep** in Namaqualand laying the copper mine under siege. Easy days follow. *But when things get too quiet for Reitz, he ties a Union Jack to his horse's tail and charges past the British post. They fire - but miss. The ragamuffin rides again.* Shortly thereafter, General Smuts has him fitted out in new clothes. Nobody recognised the 'new' boy. He accompanies Smuts to the peace talks in the Transvaal. Reitz was there at the start, he was there at the end. Deneys Reitz, after years of self-imposed exile, came back to eventually become a minister in Smuts' cabinet. He died in 1943, holding the post as High Commissioner in London, in 1943. ❑


***Source:***

Reitz, D. *Commando,* London, 1968.

# ANGLO-BOER WAR 1899-1902

09.14.1999

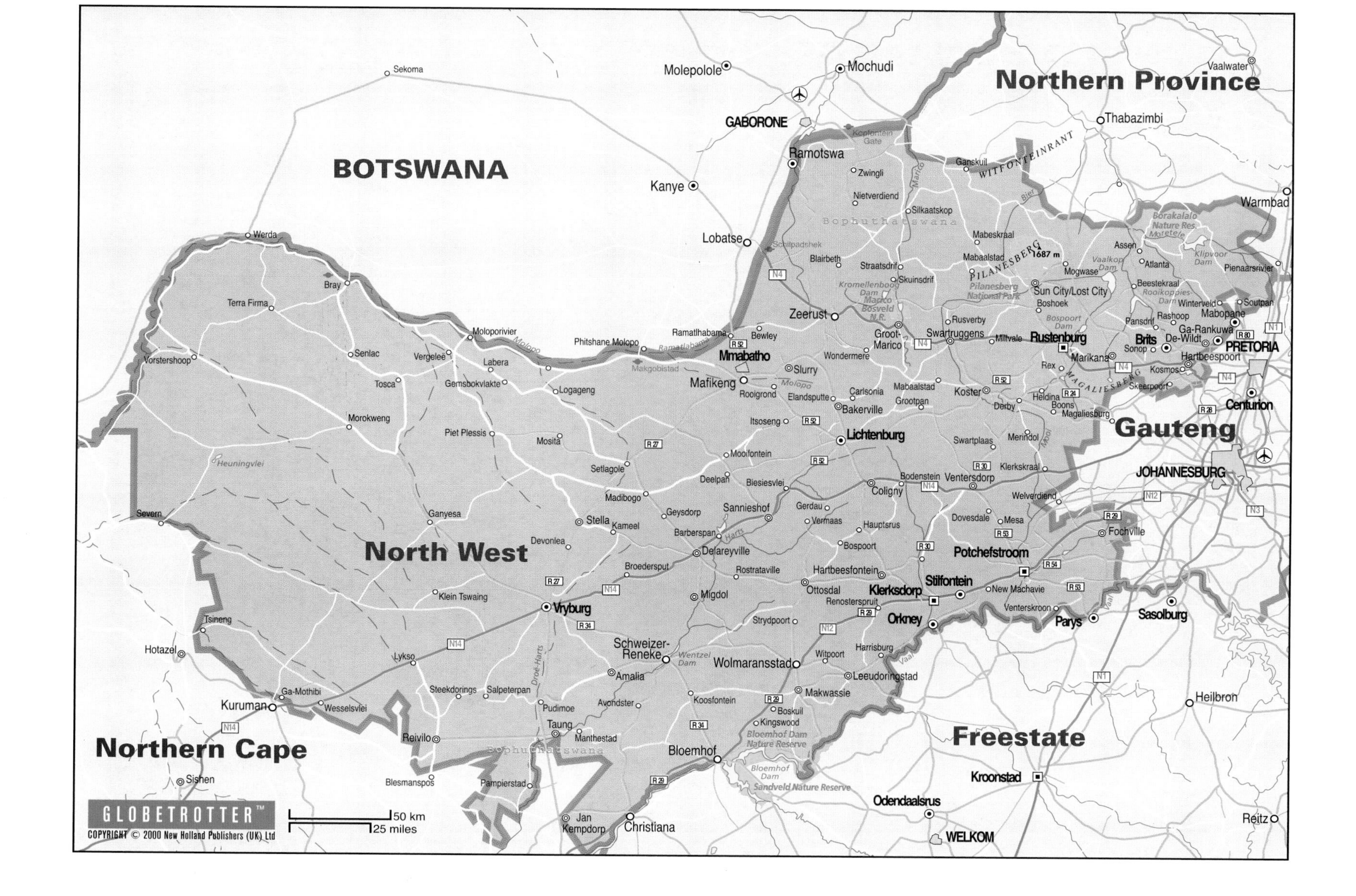

Northern Province
BOTSWANA
North West
Gauteng
Freestate
Northern Cape
GABORONE
PRETORIA
JOHANNESBURG
Centurion
Mafikeng
Mmabatho
Rustenburg
Lichtenburg
Potchefstroom
Klerksdorp
Stilfontein
Orkney
Vryburg
Zeerust
Brits
Sun City/Lost City
Wolmaransstad
Schweizer-Reneke
Bloemhof
Christiana
Taung
Kuruman
Sasolburg
Parys
Kroonstad
Odendaalsrus
WELKOM
Heilbron
Reitz
Molepolole
Mochudi
Kanye
Lobatse
Ramotswa
Sekoma
Thabazimbi
Warmbad
Vaalwater
PILANESBERG
MAGALIESBERG
WITFONTEINRANT
1687 m
Pilanesberg National Park
Bloemhof Dam Nature Reserve
Sandveld Nature Reserve
Bophuthatswana
50 km
25 miles
GLOBETROTTER™
COPYRIGHT © 2000 New Holland Publishers (UK) Ltd

To the

# Countess Georgina Howe

We, the MAFEKING MUNICIPAL COUNCIL, desire, on behalf of the Inhabitants (including Refugees) of MAFEKING, to deeply thank you for your thoughtful and indefatigable efforts, by means of which a Fund of £24,000 was subscribed by the ever-generous British Public, for the Relief of the Mafeking people, besieged by the Boers.

The monies so collected have considerably relieved the physical and pecuniary losses and sufferings of a large number of the Inhabitants, both European and Native, and have assisted most of the women, children, invalids and others to take a trip to the Coast or to Great Britain; thus enabling — what otherwise, in many cases, would have been impossible — them to recruit and recover their health after the tension and strain of the Siege.

YOU have secured the heartfelt appreciation of all sections of the Townspeople by your timely intervention, and, on their behalf, we beg of you to accept this album of Siege photos as an insignificant but very sincere expression of their gratitude for the kindness and interest displayed by you on their account.

THE Townspeople wish you every happiness and hope that you will ever continue to evince an interest in Britain's Colonists and thus help to strengthen the common bond, which, they trust, will always exist between the Old Country and her Colonies.

A. H. Friend, Mayor.

J. Aldred

C. W. Lucas

S. Smyth

Councillors.

December 1900.

"For there is no other place I know that is so heavy with atmosphere,
so strangely and darkly impregnated
with the stuff of life that bears the authentic stamp of Africa.

CHARLES HERMAN BOSMAN

**MAFIKENG TOURISM INFORMATION**

**Tel: (018) 381 3155/7 Fax: (018) 381 6058.**

**e-mail: nwptb@iafrica.com website: www.tourismnorthwest.co.za**

*How to get there* Travelling on the Lichtenburg road close to Mafikeng near Cookes Lake Reserve, and at the TIDC entrance, you will see a small thatched roof complex. Here you will find the Mafikeng Tourism Information and Development Centre. They supplies tourism information for other towns, such as, Lichtenburg, Zeerust, Groot Marico, De La Reyville, Madibogo, Itsoseng and Lehurutshe.

**Mafikeng** went through a number of name changes from ***Mahikeng*** to ***Mafeking*** to ***Mafikeng*** as it is now known. During the Anglo-Boer War it was called **Mafeking** and I hope the reader will understand the use of the the name of **Mafeking** in reference to the Boer War. When referring to the present day I will use the latest version of the name. I trust this will alleviate any confusion.

**Mafikeng** is 67 km from Zeerust, 62 km from Lichtenburg, 25 km from the Botswana border, 160 km from Gaborone (Botswana), 290 km from Johannesburg and Pretoria, 380 km from Kimberley and 460 km from Bloemfontein.

It was established in 1885 after the British annexation of the territory. The name of Mahikeng in Setswana is said to mean *'place among rocks'*. The climate is healthy with a low humidity. Dry and hot in summer (22° to 34°C), cold in winter (02° to 18°C).

The area is Malaria free and the tap water is safe to drink.

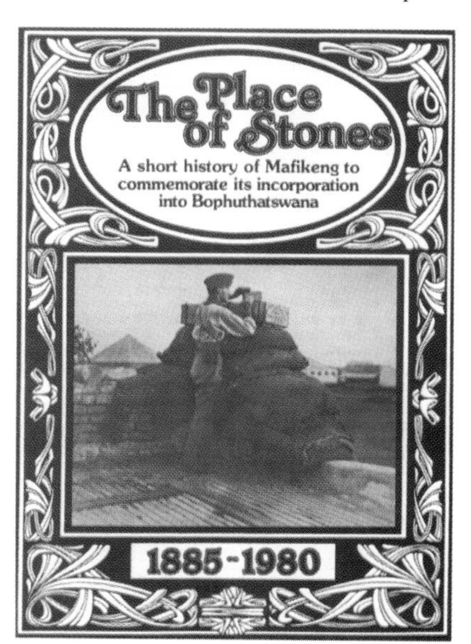


Brochure available from Mafikeng Museum.

**Mafikeng,** the Capital city of the North West Province, known as the *Platinum Province*, produces over 90% of South Africa's Platinum group metals and 40% of the world's output. One of the major attractions in the area are the game reserves which are within easy driving distance from the city. (See OTHER ATTRACTIONS )

## BOER WAR HISTORY

### *The Background*

In 1899 Mafeking was a small town with a train station, hotels, shops and other amenities; all regarded as important to both the British and the Boers; including its strategic position to Rhodesia (Zimbabwe) through Bechuanaland (Botswana).

The Boers had, for a long time, wanted to take control of the town and they constantly attacked the Barolong people. In fact, there has been an ongoing feud for many years – instigated by considerable frontier instability between the British controlled Cape Colony and the Boer Transvaal Republic.

### KRAAIPAN

Afrikaans for *'crow pan'* or *'crow depression'*. A small hamlet 70 km south-west of Mafeking.

On the night of the **12 October 1899,** just about 3 km south of the station, the Boers launched into the Second Anglo-Boer War – attacking and wrecking an armoured train. They then lay siege to Mafeking on the **14 October 1899**.

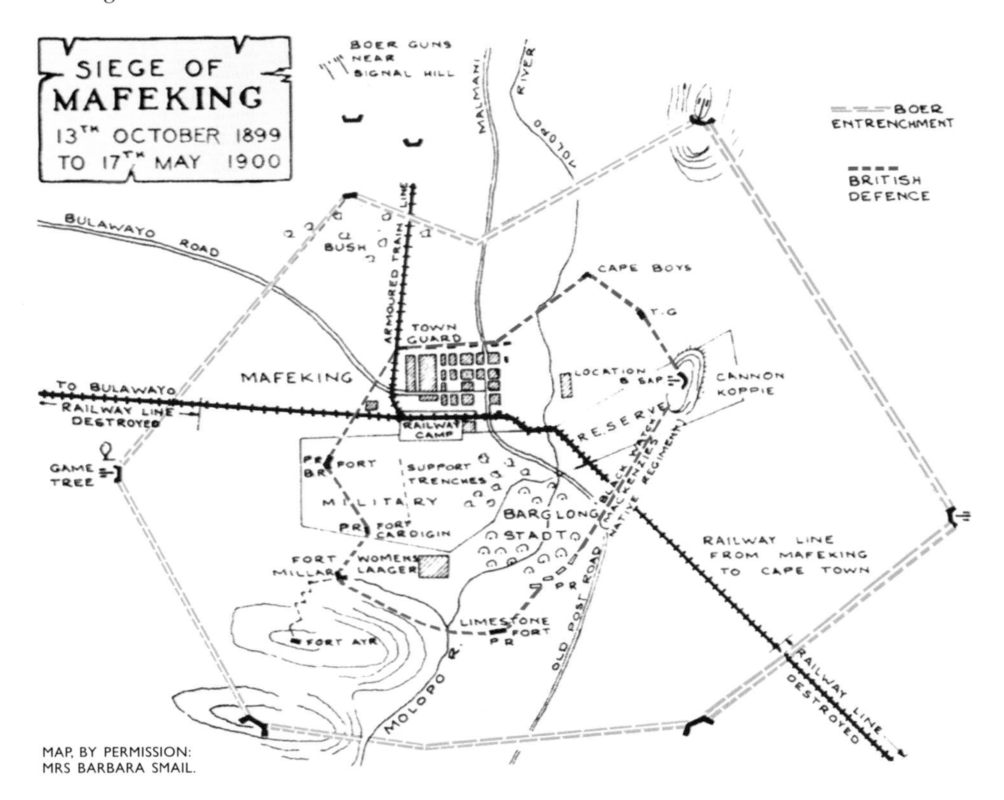


MAP, BY PERMISSION:
MRS BARBARA SMAIL.

### THE SIEGE

The siege lasted 217 days until relieved on 17 May 1900. There were about 10 000 people (men, women and children – black, coloured and white – civilians, militia and soldiers) all entrapped in the town. The siege encompassed the British town of *Mafeking* (for whites) the Tsidi town of *Mafikeng* (for local blacks and coloureds) and two *locations* for black refugees. Colonel Baden-Powell was in command of the town with a small force of 1 200 men with the support of 6 000 Barolong Boora Tshidi natives whereas General Piet Cronjé commenced the siege with 7 700 Boers – which eventually decreased to only 1 200 at the time of the Relief. Cronje realised that his Boers were becoming complacent and moved most of them into the fighting areas of the Northern Cape and later to the Transvaal Republic.

Making £1 inside Mafeking Mint.

*'Through laziness, the Boers failed to provide latrines for the men and the space around their fort was becoming rather unhygenic. It was difficult to avoid walking in waste and I was forced to put Bluegum oil under my nose to be able to breathe.'*

GEOFFREY PHILLIPS, MAFIKENG MUSEUM – ABRAHAM STAFLEU'S DIARY, 2 DECEMBER 1899.

As the Siege developed both Blacks and Whites became actively involved in the defence of their town. The Barolong raided the Boer lines and captured their cattle which, in turn, were driven back to Mafeking.

*'During a Mfengu/Barolong cattle raid the cattle at a nearby Boer farm evaded capture. Only the farmhouse was left to loot ... The Barolong found sumptuous repast on the table consisting of bread, meat, potatoes, coffee and* dop *brandy. They consumed everything they could ... including some dried peaches they found in a bag, and departed after loading themselves up with meal (maize), etc.'*

GEOFFREY PHILLIPS, MAFIKENG MUSEUM - CHARLES BELL'S DIARY, 24 MARCH 1900.

Sol Plaatje, who worked as court interpreter for Magistrate Charles Bell, wrote the famous *Mafeking Diary, a Black Man's view of a White Man's war.* This eloquently written book displays the courage and fortitude of the peoples of Mafeking during the Siege as well as the discrimination of Blacks by Whites. The success of the British surviving the Siege would have been more difficult without the help of the Barolong.

*'The ladies will now have to go about unstarched as it (starch) is also used, by the Commissariat, to thicken up the Africans' soup ...'*

GEOFFREY PHILLIPS, MAFIKENG MUSEUM - CHARLES BELL'S DIARY, 22 MARCH 1900.

One of the interesting people caught up in the Siege was Lady Sarah Wilson (pictured right) a close relative to Winston Churchill and a personal friend of Cecil John Rhodes (who was, at the time, incarcerated in Kimberley with his own problems). It has been said that Sarah Wilson was the only woman that Rhodes treated as a close confidant. Lady Sarah's husband, Gordon Wilson, was stationed at Mafeking. As she had *'become a problem'* for Baden-Powell he decided to *'evict'* her. Lady Wilson went to stay with friend on a farm at Setlagole (close to Kraaipan). On 12 October 1899, she heard the first shots of the war. Later, after an incident with carrier pigeon's, she was arrested by General Snyman and bought to the Boer Laager. She was possibly the first woman *Prisoner of War* held by the Boers; and indeed one of the most troublesome women they had come across. She helped with nursing the Boers at Vryburg but wanted to be with her husband in Mafeking.

The following is taken from a letter sent to her from her husband:

*My dear Sarah,*

*I am delighted to hear that you are being well treated but very sorry to have to tell you that Colonel Baden-Powell finds it impossible to hand over Petrus Viljoen in exchange for you, as he was convicted for horse-stealing before the war. I fail to see in what way it can benefit your captors to keep you a prisoner. Luckily for them, it is not the custom of the English to make prisoners of war of women.*

Two days later she received the following letter from Baden-Powell.

***December 5, 1899***

***Dear Lady Sarah,***

***I am so distressed about you. You must have been having an awful time of it, and I can't help feeling very much to blame; but I had hoped to save you the unpleasantness of the Siege.***

***However, I trust now that your troubles are nearly over at last, and that General Snyman will pass you in here. We are all very well, and are really rather enjoying it all.***

***I wrote last night asking for you to be exchanged for Mrs Delport but had no answer, so I have written again today and sincerely hope it will be alright.***

***Hope you are well in spite of your troubles.***

***Yours sincerely, R. Baden-Powell.***

Mrs Delport refused to be exchanged and so Baden-Powell unsuccessfully held a lottery amongst the Boer women to see if any one wanted to be exchanged for Lady Sarah.

General Snyman wanted to exchange Lady Wilson for Petrus Viljoen, who was being held prisoner in Mafeking. Although Baden-Powell initially refused to exchange Viljoen (as his knowledge of the town and its fortifications would be invaluable to General Snyman) the problem was compounded as Viljoen was reluctant to leave prison. Eventually he was persuaded by the British and the exchange took place.

The *Mafeking Mail* commented:

**'... We are sure we represent the whole of Mafeking when we offer the most hearty congratulations to Captain Wilson and Lady Sarah Wilson on her Ladyship's safe arrival in our tight little garrison, after her experiences with the Boers'. The warmest welcome came from the Boers as Baden-Powell's ... and the residents fears ... were realised. Abraham Stafleu was present when Petrus Viljoen arrived at the laager and noted that 'he was able to provide the Boers with a detailed report of conditions in Mafeking. Viljoen was also able to point out to the crews of the guns where and when to shoot to best effect'.**

**Within five minutes of her arrival, more accurate shelling was throwing death and gravel everywhere.**

*The Boy, Baden-Powell and the Siege of Mafeking*
PAT HOPKINS & HEATHER DUGMORE (p.120)

An interesting book worth reading is ***The Boy, Baden-Powell and the Siege of Mafeking*** by **Pat Hopkins & Heather Dugmore.**

This book covers the Siege in great detail – the Barolong and Baden-Powell's involvement in the siege and the background of Lady Sarah Wilson and her months of *incarceration* with the Boers. It also highlights, with considerable depth, various battles and skirmishes undertaken by both the Boers and the British during the Siege.

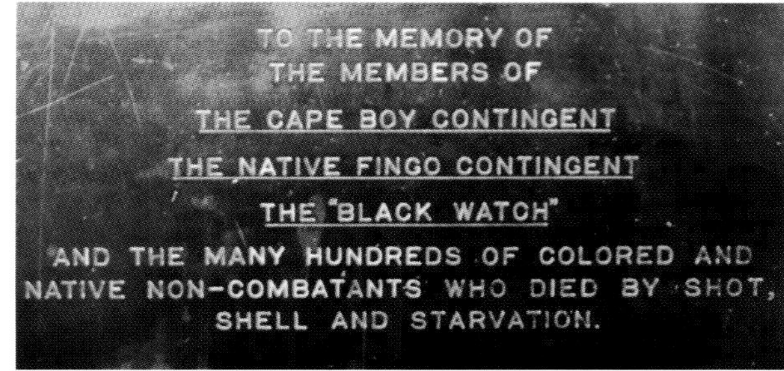


**The Cadet Corps:** During the Siege, Lord Cecil formed a Cadet Corps – young boys aged 9 to 15 years – to undertake light duties (such as running of messages, etc.). As an introduction to the army the boys were taught drill and discipline with a view to their eventual enlistment. This Cadet Corps sowed the first seeds for **THE SCOUT MOVEMENT**, which Baden-

Powell started in England in 1907 as **The Boy Scouts.** Presently the movement has a membership of over 26 million scouts in more than 150 countries throughout the world.

*The following are a few anecdotes that give an impression of the hardships that the communities of Mafeking underwent during the months of Siege.*

## Food

'Much troubled by flies which are increasing daily.
During meal times they swarm around the table like bees
and sicken one by their attention to the sweets and hot meats.
The meat itself is enough to nauseate one,
but to have it embellished with five or six
hundred flies is a test for the strongest stomach'.

Geoffrey Phillips, Mafikeng Museum – *Charles Bell's Diary*, 28 November 1899.

Meals consisted of delicasies such as curried locusts,
which were caught by the natives and baked in ovens.
they then ground the cooked locusts and ate them.
It was said by Tom Hayes that they tasted like ground meat.

Other animals that were on the menu were horses,
mules and the occasional dog. Dog owners had to keep
an eye on their pets, as an unlicenced dog was shot and
buried. The shangaans (refugees) relished dogs, they
watched the burials of the animals and disintered
the dogs, cooked and ate them!!

A sheet of corrugated iron peppered with shrapnel on view at the Mafikeng Museum.

## Watery Grave

'Tremendous rain ... flooded every hole and corner
... a volunteer fell into a grave in the cemetry where they are stationed,
and being drunk was unable to get out. He was only just rescued in time from being drowned'

Geoffrey Phillips, Mafikeng Museum – *Charles Bell's Diary*, 28 November 1899.

**The Relief:** The town was finally relieved on 17 May 1900 by Colonel Mahon; Major Karri-Davies had ridden into Mafeking during the night to ensure the route was clear. In fact, Colonel Peakman was the first to enter Mafeking in the very early hours of 17 May. The following extract from ***The Relief of Mafeking*** by **Filson Young (Methuen's Colonial Library 1900)** explains:

'In a few moments the group in advance pulled up, shouting "'Wire, barbed wire!'

We all stopped, and there were frantic calls for wire-cutters. With four reports like the snapping of big fiddle-strings the last barrier before Mafeking was removed, and we passed on again, this time at a hand-canter. In a few minutes we heard the sound of a galloping horse on the road, and a mounted man challenged us.

"Halt! Who goes there?'

"Friend."

"Who are you?" (The excitement was too high for the preservation of the proper formula.)

"Colonel Peakman, in command of the Advance Guard of the Relief Column."

"By Jove, ain't I glad to see you, Sir!"

It was an officer sent out by Colonel Baden-Powell to meet us and bring us in. We left the squadron, and the five of us went on, this time at a gallop, over trenches, past breastwork and redoubts and little forts, until we pulled up at the door of the headquarters' mess.'

If you get a copy of the book by Filson Young you will definitely find it a *worthwhile* read. He tells of the reaction of the besieged troops to the news of the relief column.

> '...how they looked with rapt faces at us commonplace people from the outer world as though we were angels, how we all tried to speak at once, and only succeeded in gazing at each other and in saying. "By Jove!" "Well, I'm hanged!" and the like ... senseless expressions that sometimes mean much to an Englishman. One man tried to speak; then he swore; then he buried his face in his arms and sobbed. We all gulped at nothing, until someone brought in cocoa and we gulped that instead. Then Baden-Powell came in, and one could only gaze at him, and search in vain on his jolly face for the traces of seven months' anxiety and strain.'

Said he of the relieving force
As through the town he sped,
'Art thou in Baden-Powell's horse?'
The trooper shook his head,
Then drew his hand his mouth across,
Like one who's lately fed.
'Alas for Baden-Powell's horse,
It's now in me,' he said.

*Drummer Hodge*, THE POETRY OF THE ANGLO-BOER WAR, M van Wyk Smith.

## BOER WAR SITES

**Concentration Camp Cemeteries:** Vryburg Road. The total number of 858 burials were recorded but only 825 marked graves were located. A smaller Concentration Camp Cemetery can be found 800 metres south of the large cemetery in the Magogoe area. During 1949, when renovating the graves it was found that there were up to four corpses in some of the graves; which compounds beliefs that many black women and children also died in the concentration camps.

**Concentration Camp Site:** Vryburg Road. This was a refugee camp which was established during the Siege. When the *Scorched Earth Policy* started Boer families and their servants were moved into the camp. It was proclaimed a Concentration Camp in July 1900 – the first in South

Africa – <u>and the worst</u>. After the Superintendent was dismissed for gross negligence, it was 'visited' by **Emily Hobhouse** on 10 April 1901.

<u>**Kanon Kopje**</u>: Next to the Hospital. One of the few areas in this flat terrain area offering an elevated view of Mafeking. The stone fort was built in 1885 by Warren's expedition. (The keys are available at the Museum.)

<u>**Kgotla of the Barolong Boora Tshidi**</u>: Prince of Wales Way. A monument to honour the Barolong who died in action during the Siege. An engraving of the Barolong totem, the Tholo (Kudu) is on the top of the memorial.



<u>**The Mafeking Cemetery**</u>: Carrington Street. This cemetery was used by both military and civilian victims. The grave of nine year old Frankie Brown, the youngest of Baden-Powell's cadets, killed by a shell. The grave of Captain Andrew Beauchamp-Proctor, the highest decorated Airman of World War I can also be found here.

<u>**Mafikeng Prison**</u>: North Street. On 28 December 1901, Arnold Renike (a Cape Rebel) and Louis Brink from the Mafeking district were publicly executed for murder. Both men stated they had acted on the instructions of their commander, General Snyman.

<u>**Maratiwa**</u>: The house, which has been renovated, was built by Silas Molema, the son of the founder of Mahikeng. Sol Plaatje stayed in the house during the siege.

<u>**Masonic Lodge**</u>: Tillard Street. Built in 1894, it was used for concerts during the Siege. After a battle on 12 May 1900, Commandant Sarel Eloff and his men (after surrendering) were imprisoned here before being exiled to St. Helena Island.

<u>**Mother and Child Monument**</u>: This monument was erected in 1935 for the Burghers and the women and children who died during the Anglo-Boer War.

<u>**Museum**</u>: (pictured overleaf) Martin Street. Built in 1902 as the Town Hall. A good place to start your tour of the sites of the Anglo-Boer War and interesting other information.

The curator Geoffrey Phillips (pictured right) has a fund of knowledge and is enthusiastic in parting with it. He will keep you spellbound with stories of the history of the area.

The Siege Room features displays of artifacts and photographs – with the famous *BP Lord Nelson gun*. ***The museum is a 'must see'***. Tel: (018) 381 6102. Fax: (018) 387 3436. The write to: Mafikeng Museum, PO Box 526, Mafikeng, 2745.

**St. John's Anglican Church:** Martin Street. Designed by Sir Herbert Baker, the church was built in commemoration the Siege. The inscription on the foundation stone reads *"To the glory of God and in memory of those who died during the Siege of Mafeking, and as an act of thanksgiving for the Relief of the Town"*.

**Victoria Hospital:** Victoria Street. Adjacent to the convent, the hospital was built in 1899 and named after Sister Victoria. While nursing her husband Gordon Wilson, Lady Sarah Wilson, was trapped under the bricks and rubble when a shell struck the convent. Fortunately she survived the ordeal.

**Warren's Fort:** Take the Main Street for 0,5 km from town. The entrance to Warren's Fort – which was used as a police post to protect the Barolong people – is through Police HQ as it is now situated on their property. During the siege 28 men (under the command of Colonel Hore) were stationed here. The Fort was captured by Commandant Eloff and 200 of his men. Within 12 hours however, it was back in the hands of the British.

Visitors are welcome and at the gate ask to see Captain B. Ngakane (pictured above). He is one of the most charming people I have come across and is only too willing to help in arranging a 'show' of Warren's Fort.

## Other attractions & Activities

There is a lot to keep you occupied in Mafikeng and the surrounding area. As it is so close to the Botswana border, why not cross over for a day trip or visit one of the various game reserves around Mafikeng.

Town Guard at Early's Corner.

**Botsalano Game Reserve:** Tel: (018) 386 2433. Cell: 083 289 5713. Situated about 20 minutes drive from Mafikeng on the Ramathla-bama border Road, the reserve is 5 800 hectares in size. The reserve has been stocked with White Rhino and has over 2 000 plains game antelope, as well as over 200 species of birds which can be found in the *Acacia* and *Karee* woodlands and on the grasslands. It is one of the oldest volcanic craters in the world – an ideal refuge for game. Accommodation facilities include camping and picnic sites as well as the **Mogobe Tent Lodge** which overlooks a waterhole.

**Mafikeng Game Reserve:** Tel: (018) 381 5611. Take the Zeerust Road out of town and before the overhead bridge turn right and follow signs to this 4 600 hectare reserve. It has ± 2 000 head of game which, due to the flat undulating plains can be easily spotted – including Giraffe, White Rhino, Zebra, Warthog and Ostrich. The birdlife is noticeable along the Molopo River. The picnic sites and open air Lapa are situated on the banks of the river. The **Manyane Game Lodge** has self-catering chalets which are located next to the reserve. Tel: (018) 381 6020.

**Madikwe Game Reserve:** Park Management: Cell/Mobile: 083 629 8282. Access to the reserve is through Zeerust where there are signposts for directions to the lodges. Self-drives around the reserve are not permitted as the **Big Five** (lion, leopard, buffalo, elephant and rhino) are to be found here. Madikwe supports over 10 000 animals and 66 mammal species – see the stunning Wild Dogs which have been successfully relocated to the reserve. For the ornithologists, over 337 bird species can also be found here.

There are a few private owned and run lodges which cater for guests:-

**Madikwe River Lodge:** Tel: (014) 778 0891. An upmarket lodge with full facilities and game drives in open vehicles.

**Tau Lodge:** Tel: (018) 365 9027. Similar to Madikwe Game Lodge also supplying game drives in open vehicles.

**Honey Guide Trails:** Tel: (011) 802 3643. A rustic bush camp which specialises in guided walks through the bush.

## Tour Operators & Tour Guides

**Kontrei Tours:** Mafikeng. Tel/Fax: (018) 381 5278. Cell/Mobile: 082 366 3435. Tours to suit the clients' every need – including day and evening game reserve trips. *Contact*: Col. L.G. Schultze.

**Tours & Trails:** Mafikeng. Cell/Mobile: 083 340 1851. Fax: (018) 381 5392. Historic Tours of Mafikeng as well as morning and evening game drives in Mafikeng or Botsalano Game Reserves. *Contact*: R.Ashman.

**Casper Steenkamp:** PO Box 248, Mafikeng 2745. Tel: (018) 381 5132. Cell/Mobile: 082 757 4330.

**Brenda Venter:** (T.5901). PO Box 2339, Mafikeng 2745. (018) 381 0935. Fax: (018) 381 0179. Cell/Mobile: 082 935 3049.

# Mafikeng

## TUSK MMABATHO CASINO RESORT, MMABATHO

This Casino Resort captures the peace and serenity of the surrounding bush and envelopes it in luxury and excitement. There are three restaurants and four bars to keep you well occupied. Relax by the pool or try your luck at the Casino.
150 Rooms from R295 pp sharing. Single R465.
Tel: (018) 389 1111. Fax: (018) 389 1746.
e-mail: www.tusk-resorts.co.za

## TUSK MOLOPO HOTEL, MMABATHO

Conveniently situated between Mmabatho and the old Mafikeng, and well positioned for visiting the Game reserves and Anglo-Boer War sites. In the evenings, enjoy a meal at one of the two restaurants, or take a five minute drive to the Casino Resort.
204 Rooms from R132,50 pp sharing. Single R265.
Tel: (018) 392 4184. Fax: (018) 392 1256.
e-mail: www.tusk-resorts.co.za

## OAKBURN LODGE, MAFIKENG

This luxurious stately thatched home is perfectly situated in the quiet suburb of Riviera Park in the old Mafikeng sector. Enjoy a relaxing pre-dinner drink at the Pool Bar. All rooms are *en-suite* with satellite TV and air-conditioning.
8 Rooms from R140 pp sharing Bed & Breakfast.
Tel: (018) 381 5963. Fax: (018) 381 5963.
Cell/Mobile: 082 771 3267.

## THE ROSE AND THORN LODGE, MAFIKENG

This lodge, with beautiful gardens and swimming pool is only 500 m from Mafikeng Game Reserve with an abundance of game. In the evenings bar/supper facilities are available for those wanting to stay in and relax or watch satellite TV.
7 Rooms from R120 pp sharing Bed & Breakfast.
Tel: (018) 381 6675. Fax: (018) 381 6675.
Cell/Mobile: 082 771 3267.

## LIZARD LEAP LODGE, RUSTENBURG AREA

Situated 36 km from Magaliesburg town and 18 km from Rustenburg in the foothills of the Magaliesberg mountain range. Lizard Leap Lodge is at Roberts Farm Horse Trails. Enjoy the experience of riding through this picturesque area. For those interested, ride the blockhouse route.
Tel: (014) 577 3332 for further information.
e-mail: rides@mweb.co.za

# Derdepoort

**MADIKWE RIVER LODGE, DERDEPOORT**

Set on the banks of the Groot Marico River, in 75 000 hectares (malaria-free) Madikwe Game Reserve. Search for the *"Big Five"* as well as Cheetah, Wild Dog and other game. Close to the site of the Battle of Derdepoort.
16 Chalets from R 850 pp sharing. Fully inclusive.
Tel: (014) 778 0891. Fax: (014) 778 0893.
e-mail: madikwe@country-escapes.co.za

# Wolmaransstad (on N12)

**LINDBERGH LODGE, WOLMARANSSTAD**

Combined with old world charm this luxury guest house offers some spectacular game viewing, as well as a visit to their own private Diamond Mine. Swimming, tennis, nearby golf course and driving range. Tours arranged.
15 Rooms from R430 pp sharing. Dinner, B&B.
Tel: (011) 884 8923. Fax: (011) 884 8925.
e-mail: lindberg@iafrica.com

**"MOSES" STORIES**

When a Boer woman was removed from her farm and forcibly taken to a concentration camp, despite of her protests, her seven year-old son and her baby were left in the farmhouse. For a week or more her seven year-old son cared for the baby, giving it goat's milk and mealie-meal porridge. (Schikkerling, 266/267).

# Baden-Powell in Mafeking

**The first shell was fired into Mafeking at 9.20 am on 16 October, 1899.** Firing continued until 2.15 pm when Cronje sent a messenger with a Flag of Truce demanding the immediate surrender of the town *"to prevent further bloodshed"*. Baden-Powell replied that *"so far the only blood shed was that of a chicken"*.

Throughout the siege he acted on the principle of letting the inhabitants have all the news possible; copies of letters between him and the Boer commandant were posted up or printed in the ***Mafeking Mail*** (a news-sheet produced daily throughout the siege and, as white paper ran short, was printed on a queer assortment of red, green, blue and orange papers intended for other purposes). The first issue appeared on 1 November with the sub-head *'Issued daily, Shells permitting'*.

The following extract from Baden-Powell's instructions set the pattern for the way he controlled the Siege of Mafeking.

*"Bluff the enemy with show of force as much as you like, but don't let yourself get too far out of touch with your own side without orders, lest you draw them on into difficulties in their endeavour to support you ... Do not always wait for orders if you see the situation demands action. Don't be afraid to act for fear of making a mistake* - 'A man who never made a mistake never made anything.' *If you find you have made a mistake, carry it through nevertheless with energy. Pluck, and dash, have often changed a mistake into success."*

Early on in the siege an unintended effect added to the Boer bewilderment. Two trucks of dynamite were in the railway siding and, as these would obviously be a constant source of danger, it was decided to get rid of them. They were pushed forward out of the town by an unattached engine which abandoned them at the top of a gradient. As the trucks slid down the line, the Boers, thinking this was another armoured train, attacked and were considerably astonished when their firing blew up the whole lot.

Another ruse may be described in Baden-Powell's own words: *"For instance, we laid explosive mines all round the place. They were contained in small boxes and were made-up by an expert in a certain building ... and were then carried with the greatest care by natives, who were warned against the disastrous explosion that would follow if they should drop one of them. These boxes were carefully buried at different points round the front of the town, and wires were laid connecting them with the central observation post. Notices were posted*

Mafeking Cadet Corps.

"A man found an unexploded shell today and while opening it to get out the powder, found in it a letter to Colonel Baden-Powell, asking him not to let his men drink all the whiskey as they (the Boers) were coming in soon." *Tom Hayes Diary,* 5 December 1899

Geoffrey Phillips, Mafikeng Museum

*in English and Dutch, warning the inhabitants that if they allowed their cattle or children to wander there, it would be at their own risk.*

*We gave notice that on a certain day a trial would be made with one or more of the mines to see that they were in working order, so people were warned to keep clear of the east front between 12:00 noon and 2:00 p.m. With everybody safe indoors, Major Panzera and I went out and stuck a stick of dynamite into an ant-bear hole. We lit the fuse, ran and took cover until the thing went off ... which it did with a splendid roar and a vast cloud of dust.*

*Out of the dust emerged a man with a bike who happened to be passing, and he pedalled off as fast as he could go for the Transvaal, eight miles away, where no doubt he told how, by merely riding along the road, he had hit off a murderous mine. The boxes were actually filled with nothing more dangerous than sand!"*

It was little use trying to keep anything secret in Mafeking – there were too many spies about who could easily pass into the Boer lines at night; so any idea which Baden-Powell wanted the enemy to know about could be passed on in the form found most useful for his own purposes. The information about the land-mines was not to be the only misleading news the Boers received.

NOTICE

SPIES.

THERE are in town to-day nine known spies. They are hereby warned to leave before 12 noon to-morrow or they will be apprehended.

By order,

E. H. CECIL, MAJOR,

C. S. O.

Mafeking,
7th Oct., 1899.

The notice issued to spies by Colonel Baden-Powell

Part of the genius of Baden-Powell was his ability to 'stimulate' others to use their wits and inventive powers. Without even a touch of jealousy in his character, he welcomed any good suggestions, whatever their source, with as much glee as he would those of his own devising. One civilian was an expert in the use of acetylene lighting; his skill was used in devising a portable searchlight made out of a biscuit tin nailed on top of a pole. It would be turned on at night at one fort, and then rushed off to another place and a few flashes made before being taken to a third position. The Boers got the impression that the place was equipped with a series of searchlights and therefore were discouraged from making the night attacks (which Baden-Powell feared most of all). He invited every one to contribute ideas – there was a public competition for the best life-sized dummies representing men from the defence forces. These had to be equipped with mechanical arms and were effectively used in the forts

## NICKNAMES

Colonel Baden-Powell was called *'bathing-towel'* by his men, known for his appearance dressed only in a towel after his baths in the field.

**To the Bitter End**, *Emanoel Lee*, 1985 Viking Penguin Inc.

Canon Kopje look-out.

and trenches to draw the fire of Boer snipers and gunners. The strain was further lessened by the observance of Sunday as 'a day of truce' on both sides which resulted in yet another bit of bluff. Baden-Powell describes how the Boers, *"... used to come out of their forts to stretch their legs. We could see that their forts were surrounded by barbed wire, because of the upright posts and the careful way in which the men lifted their legs over the wire. So we put up 'barbed wire' around ours. We had no 'barbed wire', but we put up forests of posts and then, on Sundays, when our men stepped out to stretch their legs, they lifted these posts with the greatest care and difficulty over imaginary 'barbed wire' – a performance which fully impressed the enemy watching them."*

But Sunday was the day for recreation. After morning services there was always some kind of outdoor sport or amusement and, later in the day, maybe a concert was held. *Guy Fawkes's Day* fell on a Sunday and this was celebrated in the traditional manner (after warning had been sent to the Boers that fireworks were harmless). Polo, football, sports, athletics and gymkhanas were organised and, later on, a series of exhibitions and competitions were held – similar to the already mentioned (for a dummy soldier). Another exhibition for agricultural produce which, perhaps incongruously, included a *Grand Diploma* for the Best Siege Baby! There were some people who frowned upon these 'goings-on' and one pastor was reprimanded by his congregation for playing football – he promptly resigned his charge.

In all these activities Baden-Powell took a leading part, and the sight of him masquerading as *'Signor Paderewski'*, or as a meditative coster, or attending a gymkhana dressed up like a circus director, in no way lessened his authority as commander.

The chief problem of the garrison was the lack of artillery. This was more marked when, toward the end of October 1899, the Boers brought up a 94-pounder siege-gun which was at first placed at the Jackal Tree ± 3 200 yards south of the town. This gun was known

Wolf Gun at Mafeking.

as *'Long Tom'* and/or *'Creaky'*. By a system of warnings from the lookout, the inhabitants had time to take cover before the shell hit; fortunately many of the shells did not burst and there was a rush to secure the trophy. There was indeed a regular trade in souvenirs, and the *Mafeking Mail* gave regular quotations from 'the conchological market' as it was called.

Many devices were used to overcome the disparity in guns. Hand grenades were made out of potted meat tins filled with dynamite, and one ingenious soldier found that he could fling these most effectively from line of a fishing-rod. The railway workshops made an excellent howitzer which was christened *'The Wolf'* after Baden-Powell's Matebele name. This was constructed out of the steam-pipe of an engine (reinforced with some iron railings melted down and shrunk into it) which was mounted on the wheels of an old threshing machine. The use of this queer gun is described by Baden-Powell.

*"... With home-made powder and shot,* 'The Wolf' *did not carry very far, so in order to make up for this we used to move it out in the night as silently as we could, with its wheels wrapped up in canvas and straw, till we got within its range of the enemy's camp. Then we hung up blankets all round it so that the flash would not be very visible. Then we loosened off our shots as fast as we could and lay low while*

*the enemy spent the rest of the night firing vaguely at where they thought we were – which was generally where we were not."*

Major Alexander Godley noticed that one of the gate-posts of a farm was an old gun. It was dug up and it proved to be an 18th Century carronade, and on it, by curious chance, were the initials B.P., being those of the makers. The discoverer's account of its first use is typical of the spirit in which the defenders faced their dangerous situation.

*"The resourceful railway workshops made cannon balls for it, mounted it on a wooden carriage, and we soon had it down on the eastern front ready for action. The first shot was aimed down the main road to Johannesburg, and with great interest we watched the flight of the projectile, which looked exactly like a cricket ball. It bumped down the road into the Boer laager amongst the waggons, and one old Boer tried to field it, with disastrous results to himself. The effect was that the laager moved about three miles farther back. This great piece of ordnance was appropriately named* 'Lord Nelson' (SEE PICTURES). *The plucky crew of the Nordenfeldt, not to be outdone, started to creep out at night and get within range of* 'Long Tom', *with the result that he also had to shift farther back."* ❑

**Source:**
E. E. Reynolds 1942. Oxford University Press, Amen House, E.C.4.

Baden-Powell's simple grave in Nyeri, Kenya only has his name on it and a 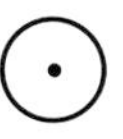 – the Boy Scout trail sign for *"I have gone home"*.

**Generals of the Anglo-Boer War**, Phillip Bateman, 1977 Purnell & Sons (SA) (Pty) Ltd

# The Imperial Reserve, Warrens Fort

The reserve is a portion of 400 morgen of land set aside by Sir Charles Warren in 1885 as a Military Reserve to serve as a buffer between the *Barolong-Boo-Rra-Tshidi* village of *Mahikeng* and the town to be established as *Mafikeng* in British Bechuanaland. It served as the Headquarters of the **Bechuanaland Border Police** from 1885 to 1895, when British Bechuanaland was handed over to the Cape Colony, which at the time was under British rule. Britain retained the Reserve as the Headquarters of the Bechuanaland Protectorate Government until 1966. It was known as the Imperial Reserve.

In 1889 the **British South Africa Company Police** was established on this Reserve to accompany the Pioneer Column on the opening up of what was to become Rhodesia. In September 1896 the Reserve became the Headquarters of the Bechuanaland Division of the **British South Africa Police of Rhodesia**. On the 12 May 1900, during the Siege of Mafeking, ***Veldkornet Sarel Eloff*** broke through the British defences and, for 12 hours before surrendering, occupied **Warrens Fort** on this Reserve. In 1966 the Imperial Reserve was transferred to the Republic of Botswana who, in turn, sold it to the South African Government. The Tswana Territorial Authority operated on the Reserve until it was handed over to the Bophuthatswana Government in 1977 as part of the Independence agreement. In 1976 the Botswana Chiefs, under the leadership of His Excellency the State President, L.M. Mangope, then Chief Minister, at a meeting on this Reserve passed a motion in favour of future independence.

On this reserve the Constitution for the future Government of Bophuthatswana was drawn up and between 1977 & 1983 various Bophuthatswana government departments were accommodated. It was handed over to the Bophuthatswana Police as the H.Q. and Training College of the Force in 1983. ❑

## ELOFF'S REQUEST

Commandant Sarel Eloff, who commands the KoiKoi laager, near the Railway Cottage at the Rietfontein Bridge, wrote to Baden Powell to say he had seen in the *Bulawayo Chronicle* that we played cricket and held dances on Sundays. As life was monotonous around Mafeking and as it was likely to remain that way for some time longer, he proposed that he should play us at cricket and join in our dances if PB would not mind letting him know when he could come.

A suitable reply was sent stating that it was 200 not out (yesterday was the 200th day of the Siege): that three bowlers, Snyman, Cronje and Botha had tried without success and that it was about time they put on another. The reply was sent through Snyman, who being a *Dopper*, will be horribly shocked at the wicked proposals of his subordinate officer.

from *Charles Bell's Diary*, Monday 30 April 1900

Geoffrey Phillips, Mafikeng Museum

*Andrew J. McLeod*

# Sol Plaatje, a man of words

Sol Plaatje was born 9 October 1876 in the Orange Free State was a great man! His parents were members of the Tswana-speaking *Barolong* people. Sol, the man, linguist, journalist, editor, political pioneer, campaigner of African people and important writer in both English and Tswana, as a child loved school and learned to read and write in English and Dutch.

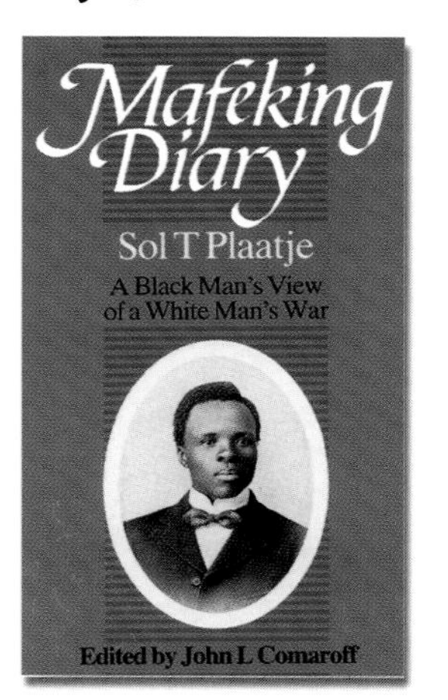


At 18 years of age he worked in the Post Office in Kimberley and used all his spare time to study on his own. Four years later he could speak six languages and write in four.

At only 23 years of age, Sol, a Tsidi-Barolong, finds him-self in the middle of a siege. First educated in a mission school, he continues studies on his own, con-centrating on languages. In court he is needed for English and Setswana, but Dutch and Xhosa come in handy. He worked in the court of law in *'white'* Mafeking. Yet he lived with his relations in the sprawling Tsidi-town, the *'stadt'*, the *black* Mafikeng. Travelling to and from the court on his pony, his life was caught between two societies.

Soon food was the major problem. With no rail contact to the south or north, Mafeking lies in a hot, semi-desert land. It is high summer. Martial law is declared. Rationing is implemented. But for the black population, luxu-ries (bread) is not allowed. Grain for horse feed was not for humans. Food was controlled by the military autho-rities with disastrous effects on the black population.

Sol was later used for work unrelated to his court duties. He could speak to the Tsidi and acted as 'go-between'. He was fiercely loyal to the British. Yes, fiercely loyal to the British, he was. Yet fair to his enemies when he says in his diary on 3 January 1900: *"The Boers*

Native runners describing the relief of Kimberley. From left to right: A runner, Mr Bell, Resident Magistrate, Sol Plaatje the interpreter, Administrator Major Gould Adams, and another runner seated on the floor.

## FROM SOL PLAATJE'S PEN

The following was published in *Diamond Fields Advertiser*, 27 March 1926:

During the War, a quarter of a century back, (in a Free State district), nine natives were court-martialled and sentenced to death, some burghers being ordered to go out and execute the sentence. The natives, having arrived at the place of execution, asked permission to say their last prayer, and began by singing what they believed was to be their last hymn on earth. But the prayers touched the Boers so keenly that when the order was given they flatly refused to fire; and their leaders went back and told the Commandant to come and do his own dirty work. The result is that all the natives are alive to tell the tale.

STEVE'S WAR STORIES

## SOL PLAATJE'S DEATH

*"After I left Mr Mahlelebe yesterday ... Mauser bullets were just like hail on the main road to our village ... one flew close to my cap with a 'ping', giving me such a fright as caused me to sit down on the footpath ... I continued my journey during which I heard a screech and a tap behind my ear; it was a Mauser bullet and as there can be no question about a fellow's death when it enters his brain through the lobe, I knew at the moment that I had been transmitted from this temporary life on to eternity.*

*I imagined I held the nickel bullet in my hand. That was merely the faculty of the soul recognising (in an ordinary post-mortal dream) who occasioned its departure – for I was dead! Dead, to rise no more. A few seconds elapsed after which I found myself scanning the bullet between my finger and thumb, to realise that it was but a horsefly."*

from *Sol Plaatje's Diary*, Wednesday 29 October 1899

GEOFFREY PHILLIPS, MAFIKENG MUSEUM

*were justified in their bragging - they have kept a town of the strongest empire on earth under siege for three months."* Surely, continued bombing from *'Ou Sanna'* (*'Long Tom'*) unnerved him ... that's what it was *meant* to do.

This gifted Barolong kept a diary of the privations encountered during the 217 days of the siege. In beautiful English he describes daily life for the people caught between the two grinding stones ... their everyday life ... the trade in shrapnel ... the value of sorghum beer ... the problem of the food, of people starving ... of the beggars that he helped. He tells the Mafeking story from the inside. The siege of Mafeking was a minor event in the total war (with intrigue and human interest stories being plentiful). Eventhough life experiences are quite different for blacks as for whites, Sol Plaatje experienced both worlds – and survived with humour and even more determination.

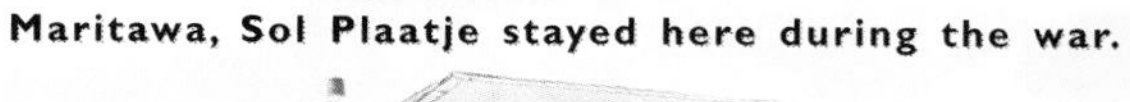
**Maritawa, Sol Plaatje stayed here during the war.**

After the Siege he wrote his Civil Service Examinations in Dutch and Typewriting. He started the first Setswana newspaper *'Koranta ea Becoana'* and, when the ANC was founded in 1912, Sol Plaatje was its first secretary. Yes, *Sol Plaatje* was *a man of words.* ❑

**Sources:**

Comaroff, J.L., *The Boer War diary of Sol T. Plaatje*, Johannesburg, 1973.

Warwick, P., *Black people and the South African War*, Cambridge, 1983.

## THINGS ARE GETTING SERIOUS

*"The pang (of hunger) has been felt all round ... I have developed a marvellously strong appetite. I long for food every evening at 10 p.m. and after taking my supper at 7 p.m. I nearly die during the night if I do not take a cup of cocoa and a few biscuits before going to bed. Things are getting serious ..."*

from *Sol Plaatje's Diary*, Thursday 8 February 1900

GEOFFREY PHILLIPS, MAFIKENG MUSEUM

# Black African War Heroes

Above, Fingoe's under Mr D. Webster.

On 12 May 1900, Boer forces under command of Sarel Eloff (a grandson of President Paul Kruger) attempted to capture Mafeking. Some of his forces invaded the tribal town (The Stad) causing much destruction, but the inhabitants fought back and contributed quite considerably to Eloff's defeat.

**RATSHIDI HEROES**

BESELE. Having located the Boers on the kopje on the eastern side of the Molopo near the Women's Laager and having been shot in so doing, Besele volunteered to guide Captain Marsh's scouts to the same place and which duty he accomplished – probably saving much loss of life on the British side.

JOSIAH MOTSHEGARE. On the first arrival of the Boers in the tribal town, he captured a kopje which had just been occupied by them, next to Minchin's garden, and held it till the arrival of reinforcements. Four Barolong were killed in taking the drift and it would appear that many more lives would have been lost but for the promptitude shown by Josiah Motshegare in resisting then repulsing them (the Boers).

JOSIAH MOLEMA. With a small party of Barolong, hemmed the Boers in the kraal which was eventually taken in the afternoon, the occupants surrendering.

This party of Boers was endeavouring to slip away from the BSAP fort (Warren's Fort) towards the Koppie from which another party of Boers were afterwards driven, but, owing to Josiah Molema's heading them off, they (the Boers) had to take refuge in the Kraal where they were trapped.

KESHUPILOE. Assisted Josiah Molema in the above attack by occupying a wall flanking the kraal towards the Women's Laager.

LETOUSE and MOTSALORE were both conspicuous in preventing the Boers from taking the koppie near the Women's Laager. They occupied positions close to the left bank of the river under heavy fire, which positions, they maintained all day. The Boers were also successfully ambushed by the Ratshidi at the rocky outcrop (small koppie) near the Kgotla. As Geoffrey Phillips of the Mafikeng Museum points out, *none of the Africans involved in the Siege of Mafikeng ever received a medal, nor did the deceased families receive compensation from the ultimately victorious British*. ❑

**Source**: *Steve Lunderstedt*, Kimberley.

Barolong Tribal Chiefs posing for photograph.

Baralong Memorial, Mafeking.

## BAROLONG KOTLA MEMORIAL

Mafeking. 'Segopotso sa Botlhe ba ba Ntshitseng Matshelo a bona sethlhabelo motlhaselong ya Mahikeng. Diphalane 1899 – Motsheganonc 1900.

Shell damaged house in which Natives were killed.

## "Grapes of Wrath" at the Magistrate's Office

*"This morning I went round for another taste (of grapes). I tried to pick only as much as necessary for tasting when the whole bunch came down in my hand ... Just when I came in I heard (the Magistrate, Charles Bell) say:*

*'Do you know who steals my grapes, Patrick?' (Patrick Sidzumo was the court messenger).*
*'No, Sir, I don't', was Patrick's reply.*
*'Do you know Plaatje?'*
*'I am Plaatje' (I replied.)*
*'Do you know who always steals my grapes?'*
*'No!' (I replied.)*
*'To steal is no answer ... By jove! It is you who always steals my grapes ...'*
*I thought that the next question might be too unpleasant and I tried to modify the flowing tide before it grew worse, so I began: 'I have only been eating ("eating" mind you and not "stealing") those in front of the stable, Sir.'*
*'I don't see why you should steal them even if they were at the back of the stable, for your father (the word "father" used here to mean the older generation) didn't steal any grapes.'*
*I successfully stemmed the tide when I interpolated: 'Well, my father didn't work for the Magistrate.' He (Charles Bell) turned around and went on with his business. He was still smiling when he eventually gave me the sweetest bunch in the garden!"*

from *Sol Plaatje's Diary*, Friday, 5 January 1900
GEOFFREY PHILLIPS, MAFIKENG MUSEUM

*John Pennefather*

# The 'Guerrilla Phase' of the North West

7 June 1900 saw the occupation of Pretoria by the British under Lord Roberts and the retreat of the Boer forces into the Eastern Transvaal. The Boer High Command then decided to embark on a guerilla campaign. With this in mind, General De La Rey and State Attorney Smuts were commissioned to reactivate the Western Transvaal Commandos which had become very dispirited and disorganised after the Boer defeats.

This was accomplished by these two formidable leaders and under the astute leadership of General De La Rey, the Boer forces waged a successful guerilla campaign by which they regained the tactical and strategic initiative until the end of the War in May 1902. The gripping story of the many battles and skirmishes which were fought in the region, is ample testimony to this. By large scale drives involving thousands of men and the erection of the blockhouse lines, the British vainly tried to contain and repel the attacks of the mobile Boer forces.

In this campaign, the rugged natural features of the Magaliesberg, the Witwatersberg and the Zwartruggens, played a key role in the tactics employed by, and the fortunes of both sides in this gripping struggle.

Prominent role players in this conflict on the Boer side were Generals De La Rey, De Wet, Beyers, Smuts, Lemmer, Kemp and Oosthuizen as well as Commandant Ludwig Krause and Burgher Deneys Reitz amongst others.

On the British side, key role players were Lord Kitchener and Generals Baden-Powell, Methuen, Cunningham, Clements, Smith Dorrien, Broadwood and Hamilton as well as Colonels Kekewich and Allenby. Lesser known, but important were Major Tunbridge of the Queensland Mounted Infantry and Captain Butters of the South Rhodesian Volunteers at Elands River. The heroic ride of an English speaking Cape Colonial girl, Miss Emily Backe, should also be remembered after the Koster River Battle.

Many famous British and Colonial regiments took part in the actions in our Region and six Victoria Crosses were won by members of the British forces.

In the Boer Army, Commandos from Pretoria, Krugersdorp, Rustenburg, Marico, Lichtenburg and Wolmaransstad saw action. At Nooitgedacht, the Waterberg and Soutpansberg Commando saw much action.

***For bookings and further information contact:***

**John Pennefather:** (T.6583) Tel: (041) 592 2844 and (041) 592 2457 Cell/Mobile: 082 8088 346

**Ron Gilbert:** (T.6581) Tel: (014) 533 2774 Cell/Mobile: 083 2675 040

**Peet Coetzee:** (T.6580) Tel: (012) 993 3157

German volunteers.

## LIST OF BATTLEFIELDS

| | |
|---|---|
| Battles at Derdepoort & Kayasepoort | 25/11/1899 & 18/02/1900 |
| Two Battles at Silkaatsnek | 11/07/1900 & 02/08/1900 |
| Battle of Koster River & the Emily Backe ride to Rustenburg | 1/07/1900 & 22/07/1900 |
| General De Wet's epic escape over the Magaliesberg | 20/08/1900 |
| Siege at Elands River | 04 - 16/08/1900 |
| Battle at Slypsteenkop (Kwaggefontein) | 31/08/1900 |
| Skirmishes at Wonderfontein (Groot Marico) | 09/11/1900 |
| Battle of Buffelspoort | 03/12/1900 |
| Battle of Nooitgedacht with Boer Cemetery | 13/12/1900 |
| Ebenhaezer Monument | 16/12/1900 |
| Battle at Cyferfontein | 05/01/1901 |
| Battle of Middelfontein | 23/01/1901 |
| Battle of Vlakfontein (Derby) | 29/05/1901 |
| Battle of Moedwil with British and Boer Cemetery at Dwarspruit | 30/09/1901 |
| Battle of Kleinfontein | 24/10/1901 |

### BATTLEFIELDS & PLACES OF INTEREST FOR VISITORS

Zeerust Military Cemetery.

British Base at Naauwpoort West and Blockhouse Lines.

Rustenburg Commando Head Quarters and Cemetery and Memorial at NG Kerk.

British Military Cemetery at Rietfontein.

War correspondents outside dug-out in Mafeking.

Ex-Naval troops.

# Action at Moedwil
## 30 September 1901

***In 1901, only one British column was left in the neighbourhood of the Magaliesberg and Zwartruggens in the Western Transvaal (North West Province), that of Colonel Kekewich.***

The Boer leaders De La Rey and Kemp, partly from a desire to replenish their failing stores of ammunition, partly to show their contempt of Kitchener's proclamation, had resolved to make some vigorous effort, and it was not long before they obtained a promising opportunity. This British column consisted of three guns of the 28th Battery, one *Pom-Pom*, the Scottish Borderers, the Derbyshire's, the 1st Scottish Horse and the 7th Imperial Yeomanry. This column which left Naauwpoort for the Magaliesberg on 13 September had a total strength of 800 infantry, and 560 mounted men. Prior to passing through Magato Nek and entering the Zwartruggens, the Scottish Borderers were at the *Farm Moedwil* on the afternoon of the 29th. At 1900 hr, a convoy of empty wagons, together with some Boer prisoners, a company of Derbyshires, one and a half squadron of Scottish Horse left on a return trip to Naauwpoort.

In the bushy broken country that the British were reconnoitring, safe sites for camping were not easy to locate. The site selected by Kekewich had strong natural advantages and one great defect. South of the main drift the river bent sharply eastwards half encircling the camp. The western side of the river created picket distribution difficulties due to the thick patches of bush.

It was on 30 September while the British camp was sleeping, that the Boers moved silently into position, they had moved so quietly that by 0430 hr, they had reached the river and had managed to conceal themselves behind the shrubs and bushes. At 0445 hr, a patrol of Devon Yeomanry searching along the river bed on the north west of the camp, came across the Boers. The patrol opened fire, and the camp was aroused. The Boers now attacked from all sections. By 0500 hr, the Boers had gained the crest of the steep bank and poured a volume of converging fire into the British camp. The British resisted fiercely and as the light of day approached the casualties increased. The Boers gained no ground. At 0600 hr, with fixed bayonets the British charged driving the Boers back. By 0615 hr, the Boers retired, they had attacked and severely crippled the column. 214 British officers and men were killed and wounded, 327 horses and several draught-beasts were lost. ❑

***Source***:
*Battlefields of the SA War 1899* by J.L. Smail.
(with kind permission Mrs Barbara Smail)

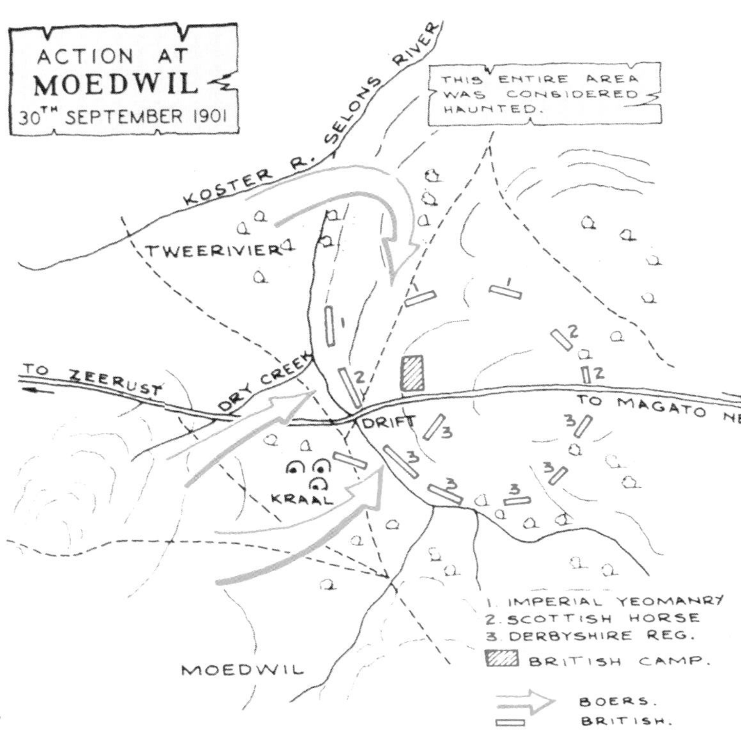

*Stowell Kessler*

# Black Concentration Camps

If we could go back in time to the days of the Second Anglo Boer War in the year 1901 when the British Army flying columns were sweeping the veld of all human inhabitants our eyes would see an amazing and sorrowful scene. In the background smoke was rising to the heavens from the burning of nearly 30 000 farmhouses. Boer women and children were walking or riding on ox wagons. Old oumas and oupas were also trudging along. Black soldiers were driving thousands of cattle, sheep and goats. Our eyes would also behold Black servants and farm workers caught up in this same forced trek. Black and White together were being compelled by military force to enter the Concentration Camps. Some of these Black civilians would end up in the White Camps and some in the Black Concentration Camps. Lord Herbert Kitchener, the Commander-in-Chief of the British forces in South Africa had ordered this done, as he said, to bring the guerrilla war of the Boers to an end. Faced with the finest horse cavalry in the world and unable to defeat the Boer forces in the field it was decided to sweep the veld clean and starve them into submission. And in the end that is exactly what happened.

The Black Concentration Camps have been forgotten and in some sense eliminated from many histories of the war. Many deny that these camps ever existed but when they are acknowledged it is often argued that they were quite different from the White Camps and that they were formed for solely humanitarian reasons. However, the historical records in the National Archives show that the Black and White Camps were formed for basically the same reason.

That reason was a military strategy to sweep the veld clean of every living creature and food producing plant to create a hostile environment. This, it was hoped, would make it impossible for the Boer Commandos to continue to attack British Army units, blow up bridges and railway lines and would, in the end, result in the defeat of the Boer forces. In particular the research of the historical record has shown that the Black workers on the Boer farms were forcefully removed to the Concentration Camps for three reasons:

1. Some Black workers were loyal to the Boer farmers and were hiding their cattle from the British Army and providing the Boer forces with intelligence;

2. Some of the Black farmworkers had livestock of their own that could be voluntarily or involuntarily commandeered by the Boer commandos;

3. As a by-product of their removal the Black men could provide labour for the British Army departments and the gold mines on the Rand. However, this was not the reason that their kraals were burned and they were removed. In the end well over 100 000 Black civilians were incarcerated in over 100 Concentration Camp sites where over 20 000 Black women and children died of the same diseases, poor sanitation, lack of adequate food, medical care and poor housing that killed over 28 000 Boer women and children.

In the beginning some Black refugees went into the areas controlled by the British Army to escape the war on the veld. With the increasing sweeps of the veld Black women and children were dumped along the railway by the British columns at the military terminal points. Lord Kitchener ordered that the servants of the Boer women and their children should be placed in the White camps with their mistresses. Others were left to their own devices. Some found their way into the

Native "*agterryer*" with horses.

existing Black locations in such places as the Waai Hoek location at Bloemfontein. Slowly Black Concentration Camps were formed in the Orange Free State and eventually came under the supervision of the White Camp administrations. These camps became mutually dependent on each other. The Black camps provided labour to maintain the White Camps (cleaning latrines, etc.) and working in the hospitals and in return the White Camp superintendents provided food and other supplies and a very minimal amount of medical service.

However in the Transvaal the organisation was much less developed. Basically, with few exceptions, the Blacks swept off the veld by the British columns were left to fend for themselves along the railway. These forced refugees received no food or medical care – the resulting deaths were not recorded. Some of the Black men stranded with their families along the railway were employed by the Johannesburg Army Labour Depot which was formed by the Director of the Imperial Railway. This system was modelled after the labour recruitment monopoly of the Chamber of Mines. The purpose of this system was to keep Black labour wages down by preventing competition for labour by the various Army Departments. In June 1901 the Army Labour Depot was closed and the Department of Native Refugees and the Witwatersrand Native Labour Association replaced it. Following the migrant labour system of the mining companies the Black women and children were moved to abandoned farms where they were required to grow food (for themselves and the British Army). Those who refused to grow crops were charged double for food. The Army Departments employed the men. The movement of the former camps to the farms caused over 7 000 deaths due to a lack of housing and medical service. This was done to save £10 000 a month that it had cost to feed and care for the Black women and children when they had been under the supervision of the White Camp administrations.

In the end nearly 50 000 women, children, elderly men and POWs died in the Black and White Concentration Camps during the Second Anglo Boer War. They died both Black and White together of epidemic disease due to concentration and poor medical care, poor sanitary facilities and contaminated water supplies and poor and inadequate food. This experience of the Black people in the Concentration Camps was one of mutual suffering with the Boers. Black people fought on both sides in the war, served as spies on both sides and died by the thousands in the Concentration Camps of the Second Anglo-Boer War. Several of the Black Concentration Camp cemeteries and camp sites are now being discovered in such places as Aliwal North, Alleman's Siding near Bloemfontein and Brandfort. Cemeteries have also been discovered at Greylingstad and Boksburg. Two cemeteries were previously known as the Vredefort Road Camp and the Koppies Camp. ❑

# Concentration Camps in the War

In early March 1901 Lord Kitchener decided to break the stalemate that the extremely costly war had settled into. It was costing the British taxpayer £2,5 million a month. He decided to sweep the country bare of everything that can give sustenance to the Boers i.e. cattle, sheep, horses, women and children.This *scorched earth policy* led to the destruction of about 30 000 Boer farmhouses and the partial and complete destruction of more than 40 towns. Thousands of women and children were removed from their homes by force. They had little or no time to remove valuables before the house was burnt down. They were then taken by ox-wagon or in open cattle trucks to the nearest camp.

Conditions in the camps were less than ideal. Tents were overcrowded. Reduced-scale army rations were provided – in fact there were two scales. Meat was not included in the rations issued to women and children whose menfolk were still fighting. There were little or no vegetables, no fresh milk for the babies and children; 3/4 lb of either mealie meal, rice or potatoes, 1 lb of meat twice weekly, 1 oz of coffee daily, sugar 2 oz daily, and salt 0,5 oz daily (this was for adults and children who had family members on commando).

Children who were under six years of age received 0,5 lb of meal daily, 1/2 lb meat twice weekly, 1/4 tin of milk daily, 1 oz sugar daily and 1/2 oz of salt daily. This very poor diet led to the rapid spread of diseases such as whooping cough, measles, typhoid fever, diphtheria, diarrhoea and dysentery, especially amongst the children.

There was a chronic shortage of both medical supplies and medical staff. Eventually 26 370 women and children (81% were children) died in the concentration camps.

The visit of the British humanitarian, **Miss Emily Hobhouse**, a delegate of the South African Women and Children's Distress Fund to the camps in the southern Orange Free State led to an improvement in the conditions. On her return to Britain the story she told of the conditions under which the women and children had to live shocked everyone not committed to believe in the inevitability of the war and the harsh measures that was to end it.

Her fifteen page report to the Committee of the Distress Fund was first circulated to MP's and published in late June. From August to December 1901 the **Fawcett Commission** visited the different camps and presented their report in December confirming in all essentials the accuracy of Emily Hobhouse's account.

They berated the camp authorities for the red tape which complicated the running of the camps, the spread of diseases that should have been foreseen, elementary rules of sanitation that had been forgotten, the vegetables that should have been provided; and the fact that medical staff should have been rushed to the scene as soon as the epidemics broke out.

Their recommendations led to improvements within the camp system. By February the annual death-rate in the camps were to drop to 6.9 percent and soon to 2 percent. ❑

Walter Mears of the Scouting Corps used to visit his fiancee in the Pietermaritzburg Concentration Camp, disguised in a British uniform. (Mears succeeded Danie Theron as Kommandant of the Corps.)

**Heidelbergers of the Boer War**, *Ian Uys*, 1981 Ian S. Uys

## NOT EVERY STORY A HORROR STORY FROM THE CAMPS

Mr and Mrs P .H. Jacobs, an old couple aged 78 and 68 years respectively, had been sent from the town of Koffiefontein to the Boer Concentration Camp at Orange River Station. Owing to their ill-health while in the camp they were sent to live with their son-in-law in Beaconsfield, then a sister municipality to Kimberley.

STEVE'S WAR STORIES

## SOUTH AFRICAN COINAGE & THE CONCENTRATION CAMP

After the Anglo-Boer War, the Boer women who had survived the Concentration camps expressed a wish to Jan Smuts and Rachel Isabel Steyn (wife of the President of the Orange Free State) that the humblest coin in the South African coinage should bear the emblem of the humble sparrow, to remind each one of us of the verses in St Matthew's gospel which tell us of our worth in the eyes of God.

Matthew 10 v 29-31: *Are not two sparrows sold for a penny? Yet not one of them will fall to the ground apart from the will of your Father. And even the very hairs of your head are all numbered. So don't be afraid; you are worth more than many sparrows.*

Their wish was fulfilled when a design of two sparrows on a mimosa branch by Kruger Gray, an engraver at the British Royal Mint, was depicted on the farthing in 1923, during Smuts' first term as Prime Minister.

The farthing depicted the sparrows until 1960 and then they were depicted on the half cent coin from 1961 until 1964. A new sparrow design by South African engraver Tommy Sasseen (based on a painting by Dick Findlay) appeared on the one cent coin from 1965 to 1990 and the half cent coin between 1970 and 1981. A design by William Lumley, based on the Kruger Gray design, has been depicted on our smallest coin, the one cent coin, since 1991.

STEVE'S WAR STORIES

## DIVINE MESSAGE

Early in the morning of the 6 February 1901, Maggie Biccard awoke in the Concentration Camp at Howick to hear an angelic choir singing her husband's favourite hymn. She knew that something had happened to Johnny. Two weeks later she heard that he had been killed during the night attack on Lake Chrissie. (Co-incidentally this lake was named after Maggie's mother, Christina, daughter of the Voortrekker Andries Pretorius). Maggie knew that her husband was gifted with second sight as, at a Sunday Service during their courtship in April 1892, he had a vision of the funeral of the presiding Minister. Rev.van Warmelo died during the following week and was buried the next Sunday.

**Heidelbergers of the Boer War**, *Ian Uys,* 1981 Ian S. Uys

# Concentration Camps in Transvaal, Free State and Natal

The concentration camps set up in Natal were for prisoners from Orange Free State and the Transvaal.

TRANSVAAL:

Barberton, Balmoral, Belfast, Heidelberg, Irene, Johannesburg, Klerksdorp, Krugersdorp, Meintjeskop, Middelburg, Mafeking, Nylstroom, Pietersburg, Potchesfstroom, Standerton, Vereeniging, Volksrust, Vryburg, v.d. Hovensdrift.

ORANGE FREE STATE:

Aliwal North, Bloemfontein, Brandfort, Bethulie, Heilbron, Harrismith, Kroonstad, Kimberley, Norvalspont, Springfontein, Vredefortweg, Winburg, Oranjerivier.

NATAL:

Ladysmith, Colenso, Howick, Pieter-maritzburg, Jacobs, Wentworth, Merebak, Eshowe, Port Elizabeth, Uitenhage and East London.

## WAR PENSIONS MOOTED FOR BLACK PARTICIPANTS

While Daniel Ontong was serving as a Native Scout for the Imperial Forces in the Koffiefontein/Jacobsdal area in 1900/1901, he was severely wounded in both legs and became totally lame in one. After the war it was suggested that £50 sterling in compensation be paid to Ontong. At least ten Native Scouts from Koffiefontein had been killed while assisting the British in the region. Likewise, another black, one Antonie Remmeline, while operating as a Native Scout for the Imperial Forces in the Koffiefontein/Jacobsdal area, was shot through both arms and an ankle and was more or less a cripple. It was suggested after the war that £50 compensation be paid. There is no record that any compensation was paid out to either Ontong or Remmeline, nor to the families of any of the deceased Scouts.

STEVE'S WAR STORIES

# Women & Child Mortality in the Concentration Camps

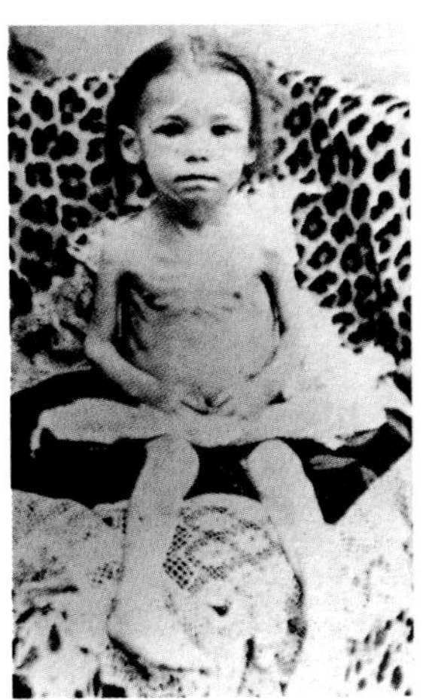

The rate of mortality amongst the women and children in the Concentration Camps of the 2nd Anglo-Boer War was considerably higher than the number of burghers who lost their lives on the battlefields (considering that the statistics do not include the figure for the men (and boys over the age of 16) who died in the Concentration Camps.

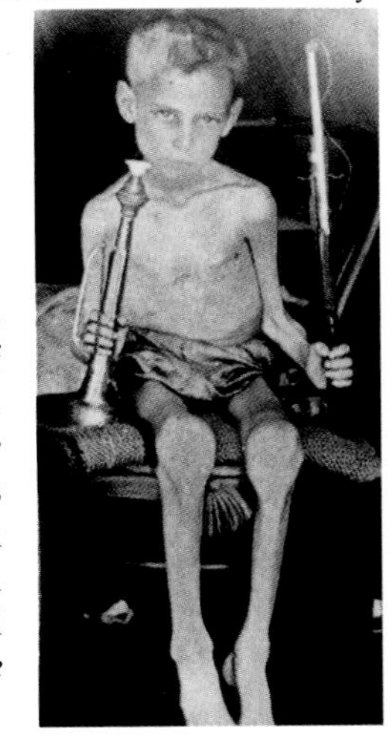

The official records show 6 189 burghers were either killed in action, died of illness or accidents or as prisoners of war. An official figure of 26 251 was given for women and child mortality but this is believed to be considerably higher than the figures collected by the head government official, Department Internal Affairs in 1914. The figure quoted was taken from the *"English Blue Book"*, kept in the government archives. ❑

Mpumalanga
SWAZILAND
Freestate
KwaZulu-Natal
INDIAN OCEAN
Volkstrust
KwaZulu-Natal
Ladysmith
Richards Bay
DURBAN
LOCATION
Battle sites are signposted with :
GLOBETROTTER™
COPYRIGHT © 2000 New Holland Publishers (UK) Ltd
= Battle Site
1 Allermans Nek
2 Wall of Remembrance
3 Convention Bridge
4 Majuba
5 O'Neill's Cottage
6 Skuinshoogte
7 Laingsnek
8 Fort Amiel Museum
9 Old Utrecht Cemetery
10 Utrecht Museum
11 Pokrowsky Memorial
12 P.L. Uys Memorial
13 Kambula
14 Scheepersnek
15 Blood River Poort
16 Bloedrivier
17 Moth Museum
18 Talana Museum
19 Talana
20 Fort Pine
21 Karl Landman Home
22 Fort Mistake
23 Rorke's Drift
24 Isandhlwana
25 Fugitives Drift
26 Helpmekaar
27 Elandslaagte
28 Siege of Ladysmith
29 Siegetown Museum
30 Saailaer
31 Rensburg Koppie
32 Tugela Heights
33 Colenso Museum
34 Colenso
35 Ambelside Military Cemetery
36 Clouston Field of Remembrance
37 Chieveley Military Cemetery
38 Bloukrans
39 Armoured Train Cemetery
40 Fort Dunfort Museum
41 Gen. Louis Botha's Birthplace
42 Ntombe
43 Holkrans
44 Hlobane
45 Lancaster Hill
46 Raadsaal & Fort
47 Prince Imperial Memorial
48 P.L. Uys Memorial
49 Ulundi
50 Ondini
51 Umgungunhlovu
52 Piet Retief's Grave
53 Dingaans Kraal
54 Italeni
55 Cetshwayo's Grave
56 Site of Shaka's Kraal
57 Coward's Bush Monument
58 Fort Kwa-Mondi
59 Nongqai Fort
60 Tugela
61 Fort Pearson
62 Shaka's Memorial
Volksrust
Charlestown
Laingsnek
Groenvlei
BALELESBERG
2277 m
Luneberg
Commondale
Grootspruit
Paulpietersburg
Pongola
Onverwacht
Candover
Magudu
Mahlangasi
Bivane
Mpemvana
Utrecht
Madadeni
Newcastle
Botha's Pass
Mullers Pass
Osizweni
Vryheid
Hlobane
Ngobeni
Ngome
Stellrand
Swart Umfolozi
Nongoma
Kingsley
Bloedrivier
Normandien
Dannhauser
Hattingspruit
Calvert
Gluckstadt
Black Umfolozi
Dundee
Glencoe
BIGGARSBERG
Nondweni
Nqutu
Nhlazatshe
Hlabisa
Wasbank
Vant's Drift
Rorke's Drift
White Umfolozi
Ulundi
Mahlabatini
Driefontein
Elandslaagte
Silutshana
Babanango
Helpmekaar
Elandskraal
Mangeni
Mtonjaneni
Ladysmith
Pomeroy
Sundays
Randalhurst
Roosboom
Qudeni
Melmoth
Nkandla
Colenso
Tugela Ferry
Dlolwana
Ndundulu
Nkwalini
Winterton
Weenen
Keate's Drift
The Ranch
Empangeni
Felixton
Frere
Loskop
Estcourt
Entumeni
Eshowe
Muden
Kranskop
Ntabamhlope
Greytown
Ahrens
Fort Mtombeni
Tugela
Amatikulu
Mtunzini
Gingindlovu
Rietvlei
Mooi River
Sevenoaks
Mapumulo
Mandini
Rosetta
Redcliffe
New Hanover
Dalton
Umvoti
Tugela Mouth
Darnall
Nottingham Road
Stanger
N
25 km
10 miles
R23
R33
R34
R66
R68
R69
R74
N2
N3
N11

# KwaZulu-Natal

*Northern KwaZulu-Natal is a tranquil countryside of cornfields, cattle ranges and pastures, dotted with small, friendly farming towns. The tranquillity of the area belies its bloody history.*

*In days gone by this land was the scene of momentous battles between Boer, British and Zulu forces which shaped the course of South African history.*

*This unique concentration of historic sites has become popular with tourists from far and wide who come to explore the period buildings, museums and monuments, and see for themselves the valleys and hills where the great battles were fought.*

*The Battlefields Route, as it is known, starts at Escourt in the south and winds north through Colenso and Ladysmith to Newcastle and Volksrust, and eastwards to Utrecht, Glencoe, Dundee, Nqutu, Paulpietersburg, Vryheid and Ulundi. It is traversed by the mighty Tugela River, which rises high in the Drakensberg mountains and flows eastwards to the sea, forming the natural boundary between the old Natal colony and what was traditionally known as Zululand. Historical attractions aside, the Battlefields Route has much to offer. For the adventurous, there are nature reserves, hiking trails, and opportunities for river rafting. There are also farm resorts, charming bed & breakfast establishments, craft industries and roadside stalls. For those interested in traditional Zulu culture, the area is a rich hunting ground. Visitors willing to venture off the beaten track will find glimpses of a way of life that has hardly been affected by the march of time.*

*KwaZulu-Natal offers the adventurous visitor a variety of game parks, nature reserves and wilderness areas where wild animals roam and the spirit of ancient Africa calls.*

*Most of the Game Parks are situated in the northern and eastern parts of Zululand, with a stunning diversity of wetlands, riverine forests, offshore coral reefs and bushveld habitats.*

*These Parks are complemented by the vastly different alpine meadows of the Drakensberg Park to the west, on the border of the rugged Lesotho mountain kingdom.*

*These Protected Areas are the cradle which will continue to sustain life as we know it in this part of the continent, and provide visitors with a unique opportunity to enjoy and appreciate the wild, untamed beauty of Africa.*

# Dundee and Elandslaagte

### Eweni Country Lodge, Dundee

Built on the edge of the 72,5 metre high Helpmekaar Falls near Dundee. Eweni is a delightful farmstyle getaway. Enjoy peace, quiet and a view of the valley below. Visit the site of the Battle of Helpmekaar. Tour the Anglo-Boer and Anglo-Zulu War Battlefields.
4 Rooms from R220 per person. Dinner B&B.
Tel: (034) 642 1841. Fax: (034) 642 1841

### House on the Park, Dundee

Situated in the heart of the Battlefields. The owner is a tour guide specialising in tours of Isandlwana, Fugitives Drift and Rorkes Drift. Chalets are en-suite with TV's. Children welcome. Swimming pool.
5 Rooms from R110 pp sharing. Bed and Breakfast.
Tel/Fax: (034) 218 1893. Cell/Mobile: 082 457 2563.
e-mail: jeremy@dundee.lia.net

### Paddock Wood Cottage, Dundee

On the site where troops were camped in 1899 at Dundee; with views onto the Mpati hills. Thatched cottage sleeps up to 5 people. 4 bedded room, lounge/kitchenette. TV, radio and swimming pool.
2 Rooms from R110 pp self-cont. R125 pp B&B.
Tel: (034) 218 2212. Cell/Mobile: 082 722 7742.
e-mail: dique@dundee.lia.net

### Thornley, Dundee

Thornley is a historical homestead and a National Monument situated in a parklike garden on the eastern slope of Talana Hill where the Boer Hospital and Headquarters were. Centrally situated for Elandslaagte and Ladysmith. Charming hospitality.
2 Rooms from R130 pp. B&B. Dinner available.
Tel: (034) 212 2738. Fax: (034) 212 2738.

### Blanerne Farm, Elandslaagte

Cattle and game farm. During the Boer War General Kock's route to Elandslaagte crossed the farm. Simpson Mitchell-Innes, the owner of Elandslaagte Colliery, was captured by the Boers. Dinner available.
2 Rooms from R150 per person sharing. B&B.
Tel/Fax: (036) 421 1747. Cell/Mobile: 083 300 0601
e-mail: blanerne@ls.lia.net

# Ladysmith, Vaalkrantz, Van Reenen and Spionkop (ENGLISH) / Spioenkop (AFRIKAANS)

### BULLER'S REST GUEST HOUSE, LADYSMITH

Situated on Cove Redoubt Hill, this luxury thatched accommodation has excellent Berg views. Dinner is available on request. Enjoy evenings in the 'Boer War' pub surrounded by militaria from the Anglo-Zulu and Anglo-Boer Wars.
5 Rooms from R175 - R225. Dinner B&B.
Tel: (036) 631 0310. Fax: (036) 637 3549.
e-mail: a.breedt@sun.co.za

### VAALKRANS BUSH LODGE, NEAR SPIONKOP.

Exclusive and unusual Bush Camp on the banks of the Tugela River at the site of the Battle of Vaalkrans and located near *Skietsdrift* where the Wen Commando passed to do battle with the Zulus at Blood River 1838. There are 2 en-suite double-Rooms *plus* 2 Beehive huts and central catering lapa. Accommodating up to 12 persons at R1 000 per night for the lodge incl. attendant.
Tel/Fax: (036) 488 1404. Cell/Mobile: 082 573 0224.

### OAKLANDS COUNTRY MANOR, VAN REENEN

Nestling in the mountains at the top of Van Reenen's Pass, Oaklands offers swimming, tennis, horse riding, fishing and hiking to their guests. Excellent cuisine with fresh farm ingredients. Boer War Battlefields tours available and can be arranged.
9 Rooms from R225 pp sharing. Dinner B&B.
Tel: (058) 671 0067. Fax: (058) 671 0077.
e-mail: oaklands@compuserve.com

### THREE TREE HILL LODGE, SPIONKOP

Steeped in Boer War history, Three Tree Hill Lodge is situated on the famous Spionkop Battlefield, overlooking the Spionkop Nature Reserve and the majestic Drakensberg Mountains. You must take a tour to the famous Battlefield. Excellent accommodation and cuisine.
6 Rooms from R500 per person sharing.
Cell/Mobile: 082 570 3764

### SPIONKOP LODGE, SPIONKOP

The original Spearman homestead visited by Buller & Churchill has been renovated to accommodate visitors. Tour Spionkop & Mt.Alice-Buller's HQ. on this 700 ha game farm. Retrace Churchill footsteps. There are Game Drives & Sundowner Cruises on 3000 ha Spionkop Dam.
10 Rooms from R475 per person full board.
2 self-catering Cottages from R475 & R675 per cottage.
Tel/Fax: (036) 488 1404. Cell/Mobile: 082 573 0224.

# Dundee environs

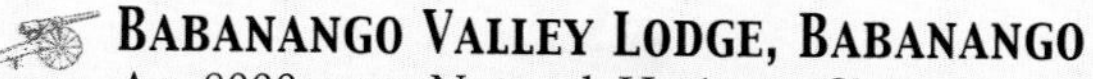

## BABANANGO VALLEY LODGE, BABANANGO

An 8000 acre Natural Heritage Site surrounded by mountains. Walks, bird-watching and guided tours available to Anglo-Zulu War sites. Close to Rorke's Drift and Dundee Boer War sites. Relax by the swimming pool with a drink.
6 Rooms from R540 pp sharing. Dinner B&B.
Tel: (035) 835 0062. Fax: (035) 835 0160.
Cell/Mobile: 082 321 7141.

## FUGITIVES' DRIFT LODGE, RORKES DRIFT

Renowned for its Battlefield tours; Fugitives' Drift Lodge is situated within a game reserve overlooking Isandlwana and Rorke's Drift, with the Fugitives' Drift Monument on the property. Enjoy the great hospitality of the staff.
8 Rooms from R875 per person sharing.
Tel: (034) 642 1843. Fax: (034) 271 8053.
e-mail: fugdrift@dundee.lia.net

## SHEPLEIGH LODGE, RORKES DRIFT

4 km from Rorke's Drift of Anglo-Zulu War fame. Sleep in stone/thatch cottage or old milking shed. Experience the Battlefields of Anglo-Boer and Anglo-Zulu Wars with Marilie, a Registered Tour Guide, specialising in battlefields.
6 Rooms from R170 pp B&B. R220 pp Dinner B&B.
Tel: (034) 642 1805. Fax: (034) 642 1805
Cell/Mobile: 082 930 1444.

## PENNY FARTHING COUNTRY HOUSE, HELPMEKAAR

Situated at Helpmekaar surrounded by Battlefields, 30 km south of Dundee. Luxury accommodation run by Battlefields Tour Guide Foy Vermaak. Antiques, memorabilia, a 'fort', birds and game to keep you occupied.
5 Rooms from R265 pp sharing. Dinner B&B.
Tel: (034) 642 1925. Fax: (034) 642 1925.
e-mail: penny@dundee.lia.net

## MANOR HOUSE & GOOSE COTTAGE, WASBANK.

108 year old farmhouse, been in the same family since 1940. Central to the Anglo-Boer and Anglo-Zulu battlefields. Self-catering, meals on request. The manor was HQ for a British garrison; also the home of *Codewyk De Jager* (Talana Museum).
9 Rooms from R150 to R300 per room.
Tel: (012) 346 3550. Fax: (012) 346 2499.
e-mail: jacana@lia.co.za

# Midlands

## Halls Country House, Mooi River

Only 4km from Mooi River and ideally situated between the Battlefields, the Midlands Meander and the Drakensberg. En-suite accommodation, a cosy pub and restaurant offering hearty country meals.
4 Rooms from R175 pp sharing. Bed & Breakfast.
Tel: (033) 263 2696. Fax: (033) 263 2697.
e-mail: hch@mweb.co.za

## Hartford Country House, Mooi River

This beautiful homestead was originally owned by Freidrich Moor, last Governor of The Union of Natal. Part of the 'Treaty of Vereeniging' was signed on the verandah. Trout-fishing, tennis and golf are offered.
11 Rooms from R245-R460 pp. Bed & Breakfast.
Tel: (033) 263 2713. Fax: (033) 263 2818.
e-mail: info@hartford.co.za

## Granny Mouse Country House, Balgowan

Close to the Private Schools. Excellent food and relaxation in the lounges or in the quaint pub. Enjoy candlelit dinners. Accommodation in thatched cottages. Swimming, river walks and birdlife.
16 Cottages from R390 pp sharing. Bed & Breakfast.
Tel: (033) 234 4071. Fax: (033) 234 4429.
Cell/Mobile: 082 443 8100

## The Coach House, Currys Post Road

Established in 1873 on the Currys Post Road which served as the main military route during the Anglo-Zulu and both Anglo-Boer Wars. Furnished with antiques and Yellowwood. Trout fishing and golf close by on the Midlands Meander Route.
6 Rooms from R150 pp sharing. Bed & Breakfast.
Tel: (033) 330 2380. Fax: (033) 330 2380.

## Old Halliwell Country Inn, Currys Post

A 4-star luxury county inn, dating back to 1830 which was used as a staging post for troops en-route to the front line. Superb cuisine and beautifully decorated rooms add to the excellence of this Inn.
15 Rooms from R320 - R550 pp sharing. B&B.
Tel: (033) 330 2602. Fax: (033) 330 3430.
e-mail: haliwell@pmb.lia.net

# Midlands

## Otter's Holt, Dargle

Comfortable en-suite accommodation on working farm. Emphasis on outdoor pursuits. Trout and Bass fishing, hiking and mountain biking. Walking distance to the site of the Battle of Willow Grange.

5 Rooms from R150 pp sharing. Bed & Breakfast.
Tel / Fax: (033) 263 2616. Cell / Mobile: 082 573 1212
e-mail: woodinn@mweb.co.za

## Briar Ghyll Lodge, Pietermaritzburg

Enjoy the ambience of a bygone era. A Victorian lodge, Circa 1865, set in 20 hectares (50 acres) of park-like surroundings, with charming accommodation. Rooms have TV, phone & tea / coffee making facilities.

5 Rooms from R210 per person sharing. B&B.
Tel: (033) 342 2664. Fax: (0331) 45 2514.
e-mail: bglodge@dialup.co.za

## Norwood Bed & Breakfast, Pietermaritzburg

A splendid Victorian home built in 1860 as the Governor-Generals' hunting lodge. On acres of garden in the quiet suburb of Oak Park. Rooms have TV, phone, fridge, microwave and tea / coffee facilities.

2 Rooms from R150 pp sharing. Bed & Breakfast.
Tel: (033) 347 3453. Fax: (033) 387 4535
e-mail: rameng@iafrica.com

## Warren's Guest House, Hillcrest

In the village of Hillcrest between Pietermaritzburg and Durban. Thatched house with English pub. Rooms have TV and private entrances, and some have self-catering facilities. Pool and secure parking.

5 Rooms from R150 pp sharing. Bed & Breakfast.
Tel: (031) 765 5470. Fax: (031) 765 5470.
Cell / Mobile: 082 455 6348.

### TO GET RID OF MOSQUITOES

Mosquitoes prefer beef blood better than they do anything that flows in the veins of human kind. Just put a couple of pieces on plates near your bed at night and you sleep untroubled by these pests – in the morning you will find them full and stupid and the meat sucked as dry as an ordinary Railway Hotel customer. Fresh beef well suited for the purpose can be obtained at the Ration Shop – free to Residents only.

*Printed & Published at Ladymith, Natal 18 November 1899*

# Vryheid

## TENDELE GUEST LODGE, VRYHEID

Thatched cottages with a cosy atmosphere. Superb African cuisine with homemade bread, butter and free range eggs, as well as farm fresh vegetables. Close to the Itala Game Reserve and the Battlefields.
5 Rooms from R180 pp sharing. Bed & Breakfast.
Tel: (034) 981 1667. Fax: (034) 981 1667.
Tendele Farm, Lowsberg Road, Vryheid.

## VILLA PRINCE IMPERIAL, VRYHEID

On two acres at the foot of Lancaster Hill, Vryheid. An elegant country house offering guests a relaxed and peaceful stay. A Tour Guide can take you to the sites of both the Anglo-Boer and Anglo-Zulu Wars as well as the Prince Imperial site.
12 Rooms from R250 pp sharing. Bed & Breakfast.
Tel: (034) 983 2610. Fax: (034) 983 2610.
e-mail: princeimperial@intekom.co.za

## PROTEA HOTEL STILWATER, VRYHEID

6 km from Vryheid on the Dundee Road. Perfectly situated for touring the Anglo-Boer War battlefields, Isandlwana and Rorke's Drift. A pleasant ladies and action sports bar, restaurant with à la carte and carvery.After a days' touring relax by the swimming-pool and enjoy a braai/barbeque for the evening.
68 Rooms from R250 single & R315 double B&B.
Tel: (034) 981 6181. Fax: (034) 980 8846.

Pictured left: Back row, standing centre: General Ben Viljoen, with Commandant H. Malan on his left and Captain Blignaut on his right. Standing at the back is Dr Visser (Red Cross).
Front row, sitting centre: Adjutant Nel wearing a straw hat.
*Note the new recruit, the monkey with the rifle.*

Pictured right: Colonial Units: Buglers.

## Coastal

### BURGUNDY BAY HOUSE, UMHLANGA ROCKS
A beach guest house 100ms from the sea, and 1,5km from Umhlanga Rocks. Mediterranean style with all the luxuries catered for. Walking distance from Umhlanga village and 30mins from the Airport.
4 Suites from R250 - R325 pp sharing. B&B.
Tel/Fax: (031) 562 9986. Cell/Mobile: 083 778 6187
e-mail: tichs@iafrica.com

### HOLLAND FARM GUEST HOUSE, BALLITO
Enjoy warm hospitality and tranquil settings amid an anthuriam flower farm set against rolling hills. Visit Shaka's Rock a mere 10 minute drive inland and on the back road to Dundee. Close to Battlefields.
6 Rooms from R250 pp sharing. Bed & Breakfast.
Tel/Fax: (032) 942 9042. Fax: (032) 942 9045.
e-mail: holland@saol.com

### GHOST MOUNTAIN INN, MKUZE
Ideally situated for trips to the Natal Game Reserves. Day and night game drives organised and acclaimed bird-watching. Close to the Anglo-Zulu Battlesites of 1879. Fishing, canoeing and boat cruises arranged.
33 Rooms from R250 pp sharing. Bed & Breakfast.
Tel: (035) 573 1025/6/7. Fax: (035) 573 1025/6/7.
e-mail: ghostinn@iafrica.com

### PROTEA HOTEL SHAKALAND, ON R66, ZULULAND
An authentic recreation of the Great Zulu Kraal overlooking the Umhlatuze Lake. Experience the lifestyle of Zulus and warriors of bygone days. Stay in first-class accommodation in *beehive huts* with en-suite bathrooms. The evening program of entertainment starts at 1600 hrs (4 pm).
48 Rooms from R575 single & R900 double DB&B.
Tel: (035) 460 0912. Fax: (035) 460 0824.

### PROTEA HOTEL SIMUNYE, ON R66, ZULULAND
In the Mfule River Valley sheltered by high cliffs.Experience a trip on an ox-wagon or by horseback. After sundowners and dinner, sit around the fire as Zulu legends unfold to the drumbeats. Soak in a private steaming rock-bath, drift to sleep in your stone-walled room.
18 Rooms from R725 single & R1 188 double.
Tel: (035) 450 3111. Fax (035) 450 2534.

## DUNDEE PUBLICITY ASSOCIATION

**Victoria Street, Dundee. Tel: (03421) 22121. Fax: (03421) 23856.**

**Talana Museum & Battlefield. Tel: (03421) 22654. Fax: (03421) 22376.**

*In the foothills of the Biggarsberg mountains, the town was named by one of its founders, Peter Smith, who came from a village near Dundee, Scotland. He first mined coal on Talana Hill and floated the Dundee Coal Company on the London Stock Exchange in 1899, beginning Dundee's long connection with coal mining in South Africa. At the heart of the Battlefields Route, Dundee has numerous historical buildings. Most of the churches date from the turn of the century and have commemorative battle plaques.*

### BOER WAR SITES & HISTORICAL BUILDINGS

**Boswells Building**: A National Monument. It was originally erected as the Biggarsberg Unity Lodge in 1898. Unique both architecturally and historically, it is the last remaining pre-1900 theatre in the province.

**Cottage Hospital**: Originally built as a Cottage Hospital. It was used as a military hospital to tend to the British wounded during the Battle of Talana.

**The Mews**: This complex of small, intimate shops was the original Williams Hygienic Bakery. The original buildings and roof have been preserved.

**Talana Museum**: One of the most impressive museums in the country. Talana Museum is situated on the site of the ***Battle of Talana***. Buildings from the time of the battle still exist and a cemetery is one of the exhibits. The founder of Dundee, Peter Smith's, homestead has been restored and refurbished to its original state. These are but a few of the extraordinary exhibits to be seen at the Talana Museum. Open Monday - Friday: 08h00-16h30. Saturday: 10h00 - 16h30 and Sunday: 12h00 - 16h30. Arrangements can be made with the curator for guided tours of the Museum and surrounding Battlefields. **Tel: (03421) 22654 or Fax: (03421) 22376.** Walk-and-Talk audio tapes of the major battlefields are available.

**Thornley Farm**: On the reverse slopes of Talana Hill. Thornley Farm was used by the Boer forces as their headquarters, hospital and mortuary during the **Battle of Talana**. Although these restored buildings are on a private farm, visitors are welcome.

### ATTRACTIONS IN AND AROUND DUNDEE

**Baskets from Africa**: Cnr. Beaconfield & Gladstone Streets, Dundee. Made with natural products, the baskets are crafted by Zulu women who live on farms in the immediate vicinity of Dundee. The use of natural materials - grasses, barks, twigs and other plant material - has created an environmentally aware work force. Tel: (03421) 23240.

**Blood River Battlefield**: On 16 December 1838 a party of Voortrekkers defeated the Zulu army here. Replica bronze wagons are set in a laager on the site of the battle.

**Fort Pine**: On the farm *Sheepmoor*. Fort Pine was built in 1878 by the Royal Engineers as a convenient place for the civilian population to gather. Contact the Talana Museum to arrange access. Tel: (03421) 22654.

**Fugitives Drift (Anglo-Zulu War)**: It is here, on this lonely hillside, that the two men responsible for saving the ***Queen's Colour*** from the ***Isandlwana Camp 1879***, lie buried. Lieutenants Coghill and Melville made their way to this spot high above the Buffalo River before they were killed by the Zulus. The site is 15 km beyond Rorkes Drift; *and Fugitive's Drift Lodge owned by David & Nicky Rattray is here. (034) 642 1843.*

**Rorkes Drift Battlefield (Anglo-Zulu War)**: Where 100 British troops repelled 4 000 Zulus, and despite overwhelming odds stood victorious after 12 hours of fighting. A record number of **11 Victoria Crosses** were awarded to the defenders. The site is 42 km from Dundee and en route to Fugitives Drift.

**Prince Imperial Memorial (Anglo-Zulu War)**: The last hopes of the Napolenic dynasty were shattered with the fatal stabbing of the ***Prince Imperial of France*** by Zulu warriors. A memorial has been erected on the site where he fell. One and a half hours drive from Dundee en route to Vryheid via Nqutu.

## Tour Operators

**Gunners Rest Battlefield, Adventure and Zulu Heritage Tours**: *Tailor-made Tours to suit your requirements. Expert guides, fully knowledgeable on KwaZulu Natal, Military History and Battlefields.* Contact: Pat Rundgren. Tel/Fax: (03421) 24560. Cell/Mobile: 082 690 7812.

**KZN Battlefield Promotions**: *Pam McFadden, the curator of the Talana Museum, has expert knowledge of Kwa-Zulu Natal, Military History and the Battlefields. Tours arranged to suit your requirements.* Contact: Pam McFadden. Tel: (03421) 22654.

**Penny Farthing Battlefield Tours**: *Vast knowledge of Anglo-Zulu Battles and Boer War battlefields.* Contact: Foy Vermaak. Tel: (034) 642 1925. English, Afrikaans and Zulu languages.

## Tour Guides

**Marilie & Henreik Bruyns:** (T.5972). PO Box 1401, Dundee 3000.
Tel/Fax: (034) 642 1805. Cell/Mobile: 082 930 1444. *Battle of Talana in Afrikaans/English. Zulu tours. Dundee & district.*

**Pam McFadden:** (T.0359). PO Box 1852, Dundee 3000.
Cell/Mobile: 082 462 6132. Fax: (03421) 22376. *Northern Kwa-Zulu Natal. Military History and the Battlefields. Tours arranged to suit your requirements.*

**Pat Rundgren:** (T.0028). PO Box 1726, Dundee 3000. Tel/Fax: (03421) 24560.
Cell/Mobile: 082 690 7812. *Tailor-made Tours to suit your requirements :– KwaZulu/Natal. Military History and Battlefields. Adventure Tours. Zulu Cultural Tours.*

**Neville Worthington**: (T.3876). PO Box 998, Dundee 3000.
Tel/Fax: (03421) 21347. *Battlefields:-Talana. Elandslaagte. Spionkop. Tugela Heights.*

Tour group with guide at Isandlwana.

## Ladysmith Tourism Organisation
## Siege Museum, Murchison St, Ladysmith.
## Tel: (036) 637 2992

***Known as Siegetown, and named after the Spanish wife of Sir Harry Smith, Ladysmith made world headlines at the turn of 20th century when it was laid besieged for 118 days by the Boer forces. Numerous cemeteries, monuments & buildings of architectural splendour stand to the memory of those who gave their lives in the struggle to 'keep the flag flying'.***

### BOER WAR SITES & HISTORICAL BUILDINGS

**Town Hall & Museum**: Queen Street. This architectural treasure, originally designed by architect Robert Selby Walker, was built in 1883. It's history is depicted in the Town Clerk's office, which is now the Town Hall Museum. Open weekdays 09h00-16h00.

**Siege Museum**: Next to the Town Hall, was erected in 1884. It was originally the Market House. It also served as a ***Ration Post*** for civilians during the siege. Acclaimed as an exceptional museum, it features photographs, artifacts, documents, uniforms and firearms, as well as a diorama of Ladysmith and its surroundings. Open weekdays from 09h00-16h00 and Saturdays from 09h00- 13h00. Tel: (036) 637 2231.

**Castor and Pollux**: Two ***6.3" Howitzers***, sent from Port Elizabeth, served the town with distinction to the extent that they engaged and damaged one of the Boer ***Long Toms*** on the Middle Hill. Not used after the relief, they stand proudly in front of the Town Hall.

**'Long Tom' Gun**: This is a replica of one the original four ***6inch Creusot 'Fortress' Guns*** ordered by the ZAR (Transvaal Republic). Three of the Pretoria guns were destined for the most important Front in Natal, viz the Siege of Ladysmith.

**12" 600lb Solid Shot**: These two giant shells pose a question as Ladysmith never saw 12" guns. In explanation, 16 of these, with chains to anchor down the platforms, stand as reminders of the frantic rush by the **Naval Brigade** to get two 4.7" guns into Ladysmith before the Boers laid siege. In adapting the 4.7's for land use, Sir Percy Scott, Captain of ***HMS 'Terrible'***, had not had time to check their stability mounted as they were on timber beams. Unnecessary as events proved, these two heavy weights do duty outside both the Town and Moth Halls. (M.O.T.H. - Member of the Order of Tin Hats).

**Platrand & Wagon Hill**: The site of the Platrand & Wagon Hill Battle. A self-guide brochure from the Information Office will assist you to discover the historical sites in the area, including a sculpted memorial to fallen Boers, various monuments to the British forces, gun emplacements and a military cemetery. Splendid view of the entire Siege area. Open daily from 06h00 to 18h00. Tel: (036) 637 2231 or (036) 637 2992.

**Monument**: 1st Battalion Royal Irish Fusiliers: Situated just off the Main Road prior to the N fly-over intersection leading to Durban/Colenso. The cross is in memory of those who died during the Siege 1899-1900.

**Statue of Gandhi**: Mohandas Karamchand Gandhi, (1869-1948) to become the Mahatma, was a stretcher bearer with Buller's Relief Forces during the Siege. Trained in Durban, by Dr Booth, Gandhi, a young advocate, saw the need, and indeed an opportunity for the Natal Indians to prove their worth, a way to justify their protection and care by the British, by convincing his fellow countrymen to qualify themselves as **Dhoolie-Bearers** in the Natal Campaign. Having trained some of the 1 100 Indians in Ladysmith, Gandhi is said to have left on the last train out, along with General French and Major Haig, who described their journey through Pieters Station as somewhat hazardous, being forced to lie on the floor to avoid being hit by Mauser bullets whizzing through the compartment! Gandhi travelled as far south as Estcourt where he then

trained Indians to become stretcher bearers. ***It was in this capacity that he saw service during the First Battle of Colenso, where according to his autobiography, he claims to have had the honour of carrying Lt. Fred Roberts VC, to his final resting place.***
Gandhi and his bearers are reported to have done stirling service during, and indeed after, the *'slaughter'* at Spioenkop. Stretchers were the only 'suitable' transport for any number of serious head wounds, and teams of 12 bearers took turns to carry patients to No. 4 Field Hospital at **Spearmans**; and some all the way back to Frere. ***The Indian Bearer Corps*** was disbanded after the Natal Campaign. Arrange with caretaker who will open the gates. Tel: (036) 637 7777.

## Restaurants

**Swainson's Restaurant**: Royal Hotel. Tel: (036) 637 2176.

**Royal Carvery:** Royal Hotel.

**Crown & Cannon:** Crown Hotel. Tel: (036) 637 2277.

**Guinea Fowl Country Kitchen & Pub:** Piazza San Marco.

## Tour Guides

**Carole Rafinetti:** (T.5985). 17 St.Augustine Avenue, Ladysmith 3370.
Tel/Fax: (036) 631 2219. *Siege of Ladysmith. Colenso. Wagon Hill. Spionkop. Tugela Heights.*

**John Snyman:** (T.0745). 64 Beacon Road, Hospital Park, Ladysmith 3370. Tel: (036) 631 0660. Fax: (036) 637 5734. *Military History-Colenso. Spionkop. Ladysmith. Capture of Winston Churchill.*

**Liz Spiret:** (T.0466). 17 President Str, Ladysmith 3370. Tel: (036) 637 7702. Fax: (036) 637 2992. *Ladysmith. Spionkop. Wagon Hill. Elandslaagte. Vaalkrantz. Tugela Heights. Colenso.*

**Piet Van Rooyen:** (T.5453). 20 Kingfisher Rd, Lynwood, Ladysmith 3370. Tel: (036) 637 3311. Fax: (036) 637 2992. Cell/Mobile: 082 887 5297. *Battlefields. Ladysmith. Colenso. Spoinkop.*

## Tour Guides in other areas of Kwa-Zulu Natal

**Warwick Baker:** (T.3667). PO Box 1188, Westville 3630. Tel: (031) 266 5480. Fax: (031) 266 9045. Cell/Mobile: 082 417 5248. *Battlefielda in Kwa-Zulu Natal, Mpumalanga and Gauteng.*

**Ken Gillings:** (T1007). 42 Broadway, Westville 3630. Tel: (031) 266 2233. Fax: (031) 267 0076. *General history of Kwa-Zulu Natal. All Battlefields from Shakanera 1856, Anglo-Zulu War 1879, Anglo-Boer War 1881, Zulu Civil War 1883-1888, Anglo-Boer War 1899-1902 and Bhambatha Uprising 1906.*

**Evan Jones**: (T.0324). PO Box 13830, Cascades 3202. Cell/Mobile: 082 807 8598.
Tel/Fax: (033) 344 3260. *Military History.*

**Scott Kirk:** (T.5319). 13 Martin Rd, Estcourt 3310. Tel: Work (036) 352 2130.
Fax: (036) 352 5664. Home (036) 352 3941. *Battles-Tugela line. Willow Grange. Frere.*

**Ron Lock**: PO Box 2388, Hillcrest 3650. Tel: (031) 765 7048. Fax: (031) 765 1244. *All Anglo-Boer and Anglo-Zulu War battles.*

**Paul McIlvenny:** (T.4455). PO Box 100884, Scotsville 3209. Tel: (033) 386 9645.
Fax: (033) 386 4601. Cell/Mobile: 082 853 1307. *Natal Battlefields. Durban. Pietermaritzburg. Mpumalanga Provincial.*

**Major Paul Nash:** (T.1319). PO Box 40034, Queensburgh 4070. Tel/Fax: (031) 463 2887.
*Military Historian on Kwa-Zulu Natal Battlefields.*

**Ngqabutho:** (T.4650). PO Box 100928, Scotsville 3209. Cell/Mobile: 082 927 2125.
Faz: (033) 342 6097. *Isandlwana. Rorkes Drift. Zwa-Zulu Natal.*

**Norman Schafer:** (T.5471). 7 Golf Gardens, 31 Adams Rd, Hayfields, Pietermaritzburg 3201. Tel/Fax: (033) 396 4716. *Spionkop. Colenso. Ladysmith.*

**Gilbert Torlage:** (T.0703). Private Bag 9050, Pietermaritzburg 3200. Tel: (033) 345 3201.
Fax: (033) 345 3207. *Anglo-Boer War 1899-1902 in Kwa-Zulu Natal.*

**Steve Watt:** (T.00286). 46 York Avenue, Scottsville, Pietermaritzburg 3201. Tel: (033) 386 5188. *Military History with field work to all sites in Kwa-Zulu Natal and Eastern Free State.*

*Pat Rundgren*

# The Queen's South Africa Medal with "Talana" bars to Colonial Units

The Queens Medal.

When the war broke out (even after a lengthy provoking of the Boers), the British, being unprepared, had to rush troops to South Africa from all parts of the British Empire. In order to do this required the use of steam ships. The coal used to power these ships came largely from the strategic collieries of Dundee and Elandslaagte in Northern Natal. The Boer strategy at the opening of the war in Natal was, therefore, to deprive Britain of these resources and thus the first two major battles of the war took place just outside Dundee, at Talana on 20th October, 1899 and at Elandslaagte the following day. It is not the purpose of this article to study the battles in any depth, but rather to take a look at the tokens of recognition that were awarded by the British with especial regard to those awarded to Colonial troops, once *all the fuss was over*. As a reward for their service in South Africa and more specifically at Talana and Elandslaagte, Imperial and Colonial troops were awarded the ***Queen's South Africa Medal***. This medal, held by a red ribbon with two narrow blue stripes and a broad central orange one, was 36mm in diameter and was awarded in silver or bronze. The bronze being awarded to Indian Stretcher Bearers and servants. The obverse showed the Jubilee bust of an ageing Queen Victoria, while the reverse showed Britannia holding a flag in her left hand and holding out a laurel wreath towards a large group of advancing soldiers, with warships offshore with *South Africa* inscribed round the top. Since it was expected at first that the war would be over very quickly, initial stocks of the *QSA* had the raised dates ***1899-1900*** inscribed at the back. Since it became clear very early on that the Boer forces were going to be much more resilient and uncooperative than expected, these first batches were withdrawn and the dates erased, so it is exceptionally unusual to find a *QSA* with raised dates.

In addition to the medal, some 26 authorised clasps were also awarded to commemorate either specific battles in which the holder had taken part, or to denote areas of operation. Two such clasps were the *'Talana'* and *'Elandslaagte'* clasps. I have yet to see one with raised dates, although I have a couple in my collection which have so-called 'ghost' dates where the dates have been incompletely removed.

## *Talana*

The *'Talana'* bar was awarded to all troops under Lieutenant General Sir William Penn Symon's command on 20th October 1899, who were north of an east-west line drawn through Wasbank Station, some 15 km south-west of Dundee, and who participate (or were at least within firing distance) from the battle of Talana. The Imperial Regiments were the Royal Dublin and Royal Irish Fusiliers; the Kings Royal Rifles; the Leicestershire Regiment; 18th Hussars; 13th, 67th and 69th Batteries Royal Field Artillery; Royal

The Kings Medal.

Army Medical Corps as well as the usual 'odds and sods'. Civilians were evacuated from Dundee over a 3-day period beginning Monday 16th October. Only members of the Town Guard; the Dundee Troop of the Natal Carbineers; municipal, Government and mining officials; clergy; Police and some storekeepers stayed behind to look after their interests. The ***'Talana'*** bar **is** therefore **very rare to South African** units. These units were as follows:

*The Dundee Troop of the Natal Carbineers: 26 men under the command of Captain C.G.Willson*

There are only two men who qualified for both the *'Talana'* and *'Elandslaagte'* bars to their QSA's, and they are both Carbineers from the Dundee Troop. Trumpeter H.A. Craig and Cpl.J. Watson were presumably dispatched with messages to General Sir George White or Major-General Sir John French at Elandslaagte the day after Talana, and thus arrived at Elandslaagte to do it all over again!

This troop lost Troopers T. Elliott, W. Buxton, R.M. Milner and W. Craighead Smith killed, as well as another seven men wounded and eleven horses killed, when a *'Long Tom'* shell fired by the Boers from Bulwana during the siege of Ladysmith burst in their quarters.

*The Dundee Town Guard: 250 men under leader W.H. Reynolds*

Under Reynolds leadership were several sub-leaders, one of whom, Harry Ryley (the local miller) was to win a Military Cross in German South West Africa in 1914 while serving in the 2nd Mounted Rifles (Natal Carbineers). Another was A.E. Allison, one of only nine men of the Natal Guides to be awarded the Distinguished Conduct Medal (DCM) while serving as a scout and field intelligence operative in that unit later on in the war.

The Medal Roll for the Natal Corps of Guides lists seven men who qualified for the *'Talana'* bar. Two, Allison and H.Wiltshire, qualify by virtue of their membership of the Town Guard at the time. The other five do not appear on the Town Guard roll, and one thus assumes that they were there as Guides. Two of them, the brothers T. and F. Loxton, also won the DCM later on in the war.

*The Dundee Rifle Association: 47 men under leader W.C. Smith*

Dugald McPhail, member of the Dundee Rifle Association.

A more colourful member of the Dundee Rifle Association was Dugald McPhail. Born in 1840, the Quarter-master of the Buffalo Border Guards, he had the good sense to leave the field of Isandlwana on 22 January 1879, just minutes before the frenzied Zulu hordes *wiped out* the entire camp. To further this streak of good judgement, he married the daughter of Peter Smith (founder of Dundee who went on to become a coal magnate of some note). His QSA, which now resides in the M.O.T.H. War Museum in Dundee, has the single bar *'Talana'* for his services on that fateful day. He later went on to fight in 1906 in the Bambatha Rebellion. In 1914, at the age of 74, he once again volunteered for duty and was most peeved to be told that he would not be required even though he maintained that he was "highly qualified"! Not to be outdone, he served as a Police Reservist at the age of 101.

Another member of the Association was the Reverend G.C.Bailey of the Anglican Church of St.James who remained behind when Dundee was evacuated and left behind a remarkable diary of the events in the town for the eight months that Dundee changed its name to 'Meyersdorp' under Boer occupation. He conducted the burial service for the late General Penn Symons, and had the Union Jack with which the General's body was wrapped under the floorboards of the church. On the relief of the town, one of the first sights to greet the troops was the selfsame flag, unearthed and flying on a tree branch outside the church.

Francis Birkett, the Town Clerk, was another member. He had strode around the town

When the Boers first entered Natal, a lot of Indians fled in panic. Sannie de Jager found an Indian baby on the banks of a river, abandoned by its parents. She cared for and reared the child who later became her maid. (Schikkerling, 267).

for three days organising the evacuation of the civilians. As the British finally withdrew from Dundee, he left a laconic note in the town Record Book – *"Just leaving the office. Boers in occupation of the town."*

It is interesting to note that there were four Smiths (A.A., R.H., S. and T.P.) in the Town Guard and another three (W.C., P.P. and D.G.) in the Rifle Association.

Similarly, between the two units there are seven Browns, four Gutridges, five Marshalls, five Harveys, and four Nurses, as well as several threesomes. Obviously television was a much needed commodity in early Dundee!

*For some unknown reason (perhaps they were lost) six men of the Cape Garrison Artillery under the command of Lt. E. C. Gates*

*The Natal Police: 48 men under the command of 431 Inspector Arthur George Petley*

A member of the Natal Police who was awarded the *'Talana'* bar, 2420 Trooper Samuel E. Johnson, qualified through membership of the Dundee Rifle Association. Three others – Troopers 1715 T.W. Leach, 2130 R. Lewis and 2072 D'Arcy Sibthorpe were subsequently discharged for bad behaviour and/or drink. Troopers C.St.J. Maynard, J.J. Willis and C.J. Beaumont died of disease during the subsequent Siege of Ladysmith. Troopers R.F. Ryan and A.W. Wright were both wounded and captured by the Boers.

*Veterinary Corps*

The medal was awarded to: Col.H. Watkins-Pitchford (Border Mounted Rifles); Captain J.P. Byrne (Natal Carbineers); Lt. W.M. Power (Border Mounted Rifles); Lt. S.T.A. Amos (Natal Mounted Rifles); Lt. F.H. Shore (Veterinary Officer, 18th Hussars, who was taken prisoner); Lt. E.B. Bartlett; Pte. W.M. Pye (Imperial Light Horse); Pte. E.A. Hollingham (Imperial Light Horse); Pte. A.F. Harber (Border Mounted Rifles) and Trooper J.W.H. Ashe (Border Mounted Rifles) – all were qualified Veterinary Surgeons.

*Natal Government Railways*

Bridge Guard P.D. Hamber; Station Master A. Hunter (under fire at Talana, Acting Pay Clerk at Rail Head) and Driver A.A. Osborne (present battle of Talana, taken prisoner through siege). ❏

This work was undertaken by Bacon in Great Britain without his having seen or experienced any action of the war in South Africa.

As can be seen the uniform colours are incorrect, as well as the topography. This was always a major problem with art, drawings, and even articles produced by persons who never visited the "countries of action".

BACON NO. 1 PRINT: Painting of the *Battle of Dundee*, 20 October 1899.

*Henk Loots*

# Medals to the Boer Side

Between 11 October 1899 and 31 May 1902 more than 90 000 men served on the Boer side. Some 35 000 of these were taken as prisoners of war, many thousands surrendered voluntarily (the so-called *'hensoppers'* or *'joiners'*) and more than 7 000 were killed in action or died on service. At the end of the war only some 21 000 *'bitter-einders'* finally laid down arms.

The two Boer Republics never had any official awards for gallantry or military service[1]. Notices, however, did appear in the ***ZAR Government Gazette*** in **May 1900** about a proposed post-war bravery award for Boer soldiers: this, for obvious reasons, did not materialise.

In 1913, Col. Skinner, Commandant of the Military School at Bloemfontein, noticed that ex-Republican officers attending a course were without medal ribbons whilst their fellow officers, who had seen Anglo-Boer War service with the British Forces, were well beribboned. He asked Defence Headquarters to rectify the matter, but due to the outbreak of the First World War nothing was done at the time. However, in December 1920, **A Decoration for Devoted Services (Dekoratie voor Trouwe Dienst** or **DTD), a Medal (Anglo Boere Oorlog Medalje or ABO)** and a **Wound Riband (Lint voor Wonden** or **LVW)** were officially gazetted.

The Decoration and Medal are both of silver: on the one side is the Coat of Arms of the ZA Republic and on the other side that of the Orange Free State. The rank, initials and surname of the recipient are impressed on the rim. The Wound Riband has no accompanying medal, but was issued with a printed certificate. All three ribbons have the colours of the two Republics (green, white, red, blue and yellow-orange) in various widths and combinations.

*The regulations restricted the awards to SA Citizens, serving or eligible for service in the SA Defence Force who, as burghers of the SA Republic and Orange Free State, had faithfully served in the field between 11 October 1899 and 31 May 1902.* This *per se* excluded men such as foreign volunteers, Cape and Natal Rebels who had also fought on the Boer side. In later years, the original conditions were less stringently enforced, with resultant medal issues to these men.

Claimants, which could include the direct descendants of a deceased Officer/Burgher, had to submit details of actions fought in, dates POW or wounded, commanding officers, units or commandos served in, etc. on official application forms. Virtually all these forms have survived, making the awards highly researchable (except in some cases where medals were issued to two or more men with the same rank, initials and surname)[2].

The award of the **DTD** was discontinued on 31 December 1946 with a total of 662 issued, the last of 1060 **Wound Riband Certificates** was approved in November 1949 and a final batch of 12 **ABO medals** was issued in 1982[3]. In total some 14 600 **ABO** applications were received, of which approximately 13 800 were approved; in comparison, there were over 12 times more **QSA (Queen's South Africa)** medals (177 000) issued on the British side! ❑

NOTES

1. A service medal, however, was **privately** issued in 1899 by the Commanding Officer of the Johannesburg Volunteer Corps. There were bars for the Jameson Raid (1895-6) and the Swaziland Expedition (1889).
2. For more details on this aspect see the OMRS publication 'Miscellany of Honours' No.9 (1992), p50-61.
3. A skimmed and renamed medal was specially issued in 1988 to a descendant of a German Lieutenant who had served in the German Corps.

*Pat Rundgren*

# The Battle of Talana
## 20 October 1899

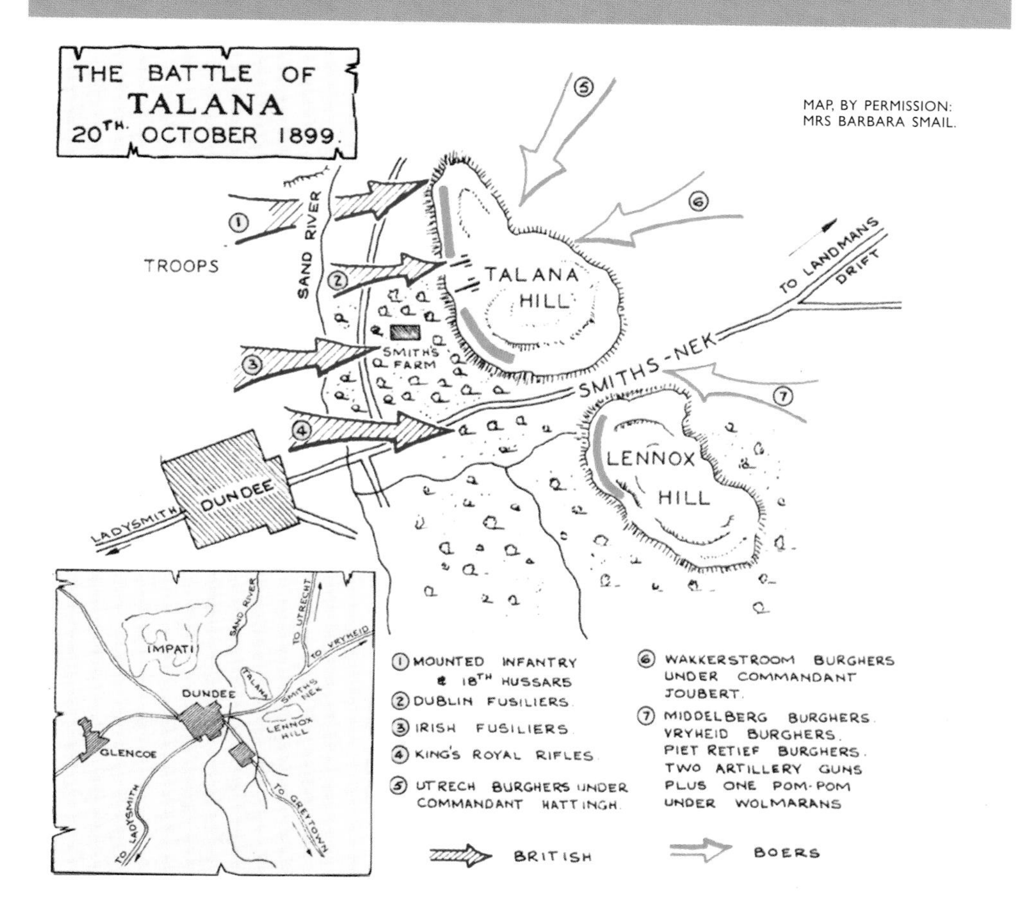


General Sir William Penn Symons in command of the British forces at Dundee was determined to hold the town. The Boer forces moving into Natal over Laing's Nek split into three columns. General Lock led the Johannesburg commando and the Hollander and German Corps directly south over Mkupe Pass towards Elandslaagte. General 'Maroela' Erasmus with 4 000 men from Pretoria, Heidelberg and Boksburg went south-east through Dannhauser and Hattingspruit. Swinging east along the line of the Buffalo frontier, General Lukas Meyer and the men under his command moved to concentrate at the Doornberg. The net was closing around Dundee.

Over confident, Penn Symons persisted in his decision to defend Dundee. Evading General White's pressure to retire to Ladysmith, he limited himself to evacuation of the civilians.

The Boers seized the railway line at Elandslaagte and Dundee was cut off. On 20 October, the Boer forces that had climbed Talana, Lennox and Mpati hills in the dark of the night, stood on the hills waiting for the mist to lift. Shortly after 0500 hr, the first shells landed in the British camp.

Within minutes the artillery were replying and spraying the slopes of Talana hill with shrapnel. Leaving the Leicesters, Natal

Carbineers, the Natal Police and the 67th Battery to defend the camp, the other troops were sent to attack the hill. It was to be a frontal attack by the Royal Irish Fusiliers, the Royal Dublin Fusiliers and the Kings Royal Rifles. The cavalry were sent behind Talana Hill to cut off any retreat by the Boer forces. The British casualties were heavy, the cross fire from Lennox and the accuracy of the Boer marksmen proving deadly.

The attack bogged down in the plantations at the base of the hill, which offered cover to the troops. In urging the troops on, Penn Symons was mortally wounded. He quietly retired, handing over command to General Yule. Led by their officers, the British now made the final assault up the hill. By noon the guns had fallen silent and the British forces were on top of Talana Hill. The reality, however, was very different. The Boer forces on Talana Hill had been steadily pulling their guns and troops back from the edge of the hill for protection. No assistance was shortcoming from 'Maroela' Erasmus on Mpati mountain and Lukas Meyer had decided to save his guns and men for another day. The Boer forces withdrew from Talana Hill and moved off towards the Buffalo River in an orderly fashion. The cavalry, under Col. Moller, found themselves in the path of the large force. With their small number they were unable to attack and moved in a northerly direction to keep out of the way. They were cornered on Adelaide farm by a group of 'Maroela' Erasmus's men and forced to surrender.

The battle was over. The British forces had driven the Boers from Talana and Lennox hills, but, 'Maroela' Erasmus' force still occupied Mpati mountain. The next morning the British forces found themselves under fire from Mpati mountain and eventually were forced to retreat from Dundee back to Ladysmith. The Utrecht and Wakkerstroom Commandos, on whom the brunt of the battle had fallen, had put up a tremendous resistance and had paid a heavy price. The first burgher to fall was Dirkie Uys of Utrecht, yet another of the ill-fated Voortrekker family, whose warrior sons had fallen in 1838 and 1879.

The British casualties were 51 dead, 203 wounded and 211 taken prisoner. The boers losses were 145 men. ❑

***Reference:***

*Pam McFadden, Talana Museum, Dundee.*
*KZN Battlefields Route Committee.*
http://www.battlefields.co.za/history/anglo-boer_war/talana/talanapam.htm
http://www.battlefields.co.za/history/anglo-boer_war/talana/talanakzn.htm

Gun on Talana Hill.

*Pat Rundgren*

# Anatomy of the re-enactment of the Battle of Talana, Dundee

## Part I

I sit here with a blank piece of paper in front of me and a simple objective: *write about how a committee of volunteers from Tourism Dundee set about staging a re-enactment of the battle of Talana as part of the commemorative functions of the Anglo-Boer War.* No sweat!

But hang on, it's not that easy. The historical facts are well known, but how does a group of enthusiastic country bumpkins with no experience whatsoever go about staging the largest Victorian battle re-enactment ever done, and an absolute first for South Africa? All this in the teeth of general public apathy, ice cold to freezing receptions from the powers that be, no funding worth a damn and no prospect of success.

Add to the equation a new Government which initially views the War as a colonial struggle by two white races who need to determine which of them would be able to suppress their black countrymen for the next century. General embarrassment from the Brits (after all, it was an unjust war engineered mainly for control of the goldfields of the Transvaal) and a burning desire for apologies from the British (remember concentration camps, scorched earth and so on? Not invented by the British but certainly refined by them.)

Ah, the plot thickens. So I guess we took a leaf out of the bumblebee's book and flew anyway. And the first event, staged on Saturday, 23 October 1999 was such a cracker, with over 130 participants and some 5 000 spectators, that we're going to do it all over again: twice! So lets begin at the beginning.

Dundee sits in the heart of KwaZulu-Natal battlefield country. Our forebears were a pretty aggressive lot, and there are thus some 68 major battle sites within an hour's drive of the town. Our main claim to fame has always been Isandlwana and Rorke's Drift (with some assistance from the film '*Zulu*' starring Michael Caine and Stanley Baker). When we set about planning the re-enactment of Talana nearly two years ago it was with the intention of attracting as many tourists as possible to the site of what was, in pure mathematical terms, a relatively minor battle as regards casualties (only 41 British dead). We had to do something out of the ordinary, other that laying a few wreaths. At the same time, we hoped like hell that no battlefields' visitor would visit Talana without going on the extra 50 kilometres to Rorke's Drift. And then we decided to stage an historical carnival. Zulu cultural festival and Boer-Brit sing-along as well just to keep them here and occupied for a little longer.

One dark night, while the Committee from Tourism Dundee hunched over a green baize

table, eye shades pulled down low and cigar smoke curling lazily towards the ceiling (well, not quite, but you get the point). It was firstly mooted that perhaps we should involve hundreds of school children wearing appropriate garb to storm Talana Hill shouting *'Bang!'* Enter the eccentric Pom called Ian Castle, who was visiting the battlefields and who does these things for a part-time living in the U.K.

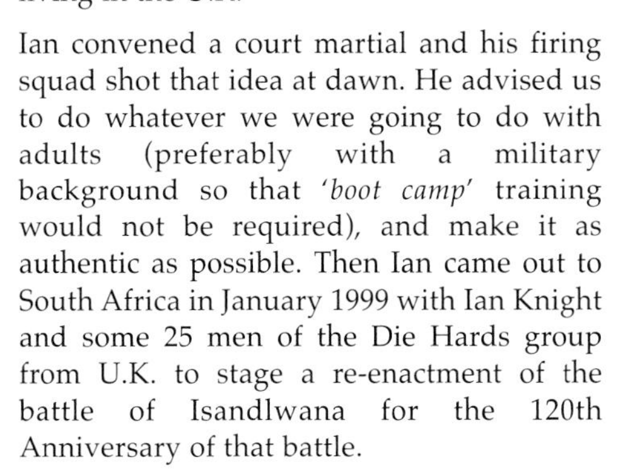

Ian convened a court martial and his firing squad shot that idea at dawn. He advised us to do whatever we were going to do with adults (preferably with a military background so that *'boot camp'* training would not be required), and make it as authentic as possible. Then Ian came out to South Africa in January 1999 with Ian Knight and some 25 men of the Die Hards group from U.K. to stage a re-enactment of the battle of Isandlwana for the 120th Anniversary of that battle.

The practice sessions were excellent, although authenticity was stretched by the odd Zulu wearing Ray Bans or Nike takkies. One was also wearing in his hair what looked like the aftermath of a serious argument with his feather duster. On the day, however, the Zulus got so carried away that they refused to die and came storming straight on in, so much so that the enactment ended in double quick time. They were also paid on the Saturday, with the result that they had all departed for home by the time Sunday's enactment was due to start, much to the indignation of tourists who had come many miles to see them! Most of the battle casualties were to be found amongst the journalists as they were jostling and swearing for position. All in all, great fun and a great learning curve for us as we watched and watched again, jaws hanging slackly on chests, and for the first time realising what we were up against!

Back to the drawing board! Living on promises of funding from public sector sources, we arranged for Ian to come out and produce the re-enactment while we set about recruiting volunteers and gnawing our fingernails to the elbow as we presented motivation after motivation to potential sponsors. Typical response:- *"So glad to see you! What? Anglo-Boer whatsit? No, not today thank you. Not politically correct, you know"*.

Undaunted, certain enthusiasts picked out their future parts, studied portraits of the characters concerned and were noted sneaking into a local ladies' hair-dressing salon to reappear some hours later with a new hair-do and highlights. The order also went out for prospective soldiers to cultivate moustache's. Suddenly upper lips around town sprouted rather reluctant, wispy moustache's (which emerged rather shyly, rather like mushroom spores under the kitchen sink), encouraged by much tugging, waxing, exhortations and chicken manure.

One can write a book about our efforts to obtain sponsorship, but that became a most painful subject and is still the stuff of wild nightmares.

As an example, we were invited to approach the local Regional Council's Tourism committee, who listened attentively and sympathetically and informed us that they had no mandate to grant any funding, and that the matter would be passed upstairs. This was duly done and budget number umpteenth presented. Result: nothing! Gentle reminder. Reply of *"What, never heard*

*of it"*. Frantic rustling of budget umpteen. *"Oh, that. Well, we'll see"*. But we never did, at least not directly!

In the meantime our Transitional Local Council came to our assistance with limited bridging finance so we could at least get the brochures out and advertising started; a courageous decision on the part of the Councillors in view of the myriad demands being made on the Council by the ratepayers.

4

Then disaster! Wheels came off in all directions as our Mayor gets the zig for some reason or other and accuses Tourism Dundee of being White Elitist and racist! Frantic lobbying, and all friends again. More money from the Council (bless their hearts) but not nearly enough.

So much red tape elsewhere that we could have used it to truss up the country (and, while we were about it, wring a few necks as well), and massive apathy elsewhere. Catch 22 situation so far as equipment was concerned; *"We've got what you want but we want your money first"*. Like Oliver, we replied that we want what you've got but we ain't got no money. And you all know the answer to that one!

So time slipped away, and eventually Ian could not wait any longer for a definitive answer as to whether the enactment would ever take place. We thus lost his expertise when he was forced to take another, more concrete contract.

General consensus was to forget the whole thing. Much gloom and doom at meetings. A public meeting called to discuss the issue had to be cancelled due to lack of public support. We set a deadline for the end of June; if we didn't have the money by then, we would cancel the whole deal. June came and went, so did July, and still we hung in there.

Mayor organises a trip to Pretoria to meet with the Department of Arts, Science, Culture and Technology. Very cordial welcome, but we come away as penniless as we arrived. Mayor redoubles his efforts and we obtain an audience with Kwa-Zulu Natal's Premier. Same again; much sympathy but nothing concrete. However, in the meantime, like shadows in a pond, things are moving elsewhere!

August, first chinks in the armour! Maybe, just maybe, all the beavering away by myriad committees could possibly result in something? Then the fantastic news; the Provincial Parliament had voted over R4 million to the province for the Centenary commemorations.

Ken Gillings, the Regional Anglo-Boer War Committee Chairman, who had taken to muttering to himself (he must have a very understanding employer) but who had also developed the patience of the proverbial saint, could leave the few remaining chunks of his coiffure alone (after having torn most of it out in frustration.) More biting to the elbows (amazing that in the days of instant electronic banking it took another six weeks for the money to make it's way down murky, mysterious Government channels towards Tourism KZN, who would act as a conduit). New budget prepared and submitted.

And on 7 September, the great news. Our sponsorship money (about one fifth of our original estimate) was in the bank and there were only six weeks to "D" day!

Start our famous headless chicken act and begin frantic running around. For my sins, I was tasked with the commissariat and getting together all the kit and equipment required for the soldiers. No kit, no soldiers. No soldiers, no re-enactment. No re-enactment, kiss Dundee's chances goodbye! Simple mathematics.

So, where on earth does one get hold of 120 Long Lee Enfields? Answer, you don't. Not in this country anyway. I manage to find 22, and had gunsmiths frantically modifying P14s, Mark 3s and 4s in an effort to get the profiles right, although that never quite materialised since we ran out of time. Mausers are not a problem, but is there any .303 and 7 mm blank ammunition available for them in the country? Dig, and dig some more. Discover that there is a difference between '*flash*' and '*smoke*' blanks, and eventually track down some .303 (but no 7 mm) at nearly R2,00 a shot and we need 30 000 of them. Half our budget! Volume of fire at the re-enactment immediately drops by half!

Then the Government changes the Firearms Act, and it becomes illegal for any person to handle a weapon which belongs to someone else unless under the direct supervision of the owner and on ground that belongs to the owner. Result is that the use of 100 year old weapons for the re-enactment becomes illegal, just in case we want to stage a coup and overthrow the Government!

Frantic lobbying with the Police, especially Director Abri Burger of the Central Firearms Registry, who rises magnificently to the occasion and grant us an exemption from the Act under some mysterious sub-section or other. They also go the extra mile and agree to assist us with the safe keeping of the weapons once we have them. Thank God for common sense and civic duty, and a medal for Inspector Sanette Kenchentin. The South African Police both at the Central Firearms Registry and Dundee go to the top of the Christmas Card list, although the duty guys steadfastly stand and watch as we daily struggle in and out of the strongroom with hundreds of heavy weapons. Help us carry some? Well, no. I don't think it's in my job description.

Right, we've got weapons. Next, uniforms. You guessed it, none available in the country at anything like sensible prices. We learn the difference between '*yellow*' and '*green*' khaki. Pam MacFadden and Frenchy Ribet learn of a camel train leaving shortly for Afghanistan (it's very big, so I hear, among the sheep herders) with all the khaki material produced in this country for the next half century. Convoy ambushed with a big cheque, and Pam's office develops a 380 metre khaki haemorrhage oozing slowly from under the door. I managed to mug one of the Die Hards of his Boer War type uniform in January, and so our local ladies, all volunteers, under the direction of Marilee Bryns, strip the uniform down, start up a sweat shop and churn out another 100 or so. Simple, eh?

African vendors innocently selling leather hats are hijacked as they pass by the museum, to emerge minutes later with a bemused smile on their faces and clutching fistfuls of money, while the wardrobe mistress adds some '*Boer hats*' to her inventory.

I consult the local gurus of British Victorian uniforms, Doug McMaster of the Blockhouse Museum in Ladysmith, and Andy May, the well known war artist. Doug's display models are ravished and end up naked and shivering while we inspect their Slade Wallace webbing, boots, gaiters, the way the jacket seams run and the amount of loose change in the pockets. What size buttons go where? Do they have a regimental of general service crest? Why do the Rifles have black webbing and everyone else has white? Where on earth does one get '*S*' type belt buckles for the Rifles, and why do they have to be different anyway?

The webbing is duplicated by Allison's Saddlery in Pietermaritzburg. On our first visit, clutching shreds of what used to be Slade Wallace equipment and dozens of photographs, Peter Jones, who plays the part of General Sir William Penn Symons in the re-enactment, falls in love with a century old wooden display horse in the shop window. Having only recently learnt which end passes manure and which end bites, Peter makes a bid for the horse

with an idea of tying string around the hooves and having it pulled around the battlefield. A hell of a lot safer than the real thing that could take off for the tall timber every time a bang goes off. But alas, it's not for sale, and Peter has to settle for the real thing.

As an aside, Peter's wife Decima, who runs the local Publicity Office, when asked what it feels like to be sleeping with a General, merely gives a derisive snort? General invites her to come and inspect his Privates instead. But glad tidings; our recruiting posters for camp followers are bearing fruit with dozens of volunteers coming forward. We lose a few after explaining just exactly what it is that a camp follower is expected to do, but are left with the enthusiastic unfazed ones under '*Madam*' Joan. During the re-enactment, one gazes around wistfully at the cavalry and expresses the wish to go for a ride. Instant retort *"There's plenty of men who'll oblige you." "No, silly, on a horse." "lucky horse!"*.

Peter and Decima attend the Pietermaritzburg Show to publicise the event. Peter is in full dress. Comments range from,*"No, dear, it's not alive, it's a dummy"* to *"He looks bloody old for a general."* Much nit-picking of the uniform by *'experts'*, but some offer surprisingly good advice and we're learning all the time. Private joke amongst us is Peter, stripped to his underpants, with his back to a wall.

Tents. Where the dickens does one get Boer War era Bell Tents for a British camp? You guessed it. Nowhere. Neville Worthington journeys by ox-wagon once more to Ladysmith armed with scraps of canvas and photographs, and comes back two weeks later with a fistful under each arm. Ladysmith Tent and Canvas also in line for a medal!

Helmets. How many do you think are available in the country? Only six. Where do we get them? From Bulawayo in Zimbabwe, of all places.

Edgar McMaster casts Victorian belt buckles fast and furiously; Brian Gavin does the same with buttons and badges. The Society for the Preservation of Militaria also do their bit. Apart from putting on a wonderful exhibi-tion at the first re-enact-ment, they somewhat rashly invite me to address their monthly meeting with Talana as my theme. Bore the socks off them, but manage to part them from several goodies which we need. Malcolm Wright and his bank of alchemists also manage to put together several hundred blank cartridges for us.

And so it goes on. We have six weeks for the Museum's Curator, Pam MacFadden, to "have several puppies" in putting together battlefield sites, constructing stone walls, putting up tents, organising toilets, water, VIP teas. The list never ends. Geoff Eave, Tourism Dundee's Chairman, grins lopsidedly, hunches his shoulders and pours diplomatic oil over troubled waters. Lisa Henry returns from honeymoon to learn the difference between a rifle and a gun, a carbine from a revolver, .762 to .303, and how to lug 100 rifles in and out of the Police Armoury.

My wife Cheryl keeps me going by listening to my whinging and whining and does volunteer work all over the place, dressed like the rest of the Tourism Dundee ladies in a green and white outfit which resembles something between a Green Peace advertisement and an apple ice lolly. My son Neale becomes a drummer boy.

Who in the blazes in this country knows how to do Victorian drill? But wait. Tourism KZN's boss man Gareth Coleman put aside money for some plane tickets. Fly three of the Die Hards Re-enactment group out and they'll lick the boys into shape. Frantic to-ing and fro-ing, and the tickets come through two days before they are due to leave. And so Craig Appleton, Tim Rose and Ian Church complete the picture by bellowing incomprehensible commands in a seemingly alien accent at groups of volunteers shivering in the pre-dusk cold. *"What in the hell is that Pommie bastard talking about?" "Buggered if I know, seems to have roasted pineapples in his mouth"*.

And at long last, the public of Dundee

respond magnificently. Men from geriatric homes tune up their pacemakers; busy professionals turn up for practice at off times; youngsters bunk school and go to the Museum to practice, fire, march and counter march and run up hills and try to avoid dying and falling into a fresh pile of horse manure that the cavalry, led by Lieutenant Mark Nebbe, have cunningly left on the battlefield (gives new meaning to the word *'land mine'*) and generally play nicely and *man, do they have a good time!* Steve and John and Ross are so keen that they make the eight hour drive from Johannesburg and back to be there. We have an ex-Colonel from the Air Force, an ex-CSM from the Artillery (does everything with a bang - just ask his wife Sheila), ex-everything from every unit imaginable.

Myriads of questions to be pondered and solved: traffic control; parking; sound systems; the colour of the tomato sauce in the hot dogs; how to keep the press under control; fencing; uninvited guests in the VIP tent; the weather, toilets, toilets and more toilets; dust suppression; simulated explosions instead of cannon fire; should the General die in front of/or behind the stone wall? and ... who cares anyway?

Duke of Kent stirs things up on a private visit to the Museum on 10 October. Soldiers are lounging around to give local colour. Posselt Louwrens the town eccentric, defies every rule of etiquette as he buttonholes the Duke (what is his first name; Harry of Igor?), thrusting a tattered moth eaten disfigured hat in his face. "*See all these notches around the brim? There's one for each damned Englishman I've shot.*" He cuts another, and presents the scrap of felt to the Duke as a memento. Everyone signs his walking stick, and the Duke passes on, considerably relieved at having survived. Debby Goldthorpe, the British Consul in Durban, looks ready to fall on her sword.

A dry run at Durban dockside on 16 October to assist Durban Metro with local colour when the troopships come in, and finally, 23 October dawns. Hot! Very hot!

Dry mouths and butterflies. Like a girl in her first party dress, we wonder amongst ourselves if anyone is going to ask us to dance? Dust hangs in the air; is that really someone coming to pay to watch? And so it is. 5 000 plus people flock into the Museum grounds, along with the Radio Hams (from the Eskort Bacon factory?); the Lotus Car Club and the Dundee/Glencoe Commando under Major Leon Lombard. Over 50 food stalls and souvenir sellers do brisk business. Mervyn Mitton stumps round in his Natal Mounted Police uniform, looking and no doubt feeling like a veteran from the Zulu War. There is a buzz in the air; smells of burning boerewors and horse manure, sweat and perfume, nervous anticipation.

Margie and Sally and Tony and Alida produce endless meals for the troops from their smoky field kitchens. Paul Garner produces tin mugs full of *'fortified' tea and ash* for the troops. The nurses give enemas, smile sweetly and refuse point blank to give mouth to mouth. Yatesh Deena and his stretcher bearers, dressed something like Casper the friendly ghost, try out the litters.

The Boers have got things better organised.

Although destined to lose, they are in good spirits as they sit around the fire drinking coffee laced with *mampoer* and slurping *boerewors* under the able command of General Lukas Meyer, alias Dirk Froneman, the former rugby Springbok. Posselt Lauwrens turns up with the tractor crankcase which he's turned into his coffin.

The local happy snappers, Terry Worley and Sanjay (fetch the Bryani) Singh, obviously suffering from lumbago, contort into fantastic poses as they capture the moment for posterity. Why is it that journalists can take a hundred pictures of the same subject from the same position and still have to re-focus their cameras each time?

Just about time for the off. But wait; check if Posselt really does have live ammunition in his bandolier or are they wooden heads? Phew, the latter. Check Oorlog as well, just in case. A herd of cows comes wandering unconcernedly across the soon-to-be field of mayhem. Marilee, resplendent in official red 'T' shirt, leaps out from the undergrowth where she has been concealing the bayonets for the King's charge, and shoos them off with a few well chosen Afrikaans phrases, all having something to do with sex and/or travel. Our first casualty! Sheila Mitchell, video camera clamped to her eye, fails to notice the rapidly approaching rear end of a rather large horse, and is dumped unceremoniously in the dust. But she's okay, just a few bruises. She landed on her chest, which husband George says is just as well as there's lots of padding there. Thank goodness the camera's okay.

Kevin Munro does the lead-in commentary, Shaun Lake sets off the first 'bang' with explosive charges and the battle of Talana, three years in the planning and six weeks in the making, kicks off. And what a hell of a time was had by all. By the way, it's a comfort going into battle knowing that one is *(a)* going to win and *(b)* survive. As Regimental Sergeant Major I'm pretty conspicuous, but I'm also big and our Indian stretcher bearers have threatened to go on strike if they have to carry me. So I'm bomb proof! ❑

***Part II***

# BOER and BRIT ... the Raw Material

Saturday, 23 October saw the first large scale re-enactment of an Anglo-Boer War battle ever staged in South Africa, at Talana just on the outskirts of Dundee in Northern Natal. After many trials and tribulations, the local committee of Tourism Dundee was on track to lure many hundreds of tourists and locals to commemorate and reflect on such an important piece of our heritage.

Apart from the re-enactment itself, there was a whole weekend's entertainment organised. There was a Boer-Brit smoking concert on the evening of Friday 21 at the MOTH Shellhole. On the Saturday, the re-enactment took place on the battle site, as well as a display by the Society for the Preservation of Militaria, another by the Dundee and Glencoe Commando; over 50 stalls catered for the inner man as well as thousands of Boer War souvenirs and genuine relics, militaria and good South Africa beer for sale. Visitors to the area with any military interest viewed the film *'Zulu'* once again and took the opportunity to visit or partake in an organised tour to Isandlwana and Rorke's Drift, only an hour away!

On Sunday 24, there was a whole programme of events organised to commemorate the battle of Elandslaagte, some 40 kilometres south of Dundee. The planning and organisation over the last 18 months had been

**'THEY SHALL GROW NOT OLD AS WE THAT ARE LEFT TO GROW OLD AGE SHALL NOT WEARY THEM,
NOR THE YEARS CONDEMN AT THE GOING DOWN OF THE SUN,
AND IN THE MORNING, WE WILL REMEMBER THEM.'**

both exciting and enormously frustrating. One pleasure, however, was the enormous amount of research required and I have stumbled across the diaries of some incredibly interesting characters from both sides, not necessarily of the ***'captains and kings'*** variety, who participated in and commented on the battle of Talana all those years ago. They have become ghostly friends, but their stories presently lie dead and buried amongst the dusty shelves of the archives. The re-enactment aimed at bringing the memory of some of those long forgotten men fleetingly back to life. This article is primarily about the Boers and Brits who actually took part in the fighting; those others who also played such an important role, for example the colonial troops, townspeople, African scouts and Indian stretcher bearers, will be the subject of another article. This is dedicated to all those extraordinary fighting men who battled it out on the boulder strewn slopes of Talana nearly 100 years ago.

The Boer Republics had some permanent military units, such as the Transvaal and Oranje Vrystaat Staatsartillerie and the Z.A.R.P.'s (permanent Police force), but their forces largely consisted of citizen soldiers. Most had little or no formal military training, but were members of so called '*commandos*' (a word now permanently grafted into the English language), which were quasi-military units based on administrative districts. Any male capable of bearing arms was called out for armed service when the occasion demanded. Their rank structure ranged from a common '*burgher*' or citizen, up to '*korpral*' then '*Veldkornet*' (roughly equivalent to a Lieutenant), '*Commandant*' or Colonel, and Vecht-Generaal (literally Fighting General.) Voted into office, ineffective or unpopular officers would be disobeyed and could just as easily be voted out again and reduced to the ranks.

Drawn from hardy frontier stock, the average Boer was used to roughing it, travelling light and living largely off the land. He was an excellent horseman and marksman. Boers fought in their everyday working clothes, with no bright uniforms to make them conspicuous. Their field craft was superb. A Boer did not believe in the concept of dying with honour; indeed, such a course would mean great hardship for his family and was to be avoided at all costs! Hand to hand combat was not to his taste, and he far preferred the hit and run tactics of a guerrilla fighter. Even the lowliest burgher was allowed his say at the war councils where strategy was planned. All of them therefore knew what was required of them, and could adapt as they went along if the plan went awry. On the debit side, Boers had the right to refuse to go into action if they did not agree with the strategy, and a constant problem was men simply packing up and going home when there were chores to be done back on the farm. Boer commanders ordering attacks or strategic movements were thus never sure of just how many burghers would ultimately answer the call.

A male Boer was responsible for providing his own equipment and horse, but the Government usually issued him with a bolt action 7mm Mauser rifle with a 5-shot magazine, imported in large numbers from Germany after the Jameson Raid. This weapon fired cartridges filled with the latest smokeless powder and was deadly accurate up to 800 m. By contrast, the British army in 1899 was very much a regular force. Its main function was to police all those far corners of the earth that compromise the British empire. Since many of these areas were populated by generally savage tribesmen who fought with stone age weapons, the average British soldier was more used to fighting enemies armed mainly with shields, spears and swords. He was not familiar with fighting a war where the use of smokeless powder made detection of the enemy very difficult and where casualties were taken at extreme ranges.

In addition, at the start of the Boer War the

British tended to fight in tight formations, the better for the Officers to keep control, but a splendid target for opposing marksmen. They relied on volley fire, and thus the standard of individual marksmanship was generally low.

By this time the British army had moved away from the scarlet and blue uniforms of the Zulu war. They wore a sandy brown colour uniform known as Khaki, which had evolved in India. These uniforms were initially of light drill cloth, but this proved inadequate for South African conditions and was later replaced by serge. They carried all of their ammunition and provisions on buff leather belts and pouches, although these were quickly camouflaged with tea or mud once it was realised what a splendid target they made.

They carried bolt action, .303 Lee Metford or Lee Enfield rifles (pictured below), with a ten round magazine. These were effective up to about 700 metres, and were fitted with a model '88 bayonet, while cavalry regiments carried a carbine and some a 9 foot Malacca cane lance. They also utilised Maxim machine guns, which had yet to realise their full potential.

### – *THE TACTICS* –

The official story of the battle of Talana is cut and dried. General Sir William Penn Symons, commanding an under strength brigade of some 4 000 men, was tempted to hold Dundee, instead of retreating to Ladysmith which would have been the sensible thing to do, firstly by the local colliery owners (protecting their financial interests) and the playing of the oft used '*Zulu*' card, the threat of a Zulu uprising should the British withdraw and cause a power vacuum.

Dundee is situated in a bowl, surrounded on all sides by large hills and mountains, and it was thus imperative that the British hold the heights in sufficient strength. However, they made no attempt to do so, which was not very sensible against an enemy comprising excellent fighters who had the audacity to ignore the rule books and ship a so called immovable 155mm Creusot '*Long Tom*' fortress gun from Pretoria by train to Hattingspruit siding and thence slog with it up Impati Mountain, where they could fire with impunity into the town, outranging the British guns by some 4 000 yards.

In short, the battle of Talana on 20 October 1899 kicked off just after 0500 hr with the discovery by the British of Boers from the Wakkerstroom and Utrecht commandos, plus three 75mm guns of the Transvaal Staatsartillerie, on top of Talana hill, situated some three miles to the east of Dundee. Unbeknown to them there were also Boers on Mpati hill to the north and Lennox hill to the south of Talana, but still hidden under a blanket of morning mist. It was determined to remove the Boers by a classic attack strategy. The Royal Irish and Royal Dublin Fusiliers, together with the Kings Royal Rifle Corps, were to make a frontal attack up the hill, supported by the 15 pounder guns of the 13th and 69th Royal Field Artillery Batteries.

While the infantry were going in, a detachment of 18th Hussars under Colonel Moller were to make their way around the back of Talana Hill from the north east and smash the re-treating Boer forces once they were driven off the hill by the infantry assault. In the meantime, the artillery were to advance to Smith's Nek and shell the retreating Boers to add to their discomfort.

It is now common cause that the attack did not go quite as planned. Subjected to both frontal fire from the top of Talana and enfilading fire from Lennox, the infantry attack stalled. In order to encourage his men, Penn Symons rather rashly decided to lead by example and stepped through a gap in a stone wall, behind which his men were taking cover. Becoming the source of undivided attention by some 800 Boer marksmen, it was a matter of seconds before he went down, mortally wounded in the groin.

Command passed to Brigadier General Yule who, with assistance from the artillery keeping the Boer heads down, revived the infantry assault up the hill. If one looks at the position today, the charge up that steep hill under concentrated rifle fire, bad enough under any circumstances, would have been suicidal without artillery support. In a pure blood and guts, sheer dogged determination hand-to-hand scrap which cost the lives of 10 officers (including the General and Colonels Sherston and Gunning) and 31 non-commissioned officers and men, with 185 officers and men wounded, the hill was carried. Some of the British casualties were caused by their own artillery, whose spotters were unable to distinguish between friend and foe once the top of the hill had been taken.

The 18th Hussars, around the back of the hill, missed a golden opportunity to stampede the Boer horses, tethered in a long line at Thornley farm. Instead, Colonel Moller detached Major Knox to the south, where he disappeared into the mist. When the retreating Boers finally came off the hill, they swept a now very under strength detachment of Hussars before them, resulting in Moller and eight other officers and 211 men being listed as missing or captured as the hunter became the hunted.

The artillery also failed to follow up the retreat from their new positions on Smith's Nek. Colonel Pickwoad, although he had a splendid view, was somewhat miffed at being blamed for firing on British soldiers on top of the hill, and declined to fire on the retreating Boers with the excuse that he was unsure as to whether they were friend or foe. ❏

***That's what the history books say ...***
***but what was it REALLY like on the ground?***

## Lieutenant M.S.W. du Toit: *Transvaal Staatsartillerie*

Michael Sievert Wiid (Mike) Du Toit was employed by the Transvaal Surveyor General's Department. Engaged in the fighting during the Jameson raid, he joined the Staatsartillerie in 1897 and immediately sent in command of an expedition to Swaziland. His grandson, Pierre, now living in Johannesburg, gave the following information. *"On 20 October, exactly 100 years ago, my grandfather, Lt.Mike Du Toit of the Transvaal State Artillery, was wounded during the first battle of the war at Dundee in Natal. I have a photograph taken some years later showing him standing at the spot where he was wounded. I visited the site some years ago and due to the 'skull-like' rock in the background was able to identify the exact position. The summit was open veldt without much cover but is today thickly covered with thorn bushes and trees. The Boer plan was to attack Dundee from three sides simultaneously at dawn on 20 October. Due to poor weather, the normal lack of discipline and the bickering of the Boer commanders only General Lukas Meyer, with a force of about 2 500, was in position on Talana and Lennox hills and ready to attack at the prescribed hour.*

*On Talana they hauled four guns to the summit but only positioned three before dawn. Two Krupp 75mm under Maj.Wolmarans and Capt.Pretorius, and a Creusot 75mm under Mike. The British camp was in plain sight below them and the first few rounds caused consternation. General Penn Symons remarked that it was "damned impudence to start shelling before breakfast!" The battle was fierce and bloody with the British succeeding in driving the Boers off Talana when the other commandos failed to attack. Mike was wounded in the leg by a piece of shrapnel and carried 'piggy-back' down the back of the hill by his friend F.L.Rothman where he was transferred to an ambulance and on to a farmhouse where the Boers had established a hospital (now Thornley Farm).*

*After the British evacuated Dundee, Mike was carried in a litter to the Scandinavian Mission church, which had been converted into a hospital where doctors from both sides were tending to the wounded. Amputation was considered but deferred, and he was transferred to a hospital train at Elandslaagte station, After the arrival of his wife, Kate, and his sister, a nurse, Dr. Harvey of Heidelberg organised a van to the Volkshospitaal in Pretoria, where the shrapnel was removed with the aid of Roentgen (x-ray) equipment. After the British entered Pretoria he was made a payroll prisoner and transferred to the Cape."*

In 1909 he became Commissioner of Police for the Orange River Colony. He commanded an internment camp at Fort Napier in 1914. Promoted as Departmental Commissioner for the eastern Cape in 1915 and in 1920 for the Transvaal, he retired in 1928 and became a Member of Parliament for Pretoria West. He died on 15 May 1938 at Sea Point, in the Cape. ❑

## Dr G. O. Moorhead

Born in Rawalpindi, India, in 1866, in spite of his background, Moorhead was working as a Doctor for the Boer forces and found himself at what is now Thornley Farm on the eastern side of Talana.

*"The farmhouse, a solid building surrounded with stone walls and stone offices, which had belonged to a farmer named Smith, presented an extraordinary appearance. The yard was full of horses standing patiently with their bridles hanging down and saddles glistening in the rain - Boers in every possible state of mind were crowded about - some stood talking; some rushed about, others sat quietly against the walls eating tinned food; some had their bandoliers and rifles, while others had neither and were hastily pinning on bits of red rag to their arms or begging us for Red Cross badges; wounded men were being helped in by their friends, carried down in blankets or overcoats; Boers were constantly arriving from the hill above, on which the rifles still cracked out. Shrapnel whizzed noisily overhead now and then. All looked angry and frightened.*

*I stepped into the house. Right opposite me, crumpled up in the passage, lay the body of Field Cornet Joubert of the Middleburgers, a little round hole in the centre of his four-coloured hatband. A room to the left was full of sopping wet and wounded Boers lying about in every attitude. In a room to the right the little German Artillery Doctor welcomed us warmly ... on a large bed lay Lt. du Toit with whom I had ridden a couple of days previously - his leg shattered by shrapnel. Beside lay an Artillery private shot through both lungs - the floor was covered with wounded - pools of water and blood lay everywhere.*

*I had noticed a young British officer with a bandaged hand, Lt. Weldon of the 1st Leicestershires ... presently I saw him strolling nonchalantly away around the hill. A stout red-faced Commandant shouted orders to the burghers to bring him back. "Leave your weapons here, he is unarmed" he added further, a kindly trait at such a moment. Hungry and tired, I pointed out a fowl running about the farmyard to my Hottentot driver, Klaas, suggesting its capture for dinner. Spattered with mud from a shell which had burst near him while minding the mules, he eyed me with disgust, rebuking me with "Sir, this is not a time to think of eating."*

*The confusion inside the hospital all this time was indescribable. Some 30 Boers whose horses had been lost, shot or stolen and who could therefore not get away, had hastily donned red crosses - they had found some drink in the house and were beyond all control, looting and destroying as soon as one's back was turned.*

*The next thing I remember was a clear English voice asking who was in charge of this hospital? I went out and found a flushed and panting subaltern of the Dublin Fusiliers outside, his helmet pushed back, a sword in one hand and a revolver in the other - at his back half a company of grimy panting soldiers with fixed bayonets. The British had taken possession - the hill was theirs! Some British wounded now came in, but room was found with the greatest difficulty, for there were over 80 people lying in one small house. I had by now annexed the key to the pantry, which still held a few stores, from the Artillery Corporal who had it - a veteran looter of many campaigns, and appointed orderlies and organised search parties for the wounded who were still lying out in the rain among the rocks. Late in the evening Lt. Crum of the K.R.R. and a mounted man were brought in badly wounded and attended to, having to lie on the ground in an outside store room. One of the officers, Lt. Cape of the 18th Hussars, had had rather a narrow escape. He had been brought in the day before, shot right through his neck from side to side. Next morning, rather to my astonishment, he was up and walking impatiently outside waiting for the Dundee ambulances, a slight stiffness of his neck being the only sign he showed of his wound.*

9

*It is interesting to know that the British artillery fired 1 237 rounds of shell and the troops 82 000 rounds of ball cartridge; it took therefore at this battle about 8½ pounds of shrapnel and over 500 Lee-Metford bullets to account for every Transvaaler. Lt. Du Toit told me that he and an artillery man named Schultz had alone worked a Krupp and a Pom Pom until they were both struck down at the same time. The British troops had attacked the hill in their best go-ahead manner and had been shot in droves, but their shell fire had been too much for Boer flesh and blood to stand (and) all discipline vanished. Several of the prominent citizens of Middelburg had sat under a stone wall near the hospital all morning smoking peacefully, alleging that they could get no orders - hundreds of others had done the same - in fact it was thought that no more than 500 men were firing during the day. The others had got behind the rocks and remained there.*

10

*A young Utrecht boy named Vermaak specially attracted my notice. Shot through the right arm, he paid no attention to his wound but sat patiently on a couch holding his grey haired father in his arms. The old man was mortally wounded in the back by shrapnel and could not lie down - out of a little body of five friends who had gone together into battle the boy and his father were the only two left alive, he told me with tears in his eyes. The old man died the next morning."* ❑

## Lieutenant H. A. Cape: *18th Hussars*

Lieutenant Cape was in command of the machine gun detachment of the 18th Hussars, who were sent around the rear of Talana to block the Boer escape.

He found an "*excellent position from which I could have raked the Boer's lead horses. Col. Moller gave the order that I was not to fire! The debacle that followed when he, with part of one Squadron and the M.I. abandoned the advanced position they held and went off into the 'Blue', in spite of his having been told by his Adjutant and others that he was going in the wrong direction, is just a lamentable example of ineptitude on the part of a man who should never have been given command of the Regiment and by his mad act brought disaster on a body of men who were second to none.*"

He subsequently became involved in a skirmish and was wounded and captured. "*I turned round and cheered on the gun and emptied my revolver at the fast approaching Boers. Waterson, one of the gun team, tells me I knocked one man over and I heard Trumpeter Salmon sing out, "Well done, Mr. Cape". I was immediately knocked out of my saddle with a bullet through my neck which just escaped my spine and came out in*

*front. I saw a Boer pointing a rifle at me but another came up and told him not to shoot. They then sent us back to the Boer hospital which had been established at the base of Talana Hill.*

*As for the Artillery, when the Boers were driven off the hill, the guns quite rightly advanced to their second position on the (nek) between Talana and Lennox Hills. When they arrived, before them were masses and masses of Boers trekking away back in disorder within close range. Here was a target! But do you think it was taken advantage of? No, not a bit. The Officer in command gave the order not to fire. At the enquiry later he produced lots of reasons why he did not do his duty, all totally irrelevant and merely confirmed the opinion held by anyone who ever met him that he too should never have been in command of anything.*

*General Symons ordered a frontal attack (on the hill) over perfectly open ground and the hill itself had to be negotiated almost on hands and knees to gain the summit, at tremendous loss. Was the frontal attack justified? In my opinion it certainly was launched much too soon and, had it been delayed somewhat, a flank attack could have been substituted for a frontal, thereby reducing the enormous number of casualties. During the attack, General Symons took almost all his Staff right up to the front line with him with the result that he was mortally wounded and all the remainder of his Staff were either killed or wounded. This is a fatal mistake in every way. A general's place, however brave he may be, is behind to direct operations. The day concluded with something like chaos in the units for want of orders. As regards the camp at Dundee this transgressed every single axiom laid down for a camp site. It was commanded on almost every side by high hills well within Boer gun range and they were unoccupied by us.*

*The only redeeming feature of the whole action was the superb gallantry of the Junior Officers and rank and file of the various units. As always the British soldier rose to the occasion and, in spite of the failure of those in high command, showed himself to be the hero he invariably proves himself in war."* ❑

1. "Sgt." Craig Appleton of the "Die Hards" and his squad of "Royal Irish Fusiliers".
2. "Officer" with revolver.
3. "Utrecht Boer Commando".
4. "Reg. Sgt. Maj." Pat Rundgren and "Sgt." Ross Dott.
5. "Kings Royal Rifles" with "British camp" in background.
6. Boers with "General Lukas Meyer" (Dirk Froneman) on the left.
7. "Officers" and "Sergeants" group.
8. Rifle inspection. "Royal Irish Fusiliers".
9. Firing line. "Kings Royal Rifles".
10. Skirmish line. "Royal Irish Fusiliers".

# Elandslaagte, today!

Elandslaagte today is a far cry from the bustling, raucous frontier-mining town that it was at the turn of the century. Far to the north the hazy slopes of the Biggarsberg mountains rise up to form a spectacular backdrop for what is now a lonely, depressing scene.

The old Victorian style station buildings have been demolished, but if one stands on the platform where they used to be and looks along the railway line in the direction of Dundee to the east, a hundred yards or so away one can pin-point where the Traveler's Rest Hotel used to stand by the few lonely trees forlornly marking the spot. It was here that Jim Price loved to waltz, his wife Dolly mothered the youngsters and itinerants and the piano tinkled out many a tune to the accompaniment of raucous singing in a dozen languages and dialects.

To the west there is the Farmer's Hall, sale pens and the Post Office. Behind them, towards the railway crossing in the direction of Ladysmith, you will discern a square of trees standing vigil over the mortal remains of 163 officers and men from all branches of the British military (including a few sailors) who died of disease and neglect at Modderspruit, Wessels Nek, Washbank and Colling's Pass during the Anglo Boer War. This is the site of the old Naval Field Hospital.

Turn right around and look south-east, and one can make out a horseshoe shaped ridge, about two miles away, rising 100 feet above the plain. The northern end of the ridge drops sharply to where the current district road disappears over a low nek, and then rises once more as a much lower ridge. Behind this lower ridge, an isolated kopje, on which stands a squat monument to those Hollanders who were torn to pieces by British shrapnel and bullets, or spitted on the lances of the British cavalry some 100 years ago, makes a distinct bump.

Concealed in the trees on the northern crest of the horseshoe ridge are another two monuments; one to the men of the Imperial Light Horse who died storming the main Boer position there, and another to their commanding officer, Col. John James Scott Chisholme.

Drive around over the railway crossing, past the Naval Cemetery, and turn left, following the battlefield signs. This dirt road will take you over the nek with the low ridge and kopje on the left, and the higher ridge on the right. Some 100 yards further on, on the right, one will see the main battlefield cemetery where the names of 13 Imperial Light Horsemen, 26 Gordon Highlanders and 14 troops of the Manchester Regiment who died in the battle are recorded on the monuments.

It is very difficult to imagine that Elandslaagte was once a thriving community at the turn of the century, some say even bigger than Ladysmith at that time. Five shafts of the Elandslaagte Coal Company stretched away westwards from the station towards Jonono's Kop, with compounds for both black and Indian mine employees. The Traveler's Rest Hotel ran by Jim and Dolly Price and the scene of many a riotous evening, McKillican's wood and iron emporium, the schoolhouse, the Mine Manager's imposing red brick residence and mine village and two large bluestone thatched rondavels which housed the Natal Mounted Police post completed the picture. The village was the focal point for teamsters by the score heading north for the Reef and east towards Delagoa Bay. Wagons carrying timber from Zululand and destined for the diamond mines at Kimberley trundled unceasingly over the Hime Bridge, and there was a constant hustle and bustle in this frontier boomtown.

British Lancer: Jason Askew.

*Pat Rundgren*

# The Battle of Elandslaagte 21 October 1899

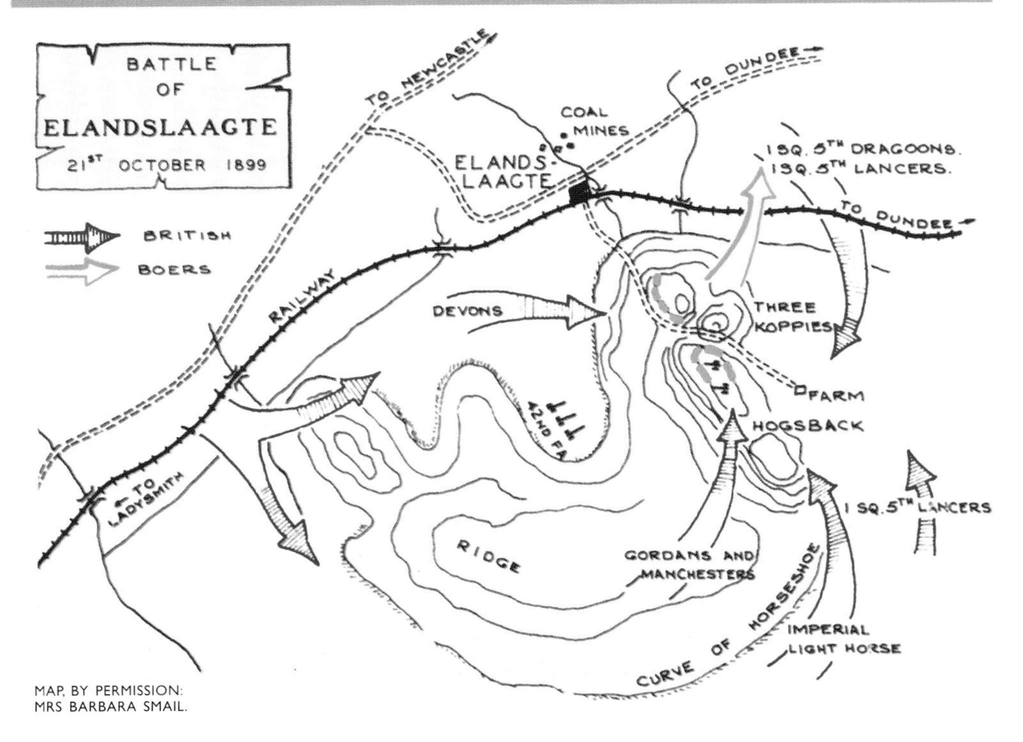


MAP, BY PERMISSION:
MRS BARBARA SMAIL.

This, then, was the unlikely scene of the second pitched battle of the second Anglo Boer War, its claim to fame being the bone crunching charge of the 5th Lancers and 5th Dragoons against the surviving Boers who quit the field of battle when they saw their resistance was hopeless.

Elandslaagte was, in the opinion of the experts, a textbook battle, where everyone did as expected, even the enemy (whoever's side you happened to be on!). It was even studied by the Imperial German Army as an excellent example of how a set piece battle should be conducted.

After the 2nd Anglo-Boer War was declared, the main body of Transvaal Boers under Comm. General Piet Joubert with some 8 000 men of the Pretoria, Kurgersdorp, Boksburg, Middelburg, Heidelberg, Standerton, Carolina and Bethal Commandos, left their base at Sandspruit near Lang's Nek on 12 October 1899 to commence their invasion of Natal.

The force split into two, with General Erasmus and General Lukas Meyer sweeping off eastwards with the objective of capturing the rich coal-mining town of Dundee, and the western one under *'Vecht Generaal'* Kock to hold a defensive line on Mkhupe Pass over the Biggarsberg between Newcastle and Ladysmith in case the British counter attacked.

Joubert succeeded in dislodging the British garrison at Dundee 3 days after the Battle of Talana on 20 October, where General Penn Symons (pictured) was mortally wounded. Col. Yule, who

Baron H. von Zeppelin, who died of wounds received at Elandslaagte, was a relation of the German airship designer. He was re-buried in the Kloof cemetery, Heidelburg.

**Heidelbergers of the Boer War**, *Ian Uys*, 1981 Ian S. Uys

succeeded in command, out-gunned by a Boer 155 mm *'Long Tom'* cannon on the surrounding hilltop of Mpati Mountain, carried out a strategic withdrawal to rejoin the main body of the British army at Ladysmith. Kock, on the western side, sent forward strong reconnaissance parties under Veld Kornets Pienaar (of the Fordsburg Commando) and Potgieter. These two, keen as mustard to get to grips with the *'Rooineks'* or *'red necks'* as the British were called (because of their tendency to succumb to sunburn) exceeded their orders to proceed only as far as the Sundays River and advanced instead up to Elandslaagte station.

***19 October 1899***

The local settlers were swept like flotsam before the advancing Boer wave. Frank Neville's farm *'Black Cray'* in the Nkunzi Valley was taken over by Schiel and his German Corps on 18 October. James Grey, his family and his parents-in-law (Peter Smith, one of the founders of Dundee) just managed to get away from his farm *'Gartmore'* and caught the last train to Ladysmith by the skin of their collective teeth. J.C. Henderson, of the farm *'Balbrogie'*, escaped with his 3 best horses just ahead of Col. Schiel's German contingent, leaving his farm manager, an itinerant named Bevan, behind. Bevan was forced to provide Schiel with an ox and a bag of potatoes for lunch, which to Henderson's fury they left uneaten as they hurried off towards Elandslaagte station after word was received that Pienaar and Potgieter had captured it.

Just after noon, David Harris, the General Manager of the Elandslaagte Colliery, was having dinner in his house with Simpson Mitchell-Innes of the farm *'Blanerne'* on the Sundays River, who was also one of the Directors of the Colliery. They saw a party of horsemen approaching the house, one of whom asked Harris if he was an Englishman? Harris replied in the affirmative, whereupon they moved away towards the station, followed shortly afterwards by about 150 more men.

The acting stationmaster, G.P. Atkinson, and D. Christie his clerk, were busy checking the goods wagons lying in the siding. One contained rice for the Indian workers at the mine; the other a load of expensive furniture from Maples of London, purchased by Harris as a gift for his new wife.

Standing panting and puffing at the platform was a train that had just arrived from Ladysmith on its way to Glencoe with a load of provisions for the Dundee garrison. Atkinson had also noticed the Boers approaching and had warned Ladysmith by wire. The train guard D.H. Mellors, frantically signaled the driver, H.W. Cutbush, who put on steam and chuffed out of the station with the Boers in hot

**These guns fired the first shots of the war for the British.**

Battle of Elandslaagte by young, South African artist, Jason Askew.

pursuit. The guards on the train, comprising an officer and 9 men of the 18th Hussars, opened fire on the Boers, shooting one in the calf and killing a horse. The Boers returned to the station, whereupon Pienaar ranted and raved at Atkinson, threatened to shoot him, and confiscated his rifle (a receipt was issued the next morning by Pienaar, who came back to apologise, explaining that he had been upset). However, luck was with the Boers as no sooner had Cutbush escaped when a following train steamed in and was promptly captured!

The Boers arrested all the officials, including two war correspondents who had been on the train, tore down the telegraph wires, commandeered some labourers from the mine to tear up the railway tracks, and then settled down to the serious business of looting the contents of the wagons! One of them contained dozens of cases of whiskey, and although orders were given that this was not to be taken, there were soon drunken Boers stumbling around the platform making a nuisance of themselves. Colonel Schiel, arriving with reinforcements for Pienaar, managed to snaffle a case which came in very handy while they were on picket duty in the drizzle that evening, covering the possibility of a British advance up the road from Ladysmith.

Harris, in the meantime, had managed to hide away most of his explosives, and had sent the mine blacksmith underground so that he would not be available to shoe any of the Boer horses. That evening, a smoking concert was held at the local hotel, the *'Travelers Rest'*, with Veld Kornet Pienaar presiding. Apparently the Boers, their prisoners and the locals had a convivial evening. In the room were 12 different nationalities, and according to Atkinson: *"The concert was opened by a comic song, rendered by a refugee from Newcastle, whose musical abilities proved of great service. He and I then rendered the old duet "All's Well", being encored, responded with the "Army and Navy"duet. A Transvaal burgher sang an Irish song as only an Irishmen can. He told us afterwards that this was his eighth campaign, but he did not know that it was his last. Next day he was dead. A German Sergeant then sat down to the piano."*

*"Sir Joseph Barnby's glee "Sweet and Low" was sung to his accompaniment ... The Boer Sergeant then played a series of National Anthems, including both "God save the Queen" and the Transvaal Volkslied. They were all played with great taste, and I certainly never expected to hear our National Anthem played or sung again under such apparently impossible conditions."*

*"While we English prisoners sang our National Anthem the Dutch present joined in..."*

At eleven o'clock Pienaar went on outpost duty. He was destined to be killed two days later.

## 20 October 1899

Daybreak found General Kock, having decided to come forward rather than order Pienaar back to Mkhupe, and the remainder of his men and 2 guns, riding in. When Schiel returned from his outpost duty, he found absolute chaos at the station. Cases of food lay open all over the place, and fearing a drunken orgy from the amount of liquor still available amongst the wreckage of the broken crates, he ordered Capt.de Witt-Hamer of the Hollander Corps to supervise a party whose task was to smash the Whiskey bottles and spill the contents on the ground.

Word of this wholesale waste of good liquor soon got around, with the Indian employees from the mine arriving in a rush to drink the dregs from the smashed bottles. Some desperate souls even knelt down on their hands and knees and slurped from the puddles and licked at the mud.

However, while some enterprising burghers also were managing to spirit away some for their own consumption later, Schiel proceeded to have a stormy interview with Kock concerning the poor defensive position that Kock had chosen for his men on the horseshoe ridge. Schiel was of the opinion, and quite rightly, that it could be outflanked at both ends, but Kock would not listen.

Meanwhile, Harris and all of the mine officials were arrested, and taken to the hotel where they were subjected to a court martial by Judge Kock (General Kock's son) and Commandant de Meilleon. While dealing with the trickier nuances of the law, the Judge took the opportunity to enjoy a roast rib of mutton, while Pienaar performed the role of Prosecutor, waving a chop in one hand and a hunk of bread in the other! All in all, the proceedings were held in a friendly atmosphere and the accused were afterwards released on parole. Harris obtained permission to remove 100 bags of rice from the station to feed his *Coolies*. He was unsuccessful, however, in persuading his black staff to go back to work.

Mr Lewis, a 75 year old veteran of *The Battle of Elandslaagte*, returns after 50 years. (Circa 1950)

### Disgrace

The Boers were the first side to suffer the disgrace of losing their guns to the enemy, when two 75 mm guns were overrun at Elandslaagte on 21 October 1899. However, the gunners had served them to the last and even General Kock (who led the invasion of Natal) was fatally wounded defending the guns. (Mcfadden, 27).

## Lost opportunity

Just before Ladysmith was besieged, the British attacked the Boers at Nicholson's Nek. They were routed and about 10 000 soldiers fled towards Ladysmith. The Boers who had superior numbers were mounted.

While General Joubert (see illustration) hesitated, General Christiaan de Wet muttered to him "*Los jou ruiters; los jou ruiters!*" (Release your horsemen!) Joubert held back and quoted a Dutch saying, "When God holds out a finger, don't take the whole hand!"

If he had let his commandos pursue the fleeing soldiers, Ladysmith would most likely have fallen that day, changing the course of the war. (Reitz, 43 /44).

*Drawing: Mounted Boer by Jason Askew.*

While all this was going on, Major Erasmus of the Staats Artillerie (Boer Artillery) had been busy setting up his canons on the rock-strewn hump of the northern end of the horseshoe ridge to the east of the station. The Boer laager was established in the space between the sharp kopje (where the Hollander monument now stands), the low lying ridge to the west of it and the "hump." Lieutenant General Sir George Stewart White V.C. (Officer Commanding, Natal Field Force) was not lying idle at Ladysmith, however. According to his official despatch: *"... on October 20th, I had pushed a Cavalry reconnaissance to Elandslaagte, and had obtained definite information that a Boer force was in position there, but apparently in no considerable strength."*

Meanwhile, Colonel Schiel had sent men, under Count Zeppelin to patrol Woodcote farm overlooking the Modderspruit road from Ladysmith. Zeppelin soon spotted the British force, and shadowed it, but the force then turned around and retired to Ladysmith. Apart from this rather timid British reconnaissance, nothing further transpired that day.

During the day the Boers discovered the mine's magazine and took some 200 pounds of dynamite, as well as 3 000 pounds of ammunition belonging to the Rifle Association. They also ransacked the mine offices, breaking open three safes which Harris had taken the precaution of emptying beforehand.

### 21 October 1899

Much has been made of General White's strategic acumen in sending out a force on 21 October to open the way for General Yule's column retreating from Dundee and to hold off the enemy driving in on the flank from the west. Although the battle did indeed have this effect, it was not known at 4 a.m. on 21 October, when the column left Ladysmith, that Yule was even contemplating retreat, having only just won the Battle of Talana on the previous day. The orders issued by White were merely to *"... clear the neighbourhood of Elandslaagte of the enemy, and to cover the construction of the railway and telegraph lines."* And to re-open direct communication with Dundee.

This force was under the overall command of Major General John Denton Pinkstone French: *"... a short powerful man with heavy jowls, a bushy moustache and a bull neck ... aged 47, son of an Irish sailor, he himself started in the Navy at the age of 14 before joining the Hussars, fought in the Sudan campaign of 1894-1895 ... he was rumoured to have run off with his Colonel's wife, consistent with his reputation as a dashing cavalryman. With him as Chief of Staff was a Major Douglas Haig."*

This force comprised of:
5 squadrons of the Imperial Light Horse under Lieutenant-Colonel John 'Jabber' Scott Chisholme, late of the 5th (Irish) Lancers (destined to be killed in the battle);
The Natal Volunteer Field Battery under Major D.W.G. Taylor.

At 0600 hr, four companies of the Manchester Regiment, under Lt.-Col. Curran, Railway and Telegraph construction companies and ancillary troops set out for Elandslaagte by armoured train and open trucks for the remainder of the men. Repairs had to be effected to the line at Modderspruit, where they arrived at about 0830 hr.

While the Manchesters were still *en route*, the I.L.H. and Volunteer Battery had reached a vantage point overlooking the railway station at Elandslaagte, where they found the Boers occupying it and every sign of them having captured the supply train on its way to Glencoe. French took his small force onto the ridge south of the Indian compound, whereupon the Natal Field Battery commenced to bombard the station. Maj.Sampson led a squadron of I.L.H. around to the north as a protective screen.

The fire from the Natal Field Battery caused no little consternation, especially on the part of Mr Walter Herald, a Manchester chemist who had been commandeered as an ambulance assistant by the Boers. He was dressing one of three Boer ambulance wagons, which were drawn up alongside each other near the railway goods shed. They were clearly marked with Red Cross flags, but as there was no breeze they could no be seen at any distance.

According to Herald: *"... the first shot ... went through the shed. The next shot struck one of our mules, and took half its head away. The third shell bust close by, and part of it went band through the wagon in which I was dressing, and was within a foot of finishing my little career. A few more shots came near us, when the Boers began to fire from the kopjes, revealing their position, so the battery turned their fire on them. After half an hour's firing, which the Boers returned with interest, the British retired over the hillside..."*

One of the "few more shots" from the battery also put the cap on what must have been, for Harris, a rather trying couple of days. This shot hit the truck in which

Elandslaagte: Charge of "C" Squadron, 5th Lancers. On the right centre is Bugler Sherlock, aged 14, who shot three Boers with his revolver. Picture, with compliments: Morley's Antiques, Cape Town.

reposed his brand new furniture, blowing it to smithereens! The Boer artillery on the ridge were not slow to respond, getting the range immediately.

A Boer shell disabled one of the N.F.A.'s ammunition wagons, and French saw that his guns were hopelessly outranged and started to fall back to Modderspruit, telegraphing for reinforcements as he got there. The Boer guns now turned their attention on the detraining infantry, but although their range estimation was excellent, many of the shells burst only after striking the ground.

In the confusion at the station, Harris, Mitchell-Innes and other white mine employees took their chances and made off across the fields towards the British lines. Atkinson and his staff climbed out of the ticket office window, where they had been held under house arrest, and did the same. Ironically, he also brought his guards along as prisoners! they were able to give French valuable information concerning the Boer dispositions.

In response to French's request for reinforcements, the following was rushed out by road:

5th Lancers under Captain Parker and Captain Oakes;
5th Dragoon Guards under Captain Derbyshire: the combined body of Lancers and Dragoons being under the command of Major St. John Gore;
Squadrons of the Natal Mounted Rifles;
Batteries of the Royal Field Artillery under Major Blewitt.

The following was rushed out by train:

1st Battalion Devonshire Regiment under by Major C.W. Park;
2nd Battalion Gordon Highlanders under Lt.-Col. William Dick-Cunyngham V.C. and Major H.W.D. Denne, who was killed in the battle);
Natal Volunteer Ambulance Corps.

On the way, the cavalry were joined by General White, with his escort of Natal Mounted Rifles. He did not, however assume command but left the conduct of the operation in French's hands. As something of an aside here, it is interesting to note that during the battle, two Natal Carbineer despatch riders, Trumpeter H.A. Craig and Cpl. J. Watson, broke through from Dundee with a message from Col. Yule to General White. Apart from having what must have been a very interesting ride, they created a little bit of history by becoming the only soldiers to qualify for both the *'Talana'* and *'Elandslaagte'* bars to their Queen's South Africa Medals by fighting at both battles.

With 18 guns, the British force finally numbered some 1 630 infantry, 1 314 cavalry and 552 gunners. Against them were about 1 000 men, including the Johannesburg Commando, under Commandant Ben Viljoen and Veld Kornets Pienaar and Potgieter. In addition to this was a troop of Z.A.R.P.'s, a Free State commando from Vrede and some 300 German and Dutch volunteers (commanded respectively by Col. A.F. Schiel – later wounded and captured – and Veldkornet P.H. Joubert – killed), with 2 x 75mm Field Guns under Major Erasmus.

Colonel Hamilton, who was later made the scapegoat for the failure of the *Gallipoli* campaign in the *First World War*, had something to prove. He had been a subaltern in the 92nd Highlanders (later the Gordon Highlanders) at the famous battle of Majuba (27 February 1881), when a Boer bullet had shattered his left wrist and he and his men were amongst those who were routed by an inferior force of Boers. He addressed the troops, explaining to them how he intended the attack to develop with the Devons going across open country for the low ridge to the north, while the rest of the infantry would work their way along the ridge from the south. He expressed his confidence that the Boers would be pushed off the hills before sunset and that the newsboys in the streets of London would be calling out the glad tidings of victory the next morning. The men cheered him, waving their hats in a frenzy of excitement and crying *"We'll do it, sir, we'll do it!"*

The attack commenced in mid-afternoon, at about 1630 hr. As the infantry appeared, the 21st Battery RFA came into action in the open on the left of the Manchesters. The 42nd Battery then coming up, the Boer guns ceased firing. The batteries were, however, enfiladed by rifle fire coming from a kopje to the right of their position.

The 21st turned their fire onto this kopje and the Boers fled, after having wounded five of the Gunners, and killing or wounding nine horses and smashing a gun wheel.

The Devons, advancing in open order across an open plain, were making for the low ridge in front of the kopje where the Hollander monument now stands, to the north of the main ridge. They halted about 800 yards out and took cover behind the termite heaps and wherever else they could, lying under heavy fire for about half an hour while they waited for the flank attack to develop.

Two newspaper correspondents, Melton Prior and Bennett Burleigh, were with the Devons. The latter began to wonder why they in particular were attracting heavy Boer rifle fire, and on looking at his companion noticed that Prior was wearing a beautifully *blanco'ed solar topee* which shone like a searchlight for all the Boer marksmen to see. Burleigh somewhat acidly asked Prior to remove the offending item whereupon life suddenly became much more pleasant with the Boer's attention being distracted elsewhere! As the infantry attack began, Colonel Scott Chisholm of the I.L.H. refused to maintain a passive role as a spectator and approached General French. French asked him *"What do you want to do?"* Chisholm replied *"I want to take that hill!"* French answered *"Very well, take it!"*

The Colonel then proceeded to do just that, his position being marked by his orderly carrying a red pennant. Col. Hamilton remarked that it was a splendid sight to see 'Jabber' Chisholme's *"little red rag going on and on."* The I.L.H. joined the Manchesters and Gordons on the ridge that they had cleared that morning, doubling out on their right. 'D' squadron of the Lancers hung back, awaiting an opportunity for further action which never came.

Toward 1700 hr the leading companies of the Gordons reached the shelter of a rocky ridge on the southern end of the horseshoe. Along its crest ran a barbed wire fence, and the men began to fall as desperate attempts were made to tear holes in the wire, Captain Haldane being one of the casualties. Lord George Murray had a pair of 'nippers' and Private Fraser tore at the wire with his bare hands until he had made a gap big enough to allow the men through. Major Denne kept his men under cover while he too went forward and used his cutters. Pt. Bobbie Hall, of 'B' Company, had his head taken off by a shell. Bullets hummed all around, and the shattering roar of the Mausers forced the ammunition carriers, with 10 full boxes and 4 000 rounds in bags, to desist in their efforts to advance, at least until the attack was resumed.

Col. Dick-Cunnyngham was early in the rush through the fence. A hundred yards further on he fell with a bullet through the arm. Waving the Adjutant on, he called *"On men, I'm coming"* before fainting.

Colonel Schiel and a handful of Germans, after successfully disengaging at Jonono's Kop and having run the gauntlet of the British artillery fire, came up from a farm behind the Boer position and made an excellent attempt at a flank attack. However, the I.L.H. rose to the occasion and drove them off.

According to Schiel: *"... Count Zeppelin had fallen. A shell fragment had inflicted a mortal head wound, also several of my brave boys lay on the ground. The enemy line of marksmen were only some 100 paces distant. From their uniforms we noticed that they were Scots. From both sides a murderous fire ensued ... a new disaster struck! A detachment of the Imperial Light Horse appeared on the extreme right flank of the enemy and covered with heavy fire the shallow depression through which Weiss and Von Albedyll had to pass to reach us. Three times they pressed forward and three times they were beaten back. We fired as fast as we could. To miss was almost impossible because we could already recognise the faces of the Scots."*

*"... Next to me lay a certain Ludwig von Borries; I admired the calmness with which he fired. Every one of his shots found its mark. He jumped up to advance a few paces, then fell back right at my feet with a bullet through his forehead. Field Cornet Potgieter knelt two paces to my half right. He used a big rock for cover. I saw him lift his rifle to take aim then suddenly his head jerked to the right and he too sank to the ground. Left and right my poor boys lay on the ground but no help was in sight."*

Schiel was wounded in the thigh, and passed out. When he regained consciousness, the firing line had passed him by: *"... How dreadful was the sight that met my eyes. All around me my brave lads were lying on the ground; only a few had made it. Scottish soldiers and our own lay intermingled. To my left lay the dead body of Herr von Borries, a pace in front of me Field Cornet Potgieter on his back; his face pale with a black beard and his large, wide opened eyes presented a dreadful aspect. His eyes were turned towards me as if he were on the point of speaking to me. Three paces behind me sat Potgieter's youngest brother with a bullet through both shoulders. Close by, two paces to my right, lay an Afrikaner...(with) a bullet through the chest and a shattered arm. A little further on lay Schmidt, a former Prussian Artillery NCO, obviously dead."*

One of the Imperial Light Horsemen, busy collecting rifles, approached. He was Trooper Greathead. Schiel greeted him *"Hello! You are one of the I.L.H. Please give my regards to Woolls-Sampson and Karri Davies."* He then gave his rifle to Greathead as a memento of the occasion. Meanwhile, both Major Woolls-Sampson and Major Karri Davies of the I.L.H. were wounded on the field, the former shot in the thigh (his leg was roughly spliced with a rifle, whose muzzle was pointing towards his armpit. The following day, it was found to be still loaded!).

During the early part of the charge Major Woolls-Sampson had observed one of his men lying down and ordered him to advance. The man retorted that he was perfectly willing to do so, but that he was paralysed with fear. The Major went on, shortly afterwards to be overtaken by the same man, this time going like a rocket. Major Sampson asked what the matter was, whereupon the Trooper showed him where his moustache and part of his upper lip had been shot away. He yelled out *"Where are the bastards? Let me at them!"* and with that he rushed away and led the charge for the rest of the action.

Colonel Scott Chisholme stopped to bandage a wounded trooper, and was shot in the ankle. He waved his men on, crying out *"My boys are doing well! My boys are first!"* He was carried to cover by Troopers (Dick) Turpin (who survived the siege of Ladysmith only to be killed later while serving in Marshall's Horse) and C. Lamb, who was severely wounded, losing a leg. However, it was to no avail as he was shot shortly afterwards in the chest, and then in the head, and was killed.

The one feature that is mentioned in all accounts of the battle is a huge black and purple thundercloud which developed behind Elandslaagte as the battle progressed, providing an apocalyptic background to the flashes of the cannon and rifles. This storm burst at the moment of the final advance, providing cover for the British troops to batter their way up the slope and get to grips with their opponents.

During this time, it was obvious to the Gunners that shrapnel fire was required to subdue the Boers. As the infantry attack went in, they advanced further to a position some

2 100 yards away on the summit of a steep, stony kopje, where they continued to fire until after 1800 hr, keeping the Boer's heads down and making their guns unserviceable.

The men reached the hollow and began the upward climb up the final slope. The rain stopped.

Lt. Monro of the Gordon's was down, as was 2nd-Lt. Campbell. Lt.-Colonel Curran and Captain Melvill of the Manchesters dropped. Captain Paton was hit when descending the hill below the wire fence. More than half of the Gordon's officers were hit and, blown from the pace of the advance, the climb and the excitement, the men were losing dash. It was at this moment that the battle hung in the balance.

The officers were equal to the occasion, however. Hamilton, galloping across from the left, where he had been directing the Devon's assault, arrived with his staff by a gap in the fence, shouting for a bugler to sound the *'Charge'*. He was later recommended for a Victoria Cross for his conduct that day, but this was rejected on the grounds that he was too senior. Earlier on in his career, at Majuba, he had also been recommended but it had once again been rejected, this time because he was too young and too junior and would have a chance to earn one later on in his career!!

Drum Major Lawrence of the Gordons rushed out into the open and headed the line, playing the call. This action later earned him a D.C.M. (Distinguished Conduct Medal). Every bugle took it up, as did the pipers and, cheering and shouting, the whole irregular surge of men rolled forward over the final crest in a savage race to the Boer guns. Various claimants came forward as having been the first there.

Private Macrae of the Gordons was said to be the first man over the crest, while Drum Major Lawrence got his hand to one of the guns an instant before Captain Newbigging of the Manchesters did the same. Lt. and Adjutant H. Fisher of the Manchesters also claimed the honour!

A Distinguished Conduct Medal (D.C.M.) was awarded to Pipe Cpl. Kenneth McLeod. According to Creswicke: *"...during the charge this gallant Scot was twice struck, once in the arm and once in the side. He however continued to pipe and advance with the Gordons to their final rush. Presently came more bullets, smashing his drones, his chanter, and his windbag, whereupon the splendid fellow had to give in."*

According to General White's despatch: *"... at length the guns were reached and captured, and the end of the ridge was gained, from which the whole of the enemy's camp, full of tents, horses and men, were fully exposed to view at fixed sight range.*

*A white flag was shown from the centre of the camp, and Colonel Hamilton ordered the 'cease fire' to be sounded. The men obeyed, and some of them moved a short distance down the hill towards the camp. For a moment, there was a complete lull in the action, and then a shot was heard, which was followed by a deadly fire from the small conical kopje to the east of the camp, and by a determined charge up the hill by some 30 or 40 Boers, who effected a lodgement near the crest line within 15 or 20 paces of our men, who fell back for a moment before the fierce suddenness of this attack.*

*Only for a moment, however, for our fire was at once reopened and, reinforced by a timely detachment of the 1st Battalion Devonshire Regiment, they charged back, cheering, to the crest line, when the remnant of the Boer force fled in confusion towards the north."*

It was during this action that four men particularly distinguished themselves, resulting in the award of Victoria Crosses (V.C.). General Kock himself was wounded in this attack. It was said that he spent most of the night on the hillside after having been stripped of much of his clothing, his money, rings and watch, by British soldiers intent on loot. He died of the effects of exposure 10 days later.

## *THE CAVALRY CHARGE*

The cavalry squadrons, which, had remained in hiding by Elandslaagte station, saw their chance as the Boers streamed away across the plain to the north of the ridge. With the Lancers on the right and Dragoon Guards on the left, the cavalry extended and charged. As they topped the rise which had concealed them, they found the Boers crossing their front at a distance of a few hundred yards. The front line of lances went down, and the cavalry smashed into the Boers, slaughtering about 40 of them. The squadrons halted after their initial attack, wheeled about and charged back again, mopping up a great many more.

*"Three times they rode right through the Boers, hacking, cutting, slashing."*

Lance Corporal Kelly of the Lancers, seeing two Boers riding away on one horse, rammed his lance through the two, killing both with one thrust, and whirled them in the air. As the Lancers charge in, Trumpeter Shurlock, aged 14, shot three Boers with his revolver. As a bugler, he did not carry a lance, and thus was issued with a revolver to protect himself.

An American boy of 18, fighting with the Boers, tells a different tale: *"... as the Lancers charged some of our men fled; a few hid. Our men – about 70 of them - who could not escape threw down their guns and cried out 'Surrendered'. From where I lay I could see those brave soldiers of the Queen ... with shouts of glee thrust their lances through men on their knees. One woman, the wife of a burgher, was with her husband at the time. (He) threw down his gun, and taking her hand shouted "We surrender." A bold, brave Lancer shouted "Stick those pigs!" and thrust first the man and then the woman ... the man who killed her took the ring off her finger as booty. She lies there today, and when the man and woman were killed three lives were given."*

Between 60 and 250 Boers were killed, including General Kock, Lt. Dr. H.J. Coster (the former State Attorney), Lt. C.G. De Jonge and Van Leggelo (a former State Prosecutor)and about 200 men were taken prisoners.

## *AFTERMATH*

The scene of the battlefield once all the action had ceased was horrible. The groans of the badly wounded, together with the cries for help from those of their comrades who were less seriously injured, created a pandemonium and babble which had to be heard to be believed. Lieutenant J.B. Neale of the Natal Volunteer Ambulance Corps and his corpsmen were stumbling around in the inky blackness, soaked through by the rain. Their lanterns glinting in the dark created an eerie effect as they searched out the living from the dead. Walking wounded made their way towards the station as best they could, often falling down the rocky hillsides.

Captain Newbigging of the Manchesters, shot in the left shoulder: *"... lay where I fell for about three-quarters of an hour, when a doctor came and put a field dressing on my wound, gave me some brandy, put my helmet under my head as a pillow, covered me up with a Boer blanket which he had taken from a dead man, and then went to look after some other poor beggar. In addition to the agony which my wound gave me, I had two sharp stones running into my back. I was soaked to the skin, and bitterly cold, and I had an awful thirst. The torrents of rain never stopped. On one side of me was a Gordon Highlander in raving delirium, and on the other side a Boer who had his leg shattered by a shell and who gave vent to the most heart-rending cries and groans. I lay out in the rain the whole of the night...my wound was dressed just seventeen hours after I was hit."*

One of the last of the wounded found was Trooper J. Hills-Jones I.L.H. (whose father was a Major General and a V.C. winner). He was found, shot through the throat and bleeding profusely, but with his monocle firmly in place. He croaked that he preferred drowning in his own blood to doing damned fatigues.

One of the ambulance bearers described a particularly tragic incident:

*"I came across an old, white-bearded Boer. He was lying behind a rock supporting himself on his elbows.*

*When I got near I saw that he was too far-gone to raise his rifle. He was gasping hard for breath, and I saw he was not long for this world. He motioned to me that he wanted to speak, and I bent over him. He asked me to go and find his son – a boy of thirteen who had been fighting by his side when he fell.*

*Well, I did as asked me, and under a heap of wounded I found the poor lad, stone dead, and I carried him back to his father...I had to turn away when the old Boer saw his dead lad. He hugged the body to him and moaned over it, and carried on in a way that fetched a big lump to my throat. Until that moment I never thought how horrible war is. I never wanted to see another shot fired. And when I looked round again the old Boer was dead, clasping the cold hand of his dead boy."*

According to General White's despatch, *"... the Boer losses were heavy, being estimated at over 100 killed, 108 wounded and 188 prisoners. Our own losses were also considerable, consisting of 4 officers and 37 men killed, 31 officers and 175 men wounded and 10 men missing. The Imperial Light Horse and the 2nd Battalion Gordon Highlanders, who encountered the severest resistance during the attack, suffered the most severely."*

The wounded Boers were robbed of many personal possessions. One prisoner jumped into a pool of water to escape two Lancers who wanted to finish him off. There was even talk that one prisoner's finger was cut off to remove a ring. Scores of riderless horses were caught and sold. Some horses, with saddle and bridle, fetched as low as five shillings. One Highlander sold his prize for a cigarette.

Ironically, though, although the action had the effect of allowing Yule through from Dundee as has already been discussed, it was largely all for nothing. After the Battles of Rietfontein and Nicholson's Nek, the Ladysmith garrison was besieged and settled down to an 118 day wait before being relieved on 28 February 1900 by General Buller battering his way forward from the south. ❏


***References:***

*Pat Rundgren, Sharp End Tours.*
Cell: 082 690 7812

http://www.battlefields.co.za/history/anglo-boer_war/elandslaagte/elandsprund.htm

Captions to pictures of graves in Elandslaagte Cemetery.
1. Memorial to Imperial Light Horse.
2. Graves for "15 Brave Boers".
3. Memorial stone to "Brave British Soldiers".

## FOOT-NOTE

An unfortunate shoeless donkey straying in the yard of the Royal Hotel walked, of his own accord, into Butler's Blacksmith Shop. Mr Butler, who naturally supposed his master somewhere in attendance, shoed the donkey. As soon as he had his shoes the donkey, acting on an understanding of the principle of commercial credit, walked off without paying and has not been heard of since. (It is conjectured he has been commandeered.)

***Printed & Published at ladysmith, Natal 18 November 1899***

# Disaster at Nicholson's Nek
## 30 October 1899

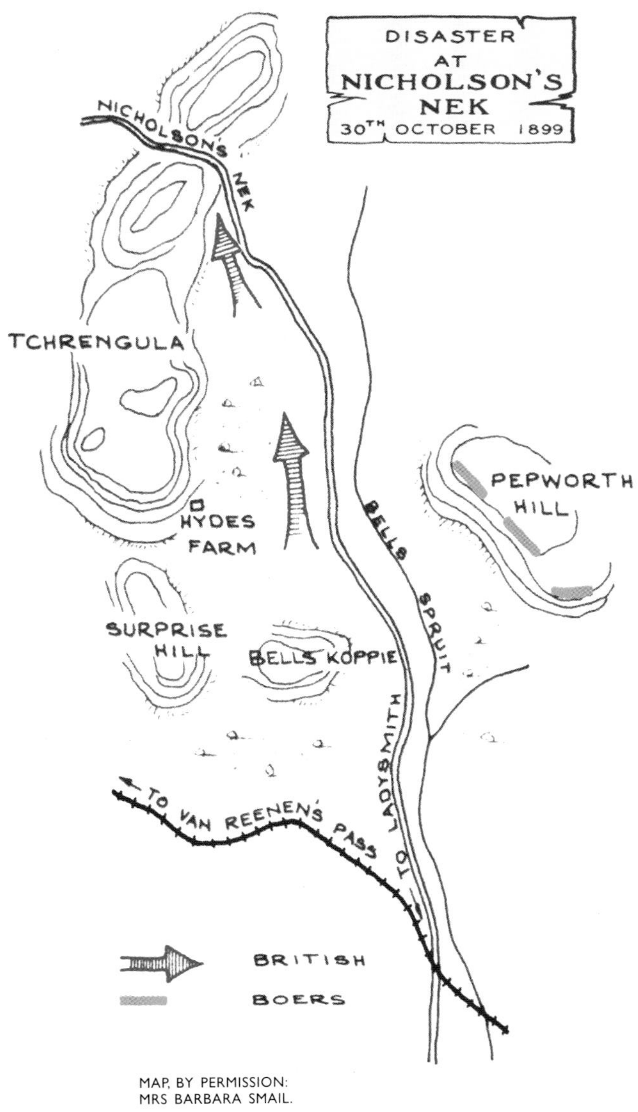


MAP, BY PERMISSION: MRS BARBARA SMAIL.

*Seven miles north of Ladysmith the road passes through a defile known as Nicholson's Nek. Here British pursuit might easily be checked by a small body of Free State Commandos that were known to be in this area.*

The plan that General White had compiled to take place on 30 October depended on this pass being kept open and the Boers occupied so as to cover up British flanking movements. The British Column for this task consisted of 520 men of the Royal Fusiliers, 450 men of the Gloucestershires Regiment and 140 men of No. 10 Mountain Battery. Besides the mules which carried the guns and ammunition there were roughly 100 mules carrying 200 rounds of reserve ammumition per man, a maxim gun, two heliographs and a few kegs of water.

The command of this column was under Colonel Carleton, but the conduct of the enterprise was mainly in the hands of Major Adye, who was well acquainted with the ground. Every precaution was taken to prevent the enemy from discovering that such a movement was to take place. Orders were sent out to observe the strictest silence during the march, no smoking allowed and the men to march as lightly and quietly as possible. No rifle magazines were to be charged, and the column, if fired upon were to march straight on in silence without returning fire. No stretchers were to be taken and if casualties occurred the men were to be left as they fell until daylight. The task of passing through the Boer lines was a tough assignment.

The advance towards Nicholson's Nek

> *For those who strew our battlefields, No passing bell shall toll;*
> *Report the living and the dead, Sergeant, call the roll!*
>
> . . . . . . . . . . . .
>
> *In the hush-tide of the gloaming, Will there come, amidst the gloom,*
> *The shadows of our loved ones, From that far-off Southern tomb?*
> *Will pictures glow in the embers, With faces fond and true,*
> *Of those who died whilst fighting, For the red, white and blue?*
>
> **Drummer Hodge:** ***The poetry of the Anglo-Boer War*** **by M van Wyk Smith**

started at approximately 1115 hr with the Royal Irish Fusiliers in front followed by their ammunition mules, the battery was in the centre followed by the Gloucestershires. The night was dark and cloudy and the pace of advance was good. As they approached Pepworth Hill great caution was exercised, as they virtually passed under the noses of the Boers on the hill.

At 0200 hr *Hydes Farm* was reached. Nicholson's Nek was now only 3 km off, but due to the late start of the column it was felt that the nek could not be reached before daylight. The commanding officer and Major Adye decided to take up a waiting position on Tchrengula Hill immediately above the farm and move up to the nek at a favourable opportunity. There were two hours before dawn. The column swung to the left and advanced up the gentle sloping ground in single file but they soon encountered loose boulders and the terrain became steeper. It was while the column was spread out in this long single file that disaster struck. The mules being handled by the fusiliers panicked and all hell was let loose as they galloped back down the way they had come, alerting the Boers who immediately opened fire.

By the strenuous effort the officers succeeded in getting the men under control. Many fusiliers had managed to get to the top of Tchrengula, the rest followed and eventually what was left of the column was re-united on the summit of the hill at about 0300 hr but without guns. The Gloucestershires saved the maxim, and with the exception of 17 boxes of ammunition, barely 20 rounds per man, all the reserve ammunition was lost including the water kegs and signalling equipment. Many men were missing and the holding of Nicholson's Nek was lost. ❑

***Source:***
*Battlefields of the S.A. War 1899* by J.L. Smail (used, permission of Mrs. Barbara Smail)

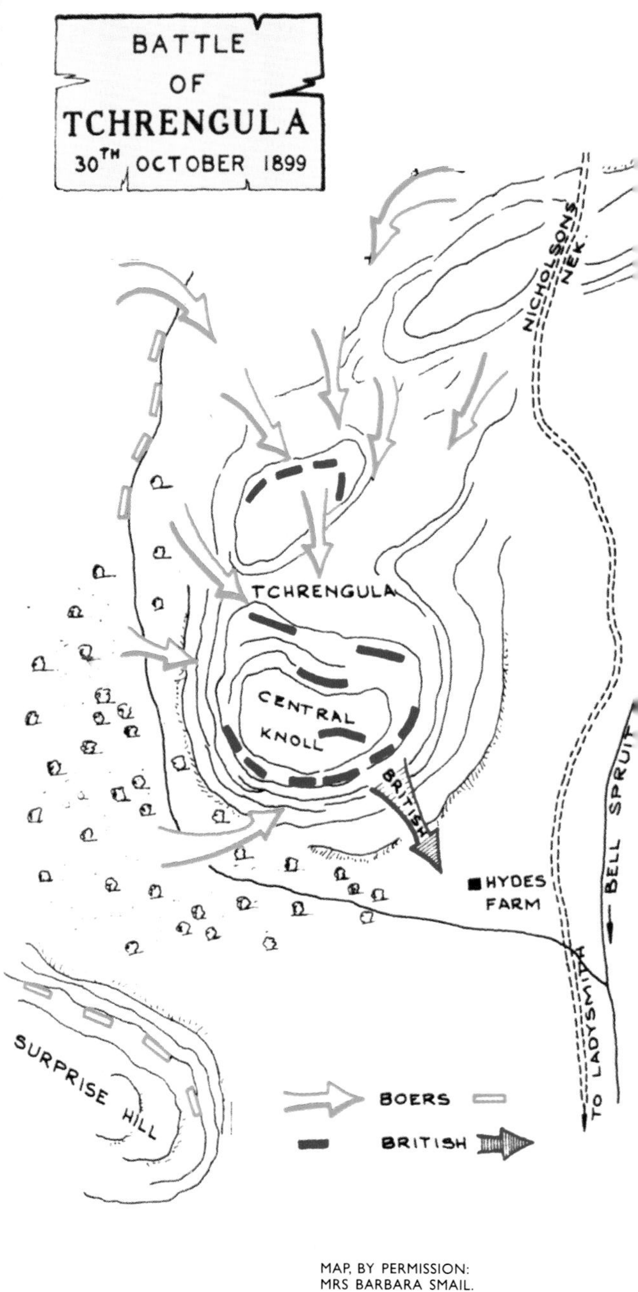


MAP, BY PERMISSION: MRS BARBARA SMAIL.

> ***The battle raged at Nicholson's Nek:***
> ***An English soldier lay,***
> ***Struck down in the dark in the deadly fight***
> ***His life-blood ebbing away.***
>
> **Drummer Hodge:** ***The poetry of the Anglo-Boer War*** **by M van Wyk Smith.**

*Pat Rundgren*

# Siege & Relief of Ladysmith
## 2 November 1899 - 28 February 1900

Although the Anglo-Boer War started on 11 October 1899 it did not reach Ladysmith until 30 November 1899 when the apparently invincible British garrison in Ladysmith under the command of General Sir George White, suffered a humiliating defeat at the Battle of Nicholson's Nek with over 1 000 casualties most of whom were taken prisoner. Fortunately the Royal Navy arrived literally in the nick of time and turned a major disaster into one of smaller proportions.

Drawings by Captain Clive Dixon: *The First Shell. The Last Shell.*

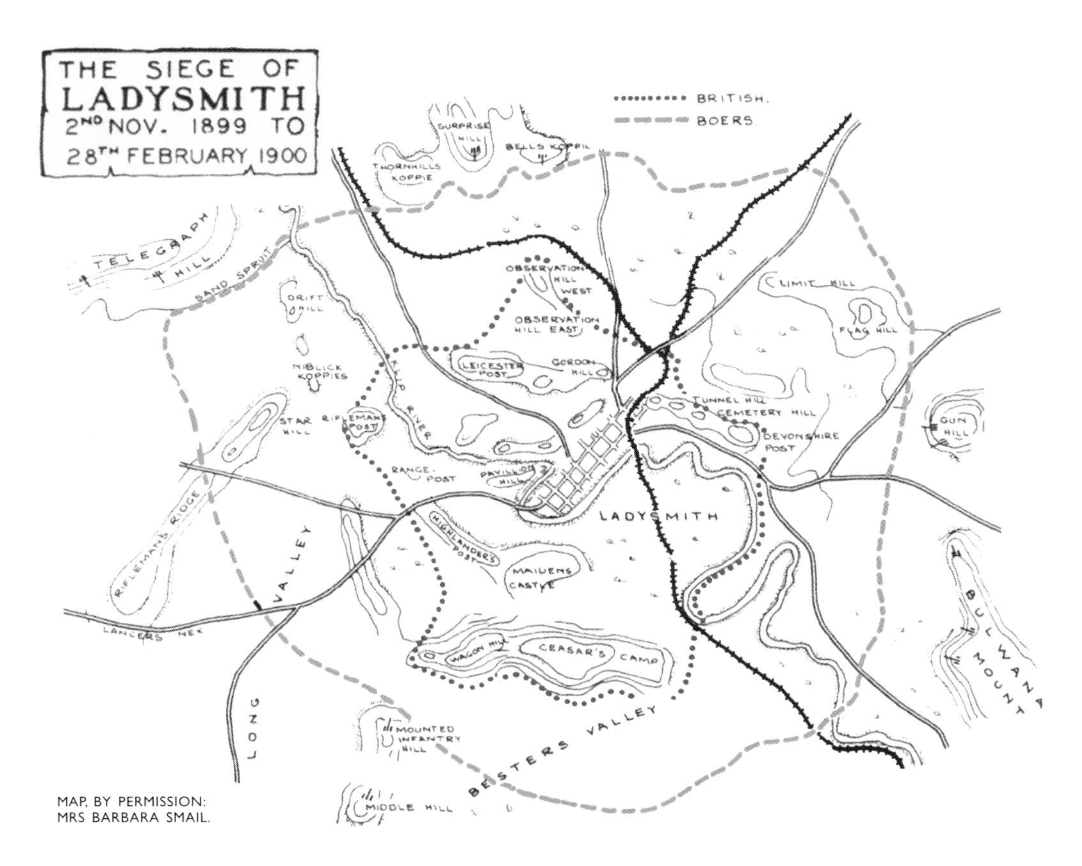

MAP, BY PERMISSION:
MRS BARBARA SMAIL.

Retreating forces from the Battles at Dundee and Elandslaagte had increased the numbers at Ladysmith which, although they gave more fighting power to Sir George White, it also meant more mouths to feed and therefore put more strain on the supplies. The internment proper began on 2 November when the telegraph lines were cut by the Boers and the railway line blown up just beyond what was to become the Intombi's Camp Hospital. For 118 days over 20 000 people, consisting mainly of military personnel but also included civilians, Indian and native helpers, were imprisoned within the town and were to suffer the ravages of disease and starvation on an unprecedented scale.

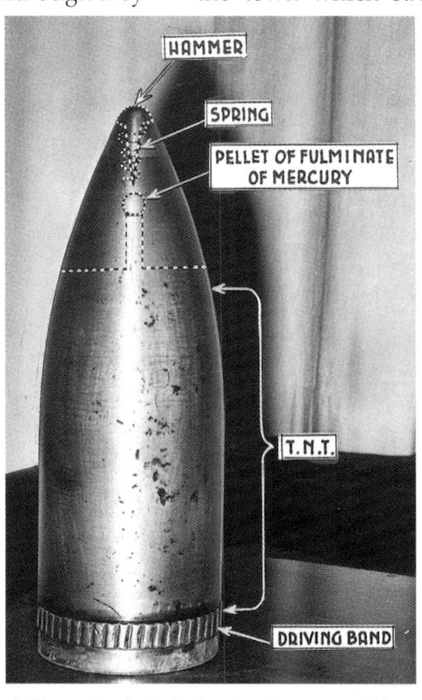

A "Long Tom" shell showing its composition.

Fortuitously someone prior to the war had had the presence of mind to horde an enormous amount of supplies in the town which saved it from an earlier surrender. However despite this, the inhabitants were people suffering the pangs of starvation long before the relief came.

In addition the Boers had cut the fresh water supply quite early in the siege and therefore the only water available was that from the Kliprivier river which became contaminated and was the cause of the high incidence of deaths from enteric (typhoid) and other diseases. Over 50% of the deaths during the siege were disease related and not from the enemy.

The Boers were not experienced in the attacking type of warfare as were the British. They contented themselves with shelling the town with their superior artillery and starving the occupants into surrender.

Several battles were to become synonymous with the Siege and Relief of Ladysmith among them Gun Hill, Platrand and the relief battles of Colenso, Spion Kop, Vaalkranz and the Breakthrough. Gun Hill was a night attack which put the dreaded *'Long Tom'* out of action and with a similar sortie 2 days later at Surprise Hill, brought a much needed boost to morale.

The Battle of Platrand was in fact two simultaneous battles at each end of the southern plateau defence line. These were called Caesar's Camp and Wagon Hill. Had these attacks not been repressed then undoubtedly the town would have had to surrender to the Boers. Casualties were high on both sides and the heroics of the British *'Tommy'* can be seen in the fact that five Victoria Crosses were awarded, Britain's highest medal for bravery. The relieving Army, under General Sir Redvers Buller, arrived in the country during November and made their first attempts to reach Ladysmith on 15 December 1899 by attacking Colenso. This was a disaster and Buller retired back to Chieveley to lick his wounds. The second attempt was at Spion Kop where once again Buller was reversed and made his way back once again to Cheiveley, on the way giving it a third try at Vaalkranz where, although successfully gaining the advantage, he decided to withdraw. By 15 February 1900, Buller had gathered his force to the east of Colenso at Hussar Hill where he made his fourth and this time successful breakthrough to Ladysmith where on 28 February 1900 a small force of Colonial cavalry arrived in the town. The official relief was on 01 March 1900. ❑

***References:***

Brian Kaighin, Ladysmith (*Brian Kaighin has accumulated information into the Siege and Relief of Ladysmith from diaries, letters including the names of over 13 000 casualties with regiments, where injured/buried, how died etc., from which those searching for relatives who took part in the siege can sometimes be found.)*

http://www.battlefields.co.za/history/anglo-boer_war/siege.htm



During the night attack on Lombards Kop outside Ladysmith, which resulted in a *Long Tom* being disabled, the British were challenged near the summit by a Boer sentry. At the loud *"fix bayonets!"* command the Boers ran away. In fact the soldiers did not have bayonets, and had tapped their rifle butts against rocks to imitate the dreaded sound. SEE PICTURE ABOVE WHICH SHOWS THE GUN ACTION CAPTURED BY THE BRITISH.

**Heidelbergers of the Boer War**, *Ian Uys*, 1981 Ian S. Uys

# The story of "Biddy" *alias Gammy*

One day during the Siege of Ladysmith, I was lying on the ground resting after two nights in the trenches, my helmet was covering my face and my right arm was extended; I felt a soft touch on my hand – it was a little mongrel bitch (in the photo) licking it. I spoke to her and gave her a pat, she then lay down beside me – from that moment she attached herself to me and remained with me wherever I went. She was a waif, neglected and hungry. I gave her the name of *Biddy* and we became fast friends. Later during the siege (which lasted 120 days) the Boers shelled my post killing eight and wounding nine of my men.

*Biddy* had her left foreleg blown off from the shoulder. The doctor who attended the wounded also attended to Biddy very successfully and she recovered – from then on she was known as *Gammy*. She remained with me and went with me to Ceylon where we escorted Boer prisoners of war. The photo was taken at the POW camp in Ceylon. Later I returned to continue the war and she accompanied me. She was killed in action near Heidelberg, Transvaal. I buried her where she fell and erected a cairn to her memory. Many years after the war I visited her grave which was still intact. The occupiers of the farm assured me it would not be disturbed.

So farewell *Biddy* alias *Gammy*.

*"If Heaven has no room for horses and dogs, then I would rather go to Hades when I die."* ❑

### STAYING COOL

Deneys Reitz accompanied his uncle on picket duty to a point just 400 yards away from the English line outside Ladysmith. They drove out on a buck-board, to which they tethered the horses, and then slept on their feather bed, complete with pillows and blankets. (Reitz, 62).

During the attack on Wagon Hill, Ladysmith, Reitz was pinned down by British fire in front of Bell's Kop. Bored, he spent the day sleeping and reading a newspaper. Boers watching from the rear thought that he was showing a white flag as he turned the pages of the newspaper, and news spread throughout the laager that his force had surrendered. (Reitz, 67).

*R. G. Reddy*

# The Indians and the War

Central to the conflict was the *Siege of Ladysmith,* played against a backdrop of human suffering and deprivation, of anxiety and tension and the prospect of all the residents (Whites, Indians, Blacks, Coloureds) and the British garrison capitulating to the Boer forces.

We examine the role of the Indian as trader, market gardener, railway worker, labourer, farm hand, domestic help – and how they survived 137 harrowing days within the confines of the town – to be under siege (or virtually cut-off from the outside world) is an unusual event for most people, but more so for people who recently emigrated to a land that promised much.

When the Boers' forces surrounded the town, many Indians left hurriedly to Port Natal on horseback, horse driven carts and on the last train that left the station. Others who worked in the district outside Ladysmith also took steps to safeguard themselves. One Indian farmer, Mohabeer (II No: 5728) (Indian Immigration Number) told the Invasion Losses Inquiry Commission after the war that he had rented ten acres of arable land from a farmer, Mr. W. Leathern, near Spionkop. He was forced to abandon his farm when hostilities broke out and he walked a distance of 30 km to the military camp at Ntombi's Camp in town. Gannapen was another 'free' Indian who farmed on Muller's Farm at Elandslaagte. Annually he drew 60 bags of mealies as well as a variety of vegetables. In his plea to the Commission he sought compensation for the loss of 40 fowls, one bag of flour, another large bag of rice presumably eaten by the Boers, and a crop

Ladysmith Hospital Corps.

Indian Medical Corps.

of Isangu (dagga/marijuana) which was mysteriously harvested. Parus Ramadoo (II No: 15032) leased 14 acres of land from an Indian Trader, Mardarsingh, who in turn had leased it from Mr. Snell in Colenso. He claimed compensation for 97 bags of grain, normally sold for £1.4s per bag (1 Pound 4 shillings) in Ladysmith, and which was expropriated by the Boers. Other Indians such as Ayasamy, the fireman at the famous Royal Hotel; Lutchman Singh, a waiter at the same hotel; Francis Murray Samuel, a cook and head waiter at the Railway Hotel, suffered personal losses during the siege. Kadir Adam, lived in Ladysmith but who worked as chief cook at the Central Hotel in Harrismith, had to flee from his place of employment when the Boer soldiers invaded the town.

Despite the deprivations suffered by the embattled citizens of the town, the local municipality maintained a constant level of services. The records of the erstwhile Ladysmith Local Board confirms that Indians were employed as lamp lighters, coolie office boys, stokers at the power station, and as scavengers in the sanitary department. The upkeep of the Town Hall, an important rallying point for the citizenry, was left in the hands of a 'reliable' Indian. Another important landmark, the Pavilion, was also placed under his caretakership. At the height of the siege, 25 additional Indian indentured workers were hired to carry out various tasks in the Sanitary Department. When the siege was lifted, 200 additional Indian workers, were hired for town cleaning purposes.

The Mudeliar Family records show that grandfather Mr. 'Gentleman' Mudeliar was employed as a Quartermaster by the British garrison, and his meticulously kept notes indicate that he handled his task in a highly professional manner. The distribution of scarce food supplies to the soldiers was a critical factor during the siege, and together with senior officers, he jealously guarded his task against lootings and theft. The Indian Interpreter at the time, Mr. David Vinden, played a significant role in facilitating communication between the British and the Indians of the town. In a letter to W.A. King, Superintendent, Indian Labour Corps in Ladysmith; the self same Vinden acknowledges the contribution of 29 Indentured Indians who were placed under the care of Major Wescott. These workers were recruited from the Durban Navigation Collieries in Durnacol. The Resident Magistrate's records also confirm that 131 Indentured Indians had been recruited from the Dundee Coal Collieries to assist the British. Mention must be made of the superlative work as medical orderlies at the La Verna Convalescent Hospital. Regrettably, this matter received a degree of prominence when the Magistrate complained to the Commander of the garrison that the orderlies who were supposed to be remunerated at a rate of 30/- (30 Shillings) had not been paid.

The South African Railways maintained a large works depot in Ladysmith, and at the time of the siege, had many Indians on their books as 'gangers' (work gangs), plate-layers, porters, signalmen, lamp attendants, pointsmen, engine cleaners and loco shopyard men. Others were used as sirdars (overseers), gate-keeping, ticket collectors, clerks and messengers. When hostilities broke out, the SAR suspended all work on their lines, and withdrew their personnel to the Railway Barracks in Ladysmith. Several Indians like Raghnooth Singh was employed as a Chief Sirdar, Baldeo Maharaj was a ganger on the railway extension to Van Reenen and Khader Khan was a conductor on the passenger line to Glencoe, Charles-town and Vryheid. Singh, Maharaj and Khan continued to play a prominent role in the Indian community in the post-war period.

Very little has been said of the contribution of the Indian traders to the town during those difficult days. At the turn of the century, the Indians had succeeded in securing over 60% of the town's trade. Their phenomenal growth was attributed to small profit margins, use of family members as shop assistants, and their specialised skill in trading with all sectors of the community. They posed such a formidable threat to the other white traders that despite restrictive legislation to curb their licenses, the town records show they helped significantly during the months of crisis. They were handsomely compensated by the military personnel. Looting was not uncommon. In support of their claims for compensation after the war, Police Inspector William MacDonald testified to the Invasion Losses Commission that he had inspected several Indian shops with a Major Ludlow. All the shops with the exception of Ebrahim Shaik Amod, Moola Mohamed Amod and Shaik Rassool had been looted, by among other soldiers, civilians and Indians. They also noted that the Military Police were also observed taking goods from Ajam Hoosen's store.

This abstract cannot conclude without some mention of the bravery and heroism of one Parbhu Singh. He was attached to the Gordon Highlanders and he was asked to stand under an umbrella on a heap of sacks. His task was to scan Umbulwane Hill for any sign of Boer military activity. When there was a puff of smoke, suggesting that a cannon had been shot, Singh would shout out in a shrill voice L-o-n-g T-o-o-m, and everyone immediately took shelter. At the end of the war his gallantry was awarded when he received a cashmere robe from the Viceroy of India. ❑


***Sources:***

Brain. J, *'Indentured and Free Indians' in Guest & Duminy: Enterprise & Exploitation.*
*Indian Immigration Papers.* II/2/5, 642/04, Natal Archives, Pietermaritzburg.
*Ladysmith Local Board, Minute Book,* 3/LDS, 1/1/1/2, 1899-1903.
*Invasion Losses Enquiry,* CSO vol. 2915, 2nd October 1901.
*Report of the Resident Magistrate, Blue Book of Natal, 1900.*


Ghandi.

*Malcolm Cobb, Durban. Tel: (031) 205 1529*

# THE ANNUAL LADYSMITH SIEGE SHOOT

## A Demonstration of practical history on the Ladysmith Battlefields

The Ladysmith battlefields area contains a wealth of interest for both the serious historian and the casual visitor, but for the real enthusiast, there is a further attraction which adds a completely different dimension to their enjoyment. Toward the close of each year, normally around the third weekend in November, shooting men forgather at Doug McMasters home on the old Van Reenens road for a weekend of competition with veteran firearms of the era of the Zulu and Boer Wars.

Although it started some twenty years ago as an informal fun shoot between the Durban Black Powder Club and the Transvaal Historical breech loaders, the shoot has taken on a life of its own with participants from as far afield as Bloemfontein, the Northern Transvaal and the Cape. The venue is perfect for the occasion as the McMasters have a double story house furnished in Victorian style, complete with a thatched roof, all built onto the side of a hill overlooking the Van Reenens road with a distant prospect of the battlefield of Spion Kop. The grounds are extensive and set with acacia trees in abundance which provide shade for those who prefer the camping option. The McMasters also accommodate visitors for bed and breakfast.

In the grounds is Doug's *'Blockhouse Museum'*, a purpose built replica of an Anglo-Boer War blockhouse which houses a private collection of relics and records of the Siege of Ladysmith that is accessible to the public. Here you will find exhibits that you won't find anywhere else in the world, plus a wealth of knowledge and plenty of help in identifying equipment, fragments of shells, empty cartridge cases or anything else connected with the Siege.

The typical **Ladysmith Weekend** begins with a guided walk around one of the many Boer War sites in the area on the Thursday and the Friday to create the atmosphere for the shoot. On the Saturday, the enthusiasts assemble on the range which is on the adjacent farm belonging to Doug's brother, Edgar McMaster. The range is 100 metres long and the firing point has been extended and now takes 12 shooters comfortably. Even the firing point has historical associations and opinion is divided as to whether it is a rudimentary fortification belonging to the Boer laager that was known to be in the area during the Siege, or it is in fact a forgotten grave site adapted to other purposes. *Don't take it too seriously, the story is mainly to psyche out visiting competitors!!*

Most of the shooting is done with the .450 calibre Martini Henry rifle, which saw service in the Anglo-Zulu and both Anglo-Boer Wars, and the long Lee Enfield in .303 calibre. Since 1995, there has also been a fair sprinkling of the Mauser Model 95 in calibre 7 mm Mauser as these rifles have become more freely available through imports. To cover the full range of weapons associated with the Siege, there is also an event for the .577 Snider and vintage handguns. To get as many people as possible shooting, the cut off

date is set at 1919 *i.e. the end of the Ist World War,* as this then allows use of the SMLE No 1 Mk III which is much easier for the average shooter to locate and is in reality not a great deal different to both the SMLE No 1 Mk 1 of 1902 and the Lee Enfield Carbine used during the Anglo-Boer War. The Lee Enfield No 4 is not allowed as the aperture sight and heavier barrel would give an unfair advantage. The 1919 date also opens up the handguns to the Luger and the Webley .455 Mk V & Mk V1 and the Smith & Wesson and Colt revolvers of similar calibre. The standard of shooting is high and shooters have to score way over 90% if possible in most events to win medals. The premier award is the ***Ladysmith Challenge Cup*** which is awarded to the captain of the winning team for the best aggregate for Martini and Lee Enfield / Mauser score.

Dress is normally modern day comfortable attire in drab khaki colours and a wide brimmed hat with not too much emphasis on historical accuracy, but such is the atmosphere at the shoot that when competitors took part in **The re-enactment of the Armoured Train Incident**, it only require the addition of a bandolier, a Free State flag or two and a pair of *verkykers* (binoculars) to look absolutely authentic for the Boer War period. This is a real opportunity for photographers as prints in black & white are indistinguishable from photo-graphs taken 100 years ago.

Saturday night sees an excellent excuse for a party and medal presentation which traditionally ends up with Doug playing the bagpipes and leading a small but determined relief column around the slumbering campers after midnight to remind them of the hazards of traditional warfare as practiced in Natal. For this reason, getting up for the Sunday morning events can also be a challenge for the survivors of the Saturday night.

However, the Sunday events themselves are slightly less serious than the Saturday events consisting of a *'3 position'* shoot (standing kneeling and prone), or hits on 6" gongs at 100 metres (far too easy); finishing off with the handgun event, in nice time for a lunchtime braai, another round of medal presentations and everyone is on the road home by 2.00 pm, and if they haven't got a medal they will have at least another fund of funny stories and pleasant experiences to carry them through until next year. ❑

***All photographs used in this article are with the kind permission of Malcolm Cobb, Durban.***

1. Shooting from kneeling position at 50 metres.
2. Prone shooting at 100 metres.
3. 100 metre range showing distance of targets.
4. Natal, Gauteng, Free State and Cape Province enthusiasts.

After the relief of Ladysmith the retreating Boers eluded their pursuers by means of a smokescreen. *"The foremost of our men had set fire in hundreds of places to the grass on either side of the road, and the smoke obscured many of us from the enemy. Had it not been for the smoke and the dust raised, we of the tail-end would have fared badly indeed."* (Schikkerling, 15).

*Tony Westby-Nunn. Tel: 083 4444 662*

# The Armoured Train Incident
## 15 November 1899

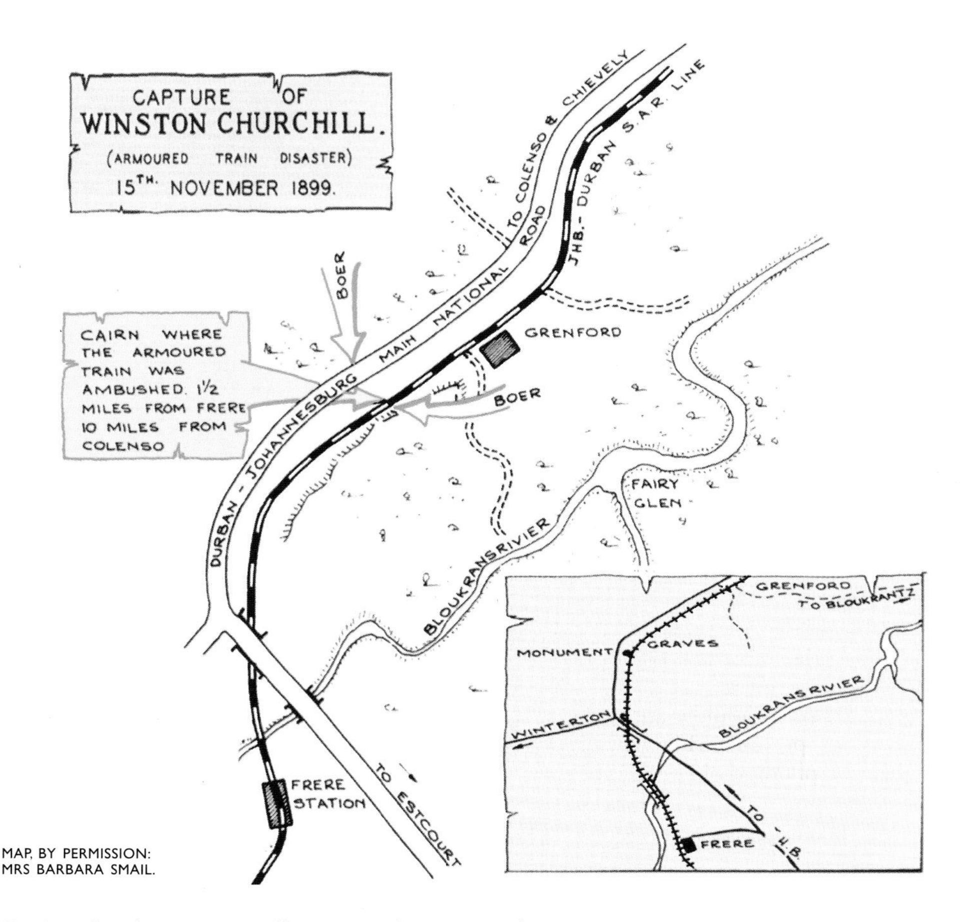


MAP. BY PERMISSION:
MRS BARBARA SMAIL.

During October 1899 small parties of Boers patrolled the hills near Colenso. Consequently the British sent out an armoured train from Estcourt, to enable them to keep an eye on developments between the towns of Colenso and Estcourt. On 1 November, there was contact between Free State commandos and the Natal Carbineers some six miles from Colenso. The Boers had also placed some guns on he slopes of Grobbelaars Kloof.

On 2 November a train left Ladysmith with Major General French and Major Haig. The Boers opened fire on Fort Wylie (covering Colenso's Railway Bridge) and an attack was made on Fort Molyneax which protected the railway bridge over the Langverwacht Spruit. The British then evacuated their positions, crossed the Tugela and withdrew to Estcourt.

In order to show some activity, the British sent out an armoured train daily and some skirmishes ensued. On 13 November 1899 the Tugela was crossed and Colenso was occupied by a force of some 3 000 Boers and four guns due to the initiative shown by Louis Botha, the Assistant General of the Boer Forces. The following day, patrols went forward to

Chieveley and to within 8 km of Estcourt. The railway line near Chieveley was also taken up. The armoured train continued to do daily excursions. There was no chance of surprising the Boers as the train could be seen and heard a long way off. On 14 November the train was fired on by the Boers and reports of a strong Boer force near the line was received, but this report was disregarded.

Thomas Pakenham in his book *'The Boer War'*, writes about Colonel Long's armoured train between Colenso and Estcourt as follows: *"With a raiding force of about the same number as the British at Estcourt but with fewer field-guns, it was not Joubert's or Botha's plan to attack Estcourt. Their primary job was to explore the country. Of course if any plum fell into their lap, that was all to the good. The next morning a large plum, in the shape of an armoured train, whose passengers included young Winston Churchill, (a reporter of the Morning Post, photographed) fell straight into their laps."*

*"Imprisoned on its vulnerable railway line, the armoured train was as helpless against field-guns in the veld as a naval dreadnought sent into battle with its rudder jammed".*

Botha, who was leading the column, must have rubbed his eyes. Soon after dawn on the 15 November he saw the train - 150 men in three armoured trucks on either side of the armoured engine, with a 7-pounder naval gun visible in one of the loop-holes steaming northward towards Chieveley. The trap was soon sprung. Chieveley was 10 miles north of the village Frere. After three miles, just beyond a bridge beyond the Blaauw Krantz River, the line swung to the right and climbed a rise. It was here that Botha's party of about 500 men, drawn from Wakkerstroom and Krugersdorp Commandos, watched (and were actually seen by the British as the train steamed passed). Then they scattered rocks on the line and waited.

The veld in this part of Natal is a rolling downland, normally silent, and the steam trains that can still be seen along this line are a delight to the ear. A plume of brown smoke, a distant musical honk and then the panting breath of the train itself, intermittently muffled as the train vanishes into a cutting. That morning, 15 November 1899, there was a thick mist, but Botha must have heard the sweet sound of the armoured train soon after 0800 hr, as it steamed back southward from Chieveley. He waited till it approached the bend close to the Blaauw Krantz River.

Winston Spencer Churchill wrote in his book *'London to Ladysmith via Pretoria'*: *"... The moment approached: but no one was much concerned, for the cars were proof against rifle fire, and this ridge could at worst be occupied only by some daring patrol of perhaps a score of men. 'Besides,' we said to ourselves 'they little think we have a gun on board. That will be a nice surprise'."*

*"... The Boers held their fire until the train reached that part of the track nearest to their position. Standing on a box in the rear armoured truck I had an excellent view through my glasses. The long brown rattling serpent with the rifles bristling from its spotted sides crawled closer to the rocky hillock on which the scattered black figures of the enemy showed clearly. Suddenly 3-wheeled things appeared on the crest, and within a second a bright flash of light - like a heliograph, but much yellower - opened and shut 10 or 12 times. Then two much larger flashes; no smoke nor yet any sound, and a bustle and stir among the little figures. So much for the hill. Immediately over the rear truck of the train a huge white ball of smoke sprang into being and tore out into a cone like a comet. Then came the explosions of the near guns and the nearer shell. The iron sides of the truck 'twanged' with a patter of bullets. There was a crash from the front of the train and half a dozen sharp reports. The Boers had opened fire on us at 600 yards with two large field guns, a maxim firing small shells in a stream, and from riflemen lying on a ridge. I got down from my box into the cover of the armoured sides of the car without forming any clear thoughts. Equally*

*involuntarily, it seems the driver put on full steam, as the enemy had intended. The train leapt forward, ran the gauntlet of the guns, which now filled the air with explosions, swung round the curve of the hill, ran down a steep gradient and dashed into a huge stone which awaited it on the line at a convenient spot."*

*"... All three trucks in front of the engine were derailed; the front truck which held some unfortunate railway workers, was completely thrown off the line and 'an armoured car crowded with the Durban Light Infantry, was carried on twenty yards and thrown over on its side."*

The fight that followed was exactly to Botha's taste. From a distance of 1 300 yards, his men poured shells and Mauser bullets into the stranded train. They soon silenced the 7-pounder ship's gun. The upturned trucks gave some cover to the British. A brisk action ensued during which Churchill led a party for an hour under fire to free the locomotive. With the wounded loaded aboard it returned to Frere Station and then on to Escourt while the rest of the detachment fought on. Some of the soldiers scattered across the veld. They were caught hiding in the railway cutting and the river-bed and were taken prisoner.

After the fight, Botha jubilantly sent a cable to his wife in Pretoria: *"Our guns were ready and quickly punctured the armoured trucks. The engine broke loose and returned badly damaged. Loss of the enemy four dead, 14 wounded and 58 taken prisoner, also a mountain gun (the naval gun) ... our loss four slightly wounded ... blood visible everywhere. Much rain. Am in good health. Publish. Greetings."*

Neither he nor Joubert mentioned what would become the famous feature of the fight: that Winston Churchill was one of the victims. Later Churchill came to believe that he had been captured by Botha in person. The man who capture him was Field Cornet Oosthuizen, known as the *"Red Bull of Krugersdorp"* – Churchill was soon to have been grateful to Botha for having given him a chance to make his name. And perhaps Botha should have been grateful to Churchill. For it was Churchill's burning desire to see a battle that helped persuade the officer commanding the armoured train, Churchill's unfortunate friend, Captain Aylmer Haldane, not to turn back when they first saw signs of Botha's trap on their journey northward. Botha and Joubert at any rate, continued their drive southward, taking a wide detour to avoid the 3 000 troops reported to have garrisoned Estcourt. Had they known how precarious was the morale of Colonel Long's troops there, they might have been more aggressive. For the intelligence report on both sides were inaccurate. In the eyes of British soldiers - and of subsequent British historians - Joubert's 2 000 men with two guns had become magnified to an expedition of 7 000 men with numerous guns, threatening Durban itself. Long had actually packed up his tents on 14 November and loaded his guns into railway wagons in preparation for a hasty retreat. As it was, Joubert had cautiously decided to split his forces into two columns: 1 500 men, led by himself and Botha; 600 men under his nephew, David. Botha's columns would converge on the railway line south of Estcourt, cutting off the garrison from its base. It rained incessantly that 16 November, and it was cold and wretched. Joubert rode in a light covered wagon – a *'spider'* – and, what with the rain, he considered calling off the whole expedition. But he had no way of com-municating with his nephew David's column, and could not leave him in the lurch. So he rode gloomily on.

The 19 November was a Sunday, and the Boer soldiers spent much time in church. The men in the Heidelberg Commando, for example, attended four church services. On Tuesday 21 November, Joubert's column at last saw ahead the thin line of telegraph posts striding across the veld. They had reached the railway. After breaking up the line, they pitched their forward tents on a kopje commanding the line close to Willow Grange, a small village a few miles south of Estcourt. At the same time, Joubert was glad to be able to join his nephew's column.

Joubert was still intensely anxious, and he had every reason to be. He had slipped his small raiding party, 2 000 men, with two guns and two Maxims, between two British Brigades,

## DOUBLY INDEBTED

A gathering of friends at an English estate nearly turned to tragedy when one of the children strayed into deep water. The gardener, hearing the cries for help, plunged in and rescued the drowning child. The youngster's name was Winston Churchill.

Young Churchill's grateful parents asked the gardener what they could do to reward him. He hesitated, then said, *"I wish my son could go to college someday and become a doctor". "We'll see to it,"* Churchill's parents promised. Years later, while Sir Winston was Prime Minister of England, he was stricken with pneumonia. The country's best physician was summoned. His name was Dr Alexander Fleming, the man who discovered and developed penicillin – the son of that gardener who had saved young Winston from drowning. Later Churchill remarked, *"Rarely has one man owed his life twice to the same person".*

ROSES ROUND UP

led by Major-General Hildyard and Major-General Barton, totalling 9 700 men, with 24 field guns. And this was only the vanguard of Buller's army Corps. The *'Roslin Castle'* docked on 12 November at Durban . Ever since that day Imperial troops had been pouring down the gang-planks to be packed onto trucks and sent up the railway line to the front in an unbroken stream. Clearly the danger now was that the two British Brigades would combine and crush Joubert and Botha.

But Barton and Hildyard, whose Brigades were about; 20 miles apart, found communication impossible while the Boers sat astride the railway line. So the British attack, that took place on the night of 22 November, died as quickly as it had started. ❑


***References:***

*London to Ladysmith via Pretoria* by Winston Spencer Churchill.

*Bushmans River Tourism Authority.*

*'The Boer War'* by Thomas Pakenham.


**THE ARMOURED TRAIN INCIDENT RE-ENACTMENT**

***Photographs of the re-enactment 100 years later.***

# Dispatches

## ARMOURED TRAIN INCIDENT

REUTERS VERSION

T.D.ZAR 16.11.1989
From Reuter, Lourenco Marques
To Standard, Johannesburg, begins
Durban 15th, 4.50p.m. Armoured train from Escourt and company which includes Durham Light Infantry proceeded beyond Chieveley unmolested, returning found Boers had meanwhile dislodged rails rounding curve - overturned trucks were violently throwing men out. Boers opened shell and rifle fire, men replied - truck tender cleared from wreckage - steamed back Escourt with few Dublins, fifteen Durhams and fifteen wounded including Captain Wylie M.L.A. Winston Churchill, Morning Post Correspondent and 150 men missing. - ends

LOUIS BOTHA'S VERSION

T.D.ZAR 17.11.1899 Confidential
From Louis Botha, H.Q. Ladysmith
To Mrs Botha
Yesterday an armoured train from Escourt surprised us; immediately the Wakkerstroom and Krugersdorp Commandants and their men sallied forth and I with them. Upon the train return, the foremost truck was derailed at a spot where our burghers had placed stones. Our guns were ready and speedily penetrated the armour of the trucks, but the badly damaged engine broke loose and withdrew. Enemy losses were four dead, fourteen wounded and fifty-eight prisoners.
We also captured a mountain gun. On our side four burghers from the above districts were lightly wounded. This took place at Blaauwkrans. Later the enemy in thick mist and rain came upon a patrol from Ermelo and killed two of our burghers. The commando went in to the attack and repulsed enemy. Their losses unknown. Blood all over the place.
Much rain. Am Well. Publish this.
Greetings - ends.

***Botha like many a man of lesser note, evidently found it as irksome to write dispatches as to write home. Here he cleverly combined the two tasks.***

WHAT GENERAL JOUBERT THOUGHT

T.D.ZAR 21.11.1899
From Commandant-General, H.Q. Ladysmith
To Government, Pretoria, begins
19.11.99 I understand that the son of Lord Churchill claims to be nothing more than a press correspondent and as such entitled to release. From a newspaper his status appears something totally different. Thus I deem it advisable that he be guarded and regarded as one potentially dangerous to our war effort. In short, he must be imprisoned for the duration of hostilities. It was through his active participation that a part of the armoured train escaped. - ends.

MORE THOUGHTS FROM GENERAL JOUBERT

T.D.ZAR 28.11.1899
From Commandant-General, Colenso
To Secretary of State, begins
I see a rumour in the papers that Lord Churchill's son Lieutenant Churchill, the Morning Post correspondent will soon be released by the Government. I strongly object to this procedure. If this person is released, so can any other P.O.W. be released. He was most active in directing the soldiers in their efforts to extricate the armoured train and while thus engaged in stultifying our operations, made a prisoner of war. He must be treated as any other P.O.W and if needs be guarded with even greater vigilance. - ends.

WHAT DANIE THERON THOUGHT

T.D. ZAR 28.11.1899
From Captain Theron, i/c Despatch-riders, Colenso
To Secretary of State, Pretoria, begins
I beg to inform you that on the 17th inst. full reports have appeared in the Natal Witness and Natal Mercury of the active and prominent part played by the press correspondent Winston Churchill in the fight with the armoured train at Frere Station. When the officers were in difficulties Churchill called for volunteers and was their leader.
According to the Volkstem and Standard Diggers News he now declares he took no part in the fight. This is a pack of lies; nor would he stand still when warned by Field-Cornet Oosthuizen to surrender or do so till covered by the latter's rifle. In my opinion he is one of the most dangerous prisoners in our hands. The Natal papers make a great hero of him - ends.

Dispatches from ***No Charge for Delivery*** by C.W.L.. DE SOUZA. Published by *Books of Africa (Pty) Ltd.*

*Pat Rundgren*

# The Battle of Willow Grange 23 November 1899

The thrust to the coast, reinvigorated by the assistance of General Louis Botha, was greatly encouraged by the success at Chieveley on the 15 November. The Boer plan was to demonstrate against Estcourt whilst some 1 000 men under Assistant General David Joubert passed it to the east through Weenen, and the main body under Botha passed it to the west through Ulundi farm. These forces were to converge at Highlands, north of Mooi River, and isolate Estcourt by cutting the road and railway.

On the 17 November, Joubert occupied Weenen without opposition and after some of his men had looted the hotel and a store or two, proceeded as intended. On the 18 November Boer patrols approached Estcourt from the north along the railway line to within 8 000 yards of the town. By this time the garrison had received substantial reinforcements. General Hildyard and staff, the 2nd Queen's, the 2nd East Surreys, the West Yorks, some of Bathune's Mounted Infantry, and the 7th Field Battery had all arrived on or before the 18 November.

On the approach of the Boers; patrols of the Imperial Light Horse reported their presence; a navel gun at Fort Durnford to the south of the town landed a shell amongst them. The Royal Dublin Fusiliers, on the right the Durban Light Infantry, and situated below the crest of the hill north of the town, fired some shots, and the Boers withdrew. They had, no doubt, served their purpose of engaging the attention of the garrison whilst the invading army operated elsewhere.

On the 19 November, Thornycroft's Horse had a skirmish with David Joubert's commandos in the vicinity of Highlands. Hesitation and indecision at Staff level failed to prevent the junction between the two Boer forces and by the 21 November they were occupying all the heights from Brynbells Ridge to Highlands and east. They had also succeeded in collecting a great amount of wagons and stock from the farms of the neighbourhood. Their situation was, however, not altogether a happy one. The garrison of Estcourt, though mainly consisting of infantry and thus greatly lacking in mobility compared with the mounted burghers were numerically superior.

At Mooi River a similar force was being rapidly built up under General Barton. The main advantage held by the Boers was that the moment things went against them, they could withdraw rapidly. Such was the position when on the 21 November, David Joubert dropped shells into the town of Mooi River. General Barton, grossly overestimating the strength of the enemy adopted an over cautious attitude.

General Hildyard in Estcourt, however, decided to strike at the enemy. Advised by Maj.Duncan McKenzie of the Natal Carbineers that the enemy were on Brynbelle in some force and that they had planted a gun there, he decided to to make a surprise night attack on the position. Thus on the afternoon of the 22 November, a column consisting of the West Yorks, the East Surreys, four companies of the Queen's, the Durban Light Infantry, the 7th Field Battery and a Naval 12-pounder, marched out of Estcourt past Fort Durnford, past the Red Cutting at Cooper's Kop, and on to the base of Beacon Hill, about 5 or 6 miles out. They were to be followed on the 23 November by the Border Regiment and the Mounted troops.

The day had been extremely hot and the late afternoon resulted in a violent thunder-storm accompanied by hailstones of unusual size, which caused damage to helmets and some injury to personnel. All troops were drenched to the skin and, when light came with at least another four storms, the ground was so drenched that rest was impossible. Furthermore, except for the lightning flashes it was so dark that visibility was nil. Old colonists and campaigners could hardly remember such a night. There were lightning fatalities on both sides.

As a result of some troops exposing themselves in the late afternoon on the side of Beacon Hill (± 5 000 yards north of Brynbelle) the Boers opened up with their big gun. The naval gun, which had been hauled up with great difficulty onto Beacon Hill, unfortunately replied, thus giving the Boers an indication that something big was contemplated.

Col. F.W. Kitchener who was to carry out the night attack with the West Yorks and the East Surreys set out shortly before midnight. The West Yorks moved on the left side, the East Surreys on the right of a stone wall which led all the way from Beacon Hill to the north eastern edge of Brynbelle. The conditions were difficult, the night pitch black, and this led to the West Yorks and East Surreys mistaking one another for the enemy. An unfortunate encounter ensued, several being wounded by rifle and bayonet.

The West Yorks made their way unnoticed by the enemy right onto the crest of Brynbelle by 0330 hr. The startled challenge of a sentry was followed, contrary to the intention, by a volley and a cheer, which gave sufficient warning to the sleeping Boers to make their escape in the darkness. Their blankets, much of the paraphernalia and a number of horses, were all there was of booty. The gun had been removed during the night.

Morning found the West Yorks occupying the highest part of the ridge and the rest of the force behind the stone wall. The Boers, reinforced, were on a ridge about 1 500 yards back. From here, led by General Louis Botha in person, they gradually advanced against the West Yorks. They were supported by two field guns and a *pom-pom*. The West Yorks had no such support. The 7th Field Battery was without orders and was in no position to help. The naval gun on Beacon Hill was out of range.

A sadly uncoordinated action followed. Left very much to himself, Kitchener ordered a withdrawal about 0900 hr. At about the same time orders were given for the Queen's and the Border Regiment to support Kitchener's left flank by advancing from Beacon Hill along the stone wall. Hildyard, who had now come on the scene, realised withdrawal was advisable and the mounted men, Imperial Light Horse leading, moved up the Willow Grange valley to assist the West Yorks. They reached the crest to find only one company of West Yorks still in position. In assisting their withdrawal Trooper. G. Fitzpatrick of Imperial Light Horse, brother of Sir Percy Fitzpatrick (author of *Jock of the Bushveld*), was killed whilst helping a wounded Yorkshireman.

The withdrawal from Brynbelle, first to Beacon Hill and then Estcourt was carried out with few casualties. It had been the intention of General Hildyard to hold Beacon Hill permanently and Lieutenant Colonel McCubbin, commanding the Durban Light Infantry had written orders to do so. The naval gun, which had been dragged with great difficulty onto the hill, had attracted a good deal of attention from the enemy guns and it was hopelessly outranged. It was said that its range was seriously affected by lack of a proper mounting. Under the circumstances the naval officer in charge decided to take it out of action. He called in the Durban Light Infantry to assist. It had to be manhandled over boulders and down steep slopes with a shoe-brake on each wheel. O'Connell records that there was a shortage of ropes and the men had to form chains by holding hands. He especially mentions the cool courage of Corporal W. Coles who stuck to his difficult task despite the grave danger that the gun was threatening to fall on top of him. Throughout the removal of the gun the party was under shellfire.

When General Hildyard learned that the gun had been removed he decided to evacuate the hill. McCubbin refrained from doing so until there was no doubt about the authenticity of the order. Thus the Durban Light Infantry were the last to leave the field. This was done by companies in single file at several paces distance and finally in extended order. Starting at 1600 hr on the 23 November the battalion arrived back in Estcourt at 1800 hr after duties which had extended from 0300 hr on 22 November – a period of 33 hours without rest.

*'The Times History'* gives the casualties of the action as 16 killed, and about 60 wounded – mostly West York's. Boer casualties were probably much less. The gallant Louis Botha had had his horse shot under him whilst conducting the counter-attack. Mr Chofoman, a local farmer, who had guided the night attack bravely and skillfully, was amongst those killed.

The operation seems to have been remarkable despite the lack of co-ordination of effort. General Barton with considerable forces at Mooi River allowed himself to be preoccupied with the small force at Highlands under David Joubert. Of the force from Estcourt *'The Times History'* (Vol.11. p.316) observed: *'as far as the British were concerned, the centre, the mounted troops in the right, and the artillery might almost equally well have been away.'*

Despite all this, the action was not without its effect. Taken with other events, Comm.-General Joubert decided not to venture any further. Indeed, he decided, to pull back to Colenso where he would be secure behind the Tugela. It was no doubt the right decision, for the British forces were mounting up against him and if he were caught on the wrong side of a Tugela in flood, and with bridges down, he would indeed be in a perilous position. By holding his main forces round the beleaguered Ladysmith at a time when there was little between him and the coast, General Joubert had lost the initiative.

By the 25 November the Boer retreat had begun. Except for a small force, which went via Ulundi the main body moved via Weenen. *'The Times History'* regards the failure of the British Army to interfere with this withdrawal as *'almost incomprehensible'*. Referring to the withdrawal it states (Vol.11. p.317):

*"It was a dangerous and difficult march. The expedition had come out lightly equipped. It returned heavy with hundreds of wagons of lost goods and droves upon droves of raided cattle, a great straggling procession whose head had almost reached Weenen before its tail lost touch with Mooi River. The roads were sodden with the heavy rains, and on one occasion their big gun stuck for 10 hours in the drift. For some miles, the track to Weenen led through a defile where a handful of men could have checked the whole force. But nothing happened".*

A curious lighter side on this is referred to in *'The Story of the Imperial Light Horse'* by GF Gibson (p.144), which reads: *'Here was opportunity for a swift stroke - the Composite Regiment took up a position on the heights commanding a narrow defile about 10 miles to the west of Estcourt through which the only available road passed. And as they were on the point of surprising the enemy and probably engaging them successfully, just such an opportunity as soldiers dream of, the OC Mounted Troops arrived on the scene and refused to allow them to fire. The OC explained to the dismayed McKenzie, in hearing of some of the equally astonished troopers, that his instructions were not to engage the enemy, but merely to shepherd them back to Colenso.'*

A footnote makes it clear that neither Lord Dundonald nor Major Gough was present. The Composite Regiment referred to included 'A' Squadron of the Imperial Light Horse and a squadron of The Natal Carbineers. The McKenzie referred to was Major Duncan McKenzie later Brig. General McKenzie K.C.M.G, C.B., C.M.G., D.S.O., Legion of Honour.

The changed outlook on the Boer side was not manifest. Up to this time all culverts and bridges had been carefully preserved, as they would be required for the advance to the coast. Now as they withdrew they destroyed the 2-span bridge, over the Blaaukrantz River at Frere, and the all important railway bridge over the Tugela at Colenso. The period of advancing and annexing the country was over. ❑

***References:***

*'Tide of Invasion Turned'* by G. Symons and Colonel Martin.

http://www.battlefields.co.za/history/anglo-boer_war/willow_grange/g_symonds.htm

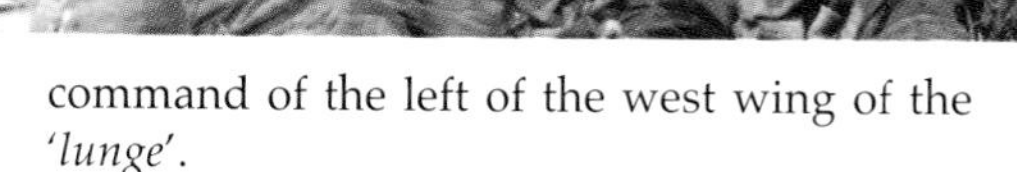

Top: Bodies, loosely buried, were found a week after the battle partially eaten by scavengers.

Right: Bodies in trench after the battle.

Once it reached the point where their resources ran out, the British forces could smash their way through in a gigantic pincer movement; first the left wing, and then followed by the right. They would consolidate behind Boer lines and spearhead a lunge for Ladysmith.

A problem for the British, however, was the size of Buller's wagon train. It was so big that it took some 13 hours to pass any given point, and thus the so-called *'dash'* was watched with interest by the Boer forces under their charismatic leader, Louis Botha. When the British moved, the Boers kept pace on the other side of the river. When they stopped, the Boers stopped too and settled down to await developments. The British were therefore constantly shadowed as they moved.

General Sir Charles Warren, a crusty eccentric individual, had been sent out after Colenso with a dormant Commission which was to be invoked if Buller showed signs of cracking under the strain. Buller intensely resented this action by his superiors, and was determined to give Warren a hard nut to crack to prove himself. If he failed, then the point that Warren was incompetent would be well proven. If he succeeded, then most of the glory would reflect on Buller as having made a good choice. In this no-win situation for Warren, Buller entrusted him with the command of the left of the west wing of the *'lunge'*.

Warren, however, failed to appreciate that his faster moving cavalry under Lord Dundonald, ranging far ahead of the baggage train, had stretched the Boer lines to breaking point by 17 January and were on the point of breaking through near Acton Homes and Bastion Hill. He instead recalled them to guard the columns oxen! On their way back, they took Bastion Hill anyway against their orders and thus opened up a second opportunity to break through the line. Warren once again testily recalled them.

Warren then followed this up with a three day artillery bombardment of the long, whale backed feature known as Thabanyama to the west of Spionkop. The Boer forces in the area had ample notice of his intentions and thus by the time the infantry assault went in, the Boers had shipped-up reinforcements, worked their magic with the spade and were well entrenched and waiting for the attack. Not surprisingly, the attack stalled. Under pressure to pull something out of the bag with General Buller looking over his shoulder; Warren, reluctant to abandon his plan of breaking through over Thabanyama in favour of Buller's plan to break through at Brakfontein to the east of Spionkop, suggested that perhaps an attack on the hill next door, Spionkop, might be the key to the

## FUTILE LOYALTY

At the height of the Battle on Spion Kop, when the combatants were shooting at each other at a range of only 20 yards, a Boer's Black servant wandered amongst the rocks looking for the body of his master. In spite of repeated warnings, the servant continued to examine the dead, and was soon shot through the brain. (Reitz, 77).

whole situation. Buller apparently somewhat in a huff, snorted *"Of course you must take Spionkop!"* The dye was cast.

Little thought, however, appears to have gone into what they were going to do with the hill once the attack succeeded. Spionkop is ringed on three sides by other hills and all these were occupied by Boer forces. It was therefore not enough to simply take Spionkop; having done so the British would be obliged to bring up heavy weaponry to protect their flanks and drive the Boers back out of rifle and artillery range. No arrangements were made until it was much too late.

The night of 23 January saw a long column of men snaking up the side of Spionkop. Right from the start the whole affair was dogged by misfortune. The column had to be led by Colonel Alex Thorneycroft of the Royal Scots Fusiliers, seconded to command an *'Uitlander'* unit comprising refugees from the Witwatersrand gold fields, Thorneycroft's Mounted Rifles. This became necessary because the African scout detailed to do so had disappeared! A large pile of sand bags at the foot of the mountain were left where they laid; no tops for the water tins; the mountain battery, so essential on the summit, was still en-route from Frere. Since it was considered that the Engineers had too much to carry and would thus be unduly fatigued when they arrived on the summit, they were allowed to leave half of their entrenching tools behind!

With Thorneycroft went the Lancashire Brigade, comprising the Royal Lancasters (The King's Own), South Lancashires and Lancashire Fusiliers, under the command of Major General Edward Woodgate, some 1 700 men in all. Under cover of the dark, the Boer picket on top of the hill was totally surprised, leaving one of their number and most of their footwear, on the slope as they departed for pastures north!

Spionkop was in British hands! However, hampered from making a proper reconnaissance by the darkness and ground mist, the British then made a cardinal tactical error. Instead of occupying either the forward of rear crest, they occupied the top of the hill and dug in as best they could. The stony ground and the lack of foresight in bringing up adequate entrenching tools restricted them to a mere 18 inch (500 mm) gash in the ground before dawn came. Once the mist dispersed, their position was totally exposed to long range rifle fire from the surrounding hills on three sides, as well as the fire from seven bigger guns, including two 155 mm *'Long Tom'* Creusot canons, 75 mm Krupp canons and Maxim-Nordenfeld 1-pounder *'Pom Poms'*. The British, of course, had neglected to bring up the heavy weapons with which they could retaliate. In addition, attacking Boer forces could climb in dead ground to within twenty yards in some places of the British trench line before having to expose themselves.

General Woodgate did not have long to rue his decision not to send scouts forward to probe for the forward crest line; by 0830 hr he was mortally wounded. For the remainder of the day, the little force was pounded from all sides while an entire British army in the valley below looked on as spectators. Apart from a gallant attempt by the King's Royal Rifles to mount a diversionary attack on Twin Peaks and desultory artillery fire, no other assistance was forthcoming to relieve the pressure on the hill. The supply train broke down totally. Wounded men lay where they fell, gasping for water in the heat, until hit yet again by Boer fire. Communications were pitiful at best, with signallers being blown away by shell fire, no oil for the lamps and messages having eventually to be conveyed by runners, who more often than not failed to reach their destinations. Not once throughout the day was the strategic importance of taking Aloe Knoll acknowledged. There was also a fiasco in the command structure with several officers believing that they were in command after Woodgate was downed. Colonel Crofton of the Kings Own knew for certain that he was the next senior officer. Colonel Hill of the Middlesex, who arrived with reinforcements in the nick of time to lead the bayonet charge that cleared the Boers out of the British trench, also thought he was in charge. In actual fact, General Buller, in a classic piece of interference, after observing the stupendous efforts made by the giant 20 stone Thorneycroft through his telescope from his forward Headquarters on Mount Alice across the river from Spionkop, *'suggested'* to Warren that Thorneycroft, a relatively junior officer, should be placed in command. This *'suggestion'* was acted upon, but the lines of command were muddled from then on because no-one else, least of all the other senior officers on the hill, were told of his promotion. Even Winston Churchill, correspondent and newly appointed subaltern in the South African Light Horse, wandered up the *'kop'* that day to see for himself what was going on. *His well meant advice to General Warren on his return down the hill not to allow another Majuba, almost resulted in him being placed under arrest!*

By nightfall; the British troops had taken an awful hammering, especially from the Aloe Knoll side (next day some 70 Lancashire Fusiliers were found in their trench with bullet holes in the right temple from enfilading fire from the Carolina Commando under Hendrik Prinsloo) and the northern face, where the Royal Lancasters had taken a pounding from Commandant Daniel Opperman and his Pretoria Commando. A portion of the British trench line had been captured by the Boers, and then taken back again. It was estimated that seven Boer shells, not to mention the long range rifle fire, hit the top of Spionkop every minute!

Thorneycroft, having fought himself to a standstill, became totally demoralised at the end of the day's fighting and ranted at the almost total lack of support and communication he had received from the rest of the army sitting on their backsides less than three miles away. He therefore determined to abandon the hill rather than have to force his men to face another such ordeal the following day. The only man on site who had the authority to stop the retreat, Brigadier Talbot Coke, was halfway down the mountain at the aid station. In view of everything else that had gone wrong that day, it seems almost inevitable that, at the crucial moment, Warren ordered Coke to leave the mountain to present a report in person to him about conditions on the summit. Coke complied with his order, but before leaving, had the foresight to instruct his Brigade Major, Captain Philips, to use his authority to stop any withdrawal from the summit. Philips, worn out by the exertions of the day, dozed off, and while he slept Thorneycroft led the last dazed survivors off the hill, past where Philips lay. Unbeknown to him, arrangements were at long last also in hand to reinforce him and send up supplies. As Thornycroft put it tersely: *"Better six good battalions safely down the hill than a mop up in the morning".*

It seems almost certain that had Thorneycroft hung on a little longer, he would have been relieved and consequently been awarded with every medal the British could pin on him in view of his stupendous efforts and outstanding leadership that day. As it happens he left too early. Although Buller tried to defend his decision to withdraw, Lord Robert's blamed Thorneycroft squarely for the loss of the hill, and the end of the war finds Thorneycroft still a Colonel and fobbed off with a Companionship of the Order of the Bath, or C.B.

The final irony is that the Boers, believing that

View of Spionkop Mountain.

The height of the Battle of Spionkop.

they had taken the worst of the beating and that the British were in total control and must at that very moment be rushing up reinforcements and supplies prior to a major thrust, had also abandoned the *'kop'* as night fell. A small group returned that night looking for bodies of dead comrades and discovered the *'kop'* abandoned by the British. Reinforcements were soon whistled up, but the British, who could have done the same, seemed to lack the will to do so and once Thorneycroft tramped off the hill with his men, meekly retired back across the Tugela.

In summary, then, a total British fiasco so far as overall command and control was concerned; a great example of inspired leadership on the part of Louis Botha, and a crying shame for the men who had fought and died for little purpose. Buller retired back from whence he came, to fail once again at Vaal Kranz at the end of the month before finally succeeding in relieving Ladysmith in the battle of Tugela Heights at the end of February.

Boer casualties from the fighting on and around Spionkop from 16 to 24 January amounted to 105 killed, including 14 from the Carolina and 24 from the Pretoria Commando. British losses were 32 officers and 290 men killed or died of wounds, 33 officers and 530 men wounded and 300 taken prisoner. Of the killed, the monument, which stands today starkly etched against the skyline with the majesty of the Drakensberg as a background, records the names of 90 Lancashire Fusiliers, 59 Royal Lancashires and 12 South Lancashires. Little wonder, therefore, that Anfield, Bolton and Blackburn football grounds had one end of the field named *'The Kop'* in memory of their brave sons. These men lie where they fell placed in their inadequate trench line and covered over. As a post scriptum, Winston Churchill discovered a friend from Harrow on top of the *'kop'*:-

*'a smart, clean looking young gentleman...had been found leaning forward on his rifle, dead. A broken pair of field glasses, shattered by the same shell that killed their owner, bore the name McCorquodale. The name and face flew together in my mind. It was the last joined subaltern of Thorneycroft's Mounted Infantry - joined in the evening, shot at dawn.'*

Pat Rundgren had the privilege of guiding the Atholl Highlanders on a battlefield tour to Spionkop in 1998. Captain Andrew Gordon stopped by McCorquodale's memorial, pulled out his cell phone and called his mother, in the U.K., who was unfortunately out in the garden and unable to take the call. He explained to us that McCorquodale had been his mother's great uncle, and it would have been poignant to phone her while standing next to where he had been killed. If one had been on the hill all those years ago, considering the shambles of the signalling arrangements, what price a cell phone then?

Organised tours to Spionkop are available throughout the year, with a full programme of commemorations, tours, wreath laying and talks scheduled in and around the Battle Sites and Winterton. For details please contact either Pat Rundgren at 03421-24560 (P.O. Box 1726, Dundee, 3000), or the Dundee Publicity Association at 03421-22121. ❑

# The Battle of Vaalkrantz
## 4-8 February 1900

*Vaalkrantz is a little flat topped hill which lay in front of Brakfontein and 3 200 m from Swartzkop, which completely dominated it from the Tugela River. Strategically the attack by the British forces on Vaalkrantz was an attempt to pierce the series of Boer positions along the Tugela River and open an access to Ladysmith.*

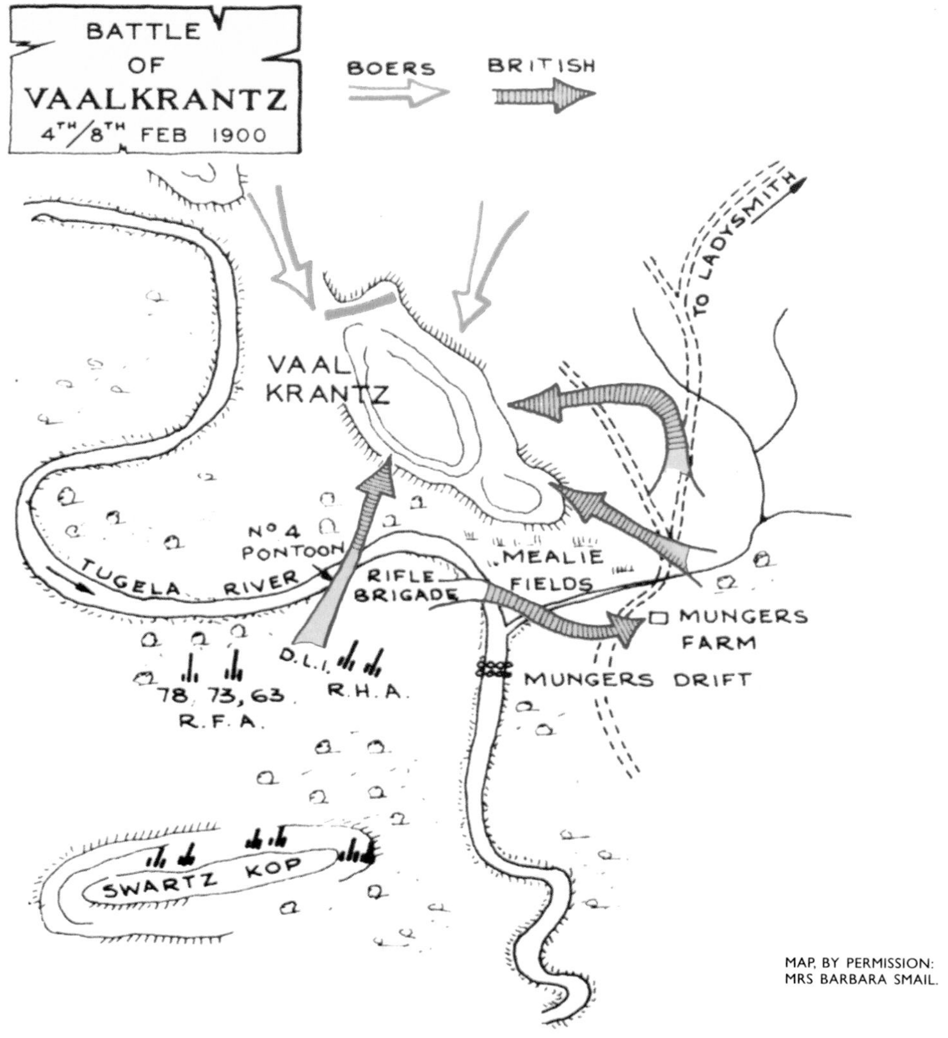


Preparations for the attack on Vaalkrantz got underway. A road and gun-slide was constructed on the southern side of Swartzkop. The Naval Brigade and Scots Fusiliers with untiring energy got six Naval 12-pounder, two guns of the 64th Battery and No.4 Mountain Battery onto the summit and carefully screened them behind bushes. Two 5-inch guns were posted on the lower spur at the western end of the hill. A pontoon bridge was constructed in front of Swartzkop. At 0915 hr on the 5th, orders were given to the guns on Swartzkop to fire on any broken ground that looked as if it might conceal

Boer bridge over Tugela River.

Boers. At 0930 hr the 63rd Battery was withdrawn and sent to cover the building of the No.4 pontoon. They were escorted by the Scottish Rifles. The bridge was completed at 1115 hr.

At 1400 hr the Durham Light Infantry moved down to the pontoon but were met with heavy fire from the Boers. After a fierce fight the D.L.I. (Durham Light Infantry) crossed the river and made for Vaalkrantz 1 100 m away. Boer guns from *'Twin Peaks'*, *'Vaalkrantz'* and *'Krantzkloof'* rained shell after shell. With superb leadership the Durham's and the Rifle Brigade were over the bank and deploying across the mealie fields. The Durhams making straight for the western foot of Vaalkrantz; the rifle brigade to clear *Mungers Farm* then to swing onto the eastern foot of Vaalkrantz.

All 66 guns in action on or below Swartzkop now concentrated their fire on Vaalkrantz which under this terrific bombardment smoked like a furnace. After this the Durham Light Infantry clambered down into a great donga. They were joined by the Rifle Brigade. With fixed bayonets the *'charge'* was on and at 1630 hr the crest was taken by the D.L.I. followed by the Rifle Brigade. Both regiments swept along the ridge for 600 m. This was on the 05 February 1900.

At 1630 hr on the 5th, Vaalkrantz was won, but could it be maintained? At noon on 06 February the Boer leader Botha arrived on the scene and at 1500 hr the Boers now infused with new energy started shelling Vaalkrantz. Taking advantage of a grass fire caused by British shells; the Boers moved forward in a smoke screen. A terrific fight ensued, but the 60th Battalion fixed bayonets and charged. The Boers retreated. This whole affair lasted about ten minutes. On the 7th, the Boer bombardment started again but no Boer attacks were made.

Buller wanted to abandon his plan but it was too late, the assault on Vaalkrantz had started. **The Battle of Vaalkrantz was lost before it started.**

Continuous firing from Boer artillery kept the British troops pinned down on Vaalkrantz, and the guns from Twin Peaks and Brakfontein were exceptionally busy.

At 1600 hr, 7 February 1900, General Buller summoned a council of war to decide on the position on Vaalkrantz. At 1900 hr, orders were issued for a *General Retirement*. On the 8th, Vaalkrantz was abandoned.❏

***Source:***
*Battlefields of the S.A. War 1899* by J.L. Smail (used with permission Mrs. Barbara Smail)

*Ken Gillings*

# The Battle of Tugela Heights 14-28 February 1900

By this stage, the Boers' morale had dropped, and there were only some 5 000 Burghers along the Thukela Line. They had taken up position along both the north and the south banks of the river, and were commanded by General Lucas Meyer.

On 14 February 1900, the Mounted Brigade, commanded by Major General The Earl of Dundonald, occupied Hussar Hill. The Boer line along the south bank stretched from Hlangwane to Cingolo Mountain. On 17 February, the British occupied Cingolo by advancing in a sweeping movement towards the East. Two more important Boer positions - Monte Cristo and Green Hill - were taken by the British on 18 February, and the key to the position (Hlangwane Hill) was occupied on 19 February, despite a spirited defence by the Burghers of the Bethal Commando. By 20 February, the British had commanded the south bank of the river.

At this stage, General Louis Botha had arrived at the Thukela Heights, and started to direct operations. Boer reinforcements were sent to the north bank, and on 21 February, the British advanced across the river. By 22 February, he had transferred 15 battalions of infantry and some 40 guns across to the north bank, and became engaged in some heavy fighting in the area known as the Colenso Kopjes, resulting in the infantry being pinned down by a determined Boer resistance.

It became necessary to extricate his troops from the Colenso kopjes, and Major General Wynne's 11th Brigade was entrusted with the task. General Wynne's objective was a low ridge, split by a gully, but which appears as three separate adjacent hills, on what are now known as the Wynne Hills.

In order to assist with the dislodging of the Boers on the next feature, Major General A.F. Hart's Irish Brigade, reinforced with troops from Colonel Norcott's brigade, attempted to dislodge the Boers, mainly from the Krugersdorp and Boksburg Commandos, from their well protected sangars along the summit of what has since become known as Hart's Hill. This fighting commenced on 23 February and was halted on 25 February, when an armistice was called to remove the dead and dying from the battlefield. During this respite, the Boers emerged from their sangars, and the combatants' swopped tobacco and drank whisky together. At the end of the armistice, however, the British gunners took range on the well camouflaged positions to which the Boers returned.

By the morning of 26 February, General Buller had positioned 76 guns across the Thukela on the south bank, and the following day, the hopelessly outnumbered Boers were subjected to a determined onslaught by virtually every brigade available to the British. It was during the course of the day that news reached both Boer and British of the surrender of General Piet Cronje at Paardeberg on this, the same

### Sporting chance

During the attack on Red Fort on Bell's Kop, Ladysmith, Robert Reinecke was under severe fire from the British whilst trying to carry a wounded comrade to safety. The soldiers, realising his predicament, ceased firing, and even allowed him to return to the firing line unmolested. (Reitz, 51).

## THE COST OF WAR!!

**1 May 1900**: Replying to a question in the House of Commons, the Rt. Hon. Hanbury said that the cost of the war in South Africa to the end of March 1900 was twenty-three and a quarter million pounds (£23 250 000).

## SOCCER

There are two versions of the story of the shell that briefly interrupted the soccer match between the Gordon Highlanders and the Imperial Light Horse during the Siege of Ladysmith. Bella Crow (a nurse) wrote in her diary on 18 November 1899 that a Long Tom shell landed in an unoccupied tent, and then buried itself between that tent and the next one, in which a number of men were playing nap. *"It scattered dust all over but they never moved, went on playing, so did the footballers"*. Griffith records that the Boers dropped a shell into the middle of the game and that, under cover of the smoke and dust, the canny Scots sneaked a goal. The Imperial Light horse objected, and even asked for a ruling from the Football Association in England.

**Thank God we Kept the Flag Flying**, *Kenneth Griffith*, 1974 Hutchinson & Co.

day that the Boers had achieved their victory at Majuba in 1881. The sheer weight of numbers, supported by the most intensive artillery bombardment in the war to date, resulted in the British overrunning the Boers' positions on Hart's, Kitcheners and Railway Hills, and on 28 February, the British broke through at Pieters, close to the left extremity of the Boers' defensive line, and later that day, a composite force of mounted infantry commanded by Major Gough rode into Ladysmith, followed by Lord Dundonald a few minutes later.

The British casualties during the battle of the Tugela Heights had been heavy, they lost some 2 259 killed, wounded and missing, compared with approximately 232 Boers according to official sources. The total strengths also vary, with most sources giving those of the British as some 28 000 (with 85 guns) to the approximately 5 000 (some reports claim as few as 3 000) Boers with 11 guns. General Buller rode into Ladysmith on 3 March to a tumultuous welcome. The Boers commenced a hasty retreat to the north, eventually taking up positions along the Biggarsberg.

It was only during May 1900 that Buller advanced out of Ladysmith, forcing the Boers back towards Lang's Nek (formerly Laing's Nek) and Botha's Pass. ❑

***References:***

http://www.battlefields.co.za/history/anglo-boer_war/tugela.htm

General Louis Botha's house in Vryheid before and after it was blown up by the British.

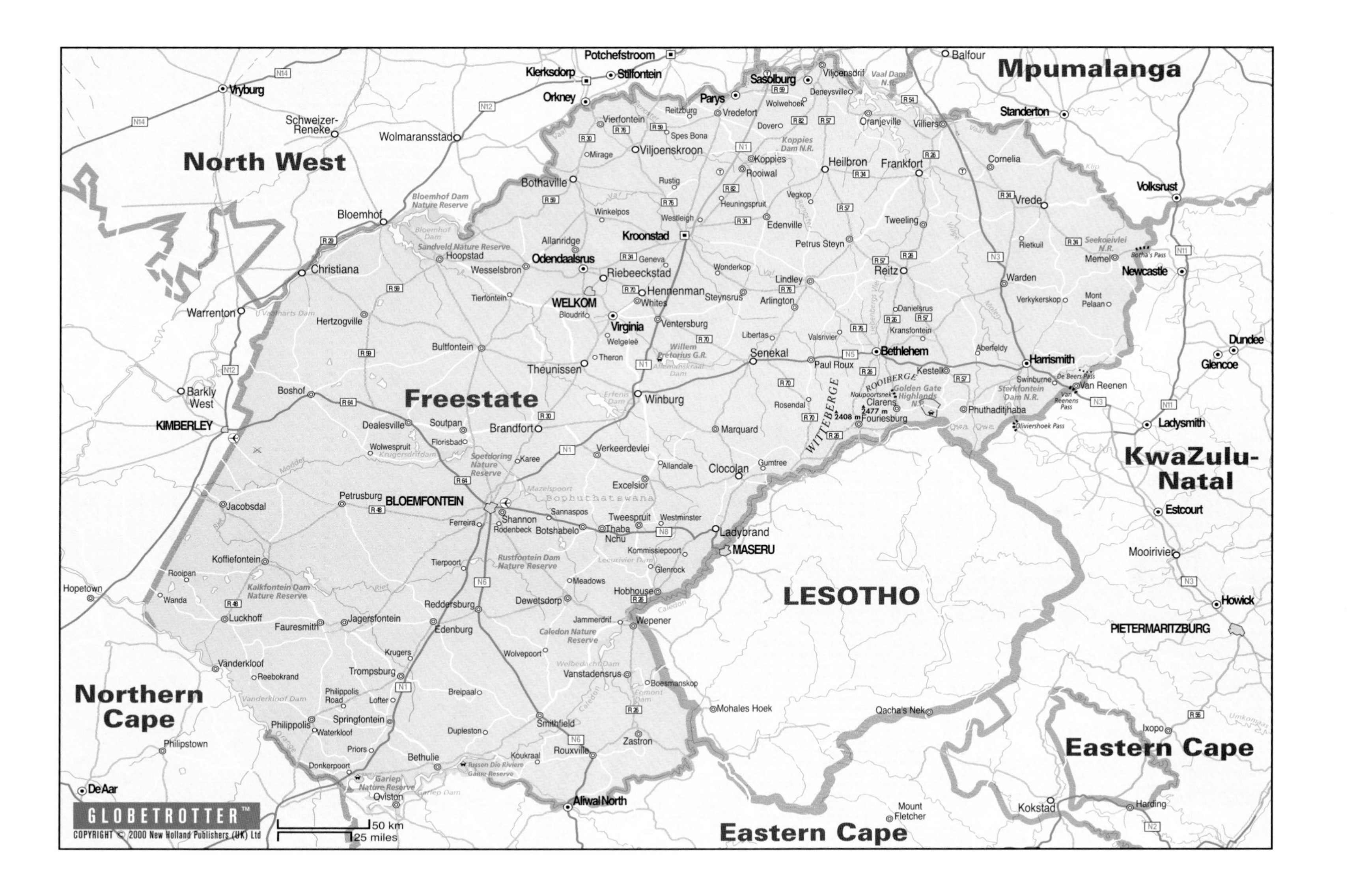

Mpumalanga
North West
Freestate
KwaZulu-Natal
LESOTHO
Northern Cape
Eastern Cape
Eastern Cape
BLOEMFONTEIN
KIMBERLEY
MASERU
PIETERMARITZBURG
WELKOM
Potchefstroom
Klerksdorp
Stilfontein
Orkney
Sasolburg
Parys
Vryburg
Schweizer-Reneke
Wolmaransstad
Bloemhof
Christiana
Warrenton
Barkly West
Hopetown
De Aar
Philipstown
Kroonstad
Bethlehem
Harrismith
Senekal
Winburg
Ladybrand
Ficksburg
Clocolan
Wepener
Zastron
Aliwal North
Smithfield
Bethulie
Trompsburg
Philippolis
Jagersfontein
Fauresmith
Koffiefontein
Jacobsdal
Petrusburg
Boshof
Dealesville
Brandfort
Theunissen
Virginia
Odendaalsrus
Bothaville
Viljoenskroon
Heilbron
Frankfort
Reitz
Vrede
Villiers
Newcastle
Volksrust
Standerton
Ladysmith
Estcourt
Mooirivier
Howick
Dundee
Glencoe
Kokstad
Harding
Ixopo
Qacha's Nek
Mohales Hoek
Mount Fletcher
Balfour
Hobhouse
Dewetsdorp
Reddersburg
Edenburg
Thaba Nchu
Botshabelo
Excelsior
Marquard
Paul Roux
Fouriesburg
Clarens
Kestell
Phuthaditjhaba
Van Reenen
Memel
Warden
Lindley
Petrus Steyn
Edenville
Koppies
Hennenman
Ventersburg
Riebeeckstad
Hoopstad
Wesselsbron
Bultfontein
Soutpan
Hertzogville
Luckhoff
Vanderkloof
Springfontein
Rouxville
Witteberge
Rooiberge
Golden Gate Highlands N.P.
Willem Pretorius G.R.
Bloemhof Dam Nature Reserve
Sandveld Nature Reserve
Soetdoring Nature Reserve
Rustfontein Dam Nature Reserve
Caledon Nature Reserve
Kalkfontein Dam Nature Reserve
Gariep Nature Reserve
Tussen Die Riviere Game Reserve
Sterkfontein Dam N.R.
Seekoeivlei N.R.
Koppies Dam N.R.
2477 m
2408 m
50 km
25 miles
GLOBETROTTER™
COPYRIGHT © 2000 New Holland Publishers (UK) Ltd

# PROCLAMATION

## To the Burghers of the Orange Free State.

The British troops under my command, having entered the Orange Free State. I feel it my duty to make known to all Burghers the cause of our coming, as well as to do all in my power to put an end to the devastation caused by this war, so that should they continue the war the inhabitants of the Orange Free State may not do so ignorantly, but with full knowledge of their responsibility before God for the lives lost in the campaign.

Before the war began the British Government, which had always desired and cultivated peace and friendship with the people of the Orange Free State, gave a solemn assurance to President Steyn that, if the Orange Free State remained neutral, its territory would not be invaded, and its independence would be at all times fully respected by Her Majesty's Government.

In spite of that declaration, the Government of the Orange Free State was guilty of a wanton and unjustifiable invasion of British territory.

The British Government believes that this act of aggression was not committed with the general approval and free will of a people with whom it has lived in complete amity for so many years. It believes that the responsibility rests wholly with the Government of the Orange Free State, acting, not in the interests of the country, but under mischievous influences from without. The British Government, therefore, wishes the people of the Orange Free State to understand that it bears them no ill will, and, so far as is compatible with the successful conduct of the war, and the re-establishment of peace in South Africa, it is anxious to preserve them from the evils brought upon them by the wrongful action of their Government.

I therefore warn all Burghers to desist from any further hostility towards Her Majesty's Government and the troops under my command, and I undertake that any of them, who may so desist and who are found staying in their homes and quietly pursuing their ordinary occupations, will not be made to suffer in their persons or property on account of their having taken up arms in obedience to the order of their Government. Those, however, who oppose the forces under my command, or furnish the enemy with supplies or information, will be dealt with according to the customs of war.

Requisitions for food, forage, fuel, or shelter, made on the authority of the officers in command of Her Majesty's troops, must be at once complied with; but everything will be paid for on the spot, prices being regulated by the local market rates. If the inhabitants of any district refuse to comply with the demands made on them, the supplies will be taken by force, a full receipt being given.

Should any inhabitant of the country consider that he or any member of his household has been unjustly treated by any officer, soldier, or civilian attached to the British Army, he should submit his complaint, either personally or in writing, to my Head-Quarters or to the Head-Quarters of the nearest General Officer. Should the complaint on enquiry be substantiated, redress will be given.

Orders have been issued by me, prohibiting soldiers from entering private houses, or molesting the civil population on any pretext whatever, and every precaution has been taken against injury to property on the part of any person belonging to, or connected with, the Army.

February 1900

**ROBERTS,**

*Field Marshal.*

Commanding in Chief,
South Africa.

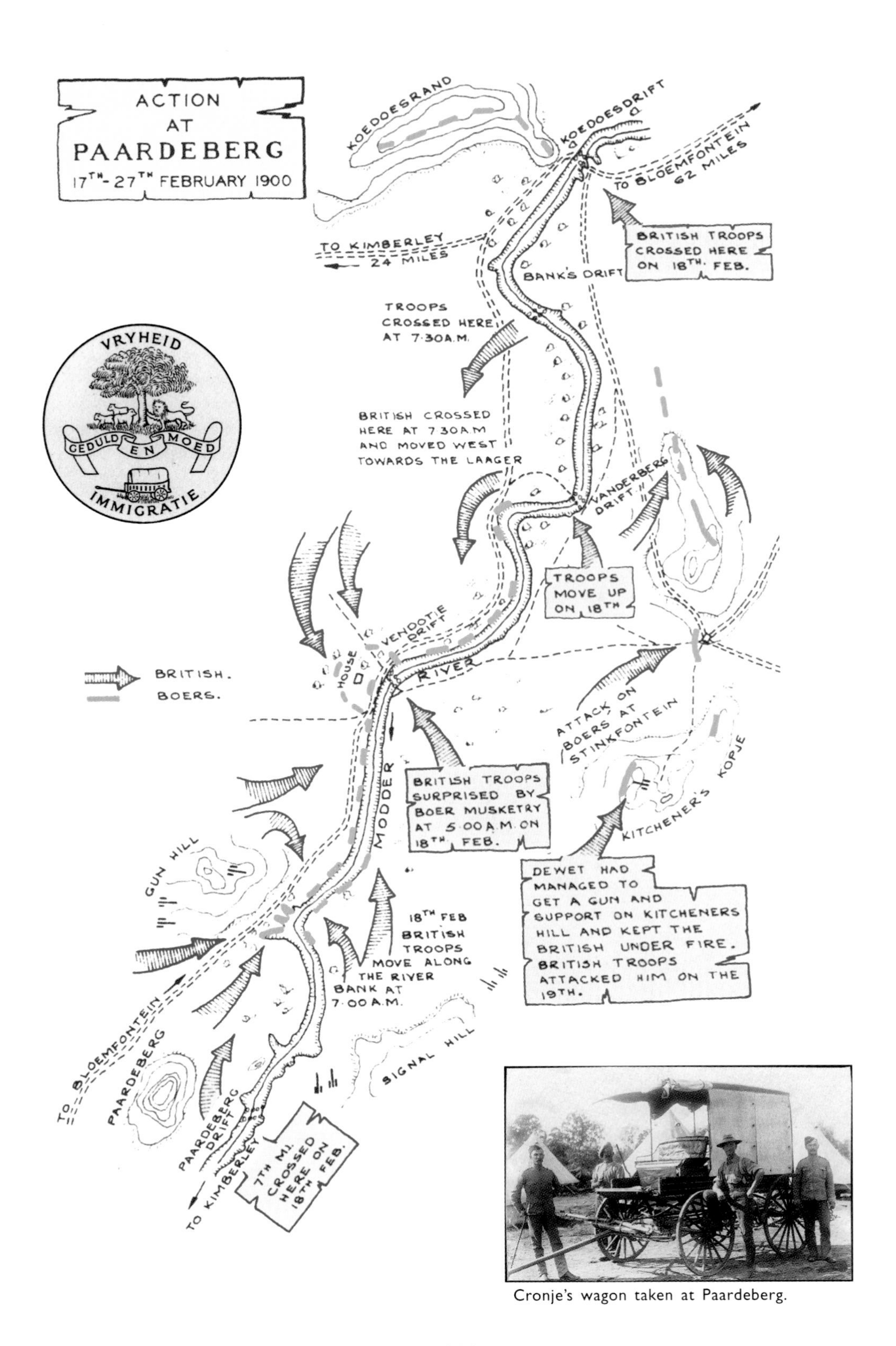


Cronje's wagon taken at Paardeberg.

After the battle of Magersfontein, the new Commander-in-Chief on the Western Front, Lord Roberts, decided to relieve Kimberley with the help of General J.D.P. French and his cavalry.

By means of a wide flanking movement to avoid the Boers at Magersfontein, French succeeded on 15 February 1900. This movement put Cronje in a precarious position in that his force of 4 000 were confronted with British soldiers to the north *and* the south of them. That left him with no alternative but to fall back to Bloemfontein along the Modder River – they were dependant on the river to obtain water for the livestock and trek oxen.

Due to the slow pace of Cronje, the British forces caught up with them at Paardeberg on 17 February 1900. They denied the Boers crossing the drift over the Modder River with the result that the Boers entrenched themselves on both sides of the river bank. On 18 February, H.H. Kitchener, who commanded the British forces for the day as Roberts had fallen ill, made a frontal assault on the entrenched Boer positions. This was fatal as the Boers were very well positioned and the result was that Kitchener suffered heavy losses. In fact, the losses on this day were the heaviest for any day during the whole of the war. After the debacle of the 18th, Roberts again took control and executed his plan of bombarding the Boer laager with military precision. He had 40 000 troops and 100 guns at his disposal against the 4 000 with only five guns. His plan was to encircle the laager and with the heavy artillery bombardment, bring them to surrender. General C.R. de Wet made an attempt to relieve the laager, but due to the women and children in the camp, the men thought it too risky to adhere to his plan.

The Siege train used at Paardeberg.

Danie Theron, a scout, crawled through the encircling soldiers to bring De Wet's plan to Cronje, but because of the aforementioned consideration, it never materialised. The heavy bombardment left Cronje with no other option but to surrender.

**18 February 1900:** Kitchener believed that the Boer forces at Paardeberg totalled approximately 10 000 strong, and that reinforcements were due to arrive at any time. The British force was 15 000 men; and Kitchener resolved to attack Cronje without delay. When dawn broke the Boer wagons were spread out in a line along the northern bank. Hasty defenses of shallow trenches were dug out of the veldt above the banks and in the river banks on both sides of the river.

At dawn both British infantry and Mounted forces worked their way along the south bank and crossed the river. At 0700 hr the main assault started down stream against the Boers around a river bend.

**19 February 1900:** On the morning of the 19th Kitchener found that only 3 km of the river was occupied. Fresh Boer reinforcements under De Wet and Ferreira were due to arrive at any moment.

**20 February 1900:** The relief of Cronje had become a dominating factor with the Boers. It was decided by Roberts not to storm the laager but to reduce it to siege with continuous bombardment from his guns.

**21 February 1900:** Strong infantry forces were posted between Kitchener's Kopje and the river. Cavalry approached in a wide arc from the south in the hope of trapping De Wet. He, however, had moved to the village of Poplar Grove. Machine guns, 50 pieces of artillery ranging from 12-pounders to four of the Naval 4.7 ins guns made movement impossible, and filled the river banks with a green cloud of lyddite fumes.

**22 February 1900:** A balloon sent up gave the Boer positions to the artillery on the accuracy of their firing.

**23 February 1900:** Cloudy weather prevented Cronje sending out heliograph messages. It

## A BLACK MAN'S WAR: CRONJE'S DEFEAT AT PAARDEBERG

Major Trollope, of the Aldershot Ballooning Department, said that the conquest of Cronje was really due to the keen eyes of a *'Cape Boy'** who had been taken up in the balloon, and who, beyond the range of English eyes, was able to tell that the artillery was firing at a dummy laager, and that the Boers were hiding in the bed of the river.

*A 'Cape Boy' in the language of the time was also known as a 'Malay' and is a person of mixed white/black parentage, or a so-called 'Coloured' person.

STEVE'S WAR STORIES

also started to rain heavily which bought relief to the laager although those in the trenches suffered the discomfort.

**24 February 1900:** All day and night it had rained. The weather made it possible for Danie Theron, who in the evening, crawled through the British lines with a message for Cronje from De Wet who had a plan to relieve him (Cronje).

**25 February 1900:** Cronje discussed De Wet's plan with his Commandants, as in the interim the river had risen two and a half metres which created a barrier of swirling water to be crossed before the British lines could be negotiated. It was decided, as there were women and children with the Boers, that no break-out was to be tried until a bridge could be built.

**26 February 1900:** The Boers started to build a bridge. The majority of Boer officers openly urged surrendered, but Cronje refused. That afternoon Roberts brought into action several Pom-Poms, showering 1-pounder shells notable for their demoralising effect, at the Boers. A siege train of four howitzers arrived and started to drop 120-pound shells. The British infantry then started to move in from the west.

**27 February 1900:** Before dawn the Royal Canadians and other Dominion forces moved to within 50 metres of the Boer trenches, but were overcome by heavy fire. They later attacked again and took possession of the Boer trenches at daybreak.

***Between 0500 hr and 0600 hr the Boers surrendered. Cronje rode out on his grey horse and approached Roberts. Majuba was at last avenged and the Western Front, with the exception of the continuous siege at Mafeking, had collapsed.***

**Casualties**

Boer: 4 085 captured and made PoWs.
British: 357 dead, 906 wounded, 61 missing.

## *from Paardeberg Museum*

# A Soldier's Protest - Colonel Ormelie Campbell Hannay

On the morning of 18 February 1900 Cronje's laager was almost completely surrounded by the British forces. Although most of the more experienced British commanders hoped to overwhelm Cronje by means of a sustained artillery bombardment, as the terrain did not lend itself to an infantry attack, Lord Kitchener, supreme commander in the absence of Lord Roberts, felt that a frontal attack would be the most effective way to force Cronje into capitulation. A full scale frontal attack commenced at 0700 hr.

Kelly-Kenny's 6th Division attacked the laager from a southerly direction whilst Colville's 9th Division attacked from the west. Colonel O.C. Hannay's (late Argyll & Sutherland Highlanders) 1st Brigade Mounted Infantry, supported by the Welsh and Essex Regiments, was supposed to cross the Modder River at Vanderberg Drift in order to attack the laager from the east. The British attackers met with fierce resistance and the concentrated Boer fire pinned them down on the plain and caused severe loss of life. By midday the British attack came to a virtual standstill.

At about 1400 hr Kitchener ordered Kelly-Kenny to renew his division's attack immediately. Kelly-Kenny resisted this order whereupon Kitchener decided that Hannay, whose men had been hindered in their advance due to an attack by a detachment of the Bloemfontein commando, should carry out the delayed eastern attack. Hannay attempted to do this but little progress was made due to the fact that his men were utterly exhausted. Still Kitchener was not satisfied; he ordered Hannay to rush the laager at all costs: *'Try and carry Stephenson's brigade on with you. But if they cannot go the mounted infantry should do it. Gallop up if necessary and fire into the laager.'* Upon receiving the order Hannay realised that most of his men would lose their lives unnecessarily as contact and co-operation with Stephenson's brigade were totally out of the question.

Kitchener's order was completely out of touch with reality and Hannay regarded it as inhuman; to Kitchener common soldiers were expendable. Hannay resolved to follow Kitchener's instruction but he also decided to protest against it in his own way. He sent his staff away on various pretexts and gathered a small group of Mounted Infantry, about 50 in total, with himself at the helm. After telling his men, led by Captain H.M.A. Hankey, *'We are going to charge the laager, follow me'.*

Hannay headed straight for the Boer trenches which were situated some 500 metres distant. Hannay had barely progressed halfway when his horse was killed under him. This did not deter him; he disentangled himself and continued his charge on foot. Some 200 metres from the laager Hannay was finally stopped after being hit several times. Hankey followed in the footsteps of his commander and met with the same fate on almost the same spot as Hannay. Most of Hannay's men were killed although some of them reached the laager where they were taken prisoner. Others swerved off to the right avoiding the laager and subsequent capture or death. The premature movement of Hannay's troops achieved nothing as was to be expected; but Hannay - in the words of Thomas Pakenham - had died just as he intended: *as a supreme act of protest against the way Kitchener sacrificed his army*. Hannay's body was only retrieved after Cronje's capitu-lation on 27 February 1900 and he was buried on the spot where he fell. Today, his lonely grave on the wide open Western Free State plain, serves as a lasting reminder of the way in which a ruthless military commander was prepared to sacrifice his army. His grave has the inscription on the front ***Darkness comes over me, my rest a stone*** and on the back of the cross ***Obedient unto Death.*** ❑

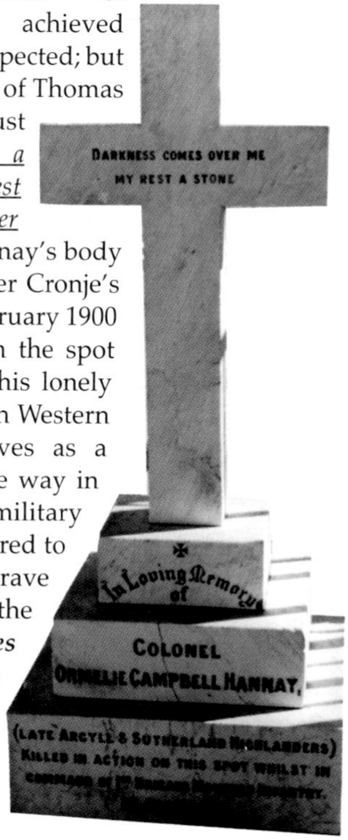

*from Paardeberg Museum*

# The British Soldier

The British Army undertook several long and exhausting marches, more often than not in the night, in order to prevent Cronje's escape. Night marches were favoured as it was hoped that this would protect the troops against the scorching heat during the day. It took much longer than day-marches due to nearly impassable terrain which sapped the soldiers' strength. Lacking sufficient knowledge of the area they often lost their way in the dark. Any chance of rest during the day was impossible as the soldiers did not have tents that could protect them against the sun.

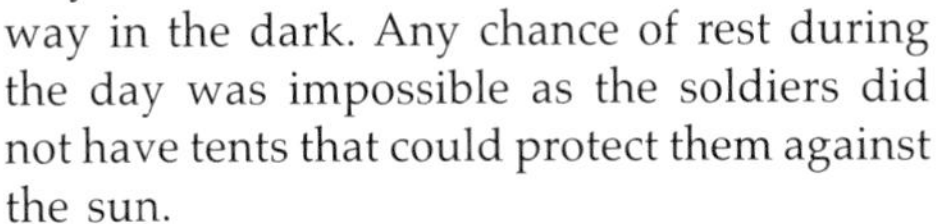

Food and water were often in short supply on the Western Front owing to numerous transport difficulties. The problem was compounded when General C.R. de Wet captured a British supply column at Waterval Drift on 15 February 1900. As a result of this the British soldiers at Paardeberg were put on half-rations for the remainder of February. After which they received 3/4 rations until the capture of Bloemfontein. During the attack on 18 February the troops had to do without food and water for more than 12 hours. Lord Roberts furthermore implemented water rationing which left the soldiers with only half a bottle of water per day. Troops unsatisfied with this measure filled their canteens with water from the Modder River contaminated with cattle carcasses.

The hardships were aggravated by the fact that worn out equipment, such as boots, was not replaced.

Medical care at Paardeberg left a lot to be desired. The fact that British soldiers had to replenish their water supply from the contaminated Modder River, their insufficient rations, and the unhygenic conditions they had to content with during the march to Bloemfontein, all contributed to a terrible outbreak of typhoid amongst the occupying force in the Free State capital.

Not much could be done to combat '*the plague of Bloemfontein*': doctors, nurses and medical facilities were inadequate and led to the neglecting of patients. At one stage nearly 5 000 soldiers in Bloemfontein suffered from the disease. During the period from March to July 1900 approximately 1 231 soldiers died as a result of disease. ❑

Top: *Mounted Infantry* by Jason Askew.
Left: Boers surrendering at Paardeberg.

### OPPIE KOPPIE, BETHULIE

Overnight in this tranquil atmosphere and enjoy spectacular views over Gariep Dam. Visit the Tussen-Die-Riviere Game Reserve and see a Black Eagle nesting site. Rooms have TV, and phone. Dinner is available by arrangement
4 Rooms from R120 pp sharing. Bed & Breakfast.
Tel: (051) 763 0388. Fax: (051) 763 0388.
Cell/Mobile: 082 923 1493.

### DE OUDE POMP SAFARI CAMP, NORVALSPONT

A Safari-Tented Camp on the banks of the Orange River at Norvalspont and 10 km from the N1. Experience luxury safari-tents with magnificent views from the decks, or stay in the sandstone cottage. Visit the Boer War sites.
2 Tents, 1 Cottage from R130 pp B&B. Dinner R40.
Tel: (051) 754 5055. Fax: (051) 754 5055.
Cell/Mobile: 083 274 4463.

### ARTISTS' COLONY KAROO GUEST HOUSE, SMITHFIELD

Restored old buildings, going back 150 years, one being a National Monument. Enjoy the character and charm of this property, and experience the atmosphere of the Free State as it was 150 years ago and during the Anglo-Boer War.
5 Rooms from R135 pp sharing. Bed & Breakfast.
Tel: (051) 683 1138. Fax: (051) 683 1138 ask.
e-mail: colony@global.co.za

### PULA HOUSE, SMITHFIELD

"Halfway to anywhere in South Africa." A Victorian Karoo house beautifully restored and on the outskirts of the town. Enjoy the warm atmosphere, grace and charm with an hospitable welcome. Easy access to the Anglo-Boer War sites.
4 Rooms from R140 pp sharing. Bed & Breakfast.
Tel/Fax: (051) 683 0032. Cell/Mobile: 083 272 3001.
e-mail: pula@acenet.co.za

### SMITHFIELD HOUSE, SMITHFIELD

This beautiful old redecorated Victorian Colonial house is situated in a quiet and secluded position on the edge of town. All rooms have en-suite showers or bathrooms. Relax at the swimming pool or on the tennis court.
3 Rooms from R150 pp sharing. Bed & Breakfast
Tel: (051) 683 0071. Fax: (051) 683 0045
Cell/Mobile: 082 450 6779

## Springfontein

### Prior Grange Guest Farm, Springfontein

Discover old-fashioned hospitality on the farm situated in the southern Free State. 6 km from Springfontein. The farm dates back to 1854, and has its own blockhouse. Owner, Blackie de Swardt, a tour guide, specialises in the Anglo-Boer War of the area.
2 Cottages & stables from R95 pp sharing. B&B.
Self-catering from R75 pp. Dinner on request.
Cell/Mobile: 083 310 3284.

## Ladybrand

### Cranberry Cottage, Ladybrand

A charming late 19th century sandstone building situated in the beautiful Eastern Free State Highlands. Only 18km from Maseru in Lesotho. Colonial style filled with antiques. Boer fugitives hid in the loft to escape capture and death.
17 Rooms from R165 pp sharing. Bed & Breakfast.
Tel: (05191) 2290. Fax: (05191) 41168.
e-mail: crancott@lesoff.co.za

### Fort Amity, Ladybrand

Close to Ladybrand which borders Lesotho, this double-storey sandstone house is set in magnificent gardens. With a tennis court and swimming pool. Undercover parking. Enjoy the charm of the guest suite with a Victorian 4-poster bed.
4 Rooms from R150 pp sharing. Bed & Breakfast.
Tel: (05191) 3131. Fax: (05191) 41633.
Cell/Mobile: 082 454 3337

## Ficksburg

### Bella Rosa Guest House, Ficksburg

A Victorian sandstone house built in 1899, in the heart of Ficksburg. Enjoy the library/lounge with open fireplace; fully licensed English pub or relax with tea or coffee on the verandah. Rooms have TV and phones. Dinners available in the restaurant.
10 Rooms from R150 - R190 per person. B&B.
Tel: (051) 933 2623. Fax: (051) 933 2623.
Cell/Mobile: 082 493 0216

# Bethlehem • Harrismith

## Bokmakierie Guest House, Bethlehem

Situated 90 minutes from the Drakensberg, 35 minutes from Golden Gate and 20 minutes from Clarens, Bokmakierie Guest House has a warm inviting ambience. Rooms cater for your every need. Self-catering accommodation available as well.
7 Rooms from R125 - R 150 pp sharing. B&B.
Tel: (058) 303 7144. Fax: (058) 303 4215.
e-mail: lhlbhm@dorea.co.za

## Fisant Guest House, Bethlehem

Situated in a quiet suburb of Bethlehem. All rooms at Fisant Guest House have DSTV, M-Net, Electric blankets and heaters for winter and fans for summer, hairdryers and tea and coffee trays. Relax in the lounge. There is secure parking.
5 Rooms from R125 - R 150 pp sharing. B&B.
Tel: (058) 303 7144. Fax: (058) 303 4215.
e-mail: lhlbhm@dorea.co.za

## Panorama Guest House, Bethlehem

Situated in a quiet suburb of Bethlehem. All rooms have a private entrance,TV, DSTV, M-Net and tea/ coffee facilities. Relax in a private lounge or by the pool. Secure parking. Close to the cinema and the shopping mall for all your requirements.
5 Rooms from R150 pp sharing. Bed & Breakfast.
Tel: (058) 303 4329. Fax: (058) 303 8471.
Cell/Mobile: 082 490 7326.

## La La Nathi Country House, Harrismith

Enjoy the ambience of the Free State Highlands in this beautiful sandstone thatched home situated on the N3 between Durban and Johannesburg. All rooms have TV, Mnet and undercarpet heating. Two luxury rooms with Spabaths and fireplaces. Dinner on request. Easy drive to the battlefields.
6 Rooms from R165 pp sharing. Bed & Breakfast.
Tel: (058) 623 0282. Fax: (058) 623 0282.

## Rooikraal Guest House, Harrismith

An old sandstone manor house 15 km north of Harrismith next to the N3. Perfect location for touring the Free State and Natal Battlefields. Rooms have TV, M-Net and Tea/Coffee facilities. Dinner on request. Visit the local Boer War sites.
4 Rooms from R120 pp sharing. Bed & Breakfast.
Tel: (058) 623 1527. Fax: (058) 622 3042.
Cell/Mobile: 082 785 2709.

# Bloemfontein

**BISHOPS GLEN, BLOEMFONTEIN**

Bishops Glen, circa 1813, near Bloemfontein was the remount depot during the Anglo-Boer War with various skirmishes on the surrounding hills. With an adjoining game farm perfect for walks and drives amongst the game.
3 Rooms from R140 pp. B&B. R200 pp. DB&B.
Tel: (051) 861 2210. Fax: (051) 861 2210.
Cell/Mobile: 082 3744986.

**DE OUDE KRAAL COUNTRY LODGE, BLOEMFONTEIN**

This historicl home was built in the late 1800's on a farm 35 km south of Bloemfontein and close to an old Blockhouse. Enjoy the peace, tranquillity and the hospitality of a Free State farm. Enjoy the superb, home-made farm dinners.
8 Rooms from R285 pp sharing. Dinner B&B.
Tel: (051) 564 0636. Fax: (051) 564 0635
e-mail: deoude@intekom.co.za

**HOBBIT HOUSE, BLOEMFONTEIN**

Winner of several awards, this charming 1924 Victorian style house, with each room decorated individually and offering good food in a tranquil setting. Each room has television, a bar fridge and tea/coffee-making facilities.
6 Rooms from R450 per Room. Bed & Breakfast.
Tel/Fax: (051) 447 0663. Cell/Mobile: 083 305 8434.
e-mail: hobbit@intekon.co.za

**JEDIDJA, BLOEMFONTEIN**

Situated in a quiet suburb close to Naval Hill from where you can watch the animals. Rooms have private entrances, television and coffee/tea-making facilities. Enclosed parking; and close to all the restaurants and shops.
3 Rooms from R110 - R130 pp sharing. B&B.
Tel: (051) 436 6584. Fax: (051) 436 6584.
e-mail: jedidja@mjvn.co.za

**PLOVER COTTAGE, BLOEMFONTEIN**

Situated 15 km north of Bloemfontein on the site of an Anglo-Boer War battlefield camp. There are excavations and artefacts to view; as well as informative tours to all the famous Battlefields in the area by a SATOUR registered tour guide.
5 Rooms from R135 pp sharing. Bed & Breakfast.
Tel: (051) 861 2136. Fax: (051) 861 2136.
Cell/Mobile: 083 262 0861.

# Bloemfontein

### Sir Grey's Guest House, Bloemfontein

In the centre of Bloemfontein, overlooking the historic buildings of Grey College, Sir Grey's Guest House takes pride in offering warm and personal service. Relax in the sitting room or around the pub.
8 Rooms from R130 pp sharing. Bed & Breakfast.
Tel: (051) 448 3744. Fax: (051) 448 3740.
Cell/Mobile: 082 375 0456.

### Protea Hotel Bloemfontein, Bloemfontein

In the heart of Bloemfontein's CBD, ideal for exploring the historic buildings of the city and a short drive to the Boer War Museum. For a culinary selection; *The Courtroom Restaurant, Judges Ladies Bar* and *Polley's Coffee Shop* to whet your appetite.
112 Rooms from R360 single & R395 double Room Only.
Tel: (051) 430 1911. Fax: (051) 447 7102.
e-mail: bloemf@iafrica.com

Mealies were the most important source of food for the Boer commandos. *"It is our meat and drink and all that sustains our animals. It is eaten green and ripe, boiled and roasted, in porridge and in cakes. It is also toasted and treated as 'coffee'. Take it away and we could not remain in the field ten days longer. Without it we would have had to abandon the war more than a year ago. A mealie cob should be on our coat of arms, to which it has more claim that all the fond images thereon."* (Schikkerling, 326).

### Nicknames

Roksak Redelinghuis acquired his nickname *"Roksak"* (pocket dress), because he always carried one of his wife's dresses with him. This served as a constant reminder of his wife, and on one occasion helped to save his life. Badly wounded, and touching the dress he remarked: *"If I die the General will take my fair-haired wife"*. (Schikkerling, 245)

### Hand grenades

Schikkerling's commando made hand grenades by filling the hollow ornamental cast-iron tops of electric posts with dynamite, as well as ink pots and baking powder tins, which were also filled with metal nuts and scraps of iron. (Schikkerling, 359)

### Escape

Cornelius Spruyt was captured on 19 February 1900, during the early phase of the Battle of Paardeberg. On his way to Cape Town he managed to untie himself and jumped out of the speeding train. Hiding during the day and marching at night, he arrived at Colesburg four days later. (Uys, 38).

Another member of the Heidelberg Commando captured at Paardeberg, Charlie Brink, escaped in Cape Town and boarded a Russian ship which took him to Lourenzo Marques. (Uys, 38,50).

## BLOEMFONTEIN TOURISM INFORMATION CENTRE

**60 Park Road, Willows, Bloemfontein.**

**PO Box 639, Bloemfontein 9300. Tel: (051) 405 8489/90. Fax: (051) 447 3859.**

The first European to settle in the area was the farmer **Johannes Brits** in 1840. He found conditions favourable around the natural spring that eventually gave the city its name. The farm purchased by **Major Warden** in 1846, became a highly-prized area of land among missionaries, hunters, Voortrekkers and settlers in these otherwise dry plains. Pioneers in the area were livid at the occupation of the ***Orange River Sovereignty*** by Warden, and another englishman, **Sir Harry Smith**, and ordered them back to the Cape Colony. The British returned and controlled the Sovereignty until 1854, during which time Bloemfontein had grown into a small town. After suffering losses to **Moshoeshoe**, the Basotho chief, and a change in Imperial policy, the British decided it would be cheaper to return the Free State to the Boers, and allow them to settle disputes between themselves, the Basothos and the Griquas.

Appeal Court, Bloemfontein.

Celebrated English author Anthony Trollope visited Bloemfontein in the 1870's and his words and heart remain; accurately describing this old colonial town: ***"The town is so quiet.. and removed from strife and want and disorder, that the beholder as he looks down upon it is tempted to think that the peace of such an abode is better than the excitement of Paris, London or New York."*** This is a place that has been fought for by many, lost by some, and won by others who saw in it something too rich to give up.

### Anglo-Boer War Sites

**Kings Park:** The two memorials in the park are the **Canadian Soldiers Memorial** and the **Scottish Soldiers Memorial**. Both can be found along the Kingsway.

**National Woman's Memorial**: Monument Road. A 36,5 metre sandstone obelisk by Anton van Wouw, dedicated to the women and children who died in the Anglo-Boer War concentration camps. The nearby War Museum houses articles and artifacts from that war.

**President Brand Cemetery**: With row upon row of metal crosses, this cemetery is a quiet devastating criticism of the sadness of war. Ironically, the majority of deaths were by typhoid which was rife in Bloemfontein during the British occupation of the Boer War.

**Queen's Fort Military Museum**: Church Street. A museum charting the military history of the Free State from 1820 to present day, including displays of all major battles and a display of the **Free State Artillery**. Near the museum is a memorial to the Boer casualties of the Basotho War of 1865/6. Tel: (051) 447 5478.

### Historical Buildings

**First Raadsaal**: St Georges Street. This modest building of dung floors and thatched roof was built by Major Warden in 1849 and has housed, at one time, almost all the city's original civil institutions, including the Parliament House and a school.

**Fourth Raadsaal**: (pictured right) President Brand Street. Completed in 1893, designed in a classical style by L. Canning. It housed the last *'model'* **Free State Republican Parliament**, the benches of which still remain.

**Old Government Building**: Maitland Street. A fine example of old Cape Dutch Architecture, housing the National Afrikaans Museum, a Research Centre and the National Acting & Drama Museum.

**The Presidency**: (pictured below) President Brand Street. The former home of Presidents of the erstwhile Free State Republic now a museum. Tel: (051) 448 0949.

**President Brand Street**: The entire street is lined with magnificent sandstone architecture and has been declared a National Conservation area.

## Other Attractions

**Loch Logan**: An innovative waterfront-style project, Bloemfontein's own waterfront.

**Naval Hill**: An extremely popular hill providing excellent views of the town. **The Franklin Game Reserve**, with many animal species, forms part of the Hill and is the only city-centre reserve in the world.

**Hamilton Park**: On the western slope of Naval Hill boasts more than 300 orchid specimens.
**Lamont Hussey Observatory**: Has been restored and now houses a cosy theatre.

## Tour Operators & Tour Guides

**Anglo-Boer War Battlefieds Tours:** Contact: Charles Williamson. Tel/Fax: (051) 861 2136. Cell/Mobile: 083 262 0861. *Paardeberg. Glen Bridge & Karee Station. Siege/Relief of Kimberley. Sannaspos. Magersfontein. Modderfontein. Monuments and Museums.*

**Mercia de Beer:** (T.2253). PO Box 169, Dewetsdorp 9940. (Dewetsdorp is 68 km south-east of Bloemfontein). Tel: (051) 541 0148. Cell/Mobile: 082 853 2022. *Anglo-Boer War specialist.*

**Bernard Connellan:** (T.4743). PO Box 17670, Bainsvlei 9385. Tel: (051) 451 1789.
Fax: (051) 451 1427. *Sannaspos and Paardeberg.*

**Sannette Greyvenstein:** (T.2268). PO Box 704, Bloemfontein 9300. Tel: (051) 447 3447.
Fax: (051) 447 1323. *Anglo-Boer War Museum. Bloemfontein. Paardeberg. Sannaspos.*

**Johan Hattingh:** (T.1364). Anglo-Boer War Museum, PO Box 704, Bloemfontein 9300.
Tel: (051) 447 3447. Fax: (051) 447 1322. *Battlefields. Blockhouses. Anglo-Boer War Specialist Guide Trainer. Magersfontein. Paardeberg.*

**Martin Lovius:** (T.2261). 13 Barnes Street, Bloemfontein 9301. Tel: (051) 447 8940.
Fax: (051) 444 0752. *Bloemfontein. Karee. Sannaspos. Paardeberg.*

**René Smith:** (T.6064). 14 High Ridge, Heuwelsig, Bloemfontein 9301. Tel: (051) 436 5945.
Fax: (051) 436 6634. *Bloemfontein. Boshof. Sannaspos. Jammersberg Drift. Dewetsdorp. Churchill route through Free State.*

**Janco Vorster:** (T.6065). Private Bag X20508, Bloemfontein 9300. Cell/Mobile: 083 407 1530.
Home Tel: (051) 522 0463. Fax: (051) 447 3470. *Bloemfontein. Sannaspos. Paardeberg.*

# Driefontein : 10 March 1900

While the battle of Poplar Grove was nothing for the Boers to be proud of, the contrary is true of the battle that followed three days later. Driefontein was the last stand they made before Bloemfontein, the Free State capital, fell to the British on 13 March 1900. General C.R. de Wet and General J.H. de la Rey had 1 500 men at their disposal to defend their positions, which reached from Abrahamskraal Drift in the north, to Bosrand in the south.

This time the burghers were ready for a flanking movement and anticipated the probability thereof. The heaviest fighting thus occurred on the southern flank and it was the Welsh and Essex positions that took the full brunt of the fighting. Under heavy artillery bombardment they advanced in overwhelming numbers on the Boers positions and succeeded in driving the Boers from their strongholds. The Boers fought with greater determination than at Poplar Grove and they only left the battlefield after a full day's fighting when they fell back to Bloemfontein.

**Casualties**

Boers: 30 dead, 47 wounded, 20 PoWs.

British: 60 dead, 361 wounded.

**Must see at Driefontein**

Monuments commemorating the fallen Burghers and the Welsh who took part.

Grave sites of casualties.

The battlefield site. Visitors must have a **Satour Specialist Tour Guide** to visit this site.

TOUR GUIDE:

Dr. Louis Bothma. Tel: 083 272 8734.

*D.A. van der Bank*

# British Occupation of Bloemfontein (13 March 1900)

The commandos of General De Wet and General De la Rey entrenched themselves in the kopjes to the west and south-west of ***Bloemfontein***, but the determined defence of the Free State capital which De Wet expected, came to naught. To avoid being encircled, the Boer forces left their positions after only token resistance and retreated northward. On 13 March 1900, the British forces entered Bloemfontein after the keys to the city were handed over by Mayor Kellner, J.G. Fraser and Magistrate Papenfus.

Lord Roberts and his staff took up residence in the presidency which was evacuated by President M.T. Steyn the day before. The advance to **Pretoria** was delayed by seven weeks due to a severe outbreak of typhoid among the troops. Public buildings such as the Fourth Raadsaal, Grey College (now Bloemfontein College), Ramblers Club and St. Andrew School (now Elizabeth le Roux Hostel of Oranje Girls' School) were set up as temporary hospitals. Some private houses, such as *Freshford* in Kellner Street, were used as regimental headquarters or to billet officers. Thousands of troops were bivouacked in and around the city and remount depots were established at Springfield and at the foot of Naval Hill, which incidentally owed its name to its occupation by the Naval Brigade. Bloemfontein's well-known landmark, the *"White Horse"* was laid out by troops of the Wiltshire Regiment on the eastern slope of this hill to serve as a marker for advancing convoys. After Lord Roberts' departure a garrison was quartered on Naval Hill and the farm, *Tempe* to the west of the city. ❑

*D.A. van der Bank*

*National Museum, Bloemfontein. Instructed by the Friends of the War Museum*

*Steve Lunderstedt*

# Day Tour into the Free State

Leaving **Kimberley** early in the morning, it was disappointing to see that the Crown and Royal Hotel at **Modder River**, the British military HQ of Lord Methuen from December 1899 to February 1900, was not open. Presumably because of the early hour!

The blockhouse guarding the Modder River bridge was in its usual position, renovated and looking good.

The town of **Jacobsdal** was soon upon us, Jacobsdal being the first Free State town captured by the Kimberley Relief Force in the form of the CIV and others in February 1900. The NG Kerk, utilised as a hospital, has a memorial to the fallen burghers of Jacobsdal, at its entrance. An unusual blockhouse guards the Paardeberg entrance to the town, while the town cemetery has within its precincts British War Graves. Among those who rest there include Gunner Rodger who won a posthumous DCM in the October 1900 Jacobsdal Market Square Battle, as well as the members of the Cape Town Highlanders who fell on the same day. It was here that General de la Rey buried his son after the Battle of Modder River.

It was on to **Koffiefontein**. After visiting the 'Big Hole' which is just that, it was on to the cemetery where lie the mortal remains of four Italian Prisoners of War of the 1939-1945 World War. In Heroes Acre lies a lonely soldier of the recent wars of Angola and SWA (now Namibia).

Next were the really beautiful villages of **Fauresmith** and **Jagersfontein**. Well worth a day drive just to admire the magnificent Victorian houses. Jagersfontein too has a 'Big Hole'. You have to pay R3.00 to look at the hole and there was nothing else in the museum except two empty houses a la Kimberley's own Mine Museum.

The Jagersfontein cemetery has a British War Graves section, while further up the hill rests General J.B.M.Hertzog's parents. A little higher is a Boer Memorial plus three graves of Commandants. Two are on Guild crosses. (Guild of Loyal Women)

One of the highlights was visiting the scene of the 1848 battle between Sir Harry Smith with his British troops (including 200 plus Griquas) and the Boers. Without going into details the British defeated the Boers. A walled cemetery encloses the British graves, while a Memorial on the small kopje is presumably built over the Boer remains. A further bit of history on the British cemetery is that Deneys Reitz slept against the wall during the guerilla stages of the Anglo Boer War. On that same trip he passed through Jagersfontein and Fauresmith. ❑

1. The blockhouse built by the British troops garrisoned in Jacobsdal. This was designed by the troops before the blockhouse system was initiated (without plans).
2. Jacobsdal church as it is today, with a spire. The church was used by both Boer and British as a hospital.
3. The cemetery at Jacobsdal has interesting gravestones, mainly to the British troops that died in the area.
4. The unique gravestone of Sgt. Roger who was awarded the DCM.

### SPRINGFONTEIN TOURISM FORUM

**Tel: (051782) 1940/2 Fax (051782) 122.**

*Mixed farming and outdoor life are the main occupations of Springfontein's residents. The town began as a crucial rail link between Gauteng and the Eastern Cape.*

**Concentration Camp**: 704 people, mostly children, died here, largely due to the severe winter of 1901.

**Concentration Camp Cemetery**: The graves of over 700 Boer and British victims of the war.

**TOUR GUIDE: Blackie de Swart:** (T.5852) Prior Grange, PO Box 11, Springfontein 9917. Cell/Mobile: 083 310 3284. Fax: (051) 783 0114. *Springfontein. Trans-Gariep. Free State.*

# Springfontein

To commemorate the centenary of the Boer War, the owners of Prior Grange Guest Farm near Springfontein in the Southern Free State, thought it a good idea to reconstruct a Rice-type Blockhouse. Approximately five of these blockhouses survived destruction and have all been moved to museums or places of historical interest.

Blackie de Swardt and his staff constructed the blockhouse on the original site. During the reconstruction, a stone was discovered with ***"A Coy, 1st Royal Irish Fusiliers, Nov 1901"*** engraved upon it. The blockhouse was reconstructed from old photos and measurements taken from plans of the Royal Engineers from the War Museum in Bloemfontein. Numerous relics from the war can still be picked up around the blockhouse. The blockhouse, with the **Union Jack** flying next to it can be seen from the N1 route about 10km south of Springfontein. It can be visited *free of charge* ***but by prior arrangement***.

Blackie de Swardt also does Anglo-Boer War tours in and around Springfontein and to blockhouses further away.

You can stay at his Guest Farm and really experience the magic of the Boer war in the Springfontein area. ❑

*Blackie and Sheryl de Swardt*
*Prior Grange Guest Farm, Springfontein*
*Tel: 051782- ask 1940. Cell: 083 310 3284.*

*Blackie de Swardt*

## Springfontein and the War

A British Military Intelligence report of 1897 described Springfontein as a place of *'about 15 houses scattered and of no tactical importance, a small church and hotel or store. There are two good springs near the church and a dam 600 yards north of the town, but the best water supply is that of the railway, which by means of a windpump and well, can water at least 30 trains a day: 30 at 1 000 gal. = 30 000 gal.'*

Springfontein, at the start of the Anglo-Boer War, was contrary to the report; it was a strategic railway junction. The railway line from Cape Town to Bloemfontein was completed seven years before the report and the one from East London joining the line at Springfontein, three years before. At the start of the war in October 1899, Boer commandos moved southwards through the town, splitting to go either to the Orange River Bridge at Norval's Pont or the one at Bethulie. Their idea being to stop the advance of the British troops making their way inland along the railway lines.

Until the arrival of Lord Roberts in January 1900, the Boer forces controlled the advance of the British Army but after Roberts took command of the Western Front and 4 000 Boers surrendered at Paardeberg at the end of February 1900, Boer resistance faltered and the commandos had to retreat back into the Free State. After Lord Roberts occupied Bloemfontein on 13 March, his forces

*Imperial Light Horse* by Jason Askew.

renewed their attacks on the southern Free State. General Gatacre moved along the East London railway line into the Free State and after a short skirmish, occupied Bethulie on 14 March. Two of his scouts, Captain Hennesey of the Cape Police and Captain Turner of Montmorency's Scouts, heard that the railway line to Springfontein was intact and unprotected. They *'stole'* a handtrolley and covered the 30 miles to Springfontein to scout the area and specifically Springfontein Junction. To their surprise they found the Boers guarding the station and small village fast asleep and so apprehended them. Hennesey and Turner took possession of two engines and 40 trucks and drove them back to Bethulie. The Boers, realising the onslaught of the British Army was imminent evacuated the town. General Gatacre's division occupied the town the next day without a shot being fired.

Springfontein was then used as a base from which British units launched two drives on General de Wet and also later to round up Boer commandos in the southern Free State. Because of this and the establishment of a concentration camp, a big permanent British camp was established.

The British defense of Springfontein was concentrated on *'Gibraltar Hill'* to the east of the railway line. The hill was encircled by a system of stone walls, sangars, trenches, sentry-posts and gun emplacements - all of which can still be seen. Between *'Gibraltar'* and the railway line was 12 General Hospital, (reputed to be the biggest medical facility in the southern hemisphere at the time), the Remount Depot and the Veterinary Hospital. Little remained of these except for the waste dump. Judging by the amount of broken beer bottles, Springfontein must have been a very hot place!!

Unusual about the cemetery at Springfontein is that Boer and Brit were buried side by side. Lord O'Hagen died on 12 December 1900 and was buried a few yards from Mattheus Hendrik Steyn, the brother of President Steyn, who died here while en route to a POW camp in Cape Town. In total, nearly 700 Boer women and children and 300 British soldiers found their final resting place in the cemetery about two km south east of the town. Interesting is that two fallen British soldiers, Lance-Corporal W. Rawbottom of the 4th Cheshire Regiment and Trooper J. Koul of the Remington Guides have the unusual honour of each having two graves. Thirty-seven unbaptised children were buried in the children's cemetery to the west of the concentration camp. The minister serving the Boers in the camp, Reverend Sandrock, b*elieved that unbaptised people were to be buried separate from baptised ones and therefore this cemetery was established.*

Towards the end of the war the Royal Engineers had constructed nearly 8 000 blockhouses along the railway lines in South Africa. In the Springfontein area the style of blockhouses were mainly the Rice-type. Many of the foundations of these blockhouses can still be spotted along the old railway lines. At one of these sites the landowners have reconstructed a blockhouse which can be visited. ❑

*Andrew J. McLeod*

# Emily Hobhouse & the Women's Memorial at Springfontein

When Emily Hobhouse, the English lady from the rectory of St Ives in Cornwall, passes the small Free State town of Springfontein she breaks her journey. It is 1 May 1901 and she is on her way home, after more than three months in South Africa. But first she wants to pay a farewell visit to the concentration camp. Before she gets there she is called to the abandoned families waiting at the railway for transportation to a camp. Due to *'red-tapeism'* nobody seemed to want control over them. They wait.

Winter is setting in and the people who have been stranded at the station for days, are without warm clothing or shelter. In her memoirs - in the form of a long letter to Mrs *'Tibby'* Steyn - she says: *"The picture (that was) photographed in my mind can never fade."*

She is first taken to an old lady stranded there with her husband. Emily writes: *"She has no skirt...slipping off my underskirt, I put it on the old woman. In those days we wore sensible clothes and an underskirt was a long full garment."*

The people used any shelter they could find. *"Sticking two or three sticks in the ground, threw the canvas over, making a crude shelter."* It was to such a shelter that she was called next. There she found a mother, sitting on a trunk, with a child lying across her knee. The mother had nothing to give it and the child was sinking fast. Emily sent to the Camp Commander for some brandy. But it was too late. They watched in reverent silence as the child drew it's last breath.

*"The mother neither moved nor wept...Dry-eyed but deathly white, she sat there motionless looking not at the child but far, far away into depths of grief beyond all tears. A friend stood behind her who called upon Heaven to witness this tragedy ... the scene made an indelible impression on me."*

When in 1908 ex-president of the Free State M.T. Steyn started the idea to erect a monument in memory of women and children who had died in the camps, he and his wife, *'Tibby'* Steyn, told Emily about this. She was taken up by the idea and it was suggested that she meet with the sculptor.

They had contracted the Pretoria sculptor Anton van Wouw for the main statue group. It was to symbolise the suffering of the women. He undertook the work in Rome. Emily was spending the winter there for health reasons. They met and he asked her opinion of his first effort. He had designed a statue of a standing Boer woman with two emaciated children sitting at her feet. This did not satisfy the *'missus'* (as her friends were want to call her). Emily saw again the vision of her experience at Springfontein. This she explained to Van Wouw. They worked together daily in creating as acceptable work of art. She was difficult to please. When all else was to her satisfaction, he still had trouble in depicting the child. She suggested that he visit a hospital to see what a dead child looked like. It worked.

When you stand at the foot of the Womens Memorial in Bloemfontein, look up at the bronze group, and remember its history. And notice that the ashes of the English woman - Emily Hobhouse - are laid under the statue of the Boer woman of Springfontein!! ❑

***Sources:***

Van Reenen, R., *Emily Hobhouse Boer War Letters*. Cape Town, 1984.

Balme, J.H., *To love one's enemies*, Cobble Hill, Canada, 1994.

*The Womens' Memorial in Bloemfontein where the ashes of Emily Hobhouse are laid.*

*"Roses Round-up"*

# The Deadliest Mauser of them all?

A Mauser in the **War Museum, Bloemfontein**, with haunting links to the Karoo and three Boer Commandants is part of an Anglo-Boer War display. All the Commandants who used this rifle died in the Karoo – two of them shortly after receiving it. Years later, the man who decided to donate it to the museum for display also died – of a heart attack. On 10 October 1902, Commandant Gideon Scheepers, the original owner of the Mauser, was captured by the British at Koppieskraal (near Prince Albert). He handed the rifle to Karel van Heerden with the request that after his execution it be given to Commandant (Judge) Henry Hugo but shortly after receiving it, Hugo was critically wounded near Beaufort West. He pleaded with his adjutant to return the rifle to Karel van Heerden (by then promoted to Commandant). Van Heerden took it to Rooiberg, a Camdeboo mountain farm about 30km from Aberdeen, where Sara (his sister, married to a Momberg) lived. She hid it in the farmhouse's loft. On 18 May 1902, Van Heerden was killed near Aberdeen.

After the Declaration of Peace, Van Heerden's brother Johannes Jacobus (Jan) approached the farmer and offered him £6 for the rifle. The farmer accepted. Van Heerden, after waiting two years to obtain a permit to transport it to his farm, Geluk in the Middleburg (CP) district, took possession of the rifle and, for years, used the Mauser as a hunting rifle. He donated the rifle to the War Museum. One day in 1934, after placing the rifle and a carefully documented history of the rifle on his desk, he suddenly collapsed – he suffered a fatal heart attack. His son, Dr Jan Van Heerden (Van Elfen), who now lives in Prince Albert says that his father's wishes were carried out. The Mauser was sent to the War Museum. ❑

Pictured: Burgher Wolhuter of the Rand Commando who grew his hair from the beginning to the end of the War.

## JAGERSFONTEIN BATTLE

On 16 October 1900 Boer forces under the command of General Hertzog, attacked and captured the town of Jagersfontein in the Free State which was being defended by the Seaforth Highlanders. This was the home town of Hertzog – his parents' home being blown up by the British nearly killing a young George Brink (later Lt.-General, of WWII fame). The Boers suffered two casualties, Commandant P.J. Visser (who was deaf and had not heard the challenge of a Highlander who then shot him dead) and a Burgher Snyman. Both are buried in the cemetery at Jagersfontein, close to the Hertzog family plot and about 100 m from the Seaforth Highlanders killed the same day.

Brink relates that after the battle he and his family stayed in the Convent, but on the second day the ladies' decided that meat was needed. A sheep had been hidden in the forage room, safe from British eyes, so George and the family domestic labourer, Anna, quietly sneaked off, killed and skinned the sheep and hung the carcass from a tree. Shortly before quartering the sheep, with George and Anna no doubt anticipating the forthcoming 'feast', two Tommies suddenly appeared and commandeered the entire sheep. Adding insult to injury, they walked off with a most cheerful *"Thank you very much, Johnny!"*

STEVE'S WAR STORIES

*Dr Gerhard M. Augustyn*

# War Sites in Eastern Free State

Taking a guess, one would think that most prospective tourists setting out to experience Anglo-Boer War sites, might be heading for those places where the larger numbers fell and the longer battles took place - around Kimberley (Northern Cape), and around Ladysmith (Kwazulu-Natal).

For the keen ABW tourist there is good news: on the way between these two destinations lie the Eastern Free State, the theatre of the hunt for *General de Wet* and his band of *Bittereinders* in the guerilla phase of the war. The stories here are 'large and long'. The mountainous area gave the Boers and their folk, chance to be a menace for the British war machine, and it made the struggle carry on longer. The full gambit of the war's impact, from humiliation, cowardice, deprivation to triumph were experienced in these parts. The local people are ready to share their humaneness with visitors, and to build a realisation of the dangers of war. Facilities are as modern as you would like, routes are amidst changing scenes on country roads. Stretch your legs whilst getting a full picture of the theatre of war. You will also find that country hospitality is a way of life.

## HARRISMITH

Harrismith was founded in 1849 by the British governor Sir Harry Smith. Just before the ABW was declared, it became the assembly point for the Boer commandos before their descent into KwaZulu Natal. The farm *'The Oaks'*, where they congregated is still in its original condition. The first Boer casualty in KwaZulu Natal was a burgher from this town *(Fred Johnson - at Besters station in Natal)*. The British occupied the town in August 1900, and the people of the town showed a kind of schizophrenia (being of Boer and British loyalties) in the times of war and those following.

The town museum displays memorabilia from all the eras of the region's history, and the remains of the British presence in the town till 1913 still adorn the vicinity (Royal Engineer's works). The beautiful Platberg Mountain has a British heliograph - station on its top, where, local rumour has it, Kitchener himself once stood; and from which the view into KwaZulu Natal and the surrounding area is breathtaking.

Dawn Patrol by Jason Askew.

## GROENKOP

This battle site just outside the town of Kestell is named after *'Vader Kestell'*, a minister of the Dutch Reformed Church *(who accompanied Pres.Steyn and General de Wet to the bitter-end)*. At this site the British army received a nasty blow on Christmas Day 1901. The story of how this site was selected by De Wet to strike a blow, how he executed his strategy, and what it meant to the Boer War effort at that late stage of the war, is worth hearing and contemplating. Recently developed by the local citizens into a tourist friendly experience, this site rewards the visitor in abundance.

## BIDDULPHSBERG

This mountain on the road between Senekal and Bethlehem, (named after an official in the administration of Sir Harry Smith) saw action on 29 May 1900, when Boer and Brit engaged in cannon fire and unfriendly exchange of rifle bullets from the top of the mountain to the plains below. Nature dealt the British a nasty hand that day. A veld fire started as a result of the cannon fire, at first it served as a smoke screen against Boer bullets. Then the wind changed direction, and the fire stormed at the *'Tommies'* in the veld, and death by burning resulted.

The local farmer has developed a nature reserve around the mountain, and history and ecology become sole mates here in this mid-eastern Free State environment.

### SURRENDER HILL/ BRAND WATER BASIN

Triumph or tragedy, depending on one's sympathies!! During June and July of 1900, the British very determinedly drove the Boer forces to the east of the Free State. The mountains of the Drakensberg region (Witteberge and Rooiberge mountains) at first looked like a refuge for the Boer forces, of over 6 000 men, with cattle and provisions. General De Wet soon realised that this haven of comfort would soon become a death trap, and made plans to move out of the area in all directions in order to go and rekindle the Boer resistance. When he left, those who had to follow his instructions quibbled amongst themselves, hesitated, and gave the British a chance to seal off the mountain passes. This inevitably led to an honourless surrender by *General Marthinus Prinsloo* and 4 000 men on 30 July 1900.

Follow the sequence of events on a drive through this beautiful basin, and imagine the hardship and the emotions in that cold winter of 1900 (the events here form the background for the highly appraised fiction written by Christoffel Coetzee: *Op soek na Generaal Mannetjies Mentz*). The local guides are well informed and would love to reveal the secrets and the implications of this surrender to the inquisitive mind. ❑

**Ambush by Jason Askew.**

## THE BLACK SOLDIERS OF JAGERSFONTEIN

George Brink relates that there were three wagon loads of bodies after the October 1900 battle in Jagersfontein – two filled with Seaforth Highlanders and another laden with the bodies of Blacks. Two of the dead blacks were known to Brink – old Jonas, the faithful prison warder and Native Constable John, messenger to Brinks' father (deposed magistrate of Jagersfontein). Both had been armed with rifles by the British and as such were treated as combatants by the Boers.

Brink had picked up much folklore from Jonas while the latter had guarded convicts outside the gaol, while John had been responsible for locking up the Magistrates office, returning the keys late each evening to the residence of Brink senior. George Brink called old Jonas one of his heroes, adding that it had been Jonas who taught him how to cook chops between two red hot stones, and to keep count of his bird 'kills' by cutting notches on his catapult.

STEVE'S WAR STORIES

# Capture of Retief's Nek : 23/24 July 1900

*After successfully deceiving the Boers of their intentions the British attack force turned west and arrived on the evening of 22 July 1900 at Boshoff's farm 5 km from Retief's Nek. At daybreak on the 23rd, after marching 3 km the Seaforths and the 76th Battery came onto a ridge looking directly towards Retief's Nek.*

*This pass is only two hundred yards across from cliff to cliff flanked on the east by a hill of white rock honeycombed with innumerable caves and crevices. From the ground the ridges rise precipitously then merge into a series of hills and high plateaux, on the west is Tuifelberg. Boer forces were well spread out and prepared for the British advance towards Fouriesberg. The Boers protected by natural fissures in the ground and with precipitous ridges all round and excellent trenches that made it felt they held an impregnable position.*

Boer positions were bombarded with well sustained artillery fire followed up by the advancement of Lovet's Scouts and Rimington's Guides supported by the Black Watch on the left flank.

The Sussex and 81st Battery moved up towards Tuifelberg on the right, the Highland Light Infantry moved against the crevassed cliff on the left of the pass.

The Seaforths with 4 guns of the 76th Battery were to capture a hill still further east of the Black Watch. Terrific fighting took place and by 0300 hr on 24 July the Boers were retreating towards Fouriesberg mainly because they did not want to be caught between two converging prongs. On the evening of 24 July a British H.Q. was established at *Retief's Nek Farm.* ❑

***Source:***
*Battlefields of the SA War 1899* by J.L. Smail (with kind permission of Mrs. Barbara Smail).

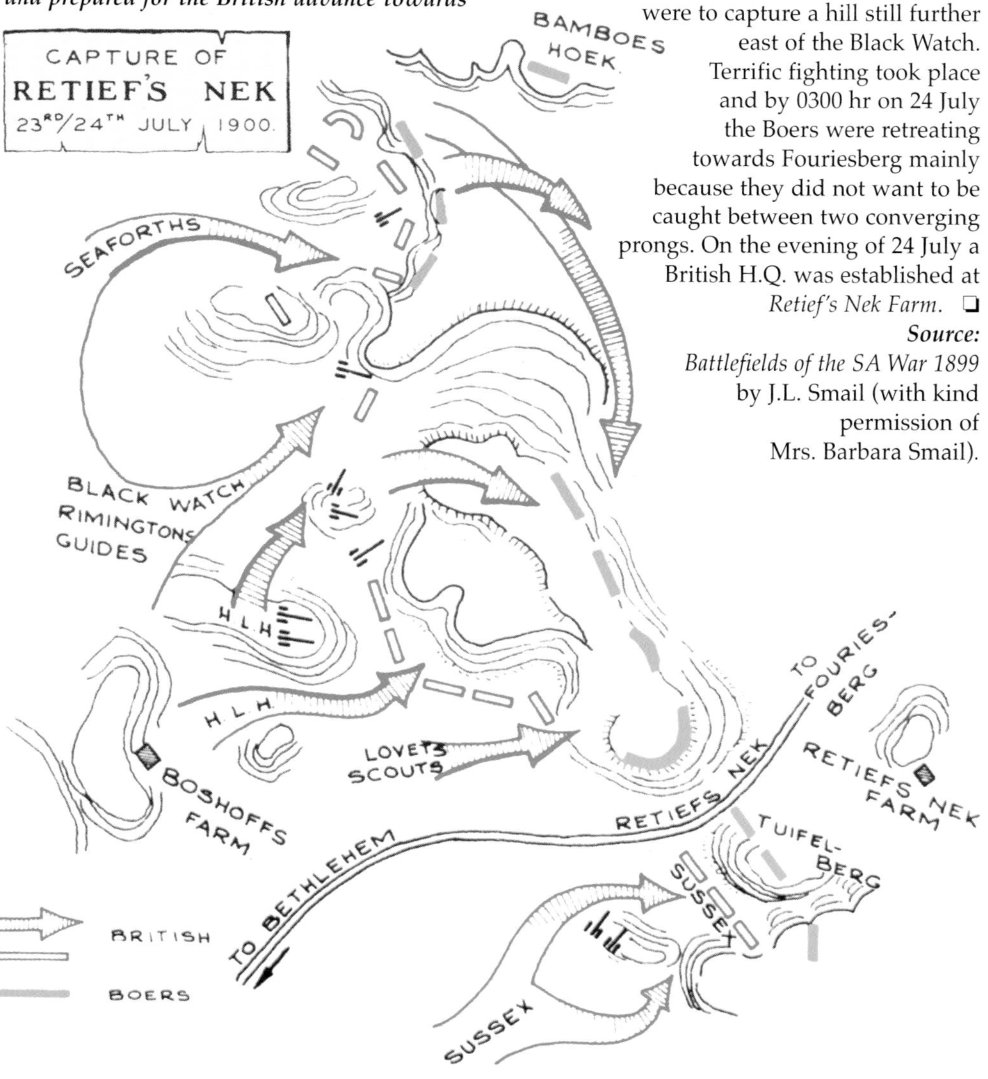

**BETHLEHEM TOURIST**

**Tel: (058) 303 5732 Fax: (058) 323 5876.**

*The fertile valleys of the Maluti Mountains inspired settling wheat farmers to name the new town Bethlehem (from* 'Beit Lechem' *Hebrew for* 'House of Bread'*). Appropriately named, it has grown from strength to strength and is now the commercial centre of the Eastern Free State. The General Athlone and Saulspoort Dams provide water to this region, which produces 65% of South Africa's wheat crop.*

**Bethlehem Museum**: (pictured on facing page) Muller Street. The history of the town is well documented by wagons, furniture, horse carriages, farming implements and an old steam locomotive.

TOUR GUIDES

**John Bailey**: (T.6070). C.L.Highland Tours,
PO Box 143, Fouriesburg 9725. Tel: (058) 223 0552. Fax: (058) 223 0166. *Brandwater Basin. Eastern Free State.*

**Rose Bailey**: (T.4742). PO Box 143, Fouriesburg 9725. Tel: (058) 223 0552. Fax: (058) 223 0166. Cell/Mobile: 083 701 9159. *Author of 'The Anglo-Boer War Centenary 1999-2002 Souvenir Battlefields Booklet'. Free State. Eastern Free State.*

**Louw van Biljon**: (T.5065) PO Box 49, Clarens. Tel/Fax: (058) 256 1195. & (058) 256 1643. *Brandwater Basin. Biddulphsberg. Groenkop. Bethlehem.*

# Bethlehem

250 km north-east from Bloemfontein and 85 km west from Harrismith is Bethlehem. During September 1899 the Free State burghers were placed on standby. On 2 October 1899 the burghers of the Orange Free State between the ages of 16 and 60 were called up. The burghers of Bethlehem also reported for duty.

The Bethlehem commando was mobilised as follows:- The burghers from the district of central Liebenbergsvlei (predominantly burghers from Reitz and Kestell vicinity) under the command of Commandant J.H. Naude. The burghers and officers left under the command of Chief Commandant Marthinus Prinsloo for the Natal border and occupied Oliviershoek Pass.

The burghers from the town and district Witteberge (a part of Fouriesburg) together with the commando of Ficksburg, Ladybrand and Wepener originally kept watch on the Basutoland border. In April 1900 they joined the rest of the commando at Dewetsdorp.

On 17 October 1899 the Boers decided to invade Natal. Three Free State commandos including a commando of 800 men made up of burghers from Bethlehem and Heilbron would lead the attack. The burghers of Bethlehem played a part in the battles of Modderspruit and Nicholsonsnek, as well as in the attack and siege of Ladysmith.

By mid-November 1899 all the burghers from Bethlehem who were in Natal were sent to the Boer positions near Colesberg to stop General French's march to Kimberley. With the advance of Lord Roberts to Kimberley, the Bethlehem commando was called back to the Modder River positions. At Norvalspont, the Bethlehem command covered the passage and were the last over the Orange River by train, a half an hour before the railway bridge was blown up. After the surrender of Cronje at Paardeberg, the Bethlehem commando joined the other Burghers at De Wetsdorp. They then proceeded with De Wet to Bloemfontein. After Roberts' capture of Bloemfontein on 13 March 1900, the Commando decided to return to their own district.

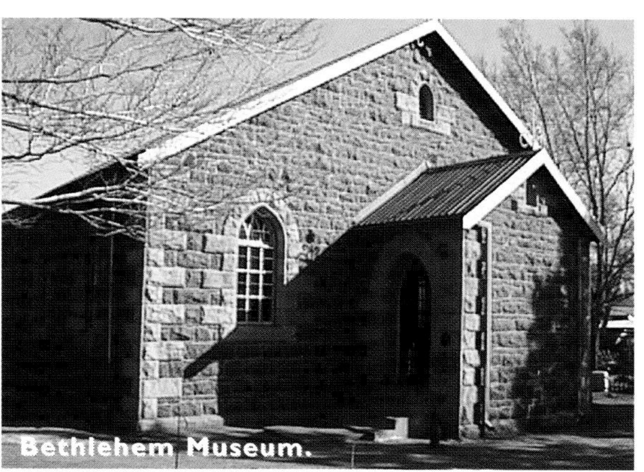
Bethlehem Museum.

The 'Klaas Gang' carried out their raids in the area. Hollow caves (where women and children sheltered) can be found all over the mountains. Here women took shelter, not just in fear of the English but also in fear of the black gangs, which as soon as the burghers had left the district, molested the women.

The Bethlehem commandos being involved in the war from the beginning, took part in various field battles in Natal and the Free State. General de Wet wrote in *The Struggle between Boer and Brit* that by June 1900 not a single Bethlehem burgher had given up the fight and that at the end of the war Bethlehem had the highest number of burghers that had fought.

Bethlehem itself was, for a short time, one of the 'hot spots' in the struggle at the end of June and July 1900, the Boer forces passed by this district in an attempt to escape the English net. Not only did the Battle of Bethlehem take place during this time but also important field battles such as the Battles of Retiefsnek and Slabbertsnek. But not just battles but also various skirmishes and other incidents occurred in Bethlehem and its vicinity during the war.

Bethlehem did not escape the devastation that came with the war. Ramsey MacDonald, later British Prime Minister, as opposition leader, after the war during October 1902 carried out an inspection tour through the Orange Free State. He wrote that in the surrounding area of the town he did not see a single undamaged farm house. About one fifth of the town was devastated. J.H. Sugden, after the war, wrote in complaint that with the exception of the N.G. Kerk, the government's offices, the Seminary and the Hospital, every house, bank and shop was plundered. Many of the pretty willow trees next to the river were used for firewood. Just like so many other towns in the Free State, the inhabitants of the town and the district had to rebuild the town after the war. Today Bethlehem is a focal point of a successful Free State. ❑

General de Wet escaped from a British trap on 23 February 1902, near Kalkkrans in the Free State by rounding up cattle and stampeding them through a guarded pass. *"Without mercy, the crazed beasts trampled on those English who could not scatter fast enough. Everybody and everything in their path, including the cannon and machine-guns, were bowled over. Utter confusion reigned. Injured English soldiers tried to crawl away from the flying hooves, whereas others were trampled to death. Those who could escape did so without firing a shot at us."*

**Heidelbergers of the Boer War**, *Ian Uys*, 1981 Ian S. Uys

## MIXED LOYALTIES

A captain told his group of Black National Scouts that they could have their pleasure, if they wished, with their female Boer captives. Botha, a National Scout fighting with them, intervened and protected the women every night until they were handed over to the Authorities. There is a Trooper Botha (who could be this man) of the *"Canadian Scouts"* is buried in the Kloof cemetery in Heidelberg. (Uys, 167).

*Andrew J. McLeod*

# De Wet ... Hunter or Hunted?

When he was 27 years old he fought in the famous battle of **Majuba (1881)**. When he was 41 years old he was just too late to take part in the smashing of the **Jameson Raid (1896).** When he was 45 years old he knew that there was a war coming. He sent his son to purchase a white horse - the well known *'Fleur'*.

De Wet started out as a burgher (a private), he ended up as acting president of the Orange Free State. At the beginning he was only a member of the *'Volksraad'*; yet he enjoyed world wide fame by May 1902. He was determined and loyal, always ready for battle, fearless, even impetuous and a daring geurilla leader. To him the world was coloured in black and white, things were right or wrong, one was either free or suppressed.

That was the hero of many opposed to the British – from the start right through to the bitter-end. That was Christiaan de Wet.

Yet, he was fearless, always spoiling for a fight. To him his mission was clear – to disrupt the British effort at every opportunity. This meant that the invading forces soon knew the name *'De Wet'*. He was around at **Paardeberg,** he scared General Broadwood at **Sannaspos,** but when he captured and burned valuable British war supplies at **Rooiwal** during June 1900, the hunt was on.

For Kitchener – to catch De Wet became synonymous with winning the war. When 4 000 Boers surrender near **Bethlehem**, De Wet and President Steyn escaped. When the British had him cornered against the **Magaliesberg,** he and his commando crossed *"where only monkeys dare roam"*. When General de Wet slips through the fortified lines and fights again. With his invasion into Cape Colony, Knox chases him for 800 miles. But ... yes, he escaped through a flooded Orange River.

At this stage the name of De Wet becomes known world wide. Eric Rosenthal writes in his book **'General De Wet'** that his name could be heard on the lips of a Cockney outside the Bank of England, used by a Frenchman in a boulevard-cafe in Paris, written in an advertisement on a sidewalk in New York, seen on a drawing in a hotel in Siberia. There were cartoons, postcards, jokes and songs. De Wet had become the icon of all pro-Boers. But would always be the *'slippery'* De Wet. Even Emily Hobhouse heard about him during her visit to the Free State during early 1901. More than once she wrote to her brother: *"De Wet has escaped again"*. She compares him with the Mexican guerrilla leader, Benito Juarez.

De Wet carries on with his mission to disrupt British war efforts. There is never any thought of surrender or coming to terms. Nevertheless his fame is due to his *'escapes'*, not his audacious attacks. The *'De Wet-hunts'* turn into *'De Wet-drives'*. The blockhouse lines and barbed wire barricades cordon him into *'kraals'*. Soon after Christmas 1901 he escapes the first *'drive'* in northeast Free State with ease. Soon after that, in February 1902, a drive (where 60 000 British troops are employed – historian Thomas Pakenham states that there was one Tommy every 10 yards), takes place in the northern Free State.

Yet, once again the hunter-hunted escapes. Kitchener's army capture thousands of cattle and horses and 778 prisoners of war. But no De Wet. At the peace talks during May 1902, in Vereeniging he argues and votes against peace. But as acting president of his republic, he co-signs the treaty. ❑

***Sources**:*

De Kock, W.J., *Dictionary of South African biography*, I, Cape Town, 1968.

Rosenthal, E., *General De Wet,* Cape Town, 1946.

Pakenham, T., *The Boer War*, London, 1997.

# Biddulphsberg : 29 May 1900

Biddulphsberg is situated near the town of Senekal. While this battle was taking place, the Boers were attacking the Imperial Yeomanry at Lindley.

These two battles were closely connected and the reason is that when the Yeomanry were besieged, Lieutenant General Rundle with his 4 000 men at Senekal tried to divert the Boers' attention from Lindley onto himself with a march from Senekal to Bethlehem. The Boers anticipated Rundle's move and placed themselves on Biddulphsberg from where they had a commanding view over the road to Bethlehem. When news reached Rundle about the Boer positions, he decided to attack the northern flank of the force. After an artillery bombardment he sent his men forward but when they were within rifle range, they came under heavy Boer fire. Meanwhile, the artillery bombardment had set the veld on fire and was at first used as a smoke screen by the attacking British soldiers. After a while, the wind changed direction and posed serious problems for the attackers. The fire swept mercilessly on the British line with the result that a lot of wounded were trapped and many died in the raging fire. This and the continuous Mauser fire proved too much for the British force and they had to retire.

The Boers were left victorious on the battlefield but later retreated to fight another battle on another day. ❑

**Casualties**

Boer: 2 dead, 3 wounded.

British: 47 dead, 130 wounded, 8 missing.

**Must see at Biddulphsberg**

Monument commemorating the battle.
The battle site.

## THE FIRST BOER CASUALTIES OF WAR

According to J. H. Breytenbach, in *Vol. VI page 8* the first casualty was one A. J. Oosthuizen who was killed near Mafeking on 14 October 1899. H.C. Hopkins in his book *"Maar een soos hy"* however, states that the first casualty was a certain Fred Johnson (a Boer of Canadian descent) who was killed on 18 October 1899 near Bester's Station. This was according to General de Wet. What is fairly certain though, if both sources are to be believed, is that Oosthuizen was the first Transvaal casualty, and Johnson the first Free State casualty.

STEVE'S WAR STORIES

*They reckon Fuzzy-wuzzy is the hottest fighter out.*
*But Fuzzy gives himself away - his style is out of date,*
*He charges like a driven grouse that rushes on its fate;*
*You've nothing in the world to do but pump him full of lead:*
*But when you're fighting Johnny Boer you have to use your head;*
*He don't believe in front attacks or charging at the run,*
*He fights you from a kopje with his little Maxim gun.*

**A.B. '*Banjo*' Paterson**
***Drummer Hodge: The Poetry of the Anglo-Boer War* by M van Wyk Smith**

# Dispatches

## INDELIBLE STEYN

*No other contemporary embodied or evoked the spirit of dour, dogged resistance than the remarkable President Steyn. Kruger might have had one eye cocked on Heaven, but he had both feet firmly on the ground. Steyn's vision, however, was on the farthest stars. It was his steadfast belief that to those that endured, without faltering, to the end was vouchsafed the perfect prize - freedom. Was not history, he asked, full of such precious precedents? It happened one day that the young Denys Reitz, riding in retreat to Kroonstad, saw and heard that venerable figure. He stood on a table in the market place, preaching his religion of resistance. As a result, Reitz and a dozen more* fled *back to the fighting. As another, did not Churchill – almost half a century later and in his country's* darkest hour *– follow, to the full, the pattern of this preaching. Judge for yourselves.*

T.D. ZAR 1.6.1900
From President Steyn, Brakvlei
To President Kruger, Machadodorp, begins
1st June 3a.m. I have received your telegram with amazement...More than half of our burghers are in the field and I have just had news of a fine action which took place on the 29th May near Senekal where the enemy were repulsed with great loss, and of a fight yesterday at Lindley where between four and five hundred prisoners were taken. Now must I understand that a Council of War is proposed by your officers in order to abandon that struggle which we began in the name of the Lord - to abandon it in a cowardly manner? Only a small part of the Transvaal is in the hands of the enemy; nearly all our land lies under his heel.
Fourteen days ago I made plain my opinion to Your Honour, and now Your Honour comes with the same proposal again. My policy remains unchanged. We must fight to the bitter end...Up to now we have heard nothing from our representatives and it was plainly agreed that until we heard something definite from them there would be no talk of a protestation.
Why was Langsnek surrendered without a fight? Did Field-Cornet Uys negotiate with Buller in terms of this letter? I shall wire Your Honour later if I go to Machadadorp. - ends.

T.D.ZAR 1.6.1900
From Chief-Commandant, President Steyn, Brakvlei
To Commandant-General Louis Botha *(pictured)*, Pretoria, begins
As a result of a telegram sent yesterday by His Honour President Kruger to our President, I am forced to the grievous conclusion that His Honour has come to the end of his courage. He alleges that his officers without exception despair of inducing the Transvaal burghers - or nearly all of them - to fight further, and so they wish to abandon the struggle.
Reading this telegram I could hardly believe my eyes, especially since our burghers here have fought so successfully during the past few days and are full of hope. I myself have had no opportunity of engaging

Dispatches from ***No Charge for Delivery*** by C.W.L.. DE SOUZA. Published by *Books of Africa (Pty) Ltd.*

the enemy, being in company with those commandos charged with conveying ammunition from Greylingstad. But now we are about to harry those forces moving up from Kroonstad and cut their communications. Brother, permit me to remind you of the situation in which we were placed after the capture of Bloemfontein. How nearly all our burghers as one man went home. How in spite of great possessions in and around Bloemfontein and everywhere in the land, we still were unwilling to give up the struggle.
However, what we did is not wholely unknown to you. We were willing to sacrifice everything as the price of our common independence. This gives me the right, I consider, to call and rely on you, whom I shall never classify among those alluded to above, to use your potent influence to the uttermost in this struggle for our cherished freedom, which cause in my opinion is not wholely lost. Think of the American War of Independence which truly appeared lost.
These men, though fighting indeed as rebels, did not lose heart and how gloriously did God crown their courage perseverance.
Brother, I too, in my position, can appreciate the heavy burden weighing on you, and the more so since it seems that President Kruger - your beloved chief - has lost heart.
Although we know the reasons used to influence him, these cannot weigh in the balance against our heritage of freedom. If needs be, let Pretoria itself fall into the hands of the enemy. Let a force threaten us through Kosi Bay and let our subsidiary communications be disrupted; even so these are no reasons to abandon the struggle. For then, like us here, you could infiltrate behind the enemy and so harass him that he would at the very least be obliged to come to reasonable terms with us. Brother, if it be asked from where we could obtain ammunition, let me point to the past. When we began our first war for independence there was an average of only thirteen rounds for each burgher. Then the Transvaal stood alone without a single cannon, and compare this with the state of our present resouces. Shall the Almighty God of yore not help our righteous cause today? Brother, when I see such a rock as President Kruger begin to waver, I feel it beyond me to utter a single word of encouragement. But just as David of old had to suffer humiliation to experience greater sorrow, so I trust and hope that this instability is by God ordained to His greater honour and glorification. May the God of our fathers use you as a Nathan in His hand and there unto be you strengthened. - ends.

*If it be asked why I should include under my heading the news of an anonymous Chief-Commandant of the Free State, I would reply that, though the hand is the hand of the Chief-Commandant, the voice is the voice of Steyn. First I would have you note that this telegram was sent from Brakvlei, the very place from where Steyn in the early hours of the morning sent his telegram of the previous day.*
*Next President Steyn could not himself seek to influence the Commandant-General of an allied state without serious breach of protocol; still less could he appear to criticize the head of it adversely.*
*But could protocol prevent permission to his Commander-in-Chief to do just that?*
*In any case, I like to think that Louis Botha was effectively moved by this impassioned plea – so full of the fervour for freedom.*
*It was a notable and noble piece of propaganda.*

# Yeomanry Hill, Lindley : 31 May 1900

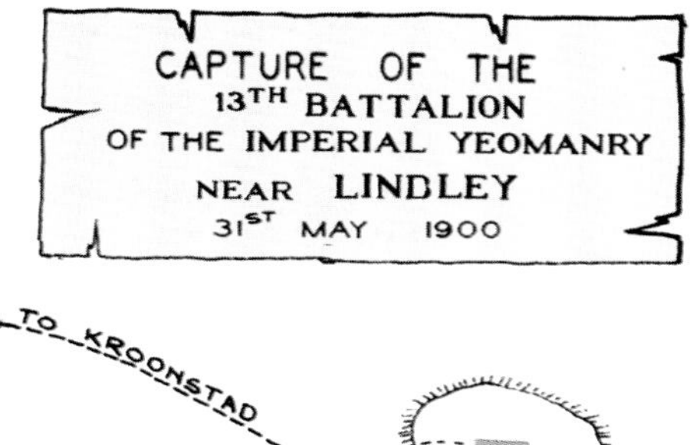


Colonel B.E. Spragge with the 13th Imperial Yeomanry was pinned down about 3 km northwest of Lindley on the Lindley-Kroonstad road. Although the Boer forces were not superior in numbers to the British forces, the Yeomanry decided to entrench themselves on 27 April 1900.

On 29 May, General C.R. de Wet arrived on the scene and the Boer numbers grew significantly to 2 000 men. As time went by, the Boers drew the net closer and on the 31st a heavy bombardment coinciding with a charge by General M. Prinsloo and his men was made on the south eastern British flank. The fierce Boer onslaught proved too much for the British soldiers and the white flag was raised. **This flag was actually hoisted without consent of the officer in charge but it had to be accepted as the Boers were already disarming most of the soldiers.** This incident proved to Lord Roberts that he could not rule the occupied territory.

**Casualties**

Boer: 30 dead, 40 wounded.
British: 25 dead, 418 POWs.

**Must see at Lindley**

Monument commemorating the battle.
The battle site.

Captured British troops slaughtering a cow.

# Battle of Groenkop : 24, 25 December 1901

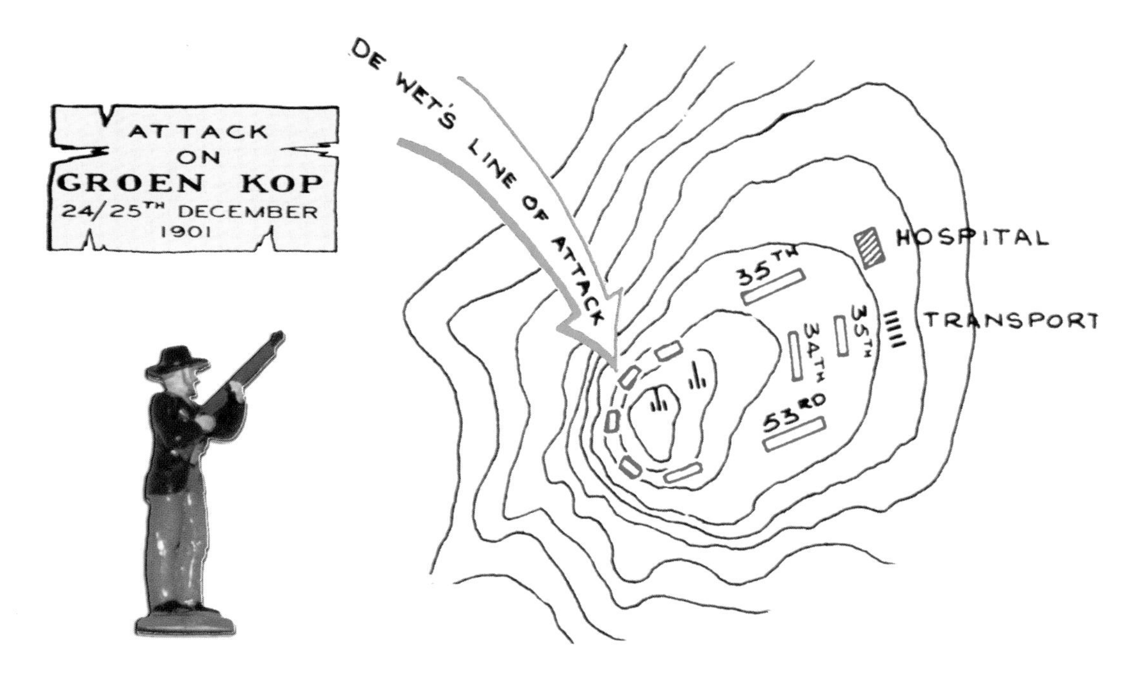


The Boers secretly gathered at *Tigerkloof Spruit* 13 km north of Groenkop. A small group remained and the rest rode to Groenkop, to the steepest side of the hill. Here two gullies were found to climb up. A few men stayed to guard the horses, and the rest not climbing up, rode around to the east of the hill to await developments.

About 450 Boers climbed bootless up the steep part of the hill at about 0200 hr. It was a moonlit night, but passing clouds and a light mist gave cover. The British knew nothing of the attack until the Boers were at the crest of the hill. In full attack the Boers moved forward through the sleeping camp.

The camp, of about 550 soldiers, comprised of the 11th Yeomanry, a gun of the 79th Battery, a Pom-Pom, the 34th Middlesex Company, the 36th West Kent Company, the 53rd East Kent Company and the 35th Middlesex Company. On the night in question the 35th Middlesex Company were deployed on outpost duty.

A third of the British fled, but the rest *'preserved a military bearing'*. They took their positions, which unfortunately lead them even more into the line of fire. The 53rd's position was about 6 ms below the southern crest, and the battle swept past them. Only after the Boers had made their way through the camp did they return to them. The last shot was fired at 0315 hr.

The first response from Rundle was at 0400 hr when a shell fell amongst the retreating wagons laden with spoils. Each of the retreating Boer soldiers had an English horse, *"...in the pink of condition for a rapid retreat"*; and nothing came of the attack.

The British recorded that the Boers, under de Wet, behaved very well, leaving men to look after the wounded. *"The real Boers were very decent chaps, and did all they could, but there were a good few foreigners with them, who were very bitter... de Wet himself sjamboked several of them freely when they attempted to loot the doctor's stores."*

The Boers left with 2 cannons, guns, ammunition, 20 loaded ox wagons, tents and 500 horses and mules. One of the wagons even had a load of spirits. What the Boers could not take they destroyed. *"...there were dead horses and men lying all over the place."*

Golden Gate, Free State.

This was the last time during the war that such a large Free State force met the British. It also represented the final failure of the British standard methods. Fighting up to now was placing immense strain on the British troops and horses, with little success.

British losses amounted to 142 dead and wounded, the monument on the hill records 67 men killed in action. 25 Black people were also killed in action. 240 British were taken prisoner by de Wet. 15 Boers lost their lives and 30 were wounded.

***Site Information***

Take the **S185** turn off on the northern side of the **N5** road between Kestell and Bethlehem. This turn off is 7 km from Kestell. The entrance onto the farm is 7 km along the **S185**, on the left hand side. Entrance is R8 per adult, R4 for children under 12 years. The battle site is on a private farm and normal courtesies are expected, such as no smoking. A tea garden is available but pre-booking is advised. **Tel: 058652 ask for Kestell 2313.** Layout maps and detailed brochures are available on site. ❑

# Surrender Hill, Roodewal : 30 July 1900

After the battle at Roodewal, Lord Roberts realised that he had to counteract the operations of De Wet. With this in mind he ordered a drive on the Boer forces which were operating in the Eastern Free State.

This driving movement succeeded in pushing the Boer forces into the Brandwater basin where they sought refuge against the British drive. The Brandwater basin is a geographical region in the Eastern Free State which offered the Boers the chance to regroup. Before Lieutenant General A.Hunter could close the routes leading out of the basin, De Wet and President M. T. Steyn escaped. There were however over 4 000 burghers left in the basin who were quarrelling over who should be their new leader. This dispute took up valuable time and before long Hunter succeeded in taking command of all the routes leading out of the basin. This led to the trapping of the Boer force in the region with the result that General M. Prinsloo, who was eventually chosen as leader, had no alternative but to surrender to the British.

The losses were a severe blow to the Boers in general, but it also had a positive outcome. The most hardy Boers who were willing to fight to the *'bitter end'* were left. **At the place where the Boers surrendered, their weapons were burnt, and to this day, grass in unable to grow on that spot.**

**Casualties**

Boer: 4 300 prisoners of war.
British: insignificant.

**Must see at Surrender Hill**

The site where the ammunition was destroyed.

Above: *"Farewell, my ancient, if inefficient comrade!"* The Surrender of Arms. Compliments: Morley's Antiques.

Below: *Skirmish at Roodewal* by Jason Askew.

## HARRISMITH TOURIST

**Harrismith Marketing Bureau PO Box 43, Harrismith 9880**

**Tel: (058) 622 3525 Fax (058) 623 0923 Cell 082 963 0050.**

*Founded in 1849 by British Governor Sir Harry Smith, because of its strategic position. The town boomed when diamonds and gold were discovered in the Transvaal and Northern Cape. This was because it was on the major transport routes from the coast to the mines. It now forms an important crossroads in South Africa's land trade routes and enjoys a serene prosperity in the matchless beauty of the surrounding rivers and mountain passes.*

**Town Hall**: (pictured below, right) A graceful sandstone and brick building built in 1907, and a National Monument.

**Township Tours**: Self drive day tours or overnight stays enable visitors to experience what was described in the dark days of the early 1900s as a township.

**Van Reenen**: Llandaff Oratory (National Monument) which seats eight people, was built in honour of Llandaff Matthew who tragically lost his life in an act of bravery in a coal mining disaster.

**Surrender Hill**: (Anglo-Boer War battlefield): After the British took Pretoria, guerrilla warfare started in earnest. Lord Roberts drove the Boers into the Brandwater Basin between Clarens, Fouriesburg and Lesotho. After the Boers had regrouped, traffic jams in the narrow exits from the basin prevented most of them from leaving. 4 300 Boers surrendered & their guns were burnt. Today, still on this spot, no grass grows.

### TOUR GUIDE

**Dr. Gerhard Augustyn:** (T.6067). 21 Olienhout Avenue, Kingshill, Harrismith 9880.
Tel/Fax: (058) 623 0258. Cell/Mobile: 083 477 1958. *Harrismith. Spionkop. Groenkop. Surrender Hill. Brandwater Basin. Biddulphsberg. Bloemfontein.*

Above: British destroying captured Boer weapons.

Right: Harrismith Cemetery

# Harrismith

Harrismith was occupied by the British forces on 4 August 1900 by General Sir Hector MacDonald. General Sir Leslie Rundle arrived two days later. No resistance was offered, and the people of the town offered gifts of socks, food, and even baths to the troops who had lost much of their baggage in veld fires.

Most of the burghers of the district were on commando, but as this followed the **Brand Water Basin Surrender**, many burghers came into town to surrender and hand over their arms. A great concert of welcome was arranged for 6 August. To quote Miss Hawkins, author of the History of Harrismith, who was a young lady at the time. *'The young girls of the town had spent much of their time preparing for the arrival of the British troops, about which they had no doubts whatever.'*

The Military left Harrismith in 1913, and had a great influence on the town, building Blockhouses, emblems on the hills surrounding the town, building dams, bridges, playing an active role in church and other civic roles. A drive around the town even today will highlight the impact they had on it.

In April 1901, a White and Black Concentration camp was founded in Harrismith. Whilst the British Military appreciated Harrismith's strategic location, its significance was not lost on the Burghers. When it appeared that war was imminent, all Free State Burghers were called to arms on Sunday, 2 October 1899.

The Harrismith commando was instructed to gather at *'The Oaks,'* the farm of Frank Mandy, an Irishman, sympathetic to the Boers. In due course 8 000 Burghers assembled there, waiting to invade Natal.

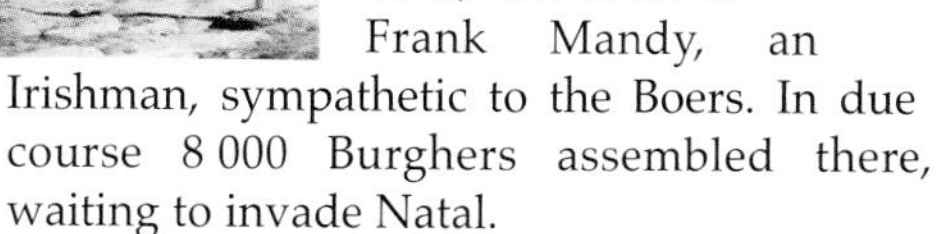

**The Harrismith Commando's finest hour was at Platrand, Ladysmith.** Around Harrismith you can see the emblems of the British troops which they marked out in stones and white washed. Many of the fallen from Groenkop / Tweefontein are buried there. Some were re-interred from the battlesite during the 1960's. It is believed that the Jewish Cemetery is unique in that it honours 3 unknown soldiers who died during the Boer War. Little is known about them, or even which side they were on.

The British built a **stone Blockhouse** to protect the town's water. It is still standing and is in the wildflower gardens. According to a British TV crew it is one of the few blockhouses still standing in a location that has not changed too much in the last 100 years. The Harrismith Commando (SANDF) has also erected an accurate replica of a **Rice-corrugated iron Blockhouse**, in the commando grounds, giving tourists an interesting comparison.

The *'military'* left many relics in Harrismith which are still visible today. Street names such as Rundle and Hector. The Anglican Church in town has many memorials to them, while the township Anglican church owes their stained glass windows to them. The majestic town hall and even the town's water supply had something to do with them. ❑

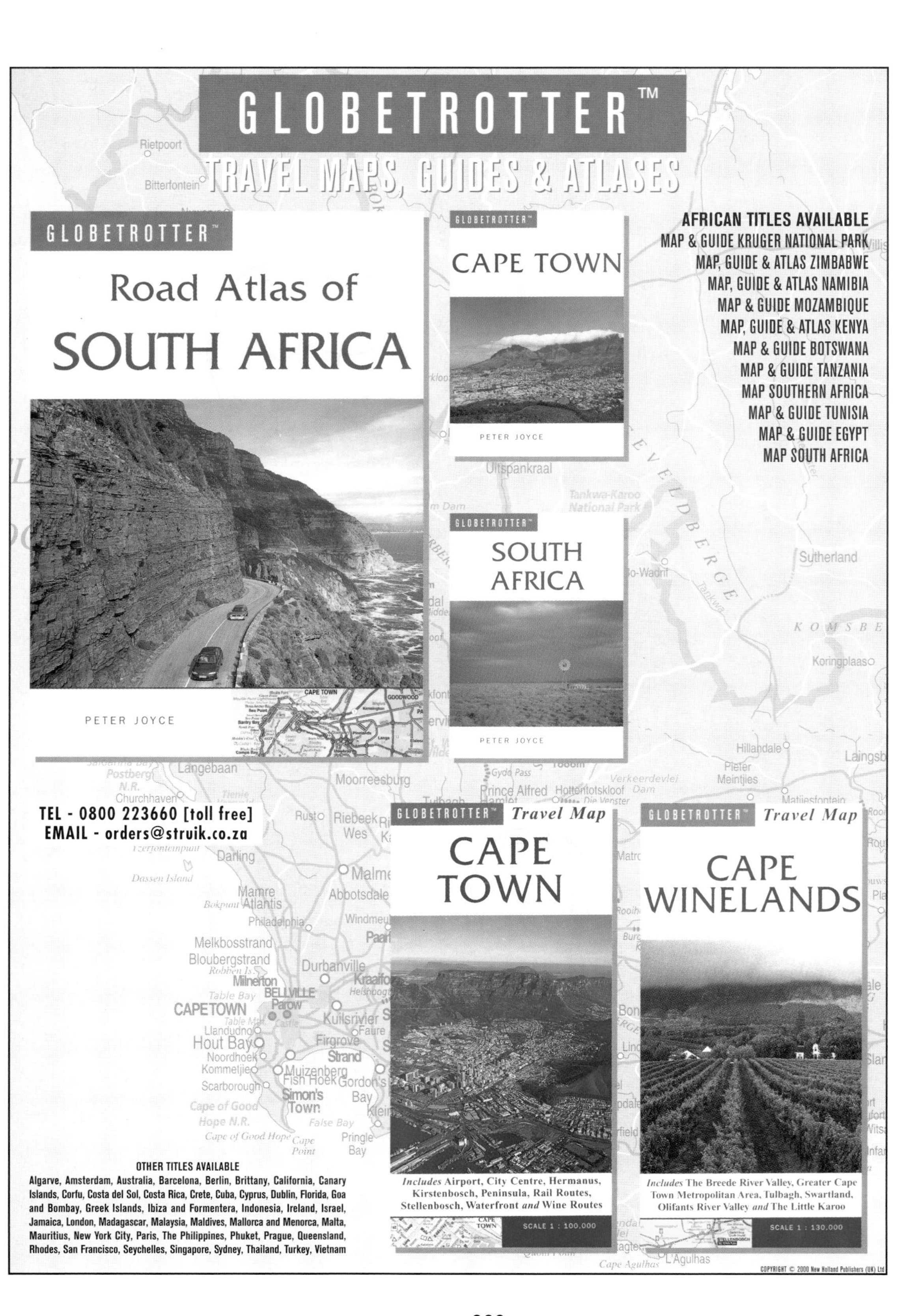

GLOBETROTTER™
TRAVEL MAPS, GUIDES & ATLASES
GLOBETROTTER™
Road Atlas of
SOUTH AFRICA
PETER JOYCE
GLOBETROTTER™
CAPE TOWN
PETER JOYCE
GLOBETROTTER™
SOUTH AFRICA
PETER JOYCE
AFRICAN TITLES AVAILABLE
MAP & GUIDE KRUGER NATIONAL PARK
MAP, GUIDE & ATLAS ZIMBABWE
MAP, GUIDE & ATLAS NAMIBIA
MAP & GUIDE MOZAMBIQUE
MAP, GUIDE & ATLAS KENYA
MAP & GUIDE BOTSWANA
MAP & GUIDE TANZANIA
MAP SOUTHERN AFRICA
MAP & GUIDE TUNISIA
MAP & GUIDE EGYPT
MAP SOUTH AFRICA
TEL - 0800 223660 [toll free]
EMAIL - orders@struik.co.za
GLOBETROTTER™ Travel Map
CAPE TOWN
Includes Airport, City Centre, Hermanus, Kirstenbosch, Peninsula, Rail Routes, Stellenbosch, Waterfront and Wine Routes
SCALE 1 : 100.000
GLOBETROTTER™ Travel Map
CAPE WINELANDS
Includes The Breede River Valley, Greater Cape Town Metropolitan Area, Tulbagh, Swartland, Olifants River Valley and The Little Karoo
SCALE 1 : 130.000
OTHER TITLES AVAILABLE
Algarve, Amsterdam, Australia, Barcelona, Berlin, Brittany, California, Canary Islands, Corfu, Costa del Sol, Costa Rica, Crete, Cuba, Cyprus, Dublin, Florida, Goa and Bombay, Greek Islands, Ibiza and Formentera, Indonesia, Ireland, Israel, Jamaica, London, Madagascar, Malaysia, Maldives, Mallorca and Menorca, Malta, Mauritius, New York City, Paris, The Philippines, Phuket, Prague, Queensland, Rhodes, San Francisco, Seychelles, Singapore, Sydney, Thailand, Turkey, Vietnam
COPYRIGHT © 2000 New Holland Publishers (UK) Ltd

LESOTHO
Freestate
Northern Cape
Western Cape
Eastern Cape
INDIAN OCEAN
Kokstad
UMTATA
EAST LONDON
Queenstown
Cradock
Graaff-Reinet
Middelburg
Aliwal North
Burgersdorp
Molteno
GRAHAMSTOWN
King William's Town
Fort Beaufort
Somerset East
PORT ELIZABETH
UITENHAGE
Port Alfred
Jeffreys Bay
Humansdorp
Plettenberg Bay
Knysna
Beaufort West
Colesberg
De Aar
Noupoort
Port St. Johns
SNEEUBERG
WINTERBERGE
BAMBOESBERG
SUURBERG
COETZEESBERGE
GROOTWINTERHOEKBERGE
BAVIAANSKLOOFBERGE
KOUGA MTNS
TSITSIKAMMA MTNS
Tsitsikamma National Park
Mountain Zebra National Park
Addo Elephant N.P.
50 km
25 miles
GLOBETROTTER™
COPYRIGHT © 2000 New Holland Publishers (UK) Ltd

# Eastern Cape

*Enjoy the warm hospitality of the Eastern Cape.*
*See the magnificent wildlife in Private Game Reserves and National Game Parks which includes the BIG 5 in a Malaria free environment.*
*Discover the ethnic culture with a splendid array of arts & crafts.*
*Steeped in history with a diversity of places to visit.*
*Swim in the warm waters of the coast and explore the trails and beaches.*

Take the N6 route from Bloemfontein in the Free State, past the historic towns of Reddersburg and Rouxville, into the Eastern Cape at Aliwal North on the banks of the Orange River. This treelined town is one of South Africa's popular inland resorts, with many historical buildings. It is here that 3 million litres of healing warm water springs forth daily. Take the R58 eastwards to Burgersdorp, the oldest town in the North Eastern Cape, sheltering in the valley of the Stormberg Mountains. Or take the R58 west from Aliwal North through the Kraai River Pass towards Lady Grey and Barkly East, and further on as it meanders through magnificent landscapes to Elliot, Rhodes and Maclear. Here visitors may pursue outdoor activities from walking trips to Bushman paintings, fly fishing, game viewing and bird spotting, backpacking, hiking, canoeing, river rafting, mountain biking, horse riding, and in the winter, skiing on the snowcovered slopes of Ben MacDhui.

Continuing on the N6 through Jamestown and onto Queenstown where you can turn off towards Tsolwana or Mpofu, two of the regions game reserves. Follow the country road to Hogsback and experience the magic of this area where it is said that it inspired Tolkien to write The Hobbit and The Lord of the Rings.

Further southward on the N6 you come to the picturesque town of Stutterheim on the slopes of the Kologha Mountains. The Kologha Forest, with its lush ferns and wild flowers, is a popular place to unwind.

As most rivers and dams in the area are well stocked with trout, why not try your luck at flyfishing?

East London is a mere 100 km from Stutterheim and the mild Indian Ocean waters are perfect for your seaside destination.

To the east you have Grahamstown, the world renowned University City (Rhodes University), and further east the magnificent beaches of Port Elizabeth with its attractions.

To the west of East London there is the Wild Coast with unspoilt beaches and coves to explore, each with its own beach hotel.

*Enjoy your trip to the Eastern Cape.*

In the cemetery at Aberdeen lies a young man who was executed for wearing khaki (which at the time was worn only by British soldiers). This incident also sparked an emotional storm. When later referring to these events, General Jan Smuts said that if Jack Baxter had not worn khaki he would have had to go about naked simply because, at that stage of the war, he had no other clothing to wear. In many other Karoo towns such as Graaff Reinet, Middelburg and Cradock there are graves of the Boer commandants who, as Cape Rebels, were tried for treason and executed.

ROSES ROUND UP

# Graaff-Reinet

### THE DROSTDY HOTEL, GRAAFF-REINET

Designed in 1804, it was initially the Magistrates Court. As part of the hotel there is Stretch's Court, a complex of 19th century cottages used as guest suites. Dinners are served under candlelit candelabras.
51 Rooms from R460 - R620 per room. B&B.
Tel: (049) 892 2161. Fax: (049) 892 4582.
e-mail: drostdy@intekom.co.za

### AVONDRUST GUEST HOUSE, GRAAFF-REINET

A Georgian style double-storey house, circa 1911, in the centre of historic Graaff-Reinet and walking distance to restaurants. Have breakfast by the pool. Enjoy relaxing with a swim or in the TV lounge.
5 Rooms from R155 per person sharing. B&B.
Tel: (049) 892 3566. Fax: (049) 892 3577.
e-mail: avondrust@elink.co.za

### CYPRESS COTTAGE, GRAAFF-REINET

Charming Karoo cottages dating back to the late 1800's, whose architecture, restoration and furnishings are typical of the Anglo-Boer War period. The property adjoins the Karoo Nature Reserve for walks.
3 Rooms from R160 pp sharing. Bed & Breakfast.
Tel/Fax: (049) 892 3965. Cell/Mobile: 083 456 1795.
e-mail: cypress@yebo.co.za

### KINGFISHER LODGE, GRAAFF-REINET

Beautifully decorated en-suite rooms with TV, M-Net, private entrances and tea/coffee facilities. The Roman suite has a 4-poster bed, perfect for that romantic getaway. Secure parking.
6 Rooms from R120 - R220 pp sharing. B&B.
Tel/Fax: (049) 892 2657. Cell/Mobile: 082 651 6280.
e-mail: kingfisher-lodge@interkom.co.za

### BLOEMHOF, GRAAFF-REINET

Step back a century into this gracious relic of colonial days. The Bloemhof homestead, surrounded by majestic Karoo countryside and a variety of wildlife, is an imposing reminder of the Ostrich-feather boom. Your hosts, the Murray Family, have been here since 1838.
3 Rooms from R110 per person B&B sharing.
Tel: (049) 840 0203. Fax: (049) 840 0203.

# Aliwal North

### Homely Guest House, Aliwal North

Close to Aliwal North's hot springs. Ideally positioned for the Free State Battlefields. The main house has two double rooms; and a cottage with one double and one single room. Karoo lamb dinner by arrangement.
4 Rooms from R135 pp sharing. Bed & Breakfast.
Tel: (051) 634 2368. Fax: (051) 634 2368.
Cell/Mobile: 083 306 8404.

### Toll Inn 1881, Aliwal North

This historical inn is situated 10 km from Aliwal North on the Lady Grey Road. When you cross the bridge built in 1881, you cross into history. Luxuriously renovated units ensure a memorable stay close to Boer war sites.
5 Rooms from R135 per person B&B.
Tel: (051) 634 1541. Fax: (051) 634 1799.
Cell/Mobile: 082 573 4113.

### Lord Somerset Guest House, Aliwal North

Antique furnished en-suite bedrooms create an atmosphere of a voortrekker museum. Sleep on a genuine old ox-wagon, the *'Boere Kar'*. Rooms have air-conditioning, TV and M-Net, electric blankets and tea/coffee facilities.
18 Rooms from R120 per person B&B sharing.
Tel: (051) 634 1114. Fax: (051) 634 1602.
e-mail: maretha@lordsummerset.co.za

Furniture looted after Boer farmers and Burghers families' were sent to concentration camps.

*The 'Wagon-bed' in the 'Boere Kar Room' at the Lord Somerset Guest House, Aliwal North.*

## Burgersdorp

**DUSK TO DAWN GUEST HOUSE. BURGERSDORP**
Each room has its own entrance, stoep, bar fridge, TV, tea/coffee facilities and splendid view of the estate. In winter guests relax in front of the fireplace. Excellent country cooked dinners by arrangement. 4 Rooms from R180 pp sharing. Bed & Breakfast.
Tel/Fax: (051) 653 0086. Cell/Mobile: 083 262 2714
e-mail: grotius@iafrica.com

## Paterson area

**ZUURBERG MOUNTAIN INN, NEAR PATERSON**
Established in 1861, a haven of delight set high up in the Zuurberg Mountains overlooking the Addo Elephant National Park. Zuurberg not only survived the Boer War, but also the great fire in 1902, after which it was restored to its former Victorian glory. 22 Rooms from R195 to R300 per person sharing.
Tel: (042) 233 0583. Fax: (042) 233 0070.
e-mail: zuurberg@ilink.co.za

GRAAFF-REINET PUBLICITY
Old Library Museum, Church Streeet, Graaff-Reinet
Tel: (049) 892 4248.
Website: http:/ /www.graaffreinet.co.za

Graaff-Reinet is situated 209 km from Beaufort West, 251 km from Port Elizabeth, 203 km from Colesburg and 56 km from Aberdeen. Founded in 1786, it was named after Cornelis Jacob van de Graaff, Governor of the Cape (1785-1791) and his wife Cornelia Reinet.

The region is dependant on pastoral agriculture with the farming of sheep, goats and game such as Springbok.

The town is is 759 metres above sea level; with hot summers (average 31°C) and cool but dry winters (average 6°C).

Graaff-Reinet lies in the centre of the 15 000 hectacre Karoo Nature Reserve with the natural wonder of the *Valley of Desolation*.

## Graaff-Reinet during the Anglo-Boer War

The invasion of the Boer Republics was considered to be unjust by the Burghers in Graaff-Reinet and after the demise of Presidents Kruger and Steyn, rebellion simmered in the hearts of the Boer supporters who had settled in South Africa.

When Kitchener declared Martial Law he sent 600 men of the Coldstream Guards to Graaff-Reinet. They arrived on 01 January 1901. Major Shute prepared the defences and certain regulations following the instructions of Colonel Haig.

*Arms, ammunition, excess stocks of food, bicycles, horses and fodder were to be handed over to the authorities. Travel was prohibited without permission. A 9 p.m curfew was imposed. Rewards of up to £20 were paid for useful information.* Most people were afraid to open their mouths. Martial Law produced more emnity and rebels than it intended.

Kitchener's *Scorched Earth Policy* created its own problems in the Cape Colony when the small bands of Commandos started to retaliate and burn the farmhouses of the pro-British.

In addition the Commandos hampered communications by cutting phone lines and blowing-up railway tracks. Towns were occupied by the Commandos and British flags torn down in defiance. The blockhouses went up and with the Mounted Infantry it was hoped that the Boers would be driven towards them and captured. Then nature decided to join in with a searing drought leaving a parched land.

No one could remain neutral. If a Burgher sided with the British he had betrayed his *'volk'*! And an English speaking person who supported the Boers was treasonous. A neighbour with a grudge could use this to his benefit and many did!! Boer sympathisers were deported and their property now unattended was stolen or destroyed. This resulted in the collapse of the farming economy.

In the meantime, the Cold-stream Guards continued with their social activities; polo, tennis, garden parties etc.

Commandant Gideon Scheepers was causing mayhem with derailing of trains, cutting communications, burning houses and taking prisoners (1 200 which were released). His great escape from Colonel Scobell and 2 000 British troops into the Camdeboo Mountains with 240 Boers was a humiliating experience for the British.

To Miss L. Muller

Office of the Civil Commissioner,

You are hereby permitted to ride your bicycle in town on the following conditions:-

I It is not to be taken out of town-

II You must carry this permit-

III A metal plate with registered number must be attached to the saddle in a conspicuous place-

IV On passing a guard or sentry the pace must be not more than six miles an hour & you must stop & dismount when ordered to do so by Civil or military police-

V A lamp must be carried between Sunset & Sunrise-

VI You are not on any account to lend your bicycle to anyone

He was eventually arrested at the Dwyka River on the 10 October 1901. He had appendicitis and was nursed back to health to stand trial. He was found guilty of murder and was shot on 18 January 1902.

## My God I'm shot!

Out on patrol two members of the Graaff-Reinet DMT approached a Boer Commando too closely. Bullets whizzed past and diving for cover they waited for the Boers to move away. Becoming bored, Arthur Kingwill tossed a stone at his companion hitting him between the shoulder blades. Alfred Thornton jumped up with fright and shouted out: *My God I'm Shot!*

***When Ants Get Angry*** by Andrew McNaughton

## Narrow Escape

Major Lord Douglas Compton of the 9th Lancers charged towards the *Paardefontein* house where Commandant Lotter was thought to be. In so doing his 'A' squadron galloped past a shed in the dark. Major Compton dropped his pistol accidentally, he swung out, dismounted, picked it up and survived. The four men following were all shot dead as they passed the shed opening. Inside were Lotter and his men.

***When Ants Get Angry*** by Andrew McNaughton

The authorities refused to allow a Boer War memorial to be erected after the war. It was finally erected on private land at the corner of Somerset and Donkin streets. It commemorates the 8 Boers who were exectuted at Graaff-Reinet.

## Historical Places

Graaff-Reinet has more proclaimed ***National Monuments*** than any other town in South Africa. It also has a conservation policy to ensure that the examples of architecture, ranging from Karoo style houses to Cape Dutch buildings, are retained and maintained.

**Dutch Reform Church:** A magnificent century old church being the focal point of the town. The Communion vessels used in the church are superb examples of Cape Silver.

**The Drostdy:** Now the Drostdy Hotel, was built in 1806 and restored to its present elegance in 1977 by the *Historical Homes of South Africa*. The picturesque cottages in **Stretch's Court**, now used as part of the accommodation for the hotel, were once occupied by emancipated slaves.

**The Hester Rupert Art Museum:** Built in 1821. Valuable works of art donated by more than 75 South African artists can be seen.

**The John Rupert Little Theatre:** Parsonage Street. It was originally the Church of the London Missionary Society. In 1975 the building was bought by Dr.Rupert and has been converted into a 150 seater theatre where an active group of amateur dramatic players perform regularly.

**Old Residency:** Opposite the Reinet House. The Residency houses the *Jan Felix Lategan Memorial* gun collection and the *Die Middellandse Regiment* collection.

**Reinet House:** Was a parsonage for almost 100 years, and was occupied by Rev. Andrew Murray and his son Charles for 82 consecutive years. Now it is a Cultural History Museum. There is a *grape vine* in the garden that was planted in 1870.

**Urquhart House:** Has an unusual gable and peach-stone kitchen floor.

## Restaurants

**The Drostdy Hotel:** There are two restaurants in the hotel; both of excellent standard. The Main Dining Room with its candlelit candelabras serves table d'hôte; and next door there is an Á La Carte Restaurant. Tel: (049) 892 2161.

**Desert Springs Spur:** Church Street. Steak House. Tel: (049) 892 3202.

## Tour Operator & Guides

**Karoo Connections Tours & Safaris:** *Contact*: David & Andrew McNaughton.
Tel: (049)-892 3978 Fax: (049)-891 1061. Cell/Mobile: 082 748 3253. *Anglo-Boer War Tours-Valley of Desolation-Karoo Nature Reserve-Horse Trails-Karoo Farm Experiences-Light Aircraft Trips.*

**Andrew McNaughton**: (T.5141). Tel: (049)-8923978 Fax: (049)-8911061. *See above.*

**David McNaughton**: (T.5140). Tel: (049)-8923978 Fax: (049)-8911061. *See above.*

**G.G.Van Niekerk:** (T.5766). Tel: 049-893 0203. Fax: (049)-893 0203. *Specialising in Boer War in and around Graaff-Reinet; and Gideon Scheepers.*

### Booysen Gets it

Piet Booysen, a pro-British Boer who had given evidence against Gideon Scheepers at his trial, was captured by the Boers and was given a severe thrashing by Commandant Van Heerden at the farm *Brooklyn*.

***When Ants Get Angry*** by Andrew McNaughton

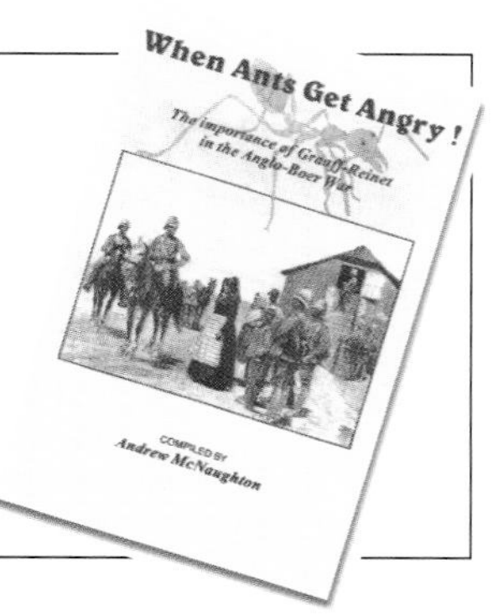

# Gideon Scheepers

Although Gideon Scheepers was executed by a British firing squad, he was not one of the Cape 'rebels'. Born in the Transvaal, Scheepers was just 17 when he joined the republic's only professional military unit, the Staats Artillerie, in 1895. During the South African War he was seconded to the Orange Free State Artillery and promoted to commandant, leading a small commando in the Cape. A fearless and popular leader, Scheepers welded his men into a tight unit. They wrecked trains, burnt the farmsteads of those unsympathetic to the Boer cause and kept the British occupied trying to capture them. Scheepers was taken prisoner on a farm near Prince Albert and tried by a military court at Graaff-Reinet on more than 30 charges (including murder). Found guilty, he was executed outside the town beside an open grave in January 1902. His body was apparently disinterred by the British during the night and secretly reburied. Many believed that a British military court was not competent to sentence a non-British prisoner of war to death during the war, and there was an outcry. ❑

***From Mrs Susie Brooks, Brooklyn, Graaff-Reinet.***

***"I have never anticipated any personal danger from the Boers, for having lived amongst them nearly all my life, I know that they are not what the press represents them to be. I feel quite sure that they will respect defenceless women and children ... Five rebels have been put to death in Graaff-Reinet in the short space of a week. They are charged with murder if they have been in an engagement where British soldiers have fallen! I am afraid the Dutch will retaliate and our soldiers will have to suffer for this".***

*Drummer Hodge.*
***The Poetry of the Anglo-Boer War***
by M VAN WYK SMITH.

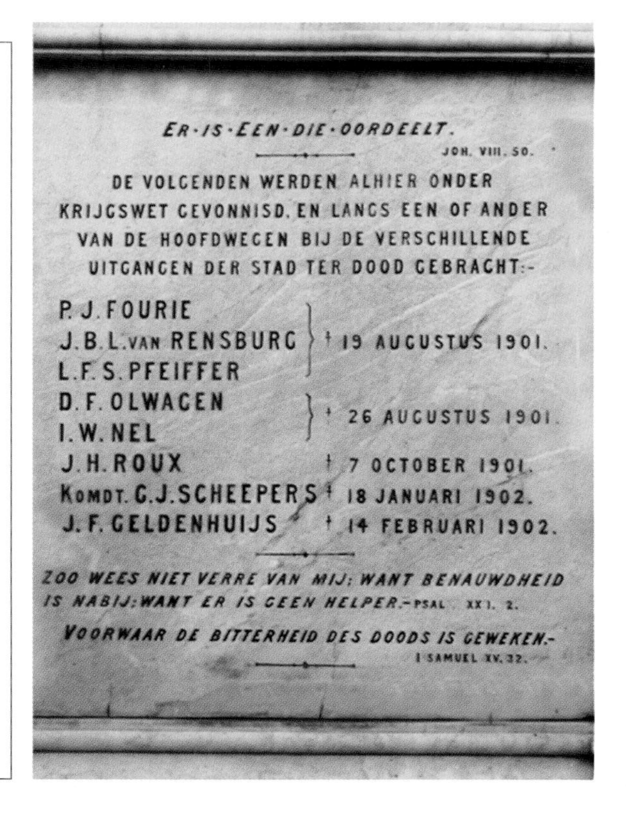

# Commandant Johannes Lötter

Johannes Lotter, 26, of Pearston, Cape Colony (Eastern Cape) a charming Naaupoort barman raised a Cape Rebel commando of Midland farmers early in 1901.

He built trenches around Compassberg to control the interior from there. Chased out, he became Com. P. Kritzinger's Second-in-Command, roving the Midlands. By August General Sir John French's men had him pinned down between the two railways which connect at Rosmead, a village 12 km east of Middelburg. In dreadful weather and heavily pursued by Lieutenant-Colonel Harry Scobell, the 9th Lancers and the Cape Mounted Riflemen, he took refuge at *Paardefontein* in the Tantjiesberg. On 9 September 1901 his commando was surprised by Scobell's column, as they lay asleep in a sheep kraal. In a skirmish 13 Boers were killed, one died of wounds and 135 men surrendered. Lotter and five of his officers were later executed.

NOTE: See the kraals and the shed later made of the roof of corrugated iron, peppered with holes, and the Boer graves at *Nooitgedacht* (now *Santesana Private Game Reserve*). The British graves of their 10 killed on site. Want to feel the Boer War? It's here.

*Santesana,* a game lodge, managed by Richard Viljoen, has its base at *Nooitgedacht.* The phone number for the lodge is (0491) 891 0879.

*Paardefontein, Spring Grove,* the neighbouring farm's new owner is Logie Buchannan, who welcomes visitors. His phone number is (0491) 891 0988.

***Source:***

DAVID & TAFFY SHEARING. Tel: (044) 343 1649 Authors of *Commandant Johannes Lötter and His Rebels;* and *Commandant Gideon Scheepers and the Search for his Grave.*

## SAVED BY AN ANTBEAR HOLE

Daantjie Jonker an '*agterryer*' (native helper or groom) with the Boers had escaped around a grove of prickly pears, when the firing started at Paardefontein. Here he found an antbear hole. Digging frantically with his hands he was able to widen it sufficiently to ease himself inside. Safe in his hiding place he heard the battle sounds die away. After three days a hungry and thirsty Jonker emerged to make his escape. He was the only member of Lotter's Commando to evade capture.

***When Ants Get Angry*** by ANDREW MCNAUGHTON

## 'HAT-TRICK' LUCK

Captain Fred McCabe, Officer Commanding of the DMT had amazing luck. While scouting in the Graaff-Reinet area he had a small piece of his ear clipped by a bullet. Then, when he raised his head to have another look, the other ear was clipped. His son Henry said the pieces missing from the ears looked as if his father had been born like that as they were a matching pair.

On another occasion Captain McCabe had his hat removed by a Mauser bullet. Pure luck to survive close encounters!! He went on to receive a Military Cross in World War I.

***When Ants Get Angry*** by ANDREW MCNAUGHTON

*A. V. Oosthuizen*

# A Guide to the Battlefields & Monuments in the North Eastern Cape

**Burgersdorp** was the railway junction of the branch line leading towards Aliwal North on main line from East London over Stormberg Junction to Bloemfontein. During the War it was well garrisoned and two blockhouses protected the town against inroads by guerrilla forces over Sanddrift into the Colony. The one guarded the northern entrance to the town and the other the railway station.

**Stormberg Junction**, was the most important strategic point in the North Eastern Cape. Boer forces occupied it in the initial stages of the war and defeated the British army in its first onslaught on the junction. The British, however, recaptured it after four months and turned it into a stronghold with two masonry blockhouses as well as many other fortifications on the surrounding hills. For the rest of the war Boer guerrilla commandos avoided this stronghold.

The Battle of Stormberg, 10 December 1899.

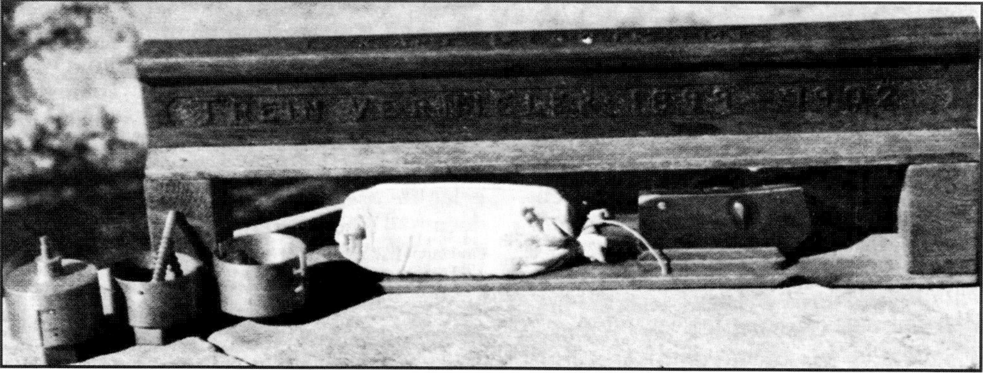

Derailment system used by the Boers in the early stages of the war.

*Pat Rundgren*

# The Battle of Stormberg 10 December 1899

**Stormberg Junction** in the north-east Cape Colony occupied the centre of a 'basin' encircled by hills through which the railway line led westward to **Steynsburg** and **Rosemead**, north-east to **Burgersdorp** and south to **Molteno** and **Queenstown**. The huge Rooi Kop towers over the south-eastern side of the basin, with a much lower ridge, the **Kissieberg,** to the south and south-west.

The Battle of Stormberg was an ill-fated and aborted attempt by Maj.-General Sir William Gatacre to drive the Boers from Stormberg railway junction. Occupied, after the invasion of the Colony, by Com. E.R. Grobler, the Bethulie (Du Plooy), Smithfield (Swane-poel) and Rouxville (Olivier) Commandos, as well as some Albert and Burgersdorp rebels under Piet Steenkamp, the occupation cut off Gatacre's lines of communication with General French. It was imperative to restore these, and Gatacre resolved to mount an attack at Kissieberg.

A tiny force, comprising 2 600 men from two battalions of the Northumberland Fusiliers and Royal Irish Fusiliers, the Berkshire regiment Mounted Infantry Company, 74th Battery Royal Field Artillery, 12th Company Royal Engineers and a detachment of Cape Police, was detailed for the attack. It was planned to take the infantry and guns as far as Molteno by train in the afternoon, followed by a night march of eight miles to rush the main position on Kissieberg at dawn. A bold and perfectly feasible plan, so long as nothing went wrong in the execution.

Disaster dogged the expedition from the start. Local intelligence gathered on the afternoon of 9 December 1899 indicated that the Boers had entrenched the south face of Kiessieberg and had constructed a wire entanglement in front of their trenches. Although the report was later found to be false, Gatacre decided to abandon a direct march and to attempt to surprise the position from one of its undefended flanks. Although a sound decision, it added a new dimension of problems to what was already a problematic situation – the night march, which would be much longer; and over unfamiliar ground, would result in the troops being exhausted rather than fresh for the assault. Also, there was a misunderstanding between Gatacre and his guides, who failed to understand what was required. The march began some two hours later than planned. Some of the force became detached even before the march began. The guides lost their way and the column, having marched for seven hours, was delivered to the wrong part of Kissieberg, where at dawn the men stumbled upon the first Boer laager (Olivier's) and lost the element of surprise. A brave attempt to storm the berg failed when men of the Royal Irish and Northumberland Fusiliers encountered a sheer cliff. The Northumberlands managed to work around the flanks, but as they crested the hill artillery fire from the 74th Battery drove their own men off it again, wounding Colonel Eager, Major Seaton and several others.

The exhausted, demoralised men were in no condition to launch an attack from the side of the Nek and as there were no reserves, Gatacre was forced to order a retreat to Molteno. The General himself was in the rear guard, and at the beginning of the retreat narrowly escaped with his life when his own gunners, mistaking them for Boers, dropped shells in the middle of them. The Boers attempted to attack the retreating troops but were repulsed by the Artillery. Although the British had only 27 men killed and seven officers and 50 men injured, a third of Gatacre's infantry spread all over and below the Nek failed to receive the order to retire. As a result, 634 men were left at Stormberg and many of them surrendered without firing a shot. Boer losses amounted to 8 killed and 26 wounded. ❏

## STORMBERG MOUNTAINS

There are places of eerie loneliness in the gaunt Stormberg range in the north-east corner of the Cape Province. For a very long time the area was only sparsely inhabited, and seemed to be shunned by white and black alike. Only the San (Bushmen), driven from the plains, took refuge in the many caves to be found among the great sandstone peaks.

Some trekboers reached the Stormberg area in the 1790s and, by the 1830s, scattered farms had been established. The big game that had once roamed there – including elephants, if local San paintings are to be taken literally – was soon shot out.

The two principal towns of the region are Molteno and Burgersdorp. Between them lies the Stormberg railway junction, the scene of a British defeat in the early stages of the Anglo-Boer War.

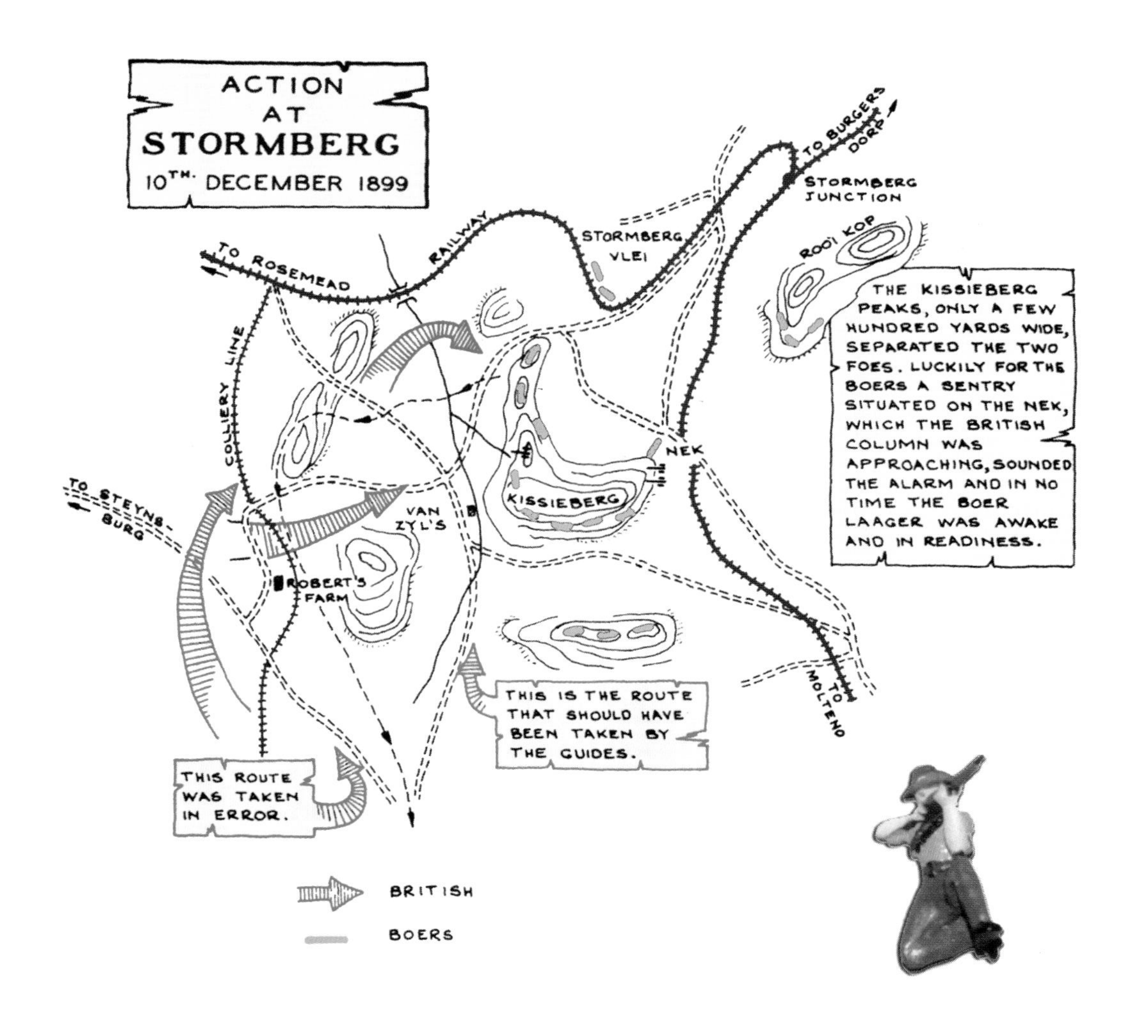

## ALIWAL-NORTH TOURISM

**Tel: (051) 633 3567. Fax: (051) 633 3569. Contact Rob Little**

Aliwal North is on the Orange River, approximately 195 km from Bloemfontein on the road to East London.

It was founded in 1849 and named by the Governor of the Cape Colony, Sir Harry Smith, to commemorate his victory over the Sikhs under Runjeet Singh at Aliwal in India in 1846.

### Boer War Sites

**Garden of Remembrance:** (pictured right)

The 138 British and Colonial soldiers who are commemorated in the Garden of Remembrance in Aliwal North were all originally buried in municipal cemeteries and farm graveyards in the districts of Aliwal North, Rouxville and Zastron. Many of them were buried just where they fell on the battlefields on outlying farms. Others were buried in town cemeteries. Most of the graves were identified by iron crosses and family or comrades put memorial stones on some graves, but others could never be located or identified.

In 1975 the S.A. War Graves Board erected the *Garden of Remembrance* in Aliwal North for the soldiers who died in these districts, as Aliwal North was the town from where all the operations in the area were carried out. Their remains were exhumed on all the remote farms and municipal cemeteries and reinterred in the Garden of Remembrance which is situated on a hilltop east of the town, next to the blockhouse.

Those who could be identified, were reinterred in separate graves. Those who could not be identified separately, were reinterred in mass graves, while those whose graves could not be located, are mentioned on the main monument in the Garden.

**Old Magistrate's Court:** (pictured below)

The Old Magistrate's Court was the headquarters of the Free State forces during their four months "annexation" of the Stormberg districts with Aliwal North as its capital. They even renamed the town **"Oliviersfontein"**. In this building hundreds of Rebels were commandeered to join the Free State forces on their way to occupy the strategic Stormberg Junction. In the same building hundreds of Rebels also surrendered to the British four months later and took the oath to neutrality. Here they were also tried in a Special Court, sent to prison, fined, disfranchised, banned and even sentenced to death. For the rest of the war it became the headquarters of the British authority and afterwards served as Aliwal North's Post Office for many years. Today it is private property and until now all attempts have failed to have it declared a national monument.

**Old Public Library**: (pictured below)

Erected in 1870, is one of the two Museums of Aliwal North. The history of the Anglo-Boer War in the Stormberg districts is one of the major projects which was launched by the Museum in recent years. The Museum has many books, documents, diaries, photographs and family records on the Anglo-Boer War. It has recently also launched a project to document the role which the Black people played in the War with special reference to the Blacks who died in the Concentration Camp in Aliwal North including those who lost their lives in military operations in the Stormberg districts.

**Old Toll House**:

When the retreating Free State commandos were too late to destroy the Frere Bridge, they shelled the bridge and the town. One bomb from their Krupp canon went through the toll house at the entrance to the bridge without exploding, but another one hit the bridge with little damage. The bridge survived the war and for many years it was used as a road and railway bridge before the new road and railway bridges were built. The Old Toll House today serves as a tourist information bureau.

**Concentration Camp Graveyards**:

The Concentration camp in Aliwal North was one of the largest in the country and almost the entire rural population, Black and White, of the districts of Rouxville, Zastron and Smithfield, was rounded up in this camp as part of Kitchener's *"scorched earth policy"* to lay waste and depopulate the entire Southern Free State. The population in the Black and White camps reached its peak in October 1901 when there were in all 4 743 people in the camp, of whom about 2 000 were Blacks. The three camps for White women and children from the districts of Rouxville, Zastron and Smithfield were situated on the banks of the Kraai River, just above its junction with the Orange River. The camp for Blacks, however, was situated five miles lower down the Orange River. The 716 women and children and a few burghers who died in the camp for Whites were buried in two graveyards on the banks of the Kraai River, while the Blacks were buried in a graveyard on the banks of the Orange River five miles away.

**Memorial Stones in the old graveyards**:

A memorial stone was erected underneath bluegum trees on the banks of the Kraai River in the original camp graveyard. This site for the graveyard was chosen, because the numerous graves could easily be dug in the soft alluvial soil. Most of the women and children who died in the camp were buried here. A second graveyard was later started a little higher up, away from the banks of the Kraai River for fear that the graves on the river bank could pollute the water of the Orange River. This was done because a pumping scheme was planned on the Orange River to supply drinking water to the town. The ground on this new site was, however, so hard that it retarded the digging of graves to such an extent that it became necessary to return to the old graveyard. Two memorial stones were also erected on this new graveyard site.

Toll Bridge at Aliwal North.

**The Concentration Camp Memorial:**

In 1980 the remains in both the original graveyards along the Kraai River were exhumed and reinterred in a mass grave in the Concentration Camp Memorial Site – situated on the hill at the southern entrance to the town next to the main road. This is also near the place where a British military camp stood during the war. All the gravestone's from the graves in the old graveyards were built into the walls of the memorial and the names of all the deceased were engraved on a roll of honour. A number of graves in the old cemeteries were not exhumed and the moulds are still visible today. These probably belonged to Blacks who either worked as servants in the camp or served as camp guards.

***Lieutenant Izak B. Liebenberg:***

Hanged in public on 11 January 1902 in the Aliwal North jail for *"murdering"* Lieutenant Leopold Neumeyer of the Smithfield police. Neumeyer was executed by order of the Boer command for burning houses and stock and harassing Boer families in the Rouxville and Smithfield districts while executing Kitchener's *"scorched earth policy"*. Liebenberg wounded Neumeyer in an ambush, and Liebenberg had to pay the price to serve as a warning to Cape Rebels. He was buried in the concentration camp graveyard, but later reburied by family on the farm *Grootfontein* in the Philippolis district. He was born in the Free State and was not a Cape Rebel.

## Restaurants

**The Pink Lady Steakhouse:**
14 Dan Pienaar Avenue. Family Restaurant specialising in steaks, pork, seafood, chicken & mutton. Cell/Mobile: 082 466 6334.

## Tour Guides

**Herman le Roux:** (T.6027).
PO Box 794, Aliwal North, 9750. Tel: (051) 634 1541. Fax: (051) 634 1799.
*General Smuts and his invasion of the Cape Colony. Stormberg, the first Battle of Black Week. the north east Cape during the Anglo-Boer War. Commandant Fouche. Concentration Camps at Aliwal North.*

**Robert Little:** PO Box 198, Aliwal North, 9750. Tel/Fax: (051) 633 3567.
*Anglo-Boer War. North Eastern Cape.*

**Sandile Bashe:** (T.6029). PO Box 198, Aliwal North, 9750. Tel/Fax: (051) 633 3567.
*Anglo-Boer War. North Eastern Cape.*

**BURGERSDORP TOURISM**

**Burgersdorp Museum. The Burgher Square.**

**PO Box 156, Burgersdorp 9744. Tel: (051) 653 1777**

There are four monuments in the central square of the town: the Burgher Monument, the original headless Taal Monument, the replica Taal Monument and the historic Old Bluegum Tree.

## Boer War Sites

**The Burgher Monument:** The names of 13 burghers who fell in the vicinity of Burgersdorp during the Anglo-Boer War are engraved on the monument. Seven of them were killed in action in the Battle of Stormberg on 10 December 1899. They were originally buried on the battlefield, but later reinterred in a mass grave in the Burgersdorp cemetery.

***Klopper(t), Petrus Willem.*** Executed in public on 20 July 1901 in the Burgersdorp goal with compulsory attendance by former Rebels. Kloppert surrendered to the British when they occupied Burgersdorp, but again joined the Boer commandos when they invaded the Colony the second time. He was taken prisoner during a skirmish in the Steynsburg district and charged for ***'murdering'*** British soldiers who died in the skirmish. Originally he was buried some distance out of town, but later reinterred in a mass grave with burghers who fell at Stormberg. The execution of Kloppert in public roused a storm of protest and was heavily criticised even in the British Parliament, with the result that public executions were stopped.

**The Historic Old Blue Gum Tree:** The Bluegum tree underneath which Petrus Kloppert was condemned to death before he was executed in public, is preserved at the entrance of Burgher Square. All historic events are engraved on a copper plaque on the massive trunk of the tree. The tree was planted at the foundation of Burgersdorp in 1848 and is today strengthened with cement as an historic treasure. Well-known artists have depicted the old trunk in their paintings.

**The Old Gaol:** In this old goal **Professor Lion-Cachet** was imprisoned and the first Cape Rebel, Petrus Kloppert, was hanged in public. As a warning to other Rebels, the community was ordered to attend the execution. The building is preserved as a National Monument and is now being restored to its original form.

**The Socio-Historical Museum:** The Museum is situated in the former Theological Seminary of the Reformed Church. It houses a remarkable exhibition of writings and books relating to the Anglo- Boer War which is of great value to the researcher. Burgersdorp was considered the ***'rebel nest'*** of the North East Cape during the War; due to Professor Jan Lion-Cachet's involvement as ***Taal Patriot*** in the Afrikaans Language movement in the Paarl, but mostly because of his students' ardent support of the Republics in their struggle for freedom.

A church in Aliwal North.

When Professor Lion-Cachet held sermons for the commandos at Stormberg, he was arrested. He was imprisoned for a long time on charges of supporting the uprising in the Colony, but ultimately was released on bail after pleas by the English and Afrikaans inhabitants of Burgersdorp. Later he was acquitted and allowed to continue with his work at the Seminary.

After the battle of Stormberg students of the Seminary took 68 wounded British soldiers in a captured ambulance to Burgersdorp. Professor Lion-Cachet personally went up to President Steyn in Bloemfontein to acquire medical supplies for the wounded. For the rest of the Boer occupation of Burgersdorp they were nursed by the staff of the Seminary, and when the British re-occupied Burgersdorp, they found their wounded in good health!

**Moordenaarspoort:** Three burghers in the commando of **General Smuts** died when they were ambushed on the farm *Moordenaarspoort* near Dordrecht on 7 September 1901. One was killed in action, while two died of their wounds in the Dordrecht hospital. They were buried in the Dordrecht cemetery. General Smuts escaped miraculously by disappearing in a donga, losing only his hat.

**Military Graves:** Of the 40 British soldiers buried in the Municipal Cemetery of Burgersdorp only two died in battle. The others all died of disease or in accidents. At least ten soldiers died in railway accidents, the worst one being the collision between two armoured trains on Stormberg Junction. In contrast with Aliwal North and other Stormberg towns where a great number of troops buried in the graveyards were from Cape Colonial regiments, only the four Cape Police buried in Burgersdorp were from the Cape Colony, whereas the rest were all from British regiments. The reason for this was that the Colonial regiments under Brabant's Horse were used mainly to combat the Cape Rebels in the Stormberg district and did not operate as far west as Burgersdorp.

Below: Steam power used for the first time in a military environment.

**MOLTENO**

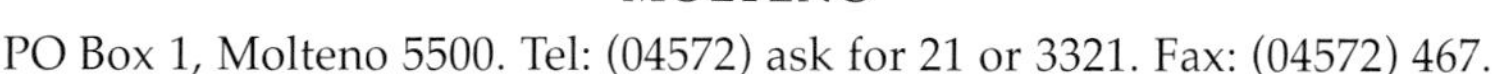

PO Box 1, Molteno 5500. Tel: (04572) ask for 21 or 3321. Fax: (04572) 467.

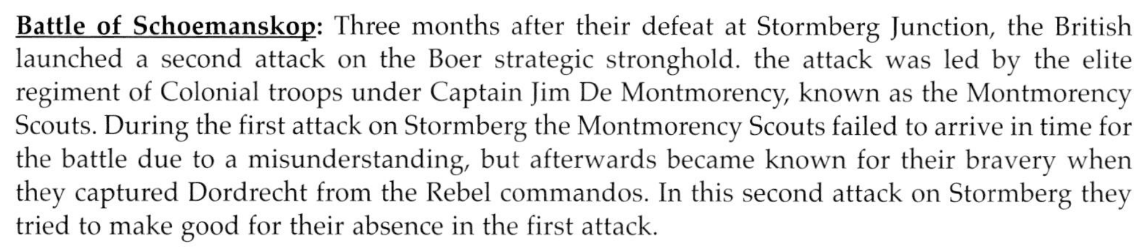

**Battle of Schoemanskop:** Three months after their defeat at Stormberg Junction, the British launched a second attack on the Boer strategic stronghold. the attack was led by the elite regiment of Colonial troops under Captain Jim De Montmorency, known as the Montmorency Scouts. During the first attack on Stormberg the Montmorency Scouts failed to arrive in time for the battle due to a misunderstanding, but afterwards became known for their bravery when they captured Dordrecht from the Rebel commandos. In this second attack on Stormberg they tried to make good for their absence in the first attack.

Captain De Montmorency and his men stormed Schoemanskop which controlled access to Stormberg Junction. The Boers reached the summit seconds before them and shot down 8 Scouts at close range, including Captain De Montmorency who stormed ahead of his comrades. The Scouts had to retreat and the second attack on Stormberg Junction also failed, but a week later the Boers retreated to the Free State without firing a shot in defence of Stormberg.

**Montmorency Hill:** A pile of stones were erected on a hill-top on the farm *Schoemanskop* where De Montmorency and his men fell. Many years later his aged sister visited South Africa to place a memorial stone on top of the pile. The hill is known as Montmorency Hill. A local farmer has laid out the Montmorency Hiking Trail on his Game and Holiday farm, *Laetitia*, approximately 11 km from Molteno.

***Vegkoppies* farmhouse:** From the front door of this house the first shot was fired which triggered the battle of Stormberg. Louis van Zyl got up before dawn to attend to his ewe's in lamb in the kraal just opposite his house when he caught some thieves redhanded slaughtering a ewe for early breakfast. He fired a shot to scare them off, not knowing they were *Tommies*. The shot rang through the early morning air and roused the attention of a Boer sentry on top of the mountain behind which the Boer laager stood. The alarm was raised in the Boer laager and they reached the summit minutes before the Northumberland Fusiliers with their drawn bayonets. Checked by a ledge of high rocks the *Tommies* were mowed down by Boer Mauser fire and a Krupp Canon; and even by their own artillery firing with the rising sun in their eyes. They never reached the top. **Only five minutes stood between victory and defeat.**

Except for a few renovations, including a Guest House, this historical farm house is still in its original form. It is only a few hundred yards from the Stormberg Memorial and overlooks the entire battlefield.

## Concentration Camps For Blacks

The guerrilla war and England's scorched earth policy rendered thousands of Blacks homeless and destitute. Initially they were put in so-called ***'Refugee Camps'***, but in due course these became **Concentration Camps**. It is estimated that up to 120 000 Blacks were kept in 66 official and over 20 informal concentration camps throughout the country and that up to 20 000 died in these camps, giving a death rate of 166 per 1 000.

The Camp in Aliwal North started as a ***'Native Refugee Camp'*** and for the first few months the blacks outnumbered the Boer women and children from the districts of Zastron, Rouxville and Smithfield. The Blacks ultimately stabilised on about 2 000 and the Whites on 2 500.

It is a well known fact that conditions in the Aliwal North concentration camp for Blacks were as appaling as in the camps for Boer women and children. However, mortality in the camps for Blacks were slightly lower than that for the Whites, because they seemed to be more immune from measles and small-pox. If the overall death rate for Black camps is applied to the camp in

Aliwal North, it can be assumed that about 330 Blacks must have died in their camp in Aliwal North. This estimation is supported by the figures laid before Parliament by **Emily Hobhouse** for all the Free State camps of which Aliwal North was considered a part.

It is likely that the first Blacks who died in the camp were buried near and even in the same graveyards as the Whites. There are still a number of graves in the Boer concentration camp cemetery along the Kraai River which were left behind untouched when the Boer women and children were exhumed. According to tradition these are the graves of Blacks who worked in the concentration camp. There are also indications that at least some Blacks of the first ***'Refugee Camp'*** were buried in the cemetery of *'Greatheads Location'* which dated well back before the war and was situated along the Orange River where the pumping station today stands. (The site was known as Greatheads Mill). All the graves in this cemetery were however exhumed in 1929 when the residential area of Arbor View was proclaimed and the remains were reburied in the *'Native Cemetery Site'* five miles lower down the Orange River.

***Blacks who died in military operations:*** Black troops formed an integral part of England's offensive in the Stormberg districts. Good pay, drought and bad economic conditions in the Stormberg districts were strong motivation for thousands of **Mfengus, Tembus** and **Basutos** to seek work in the British army. The supply was so large, that thousands had to be turned away. Initially they played only a supporting role as drivers, guards, caretakers of horses, personal attendants etc. But it soon became evident that England could not cope with the ever increasing demand on its manpower and was forced to make greater use of the vast available manpower of the Black tribes in the Eastern Cape. Ultimately these Black troops played a significant role in the **military operations** in the Stormberg districts.

The regiment of General Brabant, known as Brabant's Horse, consisted mostly of Cape Colonial Volunteer corps. However, the Black Volunteer Corps from the Eastern Cape were put under the command of white officers and also incorporated in Brabant's Horse. In the offensive against Dordrecht, Black troops were used with great success to guard the flanks of the Cape Colonials when they launched their attacks. Subsequently Black troops in Brabants Horse played a significant role in the rounding up of Rebels, of stock and of the rural population in the Southern Free State and escorting them to the concentration camps in Aliwal North.

Of even greater importance was the **Herschel Special Native Police Force** under command of **Major Hook**. 400 Basuto troops were named and later strengthened by about 100 Cape Police and white volunteers. Their duty was to guard the eastern entrance into the Cape Colony at the drifts through the Orange River and to round up guerrilla commandos in the Lady Grey and Barkly East districts. This force ultimately increased to about 1 000 and Major Hook had to shift his headquarters to Lady Grey.

The **Herschel Police Force** was so successful in fulfiling their task of protecting the eastern border of the North Eastern Cape that commandos never succeeded in getting a hold on the Lady Grey district, nor to enter the Colony through Herschel in great numbers. The only exception was General Smuts who crossed the Orange River at Kiba's Drift and passed through Herschel with his commando of 250 burghers after a brief encounter with the Herschel Police Force at the Witteberg Mission station!

The 400 km blockhouse line which surrounded the Stormberg districts consisted of approximately 500 blockhouses, each garrisoned by six black soldiers under one white officer, which means that the Stormberg region alone occupied a force of at least 3 000 Black soldiers. Many of them never returned home after the war and became permanent farm labourers on the farms where they were stationed.

Hundreds of Blacks also served in the **British Intelligence Service** and as informers for the Flying Squads whose task it was to round up Rebel forces in the Stormberg districts. The British greatly depended on information obtained from Blacks who were well acquainted with the country and could easily spy on rebels and testify against them in their trial. ❑

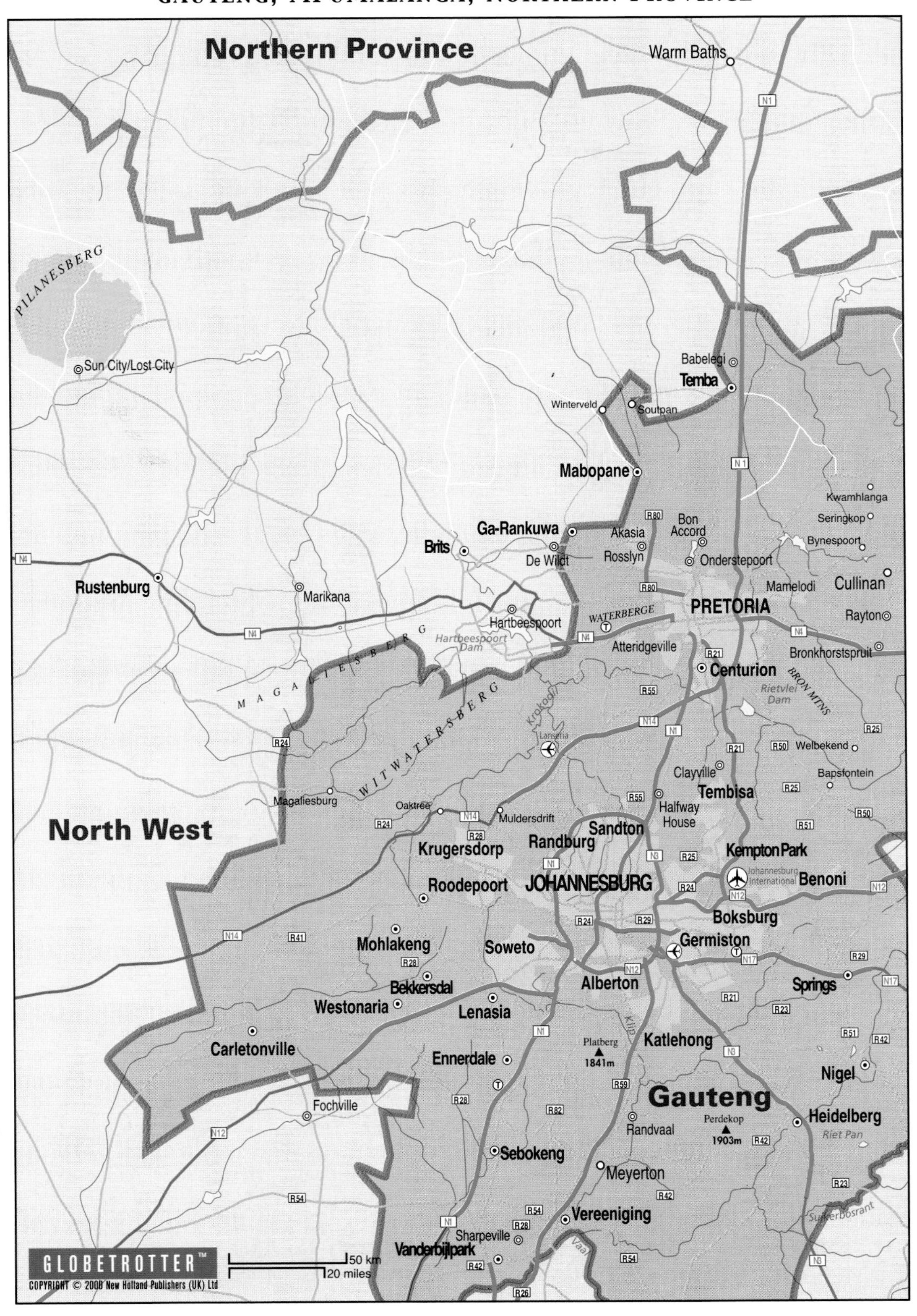
Northern Province
Warm Baths
N1
PILANESBERG
Sun City/Lost City
Babelegi
Temba
Winterveld
Soutpan
Mabopane
Kwamhlanga
Seringkop
Ga-Rankuwa
Akasia
Bon Accord
Bynespoort
Brits
De Wildt
Rosslyn
Onderstepoort
Cullinan
Rustenburg
Marikana
Mamelodi
PRETORIA
Rayton
Hartbeespoort
WATERBERGE
Hartbeespoort Dam
Atteridgeville
Bronkhorstspruit
MAGALIESBERG
Centurion
BRON MTNS
Rietvlei Dam
WITWATERSBERG
Krokodil
Lanseria
Welbekend
Clayville
Bapsfontein
Tembisa
Magaliesburg
Oaktree
Muldersdrift
Halfway House
North West
Sandton
Randburg
Krugersdorp
Kempton Park
Roodepoort
JOHANNESBURG
Johannesburg International
Benoni
Boksburg
Mohlakeng
Soweto
Germiston
Bekkersdal
Alberton
Springs
Westonaria
Lenasia
Carletonville
Platberg
1841m
Katlehong
Ennerdale
Klip
Nigel
Gauteng
Fochville
Perdekop
1903m
Heidelberg
Randvaal
Riet Pan
Sebokeng
Meyerton
Vereeniging
Suikerbosrant
Sharpeville
Vaal
Vanderbijlpark
N4
N14
N12
N17
N3
R80
R21
R55
R25
R50
R51
R24
R28
R29
R41
R23
R42
R59
R82
R54
R26
GLOBETROTTER™
50 km
20 miles
COPYRIGHT © 2000 New Holland Publishers (UK) Ltd

# Protea Hotels, Johannesburg & Midrand

## Protea Hotel Balalaika, Sandton

Established in 1949, this privately owned Premier hotel is in the heart of Sandton, walking distance to all the major malls. Comfortable and tastefully furnished air-conditioned rooms. Some of the suites have jacuzzis. Dine at *'The Colony'* restaurant.
325 Rooms from R655 single & R805 double.
Tel: (011) 322 5000. Fax: (011) 322 5021.
e-mail: balalaika@intekom.co.za

## Protea Hotel Gold Reef City Hotel, Johannesburg

6 km from Johannesburg CBD, and situated in the *Gold Reef City Theme Park* offering a unique Victorian experience. Rooms are decorated in classical Victorian decor with en-suite bathrooms. Restaurants and Pubs are walking distance.
44 Rooms from R490 single & 630 double. B&B.
Tel: (011) 496 1626. Fax: (011) 496 1636.
e-mail: grchotel@icon.co.za

## Protea Hotel Parktonian, Braamfontein

Ideally located, only a few minutes from Johannesburg CBD and 10 minutes from Sandton City. All suites have a bar and mini-safe. Health Club adjoining hotel. Excellent restaurants on site. Secure undercover parking. 24 hour transfers.
294 Suites from R485 single & R570 double B&B.
Tel: (011) 403 5740. Fax: (011) 403 2401.
e-mail: park@link.nis.za

## Protea Hotel Wanderers, Illovo

50 metres from the clubhouse founded in 1888. Brand new Premier Protea is close to the high way to the city or Sandton. Luxurious suites, and 4 restaurants to choose from. Swimming pools, Wanderers 18-hole golf course, squash, tennis & bowling greens. Access to club facilities.
231 Rooms from R625 single & R715 double.
Tel: Tollfree 0800 11 9000. Fax: (011) 419 8200.

## Protea Hotel Midrand, Midrand

Halfway between Johannesburg and Pretoria in country setting. Elegant and sophisticated with sumptuous accommodation. Sundowners on *The Terrace* with dinner in the *Palm Terrace Restaurant.* Music and drinks in *Malone's Cherrywood Saloon.*
177 Rooms from R690 single & R790 double B&B.
Tel: (011) 318 1868. Fax: (011) 318 2429.
e-mail: midrand.protea@pixie.co.za

# Magaliesberg • Melville • Pretoria

## De Hoek Country House, Magaliesberg

This Stone House set in 100 acres of indigenous bush is only an hour's drive from Johannesburg. Exceptional accommodation with superb cuisine sets the atmosphere of a retreat not to be missed.
7 Rooms from R500 pp sharing. Bed & Breakfast.
Tel: (014) 577 1198. Fax: (014) 577 4530.
e-mail: dehoek@iafrica.com

## Mount Grace Hotel, Magaliesberg

Set high on a mountain, in 10 acres of garden, this gem of Country Hotels has been a haven of tranquility and beauty for over 15 years. Tours to Nooitgedacht Battlefield can be arranged.
65 Rooms from R315 - R619 pp sharing. B&B.
Tel: (014) 577 1350. Fax: (014) 577 1202.
e-mail: mntgrace@iafrica.com

## A Room with a View, Melville, Johannesburg

A beautifully designed Tuscan styled Guest House. Overlooking the Melville Koppies Nature Museum. A few minutes stroll from the heart of Melville's entertainment centre. Pool, Sauna & secure parking.
7 Rooms from R195 pp sharing. Bed & Breakfast.
Tel: (011) 482 5435. Fax: (011) 726 8589.
e-mail: roomview@pixie.co.za

## Rozenhof Guest House, Pretoria

Rozenhof is situated in historic Brooklyn and is an experience in luxury accommodation for the visitor to Pretoria. It is within walking distance to the Brooklyn Mall. Excursions to Boer War sites can be arranged.
7 Rooms from R285 pp sharing. Bed & Breakfast.
Tel: (012) 46 8075. Fax: (012) 46 8085.
e-mail: rozenhof@smartnet.co.za

## Irene Country Lodge, Irene

A natural setting in the heart of Irene Village. A stones throw from Pretoria, Johannesburg and the International Airport. Anglo-Boer War activity took place in the village of Irene. Close to Mid-Rand.
49 Rooms from R490 pp sharing. Bed & Breakfast.
Tel: (012) 667 6464. Fax: (012) 667 6476.
e-mail: irenecl@country-escapes.co.za.

# Malelane • Pilgrim's Rest

### BUHALA COUNTRY HOUSE, MALELANE

The well known story of *"Jock of the Bushveld"* was written by Percy Fitzpatrick from the farm house. The property bordering the Kruger National Park has the original road, garages and Post Office to L.M. (Maputo)
8 Rooms from R425 pp sharing. Bed & Breakfast.
Tel: (013) 790 4372. Fax: (013) 790 4306.
e-mail: buhala@lbm.co.za

### MOUNT SHEBA COUNTRY LODGE, PILGRIM'S REST

Encircled by ancient indigenous forests, boasting 1 000 year old yellowwoods and cycads, the hotel is nestled in the mountains 25 km above Pilgrims Rest. It is close to Lydenberg and Long Tom Pass.
25 Rooms from R435 pp sharing. Dinner, B&B.
Tel: (013) 768 1242. Fax: (013) 768 1248.
e-mail: msheba@country-escapes.co.za

In Pilgrims Rest the Chief's wife bartered her honour for safety matches, which were very scarce. *"As her honour waned from full moon, so the tariff of eleven matches diminished, but never below a number that would at least yield warmth, if not fire".* (Schikkerling, 371).

# Dullstroom • Schoemanskloof

### CRITCHLEY HACKLE LODGE, DULLSTROOM

Situated in Dullstroom with its own trout filled lake. A trout fisherman's delight. Rooms have TV, a lounge and fireplace. Cosy bar and excellent dining by candlelight. Boer War Grave tours can be arranged.
23 Rooms from R495 pp sharing. Dinner B&B.
Tel: (013) 254 0145. Fax: (013) 254 0262.
e-mail: chl-wks@mweb.co.za

### OLD JOE'S KAIA, SCHOEMANSKLOOF

3 hours from Johannesburg and ideally situated en-route to Mpumalanga. Dedicated to excellent food and real personal service. Accommodation is either log cabins, rondavels or *'kaia'* rooms. A real experience.
14 Rooms from R430 pp sharing. Dinner B&B.
Tel: (013) 733 3045. Fax: (013) 733 3777.
Cell/Mobile: 082 456 0028.

# Phalaborwa

**STEYN'S COTTAGE, PHALABORWA**

Only 3 km to the Phalaborwa entrance to the Kruger National Park. Night drives to the Park available. Rooms have phones, TV, M-Net, air-conditioning and all lead onto swimming pool. Superb cuisine offered 12 Rooms from R390 per room. Bed & Breakfast.
Tel: (015) 781 0836. Fax: (015) 781 5622.
e-mail: steyncot@nix.co.za

## BETRAYAL

Troopers John Beck and Frederick Nel, amongst other National Scouts were killed in action by their former friends of the Heidelberg Commando on 24 July 1901 at Braklaagte. They were buried next to each other in the Kloof cemetery, Heidelberg.

During the same action Scheepers, Danie Maartens' brother-in-law, was badly wounded. Scheepers and a group of National Scouts had turned his sister and her daughter out of their house in nightclothes before burning it. They then drove them into the freezing veld in front of their horses for a kilometre before abandoning them.

Danie found his wife and child the following morning in a critical condition from the cold. After the Braklaagte action Danie demanded to see the wounded Scheepers, who was under armed guard. Scheepers crawled towards Danie, begging for mercy. Danie told him that he wished to hear nothing, but wanted to shoot him between the eyes. *'He aimed, fired, then climbed on his horse and rode away'.*

Two other former friends captured during this action, Piet Bouwer and Roelf van Emmenes, were tried and later executed. This was a particularly emotional execution as it was carried out by blood relatives, friends, and ex-pupils of the Schoolmaster, Piet Bouwer.

**Heidelbergers of the Boer War**, *Ian Uys*, 1981 Ian S. Uys

# Magoebaskloof

**GLENSHIEL COUNTRY LODGE, MAGOEBASKLOOF**

Elegantly appointed lodge rests amongst magnificent gardens and surrounded by rolling hills, just outside the village of Haenertsburg. The remains of a Long Tom Canon are at a site in Haenertsburg. 15 Rooms from R467 pp sharing. Dinner, B&B.
Tel: (015) 276 4335. Fax: (015) 276 4475.
e-mail: glenshiel@country-escapes.co.za

**JOHANNESBURG TOURISM**

**Ground Floor, Village Walk Shopping Centre, Cnr. Maude & Rivonia Roads, Sandown.**
**Tel: (011) 784 1354 Fax: (011) 883 4035. e-mail: marketing@tourismjohannesburg.co.za**
**Website: www.tourismjohannesburg.co.za**

Johannesburg played a very important role in the Anglo-Boer War, 1899-1902, the goldfields were essentially the cause of the war. Johannesburg boasts many famous sites and battlefields.
Should you wish to visit Museums, Johannesburg has over 60 Museums to cater for every interest. Be they Medical, Transport, Clothing, Musical, Historical or Educational, the Museums in Johannesburg are designed to educate and entertain. If its entertainment you need, look on further than Johannesburg. With some forty theatres, hosting everything from Shakespeare to the most modern and exciting South African plays, as well as restaurants catering for all nationalities everything from the most mouth-watering Japanese seafood to the delights of traditional South African Cuisine- your taste buds will want for nothing.

## Did You Know

Johannesburg's notorious Fort has a secret tunnel? It's believed to lead to an execution chamber where men were hanged as alleged traitors.

Lutyens designed the beautiful Rand Regiments Memorial. It was the model for all the World War 1 Memorials around the world.

On the site now occupied by Wits University, JS Marwick assembled more than seven thousand Zulu workers who had to be evacuated from the city. No transport was available, so he organised that they could walk home. Which they did with his guidance all the way to Natal.

During the war an armaments factory was blown up to stop it falling into enemy hands.

In and around Johannesburg are the sites of several of the concentration camps for Boers and Black workers. A hospital, still in use today, was built as a casualty hospital for British soldiers.

From June 1899, most of the *Uitlander* population left. In the last few days of September 1899, more than 4 000 people a day were leaving the city in panic.

The last set-piece battle of the war took place at **Doornkop**, outside Johannesburg on 29 May 1900. This was where the Jameson raiders were captured in 1896. The British officially occupied Johannesburg on 31 May 1900, without bloodshed. On 24 December 1901, the Johannesburg Stock Exchange reopened.

By 7 October 1899, 66 Witwatersrand mines had closed for the pending war. To obtain the last traces of precious gold the cyanide works and the plates at the mines were cleaned. Each mine yielding between £1 000 – £2 000 worth of gold.

One of the first war victims of the war was a Mrs Fourie, shot in the foot by a British flying column as she was abandoning her farm *Van Wyk's Rust.* Before May 1900, the Jewish helping hand and Burial Society were asked by the Boers to operate an ambulance service on the Rand, which they did successfully.

Cornelius Broeksma, a Boer civilian, was executed in September 1901 for smuggling information about concentration camps to the Netherlands. He is buried in the Braamfontien cemetery.

Between May 1901 and May 1902, 42 000 refugees returned to Johannesburg.

## Tour Guides

**Mindwalks:** Elsabe Brink & Sue Krige. Tel: (011) 837 2247 Fax: (011) 837 2247. e-mail: eabrink@global.co.za

**Historical Tours**: Mike Hardisty. Tel: (011) 447 8574. Fax: (011) 442 3479. Cell: 082 920 5667.

**Gold Reef Guides:** Lin Smith & Jenny Briscoe Tel: (011) 496 1400. Fax: (011) 496 1249. e-mail: guides@iafrica.com

**Parktown & Westcliff Heritage Trust:** Flo Bird. Tel: (011) 726 7528.

## Johannesburg's Anglo-Boer War Dates

6-11 October 1899 : Exodus of 7 000 Zulu workers from Johannesburg to Natal on foot.

11 October 1899 : Beginning of the Anglo-Boer War.

24 April 1900 : Explosion at Begbie Foundry.

28-29 May 1900 : Battle of Klipriviersberg.

31 May 1900 : Fall of Johannesburg. Robert's troops enter the city.

December 1900 : Establishment of Turffontein Concentration Camp.

15 March 1901 : Lord Milner takes up residence in Sunnyside.

30 September 1901 : Execution of Broeksma at the Fort. He was accused of spying.

24 December 1901 : Stock Exchange officially reopened.

31 May 1902 : Peace concluded.

1 June 1902 : Armistice announced by Reverend John Darragh.

## Historic sites identified

The Turffontein Concentration Camp; The Fort; Kilpriviersberg Nature Reserve; Sunnyside (now Holiday Inn Hotel); The Rand Club; Rand Regiment Memorial; Blockhouse site in Louis Botha Avenue; Irish-Boer Memorial; Scottish Horse Memorial; Rietfontein Hospital; Concentration Camps in Bez Valley and Boksburg.

## PRETORIA TOURISM INFORMATION

**Tourist Rendevous Building, Cnr. Prinsloo & Vermeulen Streets.**

**Tel: (012) 308 8909.**

**Palais of Justice:** Church Square, Pretoria. It was used as a British Hospital from the British occupation 5 June 1900.

**The Raadsal**: Kruger worked from here, and it was where the ultimatum was planned.

**Melrose House:** Jacob Marais street. The peace treaty was signed here on 31 May 1902.

**Fort Klapperkop:** Off Johan Rissik Avenue past Fountain Valley and follow signs. Newly renovated, it is one of four forts which were completed in 1908 for possible war. Not one shot fired was fired from the forts.

**Kruger Museum:** Church Street. This is where Paul Kruger lived and where his wife died.

**Dutch Reformed Church**: Opposite the Kruger Museum. This was the church used by Paul Kruger.

**Donkerhoek Battlefield:** East of Pretoria on the Witbank highway, past Pioneer museum boards, past Sammy Marks Museum.

## *David Panagos, Tour Guide*

# War Attractions for the Tourist

### FORTS & GUNS OF PRETORIA

Pretoria has numerous forts besides the well known Republican ones. This tour includes a visit to a Corrugated Iron Blockhouse, as well as Fort Klapperkop built by the ZAR. Then people are shown two of the large 5" guns, known as *'Cow Guns'* in the British Army, because it required a team of 16 or more trek oxen to drag them around the veld. Pretoria also has a replica of one of the famous ZAR *'Long Tom'* guns made by Schneider *et Cie*.

### BATTLE OF DIAMOND HILL: 11TH & 12TH JUNE 1900

After the occupation of Pretoria, General Botha took up positions along the eastern limit of the Magaliesberg range and was attacked by Lord Roberts on 11 & 12 June 1900. The tour takes people to a view site showing part of the 40 km length of the battlefield, and the party then moves on to the present Military Graveyard where the final events of the battle took place. The battle is also known as *'Donkerhoek'*.

### THE BATTLE OF SILKAATS NEK: 11TH JULY 1900

On the 11 July 1900 a detachment of British Dragoons, a famous cavalry regiment known as the *Royal Scots Greys*, together with three companies of the Lincolnshire Regt, and two twelve pounder guns of the Royal Horse Artillery were surprised by a Commando under General De la Rey, and were overcome in a battle which lasted all day. The Boers captured both guns.

### PRE-BLOCKHOUSE FORTS OF PIENAARSPOORT

After the battle of Diamond Hill the Boers moved off to Middelburg and were then followed by the British Army. As they moved further from Pretoria the Boers threatened the railway line and two regiments, the Royal Irish Fusiliers and the Connaught Rangers were sent back in August 1900 to fortify Pienaarspoort, where the railway passed through the Magaliesberg. Here they erected 11 major Redoubts, numerous Sangars and sheds – a total of 35 structures all built with fieldstone walling. These are all still visible today.

### BLOCKHOUSE LINE ALONG THE MAGALIESBERG

The British commenced the construction of the Blockhouse Lines in January 1901 in order to protect their lines of communication. They fortified the length of the Magaliesberg in August and September 1901 by placing blockhouses in each of the passes, stretching from Horns Nek to Olifantshoek Nek. The tour includes a fortified Police post near a masonry Blockhouse known as Barton's Folly. ❑

## LAST CASUALTIES

On 9 March 1953, more than 30 children and a schoolteacher were injured at the Crosby Afrikaans-medium School after a pupil (Jacobus Jordaan) accidentally dropped a three-pound British shell dated 1901, which he had found on a nearby kopje. It is unlikely that these will end up being the last Anglo-Boer War casualties as there must still be many unexploded shells awaiting to be unearthed. In 1981 I took a live bomb-maxim shell, found in a vlei near Dullstroom, to the Military History Museum in Johannesburg for positive identification. The munitions expert refused to even come near it, and I duly took it back to its discoverer in Dullstroom, where it is still displayed with pride above the fire-place!

**To the Bitter End,** *Emanoel Lee*, 1985 Viking Penguin Inc.

## GUNNERS

Unlike the independent, undisciplined men of the Boer commandos, the State Artillery of the Transvaal and Orange Free State fought on foot and were strong on organisation and *'spit and polish'*. Trained by officers who had served in the German Army, they wore uniforms in the German style *('drab with blue facing')* and even marched with the *goose step* when on parade. The Staatsartillerie had a strength of ± 400 in the Free State and 800 in the Transvaal.

*R. B. de Vos*

# Something interesting about the War

Next to the N4, the main road from Pretoria to Nelspruit, just a few kilometres east of Belfast, you will notice the well known monument. 'Bergendal', erected in memory of those who fell during the last organised battle of the Anglo-Boer War on 27 August 1900. It was also the last stand of the 'Zuid-Afrikaansche Republiek Polisie' (ZARP) as a unit. Of the 74 who took part, 40 were killed or wounded. A smaller monument commemorates the death of six British officers and 19 men from the 2nd Rifle Brigade, 1st Devonshire Regiment, Royal Inniskilling Fusiliers and 2nd Gordon Highlanders. Col. O.T.E. Metcalfe was one of the first to fall. The attack on 27 August 1900 was under the command of Gen.Redvers Buller who had 9 000 men altogether and 42 guns under his command.

Lord Roberts and General Buller had decided to break through the 80 km Boer lines of General Louis Botha at Bergendal. It was about 400 m south of the railway line and on the wagon route to the Lowveld, and close to Belfast. At 1100 hr, 38 guns opened fire on the position held by the ZARP. For three hours, without a pause, the bombardment continued before the British troops started their attack. The attack was witnessed by Lord Roberts from a vantage point just outside Belfast.

About 200 metres behind the monument on the remains of the kopje, stands the original farmhouse of Bergendal. Above the front door is written: *H.J. Botha – 1894*. According to his great granddaughter, Botha was already taken prisoner and at Ceylon, but his wife and children were in the house during the battle. One room was hit by a bomb and in two walls bullet marks can still be seen. The British soldiers did not bother to burn the house down after the battle. *Today it is about the only farmhouse still to be seen in the Transvaal which was not burnt down or changed since the war* and is still, to this day, occupied by a great-grandson of Botha – with only one tap in the kitchen, no bathroom or toilet and no electricity – but it still has the original floor, ceiling and roof.

Before the railway was built during 1895, the farm was used as a mail coach station. The stone stables where the horses were kept are still to be seen as well as a few of the outbuildings. ❑

## Bombardment

The British developed the creeping artillery barrage, whereby their infantry would advance behind the cover of bursting shells. The key to the Boer positions at Bergendal was a rocky ridge held by 74 men of the Johannesburg Police. *"Against this little ridge, not ninety yards in length and held by about seventy-five men, nearly 100 cannon were directed, while the English infantry were advancing under fire of their rifles. I thought everything human had perished, even to the lizards and insects in the rent and battered rocks ..."* (Schikkerling, 51).

Both sides were astounded that they were still men alive to resist the final infantry charge - in fact 32 survived the bombardment and charge, and escaped over open ground to the rear Boer positions. *"On our right stood the farmhouse and from behind it dashed a few mounted Boers; they had to ride through a heavy fire, but as we had been running hard it was rather shaky and did not stop many of them."* (Bryant, 198).

*Dries de Bruin*

# The Battle of Diamond Hill in a nutshell
## 11-12 June 1900

Take up your grandstand seat on a spot 10 km southwest of the battlefield quite near the *'Bronberge'*. The Magaliesberg mountains run east to west before you.

Louis Botha chose to defend the most Eastern outcrop of the Magaliesberg, a well chosen position to defend. It was with great difficulty that he had roped together a mere 4 000 men and 14 guns. His experience told him that Lord Roberts would make an all out attack to round his flanks. Botha spaces his men sparsely in the centre and as many as possible on the furthest points of this 40 km battleline. In your imagination you can see Lord Roberts on his kopje at *'Eerstefabrieken'*, quite near Sammy Mark's manor. He has a fine view of the entire battlefield. His instructions are straight forward.

*"Pole-Carew, with your cannons, you must hit the centre hard. Hamilton, I want you to come through well to the south, over the Bronberge, through Tierpoort and Swavelspoort, and move round the most southern end of the Boer flank. French, you must move quickly with your cavalry round the enemies right flank".*

Everything is ready to roll on the British side, 14 000 men and 68 canons. French and his cavalry move quickly and find a nice little hill, *'Louwsbaken'* unoccupied (what luck!), only to realise that 2 km down the road, De la Rey had set him a trap. All of a sudden all hell breaks loose as De la Rey starts his onslaught. So successful, that he calls for reinforcements from Botha. Remember we are viewing the battle from the southwest corner of the battlefield. You can hear and feel Hamiltons cavalry rushing past you - almost 5 000 men driving hard for the Boers left flank. Pole-Carew strikes a soggy patch as he crosses the Pienaar River, but he succeeds to place his guns. Hamilton runs into all sorts of surprises and is knocked back on occasions, but on 12 June his relentless attacks bring him success and he starts to make a breakthrough.

Botha rushes men to his left flank to plug the gap. In fact these men were earmarked to support De la Rey on the northern end. De la Rey missing a chance of a lifetime.

On 12 June after a heavy days fighting Botha realises that Roberts' superior numbers are just too much and he instructs his Generals and men to quietly move out in the direction of Bronkhorstspruit. The British Generals were of the opinion that the Boers were still in a very strong position and were surprised to find the Boer positions empty the next morning.

Casualties in the Battle of Diamond Hill were surprisingly low. What is sad in present times, is that the new housing is swallowing up this magnificent battlefield. ❑

### LONG TOMS

Among the armaments shrewdly acquired by the Transvaal Government were four 155 mm fortress guns from Creusot in France. These heavy guns – nicknamed *'Long Toms'* – were equipped with recoil mechanisms and able to hurl 43 kg shells up to 10 km away. They were so successfully applied that the British had to remove guns from some of their warships as a countermeasure. Both before and during the war, two engineers from the Creusot company advised the Transvaal Government on artillery matters and supervised the manufacture of shells at a factory in Johannesburg.

# Action at Lake Chrissie
# 6 February 1901

*The British advance had shattered General Botha's dream of invading Natal in force, but the slowness of the advance gave him plenty of time to examine the British weak points, which were obvious, and enabled him to plan his attack.*

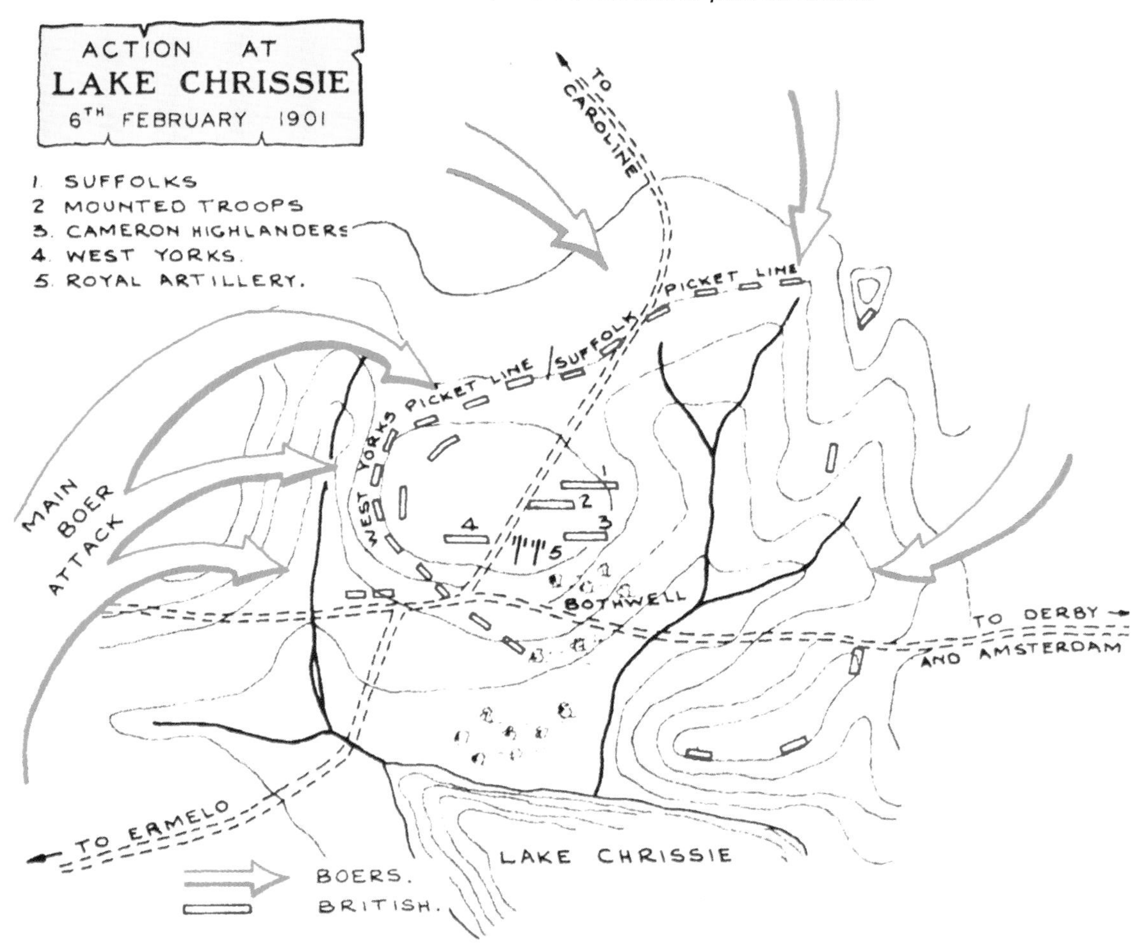


British columns under Major Generals Campbell and Smith-Dorrien were isolated, but as their lines of march converged, it was necessary for Botha to attack one or the other. On the evening of 5 February General Botha was situated between Ermelo and Lake Chrissie. On the same evening Smith-Dorrien halted at Bothwell near the northern extremity of the lake.

Lake Chrissie is little more than a glorified '*pan*' filling up in the rainy season and partially dry in times of drought. Bothwell village is close to the northern shores of this lake. It was here that the British camped. Pickets were posted, the Cameron Highlanders took the south, West Yorks the north west, and the Suffolks the north east. While the British camp slept on the night of 5 February. General Louis Botha was moving rapidly up the road from Ermelo. He positioned his forces on the north west facing the West Yorks and on the north east facing the Suffolks.

On 6 February, at 1450 hr, a tremendous fusillade broke out, followed immediately by a mounted charge, with the Boers galloping through the British camp, This caused the horses of the 5th Lancers and the I.L.H. to stampede. The Suffolks had to defend against a fierce flanking attack, while the West Yorks bore the brunt of the main attack, fierce fighting ensued, but the Boers were held at bay. Botha had staked success on surprise and a crushing volume of magazine fire, but his calculations had failed.

At 0430 hr the Boers retired. General Smith-Dorrien immediately planned a pursuit, but due to thick fog it was extremely difficult to ascertain which line to take. At 0600 hr mounted troops picked up the trail of a commando which had headed north west, this they followed for 11 km to Mooiplaats. The remainder of Botha's force went north and some south east. On the 6th, the British forces entered Ermelo to find it deserted. Botha, it is true had failed in a brilliant tactical manoeuvre, but he and the best of his forces had broken through a British encircling movement. ❑

*Source:*
*Battlefields of the SA War 1899* by J.L. Smail. (by permission Mrs. Barbara Smail).

## DIVINE MESSAGE

Early in the morning of the 6 February 1901, Maggie Biccard awoke in the Concentration Camp at Howick to hear an angelic choir singing her husband's favourite hymn. She knew that something had happened to Johnny. Two weeks later she heard that he had been killed during the night attack on Lake Chrissie. (Co-incidentally this lake was named after Maggie's mother, Christina, daughter of the Voortrekker Andries Pretorius). Maggie knew that her husband was gifted with second sight as, at a Sunday Service during their courtship in April 1892, he had a vision of the funeral of the presiding Minister. Rev.van Warmelo died during the following week and was buried the next Sunday.

**Heidelbergers of the Boer War**, *Ian Uys*, 1981 Ian S. Uys

## DEVOTION

Towards the end of September each year a package would arrive at the Post Office in Chrissiemeer in the Eastern Transvaal addressed to 'The Postmaster', with no accompanying note or even return address. The package contained a sprig of heather: one year bound with a blue ribbon, the next with a pink ribbon. This was to be placed on the grave of Lt.Arthur William Swanston of the Inniskilling Dragoons who died in action near Lake Banagher on 18 October 1900, while trying to save the life of Private J.Garlick. Instructions on what to do with the heather was handed from each Postmaster to his or her successor. *'Tannie Rensie'* Kruger, was Postmistress from 1947 to 1957 and each year placed the sprig of heather on Arthur's grave. In 1957, just before she left Chrissiemeer, she received a note with the package which she translated from English with much difficulty.

The woman who sent the heather was Arthur's fiancee, who had never married, and she said that she was very sick and that this would probably be the last time she could send heather for her beloved's grave. However, the package arrived for the next two years and 'Tannie Rensie's' successor did her duty. This touching act of devotion is all the more remarkable for the trust placed in the Afrikaans-speaking Postmasters, who would be prejudiced against the English as a result of the Anglo-Boer War, and the postal system. 'Tannie Rensie' made the comment that not a single flower of heather was ever damaged in the post!

# Action at Boschbult 31 March 1902

*Not since 1901 had Klerksdorp been such a hive of activity. Troop trains had arrived by the score following a system adopted in recent drives in the Free State. The British troops numbering ± 16 000 were split into four divisions, each consisting of 4 000 strong. One such division – under Kitchener, consisted of Canadian Mounted Rifles, Vialls's Mounted Infantry, Ducane's Column, two Battalions of infantry and a miscellaneous detachment of Mounted Infantry and Yeomanry. This force was divided into three columns. In the 3rd week of March, military intelligence reported that a large number of Boers were within 30 miles of Schoon Spruit. Kitchener successfully dispersed these Boers with 11 000 troops.*

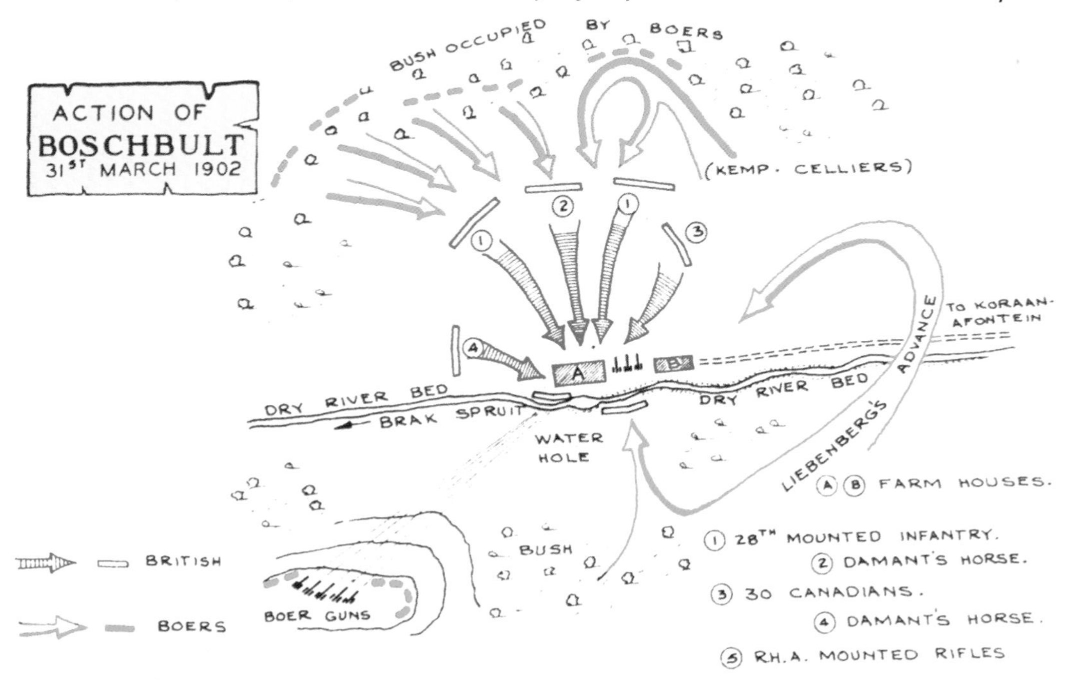


At 0200 hr on 31 March, a British force started out on a reconnaissance under Colonel Cookson. At 1000 hr, near the farm, *Doornlaagte* tracks of a Boer commando were found. This trail led the British force along the course of the Brak Spruit, an insignificant stream and at this time of year, practically dry. Giving chase the British drove the Boers westward towards Boschbult, suddenly the Boers turned and opened fire from an expanse of bush. More Boers suddenly appeared from all sides in the bush. The British force was checked on the farmlands of Boschbult at the western limit of a wide clearing in a sea of bush. As it was essential that the whole column should gain a free field of fire presented by the clearing, the R.H.A. mounted rifles, and a Pom-Pom. Entrenchment started and at 1320 hr before it was complete the Boers attacked. 4 guns and Pom-Poms opened up from the South West. Boers started to make galloping attacks, rapid firing held the Boers at bay. The outlying troops now fell back and took up a position all round the farm house, terrific firing continued and the Boers were held at bay. On 01 April after a nights rest the Boers prepared for another attack, but upon news of the arrival of reinforcements, they withheld their attack. ❑

***Source:***

*Battlefields of the SA War 1899* by J.L. Smail. (by permission Mrs. Barbara Smail)

Above: *'The Wedding'* in wood by Bonnie Ntshalintshali.

Middle: The Upside Down Tree. A Baobab tree in Northern Province.

Below: A night drive in Kruger National Park.

# Dispatches

## KEEP THE MINES WORKING

T.D. ZAR 22.10.1899
From General Cronje, Rietfontein
To Government, Pretoria, begins
(From a telegram to the Government from General Burger.) I note that the Government is embarrassed by the numerous English prisoners taken in Natal and elsewhere. I consider that these persons should be sent to Johannesburg to work in those mines still operating. They could thus work in the mines by day and be guarded in a compound by night under surveillance of the Johannesburg police...ends.

## WILD WIVES

T.D.ZAR 24.11.1899
From Assistant-General Erasmus, H.Q. Ladysmith
To Landdros, Pretoria, begins
D. van Vuuren domiciled near the European Hotel, Pretoria, has complained to General Joubert that his wife - despite numerous complaints - is suffering from want. Please investigate the matter immediately and send me a report. Enquire the whereabouts from the proprietor of the hotel; he can show you the house. We are getting complaints from the burghers from dawn to dusk. Contact the Government about the matter for the situation is intolerable - ends.

From Landdros, Pretoria
To Assistant-General Erasmus, H.Q. Ladysmith
D. van Vuuren's wife, since the 10 October has received 408 lb.of meal, as well as fish, candles, sugar, matches, soap, rice, coffee and tea. I visited her myself and she is quite satisfied. So her husband's complaints are groundless. Letter follows. The next distribution of foodstuffs is on Monday - ends.

T.D. ZAR 8.11.1899
From Assistant-General Coetzer, H.Q. Ladysmith
To Landdros, Lydenburg, begins
Your telegram received. Among others conscripted from Lydenburg who complain is Gert Visser - ends.

T.D. ZAR
From Landdros, Lydenburg
To Assistant-General, Ladysmith, begins
Visser's wife since the 11 October has received regularly each week a bucket of mealie meal plus 1-1/2 buckets of boer meal from Government sources. She also gets candles, coffee, rice, salt, soap and sugar, through a fund subscribed privately by the townsfolk. In fact, she had more than she really needs.

The families of poor burghers in the town have really nothing to complain of. The Commission would appreciate the names of all complainants. We do try to do our best for these people - ends.

T.D.ZAR 8.12.1899
From Landdros, Ermelo
To Commandant, Ermelo and Field-Cornet Ward I, H.Q. Ladysmith, begins
It is absolute bosh about the illness of Hendrik van der Merwe's wife. I myself saw her yesterday at the office. You give us officials needless trouble with these tales of sickness. Whenever a wife is sick she can first come to me or the Field-Cornet - ends.

T.D. ZAR 9.12.1899
From Special Landdros, Boksburg
To Assistant-Commandant-General, H.Q. Ladysmith, begins
I went out personally with the Field-Cornet to the house of Mrs B.J. Bester at Vlakfontein and found her in the best health imaginable. When I showed her the telegram, she was amazed to read anything like it and remarked that she never thought her husband would make such an excuse.

## NO COFFEE NO CUPS

T.D. ZAR 21.01.1900
From Captain Fort, Johannesburg
To Captain, Intendant Camp, Pretoria, begins

Police here refuse to carry out duties on account of dearth of sugar and coffee. ends.

*As the tired eyes of President Kruger fell upon this news, one can picture first his amazement, next his anger, and finally the telegraphic thunderbolt, which, as a consequence, exploded soon after in Johannesburg. The dazed recipient abjectly answered thus:*

T.D. ZAR 21.1.1900 Urgent
From Captain Fort, Johannesburg
To President, Pretoria

Your Honour's telegram received with sorrow. Never shall men under my command here in Johannesburg prize sugar and coffee more than freedom of land and people. Contritely do they now retract their words and hope with God's help and under Your Honour's direction to defend both land and people in circumstances more straitened still. I thank Your Honour for Your Honour's speedy intervention, whereby the heavy load laid upon me has been completely lifted. Shall be in Pretoria tomorrow when I hope to meet Your Honour.
- ends.

*The hope expressed in the last sentence was, I fear, a pardonable but, nonetheless, enormous exaggeration.*

*Joe West. (Tel/Fax: UK(44) 01202 887771)*

# Breaker Morant - a flawed Australian Hero

In 1980, the Australian film ***'Breaker Morant'*** appeared at cinemas throughout the world. Directed by Bruce Beresford, this highly acclaimed film purported to tell the story of a heroic Australian officer who was railroaded to his death by a firing squad in the Boer War by Lord Kitchener. This anti-British and anti-Empire film is a reflection of Australian attitudes in the 1970's and the director's prejudices produced a distorted historical picture.

In early 1901 the British Army formed a special unit called the *Bushveld Carbineers (BVC)* to operate against the Boers in Northern Transvaal. Major Robert Lenehan, a Sydney solicitor and a squadron commander in the New South Wales Mounted Rifles was appointed commanding officer and recruiting started on the 21 February 1901.

The pay for a trooper was 5 shillings per day and the only skills required were an ability to ride and shoot straight. The original target was to raise a force of 500 men but in the end about 350 were recruited. The attestation papers for the regiment are in the Public Record Office (PRO) in London and from the next of kin addresses it is possible to determine the national make up of the unit. About 32% of the soldiers were Australian, 29% British and 26% South African. The next largest contingents' were from the USA and then Ireland. However if you add the Irish to the British, plus those giving India as their address and the planter from Dominica in the West Indies, the figure for the British content rises to 33%. It is known that many of those from Australia and South Africa were born in Britain.

**Henry Harbord Morant** was almost certainly born in Bridgewater Workhouse in England on 9 December 1864, and christened Edwin Henry Murrant, the posthumous son of Edwin Murrant, the workhouse master and his wife Catherine, the matron. In April 1881 he was a tutor at a suburban London school and must have had a reasonable education. In 1883 he arrived in Australia, having sailed from Plymouth on the 1 April 1901. He married an Irish girl called Daisy May O'Dwyer at Charters Towers, a gold mining town, in Queensland on 13 March 1884. He first used the surname Morant when he was charged with the larceny of pigs in April of that year. His new bride left him shortly afterwards and *found fame and a CBE as Daisy Bates, a leading expert on Aborigines.*

Morant found work on farms and started to send poetic works to *'The Bulletin'* in Sydney and used the pen name of **'Breaker'** because of his ability with horses. He was using the names of Henry Harbord Morant by August 1895 when he wrote to **Banjo Patterson**, a fellow *'Bulletin'* poet and later notable as the author of ***'Waltzing Matilda'***. Morant picked up a reputation as a superb horseman, a hard drinker, a bush poet and a man who avoided paying his bills.

In October 1899 Morant enlisted in *South Australia Mounted Rifles* and sailed for South Africa early the next year. He served with this unit satisfactorily until his time was up in the autumn of 1900. In April 1901 Lieutenant Henry Morant joined the *Bushveld Carbineers* along with a young English officer called **Percy Hunt**. Hunt had served briefly in the 13th Hussars prior to coming to South Africa where he struck up a friendship with Morant.

In April 1901 the *BVC* went into action against the Boers. The veterinary and transport officer of the unit was Lieutenant Peter Handcock, a blacksmith, who escaping a failing marriage, had served as Farrier-Sergeant in the New South Wales Mounted Infantry. The most influential man in the area was the intelligence officer based at Spelonken. Alfred Taylor was a Captain who had been in Africa for many years and was fluent in many native dialects. The Africans called him **'Bulala'** which means **'Killer'** and there were sound reasons for this name. Taylor had served in Rhodesia with Rhodes and was an experienced soldier and, although not a member of the *BVC*, he greatly influenced many of the officers.

From early July 1901 certain officers of the *BVC* (seemingly encouraged by Taylor) **embarked on a policy of murdering Boer prisoners**. First to die were 6 surrendered Boers and then Handcock murdered an Afrikaner *BVC* trooper who had witnessed the event. On the night of the 5 August Hunt was killed in an ill-planned attack on a Boer farm. Morant and Handcock, arriving the next day, were told that Hunt's body had been mutilated and they then set off after the Boers. Eventually they captured a wounded Boer named **Visser** who was wearing items of British uniform which Morant determined had belonged to Hunt. Morant supervised the execution of Visser after arranging a travesty of a court martial.

In August Morant and Handcock murdered eight Boers, an event witnessed by a German Missionary, the **Rev.Daniel Heese**, who himself was murdered that day. After these happenings and other sinister events, Morant, Handcock and several other *BVC* officers were arrested. An intelligence officer, **Captain De Bertodano**, gathered the evidence together and in early 1902 Morant and Handcock were tried by court martial in Pietersburg and sentenced to death and shot by firing squad in Pretoria on 27 February 1902.

Today, we know that special units, such as the SAS must have rigorous selection procedures to weed out unsuitable characters and should be commanded by experienced and stable officers and NCOs. The officers of the *BVC* were a motley crew led by a weak commanding officer and were under the malign influence of the sadistic Taylor. Morant and Handcock were ***serial killers*** and it is hard to view them as heroes. In Zimbabwe Archives in the papers of Captain De Bertodano are letters he exchanged with Daisy Bates in 1945. Ironically they both knew 'Breaker' Morant well but neither knew of their mutual acquaintance. ❑

**Source**:
J.K. West. e-mail: heliwest@btinternet.com

Breaker Morant, left, with Dr. Johnston, Captain Hunt, Captain Taylor and Lt. Picton.

The night before his execution Morant wrote *'BUTCHERED TO MAKE A DUTCHMAN'S HOLIDAY'*

*No matter what end they decide – Quicklime? or boiling ile? Sir,*
*We'll do our best when crucified, To finish off in style, sir!...*
*And if you'd earn a D.S.O. – Why, every British sinner*
*Should know the proper way to go, Is: "Ask the Boer to dinner!"*

**Drummer Hodge** : ***The Poetry of the Anglo-Boer War*** by M. van Wyk Smith

*Taffy Shearing. Tel: (044) 343 1649*

# What price Khaki?

In the latter part of the 19th Century the British claimed KHAKI uniform, their 1849 invention, as their sole right. They enforced it under the Army Act of 1882. During the Anglo-Boer War a **Richard Dunbar** was sentenced in October 1900, in Kimberley, to 6 months imprisonment with hard labour for impersonating an officer and travelling without a permit. (Ref Cd 981 (56)) He was probably wearing KHAKI, but whether he was a soldier, or a civilian or a Boer isn't stated. The sentence appears moderate.

In December 1900, when Martial Law was extended throughout the Cape Colony, the Martial Law regulations included this type of notice *(Beaufort Courier, 13 March, 1901)*:

UNIFORM

NO PERSON, EXCEPT IN MILITARY OR POLICE EMPLOYMENT, IS PERMITTED TO WEAR ANY ARTICLE OF MILITARY UNIFORM, OR CLOTHING OF KHAKI COLOR CALCULATED TO HAVE THE APPEARANCE OF A MILITARY UNIFORM.

*The regulation also appeared in Dutch.*

Boers wore KHAKI uniform of the British when it suited them. **Manie Maritz** of the TVK eased his way from Aberdeen through to the north-west Cape in April 1901 by sending **Robert De Kersauson De Pennendreff** (Robert the Frenchmen), author of *Ek en die Vierkleur*, to obtain information, and in one case lodgings for the night, under the guise of a Brabants Horse officer. Boers usually claimed to be members of Colonial Corps, many of whom were lucky to be issued uniforms in the early days and whose insignia was not widely known.

No prosecutions for the wearing of KHAKI under Martial Law regulations have been traced for 1901 until **Lord Horatio Kichener** ordered Drum Head Courts Martial and summary executions of Boers dressed in KHAKI uniform in September 1901. This drastic action was taken after the 17th Lancers, surprised by Smuts' Boers at Modderfontein, Tarkastad on 17 September 1901, stated they had been conned by KHAKI-CLAD Boers pretending to be members of Gorringe's Column. This doesn't agree with the entry in the diary of 17 September of Mrs Moetie De Wet of Dordrecht: *'The Boers are wearing skins as clothing or using blankets for patches and many are without shirts'* (Ref: A.V. Oosthuizen, Rebelle van die Stormberge.)

The casualties at Modderfontein were 40 killed or died of wounds and 36 wounded. It is the highest casualty figure in the Cape Colony guerrilla warfare period, and **General French** was so furious that heads rolled. Tardy **Lieutenant-Colonel Gorringe** went home and his column was taken over by **Colonel Timsin Lukin** of the CMR and later by **Captain E.Collett.** As for the Boers, French wrote to **Lord Roberts** on 22 October 1901: *'I sent an order round the column at once ordering any prisoners taken in khaki to be tried there and then by summary court martial, and, found guilty, to be shot instantly. Three Boers have been shot in this way; now we know the boers are throwing away their khaki coats.'* (Ref: French, The Hon. Gerald, The life of Field Marshall Sir John French, London, 1931.)

The first to be executed was a straggler from Smuts' commando, the Hollander **Peit van der Ryst** or **De Rust**. An endless research in the Archives into the death of the Hollander outside Adelaide on 25/26 September 1901 has revealed nothing as yet. **Deneys Reitz** mentions the execution and some details appear in a newspaper account without mention of his name. He was apparently executed by members of the Adelaide and Fort Beaufort DMTs after a court martial on the farm *Windsor*, south of Adelaide.

Next were **Arrie van Onslen, Cornelius Vermaas** and **Henry Rittenberg**. The 3 had climbed the mountain at Brakkefontein near Glen Connor in the Eastern Cape on 3 October 1901. They were out scouting a route across the Uitenhage railway. **Deneys Reitz** and others believed that all three were executed for wearing KHAKI uniform. They were buried on Osberg and later Van Onslen and Vermaas were reinterred at Kariega and Rittenberg in the Transvaal. However local people say it wasn't quite like that.

Arrie van Oslen, according to **Steve Delport** of Kirkwood, who had entered the Cape under Smuts' **Commandant Jaap van Deventer**, had step-parents near Glen Connor. He wanted to visit the family who had brought him up and it was his birthday. He rode on ahead of Vermaas and Rittenberg and was alone when his luck ran out. He was caught in an ambush and was later found by farmers lying in the veld with a bullet in the side of his head. Van Oslen was definitely a local boy as his name appears in the *Uitenhage Rebel* list that Colonial Magistrates had to send to the Law

Department in November 1901. The entry reads: *'Van Oslen, address Uitenhage, Shot, not known when joined'*. His death, unless more information is found, can be taken as a war casualty and not as an execution. Rittenberg and Vermaas's bodies were said to be found lying side by side, shot in the temples, no attempt being made to bury them.

The next well-documented case of a Smuts Boer shot for wearing KHAKI is **Jack Baxter**. (Ref: Colvin F.F. and Gorden E., Diary of the 9th Lancers, 13 October: *'A Boer has lost his way in the mist. He was dressed almost entirely in clothes taken from the 17th Lancers....Baxter was tried by court martial and shot as we left camp.'*) Baxter wrote various letters before his execution, including one to **Commandant Bouwer** asking him to stop the Boers wearing KHAKI as they would be executed if caught. (Ref: Jordaan, So het Hulle Gesterf.)

Smuts (Ref: Smuts Papers, A1 Vol 314/5, State Archives), Commandant Ben Bouwer (The Memoirs of General Bouwer) and Deneys Reitz (Commando) all insisted that Baxter was wasn't wearing KHAKI except for a black coat to keep out the bitter cold. He was executed at Government's Vlei for it, and buried there. In the 1906 he was reinterred in the Aberdeen graveyard. Some, bits and pieces dug out of his grave, including part of his spectacles, glasses and bit of KHAKI straps from leggings, are now on display at the Graaff-Reinet Museum.

Earlier one of the Boers, **Edgar Duncker** of Bracefield south of Somerset East, confronted by **Lieutenant Watson,** claimed to be either a member of the Uitenhage Defence Force or 17th Lancers, depending on which account you read. When Watson flatly refused to believe that Duncker was a member of the SA Field Force, Duncker shot him at close range; and three others with Watson were wounded. Reitz and Bouwer thought Baxter's execution was a revenge killing for Watson, but this is unlikely as on the day of Baxter's death **Barend Fouche** of Braamfontein was captured in the Kriega area and, as a routine POW, went to India. Fouche was obviously not wearing khaki.

**Colonel Harry Scobell**, who sentenced Baxter to death, was also involved in another case. Hendrik Bester of Klerksdorp who was captured at Kingscrown, Aliwal North. Again the Diary of the 9th Lancers for 23 November 1901 *'Bester was tried yesterday evening for being in KHAKI as well as being a deserter from the Cape Police. He was shot this morning.'* He was buried at Marsh Hill and reinterred by the Rapportryers in Dordrecht graveyard in 1967 with other Boer dead.

Once the news of the deaths of the first four spread, Boers forced to wear KHAKI ripped of the insignia, added other embellishments or dyed the deadly KHAKI in BLOUBOS (Diospyros lycioides). Dye from Acacia Karroo or anything else they could find to darken the basic color.

The only other person traced who was convicted for wearing a uniform was **W J Hogan**. He was tried on 22 February 1902 in Kimberley for wearing the uniform of a lieutenant. A sentence of 112 days imprisonment with hard labour, had 28 days remitted. A further 28 days were remitted by the OC, Kimberley District. (Ref Cd 1423 no 128.)

This then is the bare bones of what, for the Boers, became a highly emotive subject. Reitz (Commando) wrote that other Smuts men were executed for wearing KHAKI, but these have all been traced to the POW or Treason Trial lists. The confusion arose when French ordered newspapers to be held back at the Post Offices. Due to the force of pursuit, the Smuts commando had long left the area and the newspapers circulating in it to be able to read about their erstwhile companions. In the long history of warfare a soldier captured in enemy uniform could only throw himself on his enemy's mercy. However, **General J C Smuts** remained angry enough about the shooting of his men for wearing KHAKI that when he became Minister of Defence after the Union he would not meet **Sir Henry Scobell**. He claimed his men wore the KHAKI clothing from necessity. ❑

*Source*:
Taffy Shearing (Co-author, *Commandant Johannes Lötter and Commandant Gideon Scheepers.*)

***She's trimmed the room with Khaki, and although it seems a shame,***
***The chairs have Khaki covers, and the table-cloth's the same;***
***Her golden hair was natural, with pride, she used to hint,***
***But now she's dyed those lovely locks a brilliant Khaki tint.***

*Drummer Hodge: The Poetry of the Anglo-Boer War* by M. van Wyk Smith

*Richard Tomlinson*

# British Blockhouses and British Forts

The blockhouses and forts erected throughout South Africa by the British forces during the Anglo-Boer War of 1899-1902 were relatively small fortifications which were designed to withstand attacks by Boer Kommandos armed with rifles and with no artillery; the difference between the two terms in this context is that blockhouses were single structures which were roofed and forts were larger complexes (sometimes incorporating blockhouses) which were open to the weather. In this country, both were fairly simple and unsophisticated structures, compared to contemporary fortifications being built in Europe and the United States for example.

## *Who built the blockhouses?*

The erection of the fortifications was undertaken by different bodies according to the method of construction, as follows:

### CORRUGATED IRON BLOCKHOUSES

The earliest rectangular examples in the eastern Transvaal (now Mpumalanga Province) were built by a civilian contractor. After that, the octagonal and the final circular patterns were designed by Major S.R.Rice, Royal Engineers, manufactured in kit form at RE factories in Middelburg (Transvaal), Bloemfontein and other centres, sent by train to the station nearest to their final site and delivered to site by ox waggon. There they were erected by infantry soldiers who dug a sentry trench round each blockhouse and surrounded the site with a barbed-wire entanglement.

### MASONRY (MORTARED STONEWORK AND CONCRETE) BLOCKHOUSES

The masonry blockhouses were designed by RE personnel using a variety of plan shapes and styles and built by civilian contractors, employing good quality mortared stonework or shuttered unreinforced concrete for the walls, timber upper floors, timber and corrugated iron roof and steel loopholes, window shutters and door. They were also usually surrounded by a sentry trench and barbed wire entanglement.

### DRYSTONE INFANTRY FORTS

These structures were irregular in plan, often incorporating natural features such as rock outcrops, and were built in dry unmortared stonework by infantry regiments, sometimes for occupation by the regiment for a limited period until it moved on, whilst others were garrisoned for longer periods.

### TOWN GUARD FORTS

This type of fort was built usually in unmortared stonework by part-time troops who served in the local Town Guard, and these forts are generally situated close to the town concerned.

## *How many were built?*

The records of returns by the Royal Engineers indicate that, by the end of the war, *a total of 7447 corrugated iron and 441 masonry blockhouses were erected*. At present, figures for the infantry and townguard forts are not known.

## *When were they built?*

During the early fluid phase of the war from October 1899 until the capture of Pretoria, capital of the Transvaal Republic, in June 1900, there was no need for static fortifications. From that time on, defences started to be built by the British, initially to protect stations on the main railway lines from the Cape Colony and Natal, which were the arteries by which their forces were supplied with food, ammunition, troop reinforcements, horses and all the other requirements of a large European army. As the guerrilla phase of the war got into gear, the Boer Kommandos concentrated on blowing up railway bridges and attacking towns so that it was found necessary for the British to protect these key points with masonry blockhouses; the earliest ones around Pretoria date from the second half of 1900 and these structures continued to appear throughout 1901 and even into 1902. The army staff soon realised that the masonry blockhouses were expensive and slow to construct and the corrugated blockhouses started to appear in early 1901. As attacks on the railway lines accelerated, it was found necessary to fortify the railway lines between the stations and bridges with corrugated blockhouses; but blockhousing with this type really increased when General Kitchener's *'drives'* started, lines of these structures at close intervals being erected across the open veld and linked with barbed wire fences against which the British cavalry could drive and capture the Kommandos. The less conventional infantry and town guard forts also date mainly from the guerrilla phase of the war.

## *How were they manned?*

The garrison for a corrugated blockhouse was usually one NCO (non-commissioned officer, usually a corporal) and 5 or 6 men; a 3-storeyed masonry blockhouse was manned by between 7 and 40 men commanded by a subaltern (junior commissioned officer) or a senior NCO, but the average was probably about 20. The number in a blockhouse garrison depended on the availability of troops and the risk of attack in the area at the time. Native (black) soldiers were sometimes employed in blockhouse garrisons.

## *What do they look like and where can they be seen today?*

Please note: Where a blockhouse or fort is mentioned by name, the new province in which it is situated will be referred to in abbreviated form as: Eastern Cape [EC], Free State [FS], Gauteng [G], Kwa-Zulu Natal [KZN], Mpumalanga [M], Northern Province [NP], Northern Cape [NC], North-West Province [NW] and Western Cape [WC]. Buildings which have been declared National Monuments and are open to the public will be designated (NM).

**CORRUGATED IRON BLOCKHOUSES**

After the war ended, most of these buildings were sold or given by the military authorities to the owners of the land on which they were built. As a result, very few examples have survived. All corrugated blockhouses have one feature in common -- the loopholed walls of galvanised corrugated iron were double-skinned and were filled to the top with shingle (coarse loose stone) to make them bullet-proof. An early rectangular corrugated blockhouse in Barberton [M] (NM) was restored a few years ago and measures 6.0 x 3.4 m in size internally (Plate 1). It may be visited by application to the local Tourist Information Office. The Rice Octagonal Pattern is represented by one on private land at Voortrekkerhoogte [G] near Pretoria, measuring 4.5 m across externally with a gabled roof and with shuttered ventilation openings in both gables. This type fell out of use because the weight of shingle caused the walls to bulge which did not happen with the circular design. The Rice Circular Pattern was a vastly superior design because the curved sheets were much stronger and therefore did not bulge, and the two skins of corrugated iron for the walls could be kept apart by small wood blocks, instead of the larger and more expensive timber framework which was required for straight walls. A reconstructed example of this type can be visited at the Boer Republics Museum in Bloemfontein [FS] and these were generally 4.5 m to 5.0 m diameter (Plate 2). Another common feature of the corrugated blockhouses was that dry or mortared stonework was built up to a height of 1.3m or so around the outside to make the building more bullet-proof (Plate 2). This stonework is often the only remaining evidence of the structure. Sometimes to save cost the full height double-skin corrugated wall is reduced to a loopholed shield 700 mm high which sits on the masonry wall instead of extending down to the ground. The loopholes in corrugated blockhouses were ingeniously formed out of flat galvanised sheet to form a *'waisted'* opening 150mm high by 75mm wide; the circular pattern would generally have 10 to 12 loopholes and the octagonal 14 (2 per side). The door was a simple wooden one, either full size or a crawl

Plate 1: Rectangular corrugated blockhouse, Barberton.

Plate 2: Rice Circular pattern blockhouse with stonework base, reconstructed at the War Museum of the Boer Republics, Bloemfontein.

door 600mm high, and in all cases the opening was protected inside by a screen constructed in the same manner as the walls.

## MASONRY BLOCKHOUSES

Because of their solid and permanent method of construction, the masonry blockhouses are the most numerous class of Anglo-Boer War fortification to have survived in good condition. Major-General E.Wood, the Chief Engineer of the British Army in South Africa, produced a design for a three-storeyed masonry blockhouse (Figure 1) which was widely used and is the archetypal and still the most easily recognised masonry blockhouse pattern. But a study of the structures has revealed a great deal of freedom given to Royal Engineers officers in designing masonry blockhouses and this in turn has created a number of different regional design types. These have been classified by the author as follows:

**Standard pattern.** This type is based on Major-General Wood's design and is found extensively along the Cape Town-Warrenton railway line, at Stormberg Junction [EC] and Burgersdor[EC] (NM) on the East London-Aliwal North railway and defending the towns of Aliwal North [EC] (Buffelspruit Blockhouse NM) and Harrismith [FS]. Along the railway lines, these structures defended major river bridges and stations. The plan size is 6.1m square externally and they were built of mortared stonework (often quarried at the site) or, in a few cases, of unreinforced

Figure 1: 'Type of two-story masonry blockhouse' (actually three-storeyed). This is Plate XIV from 'The Blockhouse System in the South African War' by Bt-Col. E H Bethell (Professional Papers of the Royal Engineers, Occasional Series, 1904, Paper XII).

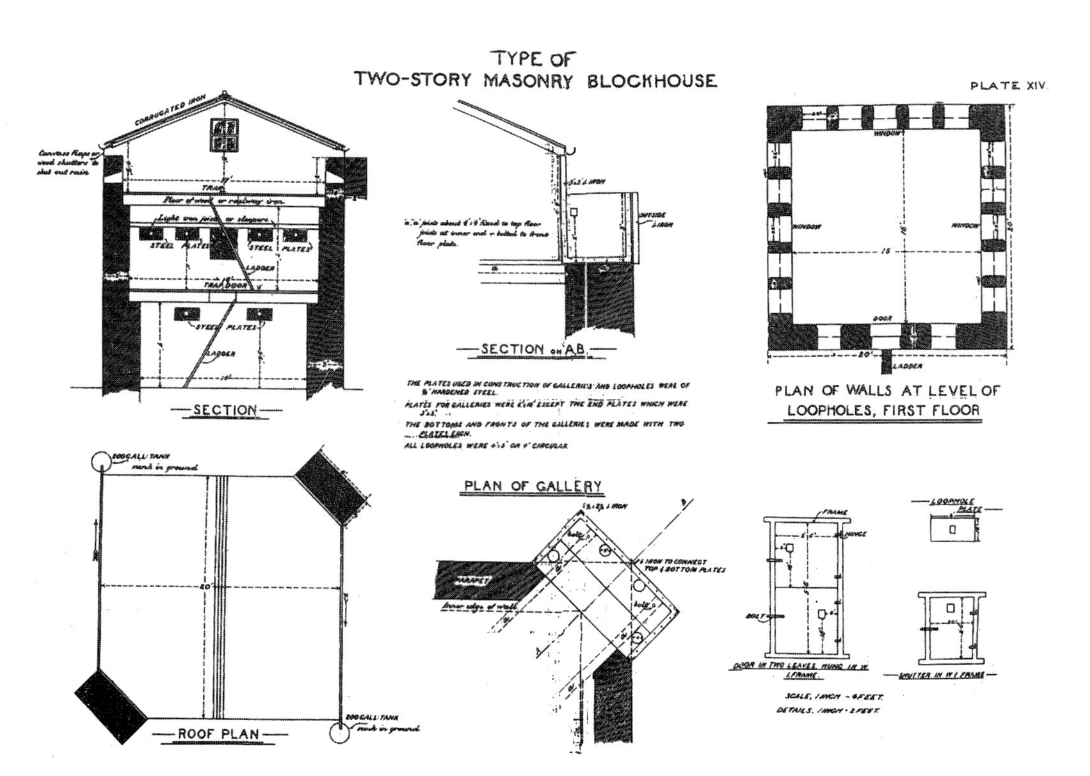

concrete. (Plate 3). Entry to these buildings is by ladder to a first floor doorway into the main living level, from where ladders led down to the ground floor storage level and up to the observation level on the second floor. (The only exception to this arrangement that the author has seen is at Orange River Station [NC] which is only two storeys high, having omitted the storage floor.) The entrance has a stable door of thick steel, steel-shuttered windows in the other three walls at this level give extra light and the walls are loopholed at all levels, the loophole plates being 12mm steel and sometimes doubled in thickness. At two diagonally opposite corners of the 2nd floor, two cantilevered steel angle galleries allowed the garrison to give flanking fire along the walls. The blockhouse is covered with a pyramid-shaped or gabled roof of corrugated iron and timber, with gutters and downpipes which collected rainwater into a tank at ground level; this often meagre supply was supplemented by the delivery of water by train or by water waggon from the nearest town, and food, mail and other necessaries were supplied in similar manner. Canvas *'drops'* were provided to close the gap between the wall top and the eaves of the roof on the 2nd floor and these could be rolled up in fine weather. (Figure 2, Plate 4). Most Standard Pattern blockhouses are accessible for inspection on the outside but, because of the high-level entrance, access to the interior is difficult without a ladder. Examples which are readily accessible inside are to be found at

Plate 3: Concrete Standard pattern at Merriman [NC].

the recently-restored ones at Beaufort West [WC], Modder River [NC] near Kimberley and the two at Burgersdorp [EC] (NM); in the Beaufort West and Burgersdorp cases, keys can be obtained by application to the local Tourist Information office. The Modder River blockhouse is open for public view and access.

**Magaliesberg pattern.** A most distinctive design is to be found defending the passes and high points of the Magaliesberg to the west of Pretoria. These examples feature crenellated parapet walls (like a mediaeval castle) rising above a flat roof, a wide range of plan shapes and the chamfering of the external angles of walls above the loophole sills to provide for additional loopholes at the angles. The group of three defending the ridge to the east of Kommandonek [NW] by Hartebeespoort Dam are, from the bottom of the hill respectively; square, T-shaped and L-shaped in plan, and Hekpoort [G] has a chevron plan. All the Magaliesberg pattern blockhouses are single-storeyed and, where built on a rounded hilltop, the site has been levelled with a terrace of dry stone. (Figure 3 (a) and Figure 3 (b), Plate 5). The flat roof at Hekpoort is of concrete poured over arched corrugated iron shuttering and supported by steel I-beams, and the lower and middle blockhouses at Kommandonek East and the one at Kommandonek West were roofed in a similar manner; however the roofs at Kommandonek East upper blockhouse and at Broederstroom [NW] were probably timber and corrugated iron. This series each had the standard steel stable door, shuttered windows and loopholes, and timber floors. One unique feature of the Broederstroom blockhouse is that it has a fireplace, a facility which unusually the author has not found in any other blockhouse in South Africa. Another feature which is associated with the Magaliesberg pattern is the construction of mule tracks to give easy access to the blockhouses in this mountainous terrain. These tracks are revetted in dry stone at the sides, sometimes to a height of 2m, and the track is finished with a bed of fine stone chippings; they are generally in good condition and still in use today.

**Daspoortrant pattern.** This type is peculiar

to the mountain ridges around Pretoria and is characterised by a regular rectangular plan (6.1 to 6.25m wide by 11.0 to 11.3m long externally) and timber ground floors. The pattern is mostly represented today only by foundations, mainly along the Daspoortrant ridge running towards Kruger's West Fort, as these structures were systematically destroyed after the war. A variant of this pattern, 6.2m square, is found in the only complete masonry blockhouse in Greater Pretoria, Johnston's Redoubt in Bryntirion. This building is single-storeyed and complete with gabled roof, door, loopholes and angle galleries, but can only be visited by special permission as it is situated in the grounds of the government house Libertas. The foundations of a second blockhouse of the same size are visible on the next ridge to the north. (Figure 4)

**Vereeniging pattern.** This very distinctive design was restricted to the main Cape Town-

Figure 2: A typical Standard pattern blockhouse, plans and section (Modder River Bridge NC).

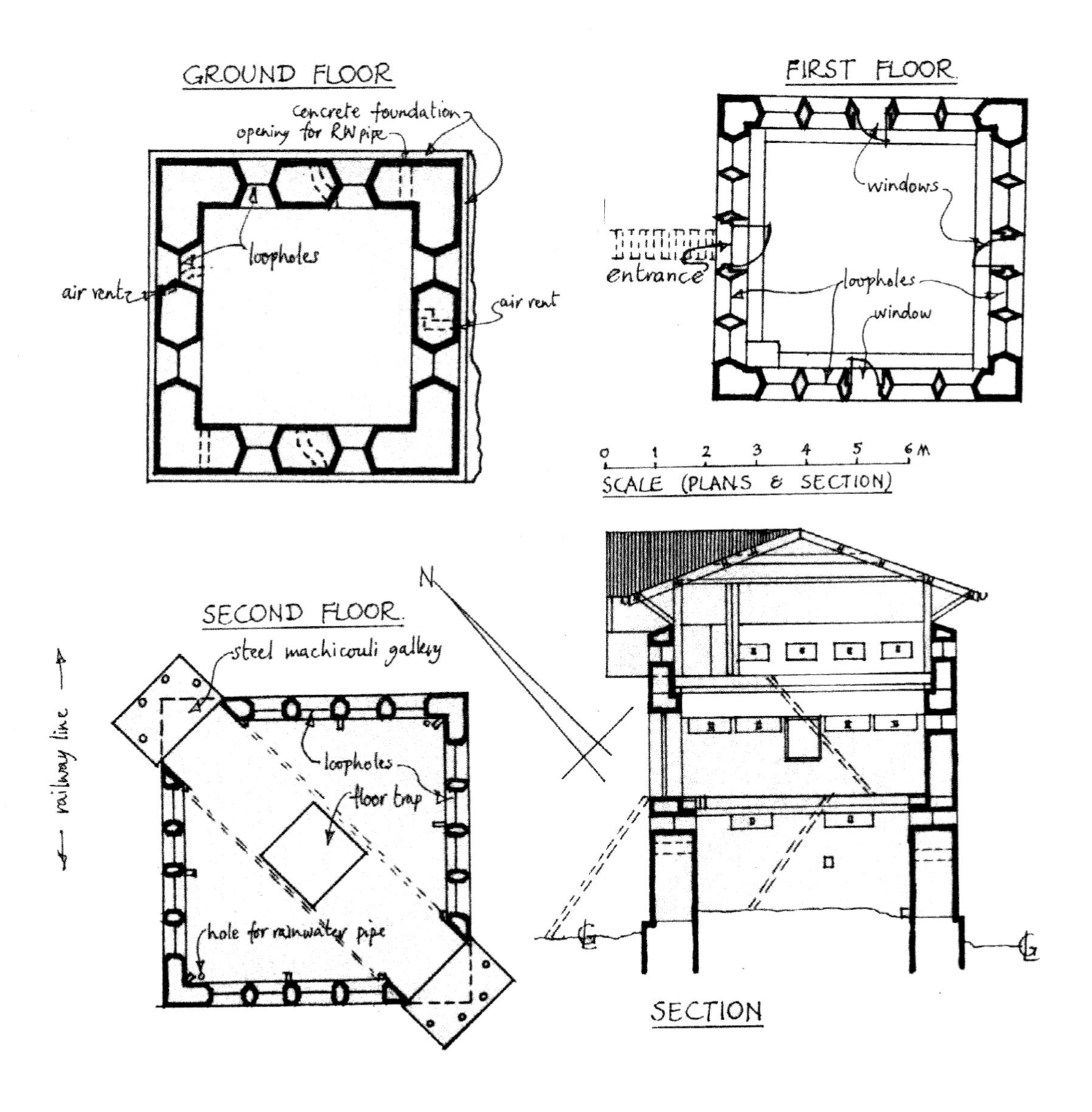

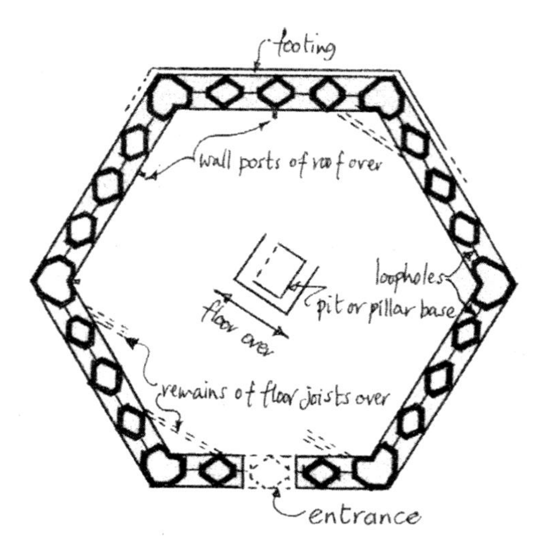


Figure 7: Aliwal Hexagonal pattern at Waterworks Hill, Aliwal North.

Plate 8: Aliwal Hexagonal pattern, Dewetsville, Aliwal North.

been used only for observation purposes. (Plate 12). The well-known small fort perched high on a rock above the R62 road at Cogman's Kloof [WC], 3km south of Montagu, is included in this category because of its mortared stonework construction and the presence of an internal stonework platform for a water tank, which seems to indicate that the building originally had a roof from which the rainwater was collected. However the 21 *'waisted'* loopholes formed in the masonry without steel plates and the simple entrance without door or screen are more consistent with a simple open fort, but it is not known how much detail has been lost in restorations. (Plate 13). Accessible at any time.

Plate 9: Warmbaths blockhouse.

We should not leave the masonry blockhouses without mentioning the two large forts in Pretoria [G] which were built by the Royal Engineers, namely Quagga Redoubt on the ridge north of the suburb of Laudium and East Fort on Strubenkop in Lynnwood. Both incorporated blockhouses in the circuit of their walls and both have been damaged by the construction of reservoirs and, in the case of East Fort, by vandals removing quantities of stone in the 1970s.

## DRYSTONE INFANTRY FORTS

Fortifications constructed by British infantry regiments using unmortared stonework are found in many parts of the country. They tend to be irregular in plan, following the contours of the ground and incorporating natural features such as rock outcrops; they are often still in good condition and many are fine examples of drystone construction. It should be borne in mind that a large proportion of the soldiers who took part in the Anglo-Boer War were civilian volunteers who came from all walks of life, including rural men who were used to building stone walls in their civilian jobs and would form the nucleus of fort-building crews in their regiments. A selection of these forts which have been examined by the author includes:

**Fort Cornwall, Irene** [G], has a small drystone structure with steeply battered outer wall faces on the crown of Cornwall Hill (the interior was filled in by the Van der Byl family after World War 2 to form the base for a monolith commemorating comrades of the SA Air Force), surrounded further out by trenches and dugouts cut into the rock of the hilltop. They were constructed by the Duke of Cornwall's Light Infantry Brigade who garrisoned the hill after Lord Roberts' army captured Pretoria in June 1900.

**Pienaarspoort** [G], where the Delagoa Bay railway cuts through the eastern extremity of the Magaliesberg 25km east of Pretoria, has a series of at least 6 forts south of the poort and a further 2 to the north of all shapes and sizes. Common features of the larger forts are right-angled screen walls protecting the entrance and loopholes neatly formed in the stonework.

**Eagles Nest Fort, Meredale, Johannesburg** [G], is a boot-shaped fort nearly 50m long by 6 to 13m wide with a screened entrance and 20 surviving loopholes in the stonework.

**Rustenburg** [NW] has a series of 6 forts on the south-eastern outskirts of the town, and a concentric circular fort still surrounded by its sentry walk defending the pass at Olifantsnek on the R30 road 16km south-east of the town.

**Heidelberg** [G] was defended by two large forts on hills to the north-east and south-east of the town. The former has a plan in the shape of a coat/trouser hanger and is protected by 3 corrugated blockhouses of which only the stonework remains; there are

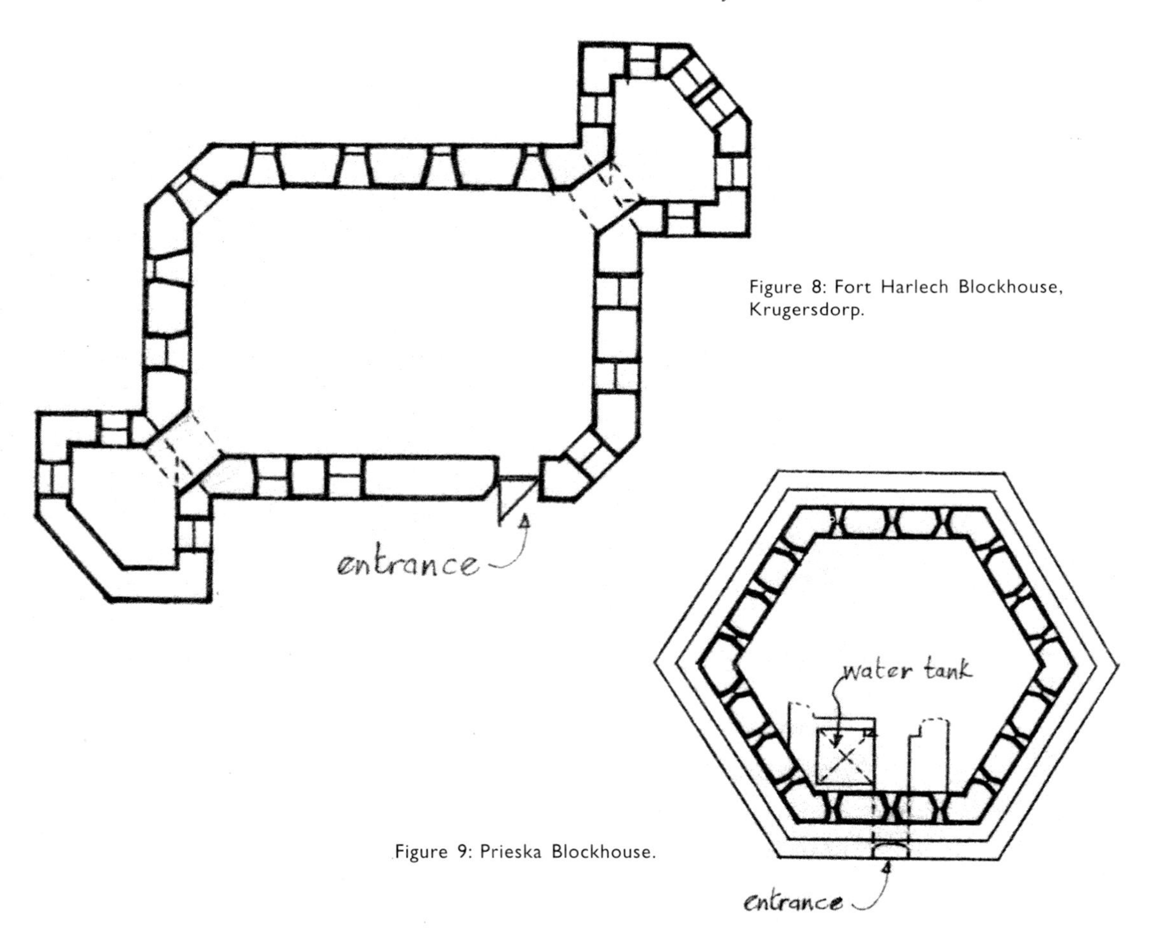


Figure 8: Fort Harlech Blockhouse, Krugersdorp.

Figure 9: Prieska Blockhouse.

Plate 11: Prieska Blockhouse.

Plate 10: Fort Harlech Blockhouse, Krugersdorp.

numerous subsidiary defences, walls blocking kloofs, etc. The south-east fort has a roughly oval plan surrounded by the remains of a drystone perimeter wall on which are placed 3 blockhouses built of large sandstone blocks without mortar, the north one being 6.2m square with walls 800mm thick and standing 2m high. There are traces of gateways and internal buildings. There are still remains of at least 3 masonry blockhouses on the hills to the north-west of Heidelberg.

**TOWN GUARD FORTS**

The author has examined the remains of several of these forts in the southern and eastern Cape. They tend to be smaller and more regular in plan, some being built of drystone like the infantry forts and others of mortared stone. In each case, they were built by the local Town Guard.

**Upper Van Stadens Dam Forts, Port Elizabeth** [EC]. These small structures are situated 35km west of the town, on the hill overlooking the dam. The higher fort is circular and 10m in outside diameter, the walls mostly surviving to 2m high with closely-spaced loopholes, the entrance protected by a loopholed external screen wall and with a paved walkway running round inside the wall. The lower fort is a rectangle with rounded ends 17m long by 7.5m wide, with closely-spaced loopholes and entrance protected by a right-angled screen wall, from which an access trench runs 22m down the hill. The forts are difficult to find in the forest and permission to visit must first be obtained from Port Elizabeth Municipality.

**Jansenville** [EC] has a fine rectangular fort measuring some 15m by 21m on a hill north of the town, the walls having loopholes and firing steps at two levels and standing to 2m or so in height, with a two-roomed internal building or enclosure. The fort and the *'noors'* (a spiny cactus) deterred the Smuts Kommando as it bypassed the town in September 1901. The fort may be visited at any time.

**Knysna Fort (Thomson's Folly)** [WC] has a plan like a small mediaeval castle, with a drystone perimeter wall following the contour of the hilltop and enclosing an area about 35 x 32m. Two wall towers and

Plate 12: Noupoort Blockhouse.

Plate 13: Cogman's Kloof Fort.

a 2-roomed garrison office in mortared stonework have survived to 2m or so high. (Plate 14). The site has been cleared and sign-posted recently by a group of local enthusiasts and may be visited at any time.

**Uniondale Fort** [WC] (NM), to the south of the town, has a circular loopholed wall about 8m in outside diameter with an external entrance passage, all built of stone with mud *'dagha'* (mortar), but the building has been considerably restored. It may be visited at any time and is a fine viewpoint. It is said to be one of 6 forts built to protect the town.

## *Conclusion*

From the foregoing, it is clear that there is plenty still to be seen by those tourists interested in the fortifications of the Anglo-Boer War and it is hoped that this chapter will give a better insight into what to look out for. These structures represent the end of a British tradition in building castles and forts in stone which stretches back 1 000 years and covers a large part of the world. The mortared masonry block-houses and some of the drystone forts are fine specimens of the stonemason's art, and the variety of designs by the Royal Engineers officers reflect the freedom for initiative which was the hallmark of previous centuries, which was largely eliminated by centralised design in the 20th century. The blockhouses are an important contribution to the built environment and to our historic heritage and remain a highly visible reminder of the war.

The story is not complete and will probably remain incomplete for many years. This is a huge country with many areas which are difficult of access and one working person can only do so much. Although this work mentions only a fraction of the fortifications visited by the author over the last two decades, he will be pleased to hear from readers of any new discoveries, demolitions, restorations or corrections to the text. ❑

Plate 14: Knysna Fort in its heyday (Photo: Knysna Museum).

*Note: All photo's and drawings are by the author, except for Plate 4 & 14 and Figure 1.*

## FROM THE SPANISH ARMADA TO BLOCKHOUSES

A Cornishman who could trace his lineage back to the time of the Spanish Armada lies buried in the Great Karoo. Richard Hastings Tremearne, born in India in 1879, was a descendant of John Tremearne, the vicar of Paul in Cornwall during the Spanish Armada. Soon after the outbreak of the Anglo-Boer War, Richard Tremearne, the British officer who supervised the building of the blockhouse lines in the Karoo, volunteered as a driver and was attached to a battery of the CIV in July 1900. He also served in columns under General Paget and General Plumer. Tremearne returned to England in November 1900 and the following year was presented with a medal and three clasps by the King. In November 1901 he received a commission in the Royal Warwickshire Regiment and joined it in the Karoo. As 2nd Lieutenant of the 5th Battalion he served in Sutherland and Beaufort West. He later moved to Carnarvon where he died of Enteric fever on 14 April 1902.

ROSES ROUND UP

# British Prisoners of War

British prisoners taken by the Boers in the early stages of the war were taken to **Pretoria** where the men were accommodated on the **Racecourse** and the officers and their servants at the **Staats Model School**. Amongst the first arrivals at the racecourse were the 243 prisoners from **Dundee** who arrived in Pretoria on 22 October 1899. They were soon to be followed by others notably those taken at **Nicholson's Nek**. By 1 November there were some 1 500 prisoners. The hospital at the Racecourse was used for wounded and sick prisoners until the fall of Pretoria. The officers remained at the **Staats Model School** until 16 March 1900 when they were moved to their new quarters known as the **Birdcage** at **Daspoort**.

The welfare of the prisoners was controlled by a board of management consisting of four persons. They were Louis da Souza, Commandant Opperman, directly responsible for the safe custody of the prisoners, Dr Gunning, who was Opperman's assistant and Hans Malan. Opperman was replaced by a Mr Westerink in March 1900. The 129 officers and 36 soldier detained at the **Staats Model School** were released on the 5 June 1900. On the 6 June Colonel T C Porter's Brigade was ordered to affect the release of the men confined at **Waterval**. A squadron of Greys under Captain Maude finally released some 3 187 men. It was found that 900 prisoners had been removed by the Boers from **Waterval** on 4 June. These men were now detained at **Nooitgedacht**. They were eventually released by the Earl of Dundonald on the 30 August 1900.

When General French entered **Barberton** in September 1900, he released the final group of prisoners namely 23 officers and 59 soldiers whom the Boers had removed from **Nooitgedacht**. Most of them had been confined in a barbed wire enclosure while some were housed in the local goal. ❑

**e-mail address** museum@anglo-boer.co.za

## THEFT

As the Boers were preparing to leave Hectorspruit to escape the victorious British Army, through what is today the Kruger National Park, they became adept at stealing from one another. *"Cattle, wagons, saddles, harness and boxes of tinned dainties, were stolen and re-stolen back and forth, countless times a day. Meeting Manie Mentz, I obtained from him for our journey, one case of cocoa, one of jam, and one of condensed milk. Then, while I went round the corner for further supplies, these were irrecoverably then stolen."* (Schikkerling, 66

## "SARIE MARAIS"

The song *Sarie Marais* is an international evergreen performed in many countries but who is the person referred to in the song?

'Sarie' was Susara Margaretha Toerien (nee Maré), daughter of Jacob Maré, after whom one of Pretoria's streets is named. In 1884, at the age of 16 she met, fell in love with and married Jacobus Petrus Toerien, one of South Africa's first Afrikaans writers – his *nom de plume* was 'Japete'. Sarie bore him 16 children, eight of whom died in infancy. Toerien staunchly identified himself with the Boer fight for freedom. At the outbreak of the Anglo-Boer War he joined the Boers and, while on commando, often sang a song he had written for his wife. It was a translation of Septimus Winner's Ellie Rhee, a ditty with roots in the American Civil War.

*Sarie Marais* has been translated into many languages, including English, Dutch, German, French, Russian and Italian. It was officially sung for the Queen in 1995 at the Royal Festival of Remembrance to commemorate the 50th anniversary of the declaration of peace in World War II.

ROSES ROUND UP

## DECEPTION

The Boer women of Heidelberg were determined that the British troops about to occupy their town would not drink their wonderful spring water, so they built a Dutch Oven over the spring. This can still be seen in the park at the corner of H.F. Verwoerd and Venter streets.

**Generals of the Anglo-Boer War**, *Phillip Bateman*, 1977 Purnell & Sons (SA) (Pty) Ltd

Kommandant Mears and Veldkornet Kamffer moved into position one night for a dawn attack on a mission station at Beerlaagte. In order to be taken for cattle, their men draped wildebeest skins over themselves and lay down next to their horses holding the reins in one hand.

**Heidelbergers of the Boer War**, *Ian Uys*, 1981 Ian S. Uys

## COMMUNICATION

Dr.O'Reilly left carrier pigeons with his patient's families on his rounds of the farms near Heidelberg so that he could be kept informed of their progress. This practice probably led to his arrest by the British and his deportation to Cape Town.

**Heidelbergers of the Boer War,** *Ian Uys*, 1981 Ian S. Uys

## FINAL WORDS

Schikkerling, a Boer commando, observed that the three words most commonly uttered by dying men are "Mother", "God", and "water". (Schikkerling, 73).

## BOER HOSPITALITY

Schikkerling and his commando took pity on the recently-released British prisoners of war making their weary way from Nooitgedacht to Waterval Boven, as the Boers were retreating down the railway line. "We made many kettlefuls of coffee for distribution, and handed them out as they passed. The Tommies relished it greatly, some of them even lapping up the grounds." (Schikkerling, 60).

***The anecdotes in this publication are used with the kind permission of Rob Milne of Johannesburg, Roses Round-up (Rose Willis of Beaufort West) & Steve's War Stories (Steve Lunderstedt of Kimberley)***

# St. Helena

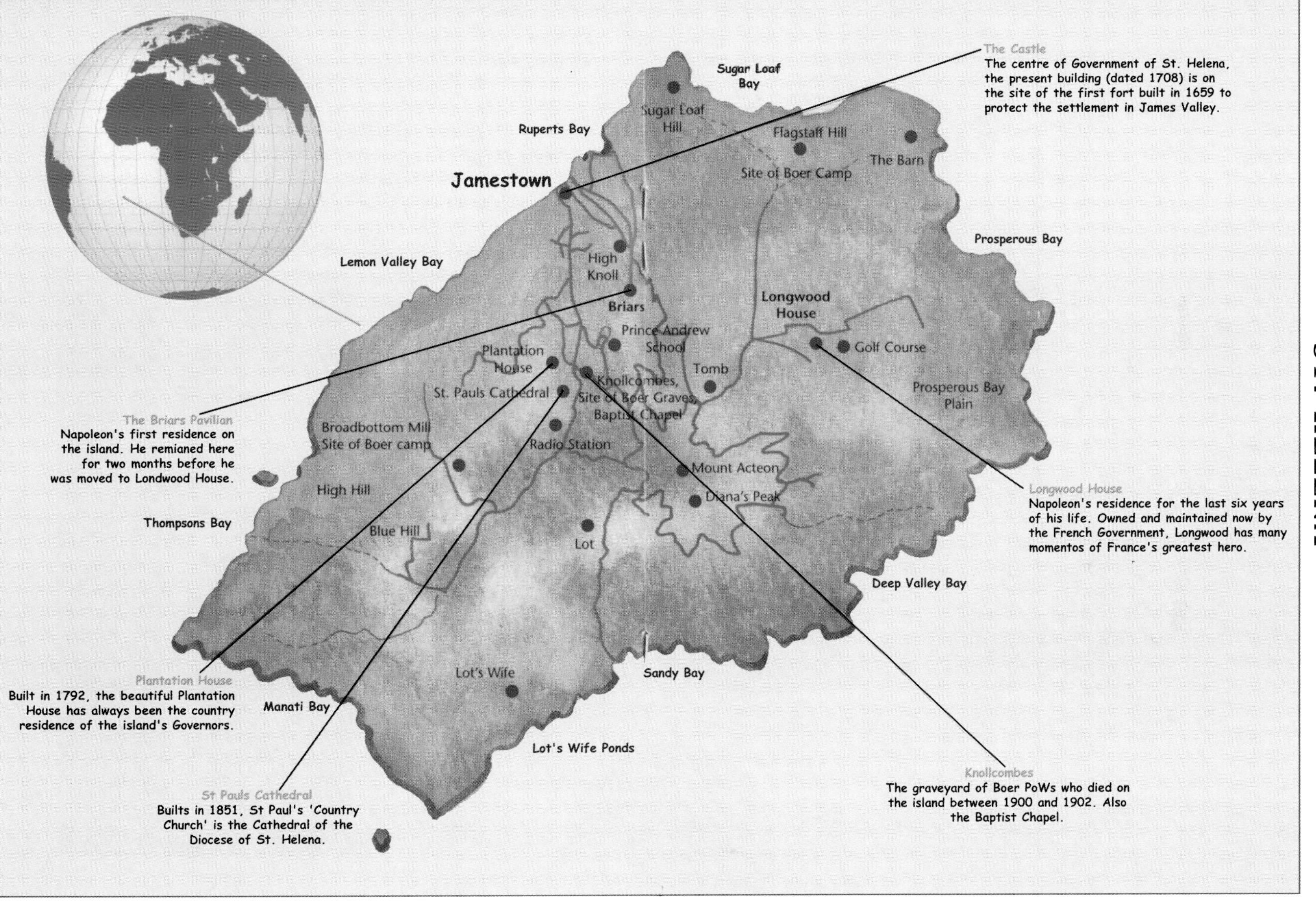

The Castle
The centre of Government of St. Helena, the present building (dated 1708) is on the site of the first fort built in 1659 to protect the settlement in James Valley.
Sugar Loaf Bay
Sugar Loaf Hill
Rupperts Bay
Flagstaff Hill
The Barn
Site of Boer Camp
Jamestown
Prosperous Bay
Lemon Valley Bay
High Knoll
Briars
Longwood House
Prince Andrew School
Golf Course
Plantation House
Tomb
Knollcombes, Site of Boer Graves, Baptist Chapel
St. Pauls Cathedral
Prosperous Bay Plain
The Briars Pavilian
Napoleon's first residence on the island. He remianed here for two months before he was moved to Londwood House.
Broadbottom Mill Site of Boer camp
Radio Station
Mount Acteon
High Hill
Diana's Peak
Longwood House
Napoleon's residence for the last six years of his life. Owned and maintained now by the French Government, Longwood has many momentos of France's greatest hero.
Thompsons Bay
Blue Hill
Lot
Deep Valley Bay
Plantation House
Built in 1792, the beautiful Plantation House has always been the country residence of the island's Governors.
Lot's Wife
Sandy Bay
Manati Bay
Lot's Wife Ponds
Knollcombes
The graveyard of Boer PoWs who died on the island between 1900 and 1902. Also the Baptist Chapel.
St Pauls Cathedral
Builts in 1851, St Paul's 'Country Church' is the Cathedral of the Diocese of St. Helena.

## ST. HELENA ISLAND INFORMATION

**South Africa:** St. Helena Line (Pty) Ltd,
1 Thibault Square (BP Centre) 2nd Floor, Cape Town.
Tel: (021) 425 1165. Fax: (021) 421 7485. e-mail: sthelena@iafrica.com
**United Kingdom:** Tel: 0171 224 5025. Fax: 0171 224 5035.
**St. Helena:** Tel: +290 2158. Fax: +290 2159. e-mail: StHelena.Tourism@helanta.sh

St. Helena Island (15.57S 5.42W) is situated in the tropical South Atlantic Ocean, 1 950 km from the coast of Africa on its east; level with the borderline of Angola and Namibia, and approximately 2 900 km from the Brazilian coast on the west. The closest land is Ascension Island at 1 125 km to the north-west. **Cape Town is 2 400 km to the south of the Island.**

It is a volcanic island of contrasts from wind eroded desert to emerald hillsides, soft pasture and lush vegetation filled valleys. The coastline has cliffs rising to 300 metres that have been carved by the pounding Atlantic Ocean.

It was discovered on 21 May 1502 by the Portuguese admiral *João da Nova* on his return voyage from India. It was popular with sea-travellers due to its climate, vegetation and wealth of fruit. The Islanders are affectionately referred to as *The Saints* and have their own charm possibly inherited from their descendants who vary from British settlers, sent out by the East India Company, slaves and indentured workers from Africa and the East. They are without doubt the most friendliest of people you will have come across; always greeting you and only too happy to pass the time of day chatting about their island.

It became a British dependency in 1834 and it still retains the early 20th century values.

St. Helena has had many famous visitors among them *Darwin, Halley, Bligh, Cook, Sir Arthur Wellesley (the Duke of Wellington) and Burchell.* The most internationally renowned figure associated with the Island is *Napoleon Bonaparte* who was exiled to the island in 1815 after his defeat at the Battle of Waterloo. He lived at Longwood House until his death in 1821. The residence is now a museum owned by the French Government.

The island is 17 km long and 10,5 km wide. It has a temperate climate with temperatures ranging from 14°C - 32°C in summer and 14°C - 26°C in winter. It is steeped in history especially military history which is evident by the profusion of fortifications and canons lying around. They date from the 1800s to the Second World War when the island was protected by a number of 6 inch guns which were never fired in anger. **There is NOT an airport on the island; and therefore the only way to get to the island is by the *RMS* *ST. HELENA*, run by the ST. HELENA LINE.**

ST. HELENA LINE INFORMATION

**SOUTH AFRICA: ST. HELENA LINE (PTY) LTD.**

2nd Floor, 1 Thibault Square (BP Centre), Cape Town.

Tel: (021) 425 1165. Fax: (021) 421 7485. e-mail: sthelena@iafrica.com

**UNITED KINGDOM: CURNOW SHIPPING LTD.**

48-50 Killigrew Street, Falmouth, Cornwall TR11 3AP. Tel: 01326 211466. Fax: 01326 212808.

e-mail: reservations@curnow-shipping.co.uk

Web site: http://www.rms-st-helena.com

The ST. HELENA LINE operates a regular passenger and cargo service from Cape Town to St. Helena Island and return. The standard voyage is 5 nights sailing to St. Helena, 7/8 nights on the island and return trip of another 5 nights. A total of 17/18 days/nights. The ship also plies between **Cardiff** and **Cape Town**, visiting the islands of **Tenerife, Ascension** and **St.Helena**.

The **RMS ST. HELENA** has 128 passenger berths in a range of categories. It is without a doubt one of the finest cruising options available with excellent, comfortable and soundproof cabins. The service of the officers and the crew is outstanding; and the food is of an exceptionally high standard. There is always something to do as the entertainment on board caters for all passengers. It is a cruise where you will most definitely make friends. ***The voyage alone is a must.***

The **RMS ST. HELENA** provides the only scheduled shipping service to the island. It is owned on behalf of the Government of St.Helena by the St.Helena Line Limited, which has appointed Curnow Shipping Limited as vessel managers and passenger agents. The service is funded in part by subsidy from HM Government's Department for International Development.

For further information on voyage dates contact the ST.HELENA LINE office in Cape Town or CURNOW SHIPPING LTD in Falmouth, UK, or visit the website: http://www.rms-st-helena.com

## ST. HELENA ISLAND

The population on the island is ± 5 500. The capital is **JAMESTOWN** where everything happens: the shops as well as the two major hotels are in Jamestown and it is small enough to walk everywhere. Very safe with zero tolerance for crime, so much so that you will find people walking in the evenings and enjoying the fresh healthy climate.

There are excellent walks to be had throughout the island from gentle to arduous. Start by climbing up the 700 steps of **Jacobs Ladder** (pictured left) (view from the top, pictured overleaf) to Ladder Hill Fort. Fish for Tuna, Marlin and Barracuda, or Dive off one of the many wrecks around the island. Bring your own mountain bike and have a challenge of a lifetime on the roads which wind all over the island. For the Golf enthusiasts there is an 18 hole course - *the remotest golf course in the South Atlantic* - which boasts a pleasurable 19th hole where you can meet some of the amiable *Saints*.

The accommodation on the island ranges from hotels to self-catering.

### Farm Lodge Country House Hotel

6.5 km from Jamestown, this hotel, built as the home of an East India Company planter (*circa* 1750), is set in six acres of lush tropical gardens with banana, avocado, date palm and coffee groves. The accommodation is luxurious and the meals are of a high standard.
3 Rooms from £50.00 per person per day. Full Board.
Tel: +290 4040. Fax: +290 2166.

### Consulate Hotel, Jamestown

This 18th century colonial building, being a mere 10 minute walk from the harbour is close to all shops and restaurants. All rooms en-suite with phone, tea/coffee facilities. Light meals, lunches and dinners available. Library with a selection of books and TV.
Rooms from £41.00 per person per day. Half Board.
Tel: +290 2962. Fax: +290 2760.

### Wellington House Hotel, Jamestown

Opposite the Consulate Hotel in the main street, run by the Yon family, the service is good and friendly. Morning tea, coffee and cakes are available for guests and visitors and the wholesome cuisine is *'St. Helena style'*. Spacious rooms with seperate bathrooms on floor above. From £39.00 per person per day. Full Board.
Tel: +290 2529. Fax: +290 2725.

## Attractions and Activities

There is a lot to do on the island to keep you occupied.

**Birdwatching:** For those interested ornithologists, The RMS St.Helena organises a special *Ornithologists Cruise* where hopefully one can see the unique two birds in their natural habitat: **Fregata Aquila** (Ascension Frigatebird) and the **Charadrius Sanctaehelenae** (St.Helenian Wirebird). The islands are home to Boobies, Noddies, Tropicbirds and Terns. The Sooty and Wideawake Tern nest in vast colonies on Ascension Island. During the sea voyage you will see an amazing number of sea-birds that seem to be following the ship; and regular sightings of Albatrosses, Petrels, Shearwaters, Skuas, Gannets and Penguins (closer to the South Africa coast) can be had.

**Boat Trips:** Take this trip and see the lee coast of the island and the imposing cliffs. Pass the small offshore islands, enjoy the birdlife and visit Lemon Valley where a quarantine camp for the Bubonic Plague was positioned during the Boer War and where General Viljoen had to remain for six weeks. On the boat trip you will see the extent of the fortifications and how well hidden they were.

**Endemic plants:** Take a tour with George Benjamin, the island naturalist, of the endemic plants of the island.

**Fortifications:** The island is literally covered with fortifications as it was established by the British as an island fortress to safeguard its lucrative early trade routes to the East Indies. You will find many a canon of different sizes and shapes lying around the fortifications. Walks from Jamestown along the coast use to be the supply tracks to the various fortifications.

**Historic Buildings:** There are a few Tour Operators/Guides who can take you to the historic buildings on the island.

The Briars.

Longwood House.

Plantation House.

Napoleon's grave

High Knoll Fort.

Dinizulu's residence

*Plantation House* (Governor's residence), Napoleon's first residence, *The Briars*, Napoleon's last residence, *Longwood*, Napoleon's Grave, The Boer Cemetery, High Knoll Fort *(where Boer irreconcilables were held)*, Dinizulu's residence *(the Zulu King was held here)*, St. Paul's Cathedral and many other old, historic buildings.

**Historical Walks:** Visit the Castle, Jacobs Ladder, The oldest Anglican Church in the Southern Hemisphere, the Museum and then have tea at Wellington House where the Duke of Wellington stayed in 1805.

**Tour in style:** Some of the best views of the island can be seen from Colin Corker's unique CHARABANC (pictured below).

## Population statistics

On 31 December 1900, it was reported that the population of St. Helena was 5 316 civilians and troops; added to which there were 2 454 Boer prisoners.

## Irreconcilables

21 October 1902

There were still 39 rebel Boer prisoners on St. Helena.

5 March 1903

Two of the five remaining irreconcilables 25614 J. J. Coetzer and 4234 W. H. Stander proceeded to England *en route* to Holland at their own request and at public expense.

20 March 1903

27655 Nicolass Van Der Walt made the Declaration of Allegiance and proceeded to South Africa.

30 April 1903

The last two irreconcilables on St. Helena, Corbett and Standen, refused to go to Europe. They had a defiant attitude. *'The Officer Commanding the troops is afraid that if these two men are allowed to remain at large on the island that they will do mischief. They are bad characters and are quite impervious to any reasonable argument or advice'.*

24 June 1903

On 30 April 1903 the last two irreconcilables, Corbett and Standen, made the Declaration of Allegiance, and sailed for Cape Town.

### Restaurants

There are a number of restaurants on the island.

### Tour Operators

**Magma Way:** Owned and run by Basil George. His grandfather was a Boer prisoner who married Mary Gunnell, a *Saint*. Basil runs a tour operating business and partakes the guiding himself. Due to his ancestral background he is extremely knowledgeable of the Boer camps on the island. He can arrange tailor-made tours to suit clients' needs.

Tel: +290 4525. Fax: +290 4924. e-mail: Busy.Bee@helanta.sh

**Charabang Hire:** Colin Corker, The owner of the *Charabanc* can arrange tours around the island on his marvellous vehicle. This is an experience to remember. Tel: +290 2518.

### Boer War Sites & Information

St. Helena was the first island that Boer prisoners were sent after their defeat at Paardeberg. The number of prisoners were too large to maintain in South Africa and with the possible threat of uniting again, it was decided to separate the prisoners and send them to the various British possessions well out of harms way.

***'The Boer Prisoners Prayer'* on board the *S.S. Lake Erie* en route for St. Helena**

**I can see the old kraal and the sheep coming in,**
**With old Jacob's loud 'hokhok' increasing the din.**
**There's the vrouw I can see, but no smile on her face,**
**But deep lines of sorrow I sadly can trace.**

The following article from the book ***St. Helena*** by **Ms. E.L. Jackson** published by *Ward, Lock & Co. London.* (pp.106 - pp.126) tells the story of the Boer Prisoners on the Island.

In 1899, the Eastern Telegraph landed a submarine cable ex SS *Anglia*, which brings the island into direct communication with England and with the Cape; during the war with the Transvaal it has been of inestimable value. It is shored at Rupert's Valley, where there also are the office and plant; but the Briars House and valley has been acquired, and offices, together with residences for the staff, are now in process of erection there.

Since the removal of the Zulu prisoners the island had been very tranquil and quiet, but on the breaking out of war in the Transvaal there arose the necessity of secure confinement for the prisoners taken in the war and St. Helena was chosen.

On 5 April 1900, *His Excellency* R.A. Sterndale, C.M.G., published the following proclamation:-

In a few days the troopship *Milwaukee*, escorted by H.M.S. *Niobe*, will arrive with prisoners of war.

No unauthorised persons will be allowed on the wharf at the time of disembarkation. The police will assist as far as they can the military, acting under the orders of the officer commanding the troops, in keeping order. *His Excellency*, the Governor expresses the hope that the inhabitants will treat the prisoners with that courtesy and consideration which should be extended to all men who have fought bravely in what they considered the cause of their country, and will help in repressing any unseemly demonstration which individuals might exhibit.

This proclamation was posted in various parts of the island, one being near the landing-steps of the wharf. I have been told by more than one of the prisoners how they dreaded landing on the formidable looking rock, how they shrank from the march through the streets of the town in view. Very many of them were able to read English, and when landed on the wharf, and while waiting for the successive boat-loads of comrades, this notice appealed so much to them after their hardships, that some few entirely broke down.

Expecting harshness, rudeness and ill-feeling from the inhabitants, they discovered from the proclamation so kindly issued by the Governor they might anticipate courtesy and respect. Not a jeering sound, or rude remark was heard from the crowds of islanders congregated to see them pass on their way to Deadwood Camp, which had been prepared for them. Amongst the number of prisoners (514) landed from the *Milwaukee* on 14 April 1900, were General Cronje with his wife.

Cronje, instead of being taken to Deadwood Camp was allowed to live at *Kent Cottage*, (pictured above) but under a strong military guard changed every day. A guard of the militia (4TH North Staffordshire) escorted them as far as Ladder Hill, where they met a guard of the Royal Garrison Artillery, who took charge of the prisoners and conveyed them to Kent Cottage, not far from High Knoll Fort. On 21 April the steamship *Lake Erie* arrived, bringing 394 prisoners, including 34 Boer officers; then on 01 May, the British transport *Bavarian* brought 1 099 to add to the increasing numbers. Another 110 including 12 officers, arrived on 26 June by the transport *Mahratta*, and in July Lieutenant-Colonel von Braun was brought by the British transport *Manchester Port*. The *Idaho*, another British transport, brought 189 men and seven officers; the last arrival in 1900 being the *Victorian*, on 10 December, with 199 prisoners; but early in 1901, on 12 January, arrived the *Columbia* with 200; on 24 January the *Bavarian* with 1 337; and on 3 February, the *Mongolian* with 649 prisoners.

For some time I had been teaching the children of the island the art of pillow-lace making, and was anxious that they should have an opportunity of exhibiting and perchance of disposing of their work. This idea, enlarged, became a scheme for the holding of an exhibition of industrial arts in the island. A committee, headed by *His Excellency* the Governor, the Bishop, the United States consul and others was formed; when, to further extend the exhibition, I proposed that the PoWs might also be allowed to exhibit. This met with unanimous approval, and after securing the consent of the Officer Commanding troops, the prisoners were asked to contribute, not as competitors, but as exhibitors with a view to sale. The idea was eagerly taken up by them, and so numerous were their exhibits that a separate room was allowed for their contributions. A committee was elected from their number on parole, and these carried out their part of the work so well that the section was a great credit to their management.

Models of carts, model of stamping machinery, carved caskets, boxes, sticks, etc., all found ready sale. The tools with which these were made were also exhibited, being old table knives made into saws, umbrella wires as fret-saws, stone hammers, etc.

The drawings, paintings, and etchings were very beautiful, as also was the writing, illuminations, manuscript music, etc. The exhibition was opened on 10 November 1900, for five days, and was a great success. Island-made pottery (by *His Excellency* the Governor), carving, models, island-made preserves, plain and fancy needlework, and pillow, Torchon, Honiton, and Point lace, photographs, painting, etc., well filled the section devoted to the islanders, the little lace-workers and wood-carver's gaining especial praise, as well as substantial remuneration for their work.

It was a pleasant change from the antagonism still going on in South Africa to the peaceful rivalry of the industrial arts, and it was a subject for wonder that such beautiful results could have been obtained from the rudest of implements and material. The exhibition caused a break in the monotony of the prisoners' lives, and caused a better feeling to spring up between them and the islanders.

On the night of 2 February 1901, a very determined attempt to escape from the island was made at Sandy Bay, by four of the Boer prisoners of war, one of them being the grandson of President Kruger (Commandant P. Eloff). The men had a quantity of provisions with them, and seized an old fishing boat at Sandy Bay. The fishermen, who had just landed, took away the oars, and a struggle ensued between the prisoners and fishermen for possession of them, the latter succeeding in retaining them. The prisoners got into the boat and tore up the bottom boards to make paddles but, finding them useless, they again landed and proceeded – to no avail – to bribe the fishermen by offering a goodly sum for the boat and oars. While this was going on a messenger sped off to report the occurrence, and in the early dawn of that Sunday morning, a guard from Broadbottom Camp arrived and took the men into custody. This attempt was an extremely foolhardy one, for the boat was in such bad condition, would surely have been in half before they were many miles from the shore. In fact, it broke in half a fortnight after the occurrence.

Another escape was attempted by two Frenchmen. They bathed from the beach at Rupert's and attempted to swim to a ship in harbour. Being seen by the guardship the guns were directed on them are they were hailed. One turned and swam back to Rupert's Beach, the other swam to the steps of Jamestown wharf, where he was taken in charge and escorted to camp.

An outbreak of ***bubonic plague*** occurred in 1901 in South Africa. All vessels touching at the Cape ports were therefore under quarantine regulations when they called at St. Helena – no passengers were allowed to land except for the island, and then only under strict quarantine. No cargo was brought by steamers, no parcel post allowed. This was a terrible loss to the island in the matter of trade.

Rats have from the earliest times been a pest on the island, and the fear of plague made the Government offer a sum of one penny per head; then of twopence, and, when they became scarcer, of threepence per head. This to a great extent cleared the country of these troublesome rodents. (See Government Notification alongside.)

Deadwood Plain, which lies due east of the island, became filled with the tents of the Transvaalers and of the 4TH Battalion Gloucester Regiment, commanded by Lieutenant-Colonel Earl Bathurst – it had then become necessary to form another camp. Broadbottom, a large plain on the western side of the island, was chosen, and here the Orange Free Staters were located.

In April 1901 Captain Meiklejohn arrived per R.M.S. *Raglan Castle*. Also in this month *His Excellency* & Mrs Sterndale left for England on 'sick leave'. Colonel Evans assumed the reins of government. Gov. Sterndale returned again in August. In January 1902 the British steamship *Orient* arrived with 1 050 prisoners, followed by the *Britannia*, which brought 39 Boer officers, amongst them General Ben

Government

**NOTIFICATION.**

Whereas it is well known that the Bubonic Plague quickly affects Rats and is by them widely disseminated it is of the greatest importance especially in the vicinity of Landing places to destroy all Rats; for the landing of a single infected rat from any ship might communicate the disease to those in the neighbourhood and they in their turn to others.

Almost every outbreak of Plague has been preceded by an unusual mortality amongst rats.

It is therefore absolutely necessary as a precautionary measure of the first class to clear our wharf and Town and the Island generally of the rats which abound. His Excellency the Governor therefore hereby gives notice that persons bringing dead rats to the Inspector of Police Jamestown, or to Police Constables Kennedy at Plantation, or Constantine at Longwood, will receive a Reward at the rate of One Penny per rat.

By command,

ROBT. R. BRUCE,
For Colonial Secretary.
The Castle,
St. Helena 23rd February 1901.

CHARLES W. BRUCE Government Printer.

Viljoen (pictured right), who had done so much for the Boers in the field!

February brought the British transport *Victorian* with the last batch of prisoners, consisting of twenty officers and 57 rebels.

The camps were nicely laid out and girdled by three separate fencings of barbed wire separated by tangled barb, and guarded on the outside by patrolling soldiers; for such a number congregated together there was very little trouble given by the majority; but, as is usual in all communities, there were bound to be agitators and ill-conditioned men. Usually the prisoners would settle their little disturbances amongst themselves, but some cases required the decision of the British commandants. Several of the untractable were confined in High Knoll, one amongst these being Eloff. Schiel also was confined there for a short time.

By degrees the moneyed men amongst the prisoners, dissatisfied with sharing tents, built for themselves snug little huts. Some of them were well constructed, the majority being composed of paraffin tins soldered together or overlapped; these, lined out in some cases with wood, in other with cloth, were most comfortable.

The commandants on parole were allowed to live outside the camp in comparative freedom with very little restriction being placed on their movements as long as they were well conducted and reported themselves at stated times.

Amongst the prisoners were clever musicians, teachers, architects, builders, engineers, carpenters, cabinet makers, as well as steady labourers – many of them obtained employment with the farmers and merchants, who were responsible for them during working hours. Camps were formed in the Government garden and in the Botanical garden in the town, so that the workers might return there after their day's work instead of having to report at Deadwood or Broadbottom, five to seven miles up in the interior. But many of good conduct were allowed to find their own lodgings on condition that they were indoors at a certain time; others, such as shop assistants, bakers, grooms and household servants lived altogether at their employers' residences.

As time went on many who had been commandeered, some who had taken arms against Britain through ill advice, and many who considered they would benefit by so doing, gave in their names

## Victoria Cross Award
## Meiklejohn, Capt. M.F.M., *Gordon Highlanders*

At the Battle of Elandslaagte, 21 October 1899, after main Boer position had been captured, some men of the Gordon Highlanders, when about to assault a kopje in advance, were exposed to a heavy cross fire and, having lost their leaders, commenced to waver. Seeing this, Capt.Meiklejohn rushed to the front and called on the Gordons to follow him. By his conspicuous bravery and fearless example, he rallied the men and led them against the enemy's position, where he fell, desperately wounded in four places. (July 20, 1900.)

to the military as being desirous of peace. It is said that a number, anxious to be on the winning side, offered if allowed to go back, to fight for Britain; and this all caused a great stir and excitement amongst those who were staunch to their own cause; naturally it was a matter for contention, and so bitter did the feeling become, that the authorities were compelled to form another camp (called No. 2 or 'Peace Camp'), where those admitting their desire to become British subjects might be located quite apart from the general camp. These men called themselves 'Loyalists' but by their fellow prisoners they were termed 'Traitors.'

A number of men were allowed liberty each day from the camp at Broadbottom and Deadwood. These in parties rambled all over the country, their rations and kettles with them; they picnicked where they pleased. In groups of ten, twenty, forty of more, they might be seen lighting their fires and boiling their coffee, grilling their steaks, and thoroughly enjoying themselves.

There were one of two disturbances with the members of No.2 camp; and then the rule was made that the liberty from the different camps should be on different days, and thus friction was avoided. As the early months of 1902 passed, the camps became greatly excited over the war news; the more enlightened amongst them, coming to the conclusion that a continuation of the struggle was futile, but the majority maintained obstinately that they could not and would not lose their independence. That seemed to be their one thought (Independence); they never contemplated terms. Owing to an absence of rain and wind, sickness broke out in the camp; this however affected the soldiers and officers more than the prisoners. A number of nurses, with additional (medical) aid arrived, and the enteric gradually declined; still, there were many deaths.

On 1 June came the cable, 'Peace,' with no mention of terms. Prisoners and British were alike loud in their demonstrations, and the stock of champagne in the island was speedily lessened. Britishers were confident the Peace was in their favour; prisoners also were quite as confident they had at last gained their independence. For hours the suspense and excitement was great; then on the following day came the terms, and with them the downfall of the Boer's hopes.

On Sunday, 8 June, thanksgiving services for Peace were offered in the Churches. At the Cathedral a detachment of Royal Garrison Artillery, who had returned from South Africa, attended, and instead of the usual organ music, the Band of the 'Buffs' accompanied the hymn, and played the National Anthem. After service the Artillery lined up near Plantation House, when *His Excellency* the Governor distributed to them the medals and clasps so hardly won in South Africa, and made them a most impressive speech.

After the declaration of Peace and publication throughout the camps of the terms by which the war was ended, notices were posted in English and Dutch throughout the island, and arrangements made for the taking of an oath of allegiance to Great Britain.

*The following Copy of Telegram from Secretary of State to the Governor, St. Helena, dated 5 June, 1902, is published for general information*

By order,

Robert R. Bruce,

For Colonial Secretary.

The Castle, St. Helena

9 June 1902

Terms of surrender of Boers are contained in the document signed 31 May, of which following is the substance. Begins:-

His Excellency General Lord Kitchener and His Excellency Lord Milner, on behalf of the British Government; and General C. Olivier, acting as the Government of the Orange Free State; and Messrs. S.W. Burger, F.W. Reitz, General Louis Botha, J.H. de la Rey, Lucas Meyer, Krogh, acting as the Government of the South African Republic; on behalf of their respective burghers, desirous to terminate the present hostilities, agree on the following:-

Article I

Burgher force will forthwith lay down arms, giving up all munitions of war, and desist from further resistance to the authority of His Majesty King Edward VII, whom they recognise as their lawful sovereign.

Article II

All Burghers in the field outside the limits of the Transvaal, and Orange River Colony, and all prisoners of war at present outside South Africa, who are burghers, will, on duly declaring their acceptance of the position as subjects of His Majesty King Edward the Seventh, be gradually brought back to their homes as soon as transport can be provided, and their means of subsistence secured.

Article III

Burghers surrendering will not be deprived of personal liberty or property.

Article IV

No proceedings to be taken against Burghers surrendering for bona fide acts of war, except in case of certain acts notified to Boer generals by Commander-in-Chief.

Article V

Dutch language to be taught in schools where parents desire it, and to be used in courts of law where necessary.

Article VI

Possession of rifles for their protection to be allowed to persons taking out license.

Article VII

Civil Government to be introduced as soon as possible, followed by representative, leading up to self-government.

Article VIII

No franchise for natives till after introduction of self-government.

Article IX

No special land-tax in Transvaal and Orange River Colony to pay for war.

Article X

His Majesty's Government will set aside 3 000 000 pounds (sterling) for restoration of population to their homes and for making good war losses. Bona fide possession of commandeering receipts, or South African Republican Government notes will be taken as evidence of war losses. In addition His Majesty's Government will make advances on loan to burghers for same purpose.
Please make these terms known to prisoners of war and inform them that preparation will be commenced as soon as possible for their gradual return, but that owing to the denuded state of the country it will take time before all can be brought back.
NOTA BENE - This is the only recognised notification.

NOTICE

From and after Wednesday, 18th inst., those burghers of the late Orange Free State and South African Republic who are desirous of taking the oath of allegiance to His Majesty King Edward VII are directed to attend at the Court House, Jamestown, between the hours of 11.00 to 1.00pm, and from 2.00pm to 4.00pm daily, Sundays and Coronation Day (26 June) excepted.
Permits for this purpose will be granted by Commandants at each camp.
The oath of allegiance will be administered by Col. A.J. Price, C.M.G., and Capt. John Proctor, C.G.A., who have been appointed Special Commissioners.
A.J. Price,
Colonel, O.C.T.

The taking of the Oath was more universal than had been anticipated, though several hung back; amongst these, Woolmarans, who urged the prisoners strongly not to take it.

On 25 June, H.M. transport *Canada* arrived, 5 701 tons, from England (Captain. Maddox), also the British steamer *Wakool*, 3 147 tons,from South Africa (Captain. Thomas); the latter was in quarantine, and brought the 3rd Battalion Royal Sussex Regiment, taking a few days later the Buffs, with their genial Colonel Theodore Brinckman. On the 26th there was great excitement in the town, when over 470 who had taken the oath came from the camp to embark on the *Canada* for South Africa. They were escorted by the band of the 3rd Wilts, and they marched down with Union Jacks flying. Before going off they assembled on the Lower Parade, where H.E. the Governor bade them farewell. He said he was glad to have an opportunity of saying good-bye, and of wishing them good luck in the future. It was a mark of regard on the side of the Government that they were being sent home first, and on arrival at the Cape they would meet the loyalists from Ceylon, and so the first one thousand men to land on their native shores would be those in whom the Government felt confidence. Had all been of their opinion, and refrained from countenancing a hopeless contest, their country would not have been in the same contest, their country would not have been in the same sad condition as it now was. He felt sure, however, that under the firm and just rule of England prosperity would come again, and that all would be firm friends. His Excellency concluded by saying: "I trust we shall always be friends and grow in prosperity day by day. You have been here now over two years and we part with you with regret. We have admired the fortitude and constancy with which you have borne exceptional trials, and I feel that amongst you I am parting with some personal friends of whose welfare in the future I shall always be glad to hear. And now I bid you all good-bye, and wish you all good fortune in the years to come." This was translated in short sentences to the prisoners by Captain Proctor, C.G.A., and was replied to by Commandant Jooste on behalf of himself and his fellow loyalists. He thanked the Governor for all his kindness to them, and then with three cheers for the King, three again for the Governor, and another three for Colonel Wright and other officers, they marched down the parade along the wharf, headed by the band playing 'Auld Land Syne.'

They were hardly able to control their excitement at the thought of seeing all those from whom they had been so long parted and of reaching their native shores after their tedious and enforced exile.

On 4 July, His Excellency received a deputation from the German residents of Deadwood Camp, late prisoners of war. Lieutenant-Colonel Hind, Camp Commandant, introduced the deputation, and Colonel von Braun presented a beautifully carved casket containing an illuminated address, which was read out by Captain Weiss as follows:-

DEADWOOD CAMP

24 June 1902

To His Excellency R. A. Sterndale, Governor of St. Helena.

YOUR EXCELLENCY,-
Having heard that peace has been proclaimed and that the prisoners of war are soon to leave the island, the undersigned take the liberty of addressing your Excellency.
In the first place we wish to express our heartfelt thanks for the kindness and consideration

shown to the prisoners of war by your Excellency in issuing to the inhabitants of the island a seasonable proclamation exhorting them to treat us with the respect due to an honourable foe.

Secondly, we beg your Excellency to convey to the inhabitants of the island our sincerest thanks for the noble manner in which they have responded to your Excellency's appeal. The kindness shown to the prisoners of war one and all by the people of the island, with very few exceptions, is a fact which all long to be remembered and cherished by them as a bright speck in the gloomy days of captivity in St. Helena.

Having received the address, His Excellency replied:-

Colonel von Braun, Captain Weiss, and Gentlemen,-
It is a most agreeable surprise, for which I thank you very much, to receive from you this beautifully illuminated address in such an elegantly carved casket, both of which will always be carefully preserved by me and my family as a valued memento of the past two years.
I thank you heartily, on behalf of myself and the inhabitants of St. Helena, for the kindly sentiments conveyed in the address, and I trust that those friendly feelings which have grown up by the intercourse of the past two years will continue to our lives' end, and bear good fruit in helping to bind our two nations in closer bonds of friendship.
As the time of your departure approaches, I feel I lose some personal friends, who will not, I trust, forget me in the time to come; and to you all I wish good fortune in the future, and a bright, happy meeting at home with those who are so anxiously looking out for a re-union after the weary time, which has now, I am glad to say, passed.

On 30 June General Cronje came into the town, accompanied by his secretary, to the Castle, and there took the oath of allegiance. At his own request, his guard was allowed to remain, as many of the prisoners, still obdurate, were very bitter against him. On 22 August, he left the island for the Cape in the transport *Tagus*, with 994 other prisoners.

Many incidents tend to show the good feeling which sprung up between the prisoners and the military staff in St. Helena.

To Dr. Casey, who was in charge of the medical ward at Deadwood Camp, was presented a very handsome album by some of his Boer patients, J. Noorthout, F. J. Fick, Max Treunissen, C. E. Schutte, and J. Frus. In accepting this, he spoke very highly of his patients. His speech shows how manliness and nobility of character were predominant throughout their time of suffering: *"I never had any patients who were more appreciative and grateful for even the slightest attention, and far from any grumbling or complaining spirit amongst them, they were more disposed to hide their troubles and suffer on in silence."*

*"Who could help admiring the fortitude of such men? Who could refuse to extend a helping hand in the hour of their need?"*

Before leaving for South Africa a public letter was written by the prisoners to the St. Helena Guardian. In this they say:-

We find it impossible to leave St. Helena unless we contribute our share of thankfulness to His Majesty's officers placed over us from time to time, for what they have done to make us take courage to fight the future. Much is owed to His Majesty's officers for the kindness and consideration accorded by them since 12 January 1901, and the conclusion has been made that the prisoners of war have been squarely and gentlemanly treated. The calm Lieutenant-Colonel Paget; the placid and

## Cost of Cronje

Over a four month period to 31 January 1901, the cost of keeping General Cronjé at Kent Cottage for carriage hire, rent and groceries came to £106-17s-7d.

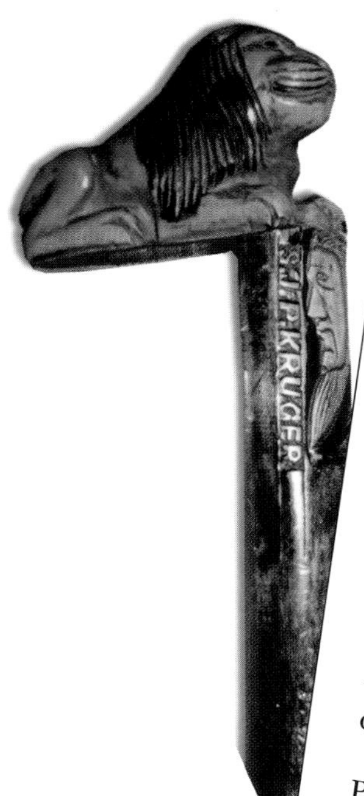

E. R.

# NOTICE.

On days when late Prisoners of War are embarking in any Ship, for South Africa or Europe, no Prisoner of War whether on parole or not, or having passes to work for Employers on the Wharf, and no late Prisoners of War, will be allowed through the Main Gate Jamestown, except those actually embarking and those who are given special passes as mentioned below in Paragraph (b.)

(a.) Those actually embarking must obtain a special permit signed by Captain PROCTOR, Staff Officer for repatriation, which must be given up to the Police on duty at the Main Gate.

(b.) Employers who wish to have Prisoners of War or late Prisoners of War on the Wharf on these days, must send in a nominal roll to the Garrison Adjutant each day.

Special passes will then be given which will be handed by the owners to the Police on duty at the Gate.

By order,

W. H. C. DAVY, Capt.,

Garrison Adjutant.

**St. Helena 16th August 1902.**

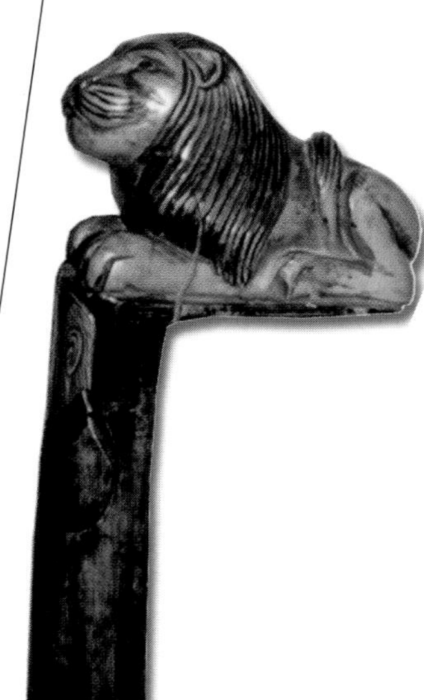

## Prisoners & Guards

At 9 March 1901 there were 5 679 Boer prisoners and guards on St. Helena.

collected Lieutenant-Colonel Barclay and Hind; the manly attitude taken up by Col. Price, C.M.G.; the even and courteous way they have received and met us from time to time - kindness that was a sweet drop in our bitter glass. Their general attitude towards us prisoners of war will always be recounted with pleasure - an attitude at once firm and manly, and worthy of admiration - and why? Because 'politeness' was evinced in all their actions and doings.

Very quickly were the preparations made for the removal of the prisoners. The special court constructed for the administering of the Oath of Allegiance, opened directly after the declaration of peace, continued till September, when it terminated according to the public notice.

By this time very few remained obdurate concerning the oath, and the greater number had already embarked after their enforced sojourn of considerably over two years. The *Golconda* in October took the last batch, and one can imagine how varied were their thoughts, while they travelled back as British subjects to the two republics which have become part and parcel of the British Empire. The ships conveying PoWs from St. Helena were:-

26 June: *Canada* – 370 (Peace Camp) and 110 other prisoners;
7 July: *Kirkfield* – 11 prisoners;
25 July: *Goorkha* – French PoWs to Europe;
1 August: *Abaka* –20 PoWs;
August: *Avondale Castle* – 20 PoWs;
21 August: *Tagus* – 994 PoWs;
21 August: *Canada* – 984 PoWs;
30 August: *Malta* – 990 PoWs;
18 September: *Goorkha* – 12 PoWs;
8 October: *Orotava* – 990 PoWs;
21 October: *Golconda* – the remaining PoWs *but the Cape rebels and a few unpardoned men remained on the island.*

General Ben Viljoen left in July, and Cronje, as before stated, in August by the *Tagus*. During the whole time the prisoners were on the island steamships were constantly arriving with live cattle (and provisions such as potatoes, onions, and the usual tinned rations, as well as medical comforts and stores). It is said each beast cost about £25 in England, which, with about £25 freight, made the sum expended in beef alone for military and prisoners no small item.

In August His Excellency Governor Sterndale had been compelled through ill-health to leave his post, the Governorship being undertaken by Colonel Price, C.M.G., O.C.T., and it was with profound and deep regret that the inhabitants received a cable announcing his death in England of sudden failure of the heart, on 3 October, for he had been expected to arrive again in the island in November. For five years he had administered the Government, and his courteous kindly manner will always be remembered by all classes of society. The fountain in the garden, the road round the West Rocks, the improved wharf, the museum, which it is greatly to be hoped will be kept up and added to, and the new drainage system will testify to his many works of improvement. In November Lieutenant-Colonel Henry Lionel Gallwey, C.M.G., D.S.O., senior division, was appointed Governor.

The West India Regiment had been ordered to St. Helena to replace those regiments stationed there during the war, but the inhabitants, having suffered before from the mutinous conduct of this regiment, petitioned against the order. The Colonial Secretary therefore refused to allow them to proceed on account of the objection raised, and the War Office accordingly decided to send two companies of South African line regiment in their place.

Cronje and his officers.

Boer camp on St. Helena Island.

## *Report by*

# GOVERNOR R. A. STERNDALE

THE YEAR UNDER REPORT has been an eventful one in the history of ST. HELENA, which from its discovery in 1502 has been destined to be a State prison. In 1511 the Portuguese banished a nobleman named FERNANDO LOPEZ to this island. Later on the East India Company sent a Rajah to be interned here but he died on the voyage; then came the memorable exile of Napoleon, which brought ST. HELENA in prominent notice, and recently when the question arose what should be done with the Boer prisoners of war, ST. HELENA naturally suggested itself as the safest and most suitable place.

Deadwood Plain.

On 10 April 1900, the Transport *'Milwaukee'*, escorted by H.M.S. *'Niobe'*, CAPTAIN A.L. WINSLOE, arrived with CRONJE (pictured right), SCHIEL, WOLMARANS and other leaders and a large number of prisoners; during the year successive transports came in with batches of Boers, till the number we have now amounts to 4 600. More would have been sent but for the difficulty of providing water in suitable spots. We have two camps, *Deadwood Plain* and *Broad Bottom*. *Deadwood Plain* is a high plateau adjacent to Longwood, treeless, and wind swept, but with a porous soil which dries up quickly after heavy rain.

Its healthiness had been tested in 1899 by encamping the West Indian troops there, and it has been well proved since by the rapid way in which disappeared the enteric fever which the prisoners brought with them, their general good health since, and their escape from influenza during the epidemic which prostrated nearly the whole of the Islanders.

If a larger supply of water could have been delivered on this plain the whole of the prisoners might have been located there, but we had hard work to increase the old supply to meet the needs of 3 000 men, including troops; the original sources were springs under *Diana's Peak*, and there was a good deal of waste, this was remedied by making concrete basins and tanks at each spring, and adding to the system other small springs that had been left out, and by renewing the old pipes, and so the volume of water was doubled.

The two camps are about five miles apart. *Broad Bottom* lies more in a hollow and is in fact a broad shallow valley about 1600 feet above the sea. The soil is more clayey than *Deadwood*, and the climate more humid, but the water supply is good, and the prisoners enjoy good health. The property is hired from the HONOURABLE G.N. MOSS, who has allowed the football teams of the camp the use of some high flat land for the game. The prisoners have a large amount of liberty, a certain number being let out under passes every day. They have been hitherto very well behaved, and I have had no complaints from the people of the Island regarding any misconduct; a number of them have been allowed to take service with farmers and others who have made themselves responsible for their safety. The Colonial Government employed, under the orders of CAPTAIN D.B. THOMSON, 28TH BOMBAY PIONEERS, about forty men, with Captain Waldeck and Baron Fagerskiold (both Prisoners of War) in the construction of the West Rocks Road and the extension of the wharf. They have been encamped in the Public Gardens in Jamestown, and their conduct has been most satisfactory. A number are also employed by the Imperial Government.

## St. Helena *Guardian* — 12 APRIL 1900

# ARRIVAL OF BOER PRISONERS

### Sailed from Cape Town on 5 April 1900 with Schiel.

The prisoners are indeed most anxious to obtain work; the pay is not so much an object as the relief from the monotony of the camp. We have relieved this as much as possible by encouraging work of all kinds, chiefly carving in wood and making walking sticks, for which purpose I have supplied them with many hundreds of sticks from the extensive thickets of privet growing in the Government House grounds. I have also given them the thinning out of fir plantations and poles of the Furcroea Aloe for the construction of recreation rooms and school houses. The Commissariat arrangements are admirable, the quality of the beef issued to the camps is first rate; some of the oxen imported have excited the admiration of the farmers of the Island.

I have in my possession photographs of two prime beasts, one of which came from Lord Rosebery's estates in Scotland, and which weighed 1250 lbs. after being slaughtered and dressed.

The gross lies which have been circulated in the Continental papers about our treatment of the prisoners have aroused considerable indignation here, even amongst the prisoners themselves.

The Boer Hospital in Jamestown is fitted up in a perfect manner, and the patients when convalescent are loath to leave.

The fair and honest among the prisoners, whilst upholding their opinion that they were right to fight and would fight again in the same cause, acknowledge that they are well treated, and there are a few who have expressed a wish to settle in the Island after the war.

As regards the benefits derived by the Colony from the presence of the Boers and troops, the increase in the Revenue is the chief one, the Customs being especially benefited by large importations by the Island merchants. The Imperial Government do not pay either duty or wharfage so that no direct advantage has accrued from the prisoners of troops. To house property there has been some benefit, for owners have availed themselves of cheap Boer labour to carry out repairs which were, in most cases, much needed. The owners of country produce have also benefited by the great demand for, and consequent high prices of, vegetables, poultry, eggs, milk, and butter; also for the hire of transport animals, viz., horses and donkeys; the price of the latter has risen from about £2 a piece to about £5.

On the other hand the Island has suffered from deforestation owing to contracts for fuel being placed locally, which is a serious matter; and the roads are cut to pieces by the heavy traffic of mule wagons, which might have been avoided had pack-mules been used, as recommended by me at the outset.

The few pack-mules we have work very well. It has, however, been a hard time for the horses and donkeys of the Island employed by the contractors for transport service.

The forces in the Colony were commanded by Colonel J.B.Leefe, R.M.A., from the arrival of the prisoners on 10 April until 7 December, when he was invalid home, and the command devolved upon Lieutenant-Colonel T.J.P. Evans, R.M.L.I. The 4th Battalion Gloucestershire Regiment is under the command of Lieutenant-Colonel Earl Bathurst.

Our Colonial forces are limited to a Company of Volunteer Sharpshooters, raised by myself in 1898. The corps is popular with the Islanders, and there would be no difficulty in increasing the number were it necessary. The men are all efficient. In order to increase the esprit de corps and to induce resort to health amusements, we have started an Institute for the Company, with billiard and bagatele tables, newspapers and magazines, which, I think, will be very popular and beneficial.

Desalination chimney.

## Smorenburg Escapee

One man succeeded in outwitting all the guards and leaving the island. He was Commandant A. Smorenburg, a tall Hollander who had settled in the Transvaal in the eighties of the last century and had served as a policeman and detective.

Smorenburg formed his escape plan when he overheard a British officer telling someone that he was sending a case of Boer curios to his address in England. Very soon Smorenburg obtained a crude packing case, and enlarged it so that he could sit inside with provisions and water. The case finally measured 4 feet in length, 2 feet 1 inch in height and 2 feet broad. Smorenburg consigned it to the address in Gloucester, England, of the officer commanding Deadwood Camp in St.Helena, knowing that this officer had already forwarded several cases of curios to his home, and hoping that one more would not arouse suspicion.

The case was marked: *'Boer curios - this side up with care'*. But Smorenburg took the precaution of fitting the case with 3 doors so that he could let himself out whatever the position of the case might be in the ship's hold. The doors were disguised with iron bands which appeared to be clamped round the corners.

Smorenburg had decided to allow himself to be loaded on board the Union-Castle steamer *Goth*, which was to call at Ascension and Las Palmas after leaving St.Helena for England. He hoped to land at Las Palmas, where the ship was to load bananas, and then make his way to Holland. To be on the safe side he allowed himself food and water for 20 days. Army biscuits, Bully Beef, Mac Connachie's rations and jam were packed in a bag weighing 15 pounds, and fastened to the floor in such a way that he could rest his knees on it when reclining. Water was carried in 2 tin containers specially moulded to fit round his chest, and he had several military water bottles as well. A few empty bottles and containers completed the equipment of the packing-case. A censors seal should have been affixed, but this was not available and Smorenburg took the risk of going without it.

It was on 20 December 1901, that the packing-case (with only the food and water inside) was taken to the hospital in Deadwood Camp and loaded on to an ambulance bound for the

---

**ST. HELENA *Guardian*** **1 MARCH 1900**

### AMMUNITION PACKED AS FRUIT

A Plymouth man serving with the forces in South Africa, in a letter written at Stormberg on 30 October to his relatives in this country, says, "*We had a very good haul this week. In a truck bound from Cape Town to the Transvaal, there were noticed two large boxes labelled* 'Dates to be kept cool'. *Someone felt inquisitive and thought he would like to sample these dates. When the boxes were lifted, they were found to be exceedingly heavy and orders were given to force the covers. This was done and lo and behold there stood a grand lot of ammunition for the Boers. So of course,* 'we kept the dates cool'."

wharf at Jamestown. This clever piece of trickery was achieved by J.W. Smorenburg, nephew of the escaper, who acted as his uncle's orderly. The plan almost came to grief, however, on the way down the steep valley road to Jamestown. The ambulance was simply a mule cart, and the driver managed to upset it and the packing-case landed in a ditch. Fortunately it did not break open. No one on the wharf suspected anything, and the case was left outside with a pile of baggage belonging to a detachment of Royal Marines who were going to Ascension Island.

Commandant Smorenburg had a parole pass which enabled him to leave Deadwood Camp during the daylight hours on 4 days to break his parole. However, the parole did not apply at night, and in the early hours of 21 December he slipped through the sentries at Deadwood Camp and reached the wharf. To his dismay he could not locate his box.

It looked as though the plan had failed. Smorenburg was a most determined man, however, and he made up his mind to search the lighters offshore before giving up the attempt. A naval vessel in harbour was using her searchlight intermittently, and Smorenburg had to avoid the beams as he swam away from the wharf. The first lighter was empty, but he was delighted to find his box under the tarpaulin in the second lighter. He pulled out the pegs which held each door in position, crept inside, and secured everything. The discomfort of wet clothes was forgotten in the excitement when he realised that the first stage of his escape had been successful. Then, exhausted after his long swim, he fell asleep.

Smorenburg awoke to the rattle of winches. They were hoisting the cargo out of the lighter, and the packing-case of 'Boer curios' landed on the deck of the *Goth* with a crash, but without breaking open. Then it was man-handled, turned over and over and lowered into the baggage-room. Some hours later the hatch was closed. Then the engines started and Smorenburg decided that it would be safe to leave the box. This was difficult, for it had been placed upside down among the marines' kit-bags. However, Smorenburg lit a candle which he had in his pocket and crawled out at last.

His first task was to move his packing-case, and the kit and heavy cases surrounding it, so that he could slip into his hiding-place at a moment's notice and come out without being trapped. This was hot work, and it had to be done as silently as possible. By the time Smorenburg had arranged everything to his satisfaction he was suffering from a raging thirst, and drank more of his fresh water supply than he could really afford.

Seamen entered the baggage-room the next day and moved some of the cases without

disturbing Smorenburg in any way. The next day was Christmas Eve, and Smorenburg could hear the passengers singing on deck. The ship slowed down early on Christmas Day, and Smorenburg knew she was approaching the Ascension Island anchorage. He had been in the habit of sitting under a ventilator and sleeping on the floor of the baggage-room; for although the whole compartment was hot, his packing case was almost intolerable. When the anchor went down, however, Smorenburg had to take cover. The hatch was removed and all the Ascension baggage was hauled out. When the hatch was closed Smorenburg felt that he was safe.

Perhaps Smorenburg would have reached Las Palmas and escaped but for the newly-laid cable between Ascension and St.

Special Pass.

P. of War W. le Roux has permission to be absent from hospital precincts from 6 a.m 12.8.'02, to 6 p.m 13.8.'02, for the purpose of proceeding to Deadwood Camp

Recommended by.

Boer Hospital.
Jamestown.
St Helena.
11.8.1902.

M.O

Helena. He had been missed at roll-call on the day after his departure, and the fact that the *Goth* had just left the island provided an obvious clue. It also seems probable that when the hue and cry was raised, some prisoner-of-war gave away the story of the packing-case. At all events a cable was sent to the naval captain in command of Ascension Island instructing him to have the case of *'Boer Curios'* opened.

Thus the unhappy Smorenburg heard the baggage-room hatch being removed for a second time. He hurried back into his case, and saw through the peep-hole an officer and a number of seamen coming down the ladder. The officer was Mr.John Attwood, who retired in 1934 as captain of the Balmoral Castle. *"I was so overcome with excitement and despair that I grabbed and drained two bottles of water,"* Smorenburg told his friends. Attwood rapped on the case, and Smorenburg called weakly: *"Stop! I'll come out."*

The surgeon of the *Goth*, Dr. Paisley, who examined Smorenburg that morning, remarked: *"I think Jonah in the whales belly had a more comfortable time than Smorenburg."* Smorenburg was in a fainting condition when he reached the deck. Attwood revived him with a brandy and soda, followed by a bath and eggs and bacon and coffee. He was sent back to St. Helena (with the packing-case as evidence) in H.M.S. *Gibraltar*. A court of inquiry was held, and Smorenburg was imprisoned in High Knoll Fort, reserved for *'turbulent Boers,'* until peace was signed. He had not broken his parole, and was not charged with any such offense. That was just as well, for an officer who breaks his parole as a prisoner-of-war is liable to the death penalty. Smorenburg's box and a number of documents bearing on the escape were presented by the Governor of St. Helena to the Africana Museum in Johannesburg some years ago. Smorenburg, I may add, became a motor-car licensing officer for the Johannesburg Municipality, a sworn translator for the Supreme Court, and a Justice of the Peace.

*"Time heals all wounds,"* wrote Smorenburg in a letter to Captain Attwood not long before World War II. *"I bear no grudge of ill-will against anyone. If the present unsettled world conditions should unfortunately result in war my services, if required, are at the disposition of the British Commonwealth of which my country forms a part".* ❑

***Reference:***

*South African Beachcomber*, Lawrence G Green (1958)

## RENT

The Saint Helenans weren't shy of charging rent for the use of the land that the British used as PoW camp sites.

**Deadwood Camp:** Mr. Deason was compensated at the sum of £50.00 per month.

**Broadbottom Camp:** Mr. Moss asked for and received £75.00 per month.

# BROADBOTTOM BREEZES

Tea-time at Broadbottom Camp.

BROADBOTTOM cannot boast of the many races and tongues which give Deadwood the appearance of a miniature Mecca of all nations.

The apparent want of variety and evident contentment might lead the careless observer to mistake our camp for the realisation of some Utopian dream, and the repeated assurances of the sentries that *"All's well"* would confirm the idea; yet once within the gates the illusion vanishes and whilst not being altogether a city of woe the majority seem to take the pleasures of prisoner of war life indifferently, if not sadly. I have not yet encountered any individual bursting with gratitude for this excursion to the tomb of *le petit Corporal*; historic associations possess little charm for the history maker, but in spite of the general depression there are to be found in this little world of Afrikaanerdom many characters and scenes rich enough to supply a philosophic nomad with food for amusement, reflection, and a bilious attack. My stable companion, the Sound Reader, does not agree with Bret Harte's gambler that one must always recognise the usual percentage in favour of the dealer; he has a habit of lying supinely on his back, but instead of hugging the delusive phantom of hope spends the time I usually set apart for a siesta in consigning to eternal perdition the inventors of barbed wire and bayonets.

Towards evening it is customary to wander forth *'with ripe meerschaum cushioned on the lower lip'* and the ramble presents more variety than is noticeable from the prosaic world beyond the deal line. The chief resort is George Moll's buffet known to the camp policeman as the Kalihara Café, where for the humble *'dubbeltje'* you may torture your inward with a 4.7 tart, or those blessed with more epicurean tastes are free to wade through some African delight known in the current vernacular as *'Boeppens'*.

Connoisseurs, however, seem to prefer the *'St. Helena Sharp-shooter'*, so styled by reason of its aimless propensities; the last named delicacy must be negotiated in skirmishing order. It may be necessary to state that your correspondent, with the happy knack of a thorough Romany, has an unpaid score at the abovementioned rendezvous hence this flattering ad. Amongst the habitue may be seen a quaint old Deutscher gentlemen alternately carving a stick and sipping tea; two well known characters discussing the possible price, after the war, of F.C. in Bloemfontein; and the ever present Othello recounting for the thousandth time the battles, sieges, and fortunes he has passed. Our camp has undergone some change during the last month. Some few of our number have transferred their domiciles to a higher altitude, others to more friendly surroundings. In camp a new town has been proclaimed to be hereafter known as *'Lappiesdorp'*, and the scene on the 19th instant, when the exodus took place recalled memories of the palmy days of the New Rush and Vaal River diggings, when towns sprung up while you waited. One row of stands has been reserved for the mercantile community and some startling advertisements are expected in the forthcoming issue of *De Krijgsgevangene*. The doings of the Debating Society are followed with the greatest interest, and the fate of kingdoms, empires, and republics are decided in the local senate with a facility perfectly refreshing. The sporting fraternity are preparing to erect a suitable Recreation Hall where members may congregate and discuss questions nearest their hearts. *'Tot weder ziens.'*

Wash day at Broadbottom Camp.

CENSOR'S OFFICE, JAMESTOWN 31 MAY 1900

To: Colonel A.J. Price. C.M.G Officer Commanding Troops, St. Helena
From: Von Anlefeldtz, Official Censor to the Boer PoWs

# MAY REPORT

This month we had rather an unusual amount of incoming letters owing to some extra steamers arriving, and the outgoing amount of letters was also a good deal larger, as many were allowed to write a few extra letters announcing to their relatives the probability of an early departure from here to Antigua. I am able to state that we have mastered our work nicely and the office is free of any accumulation.

A rather large consignment of tobacco had been detained here, owing to insufficient proof of being a free gift, and according to your instruction the import duty has been paid, amounting to over £20 this month. By the last Mailboat a still larger quantity of tobacco and cigars arrived, also other articles such as Cocoa, Margarine and various other goods, evidently for the purpose of trading. The consignee has tried his best by false statements to make believe, that the whole shipment was a free gift sent to various Prisoners in Camp, but he has not bargained that we were in possession of his letters ordering the named goods from Holland. The importation of such goods for the purpose of trading or supplying the different shops in the camps is contrary to the existing rules. All camp shops must buy their supplies from the military dry canteen, which again buy their goods too early. I am awaiting your instructions to deal with this special or any other similar cases.

The tone and feeling expressed by the Boer Prisoners of War in the outgoing letters this month, is cramped with speculations of the supported mutiny of Boer delegates and the sincere hope of peace; but of foreigners, especially Hollanders on the probability of being removed from here to Antigua and in many instances they have instructed their relatives to write no more letters to St. Helena, but to address them to Antigua, such I had mostly stopped in order to prevent letters being sent there, before we receive definite instructions. The Boer rejoices when he hears that the Hollanders may be sent away, but on the other hand many of the Dyke inhabitants are rather disheartened and would of course prefer to remain here or to be sent straight to their fatherland.

The incoming letters from the Cape unanimously speak of peace and are certain of a successful settlement, all are urging their relatives to become as soon as possible British subjects in order to return and look after their homes, we had several touching letters from fathers writing to their sons pointing out their folly.

I feel sure that soon after the departure of the Hollanders, the remaining Prisoners will give us no trouble, their great desire is to return to South Africa, and further the greater part is now convinced, that the Hollanders are to be blamed for keeping on the struggle, by everlastingly furnishing them with false hopes of foreign intervention.

The selection of such to be sent back, ought to be made very carefully, and I think that this office is in position to render great assistance in this matter, as we are getting closer connected with the views and ideas of the Prisoners of War.

A special list is kept for the purpose of showing different remarks and sentiments expressed in their letters. Should, with the batch of Prisoners to be sent to Antigua, one Censor be ordered to proceed, I consider it of great help and assistance to the authorities there.

In this case I do not consider it necessary to apply for an additional Censor in this office, should the work become too great, perhaps an alteration could be made, for the removal of one of the Staff Interpreters to Jamestown, as their work is practically nil, or an allowance could be made for overtime work, when such is needed.

No. 64
1321

E. R.

Whereas, at the time of the outbreak of hostilities between the Government of Her late Majesty Queen Victoria and the Governments of the late South African Republic and the late Orange Free State, I, the undersigned... Cai William Waldemar, Baron von Ahlefeldt Ludwigsburg

of*...... Zeerust District Marico

now residing at.... Mafeking

was a burgher of the South African Republic; and

Whereas the said South African Republic has been annexed to, and become part of, the dominions of His Majesty King Edward the Seventh; and

Whereas, I am desirous of formally claiming and securing all and sundry the rights and privileges of a British subject, which, by reason of the fact of annexation as aforesaid, I am now justly entitled to do;

Now, therefore, I hereby formally declare that I acknowledge myself to be a subject of His Majesty King Edward the Seventh, and I do sincerely promise and swear that I will be faithful and bear true allegiance to His Most Gracious Majesty, King Edward the Seventh, His Heirs and Successors according to law.

Von Ahlefeldt

Sworn and declared before me at... Mafeking...

this....7th.....day of.. January 1902

C W Wyrgan (?)

Special Commissioner.

*Fill in name of farm or town, ward and district.

[T.O.

---

**St. Helena *Guardian*** **18 December 1899**

## NEW ZEALANDERS INVOLVED IN BATTLE AT NAAUWPORT 11 JANUARY 1900

The Argentine horses now being sent to the Cape from Beunos Aires are not suitable for cavalry charges but are to be used for transport and ambulance work. The war office has ordered 950 000 lbs of corned beef from Chicago to be supplied within 10 days.

A special steamer carries it to South Africa. Ceylon are sending a gift of 30 000 LBS of tea to the troops. 40 000 000 rounds of ammunition sent by sea 22 February. There will be over 1 000 rounds per rifle.

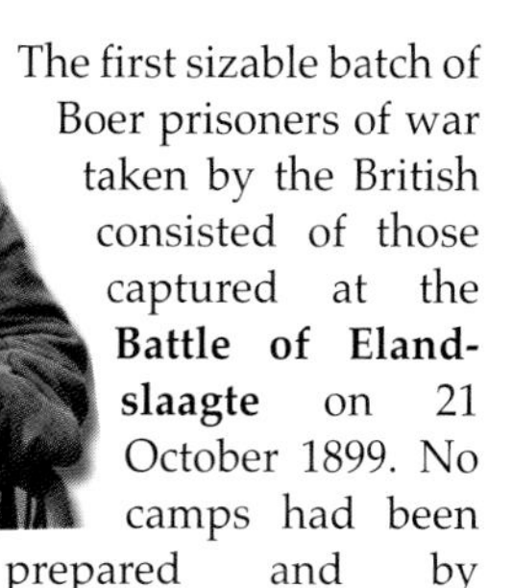

# Boer Prisoners of War

The first sizable batch of Boer prisoners of war taken by the British consisted of those captured at the **Battle of Elandslaagte** on 21 October 1899. No camps had been prepared and by arrangement with the Naval authorities these prisoners (approximately 200 men) were temporarily housed on the naval guard ship HMS Penelope in Simon's Bay. Several ships were used as floating prisoner of war camps until permanent camps were established at **Greenpoint**, **Cape Town** and **Bellevue**, **Simonstown**. The first prisoners were accommodated in **Bellevue** on 28 February 1900. Wounded prisoners were sent to the old Cape Garrison Artillery Barracks at Simonstown which had been converted into the **Palace Hospital**. The first wounded arrived on 2 November 1899.

With the first invasion of the Cape Colony – at the end of 1900 – prisoners at Cape Town and Simonstown were held captive aboard various ships. At the end of December 1900 some 2 550 men were placed on board the *Kildonan Castle* where they remained for six weeks before they were removed to two other transports at Simons' Bay.

The camp at **Ladysmith**, **Natal** was in use from 20 December 1900 to January 1902. It was mainly used as a staging camp although it had some 120 prisoners of war. Another staging camp was established at **Umbilo** in **Natal**. Prisoners of war (repatriated to South Africa after the cessations of hostilities) were sent on arrival to either **Simons' Town** or **Umbilo** where they were given with blankets and clothing before being sent by train to their final destinations. As the war developed the number of prisoners increased and the provision of accommodation raised some serious problems for the British authorities – particularly after the surrender of General Cronje and ± 4000 burghers at **Paardeberg**.

To keep large camps supplied while conducting a war over vast areas would impose intolerable strains on an already overburdened supply line. To add to this was the very real danger of insurrections in the areas bordering the camps and the risk of the release of the captives. The solution to the problem was found ... ship the prisoners overseas. The first overseas camps were opened in **St Helena**. The *SS Milwaukee* arrived off **St Helena** on 11 April 1900 with 514 prisoners on board. This was the first batch of some 5000 prisoners housed in the two camps on the island, i.e. **Broadbottom** and **Deadwood**.

Six groups of prisoners from South Africa were landed in the **Bermudas** during the period 28 June 1901 to 16 January 1902. The camps were situated on islands in the Great Sound, i.e. **Burts** (400 men); **Darrell's** (1100 men); **Hawkins** (1300 men); **Hinson's** (120 men); **Morgans** (850 men); **Tuckers** (800 men). The first batch of prisoners arrived in **Ceylon** on 9 August 1900 with others following until some 5000 prisoners had landed.

**Diyatalawa** was the main camp, **Mt Lavinia** the convalescent camp and dissidents – the *irreconcilables* were kept at **Ragama**.

A camp for prisoners on parole was opened at **Urugasmanhandiya** and **Hambantota** in September 1901. Other camps were established throughout **India** at **Abottabad**; **Ahmednagar**; **Bellary**; **Bhim Tal**; **Dagshai**; **Solon**; **Fort Govindgarh**; **Kaity-Nilgiris**; **Satara**; **Shahjahanpur**; **Sialkot**; **Upper Topa**; **Umballa** and **Trichinopol** ❑

## THE YOUNGEST SOLDIERS?

What is extremely hard to believe is the age of many Boers fighting in the field. Paging through back copies of the Cape Times of March and May 1902, it came as a shock when reading a column titled *'Boer casualties – an official War communique'* which states that W. Lyons, aged 13 years, died at the Point, Natal, on 21 March 1902, from the Harrismith district. A month later Christoffel Lombardt, from Glasgow in the Vrede district, died at Bellary from disease. Like Lyons, young Christoffel was a mere 13 years old and both were interned in Prisoner of War camps.

STEVE'S WAR STORIES

## DEPRESSION

Cor van Gogh, brother of Vincent, committed suicide whilst in a British PoW camp. He had served with the Boers in the "International Legion", which was made up of volunteers from all parts of the world.

**Generals of the Anglo-Boer War**, *Phillip Bateman, 1977*
Purnell & Sons (SA) (Pty) Ltd

***The young Joubert Reitz gave expression in this poem to the feeling of grief and longing of some 26 000 Boers who were sent to various camps, forts and gaols in Natal, along the Cape coast, St. Helena, Bermuda, Ceylon (Sri Lanka) and India as prisoners of war.***

# THE SEARCHLIGHT

When the searchlight from the gunboat; Throws its rays upon my tent;
Then I think of home and comrades; And the happy days I spent;
In the country where I come from; And where all I love are yet;
Then I think of things and places; And of scenes I'll ne'er forget.
Then a face comes up before me; Which will haunt me to the last;
And I think of things that have been; And happiness that's past;
And only then I realise; How much my freedom meant;
When the searchlight from the gunboat;
Cast its rays upon my tent.

*David Merrington. Tel: (021) 712-1641*

# 'FieldCraft' Commemorative Figurines

For those who would like a souvenir of the centenary of the Anglo-Boer War, the large-scale military figurines made by Doordrift Studio are ideal *objets d'art*, excellent gifts or items for display.

The figurines in the *FieldCraft* range are 20 centimetres in height, made of hand-painted white metal, on polished wooden bases. The range includes Regular Cavalry, Mounted Infantry, Highlanders, Naval Ratings, Boer commando riders, and other period types. These figurines are scrupulously researched, hand-made, and individually numbered, and will prove to be prized commemorative items.

David Merrington, at Doordrift Studio, Cape Town, has developed the *FieldCraft* range of figurines specially to commemorate the centenary. Merrington was a Petty Officer in the SA navy, has studied Fine Art, and has an MA in English Literature. He likes to think that this varied background enables him to produce a well-researched and well-made piece which is also invested with understanding and compassion. Some years of research into technical aspects such as uniforms, equipment, and weaponry have been necessary to do an accurate authentic job. Above all, however, it is the old photographs of faces and characters, as well as the work of war artists at the time, that really motivate Merrington's work.

The *FieldCraft* Series is produced in limited editions of 99 pieces each in order to maintain a proper commemorative value. Merrington numbers each piece and also registers ownership of each figurine. He sculpts the originals in wax and then makes a mould to cast the final pieces in a mixture of pewter and white metal. The stands are made from Jacaranda wood.

The first of the series, which is illustrated here, represents a sergeant of the Gordon Highlanders. The design was inspired by a contemporary painting after Caton Woodville, entitled *"All that was Left of Them"* which represents the Black Watch in the aftermath of Magersfontein.

Second in the series is a private of the 5TH Lancers, who came to South Africa direct from India – retaining the India pattern helmet and chain mail epaulettes. A trooper of the ILK will therefore follow the 5th Lancer in the FieldCraft series. David Merrington says that for the present cavalry figures will be presented as dismounted. He·plans to have castings of horses later this year. Among other figurines on offer during the Centenary are Boer soldiers, a naval rating, a piper, a trooper of Rimington's Scouts, and an interpretation of the *'Absent-Minded Beggar'* from Kipling's poem, which became such a popular image during the Boer War. Contemporary prints and figurines of this character are now highly prized by collectors. All the *'FieldCraft'* products are packed in sturdy and attractively labelled boxes, suitable for mailing or carrying safely in luggage. Each one includes a pamphlet describing the details of the piece and a brief history, with information about the *FieldCraft* range. ❑

### *Kimberley Engineering Works (Pty) Ltd. Tel: (053) 841 0474*

## Model of the Long Cecil

The Long Cecil model, manufactured by Kimberley Engineering Works (Pty) Ltd, known in 1899 as De Beers Workshops and producers of the original *'Long Cecil'* is on limited offer so it would be wise to place your order as soon as possible. A design model from articles from *The Model Engineer and Electrician* Vol. XXX No.662 & No.663 January 1-8, 1914 has been used. The model has been painted in the original colour of the period and stands on a wooden base with a plaque.

Visit the Kimberley Engineering Works for a tour – see the lathe that was used to turn the barrel of the original *'Long Cecil'* and a showcase of the original tooling.

In addition, a visit to George Labram's house may be possible.

For further information contact: Derek Preece, Managing Director, Kimberley Engineering Works (Pty) Ltd. Tel: (053) 841 0474 or fax (053) 842 1192. e-mail: kew@kimnet.co.za ❑

### *Cameron Blake. Tel: (021) 423 2831*

## Handcrafted Busts of British & Boer Soldiers

Cameron Blake, a 30-year old Capetonian, handcrafts busts modelled from modeller's putty in meticulous detail, with quality paint finishes (with each bust taking ±100 hours to complete). As each bust is a 'one-off' and unique unto itself (no moulding technique or casting process is used) prospective clients may (and do) request specific details. As Cameron has been a military collector for the last ten years, much essential and meticulous research goes into each bust. His books on the subject (especially the photographs therein) provide the foundation and to the best of his knowledge, each is as historically accurate as this research allows.

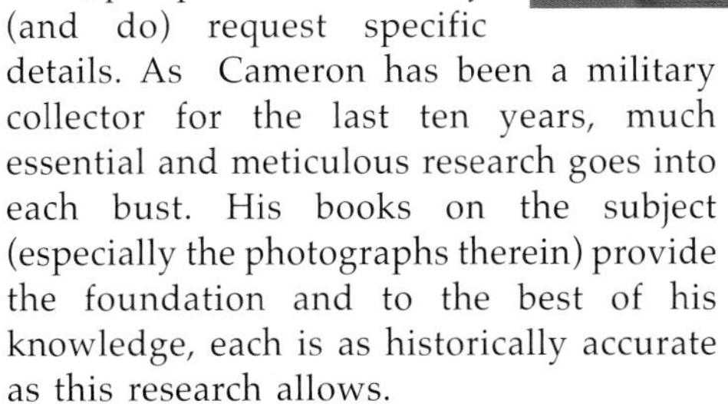

If a client wishes to have a bust depicting a British soldier from October 1899, for example, it would be very different to one depicted towards the end of the war. (By then their uniforms and accoutrements had changed slightly – in the beginning of the war pith-helmets, bearing regimental markings on one side, were the standard norm, but eventually gave way to slouch-hats and slovenly appearances.) By the same token, the client might request a bust of a smartly dressed Boer, clothed with a government equipped tunic, as opposed to (as seen later in the war) a Boer wearing a captured British tunic and *Lee Enfield* (after scavenging the battlefields for clothing and ammunition). Cameron began making the busts two years ago. Initially, they were not for sale but he decided to market his talent. His busts include subjects from the *Zulu War of 1879, 1ST & 2ND Anglo-Boer War, World War I* and *Third Reich*. The completed bust, mounted on a wooden base (overall height ± 20 cm), is accompanied by a hand-written letter of authenticity to its genuine hand-made qualities and a description of the busts' specifics. Cameron concludes that October 1999 marked the beginning of a 3-year period in which to concentrate his artistic talent and in so doing, remembers the conflict that involved so many. ❑

*Anita & Zane Palmer. Tel: (041) 32 3087*

# Handcrafted Model Cannons

*Serious collectors of Anglo-Boer War memorabilia must include the exquisitely handcrafted model cannons by **Zane Palmer** in their collection.*

Zane Palmer at 35 years of age, has been making quality model cannons for almost three decades. As a very young boy, Zane witnessed the firing of a model steel cannon and was so captured by the experience that he soon started making his own model guns. He was only six years old when he completed his first cannon at his father's *tin can and nails* factory in East London. Since then, he has perfected his skills, knowledge and techniques resulting in some of the most exquisite handcrafted model cannons available. He has travelled extensively in pursuit of information, drawings and photographs to enable him to perfect his models and widen his range. A qualified mechanical engineer, Zane intends to soon start manufacturing model cannons on a full-time basis for the purposes of exporting. His work material includes wood, steel, brass and bronze.

Except for the *'Long Tom'* and *'Long Cecil'* featured during the Anglo Boer Centenary celebrations, other models available include:

$^1/_6$ scale British Horse Artillery 6-Pounder (1846); $^1/_{10}$ scale 68-Pounder Carronade (1759-1855); $^1/_{18}$ scale 11" Dahlgren Gun (1851). ❑

---

These $^1/_{16}$ scale replicas of the War's most famous guns – the *'LONG CECIL'* and *'LONG TOM'* – are fashioned in steel and brass and will no doubt be some of the most desirable collectables attainable during the centenary celebrations.

The *'Long Cecil'* was instrumental in the successful defence of the world's richest diamond mines during the four-month siege of Kimberley by the Boers during the Anglo Boer War in 1899 to 1900. Soon after the Boers laid siege to Kimberley, the British inside the town realised that they needed a gun that could out-range the Boer artillery. Commissioned by Cecil John Rhodes and designed by the Chief Engineer of mine owners De Beers Consolidated Ltd, George Labram, the gun was manufactured in the De Beers workshops in 29 days (26 December 1899 to 23 January 1900).

The shells each had 'DE BEERS' and a diamond shaped cast into the base, while some even had 'WITH COMPTS CJR' (Rhodes initials) stamped on the body.

Its first round was fired by a woman, Mrs Pickering, wife of the Secretary to the De Beers Company – after the senior Gunner, Lt-Col. Chamier, refused (on the grounds that as a member of the Royal Regiment he was not permitted to fire guns not officially approved by the War Office).

The gun continued in action engaging Boer positions to the north and north-west of town, often targeting Kamfersdam where the Boers' most devastating weapon, a *'Long Tom'* was stationed.

During its 28 days in service *'Long Cecil'* fired *260 rounds in action*, doing more firing whilst in service than any other gun in Kimberley throughout the whole period of the siege.

Zane's models of this famous cannon are handcrafted off the original drawings which he sourced from the Kimberley Engineering Works. ❑

***Long Cecil General Information:***

Type: 4.1" Artillery
Scale: 1/16 scale
Granite base: 610 mm
Carriage width: 120 mm
Carriage height: 96 mm
Barrel length: 180 mm
Barrel diameter: 30 mm
Barrel bore: 6.5 mm

---

Manufactured by the Schneider Company at Le Creusot, Belgium in 1897, the ***'Long Tom'*** had a maximum range of 9000 metres and a calibre of 155 mm

Four *'Long Toms'*, which were also referred to as *Creusot guns*, were sent to South Africa to be erected at forts around Pretoria but were withdrawn and sent to the Boer fronts at the start of the Anglo Boer War.

It is ironic that the creator of the *'Long Cecil'*, George Labram, was killed by a shell from a *'Long Tom'* soon after it was sent to Kimberley in February 1900. The cannons were drawn from one battlefield to the next by a span of oxen, which proved a slow and tedious task. To ensure that a *'Long Tom'* never fell into British hands the Boers destroyed each gun when they could no longer outmanoeuvre the swiftly approaching British forces.

After the war pieces of the guns were collected and a cannon was assembled and sent to England as a souvenir. However, a need for steel during the First World War necessitated it being melted down.

To this day there are no drawings for the *'Long Tom'* as the factory where it was made was completely destroyed during the Second World War. The only drawings that remain are the side views that came with the guns manual. Today there are very few pieces remaining of the original guns. Four replicas of *'Long Toms'* exist in South Africa and are displayed in KwaZulu Natal and the Free State.

Zane's models of the *'Long Tom'* are based on the side views of the guns manual, consultation with other experts such as those who manufactured the existing replicas and **Prof. Louis Changuion** who has produced a book on the *'Long Tom'* and his own in depth knowledge of cannons.

***Long Tom General Information:***

Type: Fort Gun

Scale: 1/16 scale

Carriage height: 127 mm

Barrel length: 262 mm

Barrel bore: 9 mm

Each model is displayed to perfection on a granite base with a glass cover. Packaged in a wooden ammunition box, each cannon is shipped with its historical information.

As the 1/16 scale models are part of a limited edition, brass plaques are attached on which the cannon's registered number is certified. As far as possible, a register is kept by Zane of each model together with the name of its new owner. ❑

For further information please write to:
Zane R. Palmer, 14 Nathan Road, Broadwood, Port Elizabeth 6070, South Africa, or
Telephone/fax: 027 041 323087.
e-mail: apalmer@global.co.za

# Lee Enfield Rifle

*from "Classic Arms"*

Both protagonists were armed with modern small calibre high velocity weapons, the Boers with the efficient charger loading 7mm Mauser and the British soldiers mainly with their new smokeless powder Lee-Enfields.

## MAGAZINE LEE-METFORD

Before launching into the Lee-Enfield, a very brief description of its predecessor is necessary to provide some background to it and its cartridge. The Lee-Metford was Britain's first small-bore military rifle and with the advent of smokeless powder, Britain's first smokeless rifle. Initially called the **'Magazine Rifle Mk 1'**, like its predecessor the Martini-Henry, it used a black powder charge, an interim measure until the introduction of smokeless which was in the meantime being developed. The shallow-land seven groove Metford rifling system in conjunction with the new jacketed bullet was designed to surmount the problem of black powder fouling, which it did. Inherent problems with black powder as a propellant included the white smoke which was impossible to conceal and the necessity for regular cleaning was required to prevent rust from destroying the bore. With the introduction of Cordite propellant, it was discovered that after some 6 000 rounds the high burning temperature eroded the Metford rifling, especially at the lead into the rifling, resulting in deterioration of accuracy. This was to lead to the introduction of a the Enfield five groove system.

After the Jameson Raid, the South African Republic, *Zuid-Afrikaansche Republiek (Z.A.R.)* - acquired a number of captured BSA manufactured Lee-Metfords MK I and MK II which found their way to various Commandos and were sold to the Boers by the Government who also kept a stock of .303 ammunition. Lee-Metfords were popular private purchases by the Boers but not by the Orange Free State, *Oranje Vrij Staat (O.V.S.)* - however engraved and carved examples have been noted and these were most probably captured.

The Lee-Metford proved reliable and effective during active service in Sudan, the North-West frontier of the Indian sub-continent and against massed charges of spear-and-sword armies; and elusive scattered groups of rifle-armed tribesmen. the tactical system used in colonial wars was totally different in the South African war against fast-moving Boers bred to rifle and horse since childhood, adept at taking cover and now armed mainly with the latest Mausers. However, as the war developed, parity was achieved, and the more efficient Lee-Enfield was more widely used, ironically - by both sides.

## THE 303 CARTRIDGE

The well known .303 cartridge started its life in 1888, developed by Woolwich Arsenal from the 'square neck' Rubin rimless cartridge.

Approved for service in February 1889 as **'Cartridge Rifle Mark I'** but with a bottleneck and rim.

Approved in early November 1891 for the Enfield rifling, the Mk I cartridge was short lived and was suspended in July 1893 by the MK II which used the Berdan system which gave better ignition.

When in use by the Indian Army the MK II was considered inadequate against natives and the Mk V expanding bullet was developed to provide better stopping power and introduced into general service. As the conflict was against a European foe, the Mk II was used throughout the South African theatre.

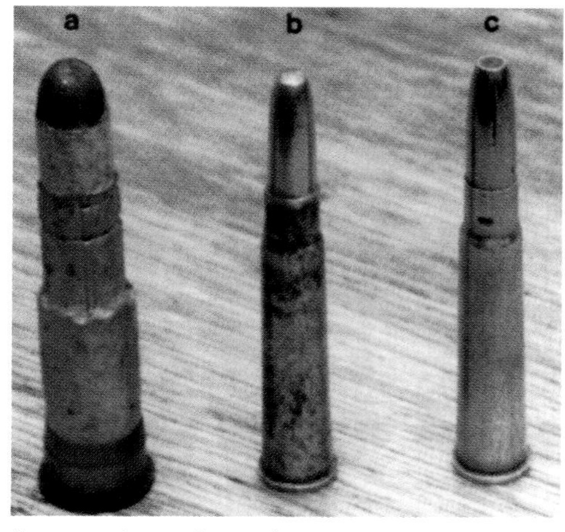


As comparisons, shown above are:
a. Boxer-Henry .450". b. .303" Cordite Mk II Berdan.
c. The Indian Army .303" 'Dum Dum'.

**DUM DUM**

British records indicate that expanding bullets were never officially used during the Boer War, however, the maligned **'Dum Dum'** did appear. The arrival of Indian contingents had brought with them the 'Dum Dum' and large stocks were captured by the Boers at the Battle of Dundee. Incidentally it was not as effective as the soft-nose 7mm Mauser ammunition of which 5.5mm of the ogive is exposed to expand on impact. It had been developed and used for hunting purposes, and possibly was used later as military ammunition stocks dwindled.

## *Conflict*

The **khaki** uniform did provide sufficient camouflage in the dusty African veld, however, as white pipe clay equipment attracted attention and made for a good aiming mark it was stained with tea or Condy's fluid to reduce visibility. For the training of British soldiers, the accent was on line formations mechanical precision, rigid dependence on orders firing strictly in volleys. They were not drilled in fighting an unseen enemy and ill-matched against such a skilled foe made almost invisible by the use of smokeless powder, who when counter-attacked melted away into the vast veldt. Although generally adapting swiftly to extended order, there were still cases of closed formation, for example, the disaster at Colenso and General Methuen's inglorious defeat at Magersfontein. When the range was not known, the Boers shooting was initially high due to the Mauser's minimum sight setting of 300 metres, but when the range was known or marked it was devastating and intense, for the Boers feared the bayonet, - like the sword they regarded them as inhuman weapons. *An oversight by the Boers as to the use of a bayonet in a role as a side-arm is highlighted in one incident where a captured group of highlanders who were not relieved of their bayonets, immediately used them to make good their escape!*

The Boers had another weapon - the spade, considered as important as the rifle, they decided it was better to dig a trench than a grave, much to the cost of the British soldier. Had the British infantry been regularly trained to the use of the spade, many difficulties would have been overcome. The use of trenches and firing at ground level across open ground created a much more effective use of the flat trajectory of the Mauser than plunging fire from a hill. These tactics were used with great effect notably by De la Ray against Methuen at Modder River where the British infantry trained to close with their enemy with bayonets found themselves powerless and pinned down, decimated by rifle fire, hugging whatever cover they could from an distant unseen enemy under a relentless African sun at a temperature of over a 100 F, lying on their rifles to keep them cool enough to use. This tactic proved so successful, it was again used by De la Ray shortly afterwards at Magersfontein hill, who had dug a 12 mile trench at its foot and bolstered by camouflaged barbed-wire entanglements. On a cold wet dawn, crowded together, a Brigade lead by the **Black Watch** was almost decimated in less than a minute.

Although technically inferior in respect to its method of magazine replenishing and cartridge in comparison to the Mauser, the Magazine Lee-Enfield was an excellent service rifle and had the misfortune of undergoing a series of teething problems in the midst of a war. It did attract some criticism when used in South Africa, much of it was deserved. The rifle was too heavy, its bolt mechanism considered too complicated, striker (firing pin) difficult to remove for cleaning; the magazine exposed and frail (but actually caused few problems in service) and slow to load were some of its failings. The long-range auxiliary sight of the Lee-Enfield was found to be of limited use, although collective volley fire was sometimes found to be effective in disrupting than actually inflicting casualties. Several well trained soldiers under ideal conditions, which generally prevailed on the veld, could bring collective fire onto an area to pin Boers down.

## Comparison between Magazine Lee-Enfield and Mauser M.93/95

| LEE-ENFIELD | M.93/95 |
|---|---|
| **Length:** | |
| 4′ 1.5″ (1 257mm) | 1 233mm |
| **Length with Bayonet:** | |
| 5′ 4.7″ (1 643mm) | Not officially used. |
| **Weight:** | |
| 9lbs 9.5oz (4,35kg) | 4,5kg |
| **Weight with Bayonet:** | |
| 10lb 4oz (4,65kg) | Not officially used. |
| **Minimum sighting:** | |
| 200 yards (182 metres) | 300 metres |
| **Sight radius:** | |
| 21.33″ (620mm) | 644mm |

It can be seen that the **M.93/95** is shorter, lighter, has a better sight radius, nevertheless the minimum sight setting is greater, and requires skills to use for precision shooting under 300 metres.

## Velocity comparison between Magazine Lee-Enfield Mk 1 and Mauser M.93/95

| LEE-ENFIELD | M.93/95 |
|---|---|
| **Velocity:** | |
| 2060fps at muzzle | 2402fps at muzzle |
| **Bullet diameter:** | |
| .31″ | 7.25mm |
| **Bullet weight:** | |
| 215 grains | 11.2 grams |
| **Powder charge:** | |
| 31.5 grains | 2.5 grams |
| **Energy:** | |
| 2026.4ft lbs | 302.8 kg/m |

The **M.93/95** bullet is lighter, has a greater velocity and produces more energy.

These tests are in no way conclusive or intended to be, and were conducted to provide some insight of the arm of the British soldier used in battle against a similarly armed opponent.

Britain had learnt many lessons from the Boer war, and when the war was over set out to modernise her Army, the result was the Expeditionary Force of 1914 boasted the best trained,best organised and best equipped army that ever went to war. Used throughout the world, the Lee-Enfield and its variants is considered one of the finest military rifles of all-time and proved to be as good as any of its contemporaries - history has proved it so!

As 7mm ammunition dwindled away by the effective British blockade, the Boers began to use increasing numbers of captured Lee-Enfield rifles. To supplement ammunition it became a practice to follow British columns and collect 'dropped' cartridges. ❑

*Source:*
Classic Arms Magazine Vol. 6 Issue 3.
Publishing fax: UK 01905 795905.

V. R.
ENFIELD
1901
L.E.
I*

Victorian marking on the right side of the test rifle butt socket denoting manufacture, date, model and Mark.

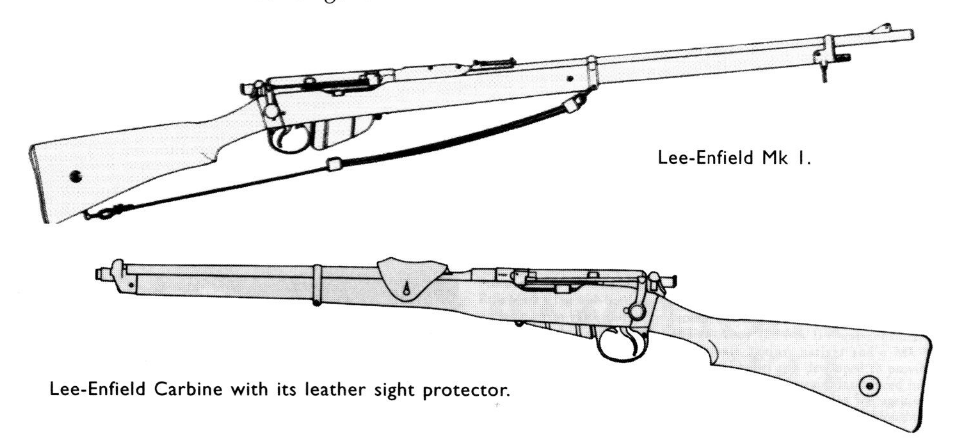

Lee-Enfield Mk I.

Lee-Enfield Carbine with its leather sight protector.

# The Victoria Cross

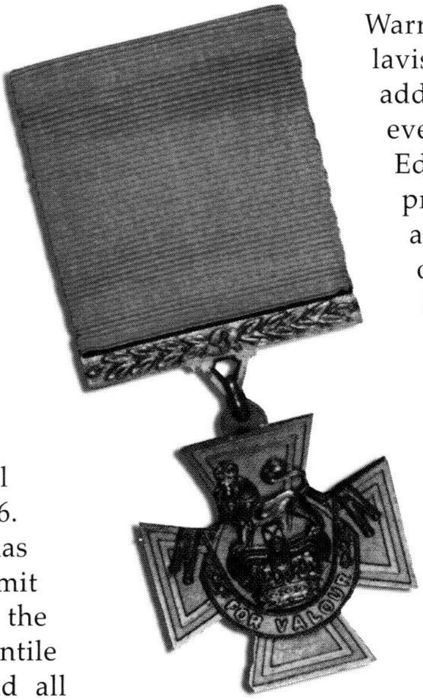

Never before had there been any decoration quite like the *Victoria Cross.* Originally intended to be awarded solely to officers and other ranks of the Navy and Army, who, serving in the presence of an enemy, should have *'performed some single act of valour or devotion to their country,'* the *Victoria Cross* was founded by Royal Warrant dated 29 January 1856. Though necessarily its scope has since been enlarged to admit other categories (such as the Royal Air Force, Mercantile Marine, Indian soldiers, and all branches of H.M.Forces, Dominion and Colonial; in addition to women and civilians in certain circumstances). It was not to be a richly be-gemmed and enamelled affair; it was not even to be a decoration of precious metal.

It was to be as near intrinsically *'worthless'* as a neatly designed bit of bronze, costing about 3d (three pence) with a scrap of coloured ribbon likely to be *'worthless'* that is, apart from its associations, and therein was to focus its value. Awarded for extreme valour, and royally conferred, it was to be utterly without reproach.

The Warrant declared the general design of the Cross, and the then colours of its ribbon, with numerous provisions. Among these was an important clause laying down that *"neither rank, nor long service, nor wounds, nor any other circumstance or condition whatsoever, save the merit of conspicuous bravery"* should *"establish a sufficient claim to the honour"* - this with the object of placing *"all persons on a perfectly equal footing in relation to eligibility for the decoration."* Its theory was as completely democratic as could be devised at the time. Pensions were granted to all recipients below commissioned rank and in the case of the Navy to below the rank of Warrant Officer, to a not over-lavish annual sum of £10, with an additional annual sum of £5 for every clasp. In 1902 King Edward VII approved the principle of the posthumous award of the Cross to certain officers and other ranks fallen in the South African War.

Designs for the new decoration were submitted to Queen Victoria who, on 5 January 1856 returned them to Lord Panmure having marked her choice with an *'x'*. The decoration was a Maltese Cross of bronze with the Royal Crest and a scroll inscribed *'For Valour.'* A V-shaped link connected it with a bar, ornamented on its face with sprays of laurel, and having on its back a space for the recipient's name. The date of the deed was engraved on the back of the Cross. More than one date may be found there.

The Cross was worn suspended from the left breast by a 38 mm wide ribbon, originally blue for the Navy and dark red for the Army, but this confusing distinction has since been abolished. From the Royal Warrant of 22 May 1920 the colour of the ribbon has been red for all services. When the ribbon only is worn, a miniature replica of the Cross is on the centre of the ribbon; a bar being indicated by an additional miniature Cross.

The *Victoria Cross* was cast until recent years from cannon captured at Sebastopol (Crimean War) and fashioned by Messrs. Hancock. The original *Victoria Cross* struck for the approval of Queen Victoria was given to the Royal United Service Museum by Lieut. Col. M.P. Hancock, D.S.O. who had it from his grandfather, who founded the firm. ❑

***References:***

A. C. Benson and Viscount Esher.
*The Letters of Queen Victoria (1907).*
*The Bronze Cross.*

# Victoria Cross Awards for Service in the Anglo-Boer War 1899-1902

| | | | |
|---|---|---|---|
| Capt. Charles Fitzclarence | Royal Fusiliers | Mafeking | 14 October 1899 |
| Maj. C. H. Mullins, C.M.G. | Imperial Light horse | Elandslaagte | 21 October 1899 |
| Capt. R. Johnstone | Imperial Light Horse | Elandslaagte | 21 October 1899 |
| Capt. Matthew Fontaine Maury Meiklejohn | Gordon Highlanders | Elandslaagte | 21 October 1899 |
| Sgt-Maj. William Robertson | Gordon Highlanders | Elandslaagte | 21 October 1899 |
| 2nd Lieut. John Norwood | 5th Dragoon Guards | Ladysmith | 30 October 1899 |
| Capt. Ernest Beckwith Towse | Gordon Highlanders | Magersfontein | 11 December 1899 |
| Lieut. H. E. M. Douglas, D.S.O. | Royal Army Medical Corps | Magersfontein | 11 December 1899 |
| Cpl. J.D.F.Shaul | Highland Light Infantry | Magersfontein | 11 December 1899 |
| Maj. William Babtie | Royal Army Medical Corps | Colenso | 15 December 1899 |
| Capt. H. L. Reed | Royal Field Artillery | Colenso | 15 December 1899 |
| Capt. H. N. Schofield | Royal Field Artillery | Colenso | 15 December 1899 |
| Capt. W. N. Congreve | Rifle Brigade | Colenso | 15 December 1899 |
| Lieut. Hon. F. H. Sherton Roberts | King's Royal Rifles | Colenso | 15 December 1899 |
| Cpl. G. S. Nurse | Royal Field Artillery | Colenso | 15 December 1899 |
| Pvt. C. Ravenhill | 2nd Royal Scots Fusiliers | Colenso | 15 December 1899 |
| Sgt. H. R. Martineau | Protectorate Regiment | Mafeking | 26 December 1899 |
| Trp. H. E. Ramsden | Pretedtorate Regiment | Mafeking | 26 December 1899 |
| Lieut. Sir John P. Milbanke, Bart. | 10th Fusiliers | Colesberg | 05 January 1900 |
| Maj. J. E. I. Masterson | 1st Devons | Wagon Hill | 06 January 1900 |
| Pvt. J. Pitts | 1st Manchester | Wagon Hill | 06 January 1900 |
| Pvt. R. Scott | 1st Manchester | Wagon Hill | 06 January 1900 |
| Sgt. J. Firth | 1st West Riding | Arundel, C.C. | 24 February 1900 |
| Lieut. Francis Newton Parsons | Essex Regiment | Paardeberg | 18 February 1900 |
| Pvt. A. E. Curtis | 2nd East Surrey Regiment | Relief of Ladysmith | 23 February 1900 |
| Lieut E. C. Inkson | Royal Army Medical Corps | Relief of Ladysmith | 24 February 1900 |
| Cpl. J. J. Clements | Rimington's Rifles | Strydenburg | 24 February 1900 |
| Capt. Conwyn Mansel-Jones | West Yorkshire Regiment | Pieter's Hill | 27 February 1900 |
| Sgt. H. Engelheart | 10th Hussars | Koornspruit | 31 March 1900 |
| Maj. Edward John Phipps-Hornby | Q.Batt. Royal Horse Artillery | Koornspruit | 31 March 1900 |
| Sgt. Charles Parker | Q.Batt. Royal Horse Artillery | Koornspruit | 31 March 1900 |
| Dvr. Horace Harry Glasock | Q.Batt. Royal Horse Artillery | Koornspruit | 31 March 1900 |
| Gun. Isaac Lodge | Q.Batt. Royal Horse Artillery | Koornspruit | 31 March 1900 |
| Capt. F. A. Maxwell | Indian Staff Corps | Koornspruit | 31 March 1900 |
| Capt. W. H. S.Nickerson | Royal Army Med. Corps | Wakkerstroom | 20 April 1900 |
| Sgt. H. Beet | 1st Derbyshire Regiment | Wakkerstroom | 22 April 1900 |
| Cpl. F. McKay | Gordon Highlanders | Johannesburg | 29 May 1900 |
| Cpl. Frank Howard Kirby | Royal Engineers | Near Pretoria | 02 June 1900 |
| Pvt. C.Ward | 2nd Yorkshire Light Infantry | Lindley | 26 June 1900 |
| Sgt. A. H. Lindley Richardson | Strathcona's Horse | Wolvespruit | 05 July 1900 |

| | | | |
|---|---|---|---|
| Capt. William Engleston Gordon | Gordon Highlanders | Doornboschfontein | 11 July 1900 |
| Capt. R. N. Howse | New South Wales Med. Corps | Vredefort | 24 July 1900 |
| Pvt. W. House | Royal Berkshires | Msilikatsi's Nek | 02 August 1900 |
| Sgt. T. Lawrence | 17th Lancers | Essenbosch Farm | 07 August 1900 |
| Sgt. H. Hampton | 2nd Liverpool Regiment | Van Wyk's Vlei | 21 August 1900 |
| Cpl. H. J. Knight | 1st Liverpool Regiment | Van Wyk's Vlei | 21 August 1900 |
| Pvt. William Heaton | 1st King's Liverpool Regiment | Leeukloof | 23 August 1900 |
| Pvt. E.Durrant | 2nd Rifle Brigade | Bergendal | 27 August 1900 |
| Lieut. Guy G. E. Wylly | Tasmanian Imperial Horse | Warmbad | 01 September 1900 |
| Pvt. J. H. Bisdee | Tasmanian Imperial Horse | Warmbad | 01 September 1900 |
| Maj. E . D. Brown-Synge-Hutchinson | 14th Hussars | Geluk | 13 October 1900 |
| Lieut. A. C. Doxat | 3rd Imperial Yeomanry | Zeerust | 20 October 1900 |
| Lieut. H. Z. C. Cockburn | Canadian Local Forces | Komati River | 07 November 1900 |
| Lieut. H. E. Holland | Canadian Local Forces | Komati River | 07 November 1900 |
| Lieut.-Col. R. E. W. Turner, D.S.O. | Canadian Local Forces | Komati River | 07 November 1900 |
| Pvt. C. Kennedy | 2nd Highland Light Infantry | Dewetsdorp | 22 November 1900 |
| Sgt. D. Farmer | 1st Cameron Highlanders | Nooigedacht | 13 December 1900 |
| Lieut. W. J. Hardham | 9th New Zealand Cont. | Naauwpoort | 28 January 1901 |
| Sgt. W. B. Traynor | 2nd West Yorkshire | Bothwell | 06 February 1901 |
| Lieut. F. B. Dugdale | 5th Lancers | Derby (Transvaal) | 03 March 1901 |
| Lieut. F. W. Bell | W.Australian Mounted Infantry | Brakpan | 16 May 1901 |
| Sgt. J. Rogers | South African Constabulary | Thaba'Nchu | 15 June 1901 |
| Lieut. W. J. English | 2nd Scottish Horse | Vlakfontein | 03 July 1901 |
| Pvt. H. G. Crandon | 18th Hussars | Springboklaagte | 04 July 1901 |
| Sgt.-Maj. A. Young | Cape Police | Ruiter's Kraal | 13 August 1901 |
| Capt. L. A. E. Price-Davies, D.S.O. | King's Royal Rifle Corps | Blood River Poort | 17 September 1901 |
| Dvr. F. G. Bradley | 69th Batt. Field Artillery | Itala | 26 September 1901 |
| Pvt. W. Bees | 1st Derbyshire Regiment | Moedwill | 30 September 1901 |
| Lieut. L. C. Magyar | 5th Victorian Mounted Rifles | Geelhoutboom | 23 November 1901 |
| Surg. Capt. T. G. Crean | 1st Imperial Light Horse | Tygerskloof | 18 December 1901 |
| Shoeing Smith A. E. Ind | Royal Horse Artillery | Tafelkop OFS | 20 December 1901 |
| Surg. Capt. A. Martin-Leake | South African Constabulary | Vlakfontein | 08 February 1902 |

The following soldiers received the Victoria Cross posthumously:

| | | | |
|---|---|---|---|
| Lieut. R. J. T. Digby-Jones | Imperial Light Horse | Wagon Hill | 06 January 1900 |
| Trp. H. Albrecht | Imperial Light Horse | Wagon Hill | 06 January 1900 |
| Sgt. A. Atkinson | 1st Yorkshire | Paardeberg | 18 February 1900 |
| Capt. D. Reginald Younger | Gordon Highlanders | Doornboschfontein | 11 July 1900 |
| Pvt. J. Barry | 1st Royal Irish | Monument Hill | 08 January 1901 |
| Lieut. G. H. B. Coulson | King's Own Scot. Borderers | Lambrechtfontein | 18 May 1901 |

References:
*For Valour.*
*The Bronze Cross.*
*The Victoria Cross.*
*The South African War 1899-1902*

## JASON ASKEW

***Young South African artist, specialising in paintings and drawings of South African wars and other military campaigns in other theatres of war around the world!***

### LAND OF HOPE AND GLORY!

Elgar's *Pomp and Circumstance March No.1* premiéred in 1901. Edward VII heard it and advised Elgar to have lyrics written. The words of *Land of Hope and Glory* were written to celebrate the King's Coronation in 1902. The lyrics are by Arthur Benson. It has become the second national anthem of Great Britain. Westby-Nunn Publishers cc

### AN AMERICAN DIES

On the 15 July 1901, an Irish American called Walter Wilson, fighting on the side of the Boers, was badly wounded in a skirmish. The British allowed Chris, his countryman and mess-mate, onto the battlefield to hear his dying words. Wilson said: *"Say good-bye to the boys, and tell them we will meet at the great Divide"*. (Schikkerling, 256/257).

JASON ASKEW

P O Box 867, Saxonwold 2132, Gauteng, South Africa
Tel: (011) 726 5698. Fax: (011) 726 5887. Cell: 083 426 9986.

*Jean Beater – National Monuments Council*

# Historical Introduction to the Commemoration of War & Armed Conflict in South Africa

## Vision

*The Country* ... Military activity, the conduct of war and armed conflict have long played a significant role in South African history. Remembrance of the human loss it caused is part of the contemporary landscape. Military graves, war memorials and monuments are tangible and symbolic reminders of our turbulent imperial and national history. While these convey different messages and meanings about the commemoration of war and armed conflict, they all recall the reality of human loss in conflict.

Moreover, through such trances of memory, we are able to contemplate past and present efforts to commemorate those who have perished, whether as combatants or as victims. Graves are often poignant reminders of how ordinary people are often unwillingly and fatally drawn into conflict. Graves and other public objects and places of commemoration form an important part of South Africa's heritage and must be conserved for future generations. As historical artefacts, they reveal ways in which the people of South Africa have sought to comprehend and to mark loss and sacrifice of casualties of wars and conflict or simply honour those who lost their lives while passing our dangerous coastline.

*and the individual* ... Graves and monuments are also tangible and symbolic reminders of individual, family and community histories of bereavement. This history is as much concerned with the record of individual loss, as with collective representation of suffering, or ideas of patriotic sacrifice or national aspirations.

*and the commemoration of those who have perished* ... The preservation and care of such important places of commemoration is an expression of respect, honour and responsibility to the memory of every individual who perished in an act of armed belligerence arising from conflict on South African soil, or to those who perished on our hostile shores as a result of shipwrecks or other causes.

## Policy

It is the responsibility of the National Monuments Council's War Graves and Grave of Victims of Conflict Division to preserve and maintain identified graves and memorials of soldiers, sailors and civilians who died (inside and outside South Africa) because of wars and armed conflict from the earliest known *modern* conflicts until 10 May 1994 (the final date for amnesty), excluding the graves of those who died in two World Wars. These graves, together with the graves of those who died in the Korean War, are cared for by the Commonwealth War Graves Commission.

The policy is that graves of conflict, war graves and cemeteries should be left undisturbed no matter how inaccessible and difficult they are to maintain. It is only when essential developments such as new roads or dams threaten a place of burial that human remains should be disinterred to another cemetery or garden of remembrance.

From a historical point of view and for research purposes, it is vital that burial sites are not disturbed. The location and marking of an individual's grave tells a life story, where he/she died defending (or attacking) a particular place and makes it easier to understand the special historical circumstances of his/her death.

## History

It was inevitable that European imperialism and the colonial settlement of the Cape in the 17TH century would bring modern casualties of armed conflict, both indigenous and European. Some individuals died in imperial clashes on South African soil, as in the late-18th and 19th century Anglo-Dutch battles of Muizenberg and

Blaauwberg. Various wars of conquest and other colonial campaigns such as the Khoisan-Dutch wars of the 17th century, the Frontier Wars in the Eastern Cape and the Anglo-Zulu War of the 1800s produced many more casualties. South African history reflects the extent to which British and colonial forces were engaged in many battles and minor skirmishes through the country. Moreover, through South Africa's imperial past, garrisons were established and families also joined soldiers, forming special military communities of loss and remembrance. Such experience was not only land-based. Naval vessels and troopships sailing around a treacherous coastline were periodically wrecked with men and families drowned.

In the contemporary era, national political conflict has played a significant part in the development of South Africa in the 20th century. This conflict took many forms such as land dispossession wars to open political opposition to the policies of the day. The conflict intensified during the 1970s and 1980s and spilt over into neighbouring countries where casualties from both sides were recorded. The opponents of apartheid were made up of a variety of organisations whilst the South African Defence Force, South African Police and other groupings assisted the Government.

Public commemoration of the dead or 'fallen' in declared wars and violent civil conflicts is essentially a 19th and 20th century phenomenon linked to the rise of democratic ideologies and the notion of common citizenship. As South Africa comes to terms with its violent past the commemoration of diverse forms of conflict or war should not be to emphasise victory or defeat, but to assist in 'bringing' the dead home, retrieving their identity and also becoming a record of our history. Assistance with the erection of memorials and the maintenance and preservation of cemeteries and graves is thus vital to the country's historic mix and memory. This function is fulfilled by the War Graves and Graves of Victims of Conflict Division of the National Monuments Council.

## The Care of War and Armed Conflict Graves

It is the policy of most armies to bury their dead where they fall. There are many cemeteries and graves at battlefields and military garrison posts throughout the country. Before the Anglo-Boer War 1899-1902, no organisation was charged with the overall care of war graves. Thus

The coffins at Turffontein.

many early and isolated graves and cemeteries suffered from neglect and some have disappeared. One example is the battlefield of Blaauwberg near Cape Town where the location of graves is now unknown.

During the Anglo-Boer War of 1899-1902 the *Royal Engineers* were given the task of recording the location of all British military graves of war. Numerous registers and lists were then compiled, of which the best known is the South African Field Force Casualty List. During the same war, an organisation known as the *Guild of Loyal Women* was formed to locate graves, erect iron crosses and compile registers for all these graves. The *South African Soldiers Graves Association* circa 1910, took over from the Guild. It administered all overseas funds that were collected for the care of graves of those who fell in the Anglo-Boer War. In 1956 a State-aided body, the *South African War Graves Board* was formed to look after war graves in the country and in 1982 the Board was absorbed into the *National Monuments Council*. The War Graves and Graves of Victims of Conflict Division operates in conjunction with a Committee. The Division has, in recent years, extended its responsibilities to include the care and recording of all graves of victims of conflict.

## Responsibilities

The Division's main responsibilities are:

- ❖ to locate, mark and maintain the graves of all soldiers, sailors, dependents and civilians who died in wars, conflict or on peacetime military service until 10 May 1994, the final date for amnesty;
- ❖ to provide assistance with the erection and maintenance of memorials to the dead and to those whose graves are unknown;

- ❖ to compile and maintain records and registers;
- ❖ to liaise with neighbouring States or their representatives regarding the care and maintenance of military graves in these countries.

## Organisation

The War Graves and Graves of Victims of Conflict Committee consists of members appointed by the Minister of Arts, Culture, Science & Technology. The Chairperson is also a member of the National Monuments Council.

The Committee usually meets twice a year to deal with policy and other matters. As the Committee members live in various parts of the country, they are able to deal with matters concerning conflict and war graves in their respective areas. The Division is based in Johannesburg at the following address:

War Graves & Graves of Victims of Conflict Division
National Monuments Council
P. O. Box 87552, HOUGHTON 2041.
Telephone (27) (011) 482-8365/6/7.
Fax (27) (011) 482-8196.

## International Interest

Considerable world-wide interest has been shown in South Africa's history from abroad with many tourists visiting cemeteries, battlefields and sites of conflict – here are a few examples:

Isandlwana, a sombre, brooding battlefield which no tourist can visit without *'feeling'* the defeat the British Army experienced here in January 1879. The Fugitive's Trail is marked by a string of whitewashed cairns, the graves of those who were overtaken and killed by the Zulu forces. Simon's Town. The names of sailors, some only boys, on the memorial in the garden of remembrance reminds one of South Africa's strategic position on an important sea route. Women's Memorial in Bloemfontein is a stark reminder of the thousands of women and children who perished in British concentration camps established during the Anglo-Boer War. ❑

## Boer War Memorial

Standing on a large, round traffic island where several roads meet, Kimberley's Honoured Dead Memorial is an impressive landmark. Erected in 1904 to the memory of those who died defending Kimberley during the four-month siege, the memorial was designed by the architect Herbert Baker, who based it on the designs of a tomb at Agrigentum in Sicily and a monument in Asia Minor.

The memorial has a base of sandstone believed to have been quarried not far from Cecil Rhodes' grave in the Matopo Hills, Zimbabwe, while the pillars and roof are of local sandstone. It bears an inscription written by Rudyard Kipling:

*This for a charge to our children in sign of the price we paid,*
*The price that we paid for freedom that comes unsoiled to your hand.*
*Read, revere and uncover; here are the victors laid,*
*They that died for their city, being sons of the land.*

## *M. van Wyk Smith*

# Boer War Literature

The Anglo-Boer or South African War (1899-1902) elicited worldwide response. For Britain and her white dominions the war was the culmination of Victorian Imperial endeavour. Britain's Imperial rivals saw the conflict as a rapacious excursion to appropriate South Africa's mineral wealth, while the Boer republics were envisioned as enclaves of heroic pastoral and patriarchal virtues.

Everywhere humanitarian, pacifist, socialist and feminist organisations rallied to the pro-Boer cause, outstanding proponents being W.T. Stead and Olive Schreiner. The black majority of South Africa, however, remained conspicuously marginalised in these contro-versies, though not in the conflict itself (see Peter Warwick, *Black People and the South African War, 1983*).

Near-universal British literacy resulting from the 1870 EDUCATION ACT ensured an 'army of a quarter million, each one almost to a man a war corres-pondent' (Bookman, 1902). Kipling's *Barrack-Room Ballads* (1892) had popula-rised the image of the common soldier (Tommy Atkins) and an infectious ballad style to express his views, while Thomas Hardy and A.E. Housman had crafted accessible modes of simple and poignant contemplation to render the more elegiac aspects of the war.

Much of the poetry was versified propaganda, but some of it anticipated Wilfred Owen's concept of 'the pity of war', notably H.D. Rawnsley, *Ballads of the War* (1900); Henry Newbolt, *The Sailing of the Long Ships* (1902); Kipling, *The Five Nations* (1903); Hardy, *Poems of the Past and Present* (1902); and T.W.H. Crosland, *The Five Notions* (1903).

Poetry protesting the war is well represented in William Watson, *For England* (1904); *Songs of the Veld* (1902); Perceval Gibbon, *African Items* (1903); Kingsley Fairbridge, *Veld Verse* (1909); and Alice Buckton, *The Burden of Engela* (1904), a remarkable articulation of empathy with the Boers.

Among soldier and journalist poets at the front the better were G. Murray Johnstone (*'Mome'*), *The Off-Wheeler Ballads* (1910); Harry Graham (*'Coldstreamer'*), *Ballads of the Boer War* (1902); and Edgar Wallace, *Writ in Barracks* (1900). The Australians A. B. Paterson, Henry Lawson and Harry (*'Breaker'*) Morant wrote sharply dissident poems about the conflict. Boer experience of the war inspired the early Afrikaans poets J. F. E. Celliers, Eugene Marais, J.D. du Toit, and C. Louis Leipoldt. In Europe spirited poetry in the Boer cause came from Francois Coppee, Edmond Rostand and Sully Prudhomme in French, Willem Kloos and Albert Verwey in Dutch, and Friedrich Lienhard and Ludwig Thoma in German.

Some 150 novels were inspired by the Boer

Painting by Emily Hobhouse.

War, ranging from imperialist romance by Ernest Glanville, Bertram Mitford and G.A. Henty to several texts more sensitive to the issues involved: Clotilde Graves (*'Richard Dehan'*), *The Dop Doctor* (1910); Owen Vaughan (*'Owen Rhoscomyl'*), *Old Fireproof* (1906); Anna Howarth, *Nora Lester* (1902); Douglas Blackburn, *A Burger Quixote* (1903); W.C. Scully, *The Harrow* (1921); and Stuart Cloete, *Rags and Glory* (1963), Kipling's enigmatic Boer War stories appeared in TRAFFICS & DISCOVERIES (1902).

Memorable personal reminiscences of the war include Emily Hobhouse, *The Brunt of the War* and *Where it Fell* (1902); Johanna Brandt, *The Petticoat Commando* (1913); C.R. de Wet, *Three Years War* (1902); Winston Churchill, *London to Ladysmith via Pretoria* (1900); M.H. Grant (*'Linesman'*). *Words by an Eyewitness* (1901); C.G. Dennison, *A Fight to a Finish* (1904); Denys Reitz, *Commando* (1929); and ... the almost sole-surviving Black account of the war ... *The Boer War Diary of Sol T. Plaatje*, ED. J.L. Comaroff (1973). For further reading, see, Rayne Kruger, *Good-bye Dolly Gray* (1959); Thomas Pakenham, *The Boer War* (1979); Peter Warwick, ED. *The South African War* (1980); M. van Wyk Smith, *Drummer Hodge: The Poetry of the Anglo-Boer War* (1978). ❑

Drawing from Drummer Hodge: *The Poetry of the Anglo-Boer War.*

## BOSMAN'S TALES OF THE BOER WAR

**OOM SCHALK LOURENS**, a simple old Boer who is really the embodiment of sly ambiguity, narrates these stories about the wars and loves, faiths and superstitions, ignorance, prejudice and insights, virtues and vices of a backveld Afrikaner community.

These tales from *Mafeking Road* and *Unto Dust*, South African literary classics and best-sellers, have made author **HERMAN CHARLES BOSMAN** and storyteller **PATRICK MYNHARDT** household names. Bosman, an English-writing Afrikaner of recognised genius, gives a unique portrait, drawn from the inside with love and wry detachment, of his controversial nation in these poetic stories, compound of satire, sentiment, realism, romance, irony and inspired clowning.

*Dr D.J. Kotze, Professor of History, Stellenbosch (circa 1960)*

# Japie Greyling

## DAPPER KINDERS VAN SUID-AFRIKA

Japie Greyling, who during the Anglo-Boer War performed a courageous deed, but because he was not part of the commandos, he could not be called *'penkop' (young boys/men who joined Commandos who had short, short haircuts).* Japie's parents lived in the district of Hoopstad and when the incident occurred, he was almost eleven years old.

A number of people tell the story of Japie Greyling: **Captain Seely**, the British officer that was in charge on the particular day in question, wrote in his book ***'Fear and be Slain,'*** published thirty years later, a detailed account of the heroic act. The famous poet, **Jan Celliers**, visited the Greylings after the war and got the story from Japie's mother and the black woman, **Sanna**, who witnessed the incident. **Uys Krige**, another famous poet, also got a firsthand account of the story, then rewrote the story into a play called ***'The White Wall.'***

The story goes that an English battalion that was a division of the Imperial Yeomanry, was encamped in April 1901 near Hoopstad in the Free State, about twenty miles away from the Greylings' farm. A spy informed the British that the Boer commandant, Japie father, and a few other Boers were spending the night on the Greylings' farm.

The British wanted to take the commandant as prisoner, and so Captain Seely went that very same night with approximately twenty men to the farm to catch him. While they were approaching the farmhouse early the next morning, they saw three Boers riding away. When the Boers noticed the British, they galloped away and the British soldiers could not catch up with them.

Captain Seely let it be known that he was furious that they had got away; as he was aware that there were various Boer commandos in the area and he assumed that the three escapees would quickly round up men and come back to attack the British. It was therefore imperative that he find out where the Boers were so as to avoid them otherwise they might get caught.

When Seely realised that the Boers had escaped, he immediately went to the farmhouse to see if there was anyone who might know where the Boer commando was situated.

Japie Greyling was in the kitchen busy making coffee when he saw the British soldiers approaching, he went outside. The spy, who was with them, could talk Afrikaans and asked Japie what his name was.

*"Ek is die seun van my vader vir wie julle nie kon vang nie,"* ("I am the son of my father which you could not catch.") he replied. After that they wanted to know where the Boers had gone.

*"Na hulle kommando toe."* ("To join their commando.") he answered.

*"Waar is die Kommando?"* ("Where is the commando?") they asked again. Japie gazed at the ground for a few seconds, looked up and answered: *"Dit kan ek nie vertel nie."* ("That I cannot tell you.")

The Officer annoyed by the impertinence of the boy, decided to force him to talk. First he threatened to shoot him if he would not answer, but still Japie would not cooperate.

*"Then I'll put you up against the wall and shoot you,"* said Captain Seely.

*"Skiet my maar dood,"* ("Shoot me, if you wish.") Japie answered.

Captain Seely then ordered his sargeant to have six men stand ready with their guns. Then two other soldiers took the boy and placed him up against the wall. The six soldiers loaded their guns and took up firing positions. Captain Seely had whispered to the sergeant that he did not really want them to shoot the boy, but he was convinced that Japie had not overhead this.

Japie's mother, brother and sisters were inside the house and could clearly hear what was going on outside. The servant, Sanna, stood about ten feet away from Japie, and when she saw what was happening, she started crying loudly and shouted to Japie's mother: *"Nooi, hulle wil vir Japie dood skiet!"* ("Madam, they want to shoot Japie!")

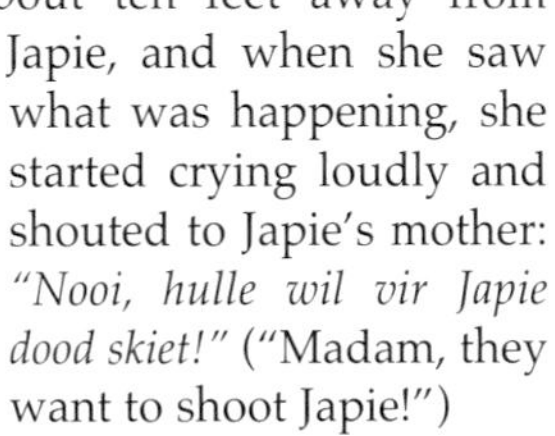

Again the officer sternly asked: "Where is the commando?" and then gave the command: "Prepare to fire!"

But then, so tells Captain Seely, Japie lifted his head up, looked the officer directly in the eye, put his hands behind his back and said with a clear distinctive voice, while his eyes glistened: *"Ek sal nie se nie!"* ("I won't tell you!")

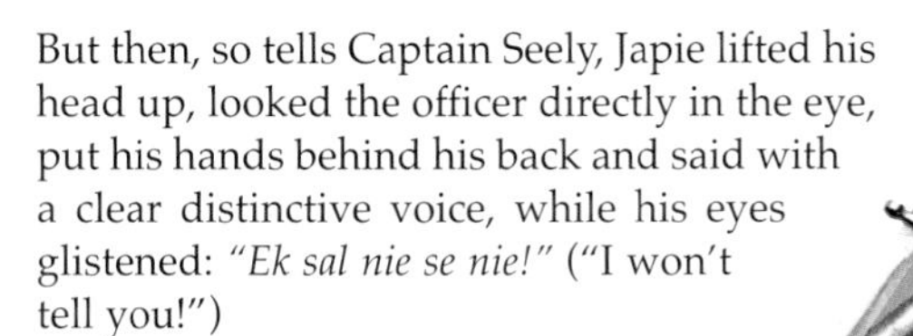

That was too much for Captain Seely. He stepped forward to the boy, took his hand and said: "I hope I will meet you again one day."

The six soldiers dropped their rifles and shortly after that the British rode away.

So goes the story of Japie Greyling as told by Captain Seely and others as they described it.

In February 1960, I and my wife visited the farm on which the Greylings' farmed, which was between Wesselsbron and Hoopstad. The farm's name was *'Smaldeel'*, but since 1901 the original farm, which had been very big had been subdivided into various small farms. The portion that the farm-buildings were on at the time of the Boer war, was always called *'Smaldeel'*; the portions that were cut off were renamed. One of these today is called *'de Rust.'*

At *'de Rust'*, we met with Japie's twin brother: **Oom Kerneels**, as he was known, was almost seventy years old. He was born on 25 June 1890. When the incident above occurred, he had been almost eleven years old. We also met an older sister of Japie, **Mrs Otto**. She lived a short distance away from there on the farm *'Fris Gewaagd'*.

Oom Kerneels and Mrs Otto told us how they had lived before and after the Boer War broke out. The Vaal River flows about a half a mile past the house. As children they often played amongst the trees on the banks of the river.

When the war broke out, their father, **Commandant B.C. Greyling**, a member of the Volksraad (Parliament) and his two eldest sons were called up. Their father was soon arrested and sent to the camp at Gordons Bay or Hermanus. The eldest son Ben and the second eldest son Abraham, remained out of the hands of the British.

When the English started sending the women and children on the farms to concentration

camps and burning the farms a scary period began for Mrs Greyling and her children. There were no men on the farms - just herself, the girls, Ben's wife and the twin boys Japie and Kerneels.

On more than one occasion they had to flee quickly to dodge the British troops. Often they sought shelter amongst the trees on the banks of the Vaal River. They also took the cattle with them. Their house was thankfully never burnt down. When they had to flee like this, all the children had to help - including Japie and Kerneels.

Now and then, when the opportunity arose, Ben and Abraham brought them something to eat. Later, when all the cattle were carried off, they brought mainly slaughter-animals. When the incident between Japie and the British soldiers took place, Ben and Abraham were across the river in the Transvaal territory, their father had already been taken prisoner.

Most books that tell the story of Japie Greyling are wrong if they state that Japie's father spent the night on the farm. It wasn't him, nor one of his sons that were part of the commandos, it was other Boers. There were often Boer commandos in the area and there were often Boer movements, but who the Boers were, nobody can say now.

Oom Kerneels and Mrs Otto also told us that Japie later farmed in the Eastern Free State on a farm near Slabbert station between Bethlehem and Fouriesburg where he lived for a long time, the farm's name is *'Sonderhout'*. Later he went to live with his daughter **Mrs Havenga** in Bloemfontein where he died in 1954. Today his son Japie still farms on *'Sonderhout'*.

The eldest brother Ben, also became a Commandant. He is still alive at the age of 86 years and lives on the farm "Duikfontein" in the district of Lichtenburg in the Transvaal. **Aia Sanna** is also still alive and is also very old. After we had chatted and drank coffee for a little while on *'de Rust'*, we all went to the farmbuildings at *'Smaldeel'* where the Greylings lived during the war. The house looks almost the same as it looked in 1901, there were just two verandahs that had been added on.

Oom Kerneels and Mrs Otto showed us the place where they had wanted to shoot Japie - it was in front of a narrow wall between the coach house door and another door at the back of the house.

While we stood there my thoughts went back to the autumn morning more than sixty years earlier, when Japie looked death squarely in the eye then; he must have known where the Boer commando was. He had not wanted to reveal it, though. In that way he had become a legend in our history.

***Japie Greyling is buried in the "Morelig" cemetery in Bethlehem. Grave No. 2322.*** ❑

# THE BOOKSHELF

*A small selection of books, CD's and video's on the Anglo-Boer War which are available at major booksellers and specialist bookshops. We have included the publishing house with each title for easy reference.*

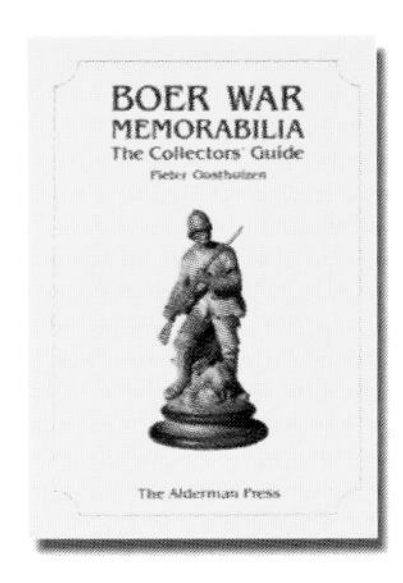

***Bosman's Tales of the Boer War.** Selected & read by Patrick Mynhardt*

Oom Schalk Lourens, a simple old boer who is really the embodiment of sly ambiguity narrates these stories about the war and loves, faith and superstitions, ignorance, prejudice and insites, virtues and vices of a backveld afrikaner community. These tales from *Mafeking Road* and *Unto Dust*; South African literary classics and best sellers, have made also Charles Herman Bosman and storyteller PATRICK MYNHARDT household names. *Obtainable on audio-tapes from: Listeners Library, Johannesburg, RSA. Tel: (011) 325 2266. Fax: (011) 341 0149.*

***The Anglo-Boer War Anniversary 1899-1999 Auction Catalogue***

**SPINK**

A magnificent catalogue for ORDERS, DECORATIONS AND CAMPAIGN MEDALS, MILITARIA AND MEMORABILIA. Excellent photos and pictures and a well researched brief history on the War. A must if you can get a copy.

*Spink & Son, 5 King Street, St. James, London.*
*Tel: UK +44 (0)20 7930 7888. Fax: +44 (0)20 7839 4853.*
*Tel: RSA (021) 761 2676. Christie's @ Cape Town.*

***Paper Currency of the Anglo-Boer War 1899-1902***

**JOHN INESON**

This book details the known Paper Currency issued during the Anglo-Boer War. Covering Boer Government notes as well as the notes produced by the besieged towns such as Mafeking, Upington, OKiep and others. Paper Currency used by the POWs in South Africa and Overseas; and more.

*Order from: Spink & Son. 5 King Street, St. James, London.*
*Tel: + 44 (0)20 7930 7888. Fax: +44 (0)20 7839 4853.*

***Victoria Cross Bibliography***

**JOHN MULHOLLAND & ALAN JORDAN**

This book is divided into 3 sections. **Part 1**. Key VC titles each with description and annotation. **Part 2**. Over 100 non-fiction and fictional books written by VC recipients but unrelated to the VC. **Part 3**. Index of every VC recipient & date of Gazette citation; and books which refer to recipients in detail.

*Order from: Spink & Son. 5 King Street, St.James, London.*
*Tel: + 44 (0)20 7930 7888. Fax: +44 (0)20 7839 4853.*

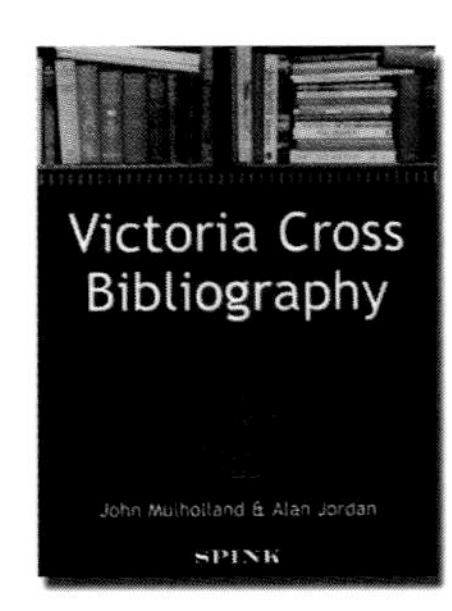

### *A Soldier's Diary. South Africa, 1899-1902*
**MURRAY COSBY JACKSON**

Corporal Jackson was one of those 'Gentleman Rankers'; offered a commission but declined to rather fight in the ranks. His diary covers many a battle and skirmish, unfortunately no places are mentioned. A very easy book to read showing how the British troops lived and fought.
*Published by: The Royal Hampshire Regiment Trustees, Serle's House, Southgate Street, Winchester S023 9EG.*

### *The Siege of O'Okiep.* GUERRILLA CAMPAIGN IN THE ANGLO-BOER WAR
**PETER BURKE**

A well researched account of the guerrilla campaign by General Jan Smuts against the British holding the vital Copper Mining town of Okiep. The siege covered two months of 1902 but there was a lot of action. It was from Okiep that Gen.Smuts travelled to the Peace talks at Vereeniging.
*Published by: War Museum of the Boer Republics, Bloemfontein. Tel: (051) 447 3447. Fax: (051) 447 1322.*

### *The Russians and the Anglo-Boer War*
**APOLLON DAVIDSON & IRINA FILATOVA**

A fascinating book on the Russians that took part in the War on the Boer side. They served in the Commandos and the Ambulance Corps. The book also covers the research that the authors undertook to obtain the information from relatives of those that took part in the war.
*Published by: Human & Rousseau, Cape Town. Tel: (021) 425 1280 Fax: (021) 419 2619.*

### *The Boy. Baden-Powell and the Siege of Mafeking*
**PAT HOPKINS & HEATHER DUGMORE**

A controversial look at the events surrounding Mafeking and the Tshidi-Barolong Mahikeng inhabitants of the native town, the *stadt*. The book looks at the role played by Sol Plaatjie and Mathakgong, cattle raider and guerrilla fighter, as well as that of Baden-Powell.
*Published by: Zebra Press (New Holland Struik Publishing Group) Tel: (021) 462 4360. Fax: (021) 465 1798.*

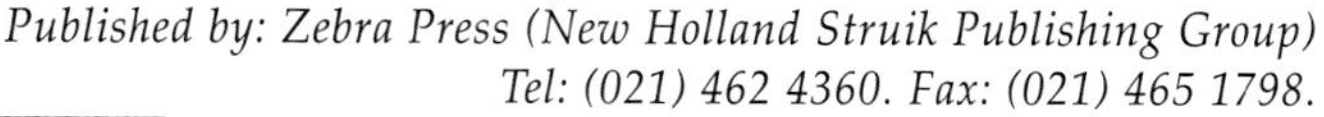

### *1899 The Long March Home*
**ELSABE BRINK**

John Sidney Marwick, Natal Native Agent, was responsible for the return to Natal, 400 kilometres, some 8 000 Zululand workers from the mines in the Transvaal. The Railways were being used for military purposes and the only alternative was for them to walk! This is the story of the *Long March Home* and of those that took part.
*Published by: Kwela Books, 28 Wale Street, Cape Town. Tel: (021) 406 3191. Fax: Tel: (021) 406 3196.*

### *Ghostriders of the Anglo-Boer War (1899-1902)*
**PIETER LABUSCHAGNE**

The first book to deal purely with the *agterryers* (coloured and native labourers). It focuses on the role played by them during the War, when 10 000 to 12 000 of them accompanied the Boers to the war front. Originally they were labourers, now they were drawn into the war by digging trenches, smuggling letters, spying and joining the firing line.
*Published by: UNISA Press, PO Box 392, Pretoria 0003.*

*Bombardment of Ladysmith Anticipated*
**ALAN CHALMERS**

The diary of George Maidment, an army orderly fresh out from the Midlands of England, recording the tedium of the siege and the bungled relief attempts as the British Army was put through its paces by a bunch of farmers. This is a story of great courage lying alongside great stupidity, of world events from the personal, intimate observations of a local boy.
*Published by: Covos-Day Books. Tel: (011) 475 0922.*

*How we kept the Flag flying*
**DONALD MACDONALD**
Similar facsimile reprint of 1st edition, (Ward, Lock & Co.Ltd 1900). This 303 page classic enduring story of the Siege of Ladysmith is the first publication by Covos-Day Books in their series of Anglo-Boer War titles commemorating the Centenary 1999-2002.
The book includes 298 illustrations and 9 fold-out maps.
*Published by: Covos-Day Books, Johannesburg, RSA.*
*Tel: (011) 475 0922. Fax: (011) 475 8974.*

*Halt! Action Front! With Colonel Long at Colenso*
**DARRELL HALL.**

The detailed account of the three batteries of the 4th Brigade Division, RFA, and the six *"Long 12s"* of the Royal Navy at the Battle of Colenso on the 15th December 1899. The three RFA batteries still serve today in the 26th Field Regiment, Royal Artillery.
208 pages with over 100 photographs, diagrams & maps.
*Published by: Covos-Day Books, Johannesburg, RSA.*
*Tel: (011) 475 0922. Fax: (011) 475 8974.*

*South African War Books - An Illustrated Bibliography*
**R. G. HACKETT**
A definitive compilation of English language publications relating to the Anglo-Boer War 1899-1902. A masterpiece and already a collector's item with only 1 200 copies printed. *"With meticulous regard for detail, this bibliography of contemporary books about the Boer War is a collector's must...a delightful insight into the mind of the bibliophile..."*The Star.
*Published by: Covos-Day Books. Tel: (011) 475 0922.*

*Fire in the Sky - The Destruction of the OFS*
**OWEN COETZER**
A shocking account of Britain's official Boer War policy of *scorched earth*, farm burning and concentration camps. More than 27 000 people, mainly women & children, died of appalling conditions. It was a mistake, Milner later wrote. But a brutal one, the consequences of which are still felt today, a century later. *Published by: Covos-Day Books, Johannesburg, RSA. Tel: (011) 475 0922. Fax: (011) 475 8974.*

***Available early 2000***

***Available early 2000***

*Mafeking!*
**MALCOLM FLOWER-SMITH & EDMUND YORKE**
Psychologically affected by the fact that it was from Mafeking that the Jameson Raid was launched, the Boers determined to regain this key town. The exceptional military leadership of Colonel Baden-Powell made him the ideal officer for the British defence. This book tells the story of the inspiration of the defenders. *Published by: Covos-Day Books, Johannesburg, RSA. Tel: (011) 475 0922. Fax: (011) 475 8974.*

**Available early 2000**

### *Anecdotes of the Anglo-Boer War*
**ROB MILNE**

An absorbing collection of true stories from the Anglo-Boer War of 1899-1902 ... some tragic ...some lighthearted ... but always entertaining – bringing humanity to the horror of war and telling the story as it was. An essential addition to the library of the Boer War collector.
*Published by: Covos-Day Books, PO Box 6996, Weltevredenpark, 1715 Republic of South Africa. Tel: (011) 475 0922. Fax: (011) 475 8974.*

### *Boer War Tribute Medals*
**M.G. HIBBARD**

The only reference ever to be published on Boer War tribute medals – it will remain the definite work on the subject for many years to come. All the medals (printed in full colour) are unknown to the collecting world which makes this book an important addition to the Boer War Numismatic collector.
*Published by: Constantia Classics Publications. PO Box 122, Fourways 2055, Sandton, South Africa.*

### *Boer Rifles and Carbines of the Anglo-Boer War*
**DR. RON BESTER**

The ultimate reference book for the Anglo-Boer War rifle enthusiast and the lover of firearms. The book also covers the decisions made by the Transvaal & Free State when acquiring their firearms. It was these decisions which determined much of the outcome of the war itself. It took 8 years to research.
*Published by: War Museum of the Boer Republics, Bloemfontein, RSA. Tel: (051) 447 3447. Fax: (051) 447 1322.*

### *The Jameson Raid - A Centennial Retrospective*
**THE BRENTHURST PRESS THIRD SERIES**

This is the first of a third series of ten volumes of limited edition Africana to be published by The Brenthurst Press. The book covers the roles and relationships between the characters of Dr. Jameson, Cecil Rhodes, Joseph Chamberlain and Paul Kruger. Also covering the Boer-Bagananwa War. *Published by: The Brenthurst Press, PO Box 87184, Houghton 2042, RSA. Tel: (011) 646 6024. Fax: (011) 486 1651.*

### *The Story of the Boer War* (*VIDEO ± 80 MINS*)

The video tells of the remarkable events of the first few months of the the war, the Sieges of Ladysmith, Kimberley and Mafeking. The shattering reverses suffered by the British at the battles of Stormberg, Magersfontein and Colenso and the bitter struggle to assert supremacy. Available from *Exclusive Books* and *Facts and Fiction* at R 79,95.
*Produced by: GTV, Sandton, South Africa. Tel: (011) 883 7060. Fax: (011) 884 5368.*

### *A Photo Album of the Anglo-Boer War* (*CD*)

More than 300 photo's of soldiers, burghers, battles, concentration camp internees, prisoners of war - all with captions. 'Page' through the album on your PC computer and print photo's for yourself or for projects. Available in English or Afrikaans for only R 99,00 each plus postage.
*Produced by: MediaMakers (Pty) Ltd, PO Box 25527, Mounment Park 0105, South Africa. Tel: (012) 428 0970. Fax: (012) 428 0975.*

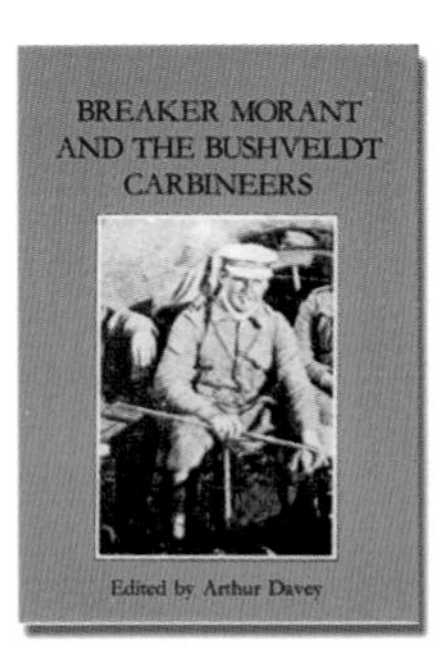


*Breaker Morant and the Bushveldt Carbineers*
**ARTHUR DAVEY**
Drawing on sources in South Africa and elsewhere, as well as publishing a large selection of important documents, Dr. Arthur Davey has sought and found definite or probable answers to a number of hitherto unresolved issues. *'Did Kitchener give secret verbal orders that no Boer prisoners were to be taken?' 'Were the Boers who were shot* "train wreckers and marauders"*?'*
*Produced by: Van Riebeeck Society, Cape Town, RSA.*

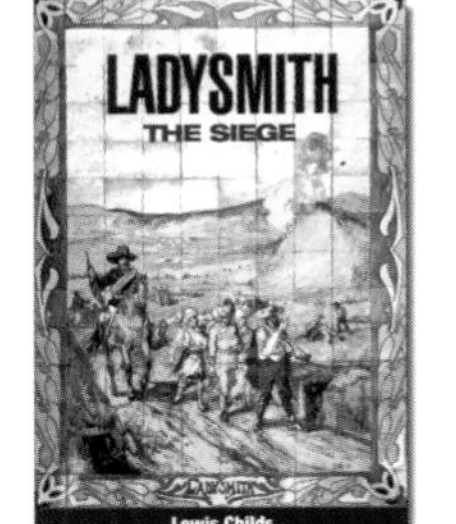


*Ladysmith - The Siege* by **LEWIS CHILDS**
This book is the companion to Lewis Child's earlier work, *Ladysmith: Colenso/Spion Kop/Hlangwane/Tugela,* and completes the story of the events in that town for the four months during which it was besieged (Nov 1899 - Feb 1900) and the engagements leading up to the siege. *Published by: Pen & Sword Books Ltd, 47 Church Street, Barnsley, South Yorkshire S70 2AS, United Kingdom.*

*Ladysmith* by **GILES FODEN**
An imperial adventure and a love story with a cast of characters ranging from Irish Republican renegades to London literary editors to some of the most famous faces of the twentieth century. At the centre is young Bella Kiernan, for whom the long siege represents an unexpected freedom: a chance to break old loyalties and establish new loves.
*Published by: Faber & Faber Ltd, 3 Queen Square, London WC1N 3AU, United Kingdom.*

*Commandant Gideon Scheepers - and the search for his grave*
**TAFFY & DAVID SHEARING**
This book documents his early life and career in the Orange Free State as a heliographer, his war record and final year in the Cape Colony. Using both new material and previously published sources, the book tries to understand something of the times and the *'victory at any price'* attitude that ruled both sides during that conflict.
*Taffy & David Shearing. Tel: (044) 343 1649.*

*Commandant Johannes Lötter - and his Rebels*
**TAFFY & DAVID SHEARING**
The book commemorates the victorious British columns and Lötter's Commando of Midland farmers who believed so faithfully that when you fight for a just cause, victory must be yours. It covers the Rebels Rise, the Special Court Trial at Graaff-Reinet to the conclusion of Lötter's execution. There are also 15 pages on the men who rode and fought with Lötter. *Taffy & David Shearing. Tel: (044) 343 1649.*

*A Century of Anglo-Boer War Stories*
**N. VAN DER MERWE & MICHAEL PRICE**
An anthology of stories and poetry written by Afrikaners, Englishmen and black South Africans, who explore the trauma of the time and place from their own varied perspectives. Amongst others, there are texts by Herman Charles Bosman, Stuart Cloete, Thomas Hardy, Rudyard Kipling, Sol Plaatjie, Eugene Marais and Olive Schreiner.
*Published by: Jonathan Ball Publishers, Johannesburg.*

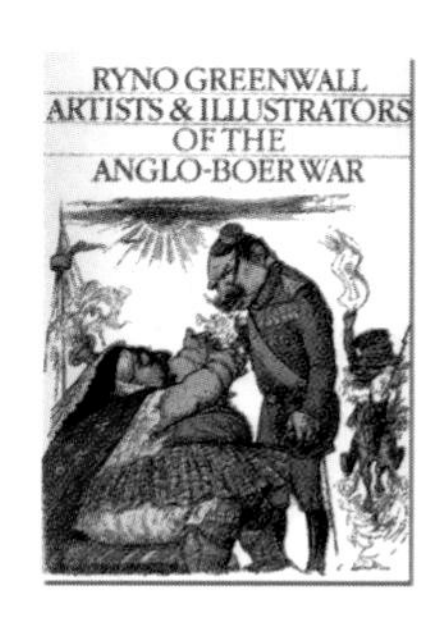


*Artists & Illustrators of the Anglo-Boer War*
**RYNO GREENWALL**
Waging war is the most destructive and ignoble of human urges; creating art one of the most sublime. When these two impulses converge and the theme is a war as bitter and destructive as the Anglo-Boer conflict, the results are usually powerful. This monumental work by Greenwall gives us a more profound understanding, than words, of the conflict.
*Published by: Fernwood Press, PO Box 15344, Vlaeburg.*

*Kleredrag tydens die Anglo-Boereoorlog*
**ANDRE MALAN & ANNEMARIE CARELSEN**
A well researched and interesting book on the clothing worn by the burghers at the turn of the 20th century. It covers *Boere-uniforms,* and *Burger-gevegsdrag,* as well as *Mansklere* and *Vrouklere.* There are patterns for those wishing to produce garments of the period.
*Orders: Protea Book House, PO Box 35110, Menlo Park, 0102 South Africa. Tel: (012) 362 5683.*

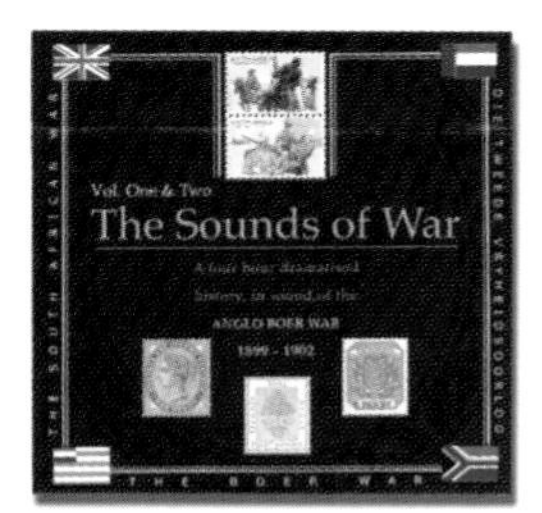


*The Sounds of War.* **A 4CD COMPILATION OF THE WAR. READ BY SOUTH AFRICAN ARTISTS**
It is also available on 4 tape cassettes. An excellent rendition of the Anglo-Boer War with effective background sounds which bring a realism to the narrative. A selection of the areas covered is: THE CAUSES. BLACK WEEK. SPIOEN KOP. KIMBERLEY & LADYSMITH. MARCHING TO PRETORIA. GUERILLA WAR. BARBARISM. ABRAHAM ESAU. And many more subjects.
*Obtainable from: Listeners Library, Johannesburg, RSA. Tel: (011) 325 2266. Fax: (011) 341 0149.*

*Drummer Hodge. The Poetry of the Anglo-Boer War*
**M. VAN WYK SMITH**
A magnificent and extremely well written book which is an unique exercise in the comparative history of 19th century English and European war poetry; with extracts of poems by the Soldiers, Boers, Prisoners of War and poets of Europe. A must for every bookshelf and collector.
*Order from: Protea Book House, PO Box 35110, Menlo Park, 0102 South Africa. Tel: (012) 362 5683.*

*Days of Horror during the Siege of Kimberley*
**CARL MEYER**
A diary of events by a German missionary presenting a unique insight to the effect of the war on social conditions at the time. Meyer was politically neutral and metered equal treatment to all persons no matter what race or political affiliation. An interesting book.
*Order from: Kimberley Africana Museum, Kimberley. Tel: (053) 830 6247. Fax: (053) 833 1954.*

*Summer of 1899. The Siege of Kimberley*
**COMPILED BY KOKKIE DUMINY, ILLUSTRATED BY JUDITH HORNER**
This magnificent book, edited by Steve Lunderstedt, is a history with anecdotes and articles written by a number of enthusiasts of the Boer War. Each chapter relates to another aspect of the Siege. An ideal coffee-table book that will keep you browsing for hours. *Order from: Kimberley Africana Museum, Kimberley. Tel: (053) 830 6247. Fax: (053) 833 1954.*

## Index